Second Edition

Money Laundering

A Guide for Criminal Investigators

Second Edition

Money Laundering

A Guide for Criminal Investigators

John Madinger

Taylor & Francis
Taylor & Francis Group

Boca Raton   London   New York

A CRC title, part of the Taylor & Francis imprint, a member of the
Taylor & Francis Group, the academic division of T&F Informa plc.

Published in 2006 by
CRC Press
Taylor & Francis Group
6000 Broken Sound Parkway NW, Suite 300
Boca Raton, FL 33487-2742

© 2006 by Taylor & Francis Group, LLC
CRC Press is an imprint of Taylor & Francis Group

No claim to original U.S. Government works
Printed in the United States of America on acid-free paper
10 9 8 7 6 5 4 3 2 1

International Standard Book Number-10: 0-8493-3395-4 (Hardcover)
International Standard Book Number-13: 978-0-8493-3395-8 (Hardcover)
Library of Congress Card Number 2005053190

This book contains information obtained from authentic and highly regarded sources. Reprinted material is quoted with permission, and sources are indicated. A wide variety of references are listed. Reasonable efforts have been made to publish reliable data and information, but the author and the publisher cannot assume responsibility for the validity of all materials or for the consequences of their use.

No part of this book may be reprinted, reproduced, transmitted, or utilized in any form by any electronic, mechanical, or other means, now known or hereafter invented, including photocopying, microfilming, and recording, or in any information storage or retrieval system, without written permission from the publishers.

For permission to photocopy or use material electronically from this work, please access www.copyright.com (http://www.copyright.com/) or contact the Copyright Clearance Center, Inc. (CCC) 222 Rosewood Drive, Danvers, MA 01923, 978-750-8400. CCC is a not-for-profit organization that provides licenses and registration for a variety of users. For organizations that have been granted a photocopy license by the CCC, a separate system of payment has been arranged.

Trademark Notice: Product or corporate names may be trademarks or registered trademarks, and are used only for identification and explanation without intent to infringe.

Library of Congress Cataloging-in-Publication Data

Madinger, John.
   Money laundering : a guide for criminal investigators / John Madinger.--2nd ed.
     p. cm.
   Includes bibliographical references and index.
   ISBN 0-8493-3395-4 (alk. paper)
   1. Money laundering investigation--United States. 2. Money laundering--United States--Prevention. I. Title.

HV8079.M64M33 2006
363.25'968--dc22   2005053190

---

informa

Taylor & Francis Group is the Academic Division of Informa plc.

Visit the Taylor & Francis Web site at
http://www.taylorandfrancis.com

and the CRC Press Web site at
http://www.crcpress.com

PREFACE

The world changed forever on September 11, 2001. In a few short minutes — the time it took for two towers to fall — thousands of lives and billions of dollars were lost. Destroyed also were illusions that had been sustained for much too long: We believed that terrorists would not strike America in its homeland, that threats made by people like Osama bin Laden were idle, that our institutions were strong enough to prevent catastrophe.

Some long-held assumptions also collapsed that day, notably the belief that terrorism could be dealt with strictly as a law enforcement problem. In previous incidents of terrorism, law enforcement responded to the scene; even before the smoke cleared, FBI evidence technicians and ATF bomb experts were meticulously combing the wreckage for clues as criminal investigators began following leads to the perpetrators. Prosecutors waited for the evidence that would lead to indictments, trials, and, hopefully, long stretches in a federal penitentiary for those responsible.

After September 11, most folks were ready to say goodbye to all that, or at least goodbye to the concept that we could afford to wait around until the next bomb blast or aircraft hijacking before taking some preemptive action. Just about everybody agreed that much more effective proactive measures were going to be needed if we were going to prevent something like the September 11 attacks (or something even worse) from happening again.

We also recognized pretty quickly that we were dealing with an enemy who was highly motivated, well trained, organized, disciplined, and, perhaps most significant, well funded. The funding aspect is so important because all the motivation, training, and discipline in the world won't get you onto an airplane unless you have the price of an airline ticket. The September 11 hijackers, of course, required a great deal more money than that, but they had all they needed. The plotters' costs, though not enormous, were substantial and included international travel, communications, flying lessons, and living expenses for two dozen or more people, probably totaling between $400,000 and $1 million.

The investigators swarming over the records after September 11 quickly followed the trail of this money to Europe and the Middle East, discovering that not only did the terrorists have enough money, they also had some left over. The investigators also discovered that many of the techniques used by the terrorists and their financial backers to move their cash were very similar, if not identical, to those used by money launderers for decades. In addition to cash, the terror networks utilized banks, wire transfers, informal banking networks, business fronts, and the financial systems of countries where secrecy is the rule. Most drug trafficking and organized crime groups would be comfortable with all of these methods of laundering money; indeed, as we shall see, they developed and perfected them.

So, although the world changed, some things did not and one of these was the need for criminal investigators to develop and perfect the techniques necessary to combat those who violate society's laws. We are trying to keep up with the criminals and, if they are playing in the financial arena, we need to be able to understand the rules of that game.

This book is, as its subtitle states, a guide for criminal investigators. It was originally written to help train task force officers and others who might be working on complex narcotics or other cases in which there was a financial component. Since the book was first written, the need for this information has only grown. Today, the Drug Enforcement Administration (DEA) and the Organized Crime Drug Enforcement Task

Force program (OCDETF) both require that the financial aspects of every case be at least addressed, if not fully investigated. DEA and other federal agencies are actively seeking investigators who can conduct financial investigations and most major cases now have some financial component.

No book can do everything for everyone, so it's a good idea to say right up front what this one is and is not. It provides a *basic* grounding in the law and theory of money laundering. It is not a "how to" guide on laundering money, although at the end the reader will know more about how launderers operate. It also is not a detailed examination of advanced or highly complex money laundering schemes. Some of these are so convoluted that even the people who designed them don't know what they're doing. If a law enforcement officer encounters one of these schemes, the advice of experts will be essential and this book will help the officer understand what the experts are talking about.

Finally, this book is a reminder that the vast majority of crimes are all about money. Some are motivated by greed for money, while in others, like the terrorist attacks of September 11, 2001, money fuels the criminals in their illegal activity. Finding the money, tracing it, linking it to the criminal, and taking it away are all essential parts of our jobs now and this book provides information to help us do those jobs. Because it is so important, I wish you the best of luck.

AUTHOR

John Madinger is a senior special agent with the Criminal Investigation Division of the Internal Revenue Service. In his 30-year law enforcement career, he has also served as narcotics agent, supervisor, and administrator. He holds a bachelor's degree in criminal justice from Indiana University and was the honor graduate in the Treasury Criminal Investigation Training Program. He is the recipient of numerous awards and citations from the Internal Revenue Service, the Drug Enforcement Administration and Organized Crime Drug Enforcement Task Forces. He has extensive experience in money laundering, forfeiture, and financial investigations; has developed training programs in these areas for the Treasury and Justice Departments; and has presented money laundering training in the United States, Europe, Asia, and the Caribbean.

INTRODUCTION

"Where large sums of money are concerned, it is advisable to trust nobody."
Agatha Christie, *Endless Night*

"Whoever profits by crime is guilty of it."
French proverb

"AS GOOD PYRATES AT LAND...": THE LEGEND OF HENRY EVERY'S SECOND BIG MISTAKE

It's been a while since Henry Every made his *second* big mistake. He should never have turned to crime to begin with, which was the first. Not that Henry and his associates were unsuccessful criminals. On the contrary, they were daring and resourceful, and they overcame tremendous hardships to further a pirate career that spanned five years and half the globe (see Figure I.1).

And what a career it was. In their last seizure alone, Every and his crew took the Portuguese ship *Gung-i-Suwaie* and its treasure valued at £325,000. As the new owner of what would be $400 million in today's money, Every is alleged to have offered to retire the British national debt in exchange for a pardon. Three hundred years later, leaders of a drug cartel would make similar offers to their government, and these, like Every's, would be refused.

No, the problem was not that Every and his men were poor criminals. Their problem was that they were *so* successful: Prosperity would lead directly to Every's second big mistake. Having accumulated a vast treasure, Every and his crew of pirates decided to divide the spoils and leave the high seas forever. Somewhat surprisingly, they chose Jolly Olde England for their retirement home.

Europe represented a civilized place to spend the loot, and there were sentimental ties, but England (and the other European countries, for that matter) had a less-than-jolly attitude toward

Figure I.1 Arch-Pirate Henry Every, from a contemporary image. Every had a successful career as a pirate in the Atlantic and Indian oceans, but legend has it that he came undone when he tried to launder his share of the treasure. (Source: National Archives)

piracy. Here, the discovery of their pirate past would result in a short ride to the end of a long rope. Every and his shipmates had radically different ideas about how to avoid that ride. Neither approach would be very successful.

Novelist Daniel Defoe (*Robinson Crusoe*) chronicled the story some years later in an account probably more fiction than fact. According to Defoe, Every's crew landed in Scotland and split up, each carrying his share of the treasure. Many of the crew members immediately drew attention to themselves by spending money freely ("Like a drunken sailor" is the phrase that comes most immediately to mind). Curious townspeople began to ask difficult questions about the background of the men and their money. This caused the crew to panic, with members offering extravagant sums for transportation out of town. Arrests ensued, followed by prompt, well-deserved hangings. One mystery remained: None of the condemned men were able to shed any light on the whereabouts of their leader, who had evidently taken a more refined approach to his financial affairs.

In Defoe's legend, Every moved quietly into the small Devonshire town of Bideford, a place with a strong maritime tradition. Up to the moment Every turned over his treasure to the Bideford merchants, his criminal career had been almost letter-perfect. Although he was the most wanted man in all of England, his travels throughout the world had kept his face from becoming well known in his home country. Those same travels had provided him with more wealth than was possessed by the entire populations of some English towns. Every had had to do some fairly unpleasant things to amass his fortune, but he was now confident that his riches would enable him to live out his days in quiet retirement. In short, he thought he was home free. The Bideford merchants had other ideas.

Every wanted to sell some diamonds, a straightforward enough request, and not unusual in Devon, the home to a large seafaring population, many of whom acquired precious stones in their travels throughout the world. What made Every stand out was the size of the sale. The retired sailor who gave his name as "Henry Bridgeman" had literally a king's ransom in diamonds, worth several thousand pounds. In a time when the average seaman might see 500 pounds over a lifetime, Every's hoard was, quite literally, a fortune.

Figure I.2 Henry Every's Big Mistake. Henry Every, arch-pirate, anxiously awaits the verdict of the Bideford merchant who is about to cheat him out of a king's ransom. The story of Every's failed career as a money launderer comes to us from Daniel Defoe, author of Robinson Crusoe. (Source: Author's collection)

The Bideford merchants put two and two together, getting exactly four. They made Every a generous offer, paid a small deposit, took all of the diamonds, and refused to give him another shilling. When Every complained, the merchants suggested he contact the local sheriff — perhaps that good man would be interested to learn of the large number of jewels brought to his quiet town. (See Figure I.2.)

Defoe says that Every, the retired arch pirate who lost his treasure to the merchants of Bideford in 1697, lived on in poverty for a number of years. He occasionally received a small sum from the merchants, whom he died cursing as being "as good Pyrates at Land as he was at Sea." (They were much better money launderers, too.)

A couple lessons from this short and unhappy career in money laundering are still valid today. First, criminals should be aware that no matter how successful they are at the crime itself, there may still be problems disposing of the loot. Every paid dearly for this wisdom. Second, the mere existence of wealth may result in exposure to the criminal. In fact, the failure to adequately explain the source of the wealth may even be fatal, as Every's crew discovered. Finally, those of us who enforce the law might take note of the fact that although the British government spent huge sums in a futile attempt to catch Every and his crew while they were pirating, it was the spending of the loot, not some fierce sea battle, that ended the pirates' careers.

Business Week magazine called money laundering "the crime of the 1990s," but it's older, of course. Certainly those who commit crimes for financial gain have gotten more sophisticated in the concealment of their wealth, but as the Every case shows, the need to dispose of the wages of sin is ancient indeed. Law enforcement today has more resources than ever to address this difficult problem, but the criminals strive to stay at least one step ahead. It is, after all, their necks (and their money) that are on the line.

Several factors have combined to make money laundering more important than ever before. Advances in communications and transportation have made the world a smaller place. Concealment of the proceeds of crime is a much easier proposition today than in Every's time. Criminals have the ability to move themselves and their stolen property between countries within hours. Funds can be wired from one world financial center to another in seconds. With centers located in different time zones, one will always be open and ready for business.

A second factor involves the internationalization of crime. Organized crime, in its various forms and assorted ethnic faces, has become a problem in countries around the globe. The home-grown syndicate has given way to a new breed of criminal, at home in many cities, able to move quickly from place to place, capable of using contacts and facilities in foreign countries. These criminals, be they members of Japan's *Boryokudan,* Sicily's *Mafia,* or Colombia's drug cartels, represent a serious challenge for law enforcement. It is no longer possible for a police officer to "know his beat" and all of those people on it. Today, a jewel thief can meet with a fence in New York on the same business day as the theft in France, get paid, and have her money in a Hong Kong bank the day before!

Drug trafficking between nations and across international borders has contributed greatly to the globalization of crime. Since the source countries for drugs such as cocaine and heroin are generally not those where the drugs are consumed, transport of the commodity is required. Customs officers worldwide are all too familiar with the almost infinite variety of methods by which drugs are smuggled. The constant testing and probing of Customs' resources by smugglers has led to an intimate familiarity with the ways and means of international travel.

Drug trafficking organizations move their product by land, sea, and air, using commercial or private facilities. Recent cases on the United States–Mexico border have led to the discovery of tunnels leading between the two countries. Smuggling by private aircraft is a common means of moving quantities of drugs quickly between nations or couriers may be employed to carry the drugs aboard commercial airliners. The sheer volume of traffic at airports and at border crossings makes detection of these efforts most difficult.

In addition to travel for the purpose of smuggling, international criminals have discovered that movement between countries is an excellent way to avoid detection by local authorities. Sensitive meetings can be scheduled for a foreign country with little anticipation that local police will follow or that those at the meeting site will be alerted or interested in the activity.

A good example is the planning session for the terrorist attacks that took place in New York on September 11, 2001. Members of the Al Qaeda terrorist organization, which was then headquartered in Afghanistan, traveled from Europe and North America to Indonesia to finalize their plans, far away from their bases and from their targets in the United States.

Finally, international organizations have learned the value of currency movement and are now as skilled and experienced at moving money from nation to nation as any financial expert in the world. Criminals have traditionally taken advantage of the confidentiality afforded by some countries' banking laws. The banks of

Switzerland have long been a haven for foreign capital, some of which stems from questionable sources. Other nations have imitated the Swiss example, creating havens for foreigners seeking to conceal wealth or income from their home governments. These offshore havens are often "dead ends" for investigators attempting to follow the money's trail. More than one investigator has seen a case go into a black hole in Switzerland, the Cayman Islands, the Bahamas, or Hong Kong never to emerge again.

IMPROVEMENTS IN LAW AND LAW ENFORCEMENT

Law enforcement has made some advances of its own. We see this progress not only in the form of new statutes enacted to deal with modern criminal activity but also in the methods used to investigate sophisticated international financial crimes.

Thirty years ago, the drug laws of the United States were relatively simple and most could easily fit on one page of the statute book. Drug offenders were charged with distribution or possession of the illegal substance and occasionally with conspiracy to possess or distribute. Today, such provisions as the Continuing Criminal Enterprise statute and much enhanced conspiracy provisions greatly improve the ability of investigators to penetrate a large organization and reach its upper echelons.

Laws directed at organized crime such as the Racketeer Influenced and Corrupt Organizations Act (RICO), "travel" or Interstate Travel in Aid of Racketeering (ITAR) Act, and similar laws have taken direct aim at the ability of criminals to combine or conspire for some nefarious purpose. Some of these statutes such as the RICO law also provide for the seizure of assets acquired by the criminal, making them even more potent weapons against crime.

In some countries, laws directed at organized crime include antimembership provisions, the banning of certain organizations, and prohibitions against association with certain groups. These laws can have a major impact on the criminal's ability to associate and they make the conduct of an illegal business more difficult and expensive.

Finally, and perhaps most significantly, the expanding use of forfeiture around the world has made life most uncomfortable for the criminal. The prospect that a government might take away all of one's ill-gotten gains, even those earned in another country, must be extremely disheartening for the mobster, drug trafficker, or syndicate hoodlum. Law enforcement has become an enthusiastic supporter of the forfeiture laws. Governments worldwide are becoming much more creative in using these provisions against all sorts of criminal activity.

All of these factors are well known to the law violator who is offered on one hand a world of much broader opportunities and, on the other, one with much greater risk. Smart criminals respond by finding ways to conceal their interest in illegal operations. In our day and age, even as in Henry Every's, this most definitely includes hiding any financial interest.

"Yeah, I'm doing twenty to life, but at least they didn't get my car."

MODERN LAW ENFORCEMENT METHODS

Just as the Information Age has increased opportunity for the criminal, so has it provided new benefits for the law enforcement officer. Agencies on the national and international level have recognized the need to adjust to and take advantage of new technology, laws, and techniques.

INTERPOL, the International Criminal Police organization, based in France, has established links to police departments and investigative agencies throughout the world. Communications via INTERPOL and other channels have steadily improved, aided by the stationing of law enforcement personnel in overseas postings. Today, representatives of at least six federal law enforcement agencies are posted in American embassies or consulates on every continent. The primary function of this foreign presence is to establish an effective liaison with law enforcement counterparts in the host nation. Many of those nations also station their law enforcement personnel in the United States, although not in such large numbers.

Law enforcement agencies all over the world have come to recognize the value of financial information in the detection and prosecution of criminal activity and many countries have established Financial Intelligence Units (FIUs) to track large and suspicious currency transactions. Not only do law enforcement officers within that country have access to this valuable resource, but the FIUs have the ability to communicate with each other about transactions having international ramifications.

By sharing ideas in all of these situations, law enforcement makes the job of the criminal more difficult. This is an especially important factor in the complex financial crimes that span international boundaries. As we draw nearer to a cashless society, the ability to track assets and unravel complicated financial schemes will challenge law enforcement personnel to be ever more sophisticated and aware. Law enforcement's response to this challenge will determine the success or failure of efforts against not just financial crimes but organized crime in general.

LAW ENFORCEMENT RESPONSE TO MONEY LAUNDERING AND ORGANIZED CRIME

The law enforcement response to money laundering and organized crime takes two forms. The first is an organizational response, in which agencies or entire governments react as a matter of policy. Perhaps the easiest response is to adopt a "business as usual" approach, one that assumes that the tried and true methods that worked in the past can be applied successfully to any new problem. Unfortunately, this response ignores the sophistication of today's criminals, as well as the rapidly changing environment in which they operate. Law enforcement officers tend to be basically conservative, slow to change, and reluctant to accept new ideas. These same attitudes and characteristics can also suffuse their organizations, bureaucracies that are naturally inclined toward doing "business as usual."

In fact, law enforcement has already made many adjustments to its changed environment. Recognition of the importance of financial investigative techniques has been emphasized by the use of forfeiture laws, first against drug traffickers and later against all manner of criminal activity. The ability of law enforcement agencies to take a flexible, integrated approach toward complex financial crimes such as money laundering will bear immediate fruit. By integrating financial investigative techniques into the law enforcement arsenal, we have the opportunity to become as flexible as the criminals we are now compelled to pursue. Law enforcement also becomes able to make better use of forfeiture statutes, to use financial information in drug or other criminal cases, and to obtain and understand financial intelligence that can be useful in future cases.

The second response is individual. Each law enforcement officer whose career will extend into the 21st century must make an honest appraisal of his or her own ability to compete on this global playing field. One of the most important messages of this book is that money laundering and complex financial crimes are going to be a part of our future. For the individual detective, investigator, or agent to properly address these crimes, he or she will need the right attitude, the right training, and administrative support.

The ability to investigate money laundering is not difficult to acquire. Most investigators already possess the necessary skills. It is not, for example, necessary to be an accountant, but a basic knowledge of financial systems, including accounting techniques, is essential. Many already have some of this knowledge through contact with banks, financial crimes, or similar job-related intercourse. (You can actually learn quite a bit about banking operations and accounting just by balancing your own checkbook. Many of the accounting functions needed to do financial investigations are no more complicated than this simple process.)

Another important individual response is the development of sources of financial information. Whether this is a reorientation of an informant to seek information about financial transactions or the development of sources within the business community, financial information is critical to the development of money laundering cases. As we will see (and without giving away too much at the beginning), there are essentially two approaches to a money laundering investigation. In option one, you can look for the crime that underlies the money laundering violation, drug trafficking for example, and then try to find out what happened to the money generated by that crime. In option two, you can look for the money and then trace it back to the crime that generated it. A surprising number of cases, many of which are going to be cited in this book, have been resolved in exactly this way.

It is definitely not the intent of this book to sell one option over the other. Both work and both work well. Rather, it is hoped that the conscientious investigator will see the merits of each approach, understand the value of financial investigative techniques in each, and use the information in this book effectively in either approach. In any case, the development of financial information, either from traditional sources (i.e. informants) or financial sources, is an important key to success.

Summing up, this text has three principal goals. First, I want to provide an understanding of how money laundering works and how it fits into the world of modern criminal activity. Second, I hope to increase the investigator's ability to conduct money laundering and financial investigations. Finally, it is hoped that the reader will recognize how valuable this knowledge will be in the investigation of organized criminal activity and be convinced to employ it in future cases.

CONTENTS

Chapter 1	Basic Concepts	1
	Money, Money, Money	1
	The Evolution of Money	2
	Money Laundering	6
	The Money Laundering Cycle	10
	Rex v. William Kidd, et al.: A Case of Piracy	11
	Money Laundering Facts	14
	Key Points to Consider	14
Chapter 2	The Historical Context	15
	Analysis of the Watergate Money Laundering Scheme	24
	More Money Laundering Schemes	26
	American Airlines	26
	Braniff Airlines	28
	George Steinbrenner and American Shipbuilding	28
Chapter 3	Federal Money Laundering Statutes	31
	The Money Laundering Control Act	34
	Title 18 U.S.C. §1956 (a) (1)	35
	The Money Was Proceeds of an SUA	36
	The Defendant Knew That the Money Was Proceeds of an SUA	37
	The Defendant Conducted or Attempted to Conduct a Financial Transaction	38
	The Defendant Acted with Intent	40
	Title 18 United States Code §1956 (a) (2): The International Transportation Offense	42
	Title 18 U.S.C. 1956 (a) (3): The "Sting" Provision	44
	Title 18 U.S.C. 1957	45
	Title 18 U.S.C. 1956 (h): Conspiracy	47
	Other Issues	47
	Venue and Statute of Limitations	47
	Sentencing	49
	Specified Unlawful Activity — Title 18 U.S.C. Sections 1956 and 1957 (Money Laundering Control Act of 1986)	49
	Frequently Asked Questions About SUAs	53
Chapter 4	The USA Patriot Act	55
	Criminal Sanctions	57

Bulk Cash Smuggling 58
Forfeiture 58
Regulatory Action..60
    Prohibition on U.S. Correspondent Accounts with Shell Banks
        (31 U.S.C. 5318 (j); Act Section 313)..60
    Availability of Bank Records 60
    Due Diligence for Private Banking and Correspondent Accounts
        (31 U.S.C. 5318 (i); Act Section 312)...61
    "Special Measures" for Certain Jurisdictions, Financial Institutions,
        International Transactions, and Accounts (31 U.S.C. 5318A;
        Act Section 311) 61
    Standards for Verification of Customer Identification (31
        U.S.C. 5318(l); Act Section 326)...61
    Suspicious Activity Reporting (31 U.S.C. 5331, Act Section 365) 61
    Forfeiture of Funds in U.S. Interbank Accounts (18 U.S.C. 981(k);
        Act Section 319) 62
    Anti-Money Laundering Program Requirement (31 U.S.C. 5318(g);
        Act Section 352) 62
    Filing of SARs by Securities Brokers and Dealers (Act Section 356) 62
    Filing of SARs by Businesses (31 U.S.C. 5331; Act Section 365) 62
    Penalties (31 U.S.C. 5321, 5322, 5324; Act Sections 353 and 363) 62
    Sunset Provisions...62
Effects of the USA Patriot Act 62

Chapter 5 Money Laundering Forfeiture..65

Money Laundering Forfeiture 67
Civil Forfeiture 70
    What Can Be Seized?...70
        Title 18 U.S.C. §981 (Civil Money Laundering Forfeiture) 70
        Title 18 U.S.C. §984 (Civil Forfeiture of Fungible Property)..........................70
    Procedures for Civil Seizures Under §981 (b) 70
        Seizure Incident to Lawful Arrest or Search 70
        Seizures Made with Seizure Warrant 71
    Administrative Forfeiture Proceedings 71
§982 Criminal Forfeiture..72
    Criminal Forfeiture Statute: 18 U.S.C. §982..72
    What Property Is Subject to Criminal Money Laundering Forfeiture? 72
    The Criminal Forfeiture Process 72
    Substitution of Assets..73
Special Forfeiture Issues 74
    Preseizure Planning...74
    Grand Jury Information in Forfeiture Cases..75
    Non-Grand Jury Information..75
    Seizure of Real Property 76
Equitable Sharing 77

| Chapter 6 | Related Federal Statutes | 79 |

Bank Secrecy Act 80
   Reports Required by the BSA...83
      Currency Transaction Report 83
      Report of International Transportation of Currency or Monetary
        Instruments 84
      Currency Transaction Report by Casinos 84
      Foreign Bank Account Report...85
      Suspicious Activity Report..85
      Report of Cash Payments over $10,000 Received in a Trade or Business...........87
   Business Registration 88
      Penalties under Title 31...89
      Investigations under Title 31 91
Racketeer Influenced and Corrupt Organizations Act 92
Illegal Money Transmitter Businesses 93
Investment of Illicit Drug Profits 94
False Statements 95

| Chapter 7 | International Money Laundering Control | 97 |

International Organizations 99
   INTERPOL...99
   United Nations 99
   British Commonwealth..99
   Financial Action Task Force..100
   Organization of American States 101
   The Egmont Group..102
   Other Initiatives 102
Impact on Law Enforcement...102
Obtaining Information from Abroad 103

| Chapter 8 | Introduction to Financial Investigation | 107 |

Case Study: Treason 108
The Importance of Context 111
A "How To" Guide to Financial Investigation 112
Looking Ahead 114

| Chapter 9 | Introduction to Books and Records | 115 |

The Capone Organization..117
Accounting Principles 135
   The Dreaded Debits and Credits...136
Analyzing the Balance Sheet 139
Analyzing the Income Statement 140
Using Books and Records in a Financial Case 143
Conclusion 144

Chapter 10 Indirect Methods of Proving Income 145

Indirect Methods 146
Net Worth 146
Defenses to Net Worth 150
Conclusion 151
Source and Application of Funds 151
Bank Deposits 152
Unit and Volume 153
Application in Money Laundering Cases 154
Crime of the Century — Laundering the Hottest Money in America 154

Chapter 11 Business Operations 161

Proprietorships 161
Partnerships 162
General Record Information 165
Terms Used in Connection with Partnerships 165
Corporations 165
Corporate Advantages and Disadvantages 166
For the Investigator 168
Corporate Criminal Liability 168
Other Business Entities 169
Summing Up 172

Chapter 12 Domestic Banking 173

Money and Banking 173
Borrowing and Lending 177
Bank Regulation and Control 178
Bank Management and Operation 179
Bank Functions 180
Making Loans 180
Receiving Deposits 181
Hold and Administer Property for Others 182
Not All Banks Are Created Alike 183
Resources on Banking 185

Chapter 13 Banking Operations 187

Making Loans 188
Consumer Loan Types 188
Mortgage Loans 188
Secured Property Loans 188
Secured Cash Loans 189
Credit Card Loans 189
Personal Lines of Credit 189
Overdraft Protection 189
Student Loans 189

| Home Equity Loans 190
| Miscellaneous Loans 190
| The Loan Process 190
| Receiving Deposits 191
| Paying Checks 195
| Check 21 — Big Changes for Banks (Almost) Everywhere 199
| Monthly Account Statements 199
| Transferring Funds 200
| Cashier's Checks 201
| Bank Money Orders 202
| Bank Drafts 202
| Traveler's Checks 202
| Certified Checks 202
| Exchange Instruments 202
| Holding and Administering Property for Others 203
| Collecting and Processing Financial Instruments 204
| Other Services 204
| Currency Exchange 205
| Services for Business 205
| Trust Department Services 205
| Bank Record-keeping and Reporting 206

Chapter 14 International Banking 209

  International Transactions 210
    Cash in Advance 210
    Documentary Letters of Credit 211
    Documentary Collection 211
    Open Account 211
  Basic Documents Used in International Trade 211
  Letters of Credit 212
    A Money Laundering Scheme Involving a Letter of Credit 213
  Documentary Collections 214
    Document Collection Process 215
    Banker's Acceptance 215
  Foreign Exchange 216
  International Banking 218
  International Banking Services Offered by U.S. Banks 220
  Foreign Bank Accounts 221
  Types of Accounts 222
  Opening a Swiss Account 222
  Account Identification 223
  Documents Available from Foreign Banks 223

Chapter 15 Money Transfers 225

  Starting Small: Licensed Money Transmitters 227
  Operation 228

  Records 229
   Use of Remittance Corporations in Money Laundering Schemes........................229
  Major Electronic Funds Transfer Systems: Fedwire, CHIPS, and SWIFT 231
   Following the Money 232
   Records Generated in a Fedwire Transfer 232
   Forms Used in Wire Transfers 233
  CHIPS and SWIFT..236
  Informal Banking Systems and Unlicensed Transmitters 238
  Money Laundering and Wire Transfers 240
  Investigating Wire Transfer Schemes...240

Chapter 16 Real Property 243

  Real Estate Transactions: Basic Anatomy 244
   Authorization to Sell 244
   Advertising 244
   Deposit Receipt Offer and Acceptance 244
   Seller Approval 245
   Escrow Papers..245
   Real Estate Ownership 246
   Corporations and Trusts 247
   Researching Real Property Records..248
   Finding Hidden Assets 249

Chapter 17 Securities..251

  Stocks: Owning a Piece of the Pie 252
   Types of Stock...252
   Making Money on Stock..253
   Market Operations 254
  Buying and Selling Stocks 256
   Information About Stock Transactions 258
    Information at the Brokerage House...258
    Information at the Transfer Agent..259
    Information at the Disbursing Agent 260
  Bonds: Owning Debt...260
   Information About Bondholders 262
  Mutual Funds: Pooling Your Money...262
  Information from Investment Firms 263
  Futures and Options: Betting the Ranch...263
  Securities and Money Laundering 265

Chapter 18 Obtaining Financial Information 267

  Risk vs. Reward...268
  Traditional Sources of Information 269
   Informants..269
   Undercover Agents 270
   Interviews...270

Surveillance Operations 271
    Physical Surveillance 271
    Mail Covers 272
    Trash Covers 272
    Pen Registers 277
From the Horse's Mouth: The Subject's Records 277
    Just Asking … 278
    Obtaining Records Through a Second Party 278
    Subpoenas and Special Exceptions 278
    Financial and Document Search Warrants 279
Preparing a List of Things to Be Seized 284
    "Permeated with Fraud": A Useful Phrase 284
Valuable Hearsay: Third-Party Records 285
    Legal Considerations 285
    Request for Production 285
    Administrative Subpoena 285
    Grand Jury Subpoena 286
        Records Requested 287
        Service 287
        Time Considerations 287
        Secrecy 287
        Payment 288
    Financial Search Warrants 288
    Tax Records 289
Information from Abroad 290
    Official and Unofficial Liaison 290
    Compelling Production 290
    Tax and Mutual Legal Assistance Treaties 291
    Letters Rogatory 291
    Subpoenas 292

Chapter 19 Sources of Information 293
    Federal Databases and Information Systems 294
        TECS II 294
        NADDIS 295
        NCIC 295
        NLETS 295
    Government Agencies and Records 295
        Federal Agencies and Records 295
            FinCEN 296
        Federal Government Departments 297
            Department of Agriculture 297
            Department of the Air Force 298
            Department of the Army 298
            Department of Commerce 298
            Department of Defense 298
            Department of Health, Education, and Welfare 298

  The Social Security Administration 298
  Department of Homeland Security 299
  Department of the Interior 299
  Department of Justice..300
  Department of the Navy 300
  U.S. Postal Service..300
  Department of State...300
  Department of the Treasury 300
  Federal Aviation Administration 300
  Federal Maritime Commission...300
  Securities and Exchange Commission 301
  Small Business Administration 301
  Department of Veterans Affairs 301
  Court Records 301
  U.S. District Court...301
  U.S. Bankruptcy Court 301
  U.S. Customs Court 301
  U.S. Tax Court 301
  State District or Circuit Courts 302
  Specialized State Courts...302
 State, County, and Municipal Governments 302
Commercial and Online Databases 303
 Commercial Databases 303
 Online Research...304
Credit-Related Sources 305
 Credit Agencies or Bureaus 305
 Other Credit Reporting Agencies...305
 International Business Ratings 306
 Specialized Commercial Credit Organizations 306
 Other Credit Issuers..306
 Credit Card Issuers 306
Business and Miscellaneous Sources 308
  Business and Industry 308
  Travel and Transportation...308
  Communications 309
  Public Utilities...310
  Insurance Companies..310
  Entertainment..311
 Miscellaneous Sources 311
  The Library...311
  Newspapers...312
 Putting Your Resource Guide Together...312

Chapter 20 Basic Money Laundering Schemes 315
 Use of a Nominee...316
  Objectives 316

- Advantages and Disadvantages 317
- Special Situations 317
- Documentation 317
- Investigation of a Nominee Scheme 318
- Sources of Information 318
- Special Situations 319
- Potential Violations 319
- Simple Business Cover 319
  - Documentation 321
  - Special Situations 322
  - Investigation of a Business Front 322
  - Sources of Information 322
  - Potential Violations 323
- Simple Banking Operation 323
  - Special Situations 323
  - Documentation 325
  - Investigation of a Simple Banking Scheme 325
  - Sources of Information 326
  - Potential Violations 326
- Banking–Business Combination 326
  - Special Situations 327
  - Documentation 327
  - Investigation of a Scheme Involving a Banking–Business Combination 329
  - Sources of Information 329
  - Potential Violations 330
- Summing Up 330

Chapter 21 Diabolically Clever Laundering Schemes 331

- Smurfs and Structured Transactions 331
  - Smurfing in the 1990s 332
  - Investigation of a Smurfing Operation 333
  - Sources of Information 335
  - Potential Violations 335
  - Black Market Peso Exchange Schemes 335
  - Investigation of a Black Market Peso Exchange Operation 336
  - Sources of Information 337
  - Potential Charges 338
  - Financial Action Task Force Description 338
- Shell Corporations 339
  - Documentation 340
  - Investigation of a Shell Corporation 340
    - What does the corporation do? 342
    - What is the capital structure of the corporation? 342
    - What do the financial statements look like? 342
    - Who are the owners of the corporation? 342
    - Who's in charge here? 342

  Sources of Information..342
  Offshore Shell Corporations...343
 Offshore Corporations and the Internet 345
  Offshore Jurisdictions 345
 Loan-Back Schemes 345
  Documentation 348
  Investigation of a Loan-Back Scheme 348
  Sources of Information..348
  Potential Violations...348
  Loan-Back 2 348
  Investigation of the Loan-Back Scheme 349

Chapter 22 Fiendishly Complex Money Laundering Schemes.................................353

 Components of Money Laundering Schemes 353
  Mechanisms for Placement 353
  Mechanisms for Layering 354
  Mechanisms for Integration 354
 Invoice Scams..354
  Underinvoicing 355
  Research on Invoice Schemes 358
  Investigating Invoice Scams 361
  Sources of Information..361
 Buy-Backs..361
  Variation on the Buy-Back Theme 363
  Investigating a Buy-Back Scheme 364
  Sources of Information..364
 Securities Manipulation...364
  Documentation 365
  Investigating a Securities Manipulation 367
  Sources of Information..367

Chapter 23 Terrorism Financing 369

 Financing the PIRA..370
  Needs of Terrorist Groups 370
  Sources of Funding 374
 Investigation of Terrorist Financing...378
  Legal Measures...378
 Money Laundering and Terrorism Financing 381
  Investigative Resources 382
   Suspicious Activity Reports 382
   Tax Returns and Tax Information 382
 Terrorist FundRaising and Financing: The Al Qaeda Terrorism Money
  Trail..384
  Investigating Al Qaeda's Funding 386
  Sources of Information..386

  Zakat Schemes..387
   United States of America v. Holy Land Foundation for Relief and
    Development..387
   Investigating a Zakat Scheme 389
   Sources of Information..389
  Hawala Schemes and Informal Value Transfer Systems 389
   Investigating a Hawala Scheme 391
   Sources of Information..391

Chapter 24 Investigating Money Laundering Cases 393

  Decisions, Decisions …..394
  Case Development Process 394
  Case Initiation..396
   What is the source of this information? 396
   Is the activity ongoing or historical? 397
  Basis for the Investigation..397
  Case Organization 398
   Questions About Participants 398
   Questions About Prosecutor Involvement...399
   Questions About the Case File 399
   Legal Considerations 399
  The Investigative Plan 399
   Evidence Collection...400
   Profiling 401
   Covert Evidence Gathering 401
   Semiovert Evidence Gathering..403
   Overt Evidence Gathering 403
   Evidence Analysis 404
   Presentation..405
  Money Laundering Undercover Operations..407
   Laundering Their Money...407
   Stings: Laundering Our Money...409

Chapter 25 The Case File 411

  Types of Documentary Evidence 412
  Introducing Documentary Evidence in a Financial Case..414
  Document Control 416
   Plan Ahead...417
   Acquisition...417
    Storage and Retrieval 417
    Security 418
    Analysis 418
    Presentation..419
  Exhibits and the Exhibit List 419
   Schedules and Summaries...419

    Case Report 419
    Conclusion 420

Bibliography 425

Appendix A Glossary of Terms Used in Money Laundering Cases 429

Appendix B Source Debriefing Guide 439

Appendix C Subpoena Templates 443

Appendix D Document Search Warrant Example 455

Appendix E Forms 461

Appendix F Federal Statutes Relating to Money Laundering Forfeiture 491

Appendix G Federal Statutes Relating to Terrorist Financing 501

Index 511

CHAPTER 1

BASIC CONCEPTS

"Money is the fruit of evil as often as the root."
Henry Fielding

"The cost of living has gone up another dollar a quart."
W. C. Fields

A stockbroker and a lawyer were sitting in a bar, chatting with the bartender. The lawyer listened as the others argued about the existence of money.

"Of course it's real," the bartender said. "My customers pay me with it. Look, I've got over a hundred bucks right here." He pulled out a wad of dollar bills. "See, you can feel it, hold it, it's real." He handed it to the lawyer, who used it to pay for the drinks.

"Big deal," sneered the stockbroker. "I handled over a million dollars today for some rich widow. Stocks, bonds, mutual funds, foreign exchange, gold, you name it. I never saw anything but little numbers on a computer screen. No way, money definitely does not exist."

Both men turned to the lawyer. "What do you think?" They wanted to know.

The lawyer thought about it. "What did you say that widow's name was?"

MONEY, MONEY, MONEY

As we start our discussion of money laundering, it's helpful to begin with a clear understanding of the nature of *money* itself. In fact, this understanding is essential. Although most of us would not question the existence of money, many would be surprised at how broad its definition has gotten over the past three or four thousand years.

Money is a concept. The idea that some object can be assigned a value and used in trade is ancient, but nearly universal. Whether or not money exists in a physical sense is probably, as our attorney friend pointed out, irrelevant. The inescapable fact is that anywhere you go on this planet, people will be working, fighting, lusting, and scheming for money, and it won't matter to any of them what form the stuff takes.

Author H. G. Wells once commented that money "means in a thousand minds a thousand subtly different, roughly similar, systems of images, associations, suggestions, and impulses." Just about everybody has a perspective on money, and it is not surprising that many of these views differ widely, especially in a world of many cultures, which grows increasingly smaller and more closely linked.

You can't understand money laundering without having a clear understanding of what money is and how it works. If you are like most people, when asked to (to borrow an overworked popular phrase) "show me the money," your first response is usually to hold up the contents of your wallet or purse. For most people, money = cash. If we get technical, though, those contents are really just pieces of paper, metal, and plastic.

Figure 1.1 *Barter in early Egypt, before the invention of money. Early civilizations such as that in Egypt relied heavily on barter as a system of exchange. The Egyptians later used money, making the transition from barter to a cash transaction system. (Source:* Banking Through the Ages*)*

All of these things might be money, but none of them have much value at all, though a credit card makes a good ice scraper in a pinch. A better definition might be, "anything that is generally acceptable as a means of settling a debt." This leaves the field wide open.

The notion of money goes back thousands of years, long before paper or printing, so we'll never know who first dreamed up the idea that some object could be assigned a value and used in trade. All commerce, now and in that distant time, is based upon exchange. Originally, trading took the form of *barter*, in which one item is directly exchanged for another (see Figure 1.1). I'll give you my hammer for your goatskin. You give me your cow for my saddle. Bartering is the most basic form of trade, one which enjoys many advantages, and continues to be practiced today. (For example, if you go to buy a car, you'll be asked if you're going to trade in another vehicle as part of the deal.) The greatest advantage to barter is that both sides wind up with exactly what they need. In the process, they each have a chance to get together, negotiate, and socialize a bit. "Doing lunch" was probably a regular feature of the early barter system.

There are a couple of drawbacks, problems that have caused bartering to be largely replaced by the monetary system of exchange. Some of the negative aspects are obvious. First, there's the fact that there are no assigned values. What if my hammer is worth more than your goatskin? Maybe that hammer is worth a goatskin and a half. But you might not want to cut up that second goatskin, and you may not agree with my opinion of the value of my hammer. I might end up hitting you with it, especially if we're trying to trade across a language or cultural barrier.

Barter is based upon a "double coincidence": You just happen to have something I need, I just happen to have something you need, *and* we're both willing to trade. This works fine when dealing in like-kind items, but things start to get a little complicated if I don't need a goatskin this week, or I do need some meat, which you don't have. If you can trade a goatskin for some meat, I would be willing to trade the hammer.

If a marketplace is available, people can engage in a number of trades, working, talking, getting the best deals they can, eventually winding up with all the things they need, and rid of all the things they don't. Maybe they've come out a little ahead, so they can come back next week. The barter process takes time and depends on goodwill and communication to work. This all works best when everybody stays pretty close to home, but less well when someone travels a long distance only to find that the items he brought to trade are not wanted or needed. Advances in transportation, notably the wheel and sails, made it possible for people to travel farther, increasing their ability to trade, but making barter a riskier proposition.

THE EVOLUTION OF MONEY

Early civilizations such as that in Egypt relied heavily on barter as a system of exchange. The Egyptians later used money, making the transition from barter to a cash transaction system.

Only one improvement was needed to revolutionize the barter system, this being the innovation of money. (Wouldn't you like to have the patent on *that* little invention?) Money has almost all of the advantages of barter, with few of the drawbacks. As stated above, money is a concept, the *idea* that some specific item has value and will be accepted in all types of exchange.

Since it's a concept, money can take any form; at various times, and in various places, almost everything imaginable has been used to represent money. Some of these things had intrinsic value. Tools, such as knives, hatchets, or hoes, were valuable because they were needed in agriculture or food production. People on the American frontier used nails, and we still use the terms "tenpenny" and "fourpenny" as a reference to their value in barter. Cattle are still used as money in some parts of the world.

Other items were valuable because of their scarcity. Gold, silver, copper, and other precious metals have been used as money. Other things, such as ivory, seashells, and whale or bear teeth, may also be scarce, but they have the additional advantage of being somewhat uniform in size and shape, or they can be carved into a specific shape. Still other items, such as tea, tobacco, pepper, and salt, have value as commodities. Easily measured or weighed, these items may also be scarce, and therefore in demand.

Salt was a very common form of money in many parts of the ancient world. Useful as a seasoning, as well as being one of the few means then available of preserving food, salt was so essential to commerce that its name became synonymous with money. "Salary," for example, is derived from the Latin word for salt.

The same Romans who used salt in commerce, paying their soldiers in this currency, also used coins made of metal (see Figure 1.2). Coins were an almost ideal form of money, a fact that has preserved their usefulness for over 2500 years. Coins can be given a precise value, assigned by weight, size, or design. They can be mass produced, with a uniform design that promotes acceptance. They can be made of durable metal, which gives them some permanence, and this metal can be scarce or precious, like gold, giving the coins value. Once again, no one is able to identify the inventor of coins, but they seem to have been common in early societies from China to Africa. The earliest known coins were minted in Lydia, a kingdom in what is now Turkey, in the seventh century BC (see Figure 1.3).

Figure 1.2 A Roman coin.

Many early coins were made of precious metals, such as gold, silver, or copper. Judas, we recall, received 30 pieces of silver for his betrayal of Jesus. One additional benefit of coins over something like seashells was that they allowed some important person — like the king — to put his picture before every member of the society. This caused the downfall of at least one such person, Louis XVI of France. Fleeing the French revolution in disguise, he was supposedly spotted by an alert guardsman who recognized the king's face from a coin. (This can't happen with American money; you have to be dead already to get your portrait on those coins.)

Gold, silver, and copper coins were widely accepted in trade because of their content. A

Figure 1.3 Seventh-century coins. *(from* Banking Through the Ages*)*.

10-g gold coin made in Rome had the same value as a coin of identical weight made in Baghdad. Because there were differences in coins from different places, money changers developed a profitable business exchanging foreign coins for local ones. This profession continued for over a thousand years. During the 16th century, European money changers and merchants kept thick books with pictures identifying hundreds of foreign coins.

But coins had some problems, too. Early mints were not very sophisticated, and their product often looked no better than the counterfeits that were extremely common. Coins could also be clipped or trimmed, some small quantity of gold or silver taken off the edges of each coin, and this minute amount then melted down for its content. Because this directly affected the value of the money and its acceptance, governments took a dim view of the practice, often hanging anybody they caught doing it.

One of the biggest problems with coins was caused by their success. Because coins had come to almost universally represent money, they were accepted almost everywhere people went to trade. It was now possible for a merchant to sail from one Mediterranean city to another, carrying the coins he would need to buy a cargo, secure in the knowledge that the merchants in the distant city would accept his money and sell their goods. Travelers knew that a *shekel* or two would buy them a room and a meal.

Other people also appreciated the value of those coins, and they employed various schemes to get their hands on some, notably piracy and highway robbery. This caused great distress for the merchants, who then, as now, had the political influence that goes along with having money. They sought assistance from their governments in reducing these depredations, and the governments discovered that armies that weren't occupied in beating up on a neighbor's army could be quite useful in suppressing the odd bandit, and that navies were perfectly suited for dealing with pirates. We're not just talking ancient history here, either. General John "Black Jack" Pershing's cavalry pursued Mexican *bandidos* prior to World War I, and navies in Southeast Asia conduct antipiracy to this day. Still, the merchants needed a better solution, and they found it on paper and in banks.

We'll get to the role of banks in promoting commerce in another chapter, but the invention of paper money is important because it takes money away from its roots, and more toward the metaphysical. After all, paper has very little, if any, value. The addition of some ink doesn't change that (though in all modesty, it's done wonders for these pages).

With the use of paper, the concept of money got a major boost. Now, money was really a *promise* to pay or provide something that had real value. In the United States, paper money was originally "backed" by gold. (This was true in Europe also, where goldsmiths made notes backed by the gold they held.) These notes or "gold backs" represented a promise by the government to redeem the bill for its face value in gold. It said so right on the bill. Later, in the 1930s, those same notes became "silver certificates," promising that the bearer could be paid in silver. Still later, the government gave up pretending that a.) everybody in America wanted or was going to demand silver for their paper money, and b.) the government really *had* all that silver stored up somewhere in the first place. Now a Federal Reserve note just says that it is "lawful tender for any debt, public or private," and "In God We Trust," which sort of sums things up nicely.

The Chinese, who probably invented paper, probably also invented paper money, and it was soon a hit everywhere. Again, these notes were promises by the issuer to pay something to the holder, and so long as it enjoys wide acceptance among the people, paper money works quite well. For example, the note in Figure 1.4, issued by the Royal Bank of Scotland in 1777, reads:

> The Royal Bank of Scotland, constituted by Act of Parliament do hereby oblige themselves to pay the Bearer on demand One pound, One Shilling Sterling.

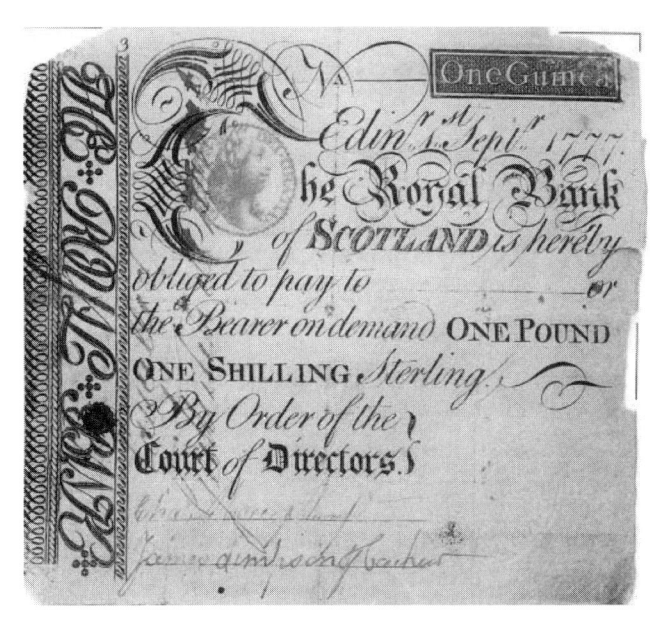

Figure 1.4 *Note issued by the Royal Bank of Scotland in 1777.*

Paper represented the first time that something with no scarcity or intrinsic value was used as money, and the fact that it could be printed up willy-nilly if the mood struck was a problem. Absolute monarchs, used to getting their way on things, could not make up some more gold, no matter how powerful they were, but they could order more bills to be printed. They quickly learned that this sort of thing had a negative outcome as inflation devalued the currency.

Though governments usually recognize the importance of keeping the promise implied on their currency, some paper promises were no good at all. Paper money issued by the Confederate States of America promised to pay the bearer in coin, 2 years after the Civil War ended. That promise and Confederate currency itself were rightly regarded as worthless by almost everybody on both sides of the battle line, even during the war.

Inflation in Germany following World War I, caused by the printing of vast quantities of currency, made the *mark* equally worthless. Mark notes with values up to 200 million were printed, and things got so bad that it was cheaper to burn bank notes than to use them to buy firewood. Figure 1.5 is a 5 million mark note from 1923.

Figure 1.5 *This bank note, with a face value of 5 million marks, was printed in Germany in 1923. Instead of printing millions of low-denomination notes, the German government opted to print bills with more zeros — so many zeros that bank tellers had trouble counting them (Source: Author's collection).*

Money evolved through the ages, but whatever physical form it took, it always retained its key characteristics. Today, money may take the form of paper currency, checks, coins, credit cards, or, increasingly, electronic blips in some computer system, a form that almost perfectly captures the "idea" of money. As we move toward the predicted "cashless society," people will become more comfortable with the idea that their money does not really exist in physical form. Very recently in fact, and for the first time ever, the amount of monetary transactions conducted by debit card exceeded that by paper checks. Not unlike a religion that requires belief in the existence of a supreme being, people will grow to take the idea of money on faith.

Why is this so important for someone learning about money laundering? We must understand that although most money laundering involves some form of currency, *anything* can be used in the laundering process. There have been cases involving diamonds, gold, credit card slips, stocks and bonds, cashier's checks, airplanes, rare coins, livestock, postal money orders, airline tickets, and wire transfers. These schemes are limited only by the imagination of their perpetrators, not by the form the money takes. Once the law enforcement officer understands the concept of money, he or she is much better prepared to recognize laundering schemes when encountered.

Case Example

Agents investigating a drug trafficking operation were told that the owner of a bar was laundering proceeds of the organization's drug sales. Bank records for the bar were subpoenaed, and deposits of several million dollars were discovered. These deposits were far larger than one would expect in a business of this size, but almost none were in cash. Most were personal checks or credit card slips, showing charges for $100 to $200 each — definitely not the usual form of payment for illegal drugs. The investigators were puzzled until an undercover agent reported that the owner kept a large stack of cash behind the bar and made cash advances for bar patrons. The customers got the dirty money, and the bar owner got a nice clean check from the bank that issued the card.

This example directly involves at least three forms of money. The first was the currency used in trade for the drugs. This money was readily accepted by the drug trafficker, and by the bar customers. Second were the credit card slips. These were readily accepted by the bar owner, who knew they would be paid by the banks that issued the credit cards. The bank recognized the credit card slips as having value when they were accepted as part of the deposit. Third was the check, sent by the card issuer's bank to the bar owner. Again, this check was readily accepted by the bar's bank. At various points during these transactions, numerous electronic impulses were sent and received, each indicating that money — in whatever form — was changing hands. (See Figure 1.6.)

Acceptance is one of the principal characteristics of money. If people are willing to accept

Figure 1.6 *Babylonian clay tablet. This tablet documents the production and sale of beer.*

it in trade, it's probably money. (It's definitely money if a bank is willing to accept it.) The economy has become so sophisticated that some really esoteric things are being accepted today. Wall Street traders might not accept a bale of tobacco, which merchants on the same site in 1650 would have taken, but they will deal in tobacco futures, tobacco options, and a variety of other tobacco-related ideas. In fact, ideas that didn't exist 20 years ago are now traded daily.

MONEY LAUNDERING

Now that we all understand the concept of money, we can turn to how exactly it is that money gets laundered. Money laundering has been defined as "the use of money derived from illegal activity by concealing the identity of the individuals who obtained the money and converting it to assets that appear to have come from a legitimate source." We can simplify things by saying that money laundering is a process to make dirty money appear to be clean. The "appearance" part is very important, because, as you will see, under American law, dirty money is never "clean," no matter how many times it goes through the rinse and spin cycle.

A few years back, a well-known stage magician performed the amazing feat of making the Statue of Liberty disappear right before the eyes of thousands of people in New York and millions more on TV. A similar stunt involves the magical transformation of a beautiful magician's assistant into a tiger or some such.

We all know that the Statue of Liberty didn't *really* disappear, although we have no idea how the magician made it *appear* to have done so. Well, money laundering is a lot like stage magic, in case you were wondering where we were going with this. The money doesn't *really* disappear, it just changes form and gets harder to find. And it never *really* gets clean — it just looks that way. The job of the money launderer is, like the magician, to use proven and secret techniques to make money obtained in one (dirty) way appear to have been acquired elsewhere.

Some money launderers are pretty good at it, too, but just as the stage magician is limited by the laws of nature, the money launderer is constrained by man-made laws, especially those governing the operation of the world's financial system. Some statutes have been specifically written to make the detection of money laundering easier. Among these are laws relating to currency transaction reporting. Other laws impose a criminal sanction for laundering money, increasing the risk factor in illegal transactions. From either side of the coin, flexibility is the key to success or failure in money laundering operations. The criminals are looking for as much flexibility as possible, and governments are trying to limit them.

The problem for money launderers is partially historical and somewhat immutable, and it relates to the methods people use to exchange goods and services. We'll call these methods exchange or transaction systems. Remember that in the beginning, there was barter. People just traded things they didn't need for other things that they did. This system worked up to a point, but it was superseded by the invention of money. Cash, in the form of coin or paper money, completely replaced barter almost everywhere. This cash transaction system worked well, and still does, but it isn't perfect, so we keep trying to improve on it.

These improvements have taken the form of financial institutions, banks, checks, records, accounting, and lots of paperwork — not nearly as much fun as going out and spending loads of cold cash. The result was a financial or business transaction system that is safer, generates detailed and often permanent records, and is widely used in businesses everywhere around the world.

Unfortunately for the criminals seeking to hide ill-gotten gains, this financial or business system of conducting transactions was not set up for concealing things; quite the opposite, in fact. In some cases, the system will accommodate the launderer, but in most instances, it is the criminal who must make concessions to the system. Even in places where bank secrecy is a rule, massive amounts of records are maintained to document transactions or financial activity. The launderer can reduce but never eliminate this exposure, often by seeking out places where law or custom afford more flexibility. See Table 1.1 for a list of the advantages and disadvantages of transactions systems to money launderers.

The anonymity of cash provides this flexibility, and, of course, the cash transaction system is used for the vast majority of illegal activity. No matter how much one might like to, it is no longer possible to live on a completely cash basis. At some point, whether it means acquiring an asset or just using a bank, you're going to have to change systems. The first major truism about money laundering is that *every money laundering scheme ever devised relies upon the movement of money. And the movement of money from a cash transaction system to a business transaction system is where the money launderer is most vulnerable.*

People who have studied the problem have characterized money laundering as a cycle, the objective of which is to have access to "clean"-appearing money at the end of the process. The Financial Crimes Enforcement Network (FinCEN) is the federal agency charged with developing money laundering responses. FinCEN describes the money laundering process as having three stages: *placement, layering,* and *integration.*

In the placement stage, the form of the money is changed or converted. Because most modern criminal activity, particularly the drug trade, relies upon cash as an initial medium of exchange, placement mechanisms usually involve either the conversion of currency into some other form or the physical movement of the currency. For example, large amounts of cash received from drug sales are converted to cashier's checks or are deposited in multiple trans-

TABLE 1.1
Advantages and Disadvantages of Transaction Systems to Money Launderers

Cash Transaction System	Business Transaction System
Advantages	*Advantages*
Everyone has cash to pay for illegal goods and services.	There is greater efficiency and security in the transfer of funds.
Lack of records makes it difficult to connect a person with a criminal activity or with the purchase of illicit goods or services.	Losses owing to employee theft are controllable.
Unreported revenues are not taxed.	Other business opportunities are available, such as legitimate investment in real estate and securities.
Currency is universally accepted.	A legitimate business is a valuable base of operations and source of cash for criminal activities.
Disadvantages	Ownership of a business permits acquisition of community standing and influence, which provides additional camouflage for illegal operations.
In large amounts, cash is suspicious, and calls attention to those who hoard it.	*Disadvantages*
Lack of records makes it difficult to prevent theft by employees.	Taxes must be paid on reported revenues.
Large amounts of cash are difficult to handle and transport.	Business records are subject to examination by authorities.
Certain assets cannot be acquired for cash without an extensive inquiry into the source.	Falsification of records is a criminal act and can lead to prosecution even without proof of other criminal activities.
	Transactions have a source and destination that can lead to the criminal activity.
	Chart reproduced from *Financial Investigations: A Financial Approach to Detecting and Resolving Crimes.*

actions into bank accounts. The form of the money has been changed, and it is now one step away from its illegal origin.

Placement of dirty money relies on businesses that deal heavily in cash, as well as financial institutions of all types. Cash, though anonymous in that it leaves no paper trail, does attract attention when used in certain situations. Large cash transactions are also subject to various reporting requirements imposed by federal law, bringing more unwanted attention. Many placement mechanisms are directed at positioning the funds in a bank or financial institution. This represents a trade-off for the launderer. Upside: All that cash has now become just another electronic blip in that vast sea of money. Downside: Once in the bank, a paper trail is automatically begun, a trail that leads in two directions from the initial deposit. (See Figure 1.7 for an early example of a paper trail.)

Figure 1.7 *Babylonian clay accounting tablet. The first known accounting records exist in the form of clay tablets from early Babylon. These records imply that money was in use, and that a "paper trail" was being created, or in this case, a baked clay tablet trail (Source:* Banking Through the Ages*).*

In the layering stage, launderers attempt to hide their tracks on the paper trail. As the name implies, layers of transactions, business entities, fronts, or other concealment mechanisms are imposed between the money and its source. These layers may involve other countries, places where bank secrecy makes following the money trail difficult or impossible.

In the United States, the paper trail can be broken only with difficulty. Federal laws and regulations govern the operation of banks, financial institutions, and even businesses that accept large amounts of cash. These statutes are specifically designed to ensure that a trail is left behind every significant financial transaction. The Bank Secrecy Act (BSA) is the most important of these anti-money laundering record-keeping laws.

The BSA, passed by Congress in 1970, required a number of records to be made or kept, not just by the banks named in the title, but also by individuals who conducted certain transactions. Specifically, the BSA required that:

- Financial institutions must maintain certain records for certain fixed amounts of time. The purpose of this requirement was strictly to guarantee that those records would be there when an investigator came looking for the proceeds of criminal activity or tax evasion. In most cases, the records were already being kept by banks, which are regulated by assorted federal and state agencies. In any case, the records required by the BSA are consistent with good business and banking practices.
- Certain cash transactions conducted at a financial institution must be reported to the Treasury Department. Deposits, withdrawals, cashier's check purchases, currency exchanges, and any other transaction involving cash above a certain amount (Treasury regulations set this amount at $10,000) require that a report be sent to the Internal Revenue Service.
- Individuals who are citizens or resident aliens who maintain an interest in, or hold signature authority over, a foreign bank account must report this fact to IRS on an annual basis. This applies if the account has a balance during the year over a certain amount, again set by regulation at $10,000.
- Individuals who transport cash or certain monetary instruments into or outside the United States must report that fact to the Customs Service if the amount exceeds a level defined by regulation. (Originally this amount was $5,000, but it was increased to $10,000, consistent with the other BSA requirements.)

All of these things were done for the sole purpose of creating a paper trail for cash transactions. In theory, at least, every large cash transaction could now be traced from the time the money first hit the financial system. The anonymity afforded by cash was to be sharply curtailed. This directly impacted the placement and layering stages of the money laundering cycle. After 1970, the deposit of large amounts of cash would trigger a report, making discreet placement of dirty cash more difficult. The recordkeeping requirements ensured that a trail would be maintained after the initial cash transaction, no matter how many layers were subsequently imposed.

Two methods have always been most popular for breaking the trail: cash transactions and use of offshore banks and businesses that aren't legally bound to follow all those recordkeeping or reporting requirements. Most layering efforts involved one or both of these methods. The BSA addressed each. People taking the money offshore were supposed to report it, and foreign bank accounts were also supposed to be reported. Any withdrawal and redeposit of cash from the system was supposed to trigger more reports. The intent of this legislation was to decrease the flexibility of the criminal, forcing him or her into more inefficient and hazardous methods of laundering dirty money.

Unfortunately, the problem is so enormous, and the financial system so huge, that much of this illegal activity goes undetected. If the place-

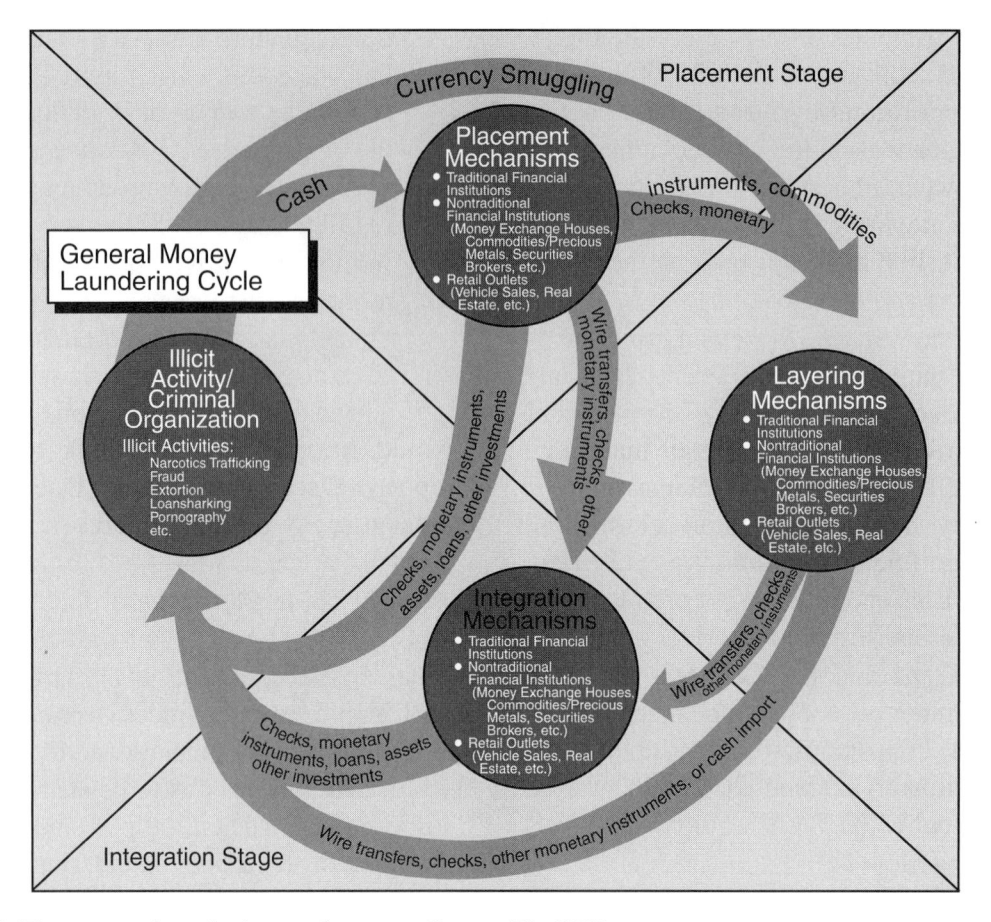

Figure 1.8 The money laundering cycle, according to FinCEN.

ment and layering stages have been successfully completed, the launderer attempts to integrate the laundered funds back into a form the criminal can enjoy. This enjoyment may entail the use of the funds to further the illegal activity, or just carefree spending.

Integration mechanisms use the same financial institutions and instruments employed in the other stages, with a slightly different objective. At this stage, the apparent *source* of the funds is the main focus. The launderer now needs to make the funds look as if their origin is legitimate, resulting in some really creative schemes and explanations that we'll explore later.

THE MONEY LAUNDERING CYCLE

The Financial Crimes Enforcement Network has developed the following model of the money laundering cycle, which includes the three stages discussed above: placement, layering, and integration. We will use an actual money laundering scheme to illustrate the three stages. (See Figure 1.8.)

Case Example

John Doe (not his real name) was a successful narcotics trafficker, whose methamphetamine business generated substantial income. Like many of his contemporaries, Doe didn't have any legitimate employment, and could not explain the wealth he had acquired from his clandestine drug sales.

Doe needed cash — his suppliers insisted on it as payment for the drugs they sold him — but he had far more cash than was necessary for purchases. Doe didn't want to lose the cash to a government forfeiture action, and he was also afraid of the questions the Internal Revenue Service might ask. Doe needed a money laundering scheme.

The scheme had to do several things. First, it had to change the form of the money from cash into something he could use without attracting attention (placement). Second, Doe didn't want to be connected to the source of the funds (layering). Finally, Doe wanted to look legit, like he'd made his money the old-fashioned way — honestly (integration).

His scheme was simple. Doe managed to get a large amount of cash, $275,000, into a bank account held by his mother. This required a number of deposits, all made in amounts well under $10,000. Some of the drug money had now been successfully placed — its form converted. He had also layered the transaction, putting another person between himself and the money. Doe could have created several other bank accounts, used some other nominees, and moved the money around some more, further insulating himself, but he didn't think it was worth the trouble. This was a mistake.

Next, Doe arranged for the purchase of a small convenience store, located on the ground floor of a large condominium/office complex. The store was acquired with the $275,000 in Mom's bank account, and her name was placed on the title. Mom generously hired her son to be the manager of the store. This provided Doe with a ready explanation for his income. He could even file a tax return, declaring the salary he earned. And it wasn't hard work. He hired a clerk to actually sell things in the store. Apparently the manager's primary duties involved going to the bank and depositing the day's receipts into the business checking account. Doe was happy to do this, especially since the business had turned so profitable immediately after he took over.

Looking at the records for the business checking account, investigators were interested to note that deposits were averaging around $3000 daily. This seemed like quite a lot of money, especially since the checks that were being written for the goods sold in the store didn't account for nearly that many sales. $3000 a day is a lot of Cheetos and Coke. The prior owner was also impressed. When interviewed, she reported that her gross sales had been more like $300 daily, or about $9000 per month. After overhead, cost of sales, and other expenses, she had been lucky to clear $2000 in profit each month, one of the reasons why she sold the place.

Doe's deposits, though almost all in cash, weren't generating any Currency Transaction Reports to IRS, because the deposits were all much less than the $10,000 that would have caused the bank to file the reports. Once in the bank, Doe used the money to pay his very liberal salary and to prepare for the acquisition of another property. Doe had documented income from a legitimate source that he could use to get a mortgage loan, buy a car, or use for whatever purpose he chose. His drug money had been successfully integrated.

This money laundering scheme is elementary, but the perpetrator managed to cover all the bases. He moved the money from one transaction system (cash) to another (business). He successfully created the illusion of legitimate wealth. In the next few chapters, we'll look at some ways of puncturing this illusion.

REX V. WILLIAM KIDD, ET AL.: A CASE OF PIRACY

As Henry Every's problems demonstrate, pirates aren't especially well known for their money laundering expertise. When most people think of pirates and their loot, they think of buried treasure. As a money laundering scheme, digging a hole and dumping a box in it doesn't go very deep into the cycle, and all the contents of that dead man's chest are still hot as a pirate's pistol. (See Figure 1.9.)

Burying the treasure is a bad plan for several reasons, not the least of which is that nobody, not even the pirate captain, has the use of any of the money while it's in the ground. This is why burying the treasure was actually not a very

Figure 1.9 *How not to launder money. This 1894 painting by Howard Pyle pictures the infamous Captain William Kidd supervising the burial of pirate treasure on a small island in Long Island Sound (Source:* Harper's Magazine, *1894).*

widespread practice in the pirate business, Long John Silver and his map notwithstanding.

The so-called "Golden Age" of piracy was a relatively short period of time a few years either side of 1700. During this time, pirates ran wild on the Spanish Main, in the Caribbean, and off the African coasts. Piracy grew with trade from Europe to the Americas, Africa, and India, and the maritime nations of Europe, especially England and Spain, recognized the growing threat to their commerce.

Serious efforts were made to curb piracy, including naval patrols and the use of convoys escorted by heavily armed naval vessels. Some pirates were killed or captured in fierce sea battles like the one that ended Edward "Blackbeard" Teach's career. Others were caught and taken to England or the American colonies, tried, and hanged.

Despite the risk, many sailors turned to piracy for the "easy" money, the freedom, or just to escape the harsh discipline of a naval or merchant vessel. Others became pirates almost by accident. Captain William Kidd originally started out as a pirate chaser, commissioned to catch buccaneers preying on British ships, one of whom, coincidentally, was Henry Every.

Kidd went "wrong," however, and soon amassed a considerable store of treasure himself. Although he is believed to have buried treasure on at least one occasion, Kidd actually had a pretty solid money laundering scam, and one which was used by most of his contemporaries.

Romantic though that "fifteen men on a dead man's chest" myth is, the fact is that most pirate loot was quickly converted to spendable cash via a money laundering scheme that involved many of the most prominent names in early America. From Charleston, South Carolina, to New York and Boston, otherwise honest merchants and government officials were cheerful participants in the scheme to launder pirate loot. In fact, some towns were heavily dependent on funds from smuggling or piracy.

Piracy was an expensive proposition. There was the cost of the pirate ship, though many of these were acquired as a result of a hostile takeover. Once acquired, the crew needed to be fed and paid, the ship maintained, and the guns stocked with powder and shot. Again, some of these needs could be supplied by theft, but many pirates obtained all they needed in friendly ports. There, merchants would provide naval stores, food, clothing, beer, wine, and ammunition, while corrupt public officials turned a blind eye to the presence of the marauders in their midst.

Frederick Philipse, a New York businessman and ship owner whose records are shown in Figure 1.10, was a good example. Philipse prospered in the money laundering business until 1698, when he was dismissed from his position as governor's councilor for suspicion of dealing with pirates. He was never prosecuted and died in 1702 still a very wealthy man.

An 18th-century author wrote about the pirates:

> They walk the streets with their pockets full of gold and are the constant companion of the chief in the Government. They threaten my life and those who were active in apprehending them; carry their prohibited goods publicly in boats from one place to another for a market; threaten the lives of the King's collectors and with force and arms rescue the goods from them. All these parts swarm with pirates, so that if some speedy and effectual course be not taken the trade with America will be ruined.

(Substitute "drug dealer" for "pirates" and you've got a fair description of the state of affairs in some parts of the world 300 years later.)

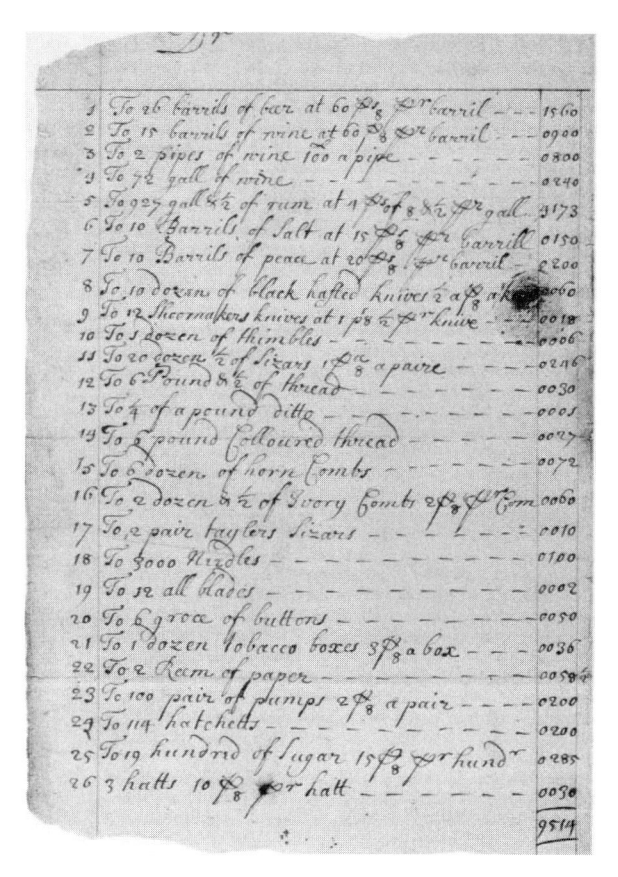

Figure 1.10 *Money laundering pirate style. This ledger, from the records of New York merchant and ship owner Frederick Philipse, records the sale of merchandise to pirates in the 1690s. Philipse, a very prominent man of the period, charged 9514 pieces of eight (Spanish coins) for items that included "26 barrils of wine at 60 pcs 8 pr barril" (Source: Government Records Office).*

None of this would have been possible if the pirates buried their loot after stealing it. Most of the pirates operating from the American colonies preyed on Spanish ships, taking "great quantities of silver coins and bullion, with rich capes, church plate and other riches, insomuch that the Spanish ambassador complained thereof." (Surveyor of customs, Pennsylvania 1697). The governors of the American colonies were not receptive to these Spanish complaints, not least because many were being well paid by those same pirates. The complicity of public officials made the task of converting all of that bullion and plate much easier.

The pirates' money laundering scheme relied upon placement of the loot with reputable Amer-

Figure 1.11 *Piece of eight. Spanish coin and object of pirate desire.*

ican merchants, who converted the Spanish pieces of eight (see Figure 1.11) and doubloons into shillings, crowns, and guineas, or exchanged them for merchandise. Captured ships' cargoes were also sold in American ports to merchants eager to buy. There was no real need for layering, since the pirates operated openly and their suppliers eagerly accepted the money offered for equipment and supplies.

Integration of the laundered funds became important only if the pirate decided to retire, as Every did, to Merry Old England. There, hanging awaited those apprehended, but lack of records made it possible for a retired buccaneer to return to England with a fortune earned in the colonies at some apparently legitimate business. Some undoubtedly did, while others enjoyed the protection their money bought in America.

What are the 300-year-old lessons these pirates provide? First, money laundering is a much easier proposition if you have the cooperation and assistance of people in government, banking, and business. Second, without an effective process for laundering money, pirates would not have been able to continue their activity. In places like England, where the pirates were not able to launder their money easily, the underlying crime was not a major problem, definitely not to the extent that it was elsewhere.

These are assuredly things to contemplate three centuries later, as we face an enormously profitable and corruptive drug trade. Keeping the criminals from enjoying their money is the whole point of forfeiture laws, and keeping that money from corrupting the financial system and government is a prime objective of today's money laundering statutes.

MONEY LAUNDERING FACTS

Some of the same locations that once served as pirate bases are now havens for money laundering activity. Coincidence? Not really. Both piracy and money laundering are directly related to legitimate commerce. Both activities profit from being located near major population and commercial centers — but not in jurisdictions that are heavily regulated

Pirates avoided places where the laws against their crime were strictly enforced, and money launderers seek out jurisdictions that do not have money laundering statutes or controls over financial activity. Another example of the old saying that "the more things change, the more they remain the same."

KEY POINTS TO CONSIDER

- Money is a concept, and its forms are limited only by the imagination.
- Money is used in two transaction systems: cash and business.
- Money laundering is a process of making dirty money appear to be clean, but laundered funds are *never* really clean.
- The movement of dirty money, especially between the transaction systems, creates vulnerabilities law enforcement can exploit.

The money laundering cycle consists of three stages: placement, layering, and integration.

CHAPTER 2

THE HISTORICAL CONTEXT

> John Dean: *It will cost money. It is dangerous. People around here are not pros at this sort of thing. This is the sort of thing Mafia people can do: washing money, getting clean money and things like that. We just don't know about those things, because we are not criminals and not used to dealing in that business.*
> Richard Nixon: *That's right.*
> Dean: *It's a tough thing to know how to do.*
> Nixon: *Maybe it takes a gang to do that.*
>
> Excerpt from President Richard Nixon's White House Tapes, April 21, 1973

White House Counsel John Dean had a couple of things right in his assessment of money laundering. It does cost money to do the job right, and it sure can be dangerous — as he and his boss were soon to find out. Money laundering *is* also the kind of thing the Mafia does, but others do it, too. In fact, as both Dean and Nixon knew, many close to the president had been laundering campaign contributions for a while and had gotten quite good at it.

Why is money laundering so important? How has it gotten to its place of prominence in organized crime today? Criminals like Henry Every knew, after all, that bad things could happen to them if their loot was traced to them. Some in history had even developed some fairly effective plans for avoiding this problem. Still, nobody was very serious until the government figured out a way to take away the ill-gotten gains.

Al Capone's troubles came as a giant wake-up call to criminals everywhere. Here was a man who had climbed to the very top of his chosen profession, creating an organization grossing an estimated $100 million annually. Capone's conviction on charges of tax evasion and his attention-getting 11-year Alcatraz vacation were milestone events in law enforcement. (See Figure 2.1.)

For the first time, criminals could be jailed, not for their participation in some murder, shakedown, or drug deal, but solely because they had made some money and didn't report it. If anyone had been paying attention (and the smart ones were), they knew by 1932 that something was going to have to change.

They tried challenging the law. Bootlegger Manley Sullivan was the first to question whether dirty money could be taxed under the relatively new federal income tax statute. The United States Supreme Court, in ruling against Sullivan, said that it saw no reason "the fact that a business is unlawful should exempt it from paying the taxes that if lawful it would have to pay." The Court also ruled against Sullivan's claim that admitting to the income would violate his Fifth Amendment privilege against self-incrimination.

After the 1927 *Sullivan* decision, the Treasury Department moved out smartly against other illegal wage earners, the most notable of whom was the King of Chicago, Alphonse Capone. Capone's defeat meant that the pro-

Figure 2.1 *Al Capone's Alcatraz mugshot pictures Capone at the end of the line. (Source: National Park Service.)*

ceeds of bootlegging, prostitution, gambling, and assorted corruption were all subject to the government's taxing authority; anyone in those businesses was now on notice that the "easy money" wasn't quite as easy any more.

Some didn't get the message. Frank Nitti, Capone's right-hand man and eventual successor, did a short stretch for tax evasion. After taking over Capone's operation, Nitti came into the sights of the tax men again and committed suicide as he was about to be arrested on new tax evasion charges. Others, however, learned the message well. One of these was Meyer Lansky (see Figure 2.2).

Born Maier Suchowljansky in Poland, the man who would become the financial genius of organized crime fought his way through the world of crime and gangs in New York City. The streets of New York were dangerous places in the early 1900s, and young immigrants from all over Europe banded together in gangs for self-defense and to profit from a wide array of criminal activity.

Lansky had a terrible and violent reputation. Although he was known for extreme brutality, including contract murders, he was also smart and politically savvy. Lansky affiliated himself not only with the Jewish gangsters, but also with Italian elements headed by Salvatore Luciana, also known as Charles "Lucky" Luciano. This alliance, forged early in Lansky's criminal career, would be the foundation of organized crime in America for the next five decades.

Meyer Lansky was more than a hired killer and cofounder of "Murder, Incorporated." Lansky understood business. He also appreciated the critical relationship between truly "organized" crime, business, and politics, this as a result of an association with another Jewish gangster from New York, Arnold "The Big Bankroll" Rothstein.

Three key elements of what would become a criminal enterprise with a worldwide reach were visible even in Lansky's earliest days in crime. First, he clearly grasped the value of businesses, both as "fronts" for illegal activities such as bootlegging and as mechanisms to launder money. One of his closest friends, Benjamin "Bugsy" Siegel, is credited with founding the gambling mecca of Las Vegas — with Lansky's financial backing. Lansky once boasted of organized crime, "We're bigger than United States Steel." It's not a coincidence that he chose a multinational corporation for comparison.

Second, Lansky, better than anyone before him, fully appreciated the usefulness of foreign countries as havens for his criminal activity. Although he is best known for his attempted takeover in 1958 of Cuba as a base for gambling and possibly drug trafficking operations, Lansky was involved in offshore activity as early as the 1920s.

He was believed to have killed Capone associate Sam Bloom, gaining control over profitable bootlegging operations in the Bahamas in 1929, and was heavily involved in bootlegging through Canada. Later in life Lansky would hold untold millions in Swiss bank accounts, using banks and corporations in Hong Kong, Israel, Switzerland,

Figure 2.2 *Meyer Lansky. (Source: FBI.)*

various South American countries, and just about anywhere else a dollar could be made or hidden.

Finally, Lansky understood the need for organized crime to work in concert with flexible government officials. Some of these, like those corrupted in the Batista regime in Cuba, were brought on board wholesale, while others were selected for their ability to assist in one area or on one issue. In this, Lansky learned well from Rothstein, whose political connections were legendary.

The intent of all these machinations was to launder hundreds of millions of dollars in mob money. This became Meyer Lansky's role later in life, as he left the more mundane aspects of crime to his associates. If there is a patron saint of money launderers, it's probably Meyer the Bug. When he died in 1983, he had beaten every tax evasion and related criminal case brought against him, never suffering a day's incarceration for the king's ransom he laundered for the mob.

Lansky's sophistication in laundering money for organized crime was instructive for his many associates. Some took the lesson, safely hiding their money, building networks of legitimate businesses, and moving their money offshore. Others were less successful. Mickey Cohen, an associate of Lansky and Siegel, received 15 years for tax evasion in 1961. Frank Costello got five years in 1954. Albert Anastasia, supposedly the head of the Murder, Inc. syndicate organized by Lansky, received a year for a tax case in 1955. Tony Accardo, who followed Frank Nitti and Paul "The Waiter" Ricca into Capone's old chair in Chicago, got six years in 1960, although the conviction was later reversed on appeal.

There were many other examples, enough that the lesson was clear: If you are going to the trouble of making all that money, you'd better find some way to hide it. Lansky lived this motto, and, ironically, we can't really tell just how sophisticated were Lansky's schemes, because most were apparently never detected. Some of the more grandiose, like his takeovers of Cuba and Paradise Island in the Bahamas, as well as his indirect influence over the entire Nevada gaming industry, hint at a laundering operation so big it almost defies imagination.

One author has commented that Lansky's schemes were not complete, in the sense that they did not fully integrate the money back into the American economy. While it's true that this would leave incomplete the cycle as described in the last chapter, the fact that many millions of dollars disappeared for decades — and have never turned up — certainly argues that Lansky figured out how to integrate at least some of the money.

By the time he died in 1983, Lansky would have known that this last step was more important than ever. By 1983, money laundering had become even more essential, and not just to the "Mafia," as John Dean put it. One word describes the reason for this new urgency: Congress.

In 1919, the year before Prohibition went into effect, there was considerable speculation in this country as to whether such a law could be constitutional. There were serious questions about the limits on the enforcement powers of the federal government, not to mention the practical consideration that federal law enforcement agencies were small, narrowly focused, and fiscally shaky. The entire Special Intelligence Unit at Internal Revenue had six agents. (Today's equivalent, the IRS Criminal Investigation Division, has almost 3000.)

The federal criminal code consisted of fewer than 100 code sections in Title 18, and very few statutes with criminal penalties existed elsewhere in the United States Code. Today, Title 18 runs over 700 pages and has hundreds of sections, and there are criminal sanctions under dozens of other titles. Once Congress decided that it had the power to make this or that illegal, it wound up making *lots* of things illegal. One of the unanticipated outcomes of all this legislating was to make the laundering of illegal money a key part of many criminal enterprises.

Much of the new legislation related to financial crime and was written to prevent certain transactions. For example, Congress passed statutes governing the financing of elections, prohibiting contributions from foreigners and corporations, and, later, prohibiting anonymous or cash donations. The *intent* of this legislation was to clean up campaign financing, making office seekers accountable for the funds they raised. The *effect* of the legislation was to force foreigners, corporations, and, later, anonymous or cash donors to launder their contributions so they wouldn't get caught.

In another example, Congress passed a statute banning the payment of bribes by American companies to foreign governments or individuals. This law didn't stop bribery — there have been several scandals and criminal cases brought since enactment. What it did do, since foreign officials didn't stop demanding bribes, was make corporations launder the bribe monies more effectively.

The same thing happened with other legislation, but the big gun that changed everybody's attitude was forfeiture. By the 1970s, billions of dollars were being made in the illegal drug trade, but none of it was forfeitable. Drugs were big business, but the profits were subject only to taxation by IRS. When, in 1978, Congress amended Title 21, Section 881 to provide for the forfeiture of the proceeds of drug transactions, being a dope dealer got a lot more complicated, and the drug business changed forever.

Congress changed some other businesses forever, too, making forfeiture a tool in the prosecution of Racketeer Influenced and Corrupt Organizations (RICO) and other crimes. Being linked to the proceeds of these crimes now became extremely hazardous, for both the criminal and the assets. Asset forfeiture is like a reverse image of a neutron bomb — it leaves the people standing but takes all their property. If you were a drug dealer or a racketeer and you weren't concerned about these developments, you were most likely in for a very rude shock.

Money laundering now became more of a necessity, an integral part of the overall scheme. Vast quantities of drug money were being laundered, increasingly traveling backward along the same routes on which the drugs were imported. And with the drug problem growing, perceptive observers could see that the money laundering situation was going to get worse.

Congress took several steps to address this new problem. One of these, the Bank Secrecy Act of 1970 (BSA), was a response to perceived problems with the movement of dirty money to tax haven and bank secrecy countries. The BSA provided for criminal penalties for the types of actions that make up most money laundering schemes — movement of funds offshore, concealing the placement of the funds in financial institutions, and the unreported holding of foreign bank accounts. The BSA also included forfeiture provisions, making violation of the statute financially as well as personally risky.

The BSA is not a true money laundering statute; those were to come later. As we'll see when we look at money laundering scams, the BSA does effectively address the mechanics of a laundering scheme, however; it's one of the legal roadblocks Congress and law enforcement have thrown up to make life harder for the criminals.

If I'm a drug dealer, my goals are pretty basic: sell the dope without getting caught. Ultimately, I'd like to stay free long enough to spend my drug money, but the government has put obstacles in the way. Now, that money becomes not only an asset but also a liability, and I have to consider that:

1. IRS will wonder how I got it and take it away.
2. DEA *knows* how I got it and will take it away.

I might decide that I'd better launder the money so that these things don't happen, but the BSA roadblocks make this path more difficult, and the laws preventing money laundering make that activity a crime, too. Congress, cleverly anticipating that I might go down that road, passed those laws to make it harder to do any of the things necessary to launder money effectively.

I can't just put it in the bank, because the banker's going to fill out a Currency Transaction Report (CTR) for all large transactions.

I can't just take it out of the country, because Customs can take it if I don't report it and fill out a Currency and Monetary Instrument Report (CMIR).

I can't just deposit it into my foreign bank account unless I report that, too.

With the passage of actual money laundering prohibitions, I can't just do a few more things, all of which serve to make my original objective — spending the money — much harder to attain. The first federal statute criminalizing money laundering itself was passed in 1986, imposing severe penalties for the conduct of financial transactions designed to launder dirty money. Under this new statute, certain crimes were identified as "Specified Unlawful Activities" or SUAs. Transactions involving the proceeds of these SUAs were now criminal offenses in and of themselves. Yet another hazard was imposed upon the criminal element.

In the almost 20 years since, many money laundering cases centered on drug trafficking, probably the most lucrative of the SUAs covered by Title 18 U.S.C., Sections 1956 and 1957. But prosecutors, recognizing the value of these charges, began using the statutes against criminals engaged in a breathtaking array of crimes. Money laundering cases have been made against arms sellers, corrupt public officials, robbers, timber thieves, and extortionists, and in crimes involving all sorts of fraud or theft. Corporate CEOs in multibillion-dollar fraud cases have found themselves looking at money laundering charges.

Since 1986, Congress has steadily expanded the number of crimes considered SUAs, added a money laundering conspiracy section, and generally broadened the scope of the statute, which also provides for the forfeiture of assets involved in laundering transactions. These statutes, combined with the provisions of the Bank Secrecy Act, are the most efficient obstacles to money laundering yet put into place. Most recently, the USA PATRIOT Act, passed after the terrorist attacks of September 11, 2001, have broadened the money laundering statutes even further and made the reach of these laws literally worldwide.

Others were watching, with the result that many states have enacted their own versions of the federal laws. Foreign governments have also begun treating money laundering as a crime, with many adopting prohibitions similar to those in the United States. The world, such a big playground for the launderer, has become a slightly more perilous place.

There is too much money at stake for the criminals to simply give up, however. Estimates of money laundering activity worldwide range from $200 to $500 *billion* annually. Because they can't just do things their way anymore, launderers' schemes have grown more complex and sophisticated. Specialists, well trained in the world of capital and finance, have come onto the scene, advising criminals on the best ways of disposing of the huge amounts of cash generated by drug crimes. Corruption of government officials or the representatives of financial institutions is rather common in some areas of the world; $500 billion buys a lot of influence and can pay for some pretty good schemes, too.

Law enforcement has responded to those schemes with financial task forces, High Intensity Financial Crimes Area (HIFCA) task forces, intelligence centers, and the Financial Crimes Enforcement Network. In the game of chess that is money laundering, the move–countermove sequence continues.

Case Study: Watergate: Money Laundering in Politics

"I am not a crook."

President Richard M. Nixon, November 17, 1973

"Follow the money."

W. Mark Felt, the informant known as "Deep Throat," to reporter Bob Woodward, in *All the President's Men*

The political scandal that would ultimately cost Richard Nixon his job didn't start out as much. A security officer found some tape on a door lock and called the police to investigate a possible burglary. Three plainclothes officers responded to the call at Washington's exclusive Watergate complex. Some of the nation's richest and most powerful people maintained apartments in the complex, which also housed a hotel and a number of office suites.

A suspected burglary at the Watergate is always taken seriously, but nobody initially had any idea just how serious this one was. Police officers checking the offices of the Democratic National Committee on the sixth floor were startled to discover five men in suits and surgical gloves, none of whom belonged there and all of whom were immediately arrested.

The scandal, now known simply as "Watergate," began on the morning of June 17, 1972. Most Americans know about the burglary and the ultimate outcome: indictments, convictions, and the resignation of the president. Many would also know that Richard Nixon was forced from office, not because of his involvement in what he called a "third-rate burglary," but because of his role in a "cover-up" of the truth about the scandal.

Fewer today are aware that the thing Nixon and all the president's men were covering up was not the burglary, but a money laundering scheme. It was money that put the Watergate conspirators in positions where they could wield vast powers, but it was money — improperly laundered money — that would bring them all down. Deep Throat's advice to Bob Woodward to follow this money was the key to unraveling the entire Watergate affair.

Over at the White House on the morning of the arrests, the news that the burglars had been busted was bad, but certainly not fatal. One of the men in custody, James McCord, was a security officer for the Committee to Re-Elect the President (officially CRP, but known to reporters as "Creep"). None of the other four, all Cuban-Americans from Miami, had any overtly embarrassing ties. One of the men had a White House phone number in his possession, not something the arresting officers saw every day, but other than this there were no obvious links to the administration.

The police had noticed that these burglars were very well equipped; they had bugging equipment and a walkie-talkie. And four were discovered to be in possession of substantial amounts of currency. Eugenio Martinez had $814 in his pockets, $700 of which was in $100 bills with sequential serial numbers. Frank Sturgis had $215, and Virgilio Gonzalez and Bernard Barker each had $230. Most of this money was also in $100 bills in sequence, and more money was found downstairs. Altogether, police recovered $4500 of the crisp, new hundreds — money the burglars had apparently brought with them to the scene of the crime.

Investigators immediately began trying to trace these funds, aided by the fact that in 1972 all American banks were recording the serial numbers of $100 bills given out to customers. They followed the money trail to the Federal Reserve Bank of Atlanta, to its Miami branch, and from there to the Republic National Bank of Miami, FL, which, coincidentally, was the hometown of four of the five burglars.

In Miami, investigators learned that the bills had been given to Bernard Barker, one of the men they'd arrested. Barker had taken this money in a series of cash withdrawals from the trust account of his company, Barker and Associates, Inc., a realty firm. Barker had made three cash withdrawals totaling $114,000 from this account: $25,000 on April 24; $33,000 on May 2; and $56,000 on May 8, 1972.

Investigators now went the other direction along the money trail, trying to find out where the $114,000 had come from. They found that on April 20, Barker had made a deposit of exactly $114,000, consisting of four bank drafts and one cashier's check. Did the bank have more information about the deposited items? Yes. The four bank drafts, in amounts of $15,000, $18,000, $24,000, and $32,000, had been drawn on a Mexican bank, the Banco Internacional of Mexico City. The name of a Mexico City attorney, Manuel Ogarrio D'Aguerre, appeared on the drafts.

The cashier's check for the remaining $25,000 had been purchased with cash by a Kenneth Dahlberg, from First Bank and Trust Company of Boca Raton, Florida. Investigators turned first to this check for additional leads.

Kenneth Dahlberg was a Minnesota businessman who maintained a home in Boca Raton. When contacted, Dahlberg acknowledged buying the cashier's check on April 8, 1972, with $25,000 in cash he had received that day on a local golf course from Dwayne Andreas. Investigators now wanted to know why Andreas had given Dahlberg the money, and how it had gotten from Dahlberg to Barker.

The first question was easy. Dahlberg explained that he was involved in fundraising in the Midwest for President Nixon's re-election campaign. Andreas, the president of Archer Daniels Midland, a huge Midwest agricultural conglomerate, had made a contribution in cash to the campaign. As for Barker, Dahlberg didn't know him. He had given the check to his boss, Maurice Stans. Stans, Dahlberg said, though the investigators already knew this, was the national finance chairman for CRP, one of the most senior members of Richard Nixon's presidential campaign team.

It had taken some time, but investigators had now followed the money backward, all the way from the burglar to its original source, a path that took the money directly to the president's top fundraising official.

Further, it appeared that this particular contribution was illegal, in that it consisted of cash. President Nixon had signed a campaign finance reform law on February 7, 1972, and this went into full effect 60 days later, on April 7. The new law specifically banned cash contributions and anonymous donations. Dahlberg's golf game with Andreas had occurred on April 8, one day *after* the law became effective, and the contribution hadn't been reported as the law required. The $25,000 was tainted money. See Figure 2.3 for a diagram of the Dahlberg–Andreas–Archer Daniels Midland path.

Meanwhile, out west, investigators were chasing down those four Mexican bank drafts. All four of the bank checks had been issued by Banco Internacional on April 5, 1972. The purchaser, Manuel Ogarrio D'Aguerre, was a Mexican attorney who represented Compania de Azuere de Veracruz, S.A., also known as CAVSA. He'd paid for the drafts with $89,000 from a total of $100,000 withdrawn from CAVSA's account at Banco Internacional on April 5.

The investigators determined that CAVSA was an inactive subsidiary of an American corporation, Gulf Resources and Chemical Company, of Houston, Texas. It was also learned that on April 3, Gulf Resources had transferred $100,000 from its account at First National City Bank in Houston to Ogarrio in Mexico City. Although the investigators appeared to have traced all of this money back to its original source as well, there were large gaps in the money trail. How had the bank drafts gotten from Ogarrio to Barker? Had these funds, like Dahlberg's check, gone through CRP first? Because many of the answers to these questions were in a foreign country, they were slower in coming, but eventually all of the gaps were filled in.

Sources told investigators that after purchasing the bank drafts, Ogarrio sent $100,000 (consisting of the $89,000 in bank drafts plus $11,000 in cash) by courier to Houston on April 5. In Houston, the money was given to an informal committee of oil men whose membership included the CEO of Gulf Resources. On the following day, April 6, the $100,000 contribution was sent by courier to Washington, where it was given to Stans at CRP, one day before anonymous and cash contributions were barred.

```
                    WATERGATE
         Laundering Illegal Corporate Campaign Contributions
         Kenneth Dahlberg - Dwayne Andreas - Archer Daniels Midland Corp.
```

Dwayne Andreas
Archer Daniels Midland

April 8, 1972
Cash $5,000

Kenneth Dahlberg
Boca Raton

April 8, 1972
Buy Cashier's Check
$25,000

1st Bank and Trust Co.
Boca Raton, Florida

1st Bank & Trust   April 8, 1972
CASHIER'S CHECK $25,000

April 11, 1972
Cashier's Check $25,000

COMMITTEE TO RE-ELECT THE PRESIDENT
Washington, D.C.

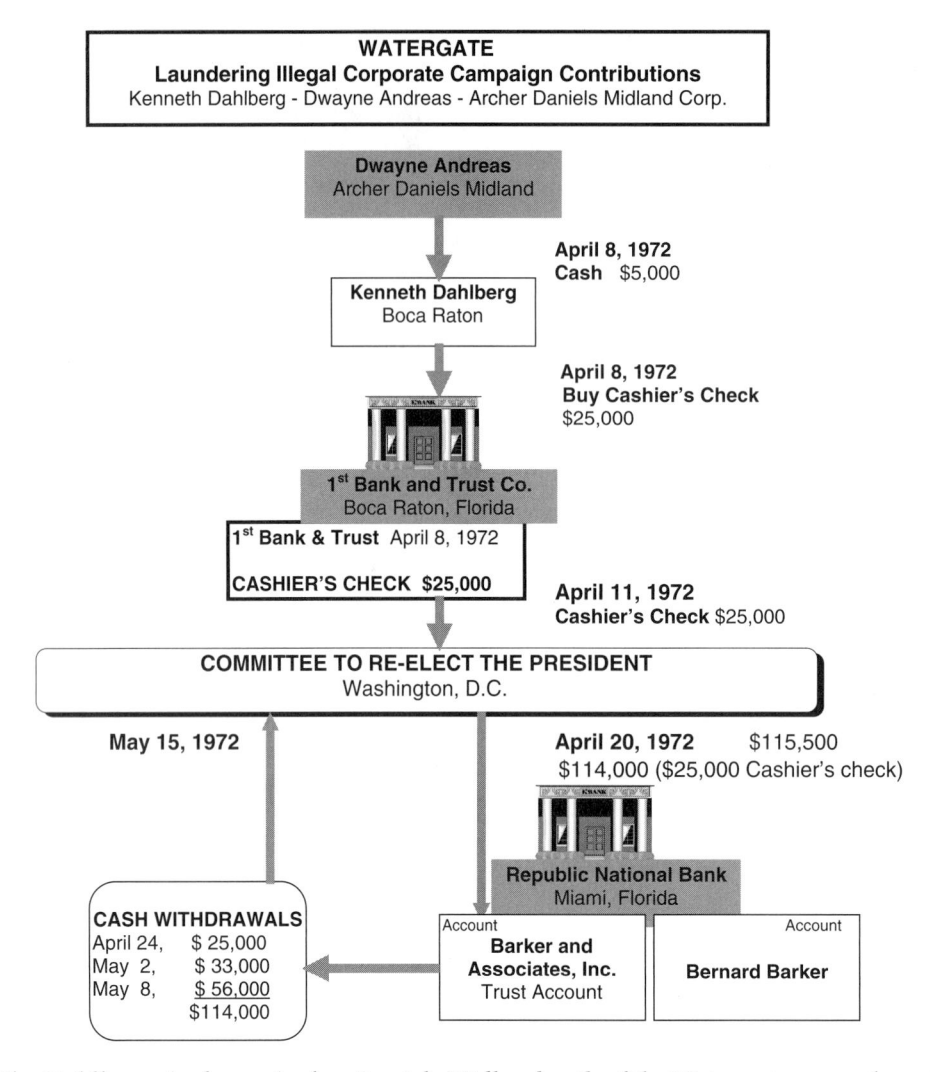

May 15, 1972

April 20, 1972 $115,500
$114,000 ($25,000 Cashier's check)

Republic National Bank
Miami, Florida

CASH WITHDRAWALS
April 24, $ 25,000
May 2, $ 33,000
May 8, $ 56,000
         $114,000

Account
Barker and Associates, Inc.
Trust Account

Account
Bernard Barker

Figure 2.3 The Dahlberg–Andreas–Archer Daniels Midland path of the Watergate money laundering scheme.

Corporate contributions were illegal even before April 7, however, and this looked very much like a donation from Gulf Resources, something that would be a violation of federal law. Robert Allen, the CEO for Gulf Resources, had another explanation. The company had previously owed Ogarrio for services performed in closing CAVSA, he said, and the $100,000 was sent on April 3 to pay these fees. Ogarrio then immediately loaned money to the Texas finance committee to make the contribution to CRP. Just by coincidence, this loan was exactly $100,000. Allen said he had given Ogarrio a promissory note documenting the loan. One author writes that investigators were "skeptical" of Allen's claim, which conflicted with Stans' statement that the money was from an American businessman who kept the money on deposit offshore. See Figure 2.4 for a diagram of the Mexican connection.

Investigators now had a much clearer picture of what had happened with both donations, but they still wanted to know how the checks had gotten from CRP to Barker. The person with the answer was G. Gordon Liddy, a White House employee who had also been at the Watergate with a walkie-talkie on the night of the burglary.

Many criminal investigations involve uncooperative witnesses, and Liddy, a former FBI agent and prosecuting attorney, was as uncooperative as he could be. This was a man who had once held his hand in a

WATERGATE
Laundering Illegal Corporate Campaign Contributions
The Mexican Connection

1st National City Bank — Houston, Texas

Account: **Gulf Resources & Chemical Co.** — Houston, TX

April 3, 1972 — $100,000

Fee - Loan Explanation

April 3, 1972
Gulf Resources pays Manuel Ogarrio, $100,000 in legal fees owed previously

April 5, 1972
Ogarrio loans the informal finance committee $100,000

April 5, 1972
Ogarrio receives promissory note for the "loan."

April 6, 1972
The $100,000 is sent to CRP in Washington

Banco Internacional — Mexico City

Manuel Ogarrio D'Aguerre

Account: **Compania de Azuere de Veracruz, S.A. (CAVSA)**

April 5, 1972 — $100,000

Bank Drafts: $15,000; $18,000; $24,000; $32,000
CASH: $11,000

COMMITTEE TO RE-ELECT THE PRESIDENT — Washington, D.C.

April 20, 1972 — $114,000 (Bank drafts - $89,000)

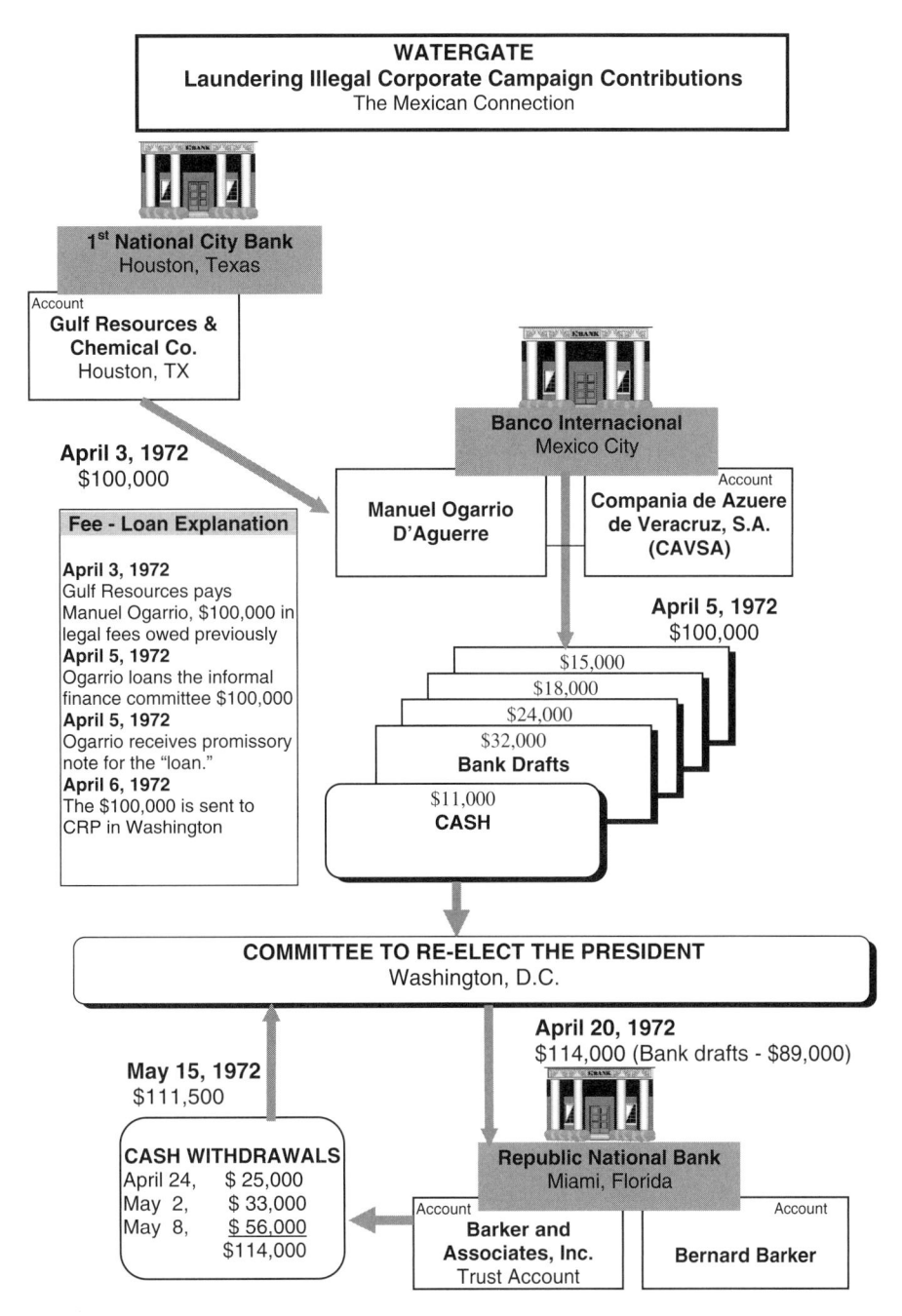

Republic National Bank — Miami, Florida

Account: **Barker and Associates, Inc.** Trust Account

Account: **Bernard Barker**

May 15, 1972 — $111,500

CASH WITHDRAWALS
April 24, $ 25,000
May 2, $ 33,000
May 8, $ 56,000
          $114,000

Figure 2.4 The Mexican connection in the Watergate money laundering scheme.

candle flame to demonstrate his indifference to pain. Liddy would, and ultimately did, go to prison without giving up his secrets. Fortunately, others at CRP were not so intransigent. From these people, investigators learned that Liddy had suggested that the bank drafts and cashier's check could be washed through Barker's Miami realty business. CRP personnel gave the checks to Liddy on April 12 or 13, and Liddy returned the $114,000 in cash, less $2,500 for unspecified "expenses," on about May 15.

At this point, the money had been tracked backward from the burglars to the source, without any significant gaps in the trail. While all this was going on, other investigators (and a horde of reporters) were learning all about the uses of the money and the illegal activities of a special unit located in the Executive Office Building, next door to the White House.

Fated to be known as the "Plumbers," the Special Investigations Unit was first established by the White House to deal with a series of news leaks that had been plaguing the administration. The Plumbers' activities grew to include spying on political opponents and a variety of "dirty tricks," almost all of which were not just dirty, but very much illegal. Liddy was closely connected with the Plumbers and had obtained a large budget from CRP to carry out the clandestine side of the re-election effort. The money given to Liddy by CRP almost invariably took the form of $100 bills. Although there was some question later about how much of the Mexican money was actually used to finance the break-in and bugging operation, there is no doubt that the burglars were carrying money that had been funneled through Barker's account.

The financial investigation of the money laundering scheme had answered many of the most important questions in the Watergate campaign-financing case. Now the investigation would turn to how much more cash was out there in CRP's coffers, how it had been raised, and, equally important, how it had been spent.

Analysis of the Watergate Money Laundering Scheme

Barry Sussman, an editor at the *Washington Post* during the Watergate years, wrote afterward in his book *The Great Coverup: Nixon and the Scandal of Watergate*, p. 77:

> It seems quite possible that had there been no Dahlberg check story, there would have been no Ervin Committee, no revelation of the existence of the tapes, and little pressure exerted to force those who knew of the cover-up to come forward.
>
> Again, such judgments cannot be made with finality. But without the work of (investigators and) newspapermen, there might have been no Dahlberg check story, for *the White House recognized the perils of the hundred-dollar-bill trail from the moment of the Watergate arrests,* and it moved immediately to block (the United States Attorney's) investigation of them." (Emphasis added.)

Clearly, CRP's effort to launder its illegal campaign funds had gone seriously wrong. An aggressive financial investigation recreated a trail that led directly from a burglary and bugging operation almost to the door of the Oval Office. To analyze the money laundering scheme and how it went wrong, we need to pretend that money laundering was a criminal act in 1972 (it wasn't) and that campaign finance violations are Specified Unlawful Activities defined by the statute. (Congress has apparently neglected to include these in the money laundering statute — go figure.) With these assumptions in place, let's ask a few questions.

Did CRP or its representatives conduct a financial transaction?

Yes indeed. They conducted quite a few, in fact. As the charts show, there were transactions at banks and among individuals, and some interstate and even international transportation of laundered funds. With regard to the $25,000 donation by Andreas, transactions included:

a. The purchase of the cashier's check by Dahlberg
b. The transfer of the cashier's check to CRP
c. CRP's providing the check to Liddy for laundering through Barker
d. Liddy's transfer of the check to Barker
e. Barker's deposit of the check in the Republic National Bank account
f. Barker's three withdrawals of cash from the same account
g. Return of the cash to CRP

With regard to the Gulf Resources contribution:

a. The transfer of $100,000 from 1st National City Bank to Banco Internacional
b. The purchase of the four Banco Internacional bank drafts by Ogarrio
c. The repatriation by courier of the $100,000 from Mexico City to Houston
d. The transportation of the $100,000 to CRP in Washington
e. CRP's providing the bank drafts to Liddy for laundering through Barker
f. Liddy's transfer of the bank drafts to Barker
g. Barker's deposit of the bank drafts in the Republic National Bank account
h. Barker's three withdrawals of cash from the same account
i. Return of the cash to CRP

As you can see, there are a number of identifiable transactions from which a prosecutor could choose. Some are quite well documented, while others rely primarily on testimonial evidence, such as the transfer of the checks from CRP to Liddy.

What was the object of the money laundering scheme, and what charges might apply?

- One objective was to further the criminal activity being conducted by the Plumbers, which could be a violation of Title 18 U.S.C. 1956 (a) (1) (A) (i).
- Additionally, the conspirators sought to conceal or disguise the source and ownership of the funds, a violation of 18 U.S.C. 1956 (a) (1) (B) (i).
- The money that was illegally mailed or transported out of the country and then transported back in again was sent in violation of 18 U.S.C. 1956 (a) (2) (B) (ii).
- The bank transactions of over $10,000 were violations of 18 U.S.C. 1957 (a).
- All of the individuals involved were aware of the object of the money laundering scheme, and a conspiracy charge under 18 U.S.C. 1956 (h) might apply.

What was the underlying criminal activity (specified unlawful activity)? How would this activity be documented?

Campaign finance violations. The campaign was taking contributions from corporations, which was prohibited by law, as well as cash contributions after April 7, 1972, also a violation. The campaign was not properly reporting the donations, thereby concealing the names of the donors from federal election officials, yet another violation.

As for documentation, the testimony of the principals, many of whom provided evidence in various court proceedings and Congressional hearings at the time, would be required.

How far did the committee get into the money laundering cycle?

Pretty far. Liddy and the "dirty tricks" people were enjoying the use of their "clean" money. The campaign had clearly made it through the placement stage, changing the form of the contributions at least once. The campaign had also layered the funds by conducting a series of transactions and again changing the form. CRP did fail to integrate the funds; aside from Gulf Resources' explanation of the Ogarrio "loan," there was no plausible, legal-appearing source for any of the money. Because reporters (and ultimately everybody else) had sources inside the campaign and the White House, the layering measures taken were insufficient to protect the whole scheme.

How could law enforcement have detected this scheme?

This scheme was not detected while in progress. It was only after the burglars were caught that the money came to investigators' attention. Although not all of the cash-reporting statutes were in effect at the time, had they been, some of the currency-reporting forms should have been prepared, any of which might have placed investigators on the money trail. (The cash transactions at the Miami banks *were* reportable to Treasury at the time.):

- A CMIR should have been prepared when the $89,000 in bank drafts and $11,000 in cash returned to the United States from Mexico on April 5.
- A CTR should have been prepared at First Bank and Trust Company in Boca Raton when Kenneth Dahlberg bought the cashier's check for $25,000 in cash on April 8.
- CTRs should have been prepared on April 25, May 2, and May 8, at Republic National Bank in Miami, when Bernard Barker withdrew $25,000, $33,000, and $56,000 in cash, respectively.
- Suspicious Activity Reports (SARs) might well have been filed by Republic National Bank in connection with the Barker transactions.
- A significant number of individuals knew of the money laundering scheme and the means by which it was being carried out. Most (with the exception of Mr. Liddy) would have been susceptible to an approach by investigators looking at the financial transactions.

President Richard M. Nixon, who once proclaimed, "I am not a crook," resigned his office on August 8, 1974, just over two years after the "third-rate burglary" at the Watergate. Pressure had been building for his impeachment for some time, spurred by revelations of conversations in the Oval Office taped on Nixon's recording system. One of these tapes, now known as "the smoking gun," proved to even the president's most loyal supporters that he had participated in the cover-up from as early as one week after the break-in. In this tape, made in the Oval Office on June 23, 1972, Nixon and H.R. Haldeman, his chief of staff, discussed the investigation:

Haldeman: Now, on the investigation, you know, the Democratic break-in thing, we're back in the problem area, because the FBI is not under control, because Gray doesn't exactly know how to control them, and they have — their investigation is now leading into some productive areas, *because they've been able to trace the money, not through the money itself, but through the bank,* you know, sources, the banker himself. And, and it goes in some directions we don't want it to go. (Emphasis added.)

Haldeman and Nixon agreed that the CIA would be used to derail the FBI's investigation on "national security" grounds. This obstruction of the money laundering investigation was a key element in the case against the president. After resisting for two years, Nixon left office immediately after the "smoking gun" tape became public.

MORE MONEY LAUNDERING SCHEMES

Three additional money laundering schemes used to make illegal campaign contributions are described below. In all three cases, the corporation making the contribution was prosecuted and fined. In one case, an officer, George Steinbrenner, owner of the New York Yankees baseball team, was convicted and fined as well.

AMERICAN AIRLINES

The laundering scheme used by American Airlines to wash a $55,000 donation of corporate funds, like the Watergate scheme, used offshore transactions and a foreign bank. At the time of the contribution, American was seeking to merge with Western Airlines and needed federal approval for the merger. Somebody suggested that a $100,000 contribution to the president's re-election campaign would be welcome, and American got the (none too subtle) hint.

American started by donating $20,000 in personal funds, turning to the corporate accounts for the rest. First, American transferred $100,000 from a corporate account at Chemical Bank in New York City to the Swiss account of Andre Tabourian, a Lebanese businessman with whom American had previously done business.

On the corporate books, this transaction was shown as a "special commission" in connection with the sale of used aircraft to Middle East Airlines, Lebanon's national carrier.

Shortly after receiving the money, Tabourian transferred the funds from Credit Suisse to his account at Chase Manhattan Bank in New York. He then withdrew all $100,000 in cash, giving it back to an American Airlines executive who kept the money in a safe in the New York office until March 1972, when $55,000 was withdrawn and given to CRP.

This type of money laundering scheme has the characteristics of an "invoice scam," long used by tax evaders. Although it looks on paper as though American Airlines paid a (tax deductible) commission on sales, the company never really lost control of that $100,000. Once Tabourian had converted it to cash, American was free to spend it on whatever it liked. In this instance, American Airlines chose to give $55,000 to the president's re-election campaign. See Figure 2.5 for a diagram of the American Airlines money laundering scheme.

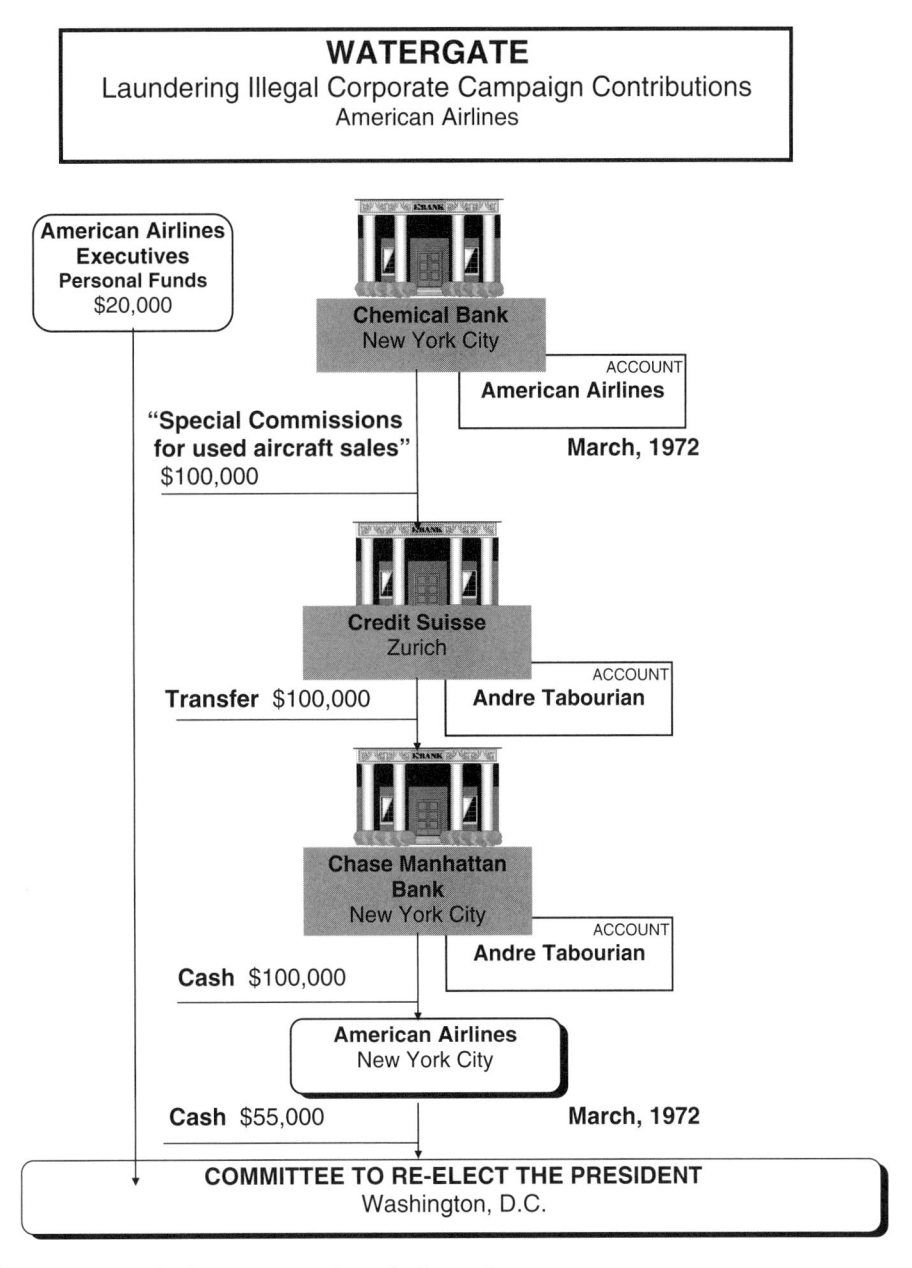

WATERGATE
Laundering Illegal Corporate Campaign Contributions
American Airlines

```
American Airlines Executives Personal Funds $20,000

                    Chemical Bank, New York City
                        ACCOUNT: American Airlines
"Special Commissions for used aircraft sales" $100,000
                        March, 1972

                    Credit Suisse, Zurich
                        ACCOUNT: Andre Tabourian
Transfer $100,000

                    Chase Manhattan Bank, New York City
                        ACCOUNT: Andre Tabourian
Cash $100,000

                    American Airlines, New York City

Cash $55,000         March, 1972

COMMITTEE TO RE-ELECT THE PRESIDENT
Washington, D.C.
```

Figure 2.5 The American Airlines money laundering scheme.

Braniff Airlines

Braniff Airlines, a regional carrier based in Dallas, Texas, wasn't nearly as big as American, but the company did have a much better money laundering scheme. At least, the *plan* was better; the company still wound up pleading guilty to campaign finance violations.

Like American Airlines, Braniff occasionally needed government assistance on a variety of regulatory matters. The company's contact with CRP began with a $10,000 cash donation from Braniff's chairman to Stans. Because this transfer involved personal funds and took place on March 1, 1972, it was strictly legitimate. The next $40,000, however, was not, and the airline knew it.

Braniff opted to use some creative accounting in addition to routing the money offshore. The company began by issuing a voucher, dated March 29, 1972, to Camilo Fabrega, the manager of Braniff's operations in Panama. Fabrega owned a Panamanian company, CAMFAB, and the voucher specified that Braniff was paying CAMFAB the $40,000 for "expenses and services."

The check was debited to Braniff's account and sent off to Panama. An offsetting credit entry showed the payment as an account receivable in Braniff's books. When he received the check, Fabrega endorsed it for CAMFAB, cashed it at a Panamanian bank, and then sent the cash, in United States currency, by courier to Braniff officials in Dallas. At this point, anyone who had been looking would have seen only a payment to CAMFAB and a receivable on the Braniff books. There was no record of the return of the money to Braniff's chairman, who gave the $40,000 to Maurice Stans. (Stans' travels to raise cash in the period just before the April 7 deadline were known as "Stans' shakedown cruise.")

Braniff now took some additional steps to layer and integrate the contribution. First, the company supplied a number of special blank airline tickets to Fabrega in Panama City. These tickets were then sold only by the Braniff supervisor at the Panama City office, and only for cash. Customers who wanted to pay by check or credit card were issued tickets from the regular stock. On the books, the proceeds of the sales of these special tickets were shown as payments against CAMFAB's account receivable. Fabrega took a total of $27,000 in cash from these sales to Dallas between April and December 1972.

In the final act of the money laundering process, Braniff wanted to eliminate the CAMFAB account in December, so Fabrega obtained a loan for the balance of $13,000 from a Panamanian bank. He gave the proceeds of this loan to Braniff and then continued to sell tickets from the special stock until he had paid back the bank loan.

This is obviously a more complicated scheme, but it illustrates several interesting points. First, not only was the use of the airline tickets as a form of currency rather creative, but it also fit right in with Braniff's regular business. Second, the use of Panama presaged that country's later role as a major money laundering center. Third, unlike the other schemes we've examined, Braniff's use of its accounting records and the airline ticket sales provided a perfectly plausible, legitimate-appearing source for the integration of the laundered funds. This is the ultimate objective of any truly successful money laundering scheme. See Figure 2.6 for a diagram of the Braniff Airlines money laundering scheme.

George Steinbrenner and American Shipbuilding

George Steinbrenner III is best known as the owner of the New York Yankees baseball team. He made his fortune in ship building and rose to become chairman and chief executive officer of American Shipbuilding. In 1972, American Shipbuilding was having a cost overrun problem with the United States Commerce Department, and it also faced an antitrust suit filed by the Department of Justice. Steinbrenner wanted some help, and he was advised that one of those $100,000 contributions to the president's campaign might get it.

Steinbrenner's money laundering scheme was simple and direct, and it cost him a conspiracy conviction and a $15,000 fine. He took $25,000 in corporate funds from American Shipbuilding and paid these to six of his employees

WATERGATE
Laundering Illegal Corporate Campaign Contributions
Braniff Airlines

[Dallas Bank, Dallas, Texas]

Account: Braniff Airlines, Dallas, Texas

Voucher
$40,000
"Expenses and services"
March 29, 1972

Camilo Fabrega
CAMFAB
Panama City

Panama Bank
Panama City

Check Cashed
Cash
$40,000
April 3, 1972

Braniff Airlines
Dallas, Texas

CASH		ACCOUNTS RECEIVABLE	
3/72 $40,000		3/72 $40,000	
	4/72 $ 8,000		4/72 $ 8,000
	5/72 7,000		5/72 7,000
	7/72 5,500		7/72 5,500
	9/72 6,500		9/72 6,500
	12/72 13,000		12/72 13,000

Airline Tickets

$40,000
Cash

Loan
$13,000
December, 1972

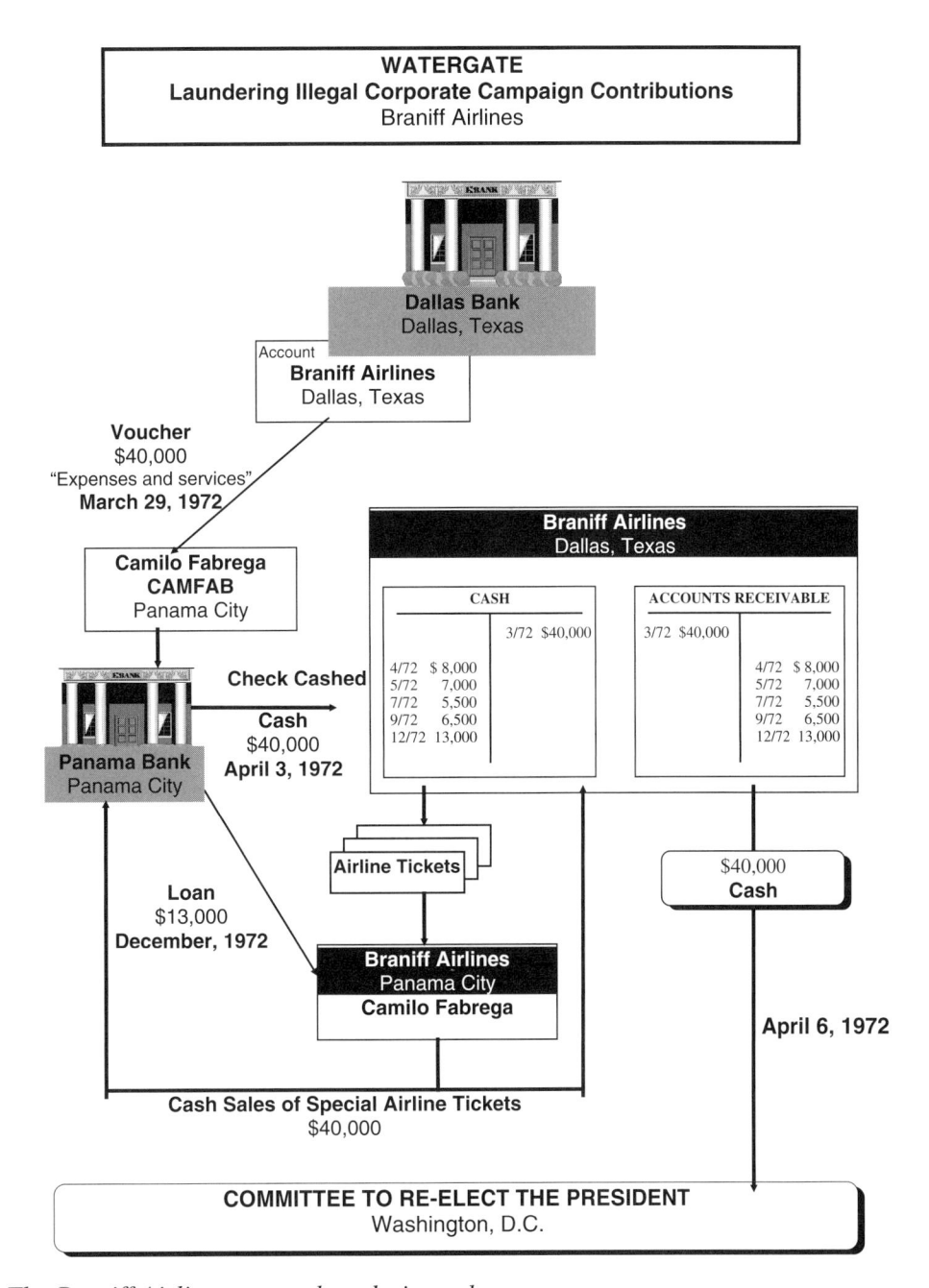

Braniff Airlines
Panama City
Camilo Fabrega

April 6, 1972

Cash Sales of Special Airline Tickets
$40,000

COMMITTEE TO RE-ELECT THE PRESIDENT
Washington, D.C.

Figure 2.6 The Braniff Airlines money laundering scheme.

as "special bonuses." Each of the employees was instructed to make a donation in the amount of the bonus to the re-election effort.

This very elementary scheme took care of the placement stage — changing the form of the corporate funds. The integration stage was also covered, as the donations from each of the six employees at least *appeared* to come from a legitimate source.

Unfortunately for Steinbrenner, he had completely failed to layer the transaction, and this failure spoiled the plan. (Variations of this scheme were also used by CRP contributors Carnation and Greyhound, as well as by contractors who were kicking back money to Vice President Spiro Agnew. It didn't work for them, either.) See Figure 2.7 for a diagram of the American Shipbuilding money laundering scheme.

WATERGATE
Laundering Illegal Corporate Campaign Contributions
American Shipbuilding

American Shipbuilding
Tampa, Florida

George Steinbrenner

"Special Bonuses" $25,000   **April, 1972**

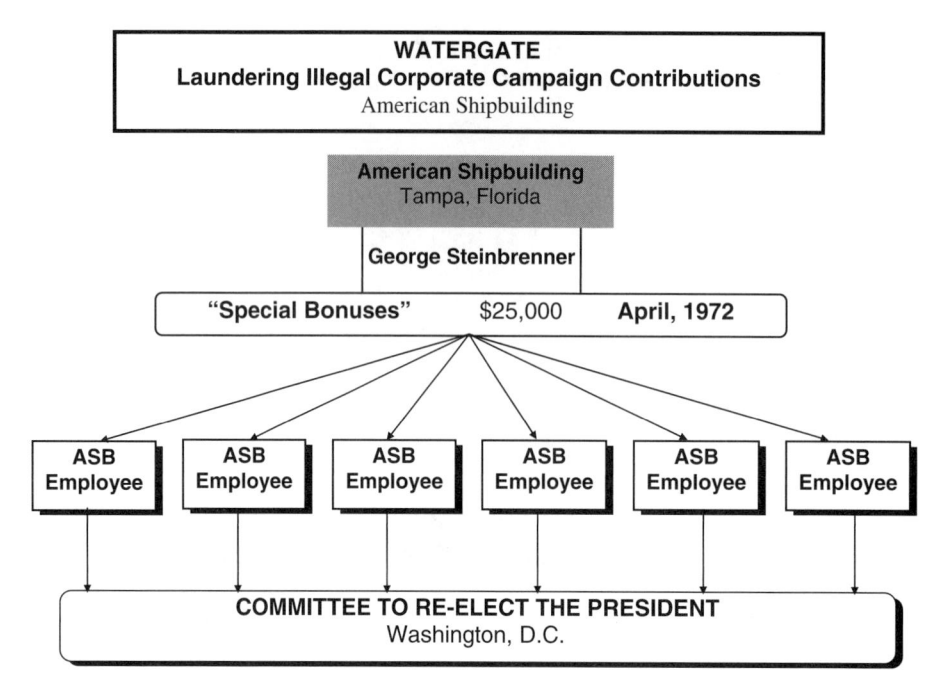

ASB Employee | ASB Employee | ASB Employee | ASB Employee | ASB Employee | ASB Employee

COMMITTEE TO RE-ELECT THE PRESIDENT
Washington, D.C.

Figure 2.7 The American Shipbuilding money laundering scheme.

CHAPTER 3

FEDERAL MONEY LAUNDERING STATUTES

"A man who has never gone to school may steal from a freight car, but if he has a university education, he may steal the whole railroad."
Franklin D. Roosevelt

Prior to 1986, the act of money laundering wasn't a crime in the United States. The financial transactions that formed a money laundering scheme might be the subject of a criminal investigation or prosecution under some other statute, but the money laundering process itself was not illegal.

By 1986, it was becoming increasingly obvious to Congress as well as the law enforcement community that money laundering had evolved into a central element of organized criminal enterprises. This was particularly true of the drug trade, where billions of dollars were being made and laundered each year.

Concerned legislators and law enforcement officials were especially aware of the corruptive influence laundered funds could have on legitimate commerce. Newspaper stories told of banks accepting duffel bags full of cash, and of bank officers winking at or even soliciting the business of criminals.

Other businesses were also affected. Simply put, it is impossible for a legitimate business owner to compete with a money launderer who has unlimited cash resources from some hidden source. Finally, the possibility that politics and government might be corrupted by laundered funds also existed. A politician or government official who could not associate with or take contributions from a drug trafficker might well be able to do so, even unknowingly, if the money was efficiently laundered.

All of these factors combined to prompt consideration in 1986 of new federal legislation directed at strengthening the government's ability to address money laundering. The law that would become the primary federal money laundering statute was enacted as the Money Laundering Control Act of 1986, Public Law 99-570. This statute was the first to actually describe money laundering, define it, and prohibit it as a crime.

Even though this development was fairly recent, attempts to address the problem posed by money laundering go back quite a ways, at least to the 1920s. The most aggressive federal efforts involved the Intelligence Unit of the Bureau of Internal Revenue. Throughout the period from 1925 through the 1960s, the Intelligence Unit repeatedly developed criminal cases against racketeers who were attempting to conceal their wealth from the taxing authority. It was in this period that the indirect methods of proving income were developed, methods such as the Net Worth, Bank Deposits, and Source and Application of Funds analyses, which would later be applied to money laundering cases and other financial crimes.

Although the penalties for tax evasion were never extreme — Al Capone received an 11-year sentence, one of the longest — the threat of prosecution was great enough to prompt mobsters into schemes to hide their income. As we've seen, Meyer Lansky, the "Mob's Accountant," pioneered many of the earliest schemes, and with his boyhood associate, "Bugsy" Siegel, developed Las Vegas into a gambling center — and a very useful money laundering tool.

The statutes enforced by the Intelligence Unit related to the evasion of taxes on income "from whatever source derived." The law was completely neutral on the source of the income; legally, IRS couldn't have cared less whether the money was clean or dirty, only whether the proper taxes had been paid.

But the law put the racketeers in something of a bind, because at this time the legal provisions for confidentiality of tax returns were not as strict as they are today, and those returns, with their damaging admissions, could be given by IRS to other law enforcement agencies. This meant that mobsters like Lansky could hardly report their income or occupations correctly, for fear of incurring even greater legal problems. Their alternative was to attempt to conceal their income, evade the taxes on it, and hope they didn't run afoul of the Intelligence Unit.

Laws against tax evasion were employed against those who directly evaded taxes, but two court decisions in the 1940s expanded criminal liability beyond the individual criminal enterprise to those persons who provided goods or services that facilitated the illegal activity.

In *United States v. Falcone*, 109 F.2d 579 (2d. Cir.), *affirmed,* 311 U.S. 205 (1940), Judge Learned Hand wrote that someone who provided lawful goods or services would not be guilty of a crime unless he or she "in some sense promoted the venture himself, making it his own (or had) a stake in its outcome." According to this rationale, someone such as a banker, having knowledge of a customer's illegal activity, might be guilty of conspiracy, even though all of the banker's actions in handling the customer's money were legal.

In a second decision, *Direct Sales Company, Inc. v. United States,* 319 U.S. 703 (1943), the Supreme Court expanded on this principle, saying that if a legitimate business or individuals (*a*) had knowledge of the illegal activity, (*b*) had some agreement or intent to further the activity, and (*c*) had some stake in the outcome, a conspiracy conviction could be sustained.

With the principle now established that those who assisted in the disposition of illegal funds could be held criminally liable for the underlying crime, the conspiracy statutes joined those relating to tax evasion in the prosecutor's arsenal against money laundering. Note, however, that both of these approaches were very indirect; neither directly punished the act of concealing the illegal source of dirty money.

In 1970, Congress enacted the Bank Secrecy Act (BSA), still a key part of the war on money laundering. Much of the BSA relates to record keeping, because its focus was the creation of paper trails where none ordinarily existed. Several reports were required as a result of the BSA, each of which addressed a separate aspect of what would later become known as "money laundering." The Bank Secrecy Act is now codified in Title 31 of the United States Code.

One provision, Section 5313, required that domestic financial institutions report certain (large) cash transactions. Regulations developed by the Secretary of the Treasury defined which transactions were to be reported, and these regulations defined a reportable transaction as one over $10,000 in coin or currency. Under the BSA, the bankers were responsible for making and submitting the reports, and they didn't particularly cherish the honor. Numerous court challenges were filed, on a variety of grounds, all of which were ultimately rejected. The courts clearly understood congressional intent in passing the statute and felt that the need for the government to have this information outweighed concerns about customer privacy, Fifth Amendment privileges, and the cost to the bankers of preparing the reports.

In a Supreme Court decision, *California Bankers Association v. Shultz,* 416 U.S. 21 (1974), the court explained the reasoning behind the statute: "Congress recognized the importance of large and unusual currency transactions in ferreting out criminal activity, and desired to strengthen the statutory basis for requiring such reports."

Other BSA provisions required reports to be filed anytime currency or monetary instruments were transported into or out of the United States (Section 5316). Originally the regulations set the reporting threshold at $5,000, but this was later increased to $10,000. Section 5314 (a) requires residents or citizens of the United States to report any interest they may have in a foreign bank account or securities overseas. Again, the interest must be over $10,000. In both of these instances, the reports are supposed to be filed by the individuals, as opposed to banks or some other institution.

The BSA imposed criminal sanctions against violators of its provisions, as well as fines and civil penalties. Added to the conspiracy and tax laws, the BSA gave law enforcement some means to track and prosecute laundering activity, although this power was still mostly indirect. Worse, the BSA, which went into effect in 1971, was widely ignored by those who were supposed to be filing the reports, including the banks. Actions against offenders were few, even though the decision in *Shultz* was only the first of many that upheld the constitutionality of the statute.

Although prosecutions were rare, enough occurred that banks eventually began filing the required reports. This led their customers to seek out ways of concealing the placement of cash. One of these was *structuring* or "smurfing" — i.e., breaking up large cash transactions into many smaller ones. This activity was especially intense in the early 1980s, when traveling road shows of "smurfs" would go from city to city, buying cashier's checks or money orders in amounts below $10,000. Because it was obvious that the BSA was being routinely circumvented in such cases, Congress amended the statute in 1986 to prohibit structuring. This legislation was part of the more sweeping money laundering control efforts in the same package as the Money Laundering Control Act of 1986.

The BSA, like the tax statutes, is neutral about the source of the cash. It was clear enough, though, from decisions like *Shultz*, that the law was aimed at criminals. Additional confirmation of this came in 1984, when BSA violations were made predicate acts under the Racketeer Influenced and Corrupt Organizations (RICO) Act.

At this point, the government had gone a long way toward addressing money laundering without legislating an outright prohibition. With Public Law 99-570, Congress went the distance in 1986. The Money Laundering Control Act of 1986, codified in Title 18 U.S.C. Sections 1956 and 1957, set out exactly what constituted "money laundering" and what the government could do about it. When combined with other federal statutes, these provisions created a very comprehensive legal response to a very old problem. In fact, the federal statutes currently on the books comprise the most effective anti–money laundering legislation in the world.

Congress has amended the money laundering statute several times since 1986, and numerous court rulings have further defined what constitutes money laundering under the Act. Some of the major legislative amendments include:

- Anti-Drug Abuse Act of 1988: addressed undercover operations involving money laundering
- Annunzio–Wylie Anti-Money Laundering Act of 1992: enlarged the definition of "financial transaction" and added a conspiracy provision
- Money Laundering Suppression Act of 1994: redesignated the conspiracy provision and amended Title 31 provisions relating to structuring
- Terrorism Prevention Act, enacted in 1996: added terrorism-related crimes as predicates for money laundering violations, as well as alien smuggling
- Health Insurance Portability and Accountability Act of 1996: added "federal health care offenses" as a specified unlawful activity covered by the money laundering act
- USA PATRIOT ACT of 2001

THE MONEY LAUNDERING CONTROL ACT

The Money Laundering Control Act (MLCA) has two key parts or elements: (1) "financial transactions" or international transportation, and (2) "Specified Unlawful Activities" (SUAs). In order for any act to be a money laundering violation, both of these key elements must be satisfied.

Before we get any further into the MLCA, it is important that this concept be understood. Your investigative approach must always provide for proof of *both* parts of this offense. Having the right mind-set on this point is critical, because the means by which these elements are proved may be (and often are) totally different.

As noted, the MLCA is divided into two code sections, §1956 and §1957. Looking at the more widely used §1956 first, we'll see that it is divided into subsections (a) through (h), with the substantive provision (a) further subdivided into three major parts relating to (1) financial transactions, (2) international transportation, and (3) undercover "sting" operations. The language of the statute is as follows:

§1956 (a) (1)

(a) (1) Whoever, knowing that the property involved in a financial transaction represents the proceeds of some form of unlawful activity, conducts or attempts to conduct such a financial transaction which in fact involves the proceeds of specified unlawful activity

(A) (i) with the intent to promote the carrying on of specified unlawful activity; or

(ii) with intent to engage in conduct constituting a violation of section 7201 or 7206 of the Internal Revenue Code of 1986; or

(B) knowing that the transaction is designed in whole or in part

(i) to conceal or disguise the nature, the location, the source, the ownership, or the control of the proceeds of specified unlawful activity; or

(ii) to avoid a transaction reporting requirement under State or Federal law, shall be sentenced to a fine of not more than $500,000 or twice the value of the property involved in the transaction, whichever is greater, or imprisonment for not more than twenty years, or both.

§1956 (a) (2)

(a) (2) Whoever transports, transmits, or transfers, or attempts to transport, transmit, or transfer a monetary instrument from a place in the United States to or through a place outside the United States or to a place in the United States from or through a place outside the United States

(A) with the intent to promote the carrying on of specified unlawful activity; or

(B) knowing that the monetary instrument or funds involved in the transportation, transmission, or transfer represent the proceeds of some form of unlawful activity and knowing that such transportation, transmission or transfer is designed in whole or in part

(i) to conceal or disguise the nature, the location, the source, the ownership, or the control of the proceeds of specified unlawful activity; or to avoid a transaction reporting requirement under State or Federal law, shall be sentenced to a fine of $500,000 or twice the value of the monetary instrument of funds involved in the transportation, whichever is greater, or imprisonment for not more than twenty years, or both.

For the purpose of the offense described in subparagraph (B), the defendant's knowledge may be established by proof that a law enforcement officer represented the matter specified in subparagraph (B) as true, and the defendant's subsequent statements or actions indicate that the defendant believed such representations to be true.

§1956 (a) (3)

(3) Whoever, with the intent

(A) to promote the carrying on of specified unlawful activity;

(B) to conceal or disguise the nature, location, source, ownership, or control of property believed to be the proceeds of specified unlawful activity; or to avoid a transaction reporting requirement under State or Federal law, conducts or attempts to conduct a financial transaction involving property represented to be the proceeds of specified unlawful activity, or property used to conduct or facilitate specified unlawful activity, shall be fined under this title or imprisoned for not more than 20 years, or both.

For purposes of this paragraph and paragraph (2), the term "represented" means any representation made by a law enforcement officer or by another person at the direction of, or with the approval of, a Federal official authorized to investigate or prosecute violations of this section.

The terms used in §1956 are defined in subsection (c).

§1956 (c)

As used in this section

(1) the term "knowing that the property involved in a financial transaction represents the proceeds of some form of unlawful activity" means that the person knew the property involved in the transaction represented proceeds from some form, though not necessarily which form, of activity that constitutes a felony under State, Federal, or foreign law, regardless of whether or not such activity is specified in paragraph (7);

(2) the term "conducts" includes initiating, concluding, or participating in initiating, or concluding a transaction;

(3) the term "transaction" includes a purchase, sale, loan, pledge, gift, transfer, delivery, or other disposition, and with respect to a financial institution includes a deposit, withdrawal, transfer between accounts, exchange of currency, loan, extension of credit, purchase or sale of any stock, bond, certificate of deposit, or other monetary instrument, use of a safe deposit box, or any other payment, transfer, or delivery by, through, or to a financial institution, by whatever means effected;

(4) the term "financial transaction" means (A) a transaction which in any way or degree affects interstate or foreign commerce (i) involving the movement of funds by wire or other means or (ii) involving one or more monetary instruments, or (iii) involving the transfer of title to any real property, vehicle, vessel, or aircraft, or (B) a transaction involving the use of a financial institution which is engaged in, or the activities of which affect, interstate or foreign commerce in any way or degree;

(5) the term "monetary instruments" means (i) coin or currency of the United States or of any other country, travelers checks, personal checks, bank checks, and money orders, or (ii) investment securities or negotiable instruments, in bearer form or otherwise in such form that title thereto passes upon delivery;

(6) the term "financial institution" has the definition given that term in section 5312 (a) (2) of Title 31, United States Code, or the regulations promulgated thereunder;

A couple of things should be obvious right off the bat. First, the government obviously means business with this statute, providing for 20-year sentences and the potential for millions of dollars in fines. Second, Congress broadly defined what types of acts could constitute money laundering, and it addresses not just the placement stage of money laundering operations but the subsequent layering and integration phases as well. Almost (but not quite) everything you could do with your dirty money is covered by this statute, no matter what form the money or the transaction might take.

Breaking the statute down even further, we'll examine each subsection separately. Section (a) (1) relates to financial transactions, listing four types of transactions that, if conducted with money from an SUA, would constitute money laundering.

Title 18 U.S.C. §1956 (a) (1)

In order to charge a violation of any of the four intents of Section 1956 (a) (1), the government must prove that:

1. A financial transaction was conducted or attempted.
2. The defendant knew that the property involved in the financial transaction represented the proceeds of some form of unlawful activity.
3. The property was in fact the proceeds of a specified unlawful activity.
4. The defendant acted with the intent to do any of the four prohibited activities listed under §1956 (a) (1) (A) and (B).

Each of these terms is described or defined by the statute, and subsequent court decisions have elaborated on what exactly constitutes the type of activity Congress intended to prohibit. The chart in Figure 3.1 shows each aspect of the

```
                    1956 (a) (1)
                 Financial Transactions

                No      ┌─────────────────────┐
    ◄───────────────────│ Money proceeds of SUA? │
    │                   └─────────────────────┘
    │                            │ Yes
    │                            ▼
    N           No      ┌─────────────────────┐
    O ◄─────────────────│ Know proceeds of UA? │
    │                   └─────────────────────┘
    V                            │ Yes
    I                            ▼
    O           No      ┌─────────────────────┐
    L ◄─────────────────│ Conduct financial   │
    A                   │ transaction or attempt to│
    T                   │ conduct financial   │
    I                   │ transaction?        │
    O                   └─────────────────────┘
    N                            │ Yes
    │                            ▼
    │           No      ┌─────────────────────┐
    ◄───────────────────│ With intent to do any of four│
                        │ prohibited activities: │
                        └─────────────────────┘
                                 │ Yes
                                 ▼
```

| Promote SUA 1956 (a)(1)(A)(i) | Conceal nature, source, location, ownership, or control of proceeds of SUA 1956 (a)(1)(B)(i) | Avoid reporting requirements 1956 (a)(1)(B)(ii) | Evade taxes 1956 (a)(1)(A)(ii) |

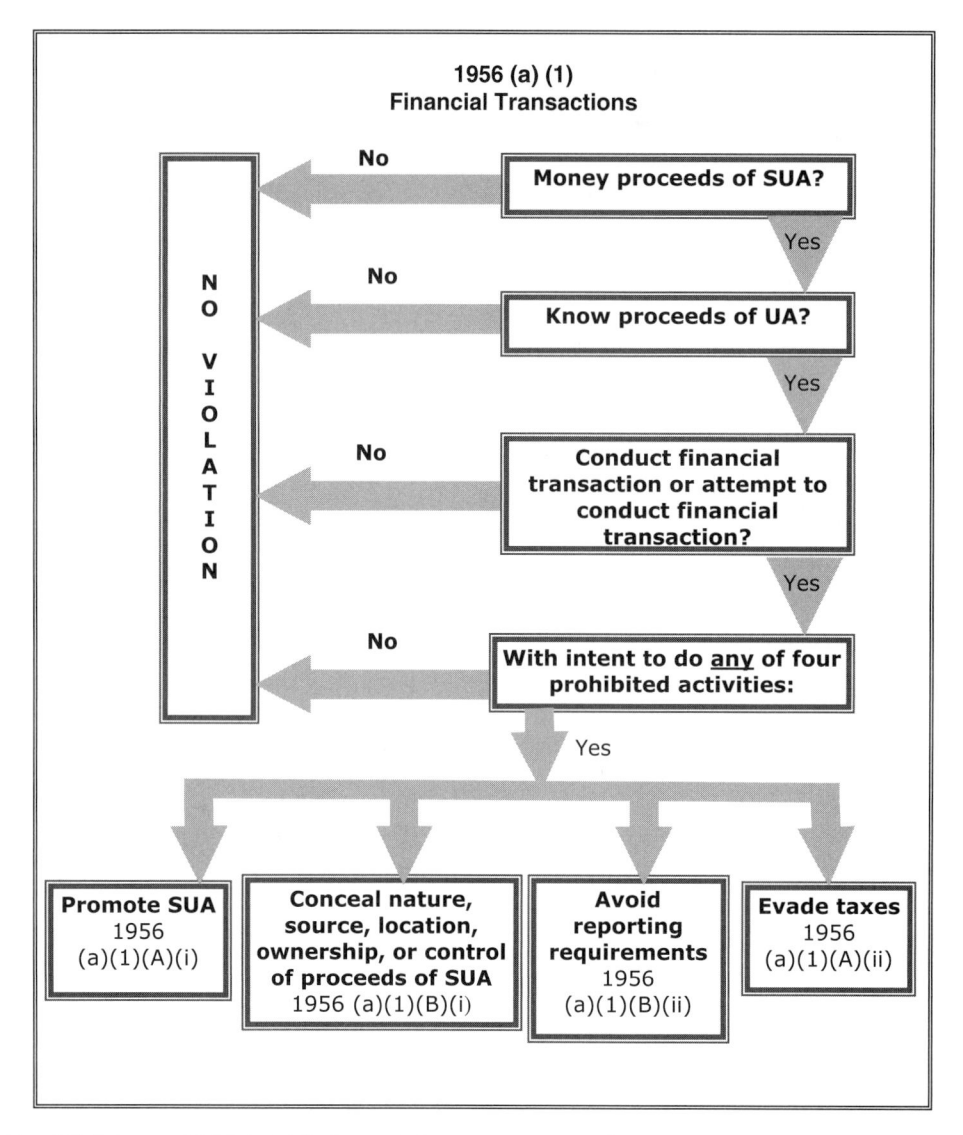

Figure 3.1 *Establishing a 1956 (a) (1) financial transaction violation.*

money laundering crime and what needs to be proved under this section.

The Money Was Proceeds of an SUA

The first question is whether the money is, in fact, the proceeds of a Specified Unlawful Activity. Subsection 1956 (c) (7) lists those crimes that constitute an SUA, a lengthy menu of federal offenses (all of which are listed at the end of this chapter), as well as predicate offenses under the RICO Act, 18 U.S.C. 1961 (1). The RICO predicates include some state crimes, such as murder, extortion, gambling, and other felonies; these too can form the basis for a money laundering charge.

Also, some violations of foreign laws or crimes against a foreign country, such as crimes involving drug trafficking, terrorism, and bank fraud, are included. As you can see, this is a fairly comprehensive listing, and the answer to the first question, *Is the money being laundered the proceeds of a Specified Unlawful Activity?*, should be either yes or no, depending on whether the activity appears on the list.

The court decisions on this issue have related mostly to the question of what constitutes "proceeds," with the conclusion being that the proceeds *do not* have to be money. Anything traceable to the original SUA can be proceeds for the purposes of the statute. Let's look at a few examples of some noncash items that qualified as proceeds in past money laundering cases:

- Real property purchased with drug money and resold. See *United States v. Rounsvall*, 115 F.3d 561 (8th Cir. 1997).
- An automobile purchased with counterfeit securities and then resold. See *United States v. Werber*, 787 F.Supp. 353 (S.D.N.Y. 1992).
- An inventory acquired in a fraud scheme. See *United States v. Griffith*, 17 F.3d 865 (6th Cir.), *cert. denied*, 513 U.S. 850 (1994).
- A fraudulently obtained line of credit, which resulted in an artificially inflated bank balance. See *United States v. Estacio*, 64 F.3d 477 (9th Cir. 1995), *cert. denied*, 517 U.S. 121 (1996).
- An automobile used to pay an illegal gambling debt. See *United States v. Davis*, 205 F.3d 1335 (4th Cir. 2000).
- A stolen diamond. See *United States v. Carcione*, 272 F. 3d 1297 (11th Cir. 2001).

Although we saw in an earlier chapter that most people tend to equate money with cash, the cases cited above broaden that definition. But how do we establish that the proceeds, in whatever form they take, are from an SUA? Circumstantial evidence can be used to link the funds to the SUA. This is where the investigation of money laundering cases follows a "two-track" strategy, track one being proof of the financial transaction, and track two being proof of the underlying offense. Because these two approaches usually require different investigative techniques, things can get a little complicated.

The courts have agreed that circumstantial evidence can be used to establish that the money is from an SUA. Some of these circumstances have included:

- The defendant's being connected to drug trafficking and paying for a car with a suitcase full of cash. See *United States v. Misher*, 99 F.3d 664 (5th Cir. 1996), *cert. denied*, 118 S.Ct. 73 (1997).
- Large quantities of cash, in small, worn bills; large transfers of money to Colombia, a source country for narcotics; a dog sniff; a co-conspirator's statement that the money was from drugs; and expert testimony about drug trafficking and money laundering. See *United States v. Saccoccia*, 58 F.3d 754 (1st Cir. 1995), *cert. denied*, 517 United States 1105 (1996).
- The defendant's receiving cash from someone who said he was a drug dealer and had no legitimate source of income. See *United States v. Isabel*, 945 F.2d 1193 (1st Cir. 1991).
- The use of information derived from a net worth analysis, showing that the defendant had insufficient legitimate income to support large cash expenditures, to demonstrate that a vehicle purchase was made with money from marijuana sales. See *United States v. Cruz*, 993 F.2d 164 (8th Cir. 1993).

In addition, the subject's actions or behavior in handling the money, including efforts to conceal the transaction, can be used to show knowledge of the underlying criminal activity, as in *United States v. Brown*, 944 F.2d 1377 (7th Cir. 1991), in which the defendant conducted elaborate, time-consuming cash transactions under $10,000.

The Defendant Knew That the Money Was Proceeds of an SUA

When it is established that the proceeds are from a Specified Unlawful Activity, the next question is: *Did the defendant know the money was the proceeds of an Unlawful Activity?*

As you might have guessed, the same sort of evidence you used to answer the first question can also be used to answer the second. What we're trying to show is knowledge, and this can be done in several ways, generally depending on the defendant's role in the transaction.

In the case of someone who is *not* the perpetrator of the SUA, there are a couple of wrinkles. First, the unlawful activity does not have to be the same activity as the SUA. It's enough that the defendant knew that some sort of unlawful activity was going on. For example, in one case, *United States v. Montague,* 29 F.3d 317 (7th Cir. 1994), the defendant knew that the money was derived from state prostitution offenses (which is not a Specified Unlawful Activity), but the actual SUA was Interstate Travel in Aid of Racketeering. Second, the unlawful activity must be a felony.

"Knowledge" can be shown by proving willful blindness, deliberate ignorance, or a conscious attempt to avoid knowledge. This issue comes up frequently in cases involving "legitimate" business people such as real estate agents and car dealers who try hard — sometimes extremely hard — not to "know" about their client's illegal activities. A good example is *United States v. Puche,* 350 F.3d 1137 (11th Cir. 2003), in which the defendant told the undercover agent, "No, no, no," telling the agent not to talk about the illegal source of the money.

Unfortunately the "I know nothing!" defense used by Sergeant Schultz in the TV series *Hogan's Heroes* doesn't cut much ice when the circumstances are plain to any reasonable person. Good examples of the failure of this defense include:

- *United States v. Long,* 977 F.2d 1264 (8th Cir. 1990), involving a car dealer
- *United States v. Campbell,* 977 F.2d 854 (4th Cir. 1992), in which a real estate agent pretended not to know the source of the (drug) money used to buy a house
- *United States v. Bornfield,* 145 F.3d 1123 (10th Cir. 1998), in which an accountant took a large amount of (drug) cash from a client whom he knew had little or no legitimate income and converted the money to check form

All of these examples are especially instructive because they involve the sort of people (attorneys, accountants, car and real estate dealers) who are essential to the money laundering process but are *not* otherwise engaged in the illegal activity generating the money. Because of this, it is helpful to show that these people profited or benefited in some way from the criminal activity or the money laundering transaction, since the courts have cautioned that investigations involving merchants and business persons not previously known to have dealings in unlawfully generated currency warrant a greater scrutiny of the evidence. See *United States v. Jewel,* 532 F.2d 697 (9th Cir.), *cert. denied,* 426 U.S. 951 (1976).

We don't have this problem when the defendant is the perpetrator of the SUA; that person clearly knows the source of the laundered funds. If this person also conducted a financial transaction, his or her goose may be cooked. In any event, if the answer to the knowledge question is yes, we move to the issue of the transaction itself, and the next question is, *Did the defendant conduct a financial transaction or attempt to conduct a financial transaction?* This question relates to the financial transaction itself, and the answer will depend on how the terms "transaction" and "financial transaction" are defined.

The Defendant Conducted or Attempted to Conduct a Financial Transaction

Section 1956 (c) (3) defines a transaction very broadly, both in general and with respect to a financial institution. The Justice Department and the courts are looking for two factors in these situations, either one of which would constitute a transaction for purposes of the statute. The first is a transfer of property from one person, and the second is some form of "disposition" of the property.

The Justice Department has taken the position, and the courts have concurred, that an exchange of cash between two drug dealers is a transaction under the general definition, i.e., a "transfer" or "other disposition." Mere possession of cash, even though it is the proceeds of some SUA, would not be a disposition and would not constitute a transaction. See *United*

States v. Ramirez, 954 F.2d 1035 (5th Cir. 1995), *cert. denied,* 505 U.S. 1211 (1991), in which the court found that constructive possession of cash in a shoe box in the defendant's brother's house is insufficient evidence of a transaction. Delivery of the cash and its storage by a third party in another location has been held to be a disposition; see *United States v. Gaytan,* 74 F.3d 545 (5th Cir. 1996).

Under this section, the transportation of funds within the United States is probably not a transaction, unless the government can show some disposition of the funds at the other end. In *United States v. Puig-Infante,* 19 F.3d 929, (5th Cir. 1994), *cert. denied,* 513 U.S. 864 (1994), the court ruled that the transportation of drug proceeds from Florida to Texas was not a transaction unless the government could show some disposition after the proceeds arrived. The possession or carrying of cash through an airport was also not considered a transaction in *United States v. Gonzalez-Rodriguez,* 966 F.2d 918 (5th Cir. 1992). However, the act of giving drug proceeds to a courier to carry somewhere was ruled to be a transaction in *United States v. Reed,* 77 F.3d 139 (6th Cir.), *cert. denied,* 116 S.Ct. 2504 (1996).

Note that in all of the above, where the government was able to show a transfer from one person to another the courts held that a transaction had taken place.

Regarding transactions involving financial institutions, the statute defines these institutions broadly, to include banks, securities brokers and dealers, currency exchanges, insurance companies, travel agencies, wire transmitters, vehicle dealers, realtors, and the Postal Service. The types of transactions included are deposits, withdrawals, transfers between accounts, exchanges of currency, loans, extensions of credit, purchases or sale of any stock, bonds, certificates of deposit, or other monetary instruments, use of a safe deposit box, or any other payment, transfer, or delivery by, through, or to a financial institution, by whatever means effected.

Court decisions have held that the financial institution does not have to be an active participant in the scheme, nor is it necessary that it contribute to or facilitate the scheme. The following have been ruled to be "transactions involving the use of a financial institution":

- Making a payment with a bank money order. See *United States v. Koller,* 956 F.2d 1408 (7th Cir. 1992).
- Writing a check to a vendor. See *United States v. Jackson,* 935 F.2d 832 (7th Cir. 1991).
- Processing credit card charges. See *United States v. Brown,* 31 F.3d 484 (7th Cir. 1994).
- Use of a safe deposit box. See *United States v. Short,* 181 F.3d 620 (5th Cir. 1999).
- Transferring money between accounts in the same bank. See *United States v. Bieganowski,* 313 F.3d 264 (5th Cir. 2002).

Other financial transactions could involve either the movement of funds by wire or other means, or the use of some monetary instrument.

Two issues of note: First, if multiple transactions take place, as in a smurfing operation, where large cash transactions are broken up into smaller cashier's check purchases, Congress intended and the courts have generally held that each transaction is a separate violation. This is true even though they are all part of one scheme.

The second question relates to the "merger" of money laundering violations with the underlying SUA. This occurs in cases in which the SUA involves financial crimes like bank fraud, wire fraud, or some securities scheme. At what point do the stolen funds become "proceeds"? In order for a money laundering violation to take place, the funds must already *be* proceeds. Thus, in a drug deal, if I buy some drugs with money I earned in my job at the burger joint, this transaction cannot be a money laundering violation; see *United States v. Puig-Infante,* 19 F.3d 929 (5th Cir. 1994). Generally speaking, the money laundering transaction must occur *after* the underlying SUA has been completed.

A final consideration is the requirement that the transaction have some effect on interstate commerce. Courts have found that drug proceeds always relate to interstate commerce, and that most other transactions, especially those involving a financial institution, also have an interstate nexus. A government claim that a $200 cash payment to a video poker establishment "affected interstate commerce," however, was rejected; see *United States v. Grey,* 56 F.3d 1219 (10th Cir. 1995), *reversing* 856 F.Supp. 1515 (D.Kan. 1994).

The Defendant Acted with Intent

Now we come to the intent of the defendant in conducting the transaction. As the chart in Figure 3.1 shows, the defendant has to have intended to do at least one of four things before the offense is complete:

1. §1956 (a) (1) (A) (i): Intent to promote the carrying on of specified unlawful activity

Examples of this situation would be paying for drugs with the proceeds from other drug sales or reinvesting the proceeds of an illegal gambling business back into that business. Circumstantial evidence can be used to show intent for this section. The government is not required to prove that a defendant intended to violate a specific statute, only that he or she did intend to promote or facilitate an activity that he or she knew to be illegal. A violation may occur even if the SUA being promoted is never completed.

A defendant can engage in financial transaction(s) that promote not only ongoing or future activity, but also prior activity. See *United States v. Montoya,* 945 F.2d 1068 (9th Cir. 1991; deposit of check that represents proceeds of state bribery offense "promotes" bribery by giving defendant use of fruits of his criminal activity) and *United States v. Paramo,* 998 F.2d 1212 (3d. Cir. July 9, 1993), *cert. denied,* 114 S.Ct. 1076 (1994; converting fraudulently obtained checks into cash promoted underlying fraud by giving defendants access to funds; intent to "plow back" funds into fraud scheme was not required).

Under Section 1956 (a) (1) (A) (i), the payment of proceeds to fraud victims to entice them to continue to invest in a fraudulent scheme or to keep quiet about an ongoing scheme could be promotion.

2. §1956 (a)(1)(A)(ii): Intent to engage in conduct constituting a violation of §7201 or §7206 of the Internal Revenue Code

Here, in essence, the defendant is trying to evade the payment of taxes on the illegally acquired funds and to conceal the income from the IRS. This subsection is not charged nearly as often as the others. Generally speaking, IRS will be directly involved in the investigation of these cases; it possesses the tax returns and other documentation needed to prove the evasion.

It is helpful to actually have the subject's tax return to show the tax fraud, but the intent can be shown even when the tax year has not yet concluded and the tax return has not been filed. However, there must be some proof that a person who engaged in a subject financial transaction was aware that the transaction related in some way to an intended violation of Section 7201 or 7206.

Section 1956 (a) (1) (A) (ii) does not limit the type of tax or the type of document submitted. Also, the tax involved need not be the tax of the person engaging in the financial transaction; the statute can apply to a person who intends to assist another person to violate the tax laws.

The Department of Justice Tax Division will not authorize a Section 1956 (a) (1) (A) (ii) charge in tax crimes involving mail, wire, or bank fraud under the following conditions:

1. When a tax return or other IRS form or document is the only mailing charged
2. When the only wire transmission to the IRS involves a tax return or other IRS form, or the transmission of a refund check to a bank account by an electronic funds transfer
3. When the mailing, wire transfer, or representation charged is incidental to the underlying violation of internal revenue laws

Tax evasion is *not* an SUA. You cannot launder money that has been legally earned, even if the taxes due were not paid.

3. §1956 (a)(1)(B)(i): Intent to conceal or disguise the nature, source, ownership, or control of proceeds of SUA

This is probably the most widely charged violation under this chapter, and much of the money laundering case law comes from these violations. This isn't too surprising, because the intent to conceal or disguise the nature, source, ownership, or control of dirty money is, after all, the very heart of any money laundering scheme and the aim of any money launderer.

Once again, the evidence used to prove this element may be direct or circumstantial, and it could include a wide variety of acts or subterfuges on the criminal's part. Some examples that the courts found to be evidence of intent include:

- Engaging in convoluted transactions. See *United States v. Prince*, 214 F.3d 740 (6th Cir. 2000), in which the defendant had victims of a fraud scheme send money through a third party, who converted the money to cash and gave it to the defendant.
- Using the names of third parties. See *United States v. Hunt*, 272 F.3d 488 (7th Cir. 2001), wherein the defendant bought a car in the name of his business and then gave it to a drug dealer for cash.
- Using a false name. In *United States v. Omoruyi*, 260 F.3d 291 (3rd Cir. 2001), the defendant deposited funds in an account opened in a false name and withdrew the funds under a false name.
- Registering a vehicle or titling real property in a third party's name. This is, as we will see, a very common (and pretty simple) money laundering scheme. Drug traffickers and others will frequently place assets in the names of their trusted associates but retain the use of the property. *United States v. Bowman*, 235 F.3d 1113 (8th Cir. 2000) was one such case, and in *United States v. Fields*, 72 F.3d 1200 (5th Cir. 1996), a truck purchased with drug proceeds was registered in the drug trafficker's brother's name.
- Structuring cash transactions. Another common scheme involves deliberately arranging multiple cash transactions to avoid the filing of government reports. In the Prince case, cited above, such structured transactions were evidence of an intent to conceal or disguise. In a similar case, *United States v. Farese*, 248 F.3d 1056 (11th Cir. 2001), the actions involved exchanging many small-denomination bills for smaller numbers of large-denomination bills. This reduces the volume of the currency, something the courts agreed would make it easier to conceal and disguise.
- Commingling funds. Yet another very common money laundering technique, commingling funds involves mixing dirty money up with funds from some legitimate source, in the hope that the tainted funds will be hidden. In *United States v. Jackson*, 935 F.2d 832, 841 (7th Cir. 1991), drug money was commingled with legitimate funds in a church bank account, and in *United States v. Ness*, 2003 WestLaw 21804853 (S.D.N.Y. 2003), cash was concealed in a shipment of gold but was not included on the shipping documents.

Some other examples are the use of codes, use of multiple safe deposit boxes, conversion of proceeds to goods or services, and falsification of documents or records.

Two other issues merit some additional discussion. First, we need to keep in mind that the scheme does not have to be elaborate, clever, or even very effective; it only has to be carried out with the *intent* to conceal or disguise. Success need not be proven. Second, we are looking for the lengths to which the criminal goes to hide the money or his or her connection to it. In many cases, the actions taken will be completely legitimate, such as registering a vehicle. The issue for investigators is *why* this action was taken, and the question can often be answered by looking at how it was done. If the criminal went to elaborate lengths or special trouble to do something that hides a connection to dirty money, the intent may be clear to the jury.

In some cases the actions taken by the criminal might have looked suspicious, but the court held that the prosecutor did not go far enough in proving intent to conceal. The best examples of this are found in *United States v. Sanders,* 929 F.2d 1466 (10th Cir. 1991) and a number of subsequent, similar cases. In *Sanders,* the court held that buying a car in your own name or that of your daughter was not a money laundering transaction, even though the funds used were the proceeds of drug transactions. The court noted that simply spending money was not prohibited by the money laundering statute and that there could be other (legal) reasons why someone would buy a car and put it in the name of a close relative.

The effect of *Sanders* and similar decisions is fairly narrow, limited to family members of the alleged money launderer. Even in those instances, the intent to conceal or disguise can be proved by other actions the launderer takes, such as the making of false statements, falsification of documents, and engaging in convoluted or multiple transactions. A good example is *United States v. Kaufmann,* 985 F.2d 884 (7th Cir. 1993).

Finally, where the defendant is *not* the perpetrator of the underlying offense, the defendant need not intend to conceal or disguise; he or she only needs to know that the perpetrator's intent is to conceal or disguise. Concealment does not have to be the only motive for the transaction.

4. §1956 (a)(1)(B)(ii) and (a)(2)(B)(ii): Intent to avoid a transaction-reporting requirement under state or federal law (includes CTRs, CMIRs, and IRS Form 8300s)

The intent here is similar to that discussed in the "conceal and disguise" section. The reporting requirements exist in the first place because the government wants large and suspicious cash transactions to be disclosed when appropriate. Crooks know this and don't want the IRS reading all about their financial arrangements, so they take steps to hide these arrangements and conceal the transactions.

These steps might include the most typical: structuring large transactions into multiple smaller ones, often using the "smurfs" we'll be meeting in later chapters. Other steps might include bribing a bank employee or providing a false name to the person preparing the report. The courts have held that the defendant must know there is a reporting requirement (see *United States v. Bowman,* 235 F.3d 1113 (8th Cir. 2000)) but need not know that structuring the transaction is illegal; see *United States v. Santos,* 20 F.3d 280 n.2 (7th Cir. 1994).

TITLE 18 UNITED STATES CODE §1956 (a) (2): THE INTERNATIONAL TRANSPORTATION OFFENSE

This section addresses the international movement of currency or monetary instruments, a prime objective of drug traffickers and others who seek to move their money offshore from the United States (and away from our forfeiture and money laundering laws).

This provision can also be used in the layering and integration phases of a money laundering scheme, when the funds are being repatriated into the United States from abroad. As you can see from the chart in Figure 3.2, one provision, (a) (2) (A), does not require that the property involved in the transportation be the proceeds of an SUA. In *United States v. Hamilton,* 931 F.2d 1046 (5th Cir. 1991), the court wrote that a foreign drug cartel could violate Subsection (a) (2) (A) by sending the proceeds of a legitimate business into the United States if the purpose was the expansion of an illegal drug business in this country.

This section is divided into two parts, both relating to international transportation. It is a violation of 18 U.S.C. §1956 (a) (2) (A) for a person to transport, transmit, transfer, or attempt to do so monetary instrument or funds from a

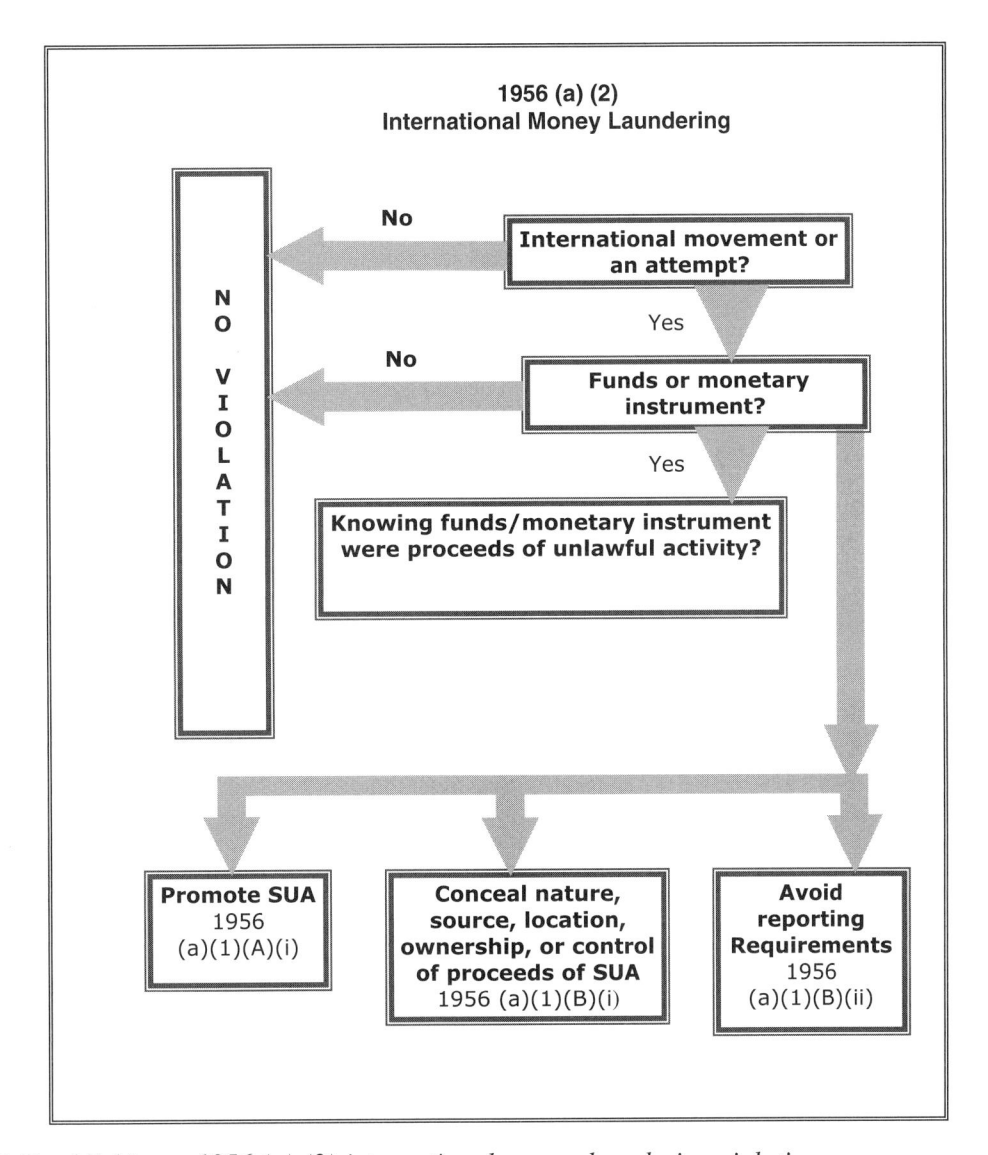

Figure 3.2 *Establishing a 1956 (a) (2) international money laundering violation.*

place in the United States to or through a place outside the United States, or to a place in the United States from or through a place outside the United States with the intent to promote the carrying on of specified unlawful activity.

It is a violation of 18 U.S.C. §1956 (a) (2) (B) for a person to transport, transmit, transfer, or attempt to do so monetary instrument or funds from a place in the United States to or through a place outside the United States, or to a place in the United States from or through a place outside the United States, knowing that the monetary instrument or funds represent the proceeds of some form of unlawful activity, and knowing (*a*) that the transportation is designed in whole or in part to conceal or disguise the nature, location, source, ownership, or control of the proceeds of Specified Unlawful Activity [§1956 (a) (2) (B) (i)] or (*b*) to avoid a transaction-reporting requirement under state or federal law [§1956 (a) (2) (B) (ii)].

The definitions used in this section are similar to those for other money laundering offenses, and court decisions have further defined what's what. "Transportation" has been found to include wire transfers; see *United States v. Piervinanzi,* 23 F.3d 670 (2nd Cir.), *cert. denied,* 513 U.S. 904 (1994), and *United States v. Monroe,* 943 F.2d 1007 (9th Cir. 1991), *cert. denied,* 503 U.S. 971 (1992). Other forms of transportation would obviously include smuggling. One case involved the unreported carrying of currency past Customs; see *United States v. Carr,* 25 F.3d 1194 (3rd Cir. 1994), *cert. denied,* 503 U.S. 971 (1992). This case also addressed the concealment and avoidance of the reporting requirement elements.

TITLE 18 U.S.C. 1956 (a) (3): THE "STING" PROVISION

Section 1956 requires that the money or property used in a financial transaction be from an SUA at the time of the transaction — with one exception. That exception relates to undercover operations. In undercover cases, the money used by the undercover agent obviously cannot be the proceeds of an SUA. For this reason, Congress created a separate section, 1956 (a) (3), to enable the government to conduct undercover money laundering investigations, some of which have been extremely successful.

See Figure 3.3 for a chart representing the requirements of this section. The salient questions are as follows:

Did the defendant conduct or attempt to conduct a financial transaction? The definition of "financial transaction" is unchanged. One issue that has been the subject of a number of court cases is the question of "attempt" and how far the defendant has to go before the act constitutes a *substantial* attempt. The general conclusion is

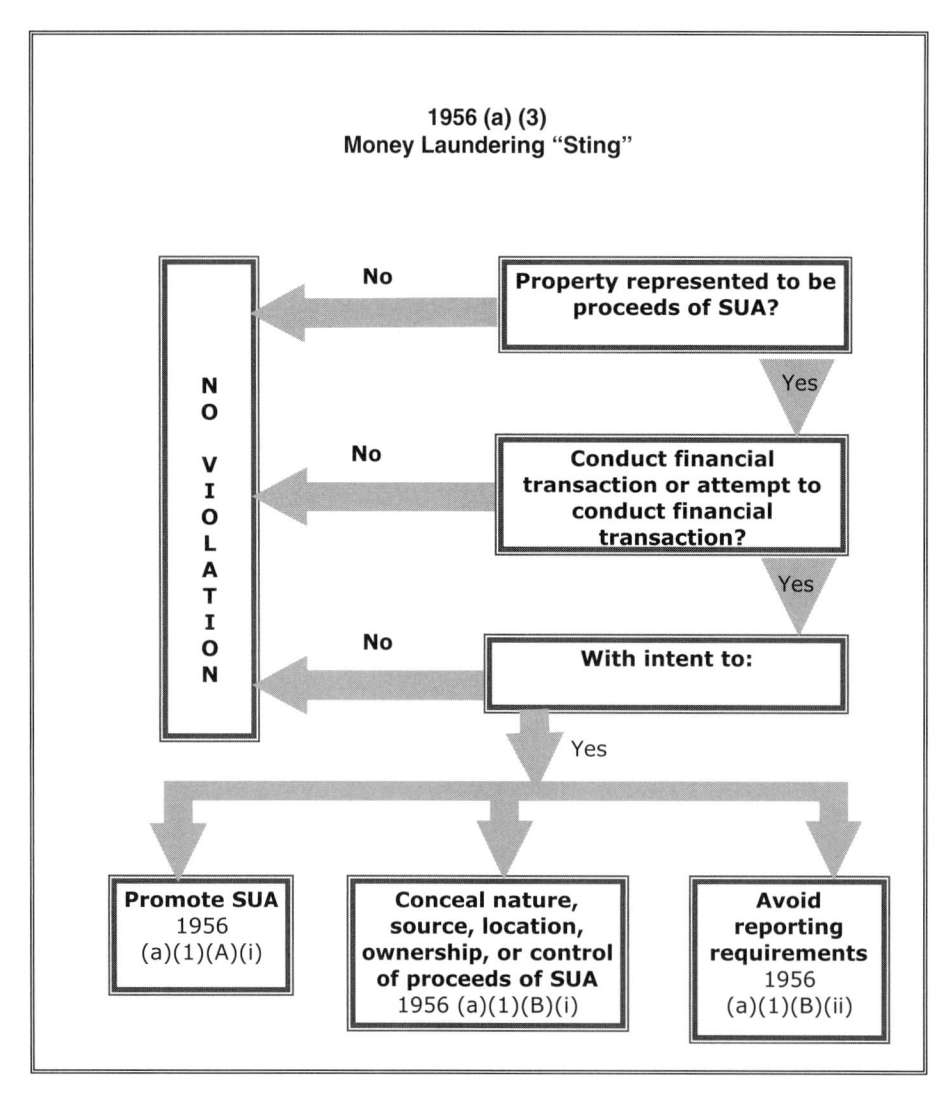

Figure 3.3 *Determining a 1956 (a) (3) money laundering "sting" violation.*

that the further along the transaction gets, the better off we are in proving what the defendant intended or had in mind.

Was the property represented by law enforcement to be the proceeds of an SUA? Did the undercover agent describe the money in such a way that the defendant could conclude that the money came from an SUA? Undercover agents have a little leeway in describing the SUA, although the United States Attorney likes to hear something like, "I told him the money came from cocaine sales." More ambiguous statements will work if the defendant's responses indicate an understanding of the illegal source; see *United States v. Breque,* 964 F.2d 381 (5th Cir. 1992), *cert. denied,* 507 U.S. 909 (1993). Alternatively, the defendant may be "aware of circumstances from which a reasonable person would infer that the property was drug proceeds"; see *United States v. Kaufmann,* 985 F.2d 884 (7th Cir.), *cert. denied,* 508 U.S. 913 (1993).

If the answers to the above questions are both yes, the defendant still has to intend to do at least one of three things in conducting the transaction. The answer to the following question must also be yes:

Did the defendant have intent to promote a Specified Unlawful Activity, to conceal or disguise the characteristics of property believed to be proceeds from an SUA, or to avoid a reporting requirement? This will be answered by the defendant's words or conduct. If the defendant takes a cash payment from the undercover agent and agrees not to file IRS form 8300, this action demonstrates intent to conceal and to avoid a reporting requirement. See *United States v. Loehr,* 966 F.2d 201 (6th Cir.), *cert. denied,* 506 U.S. 1020 (1992).

One issue raised by defendants is the question of "belief," as in, "Well, he told me he was a drug dealer, but I didn't really believe him." Juries in several cases have rejected this claim, based on circumstantial evidence that the defendant *acted* as if he or she believed the undercover agent. See *United States v. Kaufmann* and *United States v. Starke,* 62 F.3d 1374 (11th Cir. 1995).

Entrapment is obviously a factor in these cases, one that does not arise in the other money laundering crimes under Section 1956 (Section 1957 does not have a "sting" provision). The rules regarding entrapment are the same as for other federal crimes, but consider the court ruling in *United States v. Hollingsworth,* 27 F.3d 1196 (7th Cir. 1994; en banc), in which the court held that the government must prove not only that the defendant was willing to commit the money laundering offense, but also that he or she had the means to do so and only needed an opportunity, which was all that was provided by the government.

In short, the government needs to establish that even without any government involvement, the defendant was in a position to launder the money: ready, willing, and able.

TITLE 18 U.S.C. 1957

Section 1957 is sometimes thought of as the "baby brother" of Section 1956. It is less frequently used than 1956 and less well understood by agents and prosecutors. It is also simpler but has more limited applications.

Section 1957 contains an offense entitled "Engaging in monetary transactions in property derived from specified unlawful activity." In essence, §1957 proscribes the knowing receipt or disbursement of more than $10,000 in criminally derived proceeds if a financial institution is utilized at some point. In contrast to §1956, it does not require that the funds be used for any additional criminal purpose, nor is it necessary that the defendant engaged in the transaction with any specific intent.

The purpose of this part of the money laundering law is to keep dirty money out of the banking and financial system. Congress recognized that the proceeds of criminal activity can have a very corruptive influence on banks and financial institutions and that banks are key parts of most money laundering schemes. Section 1957 takes aim at money laundering that takes place in or around these institutions.

A person violates Section 1957 when he or she engages or attempts to engage in a monetary transaction in criminally derived property where the value of the criminally derived property

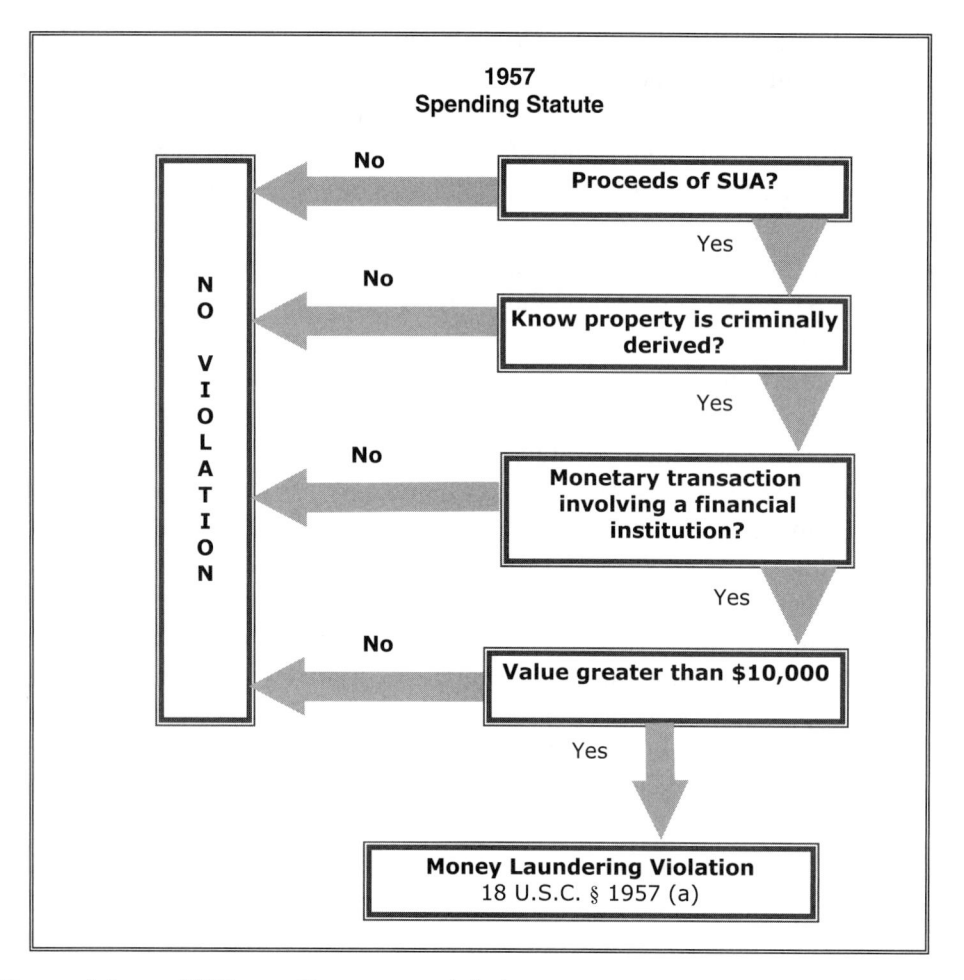

Figure 3.4 *Determining a 1957 spending statute violation.*

exceeds $10,000, the property is derived from Specified Unlawful Activity, and the person knows that the property is criminally derived.

Figure 3.4 illustrates the process of establishing a violation of Section 1957.

The first question is whether the defendant engaged or attempted to engage in a monetary transaction. The answer will depend upon the definition of "monetary transaction," a new term not used in Section 1956. Section 1957 (f) (1) defines a monetary transaction to include the deposit, withdrawal, transfer, or exchange, in or affecting interstate or foreign commerce, of funds or a monetary instrument, by, through, or to a financial institution (as defined in §1956), including any financial transactions defined by §1956 (c) (4) (B). So, pretty much everything you can do in a bank would be covered. Note, though, that Section 1957 (f) (1) states that the term does not include any transaction necessary to preserve a person's right to representation as guaranteed by the sixth amendment to the Constitution.

It is important to remember, when you are looking at potential violations under this statute, that since 1992 the term "financial institutions" includes more than just banks. Savings and loans, securities brokers, credit card companies, pawnbrokers, vehicle dealers, finance companies, real estate agents, and the Postal Service also qualify.

The second question relates to the source of the funds: *Was the transaction conducted in criminally derived property?* "Criminally derived property" means the same thing as "proceeds" under §1956; see *United States v. Savage,* 67 F.3d 1435 (9th Cir. 1995), so you would satisfy the element with the same type of information you would use in a 1956 case. Circumstantial evidence that the money is dirty can be used, such as the nature of the payment and attempts to conceal the source. The property used in the transaction *must* be criminally derived at the time the transaction is conducted, which means there is no "sting" provision for this section.

The next question is simple: *Is the value greater than $10,000?* You will recall that Section 1956 has no dollar floor for its transaction, but 1957 requires that more than $10,000 be transacted. Court rulings have been mixed as to whether the $10,000 has to be transferred all at once, but it is clear that the total has to be over $10,000. A somewhat unclear issue involves multiple sources for the funds, or the commingling of dirty money with clean. In one case, the court insisted that at least $10,000 of the total amount be traceable to a criminal source or SUA; see *United States v. Adams*, 74 F.3d 1039 (11th Cir. 1996). In another case, *United States v. Sokolow*, 81 F.3d 397 (3rd Cir. 1996), the government was not required to show that all of the money involved in a transaction was dirty when $20,000 of dirty money was commingled. It was enough that the government could show that the SUA funds had been commingled with the clean.

If a series of smaller transactions are closely related, as would be the case if a drug dealer broke a $43,000 payment into five smaller ones, all made close together in time, the payments may be considered one monetary transaction over $10,000. This type of aggregation will probably meet with Department of Justice approval, but a series of smaller deposits to a bank account, or some other transactions not so closely related to a single purpose, may not be enough to bring a case under Section 1957.

The next question is: *Is the property actually from an SUA?* Again, we are required to show that the property, which does not have to be cash, is actually traceable to an SUA. This is a factual issue, one that can be proved with circumstantial evidence, but direct tracing is mandatory.

Because so much of the other evidence in a 1957 case consists of the sort of irrefutable financial records that you normally find at a bank, the question as to the illegal source of the money is likely to be hotly contested at trial. Since this is practically the only defense available, the defendant may claim that the money *really* came from some dead uncle, a legitimate consulting contract, or some other legal source. Disproving this sort of claim is where financial investigative techniques can come in handy.

That's it. If the answers to all of the above are yes, your 1957 case is complete.

TITLE 18 U.S.C. 1956 (h): CONSPIRACY

A provision regarding money laundering conspiracy was added to Section 1956 in 1992. This subsection, originally 1956 (g), was redesignated Section 1956 (h) in 1994. It provides for a 10- or 20-year sentence for persons convicted of conspiracy to violate Section 1957 or 1956, respectively. Although the conspiracy provision does not require that an overt act be committed, the Department of Justice recommends that one be included, especially in a plea.

To prove a violation of Section 1956 (h), the government must prove that a defendant knew that transacted funds were proceeds of an SUA. In a Section 1956 (a) (3) "sting" prosecution, a court held that it is not necessary for co-conspirators to know that funds are coming from the same illegal activity, but they must know that the unlawful source is one of the prescribed SUAs. See *United States v. Stavroulakis*, 952 F.2d 686 (2d Cir. 1992). The government's role in a sting conspiracy should be limited to supplying funds, while letting the defendants be responsible for devising how the funds will be laundered. See Figure 3.5 for a chart representing the requirements of this section.

The Department of Justice has directed that conspiracy to violate 18 U.S.C. §1956 and/or 1957 will be charged under 18 U.S.C. §1956 (h) and not under 18 U.S.C. §371 — the main federal conspiracy statute.

OTHER ISSUES

Venue and Statute of Limitations

Venue in substantive money laundering cases is in any district where the financial transaction(s) took place. A new section, 1956 (i), was enacted

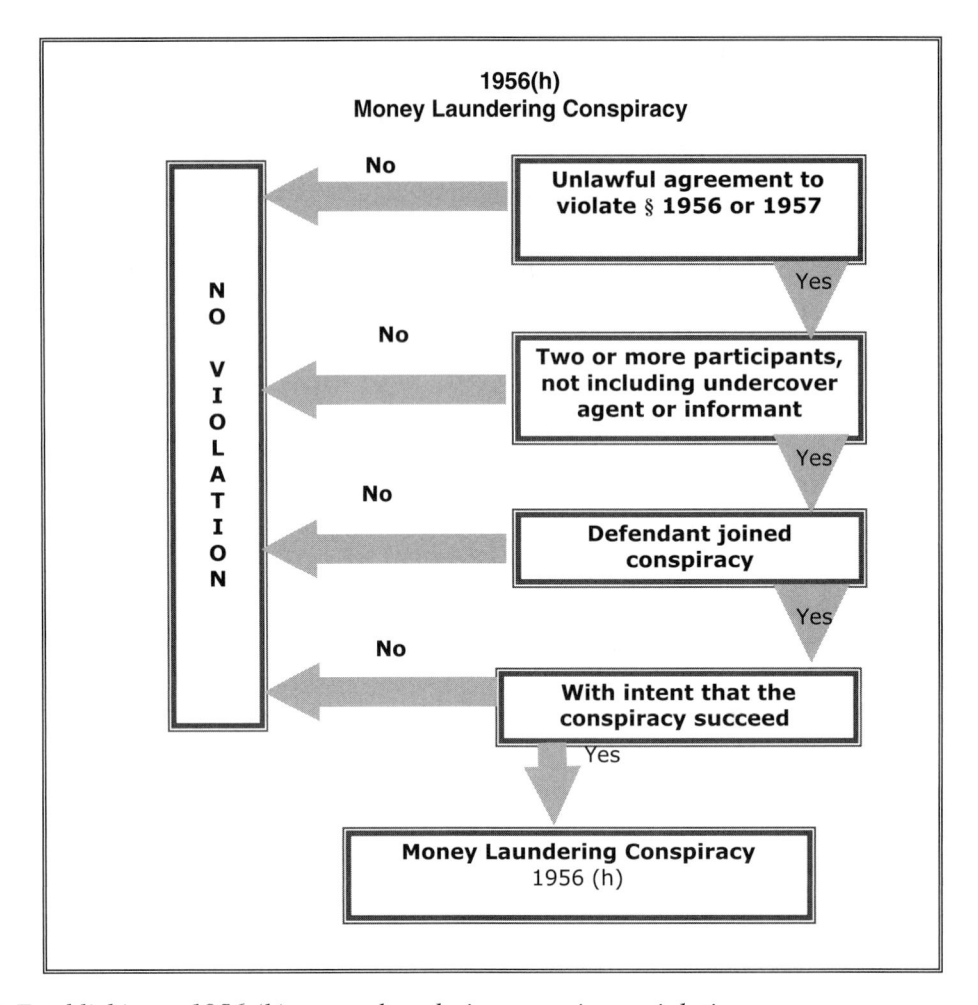

```
                        1956(h)
                Money Laundering Conspiracy

         No      ┌──────────────────────────┐
    ◄───────     │  Unlawful agreement to   │
                 │  violate § 1956 or 1957  │
 N               └──────────────────────────┘
 O                          │ Yes
 ▼                          ▼
 V       No      ┌──────────────────────────┐
 I  ◄───────     │  Two or more participants,│
 O               │  not including undercover │
 L               │  agent or informant       │
 A               └──────────────────────────┘
 T                          │ Yes
 I                          ▼
 O       No      ┌──────────────────────────┐
 N  ◄───────     │   Defendant joined       │
                 │   conspiracy             │
                 └──────────────────────────┘
                            │ Yes
                            ▼
         No      ┌──────────────────────────┐
    ◄───────     │  With intent that the    │
                 │  conspiracy succeed      │
                 └──────────────────────────┘
                            │ Yes
                            ▼
                 ┌──────────────────────────┐
                 │ Money Laundering Conspiracy│
                 │        1956 (h)           │
                 └──────────────────────────┘
```

Figure 3.5 *Establishing a 1956 (h) money laundering conspiracy violation.*

in October 2001 to clarify venue issues raised by court decisions in the past. The key issue in dispute involved where the underlying Specified Unlawful Activity took place, as opposed to where the money was actually laundered. In *United States v. Cabrales,* 524 U.S. 1 (1998), the proceeds of the SUA were transported to Florida from Missouri, the state where the SUA took place. Financial transactions occurred in Florida. The Supreme Court held that the defendant could not be prosecuted for money laundering in Missouri, even though that is where the SUA happened.

So, we should be looking for the places where financial transactions — which are the heart of a money laundering scheme — occurred. The courts tend to look at this with some flexibility, because financial transactions include "initiating, concluding, and participating in initiating and concluding a transaction," which covers a lot of ground. See *United States v. Golb,* 69 F.3d 1417 (9th Cir. 1995), *cert. denied,* 517 U.S. 1127 (1996). In this case, the court held that a violation occurred wherever the defendant traveled or made telephone calls to arrange one or more financial transactions.

The statute of limitation for crimes under 18 U.S.C. §1956 or §1957 or Title 31 is five years, and it runs from the date on which the offense is complete. This raises an interesting question: If "dirty" money never gets really "clean," when does one ever really stop laundering it?

The answer may be "never." In at least one case, an individual who made money by smuggling marijuana in the 1970s was charged with money laundering in financial transactions that occurred after 2001. He knew the assets he was moving around were originally acquired with drug money, and he was still acting to conceal them and their source from the government. The result was that, long after he left the drug business, he found himself looking at jail time for money laundering — something that wasn't even illegal back when he was a smuggler.

Proving such a crime might be difficult, but — in theory at least — investigators can reach back a very long way to catch money launderers.

SENTENCING

The bottom line for investigators and defendants alike is the criminal penalty. Those for money laundering are fairly severe. The potential sentence for a violation of 18 U.S.C. 1956 (a) (1) is a fine of up to $500,000 or twice the value of the monetary instruments involved, whichever is greater, or imprisonment of up to 20 years, or both; and for a violation of 1956 (a) (3) the potential sentence is an undetermined fine, or imprisonment of up to 20 years, or both.

The criminal penalty for a violation of 18 U.S.C. 1957 is a fine in accordance with 18 U.S.C. 3571–3574 (or up to twice the amount of the criminally derived property involved in the transaction), or up to 10 years imprisonment, or both.

Provisions for civil penalties are also included in 18 U.S.C. 1956 (b). Violators under Subsection 1956 (a) (1) or (2) are liable for a civil penalty of not more than the greater of the value of the property, funds, or monetary instruments involved in the transaction, or $10,000. The civil penalty is intended to be imposed in addition to any criminal fine. 18 U.S.C. 1956 (h) and 1957 do not carry corresponding civil penalties.

The 10- and 20-year penalties are a reminder of how far the law has progressed from the time when tax evasion, conspiracy, and Bank Secrecy Act statutes, all with five-year penalties, were the primary means of addressing this problem.

Today, when combined with these other statutes and those relating to the underlying Specified Unlawful Activities, the money laundering laws have become the extremely valuable tool Congress intended for law enforcement to have.

SPECIFIED UNLAWFUL ACTIVITY — TITLE 18 U.S.C. SECTIONS 1956 AND 1957 (MONEY LAUNDERING CONTROL ACT OF 1986)

The following are violations of federal and state or foreign law that are identified as specified unlawful activities in Title 18, U.S.C., Section 1956 (c) (7).

(7) the term "specified unlawful activity" means—

(A) any act or activity constituting an offense listed in section 1961 (1) of this title except an act which is indictable under subchapter II of chapter 53 of title 31;

(B) with respect to a financial transaction occurring in whole or in part in the United States, an offense against a foreign nation involving—

(i) the manufacture, importation, sale, or distribution of a controlled substance (as such term is defined for the purposes of the Controlled Substances Act);

(ii) murder, kidnapping, robbery, extortion, destruction of property by means of explosive or fire, or a crime of violence (as defined in section 16);

(iii) fraud, or any scheme or attempt to defraud, by or against a foreign bank (as defined in paragraph 7 of section 1(b) of the International Banking Act of 1978);

(iv) bribery of a public official, or the misappropriation, theft, or embezzlement of public funds by or for the benefit of a public official;

(v) smuggling or export control violations involving —

(I) an item controlled on the United States Munitions List established under section 38 of the Arms Export Control Act (22 U.S.C. 2778); or

(II) an item controlled under regulations under the Export Administration Regulations (15 C.F.R. Parts 730–774); or

(vi) an offense with respect to which the United States would be obligated by a multilateral treaty, either to extradite the alleged offender or to submit the case for prosecution, if the offender were found within the territory of the United States;

(C) any act or acts constituting a continuing criminal enterprise, as that term is defined in section 408 of the Controlled Substances Act (21 U.S.C. 848);

(D) an offense under section (Title 18, United States Code)

32 (relating to the destruction of aircraft),

37 (relating to violence at international airports),

115 (relating to influencing, impeding, or retaliating against a Federal official by threatening or injuring a family member),

152 (relating to concealment of assets; false oaths and claims; bribery),

215 (relating to commissions or gifts for procuring loans),

351 (relating to congressional or Cabinet officer assassination),

500 through 503 (relating to certain counterfeiting offenses),

513 (relating to securities of States and private entities),

541 (relating to goods falsely classified),

542 (relating to entry of goods by means of false statements),

545 (relating to smuggling goods into the United States),

549 (relating to removing goods from Customs custody),

641 (relating to public money, property, or records),

656 (relating to theft, embezzlement, or misapplication by bank officer or employee),

657 (relating to lending, credit, and insurance institutions),

658 (relating to property mortgaged or pledged to farm credit agencies),

666 (relating to theft or bribery concerning programs receiving Federal funds),

793, 794, or 798 (relating to espionage),

831 (relating to prohibited transactions involving nuclear materials),

844 (f) or (i) (relating to destruction by explosives or fire of Government property or property affecting interstate or foreign commerce),

875 (relating to interstate communications),

922 (l) (relating to the unlawful importation of firearms),

924 (n) (relating to firearms trafficking),

956 (relating to conspiracy to kill, kidnap, maim, or injure certain property in a foreign country),

1005 (relating to fraudulent bank entries),

1006 (relating to fraudulent Federal credit institution entries),

1007 (relating to Federal Deposit Insurance transactions),

1014 (relating to fraudulent loan or credit applications),

1030 (relating to computer fraud and abuse),

1032 (relating to concealment of assets from conservator, receiver, or liquidating agent of financial institution),

1111 (relating to murder),

1114 (relating to murder of United States law enforcement officials),

1116 (relating to murder of foreign officials, official guests, or internationally protected persons),

1201 (relating to kidnapping),

1203 (relating to hostage taking),

1361 (relating to willful injury of Government property),

1363 (relating to destruction of property within the special maritime and territorial jurisdiction),

1708 (theft from the mail),

1751 (relating to Presidential assassination),

2113 or 2114 (relating to bank and postal robbery and theft),

2280 (relating to violence against maritime navigation),

2281 (relating to violence against maritime fixed platforms),

2319 (relating to copyright infringement),

2320 (relating to trafficking in counterfeit goods and services),

2332 (relating to terrorist acts abroad against United States nationals),

2332a (relating to use of weapons of mass destruction),

2332b (relating to international terrorist acts transcending national boundaries),

2339A or 2339B (relating to providing material support to terrorists) of this title,

Section 46502 of title 49, United States Code, a felony violation of the Chemical Diversion and Trafficking Act of 1988 (relating to precursor and essential chemicals),

Section 590 of the Tariff Act of 1930 (19 U.S.C. 1590) (relating to aviation smuggling),

Section 422 of the Controlled Substances Act (relating to transportation of drug paraphernalia), Section 38 (c) (relating to criminal violations) of the Arms Export Control Act, section 11 (relating to violations) of the Export Administration Act of 1979,

Section 206 (relating to penalties) of the International Emergency Economic Powers Act,

Section 16 (relating to offenses and punishment) of the Trading with the Enemy Act,

Any felony violation of section 15 of the Food Stamp Act of 1977 (relating to food stamp fraud) involving a quantity of coupons having a value of not less than $5,000,

Any violation of section 543 (a) (1) of the Housing Act of 1949 (relating to equity skimming),

Any felony violation of the Foreign Agents Registration Act of 1938,

Any felony violation of the Foreign Corrupt Practices Act (environmental crimes),

(E) a felony violation of the Federal Water Pollution Control Act (33 U.S.C. 1251 *et seq.*), the Ocean Dumping Act (33 U.S.C. 1401 *et seq.*), the Act to Prevent Pollution from Ships (33 U.S.C. 1901 *et seq.*), the Safe Drinking Water Act (42 U.S.C. 300f *et seq.*), or the Resources Conservation and Recovery Act (42 U.S.C. 6901 *et seq.*); or

(F) any act or activity constituting an offense involving a Federal health care offense.

The so-called predicate acts under the Racketeer Influenced and Corrupt Organizations (RICO) statute, Title 18 U.S.C. 1961, are, as noted above, also SUAs for the purpose of the money laundering statutes. These predicate acts are:

(A) any act or threat involving murder, kidnapping, gambling, arson, robbery, bribery, extortion, dealing in obscene matter, or dealing in a controlled substance or listed chemical (as defined in section 102 of the Controlled Substances Act), which is chargeable under State law and punishable by imprisonment for more than one year;

(B) any act which is indictable under any of the following provisions of title 18, United States Code:

201 (relating to bribery),

224 (relating to sports bribery),

471, 472, and 473 (relating to counterfeiting),

659 (relating to theft from interstate shipment) if the act indictable under section 659 is felonious,

664 (relating to embezzlement from pension and welfare funds),

891 through 894 (relating to extortionate credit transactions),

1028 (relating to fraud and related activity in connection with identification documents),

1029 (relating to fraud and related activity in connection with access devices),

1084 (relating to the transmission of gambling information),

1341 (relating to mail fraud),

1343 (relating to wire fraud),

1344 (relating to financial institution fraud),

1425 (relating to the procurement of citizenship or nationalization unlawfully),

1426 (relating to the reproduction of naturalization or citizenship papers),

1427 (relating to the sale of naturalization or citizenship papers),

1461 through 1465 (relating to obscene matter),

1503 (relating to obstruction of justice),

1510 (relating to obstruction of criminal investigations),

1511 (relating to the obstruction of State or local law enforcement),

1512 (relating to tampering with a witness, victim, or an informant),

1513 (relating to retaliating against a witness, victim, or an informant),

1542 (relating to false statement in application and use of passport),

1543 (relating to forgery or false use of passport),

1544 (relating to misuse of passport),

1546 (relating to fraud and misuse of visas, permits, and other documents),

1581 through 1588 (relating to peonage and slavery),

1951 (relating to interference with commerce, robbery, or extortion),

1952 (relating to racketeering),

1953 (relating to interstate transportation of wagering paraphernalia),

1954 (relating to unlawful welfare fund payments),

1955 (relating to the prohibition of illegal gambling businesses),

1956 (relating to the laundering of monetary instruments),

1957 (relating to engaging in monetary transactions in property derived from SUA),

1958 (relating to use of interstate commerce facilities in the commission of murder-for-hire),

2251, 2251A, 2252, and 2260 (relating to sexual exploitation of children),

2312 and 2313 (relating to interstate transportation of stolen motor vehicles),

2314 and 2315 (relating to interstate transportation of stolen property),

2318 (relating to trafficking in counterfeit labels for phonorecords, computer programs or computer program documentation or packaging and copies of motion pictures or other audiovisual works),

2319 (relating to criminal infringement of a copyright),

2319A (relating to unauthorized fixation of and trafficking in sound recordings and music videos of live musical performances),

2320 (relating to trafficking in goods or services bearing counterfeit marks),

2321 (relating to trafficking in certain motor vehicles or motor vehicle parts),

2341 through 2346 (relating to trafficking in contraband cigarettes),

2421 through 2424 (relating to white slave traffic),

(C) any act which is indictable under title 29, United States Code,

186 (dealing with restrictions on payments and loans to labor organizations) or

501 (c) (relating to embezzlement from union funds),

(D) any offense involving fraud connected with a case under title 11 (except a case under section 157 of this title), fraud in the sale of securities, or the felonious manufacture, importation, receiving, concealment, buying, selling, or otherwise dealing in a controlled substance or listed chemical (as defined in section 102 of the Controlled Substances Act), punishable under any law of the United States,

(E) any act which is indictable under the Currency and Foreign Transactions Reporting Act,

(F) any act which is indictable under the Immigration and Nationality Act, section 274 (relating to bringing in and harboring certain aliens), section 277 (relating to aiding or assisting certain aliens to enter the United States), or section 278 (relating to importation of alien for immoral purpose) if the act indictable under such section of such Act was committed for the purpose of financial gain,

(G) any act that is indictable under any provision listed in section 2332b (g) (5) (B).

FREQUENTLY ASKED QUESTIONS ABOUT SUAS

What if the underlying offense is a gambling violation — is this an SUA? Maybe. Gambling isn't listed as an SUA, but gambling offenses may be RICO predicates. For example, Title 18 U.S.C. §1084 prohibits transmission of gambling data, and §1953 deals with the transmission of wagering paraphernalia. Section 1955 addresses illegal gambling businesses, and, finally, any gambling offense that is a felony under state law is also a RICO predicate, and, thus, an SUA. Misdemeanor gambling offenses will not qualify.

What about prostitution? No, prostitution and promoting prostitution are not SUAs or RICO predicates. However, under Title 18 U.S.C. §1952, the Interstate or Foreign Travel and Transportation in Aid of Racketeering Enterprises (ITAR) Act, prostitution is listed as an unlawful activity. You will need to prove the added elements under the ITAR statute, but there have been money laundering cases brought with this offense as the SUA.

I've got a case where someone is structuring cash transactions to avoid having the bank file a Currency Transaction Report. The money was earned legally, but structuring is a RICO predicate act. Is this an SUA? No. Even though violations of title 31, subchapter II (including structuring) are RICO predicates, they are specifically excluded as SUAs. Congress wanted to keep the focus of the money laundering statutes on money that was genuinely dirty.

What about tax fraud and evasion? Tax fraud and evasion are not SUAs or RICO predicates. Even though a tax cheat is essentially stealing money from the government, Congress did not incorporate these crimes into the money laundering statute for the same reason that structuring was not included: the focus is supposed to be on money derived from some criminal activity.

CHAPTER 4

THE USA PATRIOT ACT

"So spake the grisly terror."
John Milton

"Stand your ground. Don't fire unless fired upon, but if they mean to have a war, let it begin here!"
John Parker — command given at the Battle of Lexington

In the days, weeks, and months following the terrorist attacks of September 11, 2001, people all across America felt the need to do something. Memorials were made, tributes written to the victims, and support offered to survivors. Americans did what they could to help those affected by the tragedy, and they wholeheartedly supported their government's efforts to track down those responsible.

That effort would take place on a number of fronts, from a full-blown war in Afghanistan to criminal indictments in New York and Virginia. The government itself would undergo a massive reorganization that saw the creation of an entirely new cabinet-level Department of Homeland Security, a rebuilding of the damaged Pentagon, and the passage of legislation intended to stop terrorism.

When ordinary citizens decide they want to "do something" for their country, they may donate blood or money for relief efforts or put up yellow ribbons in honor of their soldiers. Some, like former National Football League standout Pat Tillman, join the army and make a far greater sacrifice. When Congress decides to "do something," it legislates, and in the wake of 9/11, our elected representatives wanted very badly to "do something." One result was Public Law 107-56, The Uniting and Strengthening America by Providing Appropriate Tools Required to Intercept and Obstruct Terrorism Act of 2001, also known as the USA PATRIOT Act or just the "Patriot Act."

This measure enjoyed wide, bipartisan support at the time of its passage, even getting some kind words from such unlikely allies as the American Civil Liberties Union and the Bush administration's Justice Department. Almost four years later, the rosy glow of shared good feelings has faded away as parties from all points of the political compass have discovered aspects of the act they dislike. These new objections are significant because certain provisions of the USA PATRIOT Act are designed to "sunset" or expire on December 31, 2005. By the time you read this, parts of the law may already have been effectively repealed. (Congress extended the act until February. Because the noncontroversial money-laundering provisions were in Title III, these did not sunset and are not affected by the current debate.)

Most of the controversy relates to the first sections of the Patriot Act, which outline various investigative techniques and methods law enforcement can use to "intercept and obstruct terrorism." Quite a few of the provisions address the so-called "wall" that formerly separated intelligence operations and law enforcement, preventing those working on one side of the wall from talking to those working on the other. The pre-9/11 restrictions created sometimes silly situations in which two groups in the same FBI field office would be conducting an investigation on the same individual without being able to talk to each other. As one U.S. Attorney, Patrick Fitzgerald, put it in Congressional testimony:

> I was on a prosecution team in New York that began a criminal investigation of Usama Bin Laden in early 1996. The team — prosecutors and FBI agents assigned to the criminal case — had access to a number of sources. We could talk to citizens. We could talk to local police officers. We could talk to other U.S. Government agencies. We could talk to foreign police officers. Even foreign intelligence personnel. And foreign citizens. And we did all those things as often as we could. We could even talk to al Qaeda members — and we did. We actually called several members and associates of al Qaeda to testify before a grand jury in New York. And we even debriefed al Qaeda members overseas who agreed to become cooperating witnesses.
>
> But there was one group of people we were not permitted to talk to. Who? The FBI agents across the street from us in lower Manhattan assigned to a parallel intelligence investigation of Usama Bin Laden and al Qaeda. We could not learn what information they had gathered. That was "the wall."

When the Patriot Act removed (or at least lowered) the wall, investigations of terrorist organizations resulted in indictments of groups and individuals in Portland, Oregon; Florida; and Virginia. Significantly, the use of these techniques also permitted the government to examine some of the financing mechanisms by which the terrorist groups were funded, something that relates directly to our study here. In one case, the Executive Director of the Benevolence International Foundation, based in Illinois, was indicted and convicted of using his charitable organization to obtain funds from Americans for terrorist groups such as al Qaeda and of diverting the funds to Islamic militant groups in Bosnia and Chechnya.

Other sections of the act address the types of information that investigators collect; concerns have been raised that perhaps the new law allows too much government intrusion into personal privacy, or makes it too easy for investigators to seek out personal information without independent judicial review. In fact, most of the Patriot Act's provisions in this area streamline existing procedures. For example, the act allows investigators working in multiple judicial districts to get a search warrant from one judge, rather than having to go to multiple courts in each district. The act also addresses the new technology relating to the Internet, cellular and mobile communications, and other "cyber" evidence, providing a mechanism for the government to quickly obtain warrants for electronic mail, information from Internet service providers, and voice mail messages. Because speed is of the essence in terrorism investigations, the process for acquiring warrants or court orders for this type of information was simplified, but the act did not remove the need to have an independent judicial review of each request.

There are those who find any enhancement of the government's investigative ability to be a threat to privacy and personal liberty. Others will say that people living in a nation at war must expect to sacrifice something, perhaps some privacy, in exchange for more security from terrorist attack. The Patriot Act generally tries to find a middle ground, as in the section that allows investigators in sensitive cases to conduct a covert search pursuant to warrant without immediately notifying the subject that the search took place. Investigators still have to see a judge for a warrant and have to follow other procedures designed to protect people's rights, but the law recognizes that sometimes in this fast-paced digital world, extraordinary (and speedier) measures are called for.

Ironically, the majority of the USA PATRIOT Act, with its many parts and subparts, will never affect the jobs of the average law enforcement officer or criminal investigator who is not routinely involved in intelligence, counterterrorism, or espionage-type cases. For those of us engaged in more mundane criminal investigations, the act's most relevant provisions are those that Congress tacked on because they peripherally related to terrorism cases.

Money laundering is one of these areas. About 54 pages of the Patriot Act are taken up with issues relating to money laundering and the investigation of financial crimes. Unlike the sections of the act dealing with how law enforcement can gather evidence about terrorism-related crimes, the money laundering provisions arouse very little controversy, and that in a fairly limited circle. As we will see, though, inside that circle the objections can be somewhat heated.

Within a few days of 9/11, Congress had figured out what many in law enforcement already knew: terrorism, like any other crime, is in large part about money. Mass murder was not the sole aim of the 9/11 plotters; they also intended to wreak severe economic damage on the United States, attacking one of the financial centers of the nation. They also needed money in order to carry out their plan successfully.

The financing of a terrorist plot, particularly one that was in the planning and preparation stages for years, is, investigators discovered, very similar to a money laundering operation conducted by organized criminal groups. There is an element of secrecy, financial movement and manipulation, a criminal goal, and the use of funds to facilitate the plot. What differed significantly from other money laundering cases was the source of the money itself. While there is still some question as to the actual source of the 9/11 funds, much of the financial backing for Islamist terrorism is derived from charitable contributions made in mosques and to organizations established to fulfill the Quran's requirement that Muslims give generously to the poor and needy.

Whether these contributions are made in Saudi Arabia, Pakistan, or the United States, as we have seen in previous chapters, *only* money that is derived from a crime or a Specified Unlawful Activity can be laundered in violation of federal law. The catch in the case of terrorist financing is that the charitable contributions are being used to fund an illegal and nefarious activity. Congress looked at American law and had to answer a difficult question: If money laundering is the process of making dirty money appear clean, then what do we have when crooks are using clean money — say, the proceeds of foreign charitable donations — to fund a criminal conspiracy?

Nobody, Congress included, knew the answer to that question, but everyone did know it wasn't money laundering. They also knew it shouldn't be something encouraged or even tolerated, so they took some steps to put a stop to it. One step was passage of new legislation as part of the Patriot Act relating to money laundering and terrorist financing.

Title III of the act is the International Money Laundering Abatement and Anti-Terrorist Financing Act of 2001, and the provisions in this title should look pretty familiar to anybody who has worked with previous anti–money laundering legislation. The measures taken to abate money laundering and terrorist financing fall into each of the same three general categories of actions the government used in the past: regulatory action, criminal sanctions, and forfeiture. And while nobody (except terrorists and criminals) had any great objection to the criminal sanctions or the forfeitures, some folks in the regulated industries — bankers and people in money service businesses — did have concerns about the impact of the new regulations on their operations. We'll look at those regulations and their impact, after a review of the Patriot Act and money laundering.

CRIMINAL SANCTIONS

The Patriot Act created several new money laundering crimes and increased the penalties for some offenses that were already money laundering violations. Some of these actions were taken in response to previous court decisions that had gone badly for the government, and others tightened existing statutes. Specifically, the act does the following:

- Outlaws the laundering of any proceeds from foreign crimes of violence or political corruption

- Outlaws the laundering of proceeds of cybercrime and offenses relating to the support of a terrorist organization
- Outlaws bulk cash smuggling and sets out procedures for the forfeiture of smuggled bulk cash shipments
- Revises the language of 18 U.S.C. 1960 relating to operation of illegal money transmitting businesses by eliminating the old requirement that the government had to show that the defendant *knew* the business was operating illegally. Now, anyone who "knowingly conducts, controls, manages, supervises, directs, or owns all or part of an unlicensed money transmitting business" faces criminal liability

BULK CASH SMUGGLING

The smuggling of large shipments of currency into (or, more often, out of) the United States is not an activity frequently associated with terrorist organizations. But since Congress was already making changes to Title 31 to deal with terrorist financing, it addressed a couple of other areas of concern. One of these was bulk cash smuggling, something practiced by large drug trafficking groups.

It was already illegal to fail to report to Customs the movement of a large amount of cash or monetary instruments into or out of the United States, but the Supreme Court's decision in *United States v. Bajakajian,* 524 U.S. 321 (1998), prevented the government from forfeiting large amounts of cash for this regulatory or record-keeping violation unless the government could show that the funds were derived from some illegal source. The response was to make the smuggling or shipment of large amounts of currency a separate criminal violation, a felony punishable by five years in prison. To effect this change, 31 U.S.C. §5332 was included in the USA PATRIOT Act.

The new law makes it a crime to transport or attempt to transport or transfer more than $10,000 in currency or monetary instruments into or out of the United States if the funds are both:

- Concealed on the person, in a container, or in a conveyance
- Transported with the intent to avoid the CMIR reporting requirement

See Figure 4.1 for an illustration of how this law works.

Any mode of transportation is covered, including the U.S. mail, Federal Express, UPS, and couriers. These last are especially vulnerable and can be approached for information about the source of the funds and their destination.

This new crime and revisions to the law relating to operation of an illegal money transmitter business are clearly intended to restrict the money launderer's ability to move funds offshore, where they are easier to conceal, layer, and integrate. There have already been charges brought under this statute, including some involving terrorism financing.

FORFEITURE

In the Patriot Act, Congress wielded the forfeiture hammer with great enthusiasm, creating new types of forfeitures and expanding this technique to permit confiscation of all property of an individual or entity that participates in or helps in the planning of a terrorist act. The government may also now seize any property that is derived from or used to facilitate an act of terrorism. The combined effect of these forfeiture provisions is to vastly increase the financial peril of doing business with terrorists. For individuals, groups, and businesses involved in terrorism, *all* of their assets, not just the proceeds of some criminal activity, are now at extreme risk. This is particularly significant for charitable organizations and other legitimate concerns, particularly those that are identified as "fronts" for terrorist groups.

Some of the procedures put in place under the act include:

- Providing for the seizure of property in the United States that is identified as

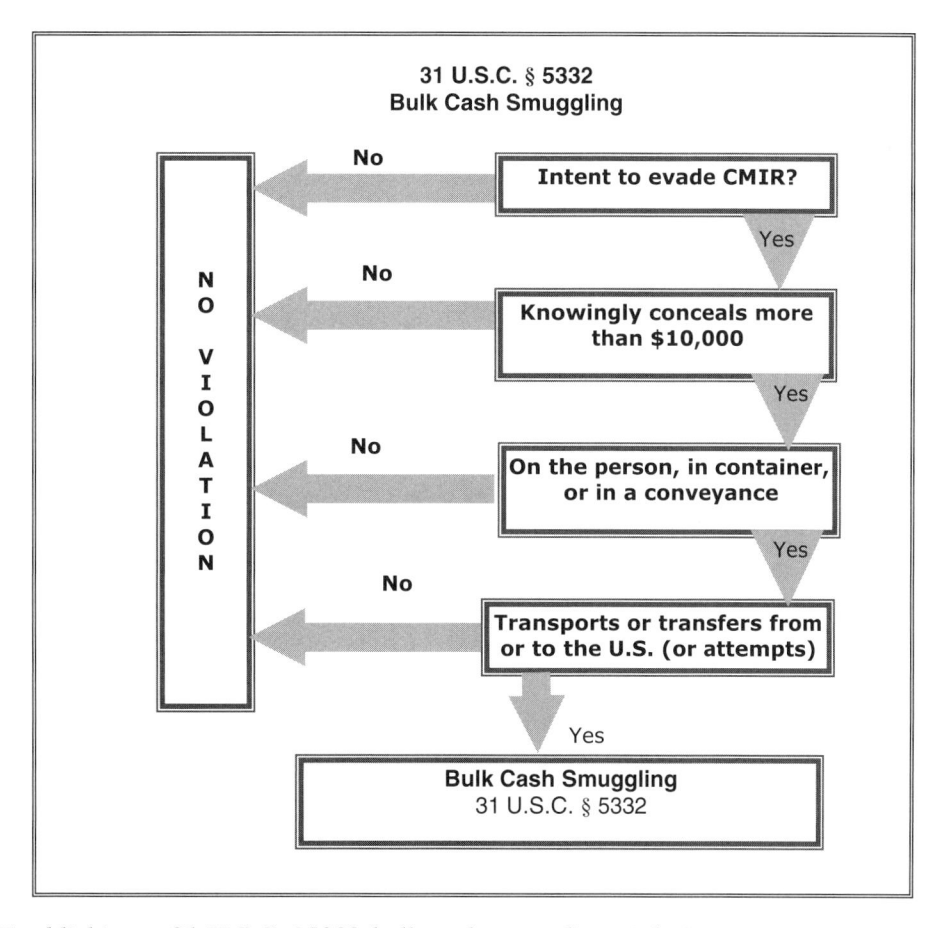

```
                    31 U.S.C. § 5332
                   Bulk Cash Smuggling

                   No    ┌─────────────────────┐
         ◄─────────────  │  Intent to evade CMIR? │
                         └─────────────────────┘
    N                              │ Yes
    O              No    ┌─────────────────────┐
         ◄─────────────  │ Knowingly conceals more │
    V                    │    than $10,000         │
    I                    └─────────────────────┘
    O                              │ Yes
    L              No    ┌─────────────────────┐
    A    ◄─────────────  │ On the person, in container,│
    T                    │   or in a conveyance    │
    I                    └─────────────────────┘
    O                              │ Yes
    N              No    ┌─────────────────────┐
         ◄─────────────  │ Transports or transfers from│
                         │  or to the U.S. (or attempts)│
                         └─────────────────────┘
                                   │ Yes
                         ┌─────────────────────┐
                         │  Bulk Cash Smuggling │
                         │   31 U.S.C. § 5332   │
                         └─────────────────────┘
```

Figure 4.1 Establishing a 31 U.S.C. §5332 bulk cash smuggling violation.

being connected with a number of foreign crimes
- Providing for domestic enforcement of foreign forfeiture orders
- Providing for seizure of correspondent accounts that are maintained in domestic financial institutions for foreign banks holding forfeitable assets offshore
- Preventing corporate entities from contesting a forfeiture if the principal shareholder is a fugitive
- Increasing American jurisdiction in forfeiture proceedings involving international businesses and individuals overseas

In another forfeiture-related action, Congress created a new criminal offense that prohibited the smuggling of bulk currency shipments. Now, if an individual smuggles or attempts to smuggle large amounts in currency out of the country without reporting the transfer to Customs, that person can be charged with a criminal offense and the entire amount can be seized and forfeited. This was in direct response to a U.S. Supreme Court decision, *United States v. Bajakajian*, 524 U.S. 321 (1998), in which the court held that such a large seizure of monies not linked to any other crime constituted an unconstitutionally excessive fine in violation of the Eighth Amendment.

These and other provisions will be examined in more detail in the chapter on forfeitures. When taken together, they expanded the scope and impact of forfeiture as a law enforcement tool, even in cases in which terrorism was not a factor.

The long arm of American law now reached much farther, and in the area of correspondent banking, it reached into a sensitive area. It is one of the few parts of the anti–money laundering provisions of the act that are at all controversial.

Losing money tends to make bankers very grumpy, and the Patriot Act provisions relating to interbank or correspondent accounts looks like a good way for banks to lose money. Because no bank is big enough to have branches everywhere, they open accounts in other banks in places where they or their customers want to do business. Thus, Bank A, located in Beirut, might open a correspondent or interbank account at Bank B in New York City. A customer of Bank A with business in New York could deal with Bank A's correspondent bank, Bank B, where funds are on deposit.

The Patriot Act now gives the government the ability to seize funds in correspondent accounts if it is unable to get at the customer's account in the foreign country. Say that an American court orders the forfeiture of the assets of a terrorist in Beirut, and the government knows (through whatever sources it may have) that the terrorist has money in Bank A. The government tells Bank A to cough up the forfeited assets, and Bank A refuses. Thanks to the Patriot Act, the American government can now tell Bank A, in effect, "Fine, we'll just take our end out of your correspondent account at Bank B in New York."

It doesn't matter that none of the money in that account belongs to the terrorist; that is now Bank A's problem. It shouldn't have been dealing with the terrorist in the first place, which is the deterrent intent of the provision. This provision is infrequently used, and it requires special Justice Department approvals, but the threat is a significant deterrent for bankers playing close to the legal line.

REGULATORY ACTION

The Patriot Act has some other provisions relating to interbank or correspondent accounts as well. These involve recordkeeping or disclosures, and most were amendments to the Bank Secrecy Act, which we'll be looking more at in a couple of chapters. Some of the more important of these amendments, most of which relate to the relationships between American banks and banks or individuals offshore, are the following:

PROHIBITION ON U.S. CORRESPONDENT ACCOUNTS WITH SHELL BANKS (31 U.S.C. 5318 (J); ACT SECTION 313)

Under this section, American financial institutions are prohibited from establishing, maintaining, administering, or managing correspondent accounts with "shell banks," which are foreign banks that have no physical presence in any jurisdiction. There are some exceptions, but for the most part, American banks have to deal with real banks that have a genuine presence somewhere.

AVAILABILITY OF BANK RECORDS

The law also assists law enforcement in obtaining records from American financial institutions — even records from overseas. Not only do these sections specify what types of records must be made available and how this is to be done, they spell out the bad things that can happen to banks that don't provide the information requested. For example, if a federal banking regulatory agency makes a request of a "covered financial institution" (an American bank) for records relating to anti–money laundering compliance or its customers, the institution has 120 hours to produce the records. This requirement also extends to the records of foreign banks with which the American bank does business as a correspondent. And the bank has to ante up pretty quickly. No more stalling for a couple of years while the diplomats and the lawyers fight it out.

The interesting part of this section is that very unpleasant things can happen to foreign banks that decide not to play ball. In the old days, they might say something like, "Sorry, the secrecy laws of our country don't allow us to give out information about our customers." That would have been the end of it for many, if not most, American investigations. Now, though, the rules have changed. Suppose the Treasury Secretary or the Attorney General summons or subpoenas information from a foreign bank relating to an account. Now, the foreign bank has seven days to pony up. If it does not comply, the Patriot Act gives the federal government the ability to direct an American financial institution to terminate its relationship with a foreign correspondent bank that has failed to comply with a subpoena or summons. If the American bank fails to terminate the relationship within 10 days, it could face civil penalties of up to $10,000 per day. This is serious business for both the American bank and its foreign cousin, because the law also requires the American banks to keep records identifying the owners of their foreign correspondents, as well as the name and address of someone in the United States who will accept a subpoena. No more hiding or game playing, and any foreign bank that wants to continue doing business in the United States is going to have to give up the information or see its interbank accounts closed.

Due Diligence for Private Banking and Correspondent Accounts (31 U.S.C. 5318 (i); Act Section 312)

The act requires any financial institution that maintains or manages private banking accounts or correspondence accounts in this country to use due diligence in ensuring that procedures are in place to prevent any money laundering through these accounts. This means that not only do American banks have to have procedures in place to prevent money laundering in their accounts, but they also have to take steps to prevent the kinds of abuses that the government knows take place in correspondent accounts or so-called "private banking." This is extra work for the banks, but it shuts off an avenue for money launderers who station themselves offshore and work through correspondent accounts to do business in the United States. Another part of this measure calls for even more due diligence for accounts with correspondent banks in countries that are "noncooperative" with international money laundering controls or that are otherwise known to be especially popular with money launderers. The Treasury Department is supposed to provide additional guidance on what types of suspicious activities might be cause for concern. As for private banking accounts, the ownership and control of these accounts must be identified, suspicious transactions reported, and if the account holder is a senior political official of a foreign government, the American bank has to take steps to ensure that monies being deposited are not derived from official corruption.

"Special Measures" for Certain Jurisdictions, Financial Institutions, International Transactions, and Accounts (31 U.S.C. 5318A; Act Section 311)

The Treasury Department is supposed to promulgate regulations for American financial institutions that deal with "particular financial institutions operating outside the United States, institutions in particular jurisdictions, types of accounts, and types of transactions, if Treasury determines that such institutions, jurisdictions, accounts, or transactions are of 'primary money laundering concern.'"

Standards for Verification of Customer Identification (31 U.S.C. 5318(l); Act Section 326)

In this provision, the government requires financial institutions to obtain verification of their customers' identity before opening an account. This "know your customer" policy seems like common sense, but it's a real asset for law enforcement, since money launderers and terrorists may use false names or identification documents to open accounts as part of their schemes. The law also permits the sharing of information about persons and entities engaged in or suspected of terrorist acts or money laundering activities between the government and financial institutions.

Suspicious Activity Reporting (31 U.S.C. 5331, Act Section 365)

These sections clarify what types of activities are suspicious, how they are to be reported, and to whom. Some of the key provisions involve safe harbor, which provides confidentiality and liability protection for bank employees that disclose suspicious activities to the government. It also specifically prohibits government employees from disclosing the fact that a Suspicious

Activity Report (SAR) has been filed. This is very important for the criminal investigator, who must take steps to conceal the fact that an SAR was filed. You should not, for example, in interviewing a suspect, tell the person that "the bank filed a Suspicious Activity Report about your transaction." Similarly, you should not tell a witness about the existence of an SAR.

FORFEITURE OF FUNDS IN U.S. INTERBANK ACCOUNTS (18 U.S.C. 981(K); ACT SECTION 319)

This was discussed above. These sections say that if a deposit of funds in a foreign bank outside of the United States is subject to forfeiture, and the foreign bank maintains an interbank account at a covered financial institution, U.S. law enforcement can seize the funds in the U.S. account as a substitute for the foreign deposit. It is not necessary to trace the funds in the U.S. account back to the foreign deposit.

ANTI-MONEY LAUNDERING PROGRAM REQUIREMENT (31 U.S.C. 5318(G); ACT SECTION 352)

This section imposes a requirement that all financial institutions have a program in place to detect and prevent money laundering within their institution and to ensure that they are in compliance with federal laws and regulations. Banks are required to have a compliance officer and employee training programs in place. Things like Know Your Customer and cash transaction reporting procedures fall into these programs, and agencies such as the Federal Reserve Board and the Treasury Department are watching to make sure the banks have their acts in order.

FILING OF SARs BY SECURITIES BROKERS AND DEALERS (ACT SECTION 356)

This topic is still pending regulation by the Treasury Department, and it is not wildly popular among the brokers and dealers who would have to do the paperwork. Designed to close a hole in the SAR net, reporting by securities dealers would enable the government to track indicators of money laundering activity in that industry.

FILING OF SARs BY BUSINESSES (31 U.S.C. 5331; ACT SECTION 365)

This section requires businesses that had previously been required to file reports of cash transactions exceeding $10,000 also to file the equivalent of a Suspicious Activity Report. Previously, these reports were made to IRS on a form 8300, which was not available to other law enforcement agencies due to federal law relating to taxpayer privacy. Now, the reports are available through the Financial Crimes Enforcement Network, giving law enforcement another valuable source of financial intelligence.

PENALTIES (31 U.S.C. 5321, 5322, 5324; ACT SECTIONS 353 AND 363)

These sections make penalties for violations of the Bank Secrecy Act stiffer, with attention-getting fines of up to $1 million for violations of the new 5318 (i) (due diligence for private banking and correspondent accounts) and new 5318 (j) (accounts with shell banks) sections.

SUNSET PROVISIONS

Sunset provisions allow for the repeal of parts of the act if Congress decides they are no longer necessary. These gestures were made in the (probably vain) hope that the "war on terror" would be won someday and the problems of money laundering and terrorist financing would go away. Unfortunately, money laundering is not likely to be vanishing anytime soon, but if it does, Congress can eliminate these new statutes and the regulations that support them.

EFFECTS OF THE USA PATRIOT ACT

So, how have things gone with the Patriot Act and, especially, with the provisions of Title III, the International Money Laundering Abatement and Anti–Terrorist Financing Act of 2001? In a July 2004 document titled "Report from the Field: The USA PATRIOT Act at Work," the Department of Justice provided a number of examples of enforcement actions and other successes. Some of these did relate to terrorism and the financing of terrorist organizations, but other cases cited were more familiar to law enforcement — child pornography and exploitation, drug trafficking, illegal weapons sales, even a kidnapping and rape case.

The tools provided by the Patriot Act have aided in the capture of fugitives, prevented acts of violence, and quickly resolved complex cybercrimes. They have also been instrumental in the investigation of terrorist plots and disruption of terrorist financing, just as they were intended. Some good examples from the Justice Department's report follow:

- The amendments to Title 18 U.S.C. §1960, relating to the business of money transmission, were valuable in resolving a case involving the Revolutionary Armed Forces of Colombia (FARC), a terrorist organization as designated by the Department of State. In this case, Libardo Florez-Gomez, a money courier suspected of laundering an estimated $1.3 million per month for FARC, was charged with being an unlicensed money transmitter in violation of 18 U.S.C. §1960. Florez-Gomez pleaded guilty and received an 18-month sentence in federal prison.
- Similar charges were brought against Mohammed Hussein, a cooperator of a money-transmitting business that accepted over $3 million in customer deposits and wired these to the United Arab Emirates without having a license to do so. Hussein also received an 18-month sentence.
- The new forfeiture provisions relating to bulk currency smuggling were employed against Alaa Al-Sadawai, a New Jersey man with connections to a foreign terrorist organization, who, with the help of his parents, attempted to smuggle $659,000 in cash out of the United States. The money, found on a commercial airline flight in a box of Ritz crackers, two boxes of baby wipes, and a box of Quaker Oats in Al-Sadawai's father's suitcase, was seized, and Al-Sadawai was convicted of conspiracy.
- In a fraud case, the government successfully used the forfeiture provisions relating to interbank accounts by seizing $1.7 million from the correspondent account of a Belizean bank in the United States. Prosecutors had identified the Belizean bank where James Gibson, indicted for conspiracy to commit money laundering and mail and wire fraud, had deposited proceeds of the fraud schemes. Unable to seize the funds due to obstruction by courts in Belize, a seizure warrant was served on the correspondent account in the United States. The government intends to return the seized funds to victims of Gibson's fraud.

The conclusion of the Justice Department's report sums up the role and value of this legislation:

> The USA PATRIOT Act has played a vital role in the Department of Justice's efforts to preserve America's system of ordered liberty for future generations. Since the Act was passed over two years ago, the Department of Justice has deployed its new authorities urgently in an effort to incapacitate terrorists before they can launch another attack, and, as demonstrated by the examples contained in this report, the Act's successes already are evident. The USA PATRIOT Act has facilitated the prosecution of terrorists and their supporters across the nation. It has authorized law enforcement and intelligence officers to share information and coordinate with one another. It has provided intelligence and law enforcement officials with the tools they need to fight terrorism in a digital age. It has assisted in curtailing the flow of funds to terrorists and terrorist organizations. And it has helped the Department to combat serious criminal conduct, such as child abduction and child pornography. For all of these reasons, the USA PATRIOT Act has made Americans safer over the course of the past two-and-a-half years, and the Department of Justice fully expects that the Act will continue to enhance the security of the American people in the future.

CHAPTER 5

MONEY LAUNDERING FORFEITURE

"What you seize is what you get."
Anonymous

"What's a thousand dollars? Mere chicken feed. A poultry matter."
Groucho Marx

Forfeiture is really the driving force behind money laundering today. You have to look at it from the crooks' perspective: They are hardly inclined to just give away all that money they worked so hard to steal in the first place. Their answer is to devise schemes to protect it from seizure and forfeiture. Law enforcement, on the other hand, has been getting better at finding and seizing, forcing the criminals to become more sophisticated in response. It is a vicious cycle, and one that probably will not end anytime soon.

One countermove in this chess game was the Congressional approval in 1986 of statutes permitting civil or criminal forfeiture of assets in money laundering cases. Although the concept was sound, the original law needed some work, and it took a couple of years to make changes clarifying exactly what could be forfeited and how. The law, as amended in 1988, sets out what can be forfeited pursuant to either the civil forfeiture statute, Title 18 U.S.C. Section 981, or the criminal forfeiture statute, Title 18 U.S.C. Section 982.

Before we get into these two laws, whose text may be found in Appendix F, we will recap the basic principles behind forfeiture for those criminal investigators who have been in suspended animation since 1975, and we will talk about some of the changes made by the Civil Asset Forfeiture Reform Act of 2000 (CAFRA).

The principle behind forfeiture is ancient, and, despite the objections of its detractors, pretty logical and fair: The criminal cannot keep the fruits of his or her crime, nor can the instruments or tools used to commit the crime be allowed to stay in criminal hands. Forfeiture is the legal process by which the government may take those items away.

In the United States, forfeiture often involved the taking of items used to commit or facilitate the commission of crimes. The very first Congress passed measures detailing how vessels used by smugglers could be taken. Historically, other items subject to forfeiture have included such things as trucks driven by bootleggers or airplanes flown by drug traffickers. In theory, these seizures deprived the criminals of the means to commit their crimes and coincidentally made a profit for the government when the items were sold at auction. While it certainly inconvenienced the crook, who now had to go out and buy a new boat or truck in order to stay in business, the profits from a thriving enterprise often made this a small problem, one easily overcome with cold cash — something a successful criminal like pirate Henry Every had lots of.

All this changed when law enforcement began targeting the *proceeds* of major crimes, particularly those derived from drug trafficking or violations of the Racketeer Influenced and Corrupt Organizations (RICO) Act. Here was where the real money was — thousands, even millions of dollars in cash, real property, and other assets that truly were the fruits of crime.

Under American law, forfeitures have traditionally been civil in nature, *in rem* actions against the property itself, rather than against the criminal. This, too, seems logical and fair: once the principle is established that criminals should not be allowed to keep the fruits of their crimes, the only question is whether those particular fruits are, in fact, crime proceeds. If so, it matters not (or didn't until CAFRA) where they are or who is holding them: they belong to the government.

In these civil forfeiture proceedings, the government could seize property based upon probable cause to believe that it was subject to forfeiture. The property owner or other interested parties (called "claimants") could contest the forfeiture by establishing that the property was not legally forfeitable or by raising some other defense to forfeiture. In doing so, the burden was on the claimant to prove his or her case by a preponderance of admissible evidence. The government, of course, presents facts of its own to the contrary, and the court makes a ruling based on the evidence from both sides.

Although the owner of forfeited property might *feel* punished, the courts have held that civil forfeiture is not a "punishment" as defined by the Constitution; the *asset*, not the owner, is the subject of the forfeiture action. This eliminates the double jeopardy issue, although the question of whether a forfeiture can be an excessive fine under the Eighth Amendment is a little trickier.

A criminal forfeiture is an *in personam* action against an individual. In a criminal forfeiture proceeding, the court or jury is asked to find not only the guilt of the defendant but the "guilt" of his assets, too. In most cases, the prosecutor will list the assets that have been used by the defendant to facilitate the crime or that have been identified as proceeds and ask that these be forfeited. If the defendant is convicted, a judgment is entered against the property, but, before that happens, the burden of proof is on the government to show beyond a reasonable doubt that the assets should be taken.

A key difference between civil and criminal forfeiture is the concept of substitute assets. In civil cases, only property specifically linked to a crime can be forfeited. I can seize a car bought by a drug dealer with drug proceeds but not one he bought with an insurance settlement. In a criminal forfeiture case, if I cannot find the first car, the courts will let me take the second one as a substitute for it. This is because the criminal forfeiture is an act to punish the criminal, and taking away his or her car — no matter how he came by it — does exactly that.

Having established that the basic purpose of forfeiture is to take either bad things away from anybody or good things away from bad people — both worthy enough goals — let's look at why Congress felt a need to "reform" civil forfeiture.

By 2000, provisions for the seizure of drug proceeds had been in place for almost 20 years, and Congress itself was adding new forfeiture provisions all the time. Two of these were Section 981 and Section 982 of Title 18, both of which allowed for civil and criminal forfeiture of assets in money laundering cases. Civil forfeiture, in particular, had become a very big business and a huge moneymaker for the government. As the drug trade grew, so did profits, many millions of which were grabbed by government investigators. This made the government, particularly the law enforcement agencies, very happy, because federal law provided for the use of forfeited money by law enforcement. Police agencies all over the country were supplementing their budgets with monies seized from drug traffickers and other criminals, and a lot of cops (the author included) were driving around in cars formerly owned by people who were now making license plates in the penitentiary.

Some folks were not happy, including the drug traffickers, their friends and families, and, notably, defense attorneys. One can speculate whether the unhappiness of the last group was the result of their clients' no longer having the funds to pay their legal bills, but, regardless, discontent was growing along with the seizures.

Something else was growing too, this being the number of iffy seizures. Although the total number of "forfeiture horror stories" is really quite small, the law enforcement focus (forfeiture opponents would say obsession) with forfeiture was generating huge numbers of cases each year. Even if only one case in a thousand was questionable, there were a lot more total cases, and the bad ones had a way of getting publicized. Thus, one story about a New Jersey prosecutor who feathered his nest with seized property or a Memphis gardener whose big roll of cash got seized in an airport had a way of attracting negative attention.

Among those who were paying attention was Congress, which liked the extra revenue generated by forfeiture but didn't like the complaints it was getting from constituents. (Notably the very vocal trial lawyers.) Some people sincerely believed that civil forfeiture did represent a threat to American liberty; they believed that the government should not be able to take somebody's property unless that person had been convicted of a crime, should not be able to seize something on an evidence standard as thin as "probable cause," and should not make the defendant prove the property's "innocence."

There were some other concerns, but this is the gist. Congress got into gear and, over some pretty strenuous objections by law enforcement, passed the Civil Asset Forfeiture Reform Act of 2000, which was supposed to change the way the police did business in the forfeiture arena. The new law put into place some strict time limits on police and prosecutors as well as protection for innocent parties, made some changes in the burden of proof, and generally addressed the bigger concerns of those lobbying for change. CAFRA did not kill off or eliminate civil forfeiture, and even today most — maybe as many as 80% of all actions — are still civil in nature.

One issue not resolved by CAFRA that directly affected forfeiture under money laundering and other statutes was the sticky Eighth Amendment question regarding excessive fines. The Constitution prohibits the imposition of fines that are unreasonable or excessive, an issue that came up in the Supreme Court decision *United States v. Bajakajian,* 524 U.S. 321 (1998), a case that began with the forfeiture of over $340,000 in currency that was being taken out of the United States. The law requires the filing of a Currency and Monetary Instrument Report (CMIR) whenever more than $10,000 in cash is brought into or taken out of the country, a requirement overlooked by Mr. Bajakajian. Customs moved to seize all of the funds, and the Supreme Court ruled that taking the entire amount was not proportional to the seriousness of the CMIR reporting offense. Unless the government could show that the funds were connected to some other illegal activity, the court said, the Eighth Amendment prohibited this type of seizure as an "excessive fine."

Congress hoped that the Patriot Act in 2001 would resolve this question when they enacted Title 31 U.S.C. §5332, making the smuggling of bulk cash shipments a criminal offense, but the question is still up in the air. One thing is certain, though: Other court decisions have consistently held that the seizure of any funds or other assets that have been traced directly to a criminal activity cannot be excessive; see *United States v. One 1988 Prevost Liberty Motor Home*, 952 F.Supp. 1180 S.D. Tex. (1996). In other words, if law enforcement can prove that the cash is the profits of a crime, it is all forfeitable.

MONEY LAUNDERING FORFEITURE

The passage of statutes aimed at laundered assets is a logical extension of the laws prohibiting money laundering itself. Nevertheless, these laws represented a significant expansion of the government's forfeiture authority. Previously, forfeiture cases almost exclusively centered on drug trafficking and the tools and fruits of that crime. By 1986, several of the states had extended their forfeiture laws to allow the seizure of the proceeds of other crimes, and the federal government wasn't far behind. Since 1988, the laws have been amended on a number of occasions to include even more crimes and Specified Unlawful Activities for which property "involved" in money laundering can be seized.

The money laundering forfeiture statutes, found in 18 U.S.C. 981 and 982, track others in federal law by permitting both civil and criminal forfeiture actions. The civil section, §981 (a) (1) (A), provides that any property "involved in a transaction or attempted transaction in violation of Section 5313 (a) or 5324 of Title 31, or of Section 1956 or 1957 of this Title, or any property traceable to such property" is forfeitable to the United States.

So, under this section, all property involved in a money laundering offense, as well as violations of the Bank Secrecy Act involving currency reporting, would be forfeitable. This includes those monies actually laundered, commissions paid to the launderer, and, in many cases, property that facilitates the laundering activity.

How "involved" does the property have to be? Under the Currency Transaction Reports and Currency and Monetary Instrument Reports reporting requirements of Title 31, money not reported is "involved" and can be forfeited; see *United States v. Real Property at 874 Gartel Drive,* 79 F.3d 918 (9th Cir. 1996). Also, forfeiture of $237,282 in currency under 18 U.S.C. §982 was not excessive under the Eighth Amendment, where currency was seized from defendants by Customs agents after defendants attempted to transport it out of the country without filing appropriate Customs forms, defendants lied to Customs agents, and defendants underreported currency that they were attempting to move outside the United States by tens of thousands of dollars. The defendants also did not establish that the currency was lawful proceeds or was intended to be used for lawful activities; see *United States v. Delgado,* 959 F.Supp. 1523 (S.D. Fla. 1997).

In Title 18 U.S.C. §1956 and §1957 cases, the proceeds of a Specified Unlawful Activity (SUA) are forfeitable if they are involved in a financial transaction. For example, if I deposit $100,000 in drug proceeds into a bank account under a false name or wire the money to Colombia to buy some more drugs, a money laundering transaction has taken place and the $100,000 is forfeitable.

This turns out to be very good news for law enforcement, because quite a few of the underlying SUAs have no provisions allowing for forfeiture of proceeds of those crimes. (This is being changed as the Congress moves toward a general forfeiture law.) For the first time, the ill-gotten gains from these crimes can be forfeited. However, you have to have a money laundering violation, and you will have to prove the elements of that offense in order to forfeit the proceeds.

What about commingled funds? After all, the commingling of funds from multiple sources is a common practice in money laundering schemes. This commingling may be part of a plan to conceal the illegal activity, or it may be an integration mechanism. Either way, the SUA proceeds are going to be forfeitable, but courts have held that the *entire* amount involved in a transaction, whether the amounts are all derived from the SUA or are from some other source, can be forfeited; see *United States v. Rodriguez,* 53 F.3d 1439 (7th Cir. 1995).

This, too, is good news. Under the other federal forfeiture laws, only the money directly traceable to the illegal activity is forfeitable. For example, under the drug forfeiture statute, 21 U.S.C. 881 (a) (6), only the proceeds of the drug sales can be forfeited. The approach in the money laundering provision is pretty logical, if you think about it, because money laundering schemes so often involve funds from varied sources and business entities.

Another category of property "involved" in a transaction is that exchanged for the SUA proceeds. If I spend my drug money on a new Ferrari, that money is long gone, but the car is still around, and it can be seized. Again, this line of thought can be good for law enforcement, because the *entire* asset is considered to be "involved" if it is exchanged. What if I spent my $100,000 on stocks instead, and they appreciated in value before they were seized? The entire amount would be forfeited, even if the government got $150,000 for the stocks.

What about the question of facilitation in money laundering cases? Property used to facilitate drug trafficking, such as cars, boats, and airplanes, has always been a big part of those cases. The money laundering forfeiture statutes do not use the word facilitation, so is property that is used to facilitate money laundering transactions considered involved? Most agents would say yes, but the courts do not see things quite so clearly.

In *United States v. All Monies in Account No. 90-3617-3,* 754 F.Supp. 1467 (D.C. Hawaii 1991), where the government asserted that the account was used to facilitate money laundering operations for Peruvian drug trafficking operation, all of the funds in a New York bank account were found to be forfeitable. This was found even though §981 does not expressly include the words facilitate or facilitating, because the statute covers property "involved in" illegal money laundering transactions, and legislative history makes it clear that "property involved in" includes property used to facilitate money laundering offenses.

If the property makes the money laundering offense easier or makes it more difficult to detect, it is probably involved (and facilitating). A business used as a front for some illegal operation, without which the financial transaction could not have occurred, would be facilitating property. A car used to drive to the bank to make a currency deposit probably would not. See *United States v. One 1989 Jaguar XJ6,* 1993 WL 157630 (N.D. Ill. 1993).

If the facilitating property was used to conceal or disguise the transaction, the connection or involvement is clearer. As with magic tricks, many money laundering schemes rely on props to perfect the illusion. The props, whether they are cars in false names or business fronts, are more likely to be seen by the courts as being involved.

This situation comes up in cases involving bank accounts. In one such case, an Immigration employee who pleaded guilty to accepting bribes in exchange for fraudulently issuing "green cards" was forced to forfeit contents of two bank accounts to the government under 18 U.S.C. §981, even though some funds in accounts were income from his employment and other legitimate sources. The court agreed with the government that the entire balance of commingled accounts is subject to forfeiture, ruling that it is precisely this commingling of tainted funds with legitimate money that facilitates laundering and enables the schemes to be successful. See *United States v. Contents of Account Numbers 208-06070 and 208-06068-1-2,* 847 F.Supp. 329 (S.D.N.Y. 1994).

For another example, consider a video rental business. We already know that if the SUA proceeds are mixed into the daily deposits with those from legitimate rentals, the funds are forfeitable. The business itself may be forfeitable as well, since the scheme could not take place without it. See *United States v. All Assets of G.P.S. Automotive Corp.,* 66 F.3d 483 (2d Cir. 1995; a business used to sell stolen auto parts and launder proceeds was forfeited under §981). The inventory of videotapes could be considered involved if it can be shown that they were acquired with commingled funds, or if the "dirty" tapes are mixed with the "clean" ones. (I'm referring to how they were bought, not the content!) The whole inventory could be forfeited. See *United States v. All of the Inventories of the Businesses Known as Khalife Brothers Jewelry,* 806 F.Supp. 648 (E.D. Mich. 1992).

Real property has been forfeited under this theory, such as when SUA proceeds were used to put up a building on some "clean" land. See *United States v. Real Property in Mecklenburg County,* 814 F.Supp. 468, (U.D.N.C., 1993), *aff'd sub nom. United States v. Marsh,* 105 F.3d 927 (4th Cir. 1997).

As a general rule, if a "clean" asset is merely incidental and does not do anything to conceal or disguise the activity, it generally is not forfeitable. Section 1957 has no "conceal or disguise" element, so the clean money probably cannot be forfeited under any of the above theories, just the dirty.

Let's analyze why and when you would want to use civil rather than criminal forfeiture. Here are some good reasons to use the civil version:

- You do not need a concurrent criminal case, so assets can be civilly forfeited even if the launderer has not been criminally charged. This is especially useful when the launderer is dead, missing, or a fugitive. Considering the number of false identities or fronts that are used in money laundering schemes, this occurrence isn't all that uncommon.
- The property was involved in money laundering generally, but specific financial transactions cannot be identified.
- You've got property held in the name of a nominee, for which insufficient evidence exists to convict, but you can prove money laundering activity.
- In a multiple count case, you do not need the money laundering conviction, but the interests of justice would be served by forfeiture of the property.

CIVIL FORFEITURE

What Can Be Seized?

The statutory language for the civil forfeiture provisions has undergone some changes over the years, as Congress has tinkered with the statute.

Title 18 U.S.C. §981 (Civil Money Laundering Forfeiture)

Any property, real or personal, involved in a transaction or attempted transaction in violation of 18 U.S.C. §1956 or §1957, or 31 U.S.C. §5313(a) or §5324(a), or any property traceable to such property, may be seized.

Title 18 U.S.C. §984 (Civil Forfeiture of Fungible Property)

In any *in rem* forfeiture action, under Title 18 U.S.C. §984, in connection with a violation of Title 18 U.S.C. §1956, §1957, or §1960 or Title 31 U.S.C. §5322 or §5324 (§5324 violations after 9/23/94), initiated within one year of the violation, in which the subject property is cash, monetary instrument(s) in bearer form, funds deposited in an account in a financial institution (as defined in Title 18 U.S.C. §20), or other fungible property:

1. It shall not be necessary for the government to identify (trace) the specific property involved in the offense that is the basis for the forfeiture.
2. It shall not be a defense that the property involved in such an offense has been removed and replaced by identical (untainted) property.

Procedures for Civil Seizures Under §981 (b)

Now that we're perfectly clear on what can be seized under these statutes, how exactly do we go about seizing it? Most criminal investigators are familiar with the process. Seizures of property involved in a transaction or attempted transaction in violation of Title 18 U.S.C. §1956 or §1957 or of Title 31 U.S.C. §5313 (a) or §5324 (a), or any property traceable to such property, may be accomplished using any of three methods prescribed in §981 (b). These methods are as follows:

1. Seizure incident to lawful arrest or search: Title 18 U.S.C. §981(b) (2) (A)
2. Seizures made with a seizure warrant issued pursuant to the Federal Rules of Criminal Procedure (F.R.Cr.P.): Title 18 U.S.C. §981 (b) (2) (B)

Seizure Incident to Lawful Arrest or Search

Property may be seized incident to a lawful arrest or search warrant, or incident to an otherwise lawful search. Most, if not all, federal agencies recommend that their agents obtain a seizure warrant, if only to protect themselves, but some situations may require action without a seizure warrant. Some examples are:

- Property that is contraband
- Property that is known to be subject to prior judgment(s) in favor of the United States
- Property that is forfeitable, but that the agent has probable cause to believe will be destroyed, concealed, or removed if it is not immediately seized
- Property that is abandoned and is taken into custody for safekeeping

Money laundering cases usually provide substantial lead time during which agents and prosecutors have advance notice that property may be seized. After all, assets are what they are looking for. This lead time permits us to obtain a seizure warrant that should protect us from civil and criminal liability growing out of seizures that go bad. Do yourself a favor: plan ahead and get a warrant.

Seizures Made with Seizure Warrant

Title 18 U.S.C. §981 (b) (2) (B) provides that seizures may be made with a seizure warrant issued pursuant to the Federal Rules of Criminal Procedure. This is the most common method used to seize property for civil forfeiture.

Seizure warrants are issued pursuant to Rule 41 of the Federal Rules of Criminal Procedure. As with search warrants, seizure warrants are based upon the probable cause affidavit of a law enforcement officer and issued *ex parte* by a Federal Magistrate Judge or a District Court Judge.

If the seizure involves real estate, however, the government must give all potential owners notice and an opportunity to be heard prior to the issuance of a seizure warrant; see *United States v. James Daniel Good Real Property,* 510 U.S. 43 (1993). Congress specifically included this requirement in CAFRA. You are going to have to have a hearing before you can take somebody's home.

In money laundering cases, the probable cause for seizures will consist of information about both the financial activity and the Specified Unlawful Activity. Both types of information must be included in the affidavit in support of the seizure warrant.

Remember, though, that much of the information obtained in financial cases comes as a result of grand jury subpoenas, and there are legal restrictions on using this information in civil forfeiture cases. This is an area that should be thoroughly explored with the Assistant U.S. Attorney *before* the seizure warrant is sought.

ADMINISTRATIVE FORFEITURE PROCEEDINGS

Federal law allows for the forfeiture of some property without any judicial involvement, a process known as administrative forfeiture. In this process, the seizing agency is responsible for properly handling the matter, using procedures set forth under the Customs laws and federal regulations. The Customs laws under Title 19 U.S.C. §§1602 *et seq.* are incorporated into Title 18 U.S.C. §981 and provide the statutory basis for the administrative forfeiture process.

Under these procedures, the seizing agency is responsible for notifying any claimants or interested parties of the government's intent to forfeit the seized property. Those parties are entitled to file a claim for the property; the claim must be accompanied by a cost bond. If this occurs, the administrative forfeiture action is automatically transformed into a judicial proceeding, since the claimant has essentially requested judicial intervention.

If no claim is made, a Declaration of Forfeiture is issued, which has the same force and effect as the Final Decree and Order of Forfeiture in a judicial case. Title to the property is transferred to the United States of America.

Keep in mind that not all property involved in money laundering offenses can be forfeited through this administrative process. Effective August 20, 1990, under the authority of amendments to Title 19 U.S.C. §1607, the following property may be forfeited through the administrative forfeiture process:

1. Any monetary instrument, defined within the meaning of Title 31 U.S.C.

§5312 (a) (3), including currency, regardless of its value

2. Personal property that has an appraised value of $500,000 or less

Real property forfeitures must always be handled as judicial forfeitures.

§982 CRIMINAL FORFEITURE

Up to now, we have been talking about seizures that are handled under the civil rules. As we have said, there are advantages to using civil procedure in some cases. There are also advantages to using the alternative — criminal forfeiture under Title 18 U.S.C. §982. Criminal forfeiture requires that the government prove its case beyond a reasonable doubt, the highest standard of proof, and, unlike with civil forfeiture, you have to (*a*) have a criminal defendant, and (*b*) convict him or her.

The most significant advantage of criminal forfeiture relates to the substitution of assets. This makes special sense in money laundering cases, since the whole investigation essentially centers on identifying the income and assets of the defendant. At the conclusion of your case, there may very well be one list of assets for which you have probable cause to seize, and a second list for which you don't. Under Section 982, you may still be able to get the assets in your second list if the defendant has hidden or transferred the forfeited assets.

CRIMINAL FORFEITURE STATUTE: 18 U.S.C. §982

Under Title 18 U.S.C. §982, the federal district court, in imposing sentence on a person convicted of a violation of Title 31 U.S.C. §5313 (a), §5316, or §5324, or of a violation of Title 18 U.S.C. §1956, §1957, or §1960, "shall order that person to forfeit to the United States any property, real or personal, involved in such offense, or any property traceable to such property." The term "traceable to" in 18 U.S.C. §982 (a) (1) has been held to mean that the government must prove by a preponderance of the evidence that property it seeks in satisfaction of the amount of criminal forfeiture to which it is entitled has some nexus to property "involved in" the money laundering offense. See *United States v. Voigt,* 89 F.3d. 1050 (3rd Cir. 1996).

Some property, however, is protected from forfeiture, namely that involved in a "case of a violation of Title 31 U.S.C. §5313 (a) by a domestic financial institution examined by a Federal bank supervisory agency or a financial institution regulated by the Securities and Exchange Commission or a partner, director, or employee thereof." This provision essentially means you cannot seize an entire bank, just because one of its accounts, or even one of its officers or employees, was involved in a money laundering activity.

WHAT PROPERTY IS SUBJECT TO CRIMINAL MONEY LAUNDERING FORFEITURE?

The list of offenses for which property is subject to criminal money laundering forfeiture has become extensive. Property that was involved in one or more of the following offenses can be forfeited under Section 982:

- 18 U.S.C. §1956
- 18 U.S.C. §1957
- 18 U.S.C. §1960, effective 10/28/92

THE CRIMINAL FORFEITURE PROCESS

In criminal forfeiture cases, the property is first indicted, just as a criminal defendant would be. The property is described in a separate forfeiture count in the same indictment that charges the defendant. Because of this marriage with the criminal case, all criminal forfeitures are governed by the Federal Rules of Criminal Procedure.

At the time the property is indicted, it may already be in the government's possession, having previously been seized civilly, or you may now have to go out and restrain or arrest the property. In either case, the rules for handling the property are somewhat different from those in civil actions.

The authorities for gaining control of the property for criminal forfeiture include:

Temporary restraining order (TRO) — Title 21 U.S.C. §853 (e) (1) provides for a TRO prior to the conclusion of a criminal investigation. You would get a TRO to make sure the property will still be available for forfeiture later. The TRO prevents or restrains anyone from transferring title or encumbering the property with loans or liens. TROs are public records and involve a hearing in court, which may result in premature disclosure of your criminal case.

Seizure warrant — A criminal seizure warrant will be issued upon (*a*) a showing of probable cause to forfeit the property, and (*b*) a showing that a temporary restraining order may not be sufficient to assure that the property will be available for forfeiture.

Once you have gained control of or restrained the property, the case must be resolved through a plea or verdict. The ball is very much in the U.S. Attorney's court at this point, but the investigator should consult on the forfeiture question.

Obviously, in any plea agreement, the forfeiture count plays a part. Negotiations with the defendant will invariably involve the assets and how much or how little he or she will agree to forfeit. Federal law allows for the pursuit of parallel civil and criminal forfeiture actions, something else that must be approved by and coordinated closely with the Assistant U.S. Attorney. In many U.S. Attorneys' offices, responsibility for these cases is split between the criminal and civil sides of the house, so more than one Assistant U.S. Attorney may be involved.

Substitution of Assets

Another question that will be the subject of consultation with the U.S. Attorney's office will involve the substitution of assets. Since this is one of the main reasons for employing criminal forfeiture in the first place, it bears a closer look.

The idea behind asset substitution is the fact that the convicted defendant in a criminal case is being punished for his or her actions. One form this punishment can take is separating the criminal from his or her ill-gotten gains. For example, a drug trafficker makes $100,000 from selling cocaine. The government is able to prove this amount to the satisfaction of a jury, through the defendant's own records, the statements of co-conspirators, and the records of the bank through which the funds were laundered. This money may be forfeited as drug proceeds or as property involved in money laundering under §981 or §982.

If the $100,000 was still in the bank, ripe for the taking, we might get a seizure warrant and go with the civil option. If not, and the money is nowhere to be found, the criminal forfeiture option begins to look more attractive. Why? Because once we have an order forfeiting the $100,000, we can forfeit substitute assets. If we can't find that specific $100,000, no problem — we can substitute any other property the defendant owns (including legitimately owned property), up to the amount of $100,000.

In order to make this scenario possible, Title 18 U.S.C. §982 (b) was revised to incorporate Title 21 U.S.C. §853 (p). Under §853 (p), a substitution of assets can take place if, as a result of any act or omission of the defendant, property subject to forfeiture:

- Cannot be located upon the exercise of due diligence
- Has been transferred to, sold to, or deposited with a third party
- Has been placed beyond the jurisdiction of the court
- Has been substantially diminished in value
- Has been commingled with other property that cannot be divided without difficulty

Keep in mind that those actions have to be taken by the defendant; you cannot substitute assets just because you don't feel like looking for the particular asset that was ordered forfeit.

Members of Congress had some problems with this provision, mostly because it did not strike them as being fair to forfeit the assets of some low-level smurf who handled millions of dollars for somebody else, none of which can now be found. It was conceivable that this person could be convicted of money laundering and ordered to forfeit a couple of million dollars that he or she never really had. So, the substitute assets provision now allows for forfeiture of those assets from a defendant who acted as an intermediary for the money launderer *if* he or she conducted three or more separate transactions totaling $100,000 or more in any 12-month period.

During the course of your investigation, you will be identifying assets that are owned or controlled by the defendant. Some of these may be traceable to an SUA or involved in the money laundering transactions. This property will be listed in the indictment as property the government is seeking to forfeit.

SPECIAL FORFEITURE ISSUES

Forfeiture law and procedure are constantly evolving. Congress continually studies major reforms or changes to the law and makes minor changes frequently. Case law can be confusing, too, as the law on money laundering forfeitures varies from circuit to circuit.

Because hundreds of millions of dollars in forfeitures take place in the United States each year, this subject has implications for people on both sides of the issue. Many cases, especially those involving money laundering and BSA violations, are hotly contested, in part because the perpetrators may be otherwise "respectable" business people, bankers, attorneys, or citizens.

Preseizure Planning

It is always a good idea to plan ahead, but this is especially true in forfeiture cases, which often involve a lot of people and agencies. Since the enactment of the Civil Asset Forfeiture Reform Act, with its various deadlines and time limits, preseizure planning is even more critical.

Many investigations involve on-the-spot decisions and seizures of property without a warrant or other process. Sometimes agents may have little or no advance notice of the existence of the property or the basis for its seizure. Not so in most money laundering and financial investigations. Some of these cases may begin with a seizure, as when a courier is apprehended at the bank, but for the most part the agent should have weeks, if not months, to get ready to seize the assets.

One purpose of a financial investigation is to identify assets and link them to their owner. As this process is ongoing, the analysis of financial records will disclose the existence of bank accounts, real property, and other assets. Frequent review of the evidence, in consultation with the prosecuting attorney, will permit decisions to be made about whether to seize the assets now or wait until later.

This review is part of the preseizure planning process. You *know* you are going to encounter property as a result of the investigation, and you *know* the law allows you to seize certain property. Why not get ready now?

There is really no excuse for not being ready. More and more agencies are formalizing this whole effort, requiring consultation early and often with a number of interested individuals. At IRS Criminal Investigation Division, preseizure planning is mandatory, with the involvement of all those who will be handling the seizure, forfeiture, and management of the property.

In federal judicial forfeiture cases, either civil or criminal, the U.S. Attorney's Office will be responsible for making sure that preseizure planning is complete and timely. In some districts, a forfeiture Assistant U.S. Attorney is designated as soon as a case that might result in forfeitures is brought to the office's attention.

In administrative forfeiture cases, the agency's asset forfeiture coordinator, its seized property officer, or the case agent will be responsible for coordinating the preseizure planning. Also included in the planning process are the property management specialists, counsel, and the Assistant U.S. Attorney.

Some seizures are more complicated (and expensive) than others, such as those involving real property, commercial businesses, and anything that eats. In those cases, the preseizure planning will be more comprehensive, as arrangements for specialists may be necessary.

Having all this planning done in advance will ensure that when it comes time to take the property into custody, all of the preliminaries will be done and the seizure and forfeiture can be completed as quickly as possible. (This is a good idea, as storage costs and other expenses reduce the value of the asset.)

Grand Jury Information in Forfeiture Cases

As a general rule, if information is obtained via the grand jury process or if it is obtained as a result of the grand jury's authority, the criminal forfeiture provisions under 18 U.S.C. §982 should be used. Obviously, this requires a criminal indictment of the responsible party for violation of 31 U.S.C. §5313 (a) or §5324 (a) or of 18 U.S.C. §1956, §1957, or §1960.

It is possible to use grand jury information in civil cases, but this requires an order under Rule 6 (e). If you are not planning to indict someone immediately, but the property is in jeopardy of being lost, this may be the only alternative.

According to the IRS *Asset Forfeiture Manual:*

> While 18 U.S.C. §981 (b) (1) states that seizures may be made pursuant to a lawful arrest or search, the secrecy provisions relating to grand juries cannot be ignored. It follows that before the property is seized for civil forfeiture, the Grand Jury information justifying such seizure will have to be made public in some fashion that would be sufficient to sustain a civil forfeiture, i.e., an indictment, complaint, Rule 6 (e) order, etc. If grand jury information has been used to obtain an arrest or search warrant, then any seizure of property pursuant to the warrant based upon this information must be seized as evidence of a crime, and not for civil forfeiture purposes. (See Section 9.7.4.5).

Your Assistant U.S. Attorney will be very cognizant of the need to preserve the secrecy of grand jury material and should be consulted about the need to use this information in an administrative case apart from the criminal investigation. Penalties for abuse of Rule 6 (e) are severe, and a challenge by the defendant's attorney can be expected.

Non-Grand Jury Information

So much in a financial investigation is developed through the use of grand jury subpoenas that it may be difficult to separate what is *not* material covered by Rule 6 (e). The problem is that while any non–grand jury information can readily be used in a civil forfeiture, little of this information may be available to you.

If you know that you are going to be seeking civil forfeiture of some assets, then administrative subpoenas, summonses, or subpoenas issued under the authority of Title 31 can be used to perfect a civil forfeiture. The problem here is that some agencies have rules against using administrative subpoenas after a grand jury investigation has been initiated. In other cases, agency procedure may require that a second agent, who has no access to the 6 (e) material, be designated to work on the civil forfeiture aspects of the case.

Another option is the use of a financial search warrant. There are drawbacks to this procedure, including the prospect of unwanted disclosure of the investigation. Still, it is something to consider if the information is not readily available otherwise.

Title 12 U.S.C. §3401 *et seq.* includes some procedures under which law enforcement agencies may obtain records from financial institutions without a grand jury subpoena. These records are required to be "relevant to a legitimate law enforcement inquiry," e.g., civil forfeiture. The procedure for obtaining information under this section is as follows:

1. A formal request is made by the agency head or his or her delegate requesting production of the records from the financial institution. (*Note:* Title 12's definition of "financial institution" is narrower than that in Title 31, but it does include banks, savings and loans, and credit unions.)

2. A copy of the request is served on the customer whose information is requested. There are forms for this notification.

If there is reason to believe that the customer notice will jeopardize the investigation, the notification can be delayed upon a showing of good cause. This requires that the case agent prepare an affidavit describing why the investigation would be "seriously jeopardized" by disclosure.

After consultation with the civil Assistant U.S. Attorney, the agent presents the affidavit, application, and any Order Delaying Notification to a U.S. Magistrate Judge or District Court Judge. If approved by the judge, the formal request and any delay of notice order are served on the financial institution. The delay of notice order will prevent the financial institution from disclosing the request for 90 days, and it must be renewed every 90 days. This is something you will want to keep track of, because as soon as your order expires, notification will be made.

Seizure of Real Property

The seizure of real estate is not an uncommon event in money laundering cases. The object of many money laundering schemes is, after all, the acquisition of houses, condos, businesses, and so forth. Not only are these forfeitures more complicated, but they are also controlled by special procedures that have been imposed by the Supreme Court to protect real property ownership rights.

A Supreme Court decision in a Hawaii case, *United States v. James Daniel Good Real Property*, 510 U.S. 43 (1993), mandated certain procedures in cases involving real property. The *Good* decision requires the government to give notice to the owner of real property and to afford that person a meaningful opportunity to be heard *before* the property is seized and taken into government custody.

An alternative to this preseizure hearing is the filing of a *lis pendens*. The *lis pendens* is filed in conjunction with a forfeiture complaint or indictment and is a legal notice that advises of a lien or pending action against the property. Because the government has not actually taken physical control of the property, the requirements of the *Good* decision are not applicable. The forfeiture complaint and *lis pendens* are supposed to protect the property from being transferred. (In fact, a *lis pendens* does not prevent the owner from selling the property, but it makes getting clear title much harder for the buyer, something that discourages interest in the sale.)

With a *lis pendens*, no preseizure hearing is required, since the property remains in the control of the owner. This saves the government from having to disclose evidence about its case prematurely, and it has the added benefit of saving the costs that otherwise would be paid for securing the property before it was actually forfeited.

The forfeiture complaint and the *lis pendens* should be filed as contemporaneously as possible. Your preseizure planning should include determining who will serve the *lis pendens*, usually the agent or a Deputy U.S. Marshal. Other potential claimants are notified by publication in a newspaper. Some claimants may be identified as a result of a title search, which should precede any real property seizure. This is an essential element of your forfeiture case and should be done professionally early on. The title report will reflect any liens or encumbrances on the property.

Additional considerations in seizing real property may include hazards on the property. Lead-based paint, the presence of hazardous chemicals, and use of the property as a drug laboratory may prevent forfeiture and in any event will cause delays in processing the matter. This should be factored into your preseizure planning.

Real property seizures are more trouble than other types of seizures, but they are usually worth it. These are very big-ticket items and the objects of many laundering schemes. Your investigation should aggressively seek out any properties owned or controlled by the defendant and attempt to link this property to either the SUA or the money laundering activity.

EQUITABLE SHARING

Assets forfeited in money laundering cases may be disposed of in several ways. One of these involves the sharing of forfeited property with law enforcement agencies that participate in money laundering investigations.

This ability of federal agencies to share the results of forfeiture cases provides a powerful incentive for participation by state and local law enforcement, which may not have their own money laundering or forfeiture provisions in state law. In many cases, state and local agencies provide invaluable assistance, without which money laundering schemes could not be fully explored.

Both the Department of Justice and the Department of the Treasury maintain asset forfeiture funds, into which the proceeds of money laundering cases are deposited and from which equitable sharing payments are made. The amounts distributed in this program have increased each year. A high percentage of money laundering cases are task-force or multi-agency investigations.

By law, the amount of money distributed after a forfeiture as part of the equitable sharing process is governed by actual participation. The agency that is applying to share in the proceeds of a forfeiture case must have been an active participant in the investigation. Contributions generally involve employee hours, but other considerations include special resources or information that the contributing agency brought to the party.

Application for equitable sharing must be made within 30 days of the date of seizure and must be made to the lead federal agency in the case. The Justice and Treasury departments each have a different form to be used in the equitable sharing application. The agency applying to receive funds must also be registered with the Justice and Treasury Executive Offices for Asset Forfeiture (EOAF and TEOAF, respectively) before the sharing request will be approved.

Equitable sharing is a good way to draw other law enforcement agencies into money laundering investigations, which can be time consuming and require the resources or abilities of several different agencies.

Whether or not assets are shared, the forfeiture is an essential ingredient in a money laundering case. It simply stands to reason that if criminals have enough money to launder, it is money we should be trying to take away from them.

The forfeiture provisions of 18 U.S.C. §981 and §982 may be found in Appendix F.

CHAPTER 6

RELATED FEDERAL STATUTES

"No brilliance is needed in the law. Nothing but common sense, and reasonably clean finger nails."
John Mortimer, British author (and lawyer)

The American anti–money laundering effort rests on the three pillars of regulation, compliance, and enforcement. The foundation for these pillars is not just the civil and criminal provisions of the money laundering laws we have already examined. A number of other laws and regulations create the basis for a comprehensive attack on money laundering, one that aims not only to capture and punish those who violate the law but also to prevent lawbreaking in the first place.

When this chapter was first written in 1999, the American model was almost unique. In the intervening years, governments around the world have used that model as the basis for their own anti–money laundering regimes, many of which are as comprehensive and effective as the original example. Other nations have some distance to go, and a few are largely part of the problem rather than the solution, but the overall trend is clear.

The network of statutes that combine in America to create a comprehensive anti–money laundering package is centered on the Bank Secrecy Act (BSA), which we have already looked at to some extent. Other laws provide for record-keeping and reporting and set out criminal penalties for acts that money launderers typically incorporate into their various schemes. It is important for investigators to recognize that all of these various statutes can play a part in any money laundering probe, and we should have a clear understanding of how the laws and regulations can help in our investigations.

In the period immediately after the September 11, 2001, terrorist attacks, Congress took a number of steps to enhance the government's ability to combat money laundering and terrorist financing. A review of the legislation enacted in the wake of 9/11 reaches the surprising finding that most of the changes came not to the criminal money laundering statutes in Title 18, Section 1956 and Section 1957, but in such laws as the Bank Secrecy Act. By addressing gaps or holes in the regulatory and compliance components of the anti–money laundering effort, Congress strengthened the entire structure. Terrorism-related offenses and other crimes were added as Specified Unlawful Activities, but much more mundane issues, such as how and when certain types of financial transactions would be reported, dominated legislation such as the USA PATRIOT Act.

The overall effect has been to greatly increase the role of the private sector and specifically the financial services industry in the anti–money laundering effort. Today, prompted by federal legislation, every bank has at least a BSA compliance officer, if not a fully staffed office. An entire industry has developed to supply financial institutions with the personnel, training, and especially the computer software to effectively monitor compliance with the BSA and other statutes.

In addition to providing employment to a large number of former IRS, FBI, and other federal agents, these compliance programs have made life much more difficult for the would-be money launderer and much easier for the investigator.

The money launderer's goal is to hide illegal activity and conceal the source and disposition of criminal proceeds. The BSA and related statutes combine to narrow the criminal's options and complicate the money laundering schemes. The net effect for the investigator is to provide new avenues for investigation, better sources of reliable financial information, and improved methods of tracking the flow of dirty money. Although we have already covered some of these changes in the chapter on the Patriot Act, we need to look at the overall package to get the best idea about how to use these laws to our advantage.

BANK SECRECY ACT

What has become known as the Bank Secrecy Act, Titles I and II of Public Law 91-508 (October 26, 1970), was passed by Congress in an effort to assist federal law enforcement agencies in the investigation of illegal activities such as drug trafficking and tax evasion. As the Supreme Court wrote, "Congress recognized the importance of large and unusual currency transactions in ferreting out criminal activity, and desired to strengthen the statutory basis for requiring such reports"; see *California Bankers Association v. Shultz*, 416 U.S. 21 (1974). Simply put, criminals deal in cash, and because cash leaves no paper trail, Congress created one.

The BSA consists of two major "titles," one requiring certain records to be maintained by financial institutions and one requiring certain reports to be made by designated parties to the Secretary of the Treasury. In typically complex government fashion, these two titles were placed in different parts of the United States Code.

Title I of the BSA is found in 12 U.S.C., with Section 1829b and Section 1953 giving authority to the Secretary of the Treasury to issue regulations requiring certain records to be maintained by financial institutions. The Secretary also has the opportunity to define "financial institutions," and this definition has come to include far more entities than banks. Most investigators would never have anything to do with these provisions, except that the law and its regulations describe the records that banks and other entities must maintain. These are exactly the records that we will need to do a money laundering or financial investigation.

Title II of the BSA is found in 31 U.S.C., with Sections 321, 5313 (a), 5314, and 5316 giving authority for the Secretary of the Treasury to require reports of currency and foreign transactions. These reports, such as the Currency Transaction Report (CTR) and Suspicious Activity Report (SAR), provide important leads to illegal financial transactions and document some of the large cash transactions conducted by criminals in their money laundering schemes.

The Internal Revenue Service and the Bureau of Immigration and Customs Enforcement share primary responsibility for enforcement of these provisions, but a number of other federal agencies, notably the Financial Crimes Enforcement Network (FinCEN), are also involved in regulatory activity. FinCEN has a critical role in collecting the BSA information and in disseminating it to law enforcement.

IRS is charged by 31 CFR 103.46 (b) (8) with the authority to examine all of those financial institutions that are supposed to be complying with the BSA, except those that are (*a*) currently examined by federal bank supervisory agencies or (*b*) brokers or dealers in securities. This includes money transmitters, casinos, and other nonbank financial institutions (NBFI) or so-called money services businesses. There are quite a few of these. The regulatory breakdown is something like this:

Responsible Agency	Number of Institutions (1999)	Type of Institutions
IRS Examination Division	200,000	Money services businesses
United States Postal Service	37,000	Post offices

Responsible Agency	Number of Institutions (1999)	Type of Institutions
NCUA	9,369	Credit unions
FDIC	7,277	Banks
SEC	5,200	Securities brokers
Comptroller of the Currency	3,377	Banks
Federal Reserve Board	1,688	Banks
Office of Thrift Supervision	1,669	Savings and loans
Casinos	350	Casinos and card clubs

Title 31 is all about reports to the government — who makes them and when and how and under what circumstances. The penalties in Title 31 are all about not filing the reports, and they range from a couple of years in jail to a "death penalty" for financial institutions. Title 31 is several score pages long, and the regulations in 31 CFR are a couple of hundred more. We are not going to delve very deeply into this material. If you are really interested, the law and regulations are available in libraries.

What the title boils down to is those required reports, and these number only six:

Currency Transaction Report	FinCEN Form 104
Currency and Monetary Instrument Report	FinCEN Form 105
Currency Transaction Report — Casinos	FinCEN Form 103
Foreign Bank Account Report	Treasury Form TDF 90-22.1
Suspicious Activity Report (two versions)	Treasury Forms TDF 90-22.47 and 56
Report of Cash Payments Over $10,000 Received in a Trade or Business	

Thousands of report forms required by the BSA are submitted to the Treasury Department every day. Most are the Currency Transaction Report. Far fewer of the other forms are turned in, but the numbers are growing. Table 6.1 sets out the totals for four of the forms from 2004.

TABLE 6.1
BSA Compliance

IRS Form 4789 (CTR)	13,674,113
IRS Form 8300	151,998
Suspicious Activity Report	663,655
Report of Foreign Bank and Financial Account	218,667

Source: FinCEN 2004 Annual Report.

Sample copies of all of these forms may be found in Appendix E. Before we discuss each one and how it relates to a money laundering investigation, we will examine some definitions to find out who is supposed to be doing the reporting. Bear with me for a couple of pages while we sort this out.

The following are defined in the statute or under Title 31 CFR:

Bank

Each agent, agency, branch or office within the United States of any person doing business in one or more of the capacities listed below:

(1) A commercial bank or trust company organized under the laws of any state or of the United States;

(2) A private bank;

(3) A savings and loan association or a building and loan association organized under the laws of any state or of the United States;

(4) An insured institution as defined in section 401 of the National Housing Act;

(5) A savings bank, industrial bank or other thrift institution;

(6) A credit union organized under the law of any state or of the United States;

(7) Any other organization chartered under the banking laws of any state and subject to the

supervision of the bank supervisory authorities of a state;

(8) A bank organized under foreign law;

(9) Any national banking association or corporation

Broker or dealer in securities

A broker or dealer in securities, registered or required to be registered with the Securities and Exchange Commission under the Securities Exchange Act of 1934.

Financial institution

Each agent, agency, branch, or office within the United States of any person doing business, whether or not on a regular basis or as an organized business concern, in one or more of the capacities listed below:

(1) A bank (except bank credit card systems);

(2) A broker or dealer in securities;

(3) A currency dealer or exchanger, including a person engaged in the business of a check casher;

(4) An issuer, seller, or redeemer of travelers checks or money orders, except as a selling agent exclusively who does not sell more than $150,000 of such instruments within any given 30-day period;

(5) A licensed transmitter of funds, or other person engaged in the business of transmitting funds;

(6) A telegraph company;

(7)(i) Casino. A casino or gambling casino duly licensed to do business as a casino or gambling casino in the United States and having gross annual gaming revenue in excess of $1,000,000. The term includes the principal headquarters and every domestic branch or place of business of the casino.

(ii) For purposes of this paragraph (7)(i), gross annual gaming revenue means the gross gaming revenue received by a casino, during either the previous business year or the current business year of the casino. A casino or gambling casino which is a casino for purposes of this part solely because its gross annual gaming revenue exceeds $1,000,000 during its current business year, shall not be considered a casino for purposes of this part prior to the time in its current business year that its gross annual gaming revenue exceeds $1,000,000.

(8) A person subject to supervision by any state or federal bank supervisory authority;

(9) The United States Postal Service with respect to the sale of money orders.

Foreign bank

A bank organized under foreign law, or an agency, branch or office located outside the United States of a bank. The term does not include an agent, agency, branch or office within the United States of a bank organized under foreign law.

Person

An individual, a corporation, a partnership, a trust or estate, a joint stock company, an association, a syndicate, joint venture, or other unincorporated organization or group, and all entities cognizable as legal personalities.

Structure (structuring)

For purposes of section 103.53, a person structures a transaction if that person, acting alone, or in conjunction with, or on behalf of, other persons, conducts or attempts to conduct one or more transactions in currency, in any amount, at one or more financial institution(s), on one or more days, in any manner, for the purpose of evading the reporting requirements under section 103.22 of this part. In any manner includes, but is not limited to, the breaking down of a single sum of currency exceeding $10,000 into smaller sums, including sums at or below $10,000, or the conduct of a transaction, or series of currency transactions, including transactions at or below $10,000. The transaction or transactions need not exceed the $10,000 reporting threshold at any single financial institution on any single day in order to constitute structuring within the meaning of this definition.

Transaction in currency

A transaction involving the physical transfer of currency from one person to another. A transaction which is a transfer of funds by means of bank check, bank draft, wire transfer, or other written order, and which does not include the physical transfer of currency is not a transaction in currency within the meaning of this part.

Business day

Business day, as used in this part with respect to banks, means that day, as normally communicated to its depository customers, on which a bank routinely posts a particular transaction to its customer's account.

Whew! That's government for you. Two or three lines of verbiage to tell you what a "person" is.

Reports Required by the BSA

Currency Transaction Report

What exactly is the responsibility of all these "banks" and "financial institutions," with respect to this law? It turns out that they are required by the statute to report certain of those transactions in currency, to the Secretary of the Treasury, within 15 days of the transaction, on the FinCEN Form 104, formerly the IRS 4789. This form is known as the Currency Transaction Report, or CTR. The CTR is used to report all large cash transactions, anything over $10,000 in currency, every time they occur at the bank. (There are some exceptions, for qualifying businesses that are exempt and for government agencies.)

A couple of key points: First, it is the financial institution, *not* the customer, who is required to prepare and submit the CTR. The bank, not the customer, will be held responsible if the form is not properly prepared and submitted.

Second, in order to complete the form, the financial institution is required to verify and record the name and address of the person presenting a transaction, as well as the identity, account number, and social security number or taxpayer identification number, if any, of any person for whom a transaction is to be effected. This verification must be made with some identity document, such as a driver's license or passport, other than a bank signature card. The purpose, obviously, is to make sure of the customer's correct identity, taking the anonymity out of cash transactions.

Similar rules apply to the purchase of bank checks, cashier's checks, money orders, and travelers checks. In these cases, the institution is required not only to verify the identification but also to keep a record or log of all cash transactions between $3,000 and $10,000, even though they do not have to be reported.

Under 31 U.S.C. 5325 and 31 CFR 103.29 (revised September 20, 1994), commonly referred to as the "Know Your Customer rule," financial institutions are not even supposed to conduct these types of transactions unless either the customer is known to them (has an account relationship) or information about the person is recorded and kept in the log.

These records have to be kept for five years, and multiple purchases on the same day are treated as one purchase. These regulations are aimed directly at smurfs, the money laundering couriers who use financial instruments such as cashier's checks in amounts under $10,000 to avoid the CTR requirement. This "structuring" of cash transactions is also covered by the regulations and is the subject of criminal penalties as well. It should be noted that banks are getting very good at detecting this type of activity through the use of computer programs that "mine" all of the day's bank transactions for any suspicious activity.

The effect of the regulations relating to reports by financial institutions is to restrict the use of banks and the like by money launderers. If they are going to do business at these institutions, the criminals will be forced to provide identification information and probably to maintain some sort of banking relationship.

Note that the statute does not prohibit large cash transactions, it just requires that they be recorded or reported, depending on their size. Also, the statute does not "care" where the money came from or whether it is clean or dirty — only that it be reported properly.

Report of International Transportation of Currency or Monetary Instruments

The second report required by the BSA is the Report of International Transportation of Currency or Monetary Instruments, which is made on a Currency and Monetary Instruments Report (CMIR; FinCEN 105, formerly Customs Form 4790). The CMIR is supposed to document every movement of more than $10,000 into or out of the United States, although banks and some other businesses are exempt from filing. All of the statutory provisions in this part of the BSA are enforced by the Bureau of Immigration and Customs Enforcement and the Bureau of Customs and Border Protection; the latter actually collects the CMIR forms from international travelers.

The statute and 31 CFR 103.23 require that each person who physically transports, mails, or ships, or causes to be physically transported, mailed, or shipped, or attempts to physically transport, mail, or ship, or attempts to cause to be physically transported, mailed, or shipped, currency or other monetary instruments in an aggregate amount over $10,000 at one time from the United States to any place outside of the United States, or into the United States from any place outside the United States, must file a CMIR.

Additionally, each person in the United States who receives currency or other monetary instruments in an aggregate amount over $10,000 at one time, which have been transported, mailed, or shipped to the person from any place outside the United States with respect to which a CMIR has not been filed, whether or not required to be filed, shall file a CMIR stating the amount, date of receipt, the form of instrument(s), and the person from whom received.

Note that in the case of the CMIR form, it is the individual conducting the transportation who is responsible for preparing the report, and Customs asks inbound passengers about United States or foreign currency they are carrying. If the amount goes over $10,000, the individual is supposed to fill out the CMIR.

Another noteworthy difference between this provision and that relating to CTRs is that the definition includes "monetary instruments" in addition to currency. These instruments could be any type of negotiable checks, travelers checks, or another bearer-type money equivalent. For example, a personal check, written to "cash" and endorsed, would be a negotiable instrument.

CMIR forms are kept by FinCEN and can be obtained by contacting your local ICE office or FinCEN.

Currency Transaction Report by Casinos

The next report is the Currency Transaction Report by Casinos (CTRC; FinCEN Form 103). As its name implies, this is a report prepared and submitted by casino, card club, and gaming operations throughout the United States. 31 CFR 103.22 (a) (2) requires that a casino file a CTRC when a person conducts a currency transaction of more than $10,000 with the casino. The report must be filed with the IRS Detroit Computing Center by the 15th day after the transaction date.

This provision applies to licensed casinos with gross annual gaming revenues in excess of $1 million. Those casinos with gross annual gaming revenues of less than $1 million have to report large cash transactions under Section 6050I of the Internal Revenue Code (Report of Cash Payments Over $10,000 Received in a Trade or Business).

Interestingly, the Department of Treasury has allowed Nevada casinos to file their CTRCs and related records with the Nevada Gaming Control Board, which in turn forwards the reports to the Detroit Computing Center. Everybody else, including Atlantic City casinos, riverboats, and Indian casinos, is supposed to file directly with IRS in Detroit.

Casinos have long been used for money laundering, and, of course, they do a lot of large cash transactions. One launderer's technique involves going to a casino, buying a large amount of chips with the dirty money, playing a couple of hands, then cashing the chips in for clean money or even for a check from the casino. Coming in or going out, any transaction like this over $10,000 is supposed to be reported by the casino on a CTRC.

Again, it is the casino, not the patron, who is responsible for filling out and submitting the form. Identification is required, in the form of a driver's license or passport, and most casinos have these transactions on videotape, as well — something you should include in your subpoena.

Foreign Bank Account Report

The Report of Foreign Bank and Financial Accounts (Treasury Form 90-22.1), also known as the Foreign Bank Account Report or FBAR, is required of each United States person who has a financial interest in or authority, signatory or otherwise, over one or more banks, securities, or other financial accounts in a foreign country. The report must be filed for each calendar year on or before June 30th of the succeeding year. Like the CMIR, it is the account holder who is responsible for submitting the report to IRS.

Note that a "United States person" is defined as a citizen or resident of the United States, as well as a domestic partnership or corporation or a domestic estate or trust. Persons required to file federal income tax returns must answer the question on the return as to whether or not they had a financial interest in a foreign account.

What this provision means is that any American who has an interest in a foreign bank account must report that fact to IRS, something that probably takes all the fun out of having something like a Swiss bank account in the first place. Failure to do so is grounds for criminal sanctions, however. If it comes to light in your case that your suspect has foreign interests, checks should be made to establish whether these interests have been properly reported.

Suspicious Activity Report

Perhaps the most important form, a catch-all for suspicious activity of any kind, is known as the Suspicious Activity Report (SAR). Also known as "the form of a thousand numbers," the SAR was created to replace multiple reports, all with different identifying numbers, filed by several different regulatory agencies, including IRS, the Federal Deposit Insurance Corporation (FDIC), National Credit Union Administration (NCUA), and the Comptroller of the Currency. All of these agencies had forms that they used to report suspicious or criminal activity, and in a remarkable (for the government) display of unity, these agencies combined, through FinCEN, to create one standard form, the SAR. The report is now processed through FinCEN as the TDF 90-22.47.

The purpose of the SAR is deadly serious for those required to file it, because *any* suspicious financial transaction or activity must be reported to the regulatory agency. What is considered suspicious? This is largely left up to the filer, but some things, such as suspected embezzlement, theft by employees, and fraud, are definitely reportable.

The vast majority of SARs are submitted in connection with suspected money laundering activity. Transactions that are suspected of being structured to avoid a reporting requirement account for 80% of the reports made by financial institutions. In other cases, the bank might report a suspicious pattern of deposits and withdrawals or receipt of currency that smelled of marijuana. Table 6.2 provides a frequency distribution of SAR filings by characterization of the suspicious activity they concern, for April 1, 1997, through June 30, 2003.

The law, as amended by the Patriot Act, provides that no financial institution or employee

TABLE 6.2
Frequency Distribution of SAR Filings by Characterization of Suspicious Activity — April 1, 1997, Through June 30, 2003

Violation Type	1997	1998	1999	2000	2001	2002	2003
BSA/Structuring/Money Laundering	35,625	47,223	60,983	90,606	108,925	154,000	72,462
Bribery/Gratuity	109	92	101	150	201	411	261
Check Fraud	13,245	13,767	16,232	19,637	26,012	32,954	16,803
Check Kiting	4,294	4,032	4,058	6,163	7,350	9,561	5,333
Commercial Loan Fraud	960	905	1,080	1,320	1348	1,879	934
Computer Intrusion[a]	0	0	0	65	419	2,484	3,605
Consumer Loan Fraud	2,048	2,183	2,548	3,432	4,143	4,435	2,271
Counterfeit Check	4,226	5,897	7,392	9,033	10,139	12,575	6,445
Counterfeit Credit/Debit Card	387	182	351	664	1,100	1,246	659
Counterfeit Instrument (Other)	294	263	320	474	769	791	615
Credit Card Fraud	5,075	4,377	4,936	6,275	8,393	12,780	6,037
Debit Card Fraud	612	565	721	1,210	1,437	3,741	4,575
Defalcation/Embezzlement	5,284	5,252	5,178	6,117	6,182	6,151	2,887
False Statement	2,200	1,970	2,376	3,051	3,232	3,685	2,316
Misuse of Position or Self-Dealing	1,532	1,640	2,064	2,186	2,325	2,763	1,564
Mortgage Loan Fraud	1,720	2,269	2,934	3,515	4,696	5,387	3,649
Mysterious Disappearance	1,765	1,855	1,854	2,225	2,179	2,330	1,264
Wire Transfer Fraud	509	593	771	972	1,527	4,747	4,317
Other	6,675	8,583	8,739	11,148	18,318	31,109	15,854
Unknown/Blank	2,317	2,691	6,961	6,971	11,908	7,704	2,290
Totals	88,877	104,339	129,599	175,214	220,603	300,733	154,141

[a] The violation of Computer Intrusion was added to Form TD F 90-22.47 in June 2000. Statistics date from this period.

Source: International Narcotics Control Strategy Report, 2003. Released by the Bureau for International Narcotics and Law Enforcement Affairs in March 2004.

can be sued for filing an SAR, a policy that encourages suspicions to be reported. The law also treats SARs as confidential communications between the financial institution and the government, something that is to be taken extremely seriously by the criminal investigator. Title 31 U.S.C. §5318 (G) (2) (A) clearly states that disclosure of an SAR is prohibited, which means that it cannot be referenced in a report or affidavit in support of a search warrant, cannot be shown to a witness or to the subject of the report, and cannot be shared with anyone outside the investigation. The same section also prohibits the financial institution from notifying its customer that the SAR was made. Unauthorized disclosure carries a penalty of five years in prison and a $250,000 fine (31 U.S.C. §5322), so do yourself a big favor and treat these reports with the confidentiality and respect they deserve.

These forms can be extremely valuable in criminal investigations. Money launderers know that certain transactions will trigger the filing of a CTR or other report and will devise schemes specifically to keep that from happening. SAR filings may show patterns of activity and series of transactions that would otherwise not come to our attention and that may lead to a broader money laundering scheme. Because the financial institutions that file these forms do not tell the customer that they have done so, SARs provide a secret insight into ongoing activity and a great opportunity for the investigator.

Many federal districts now have SAR Review Teams comprised of members from various federal law enforcement agencies who go over the SARs and collate them with data from other sources, such as other BSA forms. The results of the analyses may be shared with other law enforcement agencies. FinCEN and IRS maintain a database for these forms, and the forms may also be sent to the FBI, the Secret Service, and the regulatory agencies.

Report of Cash Payments over $10,000 Received in a Trade or Business

One other form, the Report of Cash Payments Over $10,000 Received in a Trade or Business, known as the 8300 form, needs to be covered. This report was designed to catch a type of large cash transaction that would otherwise have gone unnoticed — those that occur not in financial institutions but in other cash-intensive businesses. This represented a big hole in the paper trail; the point where the dirty cash enters the financial system isn't always a bank, sometimes it's a jewelry store or a car dealership or a real estate broker. If the reporting system works properly, that cash is reported when the jeweler or the car dealer deposited it into a bank account, but the question of who provided the money to the merchant would be unanswered.

Because buying "toys" is one of the better parts of being a drug dealer, extortionist, or alien smuggler, large cash transactions involving these people are not exactly uncommon. After all, these criminals "worked hard" for that money, and if they want to spend it on a new Mercedes, well, they think, that's what the money's for. After some years of ignoring this (pretty obvious, if you think about it) phenomenon, Congress fixed things by passing an amendment to the Internal Revenue Code in 1984 that required the reporting by trades or businesses of all large cash transactions.

Title 26 §6050I was actually recommended by the American Institute of Certified Public Accountants, not as a tool for criminal law enforcement, but as a means to identify taxpayers with large cash incomes. This is why it started out in the Internal Revenue Code, instead of the BSA.

The law requires that any person who is engaged in a trade or business, who receives in the course of that business more than $10,000 in cash in one transaction or a series of two or more related transactions, make a return to the Secretary of the Treasury. Regulations prescribed that this return be on IRS Form 8300 and filed within 15 days of the date of the transaction.

Notice the difference in terms used: §6050I uses "return," where the BSA forms are "reports." That's because §6050I is a tax statute. The difference is important because of the confidentiality of tax returns, including 8300 forms. Basically, once that return got to IRS, it could not be shared or disclosed outside IRS, which meant a lot of good law enforcement leads — drug dealers' buying cars with cash, smugglers' paying for boats, and crooks' paying for their lawyers — never led anywhere.

The 9/11 terror attacks put a stop to that situation. Congress, recognizing the need for this type of information to be available more widely, included in the Patriot Act an amendment to the BSA (31 U.S.C. §5331) that essentially duplicates the filing requirement in the tax code. Now, any transaction over $10,000 is reported on FinCEN Form 8300 and can be disseminated to law enforcement officers who need to know. This applies to any 8300 filed after 12/31/2001.

What trades or businesses are required to file the return? The requirement applies to all trades or businesses that are not designated as financial institutions by the BSA. This includes car dealerships, pawnbrokers, dealers in precious metals, jewelers, travel agencies, boat dealers, real estate agents, escrow companies, aircraft dealers, loan companies, credit card systems, and attorneys, along with just about anybody else in the yellow pages that isn't a bank.

If any of the above receives more than $10,000 in cash in the course of business, the firm is supposed to report that fact within 15 days. This applies only to regular business transactions. If I am a jeweler, and I sell my personal car for $12,000 in cash, I don't have to report that fact.

If multiple cash transactions are related, these are to be reported as such as soon as they go over $10,000. This provision kicks in if someone goes to a car dealership and makes an initial down payment of $7,000 in cash and then comes back a few days later with the balance of $5,000.

"Cash" can be not only coin and currency but also foreign money, cashier's checks under $10,000, bank drafts, travelers checks, and money orders, if those financial instruments are used to buy travel, durable consumer goods such as cars, or collectibles.

Services are included, something that did not make the defense attorneys very happy. As things stand, they are not exempt from filing the 8300 form, even though they have claimed the attorney–client privilege protects this information. The court reaction to this claim has been generally negative. In *United States v. Goldberger and Dubin*, 935 F.2d 501 (2nd Cir. 1991), two New York law firms filed 8300 forms that withheld information about the person providing the money, claiming disclosure violated the privilege and the Sixth Amendment right to counsel. The court did not agree, saying the clients were free to pay by some means other than cash.

In another case, a Florida attorney was indicted on BSA violations after he structured deposits into his firm's client trust account. The court emphasized the attorney's duty to abide by the BSA regulations relating to the source of the funds. See *United States v. Belcher*, 927 F.2d 1182 (11th Cir. 1991).

The information required on the 8300 form is similar to that on a CTR. It includes the following:

- Name, address, and taxpayer identification number of the person from whom the cash was received
- Name, address, and taxpayer identification number of the person on whose behalf the transaction was conducted
- The amount of cash received
- The date and nature of the transaction

Not nearly as many 8300 forms are filed with IRS each year as CTRs. This raises interesting questions. For example, what are we to infer if a bank reports $4 million in deposits from a car dealership on 200 CTRs, but the dealership does not file any 8300 forms? It is certainly possible that the dealership is receiving large amounts of cash from its customers and not reporting this fact as required. This example illustrates the original purpose of this statute — the completion of the paper trail for large cash transactions. The bank is doing its job and properly reporting the cash deposits, but the trail is not complete unless the dealership holds up its end.

Penalties for violation of this statute are linked to those in the Internal Revenue Code for failing to file a tax return (26 U.S.C. 7203) and causing a false return to be filed [26 U.S.C. 7206(1)], as well as to the Bank Secrecy Act. The penalty for each violation is up to five years in prison. Civil penalties can also be levied against violators, potentially taking the profit out of those big-ticket sales.

A number of cases have been made under this section, generally with IRS as the lead agency. Businesses not in compliance have included car dealerships, jewelers, and attorneys. In the grand scheme of money laundering enforcement, these cases do not represent a big piece of the action, but two potential benefits should be considered. First, those conducting the transactions at the businesses are criminally liable for their conduct, which may well represent an incentive for them to assist in the investigation of the money laundering itself. Second, information from the 8300 form may be used in establishing wealth or income. Court decisions have held that evidence of unexplained wealth can be used, even when the money cannot be directly traced. See *United States v. Magano*, 543 F.2d 431 (2nd Cir. 1976), and *United States v. Jackskion*, 102 F.2d 683 (2nd Cir. 1939), *cert. denied*, 307 U.S. 683 (1939).

BUSINESS REGISTRATION

That's it for the forms, but the BSA is also about regulating industries that engage in financial services. For example, the act contains some provisions for the registration of businesses that engage in money transmission.

According to 31 U.S.C. 5330 (September 23, 1994), any person who owns or controls a money-transmitting business (licensed with any state or unlicensed) must register the business with Treasury by March 21, 1995, or within 180 days beginning on the date of being established, by providing:

- The business name and location
- The name and address of each person who either owns or controls the business, is a director or officer of the business, or otherwise participates in the conduct of the affairs of the business
- The name and address of any depository institution where the business has a transaction account
- An estimate of the business volume in the coming year (to be reported annually)
- Any other information requested by Treasury regulation

Section 5330 also requires that a money-transmitting business maintain a list of the names and addresses of all persons authorized to act as its agent and make the list available to any appropriate law enforcement agency.

Under Section 5330, "money-transmitting business" means any business, other than the United States Postal Service, that provides check cashing, currency exchange, or money-transmitting or remittance services, or issues or redeems money orders, travelers checks, and other similar instruments; is required to file reports under 31 U.S.C. 5313; and is not a depository institution.

The term "money-transmitting service" includes accepting the currency or funds of any country and transmitting such (or the value thereof) by any means through a financial agency or institution, a Federal Reserve Bank or other facility of the Board of Governors of the Federal Reserve System, or an electronic funds transfer network.

These businesses and currency exchanges, many of which are also regulated by the states, are considered nonbank financial institutions and are regulated by the IRS Examination Division. They are required to keep certain records of their business, just as banks are, and to report large cash transactions, just as banks would. Customer identification is required for transactions over $1000, and the business must record the customer's name and address (and passport number or TIN unless the funds are received by mail or common carrier); transaction date and amount; and currency name, country, and total amount of each foreign currency.

Penalties Under Title 31

Punishment for violation of Title 31 includes criminal and civil penalties. Forfeiture may be an option in some cases as well. Violations of Title 31 are codified in Titles 12 and 31 of the United States Code, and 31 CFR 103.47 and 103.49 prescribe civil and criminal penalties. Title 12 is the civil and criminal statutory authority for the recordkeeping requirements, and Title 31 is the civil and criminal statutory authority for the reporting requirements of currency and foreign transactions.

The criminal penalties for willful violations of the reporting requirements [31 U.S.C. 5322 (a) and (b)], except for reports required for foreign currency transactions (31 U.S.C. 5315) and "structuring" transactions to evade reporting requirements (31 U.S.C. 5324), are as follows:

1. A fine up to $250,000 or up to five years in prison, or both
2. A fine up to $500,000 or up to 10 years in prison, or both, when the violation is committed while violating another federal law, or is part of a pattern of any illegal activity involving over $100,000 in a 12-month period

Structuring transactions to evade reporting requirements is dealt with in 31 U.S.C. 5324. The following are prohibited under 31 U.S.C. 5324 (a):

1. To cause or attempt to cause a domestic financial institution to fail to file a CTR, or fail to make a log entry for purchases of bank checks and drafts, cashier's checks, money orders and travelers checks over $3000
2. To cause or attempt to cause a domestic financial institution to file a CTR, or make a log entry for purchases of bank checks and drafts, cashier's checks, money orders and travelers checks over $3000, that contains a material omission or misstatement of fact
3. To structure or assist in structuring, or attempt to structure or assist in structuring, any transaction with one or more domestic financial institutions

31 U.S.C. 5324 (b) prohibits a person to fail to file a CMIR or attempt to cause a person to fail to file a CMIR; to file or cause or attempt to cause a person to file a CMIR that contains a material omission or misstatement of fact; or to structure or assist in structuring, or attempt to structure or assist in structuring, any importation or exportation of monetary instruments. CMIR violations are within the jurisdiction of the Bureau of Immigration and Customs Enforcement.

31 U.S.C. 5324 (c) (1) and (2) exclude a "willfulness" requirement to show a violation under Sections 5324 (a) or (b) and provide the following criminal penalties:

1. A fine in accordance with Title 18, or up to five years in prison, or both
2. A fine for twice the amount provided in 18 U.S.C. 3571 (b) (3) or (c) (3), or up to 10 years in prison, or both, when the violation is committed while violating another federal law or is part of a pattern of any illegal activity involving over $100,000 in a 12-month period

Failure to maintain records is covered in 12 U.S.C. 1956 and 1957. Penalties are as follows:

1. Whoever willfully violates any regulation relating to records to be maintained under 12 U.S.C. Chapter 21, Financial Recordkeeping, shall be fined not more than $1000, or imprisoned not more than 1 year, or both.
2. 12 U.S.C. 1957 increases the penalty to a fine of not more than $10,000, or imprisonment for not more than five years, or both, when the violation is committed in furtherance of the commission of any other felony under federal law.

In addition to criminal sanctions, civil penalties can be assessed for violation of the following sections:

- 31 U.S.C. 5321 (a) (2): failure to file a CMIR, or filing a CMIR with a material omission or misstatement.
- A person who does not file a CMIR or files a CMIR with a material omission or misstatement may be assessed an additional civil penalty, in addition to a penalty under 31 U.S.C. 5321 (a) (1), up to the amount of the monetary instrument involved, to be reduced by the amount of any related forfeiture.
- 31 U.S.C. 5321 (a) (3): failure to file a report related to foreign currency transactions. Anyone who does not file a report related to foreign currency transactions may be assessed a penalty up to $10,000.
- 31 U.S.C. 5321 (a) (4): structuring of transactions. A person who willfully structures transactions in violation of Section 5324 (a) and (b) may be assessed a penalty up to the amount of the currency or monetary instruments involved, to be reduced by the amount of any related forfeiture.
- 31 U.S.C. 5321 (a) (5): willful violations related to reports and recordkeeping requirements for foreign financial accounts and transactions

(excluding foreign currency transactions). A person who willfully fails to file a FBAR or files a FBAR with a material omission or misstatement, or does not make and retain records for interests in foreign financial accounts, may be assessed a penalty not to exceed the greater of the amount equal to the account balance at the time of the violation (up to $100,000) or $25,000.

- 31 U.S.C. 5321 (a) (6): negligent violation of any reporting or record-keeping requirement of Title 31. A penalty of up to $500 may be assessed on any financial institution that negligently violates any reporting or recordkeeping requirements of Title 31 and of up to $50,000 for a pattern of negligent activity by a financial institution.
- 31 U.S.C. 5330 (e): failure to register a money-transmitting business. A $5000 penalty may be assessed for each time that a person fails to comply with the registration requirements for money-transmitting businesses under Section 5330.
- 12 U.S.C. 1955: willful violation of record-keeping requirements. Any person or partner, director, officer, or employee of a domestic financial institution who willfully or through gross negligence violates any regulation under 12 U.S.C. Chapter 21, Financial Recordkeeping, may be assessed a penalty up to $10,000.

Investigations under Title 31

The two agencies that will have the most interest in these violations will be the Internal Revenue Service and the Bureau of Immigration and Customs Enforcement. Because it is their jurisdiction, any violations of these statutes should be brought to their attention and a joint investigation undertaken. This makes practical sense, too, because these agencies will have access to the computerized databases containing the various reports. Both agencies have developed profiles and methods of analyzing this data that can be used to further Title 31 cases.

The BSA is aimed at the placement stage of the money laundering cycle, where the launderer is most vulnerable to detection. It is here that the bulk of currency is reduced in size or changed in form. The BSA addresses every avenue by which this placement can occur, by requiring that reports of the activity be submitted.

The BSA has gotten stronger since 1970 and was further improved after 9/11. Although compliance was poor in the period up through 1985, things have changed as Congress and law enforcement became more conscious of the money laundering threat. Banks in particular have developed a whole new attitude toward currency reporting, aided by provisions such as that enacted in 1994 which provided for revocation of a bank charter for violations of the BSA. This "death penalty" is a real threat, one that no legitimate banking operation can afford to ignore.

IRS and the other regulatory agencies spend considerable time and energy promoting compliance among the financial institutions required to file reports. This effort, along with enforcement actions, has forced launderers away from banks and toward nonbank financial institutions (NBFIs) or direct currency movement offshore. It seems likely that continuing law enforcement attention to the BSA will prompt other changes, but it is still incumbent on us to use the tools provided by this statute.

The information is certainly there. More than 15 million CTRs are filed each year, with the number increasing annually. The number of SARs — 663,000 in 2004 — is also growing, and investigators have observed trends in money laundering operations that indicate improved compliance by financial institutions and earlier detection of laundering schemes. New exemptions in the regulations will have the effect of decreasing the numbers of bank transactions in which the CTR is required to be filed, but you will probably agree that 15 million forms represent a lot of information about bank customers and transactions.

Obtaining this information and using it properly are the goals of Title 31 investigations. One important consideration is the possibility that a money launderer might qualify under this act to be a nonbank financial institution, a wire transmitter, or a money service business. If so, the BSA regulations and statutory provisions would apply to this person. Each scheme you encounter that deals with the movement, transfer, or transportation of funds should be examined to determine whether the operator is functioning as an NBFI or other enterprise that should be regulated.

The Bank Secrecy Act works as advertised. It puts a severe crimp in the ability of criminals to use the most efficient entities — banks — in money laundering schemes. It forces them either to expose themselves or to violate the law if they want to accomplish their schemes. It provides law enforcement with tools for detecting the placement of laundered funds, and it documents many of the large cash transactions that would previously have been anonymous.

When it is combined with the money laundering statutes, as Congress intended, and with laws against the underlying SUAs, Title 31 can be a real aid in your investigations.

"Gee, if you're withdrawing over $10,000 in cash, I have to report it to the IRS. Could I see some ID, please?"

RACKETEER INFLUENCED AND CORRUPT ORGANIZATIONS ACT

Another federal statute, relating closely to the money laundering laws, is Title 18 U.S.C. Sections 1961, 1962, and 1963, the Racketeer Influenced and Corrupt Organizations Act (RICO).

As you might guess from the title, RICO is directed at organizations, or, as the statute defines them, racketeering enterprises. Since its enactment, RICO has been used against many enterprises that do not fit the conventional notion of organized crime. The act defines an enterprise to include individuals, partnerships, corporations, associations, other legal entities, and any union or group of individuals associated in fact although not a legal entity (the Mafia, for instance) that is engaged in or the activities of which affect interstate commerce.

That's painting with a pretty broad brush, which is apparently what Congress wanted, since the courts have upheld RICO convictions against gangs, syndicate leaders, corrupt public officials, drug dealers, labor unions, and a lot of other folks who got together to commit some crime.

The law addresses the enterprise affecting interstate commerce, not the criminal activity itself. This is an important distinction, especially in money laundering cases, because laundering schemes so often employ those legal entities just defined above to effect their objectives. For this reason, you should look for any overlap between RICO and the money laundering statutes when you are putting your case together.

The enterprise can affect interstate commerce through what the act calls "a pattern of racketeering activity" consisting of at least two acts of racketeering activity within 10 years. (Note that this can extend the effective statute of limitations on federal crimes by quite a bit.)

Racketeering acts include the following:

- Any act involving murder, kidnapping, gambling, arson, robbery, bribery, extortion, dealing in obscene matter, or

dealing in a controlled substance which is a felony under state law
- Specific violations of federal law, including money laundering, violations of the BSA, and mail and wire fraud, among others
- Labor offenses in Title 29 U.S.C.
- Securities fraud in Title 11, or narcotics crimes in Title 21

If an enterprise exists and the racketeering activity (also known as predicate offenses) is confirmed, RICO prohibits four types of conduct:

1. Acquisition of an enterprise with illegal funds obtained through a pattern of racketeering activity or the collection of an unlawful debt
2. Acquisition of an enterprise through a pattern of racketeering or the collection of an unlawful debt
3. Use of an enterprise through a pattern of racketeering activity or the collection of an unlawful debt
4. Conspiracy

In the first instance, dirty money is used to acquire the enterprise, as when drug money is used to buy a business front. In the second, illegal means are used to acquire the enterprise. This would occur when a business is acquired through fraud, extortion, or possibly through money laundering. The third conduct involves use of an enterprise in any illegal fashion. In a money laundering scheme, a RICO violation could occur if the business were used to launder the funds.

RICO is a very powerful statute because of its wide application. It carries potential 20-year prison terms for violations, huge fines, and forfeiture provisions as well. Because the list of predicate offenses is so long, and because the definition of "enterprise" is so broad, RICO will apply to many money laundering schemes. In fact, RICO and money laundering are practically joined at the hip, since money laundering is one of RICO's predicate acts, and the RICO predicates are all Specified Unlawful Activities under the money laundering statute.

Special approval may be needed to prosecute RICO cases, most of which are processed through Strike Force attorneys in the United States Attorney's Office. If your money laundering scheme involves an enterprise as defined by RICO, you may want to look into prosecuting this charge as well.

ILLEGAL MONEY TRANSMITTER BUSINESSES

Title 18 is another statute that underwent some radical changes with the passage of the USA PATRIOT Act. Title 18 U.S.C. Section 1960 (a) formerly stated that, "Whoever conducts, controls, manages, supervises, directs, or owns all or part of a business, *knowing the business is an illegal money transmitting business,* shall be fined in accordance with this title or imprisoned not more than 5 years, or both" (emphasis mine).

I emphasized the "knowing" part of the statute because proving this element turned out to be trickier than Congress anticipated when it included it. As you can imagine, those charged came in saying things like, "Gee, officer, I didn't know my boss never registered …" or, "I thought for sure somebody filled out the proper forms."

After October 26, 2001, however, "whoever knowingly conducts, controls, manages, supervises, directs, or owns all or part of an unlicensed money transmitting business, shall be fined in accordance with this title or imprisoned not more than 5 years, or both." This change means that the government can focus on what the person actually did — operate a business that was unlicensed.

We still have to show either that the business was not licensed, in "a State where such operation is punishable as a misdemeanor or a felony under State law," or that it failed "to comply with the money transmitting business registration requirements under Section 5330 of Title 31, United States Code." And it no longer matters whether or not "the defendant knew that the operation was required to be licensed or that the operation was so punishable."

The government also has the option of showing that the funds transmitted were known to the defendant to have been derived from some criminal activity or were intended to be used to promote or support the unlawful activity.

In addition, the definition of "money transmitting" is pretty broad, including "transferring funds on behalf of the public by any and all means including but not limited to transfers within this country or to locations abroad by wire, check, draft, facsimile, or courier." That last part is important, because it may be possible in some cases to charge bulk currency shippers and others who are moving large sums of cash across state lines or internationally with violations of this statute.

The transmission of funds by wire is a common tactic employed by money launderers. Getting large amounts of dirty money placed with a business that can instantly move the funds anywhere in the world is a dream come true. Killing that dream is why Congress passed a law making sure those in the money-transmitting businesses played by the rules.

The way things now stand, wire transmitters are supposed to be registered with the Treasury Department and regulated by IRS, as are other nonbank financial institutions, such as currency exchange businesses and casinos. All are required to abide by Title 26 and Title 31 cash-reporting requirements, as well as by regulations pertaining to record-keeping and the identification of their customers.

Title 18 was aimed directly at such informal value transfer (IVT) systems as the Chinese *fei chi'en*, the *hundi,* and particularly the *hawala*, all of which are known to transmit very large amounts of money under extremely secret circumstances. Almost none of these IVT systems are actually licensed as the law requires, and all are potentially subject to Section 1960 — if you can find them.

There have been some prosecutions under this statute, both stand alone and as part of wider money laundering or financial cases. The penalty of five years is not severe, but that isn't really the point. The objective of the statute, when combined with the Bank Secrecy Act, is to regulate these businesses and make sure that they are reporting cash transactions in the placement stage of money laundering operations.

This section would be especially applicable in a case in which a professional money launderer was assisting in the transmission of money overseas and charging a commission for these services. That launderer would also be considered a nonbank financial institution by the BSA and would be subject to those provisions as well.

INVESTMENT OF ILLICIT DRUG PROFITS

Title 21 U.S.C. Section 854 prohibits the investment of illicit drug profits. This provision reads:

It shall be unlawful for any person who has received any income derived, directly or indirectly, from a violation of this subchapter or subchapter II of this chapter punishable by imprisonment for more than one year in which such person has participated as a principal within the meaning of section 2 of Title 18 to use or invest, directly or indirectly, any part of such income, or the proceeds of such income, in acquisition of any interest in, or the establishment or operation of, any enterprise which is engaged in, or the activities of which affect interstate or foreign commerce. A purchase of securities on the open market for purposes of investment, and without the intention of controlling or participating in the control of the issuer, or of assisting another to do so, shall not be unlawful under this section if the securities of the issuer held by the purchaser, the members of his immediate family, and his or their accomplices in any violation of this subchapter or subchapter II of this chapter after such purchase do not amount in the aggregate to 1 per centum of the outstanding securities of any one class, and do not confer, either in law or in fact, the power to elect one or more directors of the issuer.

The penalty for violation is a fine of up to $50,000 and a prison term up to 10 years, and the definition of "enterprise" is similar to that in the RICO act.

The purpose of this section is obviously to prevent drug traffickers from using their dope money as leverage to obtain control of businesses and corporations. This statute is quite similar to the money laundering statutes, in that you will have to prove two key elements: the investment or transaction, and the illegal source of the funds.

Also of note is the phrase "establishment or operation of, any enterprise." This implies that if a drug trafficker were to use or invest drug money in the continuing operation of an enterprise, this, too, would be a violation. Thus, the creation of a front business or the operation of an established front would constitute a violation, even if drug money were being used only to pay the rent or utility bills.

Where the law differs somewhat from the money laundering statutes is that no intent to do anything is required, merely the "use or investment" of the money in the first place. In contrast, in §1956 (a) (1), the launderer must intend to promote the SUA, evade taxes, conceal his or her interest, or avoid a reporting requirement.

Which statute to use? It probably depends on the facts. If none of the four intents can be proved, and if drug sales are the underlying crime, this section might be the preferred alternative. It's something to consider.

FALSE STATEMENTS

False statements are an essential part of money laundering schemes, thanks primarily to the BSA. Most criminals aren't wild about the idea of putting accurate information into a report that's going to IRS or Customs. The statutes recognize this problem by making it a crime to cause the filing of a false report, but other statutes can come into play in money laundering cases as well.

One of these is Title 18 U.S.C. Section 1001, relating to fraud and false statements generally. This statute states the following:

> a. Except as otherwise provided in this section, whoever, in any matter within the jurisdiction of the executive, legislative, or judicial branch of the Government of the United States, knowingly and willfully

> 1. falsifies, conceals, or covers up by any trick, scheme, or device a material fact;

> 2. makes any materially false, fictitious, or fraudulent statement or representation; or

> 3. makes or uses any false writing or document knowing the same to contain any materially false, fictitious, or fraudulent statement or entry;

> 4. shall be fined under this title or imprisoned not more than 5 years or both.

All of the forms that are required under the BSA are exactly the types of "matter within the jurisdiction of the executive" that the law covers. For example, if a smurf used false identity documents to purchase cashier's checks or to establish an account with a bank or NBFI, this act could be charged as a violation of §1001. It might also be a violation to make a false statement to a federal agent who was investigating a money laundering or BSA violation, such as a bank employee or wire transmitter agent.

A big brother of this statute is 18 U.S.C. Section 1005, which relates to fraud and false statements in bank entries, reports, and transactions. Where §1001 carries a five-year penalty, §1005 brings an attention-getting 30-year sentence and $1 million fine. The section reads in part:

> Whoever with intent to defraud the United States or any agency thereof, or any financial institution referred to in this section, participates in or shares in or receives (directly or indirectly) any money, profit, property, or benefits through any transaction, loan, commission, contract, or any other act of any such financial institution

> Shall be fined not more than $1,000,000 or imprisoned not more than 30 years, or both.

A related provision, §1014, relates to loan and credit applications generally. It reads in part:

Whoever knowingly makes any false statement or report, or willfully overvalues any land, property or security, for the purpose of influencing in any way the action of ... a Federal Reserve bank, a small business investment company, a Federal credit union, an insured State chartered credit union, any institution the accounts of which are insured by the Federal Deposit Insurance Corporation, the Office of Thrift Supervision, any Federal home loan bank ... upon any application, advance, discount, purchase, purchase agreement, repurchase agreement, commitment, or loan, or any change or extension of any of the same by renewal, deferment of action or otherwise, or the acceptance, release, or substitution of security therefor, shall be fined not more than $1,000,000 or imprisoned not more than 30 years.

This statute essentially means that a false statement on a loan application can result not only in being declined for the loan but also a long stretch in the federal joint. Both of these sections are designed to protect banks and the taxpayers who insure deposits at those banks.

False statements are rather common on loan applications, however, as people adjust their income figures to whatever level they think will assure them of the loan.

Submission of false documents is also not uncommon in bank transactions. Many banks require copies of income tax returns for three years to accompany a mortgage loan application. These returns may be faked to show more income in order to qualify for the loan. Another scheme is the listing of a false source of income, such as an employer, when none exists. The applicant might even arrange with an associate to show the applicant "on the books" as an employee, in case the bank asks.

What is the relationship to money laundering? If the launderer has submitted false documents in connection with his or her activities, there may come a point in your investigation when you might like to direct the person's attention to the 30-year penalty. This could have an effect on his or her willingness to cooperate in exposing other members of the organization or the higher-ups.

CHAPTER 7

INTERNATIONAL MONEY LAUNDERING CONTROL

"This is the night Mail, crossing the Border
Bringing the cheque and the postal order."
W.H. Auden, British poet, from an ad for the British postal service

"For my part, I travel not to go anywhere, but to go. I travel for travel's sake.
The great affair is to move."
Robert Louis Stevenson, *Travels with a Donkey*

In the world of modern money laundering, Stevenson's romantic view of travel has been somewhat superseded. The money getting laundered in today's global economy can definitely take some long and roundabout trips, but not just for travel's sake.

Money laundering has gone international in a major way. Capital flight, money from criminal enterprises, and the looted treasuries of nations join every day with the billions of dollars in international commerce. Separating the licit from the illicit has not always been a priority among all nations, but this situation is beginning to change.

If the change is slow, it is because the recognition that dirty money has immense power to corrupt has come slowly to places where laissez faire capitalism is cheerfully practiced. In business and banking centers around the world, especially those that actively solicit international business, the prevailing philosophy has always been, as one banker put it, "There is no dirty money or clean money, only money." This attitude, together with a desire to protect the privacy of banking customers, led to the creation of bank secrecy and tax havens around the world.

Times change, and as the technology has advanced to speed the transfer of funds between nations, governments have acted to put the brakes on. Ironically, much of this action comes as even more launderers seek out the shelter of a foreign jurisdiction for their funds. As money laundering statutes and the threat of forfeiture increased the pressure on drug traffickers in the United States, anywhere offshore started to look better and better.

Certain places looked better than others. Switzerland, with its rock-solid stability and strict secrecy provisions, was the early favorite in the offshore money sweepstakes. Closer to much of the action in the Americas were Switzerland clones such as Panama, the Bahamas, the Netherlands Antilles, and the Cayman Islands. Money from ten thousand scams disappeared into these places, where the laws were specifically written to accomplish exactly that disappearance.

Attempts by American law enforcement to penetrate bank secrecy were met with a standard official response: "Our law forbids release of that information without the customer's permission." The unofficial response was that the problem was an American one, and that the source of the money was of no concern to a banker in another country.

When the latter, unofficial view began to change, change in the former one followed, though not exactly at the speed of light. Bankers are pretty proud of both their status in the community and their reputations, which are almost never enhanced by close association with drug smugglers and fraud artists. One international institution, the Bank of Credit and Commerce International (BCCI), became known informally but rather widely as the Bank of Crooks and Criminals International. Not only did this association sting the bankers' pride, but it caused governments, through their central banks and regulatory authorities, to take a much harder look at the activities of institutions like BCCI.

The unsurprising (from an American point of view) outcome was the conclusion that maybe dirty business wasn't always in the best interests of the country receiving that business. This shift in attitude was helped along by two other factors. First, the United States, still the world's largest economy and the source of a lot of legitimate offshore investments (along with some not so legitimate ones) began taking a greater interest in the offshore movement of drug money.

By the 1970s and 1980s, much more of the drug trade was being run from offshore havens, and that's where the money was going. Government agencies, notably DEA and Customs, were being frustrated in their efforts to track this money and were making demands on the State, Justice, and Treasury departments to secure more cooperation from foreign governments. Not always happily, the American government began diplomatic attempts to get more access to information from foreign countries. Some of these efforts resulted in Mutual Legal Assistance Treaties (MLATs), bilateral agreements between governments to permit release of otherwise secret information in certain cases. Diplomatic pressure could get intense, and American displeasure with money laundering was cited in at least one instance in which diplomatic pressure gave way to military action, this being the 1989 invasion of Panama.

On the "carrot" side of the equation was the other factor that aided in the shift of attitudes — the increasing use of forfeiture in criminal cases and the willingness of the American government to give cooperative foreign governments a share of the assets forfeited from offshore locations. Since 1989, when the first international asset sharing took place, the United States has transferred well over $100 million abroad to foreign governments such as the Bahamas, the Cayman Islands, Costa Rica, Colombia, and the United Kingdom. Somewhat ironically, given their early role in the whole secrecy business, Switzerland has been the recipient of the most money shared in this fashion, over $25 million to date, and it is currently America's biggest overseas forfeiture partner.

After a not always enthusiastic start, international cooperation in anti–money laundering efforts has picked up steam. As we'll see, this new attitude toward dirty money is manifested in many ways, such as treaties, bilateral and executive agreements, closer law enforcement cooperation, and the work of international organizations such as the United Nations and INTERPOL.

Most of this activity takes place at diplomatic levels far above the heads of the law enforcement officers laboring in the trenches on a financial case. Why even discuss something that we investigators have little power to control? Mainly because these activities are a sign that the landscape is changing, and that the old truism — if your case went offshore it was as good as dead — is no longer so true.

We'll look at some of the ways international cooperation has aided in money laundering cases in the past, and we'll see how information can be obtained under a Mutual Legal Assistance Treaty.

Things aren't as bad as they used to be, although almost nobody's money laundering statutes are as effective as those in the United States (Australia's, maybe, and the United Kingdom is catching up fast). The chances of obtaining foreign cooperation in your case are better than ever before.

INTERNATIONAL ORGANIZATIONS

Several international organizations have been created or assigned to deal with the money laundering threat. These groups tend to address the legislative or diplomatic questions relating to the issue, although at least one is more closely related to the law enforcement end of things.

INTERPOL

The International Criminal Police Organization (INTERPOL), headquartered in France, functions as a means for exchanging information about crime and criminals among its 168 member nations. Each member state coordinates activity with INTERPOL through a National Central Bureau (NCB), which is where your request for INTERPOL assistance should be forwarded.

INTERPOL has taken an aggressive stance toward money laundering and asset forfeiture, developing model legislation for member states, assisting with the implementation of anti–money laundering programs, and providing training in these areas to interested parties. INTERPOL also works with governments and private groups, such as bankers, to put effective money laundering control measures in place. Strategic and tactical intelligence on drug trafficking and related crimes is processed through subdivisions at INTERPOL.

The United States government is working through INTERPOL and other organizations to obtain an international agreement for the collection of information on large cash transactions, sort of a global CTR/CMIR system. The crisis of terrorist financing has definitely stimulated INTERPOL and governments around the world to faster action on this front.

UNITED NATIONS

The United Nations Narcotics Convention of 1988, also known as the Vienna Convention, requires that signatory nations make money laundering a criminal offense, and an extraditable one. Article 7 of the Convention also requires that signatories provide assistance and cooperation in resolving such matters. There is no enforcement mechanism, but the Convention requires that the signing governments change their laws to comply with the agreement. Quite a few governments have not signed the Convention, including some that are major financial and bank secrecy centers.

In the article relating to mutual legal assistance, the signatories agree to provide "the widest measure of legal assistance in investigations, prosecutions, and judicial proceedings," including the following:

- Taking evidence or statements from persons
- Effecting service of legal documents
- Executing searches and seizures
- Examining objects and sites
- Providing information and evidentiary items
- Providing originals or certified copies of relevant documents and records, including bank, financial, corporate, or business records
- Identifying or tracing proceeds, property, instrumentalities, or other things for evidentiary purposes

By signing the Convention, a government is pledging its cooperation in drug-related money laundering investigations, at least in theory. The United Nations has also used a number of expert group studies to evaluate global drug trafficking and money laundering patterns and to make recommendations about possible responses.

BRITISH COMMONWEALTH

The British Commonwealth countries include a number that have historically been associated with money laundering activity. Some have deliberately created legislation to solicit flight capital or banking customers seeking the highest degree of secrecy.

In a series of Commonwealth initiatives, member nations have established a Commonwealth Scheme for Mutual Assistance in Criminal Matters, which directly attacks international money laundering activity. The individual members are pledged to assist each other in criminal investigations, to include identifying, locating, and assessing the value of, property believed to have been derived or obtained, directly or indirectly, from, or to have been used in, or in connection with, the commission of an offence and believed to be within the requested country.

Forfeiture has become a major issue within the Commonwealth, and provisions for the confiscation of the proceeds of crimes such as drug trafficking are now on the books in many Commonwealth nations.

Financial Action Task Force

The Financial Action Task Force (FATF), an international organization formed in July 1989 by the G7, is comprised of the seven largest industrialized nations (the United States, Canada, Britain, Germany, France, Italy, and Japan) the European community, and eight other nations.

The FATF has analyzed international money laundering and examined a number of alternatives or remedies that the member states could adopt to curb the activity. The task force has issued a series of reports recommending changes in legislation regarding criminal law, banking regulations, and international cooperation. Most recently, the FATF has concentrated not only on money laundering but also on terrorist financing, and it has made new recommendations concerning that activity.

The first task force report, FATF I, recommended that members do the following:

- Criminalize money laundering
- Include other offenses besides drug trafficking as money laundering predicates
- Require banks to "know their customers" and to identify people conducting bank transactions
- Adopt currency transaction reporting requirements to track cash transactions
- Develop mechanisms for reporting and tracking suspicious transactions

Following the September 11, 2001, terrorist attacks, the FATF issued eight Special Recommendations on Terrorist Financing. These complement the first 40 recommendations regarding money laundering, and suggest that countries do the following:

- Ratify United Nations conventions regarding terrorist financing
- Make provisions for reporting suspicious transactions that relate to terrorist financing
- Criminalize terrorist financing and make provisions for the seizure of terrorist assets
- Pass laws to license and regulate persons involved with so-called informal value transfer systems, which bypass normal wire transfer networks
- Review and, if necessary, strengthen laws that prevent misuse of the non-profit and "charitable" organizations that have served in the past as fronts for terrorist groups

FATF has also sponsored regional cooperative efforts, including the Caribbean FATF, which have involved a number of governments with strong bank secrecy provisions in the area. The United States has been very active in FATF; its delegation is headed by the Deputy Secretary of the Treasury. The Financial Crimes Enforcement Network (FinCEN) also participates in FATF programs.

In its assessment of drug-related money laundering, the FATF made a number of interesting conclusions, based on what was probably the first really international assessment of the problem. The following is excerpted from the *Report of the Financial Action Task Force on Money Laundering* (Paris, February 7, 1990):

> It would be impossible to list the entire range of methods used to launder money. Nevertheless, the Task Force reviewed a number of practical cases of money laundering. It stated that all of them share common factors, regarding

the role of cash domestically, of various kinds of financial institutions, of international cash transfers, and of corporate techniques. These common factors indicate clearly where the efforts of the fight against money laundering should focus....

The form of the money obtained through drug trafficking must be changed in order to shrink the huge volumes of cash generated: unlike the proceeds of some other forms of criminal activity, drug cash usually comes in the form of large volumes of mixed denomination notes, and at least in the case of heroin and cocaine, the physical volume of notes received from street dealing is much larger than the volume of the drugs themselves.

Drug criminals are faced with major difficulties when in possession of large amounts of cash, and when large transactions cannot be performed in cash without arousing suspicion. A completely cashless economy where all transactions were registered would create enormous problems for the money launderers. Similarly, a rule that cash transactions were illegal above a certain amount for all but certain types of business regularly operating in cash would also create problems for launderers.

The report goes on to note that the role of banks is critical in money laundering schemes and that, in international operations, the use of unregulated banks or "letter box companies" provides launderers with opportunities. The report states:

Drug dealers must conceal the true ownership and origin of the money while simultaneously controlling it. To this end, they can use various corporate techniques.

Offshore companies can be used by launderers in ways other than simply as depositories for cash. Launderers can set up or buy corporations, perhaps in a tax haven using a local lawyer or other person as a nominee owner, with an account at a local bank. They can then finance the purchase of a similar business at home through a loan from their corporation abroad (or the bank), in effect borrowing their own money and paying it back as if it were a legitimate loan.

The technique of "double invoicing" can be used whereby goods are purchased at inflated prices by domestic companies owned by money launderers from offshore corporations which they also own. The difference between the price and the true value is then deposited offshore and paid to the offshore company and repatriated at will. Variants of the "double invoicing" technique abound.

All these techniques, however, involve going through stages where detection is possible. Either cash has to be exported over a territorial frontier and then deposited in a foreign financial institution or it requires the knowing or unknowing complicity of someone at home not connected with the drug trade, or it requires convincing a domestic financial institution that a large cash deposit or purchase of a cashier's check is legitimate. Once these hurdles have been cleared, the way is much easier inside the legitimate financial system.

Hence, key stages for the detection of money laundering operations are those where cash enters into the domestic financial system, either formally or informally, where it is sent abroad to be integrated into the financial systems of regulatory havens, and where it is repatriated in the form of transfers of legitimate appearance.

This analysis forms the basis for FATF's understanding of the problem, and actions taken by the group in response are addressed to these factors. Because the member nations have such economic and political clout, the FATF has the potential to be a leader in international money laundering control efforts.

ORGANIZATION OF AMERICAN STATES

The Organization of American States (OAS), formed in 1890, is comprised of 32 nations in North and South America and the Caribbean. A regional Inter-American Drug Abuse Control Commission (CICAD) was formed in 1986 to examine measures that could be taken against the drug trade. These measures eventually addressed money laundering activity, and a series of recommendations were made for member states to use in drafting legislation and regulations.

One of the results of the OAS initiative was a set of Model Regulations on Crimes Related to Laundering of Property and Proceeds Related to Drug Trafficking. Within these model regulations are forfeiture provisions, a requirement that financial records be made available in criminal cases involving drug money laundering, and requirements that financial institutions report large and suspicious transactions.

THE EGMONT GROUP

The Egmont Group is an association of Financial Intelligence Units (FIU) from countries around the world. FIUs are intended to be the collectors and custodians of information about suspicious financial transactions, money laundering activity, and terrorist financing. The Egmont Group was created 10 years ago to promote the sharing of information between FIUs. America's representative to the Egmont Group is FinCEN.

About 85 FIUs are currently represented, and other countries are in the process of signing up. The FATF's 40 recommendations state that countries should establish FIUs and take other measures to prevent money laundering and to cooperate in anti–money laundering efforts. As the list below shows, quite a few countries that are often thought of as money laundering havens are participating to some degree in the Egmont Group.

Albania	Bahrain	Cayman
Andorra	Barbados	Islands
Anguilla	Belgium	Chile
Antigua and	Bermuda	Colombia
Barbuda	Bolivia	Costa Rica
Argentina	Brazil	Croatia
Aruba	British Virgin	Cyprus
Australia	Islands	Czech
Austria	Bulgaria	Republic
Bahamas	Canada	Denmark
Dominica	Latvia	Serbia
Dominican	Lebanon	Singapore
Republic	Liechtenstein	Slovakia
El Salvador	Lithuania	Slovenia
Estonia	Luxembourg	South Africa
Finland	Malaysia	Spain
France	Malta	St. Vincent
Germany	Marshall	and the Grenadines
Greece	Islands	
Guatemala	Mauritius	Sweden
Guernsey	Mexico	Switzerland
Hong Kong,	Monaco	Taiwan
China	Netherlands	Thailand
Hungary	Netherlands	Turkey
Iceland	Antilles	Ukraine
Ireland	New Zealand	United Arab
Isle of Man	Norway	Emirates
Israel	Panama	United Kingdom
Italy	Paraguay	
Japan	Poland	United States
Jersey	Portugal	Vanuatu
Korea,	Romania	Venezuela
Republic of	Russia	

OTHER INITIATIVES

In addition to those cited above, other regional international initiatives have taken place with a view toward money laundering control. Some of these are:

- Gulf Cooperation Council
- European Community
- Caribbean Drug Money Laundering Conference
- Caribbean Community and Common Market
- Basle Committee on Banking Regulation and Supervisory Practices
- Asian Development Bank Money Laundering Initiatives

IMPACT ON LAW ENFORCEMENT

The impact of all this attention is that as nations around the world become more aware of the problem, their laws and procedures for dealing with the problem change. Whereas, once, money going to the Cayman Islands may as well have been going to the moon as far as law enforcement was concerned, there are now mechanisms in place all over the world for information — and even the money itself — to be retrieved. Surprisingly, some of the biggest players in the money laundering arena are now on the law enforcement team — at least with respect to certain crimes. Switzerland, a model of bank secrecy for decades, has assisted in the recovery of financial information and the tracing of laundered proceeds.

As more nations pass laws against money laundering, the chances that your suspect will be prosecuted for that crime in a foreign country increase. And, with those countries that have extradition treaties, the addition of a money laundering crime as an extraditable offense means that your chances of getting the launderer back are also improved.

Another possibility is that laundered assets seized overseas in a joint investigation with an American law enforcement agency could be equitably shared with that agency. So far, most of the international asset sharing — which is a part of almost all the agreements discussed above — has gone the other way. A typical case involves criminal activity in the United States that generates proceeds that are moved to a foreign country, such as Switzerland. When these assets are traced, the Swiss seize them on the American initiative. When the forfeiture case is concluded, the Swiss apply for a share of the proceeds — which, by agreement, is 50% — and the case is concluded.

OBTAINING INFORMATION FROM ABROAD

In another chapter we will discuss some of the means whereby information is obtained; however, because the emphasis in all of these international initiatives has been mutual legal assistance, this chapter is a good place to look at the Mutual Legal Assistance Treaty as a means for getting information.

The Mutual Legal Assistance Treaty or MLAT is a bilateral agreement between two countries to assist each other in specified legal matters. The United States has been most aggressive in pursuing these agreements and currently has MLATs with more than 50 countries. These are:

Anguilla	Grenada	Russia
Antigua/	Hong Kong	South Africa
Barbuda	Hungary	South Korea
Argentina	Inter-	Spain
Australia	American	St. Kitts-
Austria	Convention	Nevis
Bahamas	(OAS	St. Lucia
Barbados	Convention)	St. Vincent
Belgium	Israel	and the
Belize	Italy	Grenadines
Brazil	Jamaica	Switzerland
British Virgin	Latvia	Thailand
Islands	Lichtenstein	Trinidad and
Canada	Lithuania	Tobago
Cayman	Luxembourg	Turkey
Islands	Mexico	Turks and
Cyprus	Montserrat	Caicos
Czech	Morocco	Islands
Republic	Netherlands	Ukraine
Dominica	Nigeria	United
Egypt	Panama	Kingdom
Estonia	Philippines	Uruguay
France	Poland	Venezuela
Greece	Romania	

In the United States, money laundering investigations that have international aspects are conducted by the Justice, State, and Treasury departments, following all of the diplomatic and procedural niceties that the laws or treaties prescribe. All official requests for information or assistance from overseas are supposed to go through proper channels, although several federal law enforcement agencies maintain an overseas presence in various locations to facilitate law enforcement matters that do not involve treaty requests.

These things take time, however, in addition to all sorts of paperwork, so don't expect results on your request tomorrow. Still, things could be worse, and all of this international activity has made it more difficult for the money launderer to operate freely.

An exemplar for a Swiss MLAT information request, furnished by the Asset Forfeiture and Money Laundering Section, United States Department of Justice, may be found in Figure 7.1.

To: The Central Authority of Switzerland
Subject: Request for Assistance in the Investigation of John Doe

The Central Authority of the United States requests the assistance of the appropriate authorities in Switzerland pursuant to the Treaty on Mutual Assistance in Criminal Matters. The prosecutor for this matter is the United States Attorney for the District of _____.

Description of the Investigation

The prosecutor is conducting a grand jury investigation into the activities of John Doe, who is suspected of defrauding investors in a business venture ostensibly designed to establish and operate a foreign bank. Doe represented to investors that certain funds were to be held in escrow in a Swiss bank account.

Assistance Being Requested

The prosecutor needs Swiss bank records to determine whether investors' funds were ever deposited into such an account, and, if so, the disposition of those funds. The prosecutor further requests that any funds traceable to the subject matter of this request be frozen to prevent their removal or dissipation and to afford the victims of the fraud with an opportunity to seek recovery through the initiation of a civil action in Switzerland.

Facts

In 1988, John Doe, doing business as Capital Trust, Ltd., solicited funds for a business venture from medical doctors in Iowa. The venture involved the formation, capitalization, and operation of Today's Bank, which was to operate as a banking facility in Vanuatu. Today's Bank was to be capitalized through the sale of its shares, a total of 100. Each potential investor was offered up to 10 shares at $25,000 each. Proceeds from the sale of shares were to be placed in an escrow account at the Credit Suisse, Zurich, Switzerland. The escrow account was to earn interest at a rate of approximately 20 percent until all 100 shares were sold, at which time the share purchase money was to be placed in a working fund account at the Bank of Canada and the interest earned was to be paid to the investors.

[Additional information about the case, including the role of Swiss banks in the scheme, has been deleted.]

Offenses

18 U.S.C. §1341 Frauds and Swindles

Whoever, having devised or intending to devise any scheme or artifice to defraud, or for obtaining money or property by means of false or fraudulent pretenses, representations, or promises, ... for the purpose of executing such scheme or artifice or attempting to do ... (uses the Postal Service, or causes it to be used) ... shall be fined not more than $1,000 or imprisoned not more than five years, or both.

John Doe violated §1341 if he either obtained investor funds that he knew would not be used for Today's Bank or converted the money from Today's Bank to an unauthorized use. The prosecutor, a Federal official, has jurisdiction to prosecute John Doe for the fraud if he used the Federal mail system in furtherance of the scheme.

Person and Entity Involved

1. JOHN DOE
   - Date of Birth: January 1, 1954
   - Place of Birth: Turkey
   - Citizenship: United States/French
   - Race: Caucasian

Figure 7.1 *Swiss MLAT Exemplar*

Sex:	Male
Height:	5 feet 10 inches
Weight:	210 pounds
Eyes:	Green
Hair:	Black
Passport Number:	(United States) 012345678
	(French) Unknown
Social Security Number:	000-00-0000
Address:	1313 Integrity Way
	Des Moines, Iowa
	123 Rue de Day
	New Orleans, Louisiana
Present Location:	Unknown

2. CAPITAL TRUST, LTD.

Place of Incorporation:	Fort Madison, Iowa
Address:	1313 Integrity Way
	Fort Madison, Iowa

The prosecutor has no additional information regarding Capital Trust, Ltd., except that it began operations in Iowa in June 1988 when John Doe moved to Fort Madison from New Orleans, Louisiana.

Persons Affected

The only known persons potentially affected by a grant of assistance are the following victims whose names may be reflected in the records of the escrow account at Credit Suisse, Zurich, Switzerland, if such account exists:

1. (Name and address if available)
2. (Name and address if available)

Need for Assistance

The prosecutor suspects that John Doe opened an account at Credit Suisse in Zurich, Switzerland. The absence of an account will assist in proving that he defrauded the investors. However, even if the account was opened, the records of the account will show whether he invested the funds as claimed and whether the funds were then transferred to the Bank of Canada. If any substantial funds remain in such an account, the investors are prepared to initiate civil litigation in Switzerland to recover them.

Documents Needed

Please provide complete records of any and all accounts at Credit Suisse, Zurich, Switzerland, and at any other bank in Switzerland traceable to the subject matter of this request for assistance, relating to:

1. John Doe
2. Capital Trust, Ltd.
3. Today's Bank

Records should be for the period between September 1988 and the present, and should include, but not be limited to:

1. Original signature cards (regardless of the date the account was opened)
2. Documentation of account opening (regardless of the date account was opened)
3. Account ledger cards

Figure 7.1 Continued.

4. Periodic account statements
5. Records (copied front and back) of all items deposited, withdrawn, or transferred
6. Wire transfers
7. Correspondence to, from, or on behalf of the account holder
8. Memoranda related to the account

Testimony Needed

Please identify the official(s) of Credit Suisse, Zurich, Switzerland, or of any other bank in Switzerland connected with the subject matter of this request for assistance, who opened an account in the name, or for the benefit, of any of the above-named parties, or who has personal knowledge of any transactions reflected in the records of such account. Please interview such official(s) regarding the following points:

1. The identity of the person(s) who opened each account, and provide a proces-verbal pursuant to article 1 (4) (b), 10, and 12
2. The circumstances under which each account was opened
3. The nature and structure of each account (e.g., escrow account)
4. The disposition of the funds in each account
5. The identity of the person(s) ordering such disposition

If no account exists at Credit Suisse, Zurich, Switzerland, please identify the official(s) who can testify to that fact.

Procedures to Be Followed

Ask the Cantonal magistrate to do the following:

1. Interview the appropriate bank officials and provide a proces-verbal pursuant to article 1 (4) (b), 10, and 12
2. Require production of original or true copies of the documents from the bank pursuant to articles 1 (4) (c) and 18 (1)
3. Attach to the documents a Certificate of Authenticity of Business Records completed and signed by the person producing the documents pursuant to articles 1 (4) (e) and 18 (2)
4. Affix his or her seal (or stamp) upon the certificate pursuant to article 18 (3) if satisfied that, under the procedure followed, a false statement on the certificate would subject the person who completed and signed it to criminal penalty under Swiss law
5. Invite the bank official(s) giving testimony and producing the documents to appear at some future date at _____, at the expense of the United States government, to testify before the grand jury and/or at trial pursuant to article 23 (2). If any witness chooses not to appear in the United States, a formal deposition of the witness at some future date is requested pursuant to articles 10 and 12.

Please do the following with respect to official records:

1. Secure true and correct copies thereof
2. Have the official providing the documents attach an attestation that the documents are official records provided in her or her official capacity, or in the event that the official does not have a formal certificate, stamp, or seal of attestation, have him or her complete an Attestation of Authenticity of Official Records (enclosed) certifying the authenticity of the signature of the official who provided the official records

_____
(Name)
Director
Office of International Affairs

Figure 7.1 *Continued.*

CHAPTER 8

INTRODUCTION TO FINANCIAL INVESTIGATION

"I was planning, rather vaguely, but planning to do some serious money laundering."
Aldrich Ames, traitor

"There is a strong family resemblance about misdeeds, and if you have all the details of a thousand at your finger ends, it is odd if you can't unravel the thousand and first."
Arthur Conan Doyle, *A Study in Scarlet*

We have already seen that federal money laundering statutes require that we show both a Specified Unlawful Activity and a financial transaction or transportation. Most law enforcement officers are comfortable with the former. Proving that an unlawful activity took place and that the defendant did the crime is their job, after all. It is the financial side of things that may be somewhat intimidating. But this needn't be so.

A financial investigation is a blend of the more traditional investigative techniques and those used by auditors for 3000 years. The techniques are actually very similar. Knowing this may not make a financial case any more attractive to the law enforcement officer who has no background in accounting, but there is no getting around the fact that somebody is going to have to prove up that second, financial half of the money laundering equation.

The good news is that the financial investigative techniques used in proving a money laundering case can be employed effectively in many other investigations. As we will see shortly, they are not very hard to learn, and they open whole new vistas to those who can apply them. Even if you would not want to do financial investigation full time, it is something all criminal investigators should be at least familiar with.

In this text, I give a number of examples to demonstrate the value of the financial approach, not just in crimes such as drug trafficking, but also in cases where most people would not ordinarily think it would be much help. Crimes such as piracy, kidnapping, murder, political corruption, campaign finance violations, bootlegging, alien smuggling, and, in this chapter, espionage, are all used to illustrate the point. There are hundreds of other examples, but all involve the melding of financial and "traditional" investigative techniques.

What makes financial investigation any different from the other techniques used by law enforcement? The answer is, probably not as much as you might think. People have been auditing the financial transactions of others for at least 5000 years. The whole point of creating a paper trail in the first place is to enable someone to reconstruct what happened, to whom, and when. Audit techniques, also, are similar to those used by criminal investigators. Although much of an auditor's time is spent reviewing financial documents, quite a bit is devoted to interviewing people, asking questions about the records and about specific transactions.

Auditors follow set procedures to look for violations of Generally Accepted Accounting

Figure 8.1 Aldrich Ames.

Principles, which form a sort of statute book for accountants. The end result of an audit is a report — again, not so different from what the criminal investigator is used to.

But where the auditor is recommending changes for management or detecting problems that might cost the company money, the criminal investigator is concerned with narrower issues of guilt and proof beyond a reasonable doubt. There are enough similarities in the work that auditing translates fairly well to a financial investigation, and what we think of as "traditional" investigative techniques only make that case stronger.

Let's examine a criminal investigation that relied heavily on financial evidence. Keep in mind as you read the story of Aldrich Ames, traitor and Russian spy (see Figure 8.1), that Ames did both of the following:

1. He initially called attention to himself by his unexplained wealth.
2. He left a wide paper trail for the investigators to follow.

CASE STUDY: TREASON

You can't read about Aldrich Ames and not get really angry. It is hard to know who to be madder at — Ames, whose cold-blooded treachery sent at least 10 men to their deaths, or the incompetent superiors whose negligence allowed the spy to continue his espionage career for over eight years.

It wasn't as if Ames was a really good spy. Everybody agreed that he was spectacularly bad, in fact. He was lazy, drunk, careless, and indiscreet. You would think these character traits would have caused his undoing long before they did, but these little foibles were evidently not sufficiently outstanding at the Central Intelligence Agency, where Ames was employed, to arouse any suspicion.

Over an eight-year period, from 1985 to 1993, Ames received approximately $2.7 million in cash from the intelligence service of the Soviet Union, the notorious KGB. The KGB evidently feels it got its money's worth: Ames provided information that led to the unmasking of at least 12 Soviet citizens who were spying for the United States. Most of these men were executed as a result.

It was this money that should have been Ames' downfall. He was incredibly obvious in his spending of the cash he received from the KGB. In disposing of the money, Ames did everything to call attention to himself except wear a signboard reading, "Hi! I'm Rick, KGB Mole."

Ames began spying for the Russians in 1985 during a frustrating and disappointing career with the CIA. Although Ames held positions with tremendous access to classified material — at one point he was the head of counterintelligence operations against the KGB — he saw his career approaching a dead end. Ames had recently married a Colombian national, Rosario Casas Dupuy, who had expensive tastes but not much money. Ames, a GS-14 civil servant, had little enough himself, and he wanted more.

Ames contacted the Russians and offered secrets they could obtain nowhere else. The KGB knew a good thing when they saw it and gladly met Ames' demands for money. The pleased Russians paid their new spy in cash, ultimately forking over almost $3 million. (See Figure 8.2.) Although Ames wanted the money up front, the KGB refused, so he was forced to accept frequent large cash payments, which he laundered himself. As the quote at the chapter

```
Dear Friend,
this is Your balance sheet as on the May 1, 1989.

* All in all You have been apprpriated ---- 2,705,000 $
* From the time of oppening of Your
  account in our Bank (December 20,
  1986) Your profit is ------------------- 385,077$ 28c
(including 14,468$ 94c as profit on bonds, which we
bougnt for You on the sum of 250,000$)
* Since December 1986 Your salary is ------ 300,000$
* All in all we have delivered to You ----- 1,881,811$ 51c
* On the above date You have on Your
  account (including 250,000$ in bonds) --- 1,535,077$ 28c

P.S. We believe that these pictures would give You some
idea about the beautiful piece of land on the river bank,
which from now belongs to You forever. We decided not to take
pictures of housing in this area with the understanding that
You have much better idea of how Your country house (dacha)
should look like.

Good luck.
```

Figure 8.2 Ames' "W-2 form" from his Russian masters. FBI agents who searched Ames' house found this account of the money paid by the Russians to Ames. The record says that as of May 1, 1989, "All in all we have delivered to you... 1,881,811$ 51c." This was the type of evidence that sent Ames to prison for life.

head shows, he was aware of the need to do this, and to do it discreetly. Ultimately, however, he failed at this, just as he had at so many other things in his life.

Ames knew he had to come up with some explanation for the tens of thousands of dollars he was earning and spending, and he actually developed several cover stories, mostly revolving around his wife's "wealthy family" in Colombia. In fact, some of Ames' associates in the CIA were aware that Rosario's family was not wealthy, but nobody seemed too interested. Ames used this story to explain his purchase of an upscale home in Arlington, Virginia, for $540,000 in cash. He made similar allusions to explain the 1992 Jaguar he drove to work every day — again, paid for with $50,000 in cash.

Everything Ames did with his dirty money practically screamed for attention. During an overseas posting to Rome, he and his wife ran up phone bills of $5,000 per month, mostly for Rosario's calls to her family in Colombia. Together, the Ameses had credit card purchases as high as $30,000 per month, and they employed a maid at their Arlington home.

Ames made $1.5 million in cash deposits to his bank account, some of which were reported on Currency Transaction Reports (CTRs) to IRS. Other deposits were structured to avoid the reporting requirements. He had two accounts at Credit Suisse in Zurich, into which he deposited $25,000 per month and as much as $950,000 during his tour in Rome. Wire transfers from this account replenished his account in Virginia.

In interviews after his 1993 arrest, Ames acknowledged that he had not handled the money very well. He told interviewers that neither the Russians nor anyone following in his footsteps would be likely to make that mistake again, but the fact is that Ames was not the first spy to have drawn attention to himself through careless spending, and he probably won't be the last.

It is a rather chilling thought, but it is possible that if Ames had implemented a money laundering plan, he might have continued his double career until retirement. As it was, he faced the placement problem of converting large amounts of U.S. currency. Although he made several cash deposits over $10,000, causing CTRs to be generated, many of his transactions were conducted in amounts under the reporting threshold. On August 1, 1989, Ames exchanged 28 million Italian lire to $22,107, which he deposited into his bank account in Virginia. He had previously deposited $15,660 and $13,500 into this account on February 18, 1986, and October 18, 1985, respectively, shortly after he started his career in treason.

FBI agents investigating Ames learned that he had received $150,000 in cash at a meeting with his KGB handlers in October 1992, and he subsequently deposited $86,700 into his bank account in a series of transactions under $10,000. This was apparently Ames' (not very impressive) solution to the problem of placement.

As for layering, Ames did open two bank accounts at Credit Suisse, a Swiss bank in Zurich. During the time he was stationed in Rome, Ames deposited $950,000 in cash, telling his banker that the funds were from the liquidation of property his wife's family owned in Colombia. One of the accounts was held by Ames as a trustee for his mother-in-law, Cecilia Dupuy de Casas.

There was no layering at all between the KGB's money and Ames' purchase of a house at 2512 N. Randolph Street in Arlington, Virginia. Ames simply paid $540,000 for the place, and then he spent another $99,000 on renovations. He created some documents purporting to show that his mother-in-law had given Ames and his wife the money for the house, and at another time he said that his wife's uncle in Colombia had bought the house as a birthday present for the Ameses' son, Paul.

Integration of the laundered funds was solely based on the "wealthy family" cover story, which did not hold up to even casual scrutiny by the FBI (although the CIA bought it for years). Ames said he had originally planned to create a dummy corporation in Colombia, placed in his mother-in-law's name, which could then have been used as an explanation for where *she* had gotten the money she was supposedly giving him. This would have been a much better plan from both the layering and integration perspectives, but Ames was either too lazy or too careless to carry it out.

Ultimately Ames was sentenced to life in prison for espionage, conspiracy, and tax evasion. His wife received 63 months for conspiracy and tax evasion. This is not a happy ending to a case that should have been concluded much earlier — would have been if only the financial signs were read properly.

In its investigation of Ames, the FBI recognized the importance of the financial evidence. Where the CIA had assigned an untrained investigator to do the background check on Ames' alibi for the money, the FBI assigned an accountant to the team that did the investigation. The accountant had lots to do. Ames had opened numerous bank accounts in Virginia and in Switzerland, and he made deposits shortly after each meeting with his Russian handlers, leaving a paper trail a mile wide.

The FBI's case is a perfect example of the integrated approach to these financial cases. The FBI agents had to prove the underlying activity; they needed to show that the money was coming from a foreign power, namely Russia. They also wanted to prove that this activity was the reason for Ames' profligate spending and substantial net worth.

In proving the former, the agents relied on traditional investigative techniques, such as the following:

- Physical surveillance of Ames and his wife
- Electronic surveillance, including wiretaps of Ames' home telephone
- Recovery of physical evidence by means of a search warrant
- Trash cover
- Interviews of witnesses and post-arrest interrogation of Ames and his wife

All of these techniques paid off, providing the government with hard evidence of Ames' treachery.

The financial case was equally productive. Ames' own records were seized and examined, but the agents already had most of the information

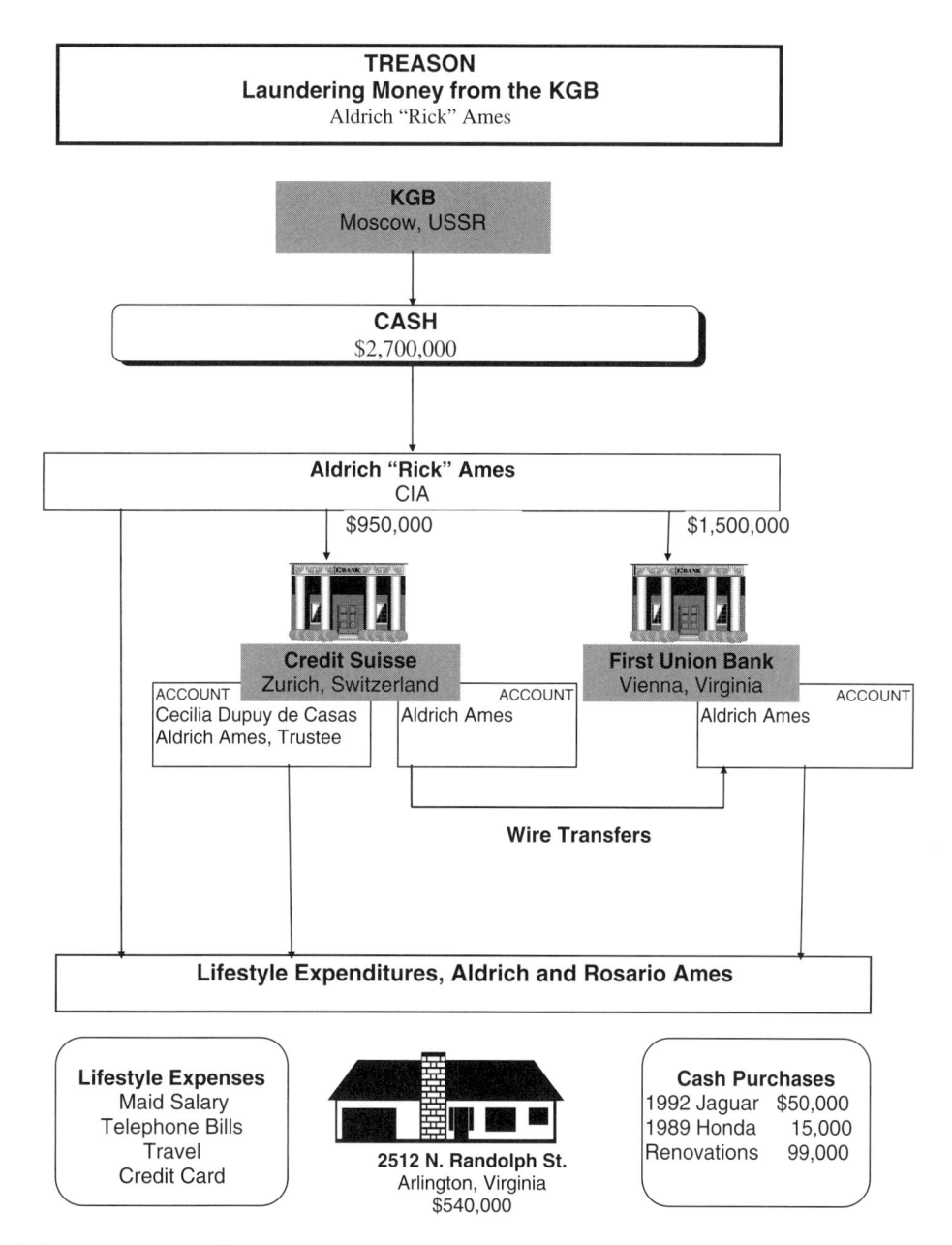

TREASON
Laundering Money from the KGB
Aldrich "Rick" Ames

KGB — Moscow, USSR

CASH — $2,700,000

Aldrich "Rick" Ames — CIA

$950,000 → **Credit Suisse**, Zurich, Switzerland
- ACCOUNT: Cecilia Dupuy de Casas, Aldrich Ames, Trustee
- ACCOUNT: Aldrich Ames

$1,500,000 → **First Union Bank**, Vienna, Virginia
- ACCOUNT: Aldrich Ames

Wire Transfers

Lifestyle Expenditures, Aldrich and Rosario Ames

Lifestyle Expenses:
- Maid Salary
- Telephone Bills
- Travel
- Credit Card

2512 N. Randolph St., Arlington, Virginia — $540,000

Cash Purchases:
- 1992 Jaguar $50,000
- 1989 Honda   15,000
- Renovations   99,000

Figure 8.3 Schematic of Aldrich Ames' money laundering scheme.

from the banks, credit card companies, and businesses where Ames conducted transactions. There were CTRs on file but no CMIRs, which should have caused some questions to be raised, given Ames' story about getting the money from his in-laws in Colombia. See Figure 8.3 for a schematic of Aldrich Ames' money laundering scheme.

THE IMPORTANCE OF CONTEXT

It was the marriage of the financial and the traditional approaches that made the case against Ames so strong. Why? Because each provided context for the other. The money all made perfect sense if you knew that Ames was selling secrets to the Russians. The spying made perfect sense if you knew about the money — Ames' motive was certainly clear enough.

In this type of case, the financial approach is used to resolve several questions:

1. Where did he or she get the money?
2. How much money did he or she get?

3. Where is the money going?
4. How is the money moving?
5. Is he or she keeping the money, or is he or she just a conduit to someone else?

These are the questions a financial approach is intended to answer, and the answers provide context for the investigation of the underlying criminal activity. In getting the answers, the financial investigator relies on documents and records, and the analysis of these records in context with the rest of the case.

For example, let's say a suspected drug trafficker makes a $20,000 cash deposit into a bank account. Does this tell us anything or answer any of the above questions? Not really, although it does provide some information. How can the context of this transaction be established? The answer is, through further investigation, using both the financial and traditional approaches. The investigator will ask:

- What was the subject doing right before the transaction? (surveillance, informants, undercover, other documents)
- Was other financial activity involved, such as access to a safe deposit box or the sale of a vehicle? (analysis of financial records)
- Is the transaction part of a pattern that would indicate an ongoing scheme? (both approaches)

With additional information, we are able to put the $20,000 deposit into its proper context. Standing alone, neither approach is as strong, but when the evidence from both is combined, we might have something much more conclusive, such as:

"Three days after returning from a trip to Miami, the subject made a cash deposit of $20,000 into bank account A. In the three days prior to the transaction, the pen register on the subject's phone disclosed numerous calls to individuals believed to be distributors of the subject's cocaine. Informants ..." You get the picture.

We can also foreclose claims and defenses that might come up at a later time ("I won the money in Las Vegas" or, "My uncle died and left me a lot of money"). Analysis of the financial records will tell us whether the transaction is the type of isolated incident consistent with some innocent explanation such as "I sold my car" or whether there is some ongoing pattern or scheme.

A "HOW TO" GUIDE TO FINANCIAL INVESTIGATION

If we accept that a financial investigation isn't all that different from the regular type, and that it's a good thing to do in connection with financial crimes, how can we use the technique in our cases? One way is to assign an accountant, auditor, or trained financial investigator to the case, as the FBI did with Ames. If you don't have this luxury, not to worry, the concept isn't that difficult. If things get complicated, you may want to have an expert check your work.

A financial case is about "accounting." Not the really boring stuff you learned (or heard about) in college Accounting 101, but "accounting" in the sense that your investigation is trying to *account* for different events or facts. Where did the criminal get the money? How much money did he or she get? What did he or she do with the money? How do we account for that $20,000 deposit, for example, in the overall context of the case?

In performing this type of accounting, some of the same rules and the same terms from conventional accounting are used, such as:

- *Asset:* money or anything that can be turned into money
- *Liability:* an obligation or claim against an asset (Somebody's house is an asset. The mortgage owed to the bank is a liability.)
- *Net worth:* what you've got after you subtract the liabilities from the assets; also known as equity or capital
- *Income:* money received for goods or services

- *Expenses:* costs of living or doing business

Just about everything in accounting starts with these five simple terms. Take Ames, for example. Investigators knew that his *income* was that of a GS-14 civil servant, around $69,000 per year. His wife didn't work, and he reported no other income. Investigators also knew Ames' *expenses*, because he charged a lot of purchases and paid those bills in cash.

From these two figures, an *income statement*, one of the two basic accounting reports, could be prepared:

Income Statement — Aldrich Ames, Jan–Dec 1992

Income	$69,000
– Expenses	– 110,000
Net Income (Loss)	$(41,000)

This means Ames spent $41,000 more in one year than he could account for by his government salary. There are only two possible explanations for this situation. Either he has another source of income he's not disclosing, or something's going on with the assets and liabilities. For instance, he could have sold an asset sometime during the year that brought him the extra $41,000.

Assets and liabilities form the basis for a *balance sheet*, the second basic accounting report. Where the income statement tracks activity over a period of time (a year, in the example above), the balance sheet is a snapshot of someone's net worth at a given moment in time.

The balance sheet equation is:

Assets
– Liabilities
Net Worth

In Ames' case, his *assets* were impressive. He owned a $540,000 home with no mortgage, a $50,000 Jaguar, a Honda, three properties in Colombia, expensive furnishings, and several bank accounts with huge balances. On the liability side, Ames had substantial outstanding balances with credit card companies and department stores. Because he paid cash for many of his purchases, Ames owed relatively little. His balance sheet might have looked like this:

Balance Sheet — Aldrich Ames, 12-31-92

Assets	$2,300,000
– Liabilities	–50,000
Net Worth	$2,250,000

Like the income statement, the balance sheet also has to be taken in context. It is almost invariably combined with some sort of income statement. Look at the application next time one of those preapproved credit card mailings comes to your house. The form asks you to list all of your major assets and what you owe to others (liabilities). It also asks for your monthly income and sometimes for expenses. This is because a person's financial picture isn't complete without information about all four terms.

The income statement showed Ames was spending far more than he was making as a CIA employee. The balance sheet showed that he was worth a lot more than your average GS-14. When balance sheets for several years are combined, it is possible to establish a much clearer picture of the subject's finances. You will also have several of the answers to the questions we asked earlier:

1. *Where did he get the money?* In Ames' case, our financial analysis can't say, but it can say that he (a) didn't get it from his government salary, (b) didn't get it from any relatives living abroad, and (c) got it all in cash. This combination of circumstances creates a powerful inference, one that the courts have said can be used in financial cases. Courts have held in numerous cases that evidence of unexplained wealth, especially large amounts of cash, can be evidence of criminal activity.

2. *How much money did he get?* Again, we can't be absolutely certain, but from

Ames' own records, including that "W-2" form from the Russians, and his own statements, the best evidence indicates at least $2.7 million. As we'll see later on, this figure could also be arrived at indirectly.

3. *Where is the money going?* Every asset acquired by Ames was tracked down, and most were seized and forfeited.

4. *How is the money moving?* Ames made numerous deposits into various bank accounts, and investigators looking at the pattern of these transactions noted that many came within days of his return from an overseas trip or a reported contact with a Russian. Once in the bank, the flow of the funds to acquire other assets was easily tracked.

5. *Is he keeping the money, or is he a conduit for someone else?* There wasn't much doubt as to who was keeping the money in Ames' case. In money laundering investigations, this question may be somewhat more difficult to resolve.

As you can see, we have been able to answer all of the questions using accounting/financial investigative techniques.

LOOKING AHEAD

The next chapters cover the types of accounting and financial investigative techniques you'll need to resolve financial crimes such as money laundering. Because these techniques rely on analysis of books and records, these are explained in some detail, as are the banking operations that generate so much of the paper used in one of these cases.

If you have the subject's records, re-creating his or her income or expenditures and tracing his or her assets is a fairly simple proposition. If not, you'll need to re-create that income through indirect methods. This isn't as hard as it sounds, and the courts have given their blessing to the use of these methods in criminal cases. Finally, the process of tracing the various assets that are acquired in the course of financial crimes is discussed. With the increasing emphasis on forfeiture, investigators and prosecutors have become much more conscious of assets and how they are acquired.

All of these topics combine to give you a more complete picture of the financial investigative technique, a different way to get answers to some old questions.

CHAPTER 9

INTRODUCTION TO BOOKS AND RECORDS

"'What is the use of a book,' thought Alice, 'without pictures or conversation?'"
Lewis Carroll, *Alice's Adventures in Wonderland*

"Perfection has one grave defect; it is apt to be dull."
W. Somerset Maugham, *The Summing Up*

There is only one place you will find any pictures or conversation in the kinds of books accountants keep, this being the Annual Report to Shareholders of a corporation. Otherwise, and I'll be right up front about this, accounting books and records *are* pretty dull. Perhaps this is because accountants try awfully hard for perfection, coming lots closer than most professions, such as doctors or lawyers.

In this chapter, we're going to cover some basic accounting principles and examine some of those perfect books and records that accountants keep. Despite the fact that the material may be dull, it's good to have an idea of how these things work. Later on, when you're looking at the balance sheet of a corporation and wondering whether it's a shell or some kind of a scam, you may be able to use some of this knowledge.

Also, if you're into investing, this chapter covers the basics of what you need to know to evaluate a company to make that investment decision. In fact, that's exactly what those fancy annual reports are really all about. Why should you, the stockholder, buy or keep our stock? Here, check out our slick, full-color, multipage report. Lots of pictures and even some conversation: the Message to Our Shareholders.

Actually, the reports prepared by accountants, all of which follow a very rigid set of clearly defined rules, are used for a variety of purposes. Banks use them in making loan decisions; businesses use them in making all sorts of decisions — whether to buy or sell, whether to extend or refuse credit, whether to acquire or divest. Reports such as the balance sheet and income statement are used to track progress and to compare performance against other periods, divisions, or businesses. The accountants' work is like a Swiss Army knife for business — it has a thousand uses.

Because the accuracy of their reports is so important, the accountants' club, in this case the

"You don't seem to have the usual qualifications we're looking for in an accountant."

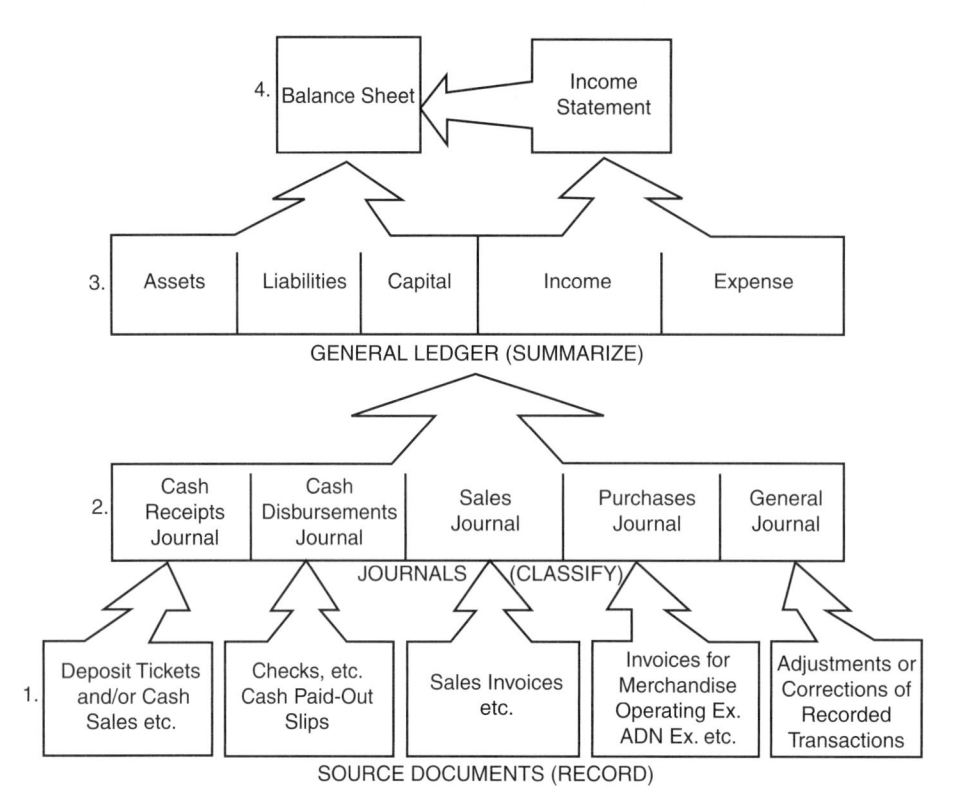

Figure 9.1 The process of creating an audit trail.

American Institute of Certified Public Accountants (AICPA), has set forth a long list of rules and regulations to be followed by all their members. These rules, known as the Generally Accepted Accounting Principles (GAAP), dictate how records are to be kept and results reported. Since everybody's supposed to follow the same rules, you can look at the balance sheet of a car parts business in Florida and one from a timber business in Idaho, and you can be fairly sure that they will allow you to make a reasonable comparison.

Everything leading up to the bottom line on that balance sheet is covered by those GAAP rules. All of the numbers on that sheet are traced backward to the original transactions that created them, and always (at least in theory) in the same consistently reliable way. Again (in theory), an accountant should be able to walk into a corporation with the annual report and work backward from there, verifying every number along the way. They really do this, by the way; it's called an *audit*.

An audit is made possible by something called an *audit trail*, and the GAAP rules dictate exactly how this path is to be laid. The trail is created with documents created in a set pattern and sequence, in which financial transactions are recorded, classified, summarized, and reported. Figure 9.1 illustrates this process.

Instead of starting at the bottom of the pyramid, we're going to begin with the top, looking at the financial reports of a corporation, and work our way down from there. For our in-depth review of how everything flows to the preparation of these two reports, we're going to use an example from real life — the books and records of Chicago gangster Al Capone. Al's business, Alphonse Capone Second Hand Furniture, Inc., was selected to make things more interesting. Trying to put Al's books together while retaining as much historical accuracy as possible was an enjoyable exercise. See Figure 9.2 for some notes about this process and the presentation of the information.

One or two things to keep in mind in reviewing the annual report of any publicly held corporation: First, the company is required by law to prepare these reports, to keep the owners (i.e.,

INTRODUCTION TO BOOKS AND RECORDS

> **Alphonse Capone Second Hand Furniture, Inc.**
>
> A couple of notes about our presentation of the books and the annual report of Alphonse Capone Second Hand Furniture, Inc.
>
> - All of the figures on the Annual Report are, of course, speculative, but most have been taken from estimates made at the time or actual accounting records obtained from the Capone organization over the years between 1925 and 1932. The figures in some of the journals and ledgers are taken directly from those same books kept by Capone's bookkeepers.
> - All of the names used are those of real people who occupied the positions described. They're all dead now, so I don't think they'll be complaining.
> - All of the statements attributed to Mr. Capone, including his entire Message to Shareholders, were actually made by him and published somewhere. Many of the quotes are taken from press conferences given by Al, in which he said some pretty astonishing things, given his occupation.
> - The only business cover Al Capone ever used officially was that of a second hand furniture dealer. He had business cards printed up to prove it.
> - Al Capone was making some SERIOUS money. In a time when you could get a full meal for a quarter and see a movie for a nickel, his organization was grossing over $100 million a year. That would be something like $10 *billion* today. It wasn't all profit, but it is still sobering to think of the kind of corruption and assorted evil that kind of money could buy.

Figure 9.2 *Notes on the books and the annual report of Alphonse Capone Second Hand Furniture, Inc.*

shareholders) and the government (i.e., Securities and Exchange Commission) informed about what's going on with the company. After the recent scandals involving Enron and other big corporations, the government is paying very close attention to how these reports are prepared. The reports are required to be accurate, and they are invariably reviewed by an independent CPA firm, which will include a statement as to its opinion about the books.

Second, annual reports *must* be compared in order to be useful. You compare them against another year for the same company and against another company for the same year; within the report, you can compare divisions or segments of the corporation to see how they are doing relative to each other. This comparative process gives you the real story of the company's operations.

Third, although the pictures and the text may be unique, the financial reports, especially the balance sheet and the income statement, will always be structured in the same "generally accepted" way. To prepare the two statements, the company's accountants first have to have some figures. As our chart shows, these figures come a long way to reach the bottom line of the balance sheet or the income statement. Along that way, the figures pass through a number of books, known as *journals* or *ledgers*, and they are documented with other bits of paper as well. Because licensed CPAs all follow GAAP, Al Capone's accountants, if they had developed an annual report for Al Capone Second Hand Furniture, would have done those parts of their report exactly the same way as accountants at Ford or IBM.

Although Al Capone never produced the type of annual report we will examine in this chapter, he and his organization maintained a wide variety of books and records, extensively documenting the financial affairs of the organization. Before we look at how those books could have been used to make an annual report, let's review a little (real) history on Mr. Capone.

THE CAPONE ORGANIZATION

Alphonse Capone (see Figure 9.3) moved to Chicago from Brooklyn in 1920, quickly rising to the top of the underworld in America's second largest city. His ascent coincided with Prohibition, and most of the money made by the Capone organization came from the sale of bootleg alcohol. He also expanded his operations, getting into prostitution, gambling, and racketeering, building a base for organized crime in Chicago that persists to this day.

Capone's operations were centered on the South Side of Chicago and in several of the small towns that were part of the city's suburbs. Cicero

Figure 9.3 Al Capone (Source: National Archives).

was Capone's headquarters for years, but he and other gangsters fought constantly for control over each other's territories. Madison Street was the dividing line between Capone's Southside gang and the Northsiders of Dion O'Banion and Bugs Moran, bitter Capone rivals. Capone's boys killed O'Banion and almost got Moran on St. Valentine's Day, 1929.

What set Capone apart from other gangsters before him was his wholesale corruption of the political and government processes in Cook County. It was estimated that bribes and kickbacks to politicians and law enforcement officials exceeded $30 million per year in Capone's heyday — a full third or more of his gross revenues.

The Capone organization, like many groups operating illegal enterprises, kept very good records, tracking receipts and expenditures. Why? Because none of Capone's underlings wanted to lose an argument over money with Al, who had been known to terminate such discussions with a baseball bat.

Many of these records, including the ledgers that would form a key part of the tax case against Capone, were seized in police and even vigilante raids against Capone-owned brothels, gambling joints, and liquor manufacturing plants. (For the sake of our study, we'll pretend that these records were kept in double entry form, which the originals weren't.)

In September 1925, raiders from assorted law enforcement agencies searched a number of Capone establishments, including "The Barracks," a dive in the Chicago suburb of Burnham.

Among the items taken were ledger books that described the operations on the premises, including income and expenses. For the week of September 6, 1925, the ledger read:

Slot machines	$ 906.00
Piano	55.25
Rooms (prostitution)	5,891.00
Bar	2,677.10
Tables (gambling)	1,800.00
Gross revenues	$11,329.35
Paid out 10% (protection)	1,133.00
	$10,196.35
Expenses	8,450.00
Net	$1,746.35

(Incidentally, this is an income statement — we'll read more about these reports shortly.) Capone had more than 25 of these "resorts" at the time, The Barracks being one of the smaller ones, and the weekly net to Capone was a tidy $75,000, or $4 million per year.

Looking back at the chart of the accounting cycle, notice that the top segment of the chart has the balance sheet and the income statement at the top. Now look at Al Capone's annual report, in Figure 9.4. Sure enough, Al's business uses two financial statements in its annual report — the balance sheet and the income statement. As the chart shows, five different segments or types of accounts make up these two statements. Assets, liabilities, and capital, also known collectively as equity or net worth, make up the balance sheet. Income and expenses make up the income statement. The two statements are different but related, and both are necessary to get a good picture of the business.

Basically, the balance sheet tells you what a business or individual *has*, and an income statement tells you what the business or individual is *doing* (and how well or badly). You will find variations of these statements all over the place. For example, as mentioned earlier, if you apply for a personal loan, you'll be asked to list your assets and liabilities (balance sheet items), and the lender will also want to know about your income and expenses (income statement items). These reports are not limited just to corporations

**ALPHONSE CAPONE
SECOND HAND
FURNITURE,
Inc.**

CHICAGO, ILLINOIS

ANNUAL REPORT
1930

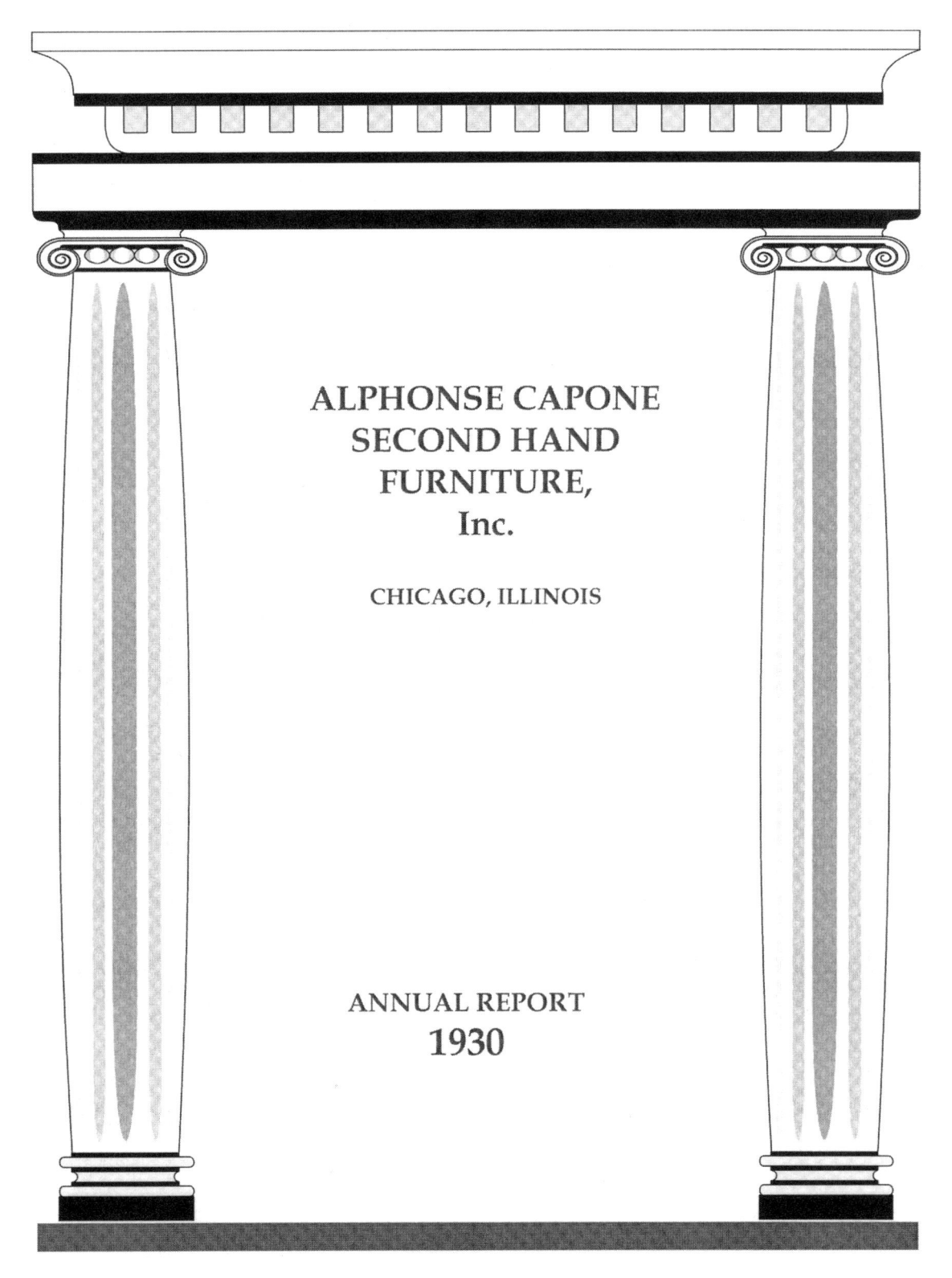

Figure 9.4 Annual Report of Alphonse Capone Second Hand Furniture, Inc. (The photos of Al Capone, Jack McGurn, Jake "Greasy Thumb" Guzik, Sam "Golf Bag" Hunt, Murray Humphreys, Tony Lombardo, Johnny Torrio, and Rocco Fischetti are courtesy of United Press International. The photo titled "Corporate Citizenship" is courtesy of National Archives. The photos of Ralph Capone, Frank "The Enforcer" Nitti, and the photo titled "Our chairman" are courtesy of the Chicago Historical Society.)

CONTENTS

2	Contents
3	Financial Highlights
4	Letter to Shareholders
5	Review of Operations
6	Beverage Division
7	Gaming Division
8	Entertainment Division
9	Insurance and Industrial Relations
10	Board of Directors
12	Mergers and Acquisition
13 - 16	Financial Report

Alphonse Capone Second Hand Furniture, Inc.
affectionately known to its customers and employees as "The Outfit," is a diversified corporation providing a wide variety of goods and services (some of them legal) throughout the Greater Chicago area. Operating from its headquarters in the ~~Metropole~~ Lexington Hotel in Chicago, the majority of the outfit's operations are centered in Chicago, Cicero, and Miami, Florida. Principal business segments are:
- **Beverage Manufacture and Distribution**
- **Gaming**
- **Entertainment Services**
- **Insurance and Industrial Relations**

Alphonse Capone Second Hand Furniture was founded in 1920 and incorporated in 1924. Common stock used to be traded on the New York Stock Exchange under the symbol BIGAL, until he found out holders of common stock got to vote on things. Now all the outstanding stock is Preferred, and he prefers to hold most of it himself.

Corporate offices are located at
Lexington Hotel
Michigan Avenue at 22nd Street
Chicago, Illinois
Phone: None of your business. If he wants to talk to you, he'll call you.

Figure 9.4 Continued.

Alphonse Capone Second Hand Furniture, Inc.
1930 Annual Report

Financial Highlights

	1930	1929
Revenue	$ 105,487,000	$ 97,350,000
Net Income	$ 491,000	$ 927,000
Per Share	$ 4.91	$ 9.27
Cash Dividends	$ 32,500,000	$ 26,000,000
Per Share	$ 3,250	$ 2,600
Average Shares Outstanding	100,000	100,000
Total Assets	$ 165,985,000	$ 163,414,000
Shareholder's Equity	$ 67,013,000	$ 64,125,000
Per Share	$ 67.13	$ 64.12
Return on Beginning Shareholder's Equity	4.4%	2.8%
Current Ratio	82 to 1	75 to 1
Employees	25,200	29,350

1930 figures reflect the adoption of Statement of Financial Accounting Standards No. 106, "Employers' Accounting for Postretirement Benefits Other Than Pensions" – such benefits consisting mostly of floral arrangements and a nice sympathy card from Al.

1930 figures reflect the results of mergers and acquisitions of both the O'Banion and the Genna corporations, which were begun in other accounting periods.

Figure 9.4 *Continued.*

To Our Shareholders

Alphonse Capone
Chairman of the Board and
Chief Executive Officer

Fellow Shareholders

These are hard times in Chicago, and I'm just like the next guy, trying to get by. Sure, I'm a bootlegger, some of our best judges use my stuff. They call Al Capone a bootlegger. Yes, it's bootleg while it's on the trucks, but when your host at the club, in the locker room, or on the Gold Coast hand it to you on a silver tray, it's hospitality. I supply a legitimate demand. Some call it bootlegging. Some call it racketeering. I call it a business. They say I violate the Prohibition law. Who doesn't? You can't cure a thirst by law.

Yes, I think Prohibition will be done away with, and I'm all for that time to come. Prohibition has made nothing but trouble – trouble for all of us. Worst thing ever hit this country.

People respect nothing nowadays. Once we put virtue, honor, truth, and the law on a pedestal. Our children were brought up to respect things. But now, look what a mess we've made of our lives. Reform did not end prostitution. Now the girls are no longer inspected once a week by the Health Department doctors. Now they are not concentrated down on the Levee. Instead, they are living in the swank apartment houses, associating with the wives and daughters of the best people in town. They simply went underground.

I got nothing against the honest cop on the beat, the kind you can't buy. You just have them transferred someplace where they can't do you any harm. But don't even talk to me about the honor of police captains or judges. If they couldn't be bought, they wouldn't have the jobs.

There's a lot of people in Chicago that have got me pegged for one of these bloodthirsty monsters you read about in the storybooks – the kind that tortures his victims, cuts of their ears, puts out their eyes with a red-hot poker, and grins while he's doing it.

I'm no angel. I'm not posing as a model for youth. I've had to do a lot of things I didn't like to do. But I'm not as black as I've been painted. I'm human. I've got a heart in me. I'll go as deep in my pocket as any man to help any guy that needs help. Many a poor family in Chicago thinks I'm Santa Claus.

Our soup kitchens feed three thousand people a day. I don't take credit to myself for being charitable. Just to show I'm not the worst person in the world.

I'm a businessman.

Figure 9.4 *Continued.*

GENERAL OPERATIONS

Revenues in all divisions topped $100 million for the first time since 1928. The beverage and gambling sectors continued to be strong performers, with earnings high in both sectors.

Total Revenues
(by Division)
Total revenues from all sources were over $105 mill, serious money in anybody's book!

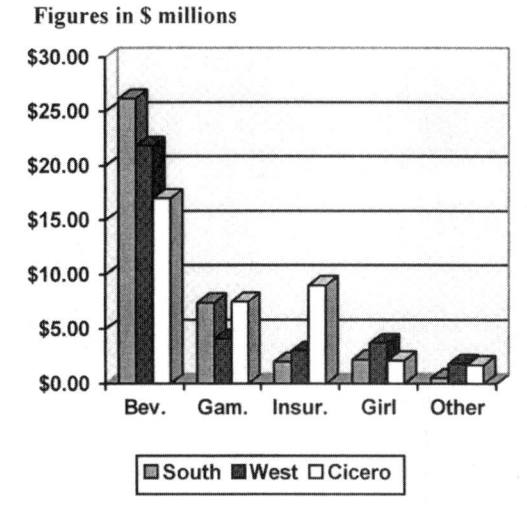

Figures in $ millions

CORPORATE CITIZENSHIP
Soup kitchens sponsored by the corporation feed 3,000 to 5,000 hungry people in Chicago every day,

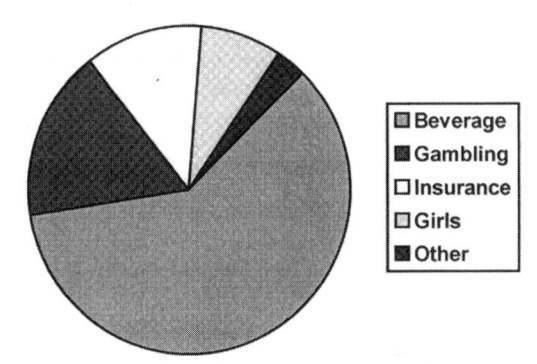

SOURCES OF REVENUE
(By Division)

Additional emphasis was put on the Insurance Division during the year, in anticipation of changes in government rules with respect to beverage distribution.

APPLICATION OF FUNDS

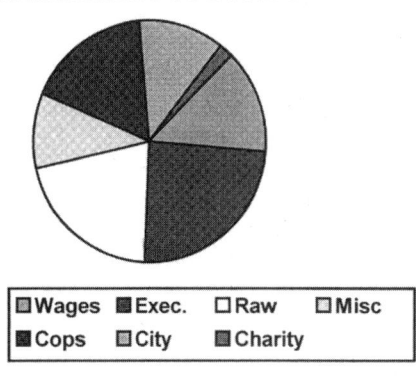

Funds were applied during the year for a variety of purposes. The largest expenditures were for government services. Over $30 million was expended for this purpose, but we got our money's worth. Executive compensation was down a little from last year, but everybody's gotta tighten their belt a little – there's a depression on.

Expense Category	%	$ Amount
Wages	21	$14.5 m
Exec. Comp.	24	26 m
Raw materials	21	22 m
Miscellaneous	10	10.5 m
Payoffs-cops*	12	17.7 m
Payoffs-city hall	10	12.3 m
Charity	2	.4 m

* Includes Prohibition agents

Figure 9.4 Continued.

BEVERAGE DIVISION

1930 proved to be another outstanding year for our brewing and distilling operations throughout the Chicago area. Sales rose for an eighth straight year, as did per capita consumption. We added to our loyal customer base by judicious mergers and acquisitions on the North Side and in the suburbs. Many new distributors joined this thing of ours after being suddenly abandoned by Dion O"Banion's organization. Rest in peace, Deanie.

The details of our bottling operations are not composed only of dry statistics, but of the personal stories of our thousands of employees and independent contractors, whose tireless efforts make the outfit a "people oriented" business. As our Chairman put it, "I'm for the little guy, the working man. If he needs a product, I provide it. What's wrong with that?"
What indeed?

Market Share
As most everyone knows, the boss is very strong on strengthening our position in the marketplace. In boardroom discussion, he can frequently be heard to inquire, "Do we own it all, yet?" The answer is still, "almost", thanks to our acquisition of the O'Banion brewing and hijacking operations, and the Gennas' alky cooking enterprises. We were looking for a friendly little merger, but they turned it into a hostile takeover, which cost the outfit time and money. It cost them a lot more, as those seven guys who bought it on St. Valentine's Day can attest!

Anyhow, our share of the beer market in Chicago, relative to that of our major competitors, is shown in the chart below. When the whole chart is blue, the boss figures we'll be positioned about right.

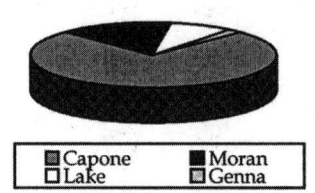

☐ Capone ■ Moran
☐ Lake   ☐ Genna

As for Distilled Spirits, we've got the market just about cornered on quality stuff smuggled from Canada, and 75% of the rotgut is ours, too. Our training program for associate distillers has eliminated a lot of the quality control problems, which, in years past, led to unpleasantness like poisonings and blinding. The boss don't tolerate that sort of thing, and lets people know it.

"Bathtub" Mike Flynn, an associate distiller on the South Side talks about the human resources policies of the organization. *"They take good care of me. My materials are always delivered on time, and the outfit comes to pick up a batch as soon as you call. A couple of times, I was late with my franchise payment, and the boys didn't even kill me, only ran my wife's hand through the laundry wringer. That kind of personalized service you don't get with just any company. And hey, in these tough times, I'm lucky to be working at all!"*

BREWING & BEER SALES

Brewery output increased, despite a number of unexpected plant closings. Excessive government regulatory action, particularly by that dirty S.O.B. Ness, resulted in slowdowns in deliveries, and the movement of equipment and supplies to more business friendly locations.

	1930	1929
Total # Breweries	14	8
South Side	7	4
Central	3	1
Cicero	3	3
Berwyn	1	0
Daily output (1,000 gallons)	45	42
Daily sales volume (x 1,000)	105	101

DISTILLED SPIRITS

Distilling operations declined slightly, due in part to the same government harassment that affected beer production. Rather than risk large losses associated with centralized production, an executive decision was made to diversity into smaller producers.

In a bit of quality related good news for Chicago consumers and the outfit, only 297 people died or were blinded by denatured or wood alcohol during the year, down from 320 the year before. That's 23 more people still alive and drinking!

	1930	1929
Total # Major distillers	57	75
Daily output (x1,000 gal)	30	95
Daily sales (x $1,000)	20	65
Total # Small distillers	1,100	720
Daily output (x1,000 gal)	20	14
Daily sales (x $1,000)	40	42

Figure 9.4 *Continued.*

Gaming Division

At the track, in a bust out joint, or in the parlor of one of our swank gambling spots, Chicago came to Capone for entertainment in 1930. Gaming (the boss likes this term more than "gambling") operations now form a full 17% of our gross sales revenues, almost all of which, except for payoffs to the local coppers, is profit to the organization.

In a couple of exciting additions to the gaming division, 1930 saw Eddie O'Hare join in with the outfit in a joint venture at the dog races. Eddie's Cicero dog track merged with our own Hawthorne Kennel Club, giving us a lock on dog racing in Chicago. Eddie also owns the patent on that mechanical rabbit that the dogs follow around, so we get a piece of that action all over the country.

Eddie was a bit reluctant at first, but our management team was persistent, as always.

Gaming action in town continued to center on our twenty five outstanding spots, notably the Ship, the Stockade, the Barracks, the Hawthorne Inn, and the ever popular Colosimo's, still carrying the name of its late owner.

Management was very concerned that the troubled economic times might adversely affect gaming revenues, but everyone breathed a sigh of relief when gambling income remained steady.

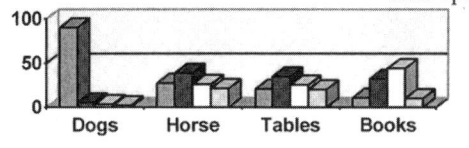

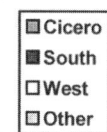

At one of our premiere joints, the Stockade, the weekly gross was up to the 1925 high of $35,000, or $1,820,000 per year. The Big Guy was very pleased, and rewarded Gaming Division Vice President Ralph Capone with a big bonus.

One of the big goals for 1931 is collection of a higher percentage of gambling debts. Nothing annoys the boss more than a welcher, and he's instructed "Machine Gun" Jack McGurn to apply the full resources of his division to this thorny problem.

Knowing Jack, we're sure the solution is right around the corner.

In geographical diversification, Al obtained control over some prime horse tracks in Florida, to where we now control eight different tracks across the country, not to mention all the employees we've got working on our behalf at the rest.

Gaming Operations
1930 figures do not include revenues from the out-of-state operations.

Gaming Revenues		
Gaming revenues (millions)	1930	1929
• Horses	7	7
• Dogs	5	3.5
• Tables	3	3
• Numbers	2	1.5
• Sports Bookies	<u>1</u>	<u>1</u>
Total	18	16

Figure 9.4 *Continued.*

ENTERTAINMENT DIVISION

General Operations

The moralists were all over us in 1930, the lousy hypocrites. As if none of them ever, well, you know. We added a few new brothels to beef up income in this area, and you'd think the world was coming to an end! And the feds with this Mann Act-White Slave thing; suffice it to say that the Entertainment Division was under a lot of pressure during the year.

Unfortunately, Division Vice President Mike "De Pike" Heitler failed to measure up to the challenge and had to be "fired." Al was shocked to hear that Mike's body was found in a burning car outside of town. Other executives immediately redoubled their efforts toward profitability.

Prostitution continued to be a clean, well organized, mostly indoor business. Members of the audit committee frequently inspected the 62 establishments under their supervision, assuring Chicagoans of the highest standards of quality and cleanliness.

At our prime resort locations, prostitution continued to represent about 50% of gross sales. For example, at the Stockade, room rentals for one week accounted for $5891 of a total of $11,329.35, or 52% of the gross. Labor costs eat into the profits, but the impact can be minimized through aggressive management and higher productivity.

Sports were supported by the outfit throughout the year, including sponsorship of several contending fighters and a number of athletes in sports such as baseball.

Our chairman, chatting with Chicago Cubs star Gabby Hartnett before a game. "I don't bet on baseball," Al commented, "not after that thing in 1919". I suppose they'll blame me for that, too, even though I wasn't even in Chicago when the Series was supposedly fixed." The boss has been to bat once or twice, and he's known as a power hitter, going two for two against the late John Scalise and the late Albert Anselmi after dinner one night. "Batter up!"

Stage and Screen performers headlined many acts at our clubs, notably Joe E. Lewis. Funny guy, he originally said he'd rather play some of the competition's clubs. Nobody was laughing when Joe got pistol-whipped and his throat cut. He's working for us now.

Revenues
Clubs generate income from several sectors. Slot machine action was a steady earner. Short term room rentals were the biggest money makers, usually followed by sales of food and beverages. Two other areas, performance fees and money from the piano were also included in this year's summary.

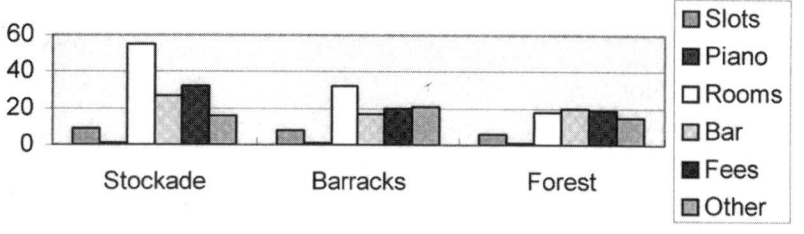

Figure 9.4 *Continued.*

INSURANCE AND INDUSTRIAL RELATIONS

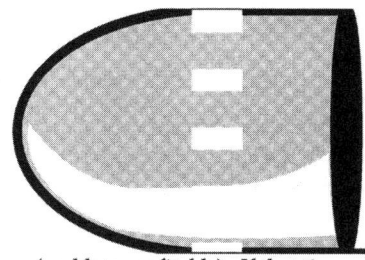

Insurance Division

Our insurance operations gained strength on new sales, as the very creative executive staff in this division explored new avenues for expansion.

"It's incredible, all the bad things that can happen to a business," one of our insurance executives commented. "Why, in one month alone, 50,000 tires were slashed in Chicago parking lots. Not one of them was in a lot operated by a dues paying member of the Midwest Garage Owners' Association".

Coincidence? We don't think so. MGOA members pay the outfit $1 a month for every car handled, and they obviously got their money's worth.

Insurance Division revenues now form twelve percent of the outfit's gross sales, a figure that is climbing steadily. What is more important than the money is the community outreach these programs afford. Through our insurance operations, the outfit is able to touch almost every Chicagoan in some personal way. "Some would call it racketeering," the boss says, "but I call it business." These expanded business relationships help prepare the outfit for a time when established segments like beverages may be more legal (and less profitable). If that time comes, we'll be ready.

Insurance Operations

Of special note during 1930 was our Electric Sign Club, pulling in membership dues from theater owners of $1,500 - $2,000 a month. Membership soared after a non-payer's theater was flooded with gasoline and burned.

Over ninety different unions or associations are now affiliated in some way with the outfit, including people selling food, fruit, junk, glass, bread, ice cream, flowers, and fish, as well as distilled water, milk, and soda pop. If it's liquid, and Chicagoans are drinking it, the outfit gets a piece of the action.

INDUSTRIAL RELATIONS

Within our primary industry, the outfit continued to maintain its reputation for firmness at the bargaining table. Wage rates stayed about even with last year, but most important, our competition was forced into some important concessions over territory and workforce. Normal attrition enabled the outfit to assure that only a few of our employee's were involuntarily separated from their jobs during the year. This was not the case at some of our competitor's establishments, where massive downsizing was practiced. On St. Valentine's Day, seven of Bugs Moran's people got downsized - six feet down. We avoided this type of disruption in our own labor force.

Also on the industrial relations front, hijackings of our beer and whiskey deliveries were up slightly, although we made up for it by taking more of theirs.

Figure 9.4 *Continued.*

OFFICERS AND DIRECTORS

CHAIRMAN OF THE BOARD

Alphonse Capone
Now residing part time in Florida, our Chairman still takes a "hands on" approach to the running of the company he founded ten years ago. His motivational techniques are legendary.
Despite the rumors that he might retire, or move to someplace like Canada, where they haven't got this stupid income tax law, Al promises to be around for a long, long time. "I don't even know what street Canada is on," he says.

Executive Vice President

Frank "The Enforcer" Nitti
Frank's back from a short stretch on a tax beef, and still as canny as ever. Insiders predict he'll go far, (but not too far).

Vice President

Ralph Capone
Head of the Gaming Division and a loyal representative of the boss when he's not around. Also the boss' brother.

VP - Human Relations

Jack McGurn
Jack, who says he got his nickname "Machine Gun" due to his rapid manner of speaking, takes on the toughest of the outfit's personnel problems. He says he had nothing to do with that St. Valentine's Day thing. And nobody's disputing him.

Comptroller - Director

Jake "Greasy Thumb" Guzik
Financial wizard and head of the accounting department. Jake set up the bookkeeping and accounting system now employed by all our finer establishments

Figure 9.4 Continued.

VP - Entertainment(Deceased)

Mike "De Pike" Heitler
Entertainment Division
Sad case of executive burn out. Al's comment that "I hadda fire the guy," should <u>not</u> be taken literally, despite the coincidence of his demise.

Director, Consigliere

Tony Lombardo
Tony's slated for bigger and better things. An innovator and effective schmoozer, he's our liaison to the Sicilians.

Director

Frank "Diamond" Maritote
Advancement in the outfit has absolutely nothing to do with the fact he's married to the boss' sister.

Director - Labor Relations

Sam "Golf Bag" Hunt
Known for his impish sense of humor and for carrying a shotgun in a golf bag. Like he says, "You never know when you might want to make a hole in one".

Director

Charley Fischetti
Boss's first cousin and loyal follower from the old neighborhood. Motto: "Whatever you say, boss."

Director - Chief Bagman

Rocco Fischetti
Charley's brother and Al's cousin. Handles cash disbursements.

Director - Appropriations

Murray Humphreys
Murray "The Camel" has one of the more colorful nicknames, and quite a rep in the hijacking and robbery end of the business.

PAST CHAIRMAN

Johnny Torrio
Ever the gentleman, now retired John Torrio knows his successors are carrying on the traditions he established. Occasionally consulted on matters of minor importance, his wisdom is appreciated.

Figure 9.4 *Continued.*

MERGERS AND ACQUISITIONS

ACQUISITIONS during the year included big parts of what used to be the Gennas'' alky cooking enterprises. As can be seen on the map, our territory now encompasses almost all of the South and West Sides, with Bugs Moran being the major problem for the time being.

As the boss is fond of saying, "You can get more with a kind word and a gun than you can with just a kind word." With this in mind, we were forced into a couple of situations that did turn into hostile takeovers during the year.

One notable exception was Meadowmoor Dairies, which was acquired through the efforts of Frank "Diamond" Maritote. The boss was amazed to find out that milk has a bigger markup than beer, and he confided to Frank (right before giving him a big bonus) "Honest to God, we've been in the wrong racket all along."

We also acquired control of the *Cicero Tribune* in a leveraged buyout, and a good bit of inventory in hostile takeovers of competitor trucks and carts. Inventory is handled on a First In, First Out, basis; it doesn't pay to keep this type of stuff sitting around for too long.

MERGERS during 1930 included a big one with Eddie O'Hare, who didn't bring any territory, but did have a dog track in Cicero, the Lawndale Kennel Club. We also got the rights to Eddie's mechanical rabbit, something you gotta have if you're running dogs anywhere, so this was a really sweet deal for both sides.

At least one effort was made during the year to merge the outfit with New York syndicates. But the four guys who were sent down to push the merger all died suddenly, and so did the takeover effort.

New Units Added to the outfit, 1929-1930

☐ Meadowmoor Dairy
☐ Lawndale Kennel Club
☐ Former Druggan territory, West of Michigan Ave.
☐ The *Cicero Tribune* newspaper
☐ 72 Speakeasies, formerly associated with the Gennas
☐ Lakefront Laundry
☐ Chicago Wet and Dry Laundry Association
☐ Undertakers' Association of Chicago
☐ 115 trucks and cars, mostly formerly belonging to Bugs Moran

Leadership of the Mergers and Acquisitions Division, Hostile Take-Overs Section
William "Klondike" O'Donnell, William "Three Fingered Jack" White, Murray "The Camel" Humphreys, Marcus Looney, and Charlie Fischetti

Figure 9.4 *Continued.*

CONSOLIDATED FINANCIAL STATEMENTS

Balance Sheet
Alphonse Capone Second Hand Furniture, Inc.

December 31,	1930	1929
ASSETS		
Current Assets:		
Cash and cash equivalents	$ 67,131,000	64,976,000
Marketable securities at cost		
(Market value: 1930 $13m, 1929 $13m)	11,408,000	12,315,000
Accounts Receivable	6,733,000	2,167,000
Less: Allowance for bad debt:		
(1930 $0, 1929 $0.)	0	0
Inventories		
- Beer	6,210,000	7,342,000
- Whiskey and distilled spirits	5,191,000	8,350,000
- Materials and supplies	3,576,000	2,019,000
Real estate held for sale	532,000	0
Deferred income taxes	0	0
Prepaid expenses and other assets	0	0
Total current assets	$100,781,000	97,169,000
Investments	$ 36,210,000	38,102,000
Property		
Land		
- Chicago area	$ 14,962,000	12,794,000
- Miami, Florida	2,100,000	216,000
Buildings	3,211,000	3,080,000
Vessels - speedboats	150,000	150,000
Trucks and cars	1,008,000	1,103,000
Machinery and Equipment		
- Brewing	4,910,000	6,237,000
- Distilling	6,575,000	8,648,000
- Machine Guns	50,000	45,000
Total	$ 32,966,000	32,093,000
Less: Accumulated depreciation and amortization	(14,822,000)	(14,000,000)
Property – net	$ 18,144,000	18,093,000
Intangibles		
Patents and trademarks	850,000	50,000
Goodwill	10,000,000	10,000,000
Total	$ 10,850,000	10,000,000
Total	$165,985,000	163,414,000

Figure 9.4 Continued.

December 31,	1930	1929

LIABILITIES AND SHAREHOLDERS' EQUITY

Current Liabilities

Current portion of long-term debt	$ 1,500,000	1,300,000
Short-term commercial paper borrowing (loan sharks)	3,200,000	3,721,000
Al's losses at tracks we don't own	4,450,000	3,158,000
Accounts payable	42,151,000	46,214,000
Payrolls and vacation pay	3,106,000	2,927,000
Uninsured claims	0	0
Income taxes	220,000	0
Total current liabilities	$ 53,627,000	57,320,000

Long-Term Liabilities

Long-term debt	20,000,000	20,000,000
Post-retirement benefit obligations	19,245,000	15,460,000
Accrued and other	6,100,000	1,850,000
Total long-term liabilities	$ 45,345,000	35,310,000

Shareholder's equity

Capital stock – common stock without par value: authorized 150,000 shares ($1.00 stated value per share); outstanding 0 shares in 1930 and 0 shares in 1929.
Preferred stock without par value: authorized 100,000 shares, cumulative convertible preferred stock ($1.00 stated value per share); outstanding 100,000 shares in 1930 and 100,000 shares in 1929.

	$ 40,000,000	40,000,000
Additional capital	6,101,000	1,070,000
Retained earnings	20,912,000	29,714,000
Cost of treasury stock	0	0
Total shareholders' equity	$ 67,013,000	64,125,000
Total	$ 165,985,000	163,414,000

Figure 9.4 Continued.

Statements of Income
Alphonse Capone Second Hand Furniture, Inc.

Year Ended December 31,	1930	1929
Revenue:		
Net sales, beverage products	$ 62,932,000	55,195,000
Net sales, entertainment services	8,420,000	10,933,000
Gaming revenues, net of losses	18,851,000	18,470,000
Insurance sales	12,791,000	11,734,000
Less: Association commissions:		
(1930 10%, 1929 10%)	(1,260,000)	(1,173,000)
Rentals and other services	2,741,000	2,191,000
Gain on sale of property	1,312,000	0
Dividends	0	0
Interest	0	0
Total revenue	$ 105,487,000	97,350,000
Costs and Expenses:		
Cost of goods sold	$ 21,847,000	20,005,000
Cost of services	14,563,000	12,361,000
Selling, general and administrative	10,411,000	9,799,000
Interest	0	0
Payoffs to politicians	12,476,000	11,376,000
Payoffs to police	17,687,000	16,504,000
Executive Compensation	24,962,000	23,161,000
Charitable contributions	2,800,000	2,800,000
Total costs and expenses	$ 104,776,000	96,006,000
Income Before Income Taxes	$ 711,000	1,344,000
Income Taxes	$ 220,000	416,000
Net Income	$ 491,000	927,000
Earnings per Share of Preferred Stock:	$ 4.91	9.27
Average Shares Outstanding:	100,000	100,000

Figure 9.4 *Continued.*

Notes to Financial Statements
Alphonse Capone Second Hand Furniture, Inc.

Summary of Significant Accounting Policies

Basis of Consolidation: The consolidated financial statements include the accounts of Alphonse Capone Second Hand Furniture, Inc., after elimination of significant intercompany amounts.

Cash and Cash Equivalents: The Company considers highly "liquid" investments acquired from competitors at no cost (via hijacking) to be cash equivalents, and turns these into cash as quickly as possible.

Inventory: Beer and distilled spirits inventories are stated at the lower of cost (first-in, first-out) basis or market.

Depreciation: Depreciation is computed using the straight line method. Depreciation expense includes amortization of assets under capital leases, and spare parts for vehicles damaged by explosions, machine gun fire, or accidents in car chases.
Estimated useful lives of property are as follows:

Buildings	1 - 5 years
Tank trucks	1 - 2 years
Brewing and distilling equipment	1 - 2 years
Machinery and equipment	1 year
Gambling equipment, racehorses, prostitutes, tommy guns	Who knows?

Income Taxes: Income tax expenses are based on a conservative estimate of what would happen if the boss loses his tax cases. This doesn't look too likely, but we'll play it safe anyhow.

Bad Debt Allowance: The boss don't allow for no bad debts. Somebody's gotta pay.

Independent Auditor's Report

We have audited the accompanying balance sheets of Alphonse Capone Second Hand Furniture, Inc. and its subsidiaries as of December 31, 1930 and 1929, and the related statements of income for each of the two years in the period ended December 31, 1930. These financial statements are the responsibility of the company's management. Our responsibility is to express an opinion on these financial statements based on our audits. Our opinion is: everything looks swell, Mr. Capone, just swell.

In our opinion, such financial statements present fairly, in all material respects, the financial position of Alphonse Capone Second Hand Furniture, Inc., and its subsidiaries at December 31, 1930 and 1929, and the results of their operations and their cash flows for each of the two years in the period ended December 31, 1930 in conformity with generally accepted accounting principles.

REIS and SHUMWAY,
Public Accountants

Figure 9.4 Continued.

or businesses; for example, both of these statements are prepared by the parties in a divorce action. As we'll see, in financial investigations we use the same information in the same format to track the assets we're trying to seize and the financial activity the crook is trying to conceal.

So, how do these assets, liabilities, income, and expenses make it into the financial report? Rules govern the process.

ACCOUNTING PRINCIPLES

The accountant's objective is to present a summary of the results of financial transactions. The accountant does this by using one of two accounting systems.

Single-entry bookkeeping is the older, simpler, and less precise system. As its name implies, one entry is made for every transaction, usually in a columnar form. The single-entry system is still used in small businesses and by individuals balancing their checkbooks. It is also the system of choice for the books of illegal businesses such as drug trafficking. Al Capone's bookkeepers were instructed by Jake "Greasy Thumb" Guzik to use this system. Big business accountants don't use it much, because there is no way to "balance the books" or check the accuracy of the figures.

Double-entry bookkeeping operates on the theory that every financial transaction always affects at least two aspects of a business' life. For example, if Al buys a barrel of beer for $55 in cash, he gained something — the beer, but he lost something too — the cash. In a single entry system like your check register, only one notation would be made of this fact: You subtract $55 from the previous balance and get a new balance. Under the double-entry system, an entry would be made in *all* of the accounts affected by the transaction. Numerous accounts are established in a double-entry system, and each transaction is classified as to how it affects the various accounts. In the beer purchase example, money would be taken from one account, called Cash, and something (the beer) would be added to another account, say, Inventory. Granted, we have to make twice as many entries in our books, but the double-entry system does do a better job of describing exactly what happened.

To make the system more precise, a fundamental equation is used. The first part of the equation holds that everything of value is owned or claimed by someone. Thus, the equation reads:

Items of Value = Claims

The items of value (on the left side of the equation) are called *assets*. These include cash, securities, real property, inventory, supplies, equipment, resources, and lots of other tangible items. Some assets are intangible, such as an I.O.U. or a copyright. If it has value to the owner, it's an asset.

There are two kinds of claims against assets. In our beer example, Al is now claiming ownership based on the fact that he's got 55 bucks invested in that asset. (And who's going to dispute him?) His investment is also known as his *equity* or *capital*, and sometimes *net worth*. In this very simple example, Al's equity in this item is $55.

The other type of claim against assets doesn't apply to the beer example, because Al used his own money (capital) to pay for it. If he had used someone else's money, he would owe that person for the amount. He would be liable for the debt, which is why this kind of claim is called a *liability*.

Now the formula can be converted to the fundamental accounting equation:

Assets = Liabilities + Equity (or capital)

or

$$A = L + E$$

Keep in mind that this is an *equation* — the items on the left side of the equal sign must always equal those on the right. In a double-entry system, (at least) two entries are always made, one to each side of the equal sign, so that the total of assets always equals the total claims.

TABLE 9.1
Transaction Changes

The Change	The Result
Increase in an asset	Decrease in another asset, or
	Increase in a liability, or
	Increase in an item of net worth
Decrease in an asset	Increase in another asset, or
	Decrease in a liability, or
	Decrease in an item of net worth
Increase in a liability	Decrease in another liability, or
	Increase in an asset, or
	Decrease in an item of net worth
Decrease in a liability	Increase in another liability, or
	Decrease in an asset, or
	Increase in an item of net worth
Increase in an item of net worth	Increase in an asset, or
	Decrease in a liability, or
	Decrease in another item of net worth
Decrease in an item of net worth	Decrease in an asset, or
	Increase in a liability, or
	Increase in another item of net worth

In our beer example, the equation would look like this:

$$A = L + E$$

$$\$55 = 0 + \$55$$

The transaction balances.

If only one entry is made, or if one entry is accidentally made twice to one side of the equation, or if an error is made in one of the entries, the equation will not *balance*. This "balance" is the perfection accountants seek. All kinds of changes can be made to the various accounts, but the changes must always be made according to a set of rules. How the changes affect the equation depends on the transaction. Table 9.1 outlines the ways these changes are to be made.

Clear? Not yet? Look at the beer example again. In buying the beer, Al decreased one of his asset accounts, Cash, by $55. This transaction, a decrease in an asset, means he has to offset another account. He chooses to increase another asset account, Inventory, by $55, and the books balance.

The point again, is as follows:

- All balance sheet accounts fall into one of three basic categories: assets, liabilities, or capital/equity/net worth.
- An entry to one account always affects another one.
- The entry must be balanced by a second, offsetting entry.

THE DREADED DEBITS AND CREDITS

Debits and credits make everybody nervous. How do you know which is which, and when to use either? Good questions. Most people, when they think of debits, associate the word with "debt" — owing something or paying something. When you "debit" your account, you're taking money *out* of it, right? Try to forget this association, or it will make you crazy.

The explanation is a lot simpler than you'd think. Accountants had to figure out some way of keeping track of the increases and decreases

DEBIT	CREDIT

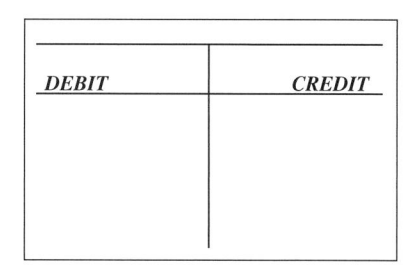

Figure 9.5 Debit and credit.

to either assets or claims. They devised a system that was based on their equation, one that is represented with two columns and a line down the middle representing the equal sign. They had to give a name to each column, so they decided the one on the left would be the "debit" column, and the one on the right, the "credit" column. See Figure 9.5 for an illustration.

"Debit" refers *only* to the left column, "credit" *always* to the right — the terms do *not* refer to adding or subtracting.

The rules dictating how increases and decreases to accounts are recorded are as follows:

Asset Accounts

Increases on the left (debit)
Normal balance

Decreases on the right (credit)

Liabilities and Net Worth (Capital)

Decreases on the left (debit)

Increases on the right (credit)
Normal balance

Income

Decreases on the left (debit)

Increases on the right (credit)
Normal balance

Expenses

Increases on the left (debit)
Normal balance

Decreases on the right (credit)

When you are looking at accounting transactions, you will follow the rules outlined above in the following situations:

- Determining which accounts are affected by the transaction
- Deciding how the account is affected — whether it is an increase or decrease
- Recording the transaction in the appropriate column as a debit or a credit

Remember — the system is an equation; debits must equal credits. For each transaction, a debit must be accompanied by a credit.

How will the beer purchase fit these rules? Al decreased one asset account, Cash. Looking at the rules above, we see that a decrease to an asset account is a credit. We'll post that entry to the right of the line, where it belongs. Now our equation is unbalanced. We have to put a corresponding entry in some other account. Al already decided to increase another asset account, Inventory, so we find the rule about recording an increase to an asset account, and sure enough, it's a debit. Figure 9.6 shows what our book entries look like now.

We're not going to get more complicated than this, having already established that: (*a*) accountants create accounts to account for things, with a system of debits and credits to do the actual accounting, and (*b*) in our example, the debits match the credits.

That is how the figures arrive on a balance sheet, which is always a statement of a condition as of a certain time. The date always appears somewhere in the report. In Al Capone's case, the date is December 31, 1930. Many balance sheets are prepared as of the date of the company's fiscal year end.

The other principal financial statement is the income statement, also called a profit and loss statement. This report covers a period rather than reflecting a condition as of a specific date. The accounts found in an income statement are different from those on a balance sheet, because they represent changes, rather than a fixed position. Accounts reported on an income statement are categorized as revenues or expenses. Once you have identified which is which, the rules as outlined in Table 9.1 can be applied to determine whether the entry will be a debit or a credit to those accounts.

INVENTORY (Asset acct.)	
DEBIT	*CREDIT*
$ 55.00	

Asset account (Inventory) <u>in</u>creased by $55.00 -- Debit

CASH (Asset acct.)	
DEBIT	*CREDIT*
	$ 55.00

Asset account (Cash) <u>de</u>creased by $55.00 -- Credit

Figure 9.6 *Double entry bookkeeping for a beer purchase. The asset account Inventory increased by $55.00, a debit. The asset account Cash decreased by $55.00, a credit.*

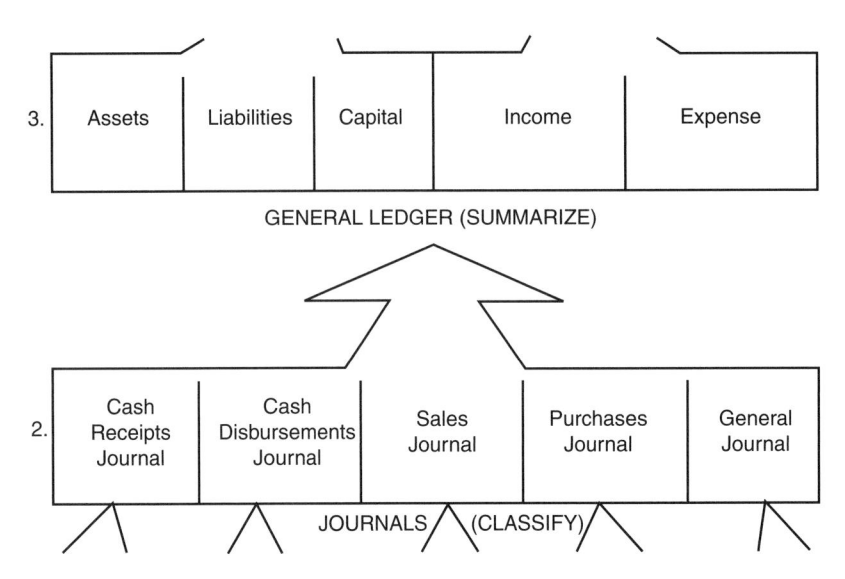

3. Assets | Liabilities | Capital | Income | Expense

GENERAL LEDGER (SUMMARIZE)

2. Cash Receipts Journal | Cash Disbursements Journal | Sales Journal | Purchases Journal | General Journal

JOURNALS (CLASSIFY)

Figure 9.7 *Journals and ledgers where transactions are classified and summarized for the financial statement.*

In the middle of the audit trail pyramid, we find the *journals* used to classify transactions. This is where the determination is made about which accounts will be affected by a given transaction. Journals are the records maintained at or near the front line of the business. Certain journals are common to almost all businesses, and they have equivalents in our personal lives as well. The Cash Disbursements journal kept by a business is not much more than a check register like the one most of us maintain. In our chart, there are five journals. (See Figure 9.7, above.) Transactions entered into these journals are *classified* so that they can be accurately reported later on either the balance sheet or the income statement. Nobody actually sits around deciding this transaction goes here, and that one there; this is all set up by the accountants beforehand, and nowadays computers do most of the work automatically.

At the bottom of the records pyramid are the source documents used to record actual transactions. (See Figure 9.8.) Most illegal enterprises don't keep these kinds of records, but we're pretending Capone's did. What kinds of source documents might we expect to find? Sales and purchases are the heart of the business, and they create the following source documents:

- Sales of either goods or services generate deposit tickets, customer receipts, and items such as checks and credit card slips for deposit into the bank. These transactions will affect accounts

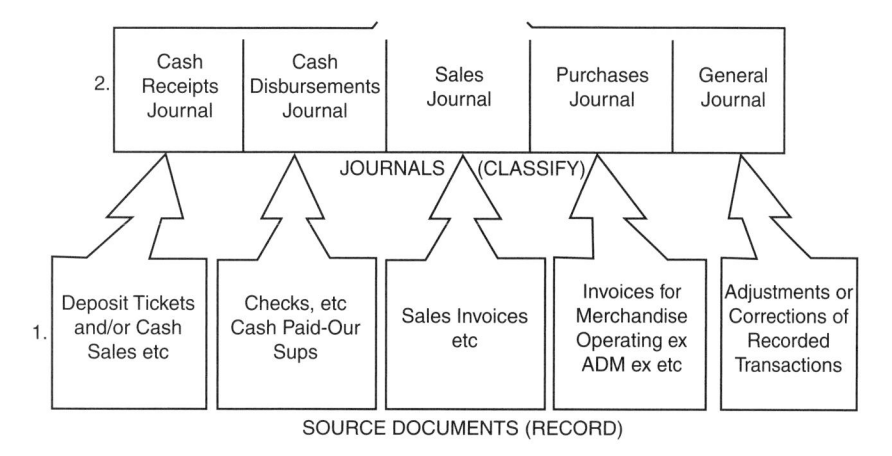

Figure 9.8 Source documents and their classification.

in both the balance sheet and the income statement.
- Purchases require that checks be written or that slips be made out noting the payment of cash. Again, both types of statements are affected.

ANALYZING THE BALANCE SHEET

So, transactions move through the system, documented at every stage, from the time money is first paid or received to the time the financial statements are prepared. What appears on the balance sheet?

In the reports of most corporations, the Assets category is subdivided further. In the Current Assets category, any asset that could be converted into cash within one year of the statement date would be listed. In the Capone Balance Sheet, Current Assets include:

- *Cash:* currency and coin, as well as money deposited in a bank
- *Securities:* stocks, bonds, and similar noncash items that can quickly be converted into cash
- *Accounts Receivable:* money owed by customers for goods or services provided by the business, including credit sales not yet paid for (An allowance for bad debts is usually calculated into this account. In Capone's case, he doesn't allow bad debts.)
- *Notes Receivable:* any debt owed to the business and documented by a promissory note; these are usually due within 1 year (not included on Capone's statement)
- *Inventories:* the merchandise available to the business for sale to its customers; usually described in terms of raw materials, finished goods, and goods ready for shipment (The value of inventories is set at either the cost of the items or the market value, whichever is *lower.*)

Longer-term assets include Investments — assets held for longer than one year that cannot be converted quickly to cash — and Property or Fixed Assets. These are the things used by the business to produce or sell its products. Capone's property includes:

- *Land:* real property on which breweries, race tracks, brothels, or gambling joints are located
- *Buildings:* the buildings, not necessarily on land owned by the organization, that house operations
- *Vehicles:* vessels, trucks, cars, and any vehicle used to move raw materials or finished goods (Capone actually used tank trucks to move his beer from large breweries to warehouses and distributors.)

- *Machinery and Equipment:* brewing and distilling equipment; equipment used to make gambling devices, and those devices themselves, such as slot machines; machine guns and other tools of the trade

These assets are all subject to *depreciation*, the recognition that these items have a limited useful lifetime and lose value over time. Since all of these items are valued at their original cost, the depreciation is figured into the asset calculation.

Intangible assets are things that do not have a physical existence but still represent something of value to the company. Franchises and copyrights are examples. Capone's intangible assets would have included the following:

- *Patents:* for example, Eddie O'Hare's mechanical rabbit, used at greyhound tracks; these can be quite impressive income producers
- *Goodwill:* the company's name recognition and position in the community; most corporations recognize that this is difficult to calculate, so they typically value Goodwill at $1 (At $10 million, Capone was proud of his.)

On the other side, Liabilities are also divided into Current and Long-Term. Current Liabilities are usually those due within a year. They include the following:

- *Accounts Payable:* amounts owed by the business to its regular suppliers and creditors, for the materials used in producing the goods for sale
- *Notes Payable:* money owed to a bank or other lender and documented by a promissory note; usually due within one year
- *Other:* commitments made but not yet paid, such as accrued vacation pay for employees or income taxes incurred but not due until April 15

Long-Term Liabilities are the debts due after one year from the balance sheet date. These might be long-term loans or corporate bonds issued. Nowadays, this category includes pension plans and post-retirement benefits.

Once you know what you *have* (assets) and what you *owe* (liabilities), simple subtraction will tell you what you *own* (equity). If you have a home with a mortgage, you can subtract the amount you owe on the mortgage from the value of the property to find out your equity — how much you own, as opposed to what the bank or mortgage holder owns.

In the Equity section of the statement, the shareholder's interest is outlined. It includes the following:

- *Capital stock:* the shares of ownership issued by the company. Each stock certificate represents a *share* in the company; in the case of Al Capone's business, a 1/100,000th slice. Stock is either common or preferred, a distinction that relates to the payment of dividends and voting rights
- *Additional Capital or Capital Surplus:* the amount above par value paid by shareholders. If the par value for the stock is $10.00, and it is selling on the stock market for $15.00, the extra $5.00 is Additional Capital for the corporation
- *Accumulated Retained Earnings:* the amount left over each year after dividends are paid to the stockholders

That's it. Add it all together, and you know the financial condition of the company as of the date of the balance sheet (in Al Capone's case, December 31, 1930). This figure can be compared with the one from the year before to see what trends might be developing, but in order to get a clearer picture, you need to see the income statement.

ANALYZING THE INCOME STATEMENT

Remember that the income statement is a statement of change; it describes what happened to the business during the reporting period. An example of a very tight little income statement is the one seized from The Barracks in Burnham, covering the week of September 6, 1925:

Slot machines	$906.00
Piano	55.25
Rooms (prostitution)	5,891.00
Bar	2,677.10
Tables (gambling)	1,800.00
Gross revenues	$11,329.35
Paid out 10% (protection)	1,133.00
	$10,196.35
Expenses	8,450.00
Net income	$1,746.35

The information on income statements is divided into two basic categories: *Revenue* (or *Income*) and *Expenses*. As with the balance sheet, a standard formula is used to reach the bottom line, *Net Income*. This formula is:

Revenue − Expenses = Net Income

At The Barracks, for the period in question, revenue from all sources was $11,329.35. Expenses, including payoffs and other costs, totaled $9,583. Applying the formula:

R − E = Net

$11,329.35 − 9,583.00 = $1,746.35

Capone's annual report isn't much more complicated; it includes categories (and subcategories) for Revenue items and for Costs and Expenses. These include:

Sales: Net Sales, or Operating Revenue in the case of a service business, represents the primary source of money for the corporation. Bootlegging was Capone's main source, so this figure is listed first. "Net" refers to the total sales minus returns and allowances for price reductions or discounts. Right off the bat you are able to compare 1930's figures against those for 1929 and see that beverage sales were up by $7 million. This would be important information for the investor.

- *Cost of Goods Sold:* Usually the largest item and the first listed, this figure includes raw materials, labor, and overhead items such as rent and electricity.
- *Cost of Services:* This category includes other costs associated with operating the business and making a profit.
- *Selling, General, and Administrative Expenses:* Salesmen's salaries, advertising, promotion, travel, and entertainment, as well as executive salaries, are included in this category. In our example, Capone's executive compensation was so large that it was given a separate heading.

At this point, an initial calculation is performed, subtracting Costs and Expenses from Revenue and arriving at Income Before Taxes. Income taxes are then subtracted to arrive at the bottom line, Net Income. In Capone's income statement, his net income from 1929 to 1930 declined, which would be a big caution signal for investors. You would want to review the income statement further and compare its figures against those for previous years to determine the reason why the company didn't do as well. Was it a drop in sales? Higher expenses? A really intense look at the company would involve going behind the income statement to the books themselves, to see how the change occurred. You would also want to look at the balance sheet and see how it was affected by the changes, because, as we noted earlier, all of these accounts are related. Table 9.2 shows how the balance sheet accounts and the income statement accounts are related.

Looking at the books themselves means studying the journals, the books of original entry. Here, each transaction is classified by type and by the accounts it affects. In the case of a beer purchase, the Cash Disbursements Journal or Check Register would be the primary entry point. The journal has a number of columns, enough to cover all of the various accounts affected. Capone's looks like this:

The transactions that we see here are as follows:

TABLE 9.2
Table of Relationships

Balance Sheet Account	Income Statement Account

Current Assets

Cash	Sales, Cash Paid Out, Expenses (any form of cash outlay)
Notes Receivable	Interest Income
Accounts Receivable	Sales
Allowance for Bad Debts	Bad Debt Expense
Inventory	Cost of Goods Sold
Prepaid Expenses	Assorted expense accounts, e.g., Rent, Insurance, Supplies

Fixed Assets

Furniture and Fixtures	Depreciation, Interest Expense, Repairs, Sales of Furniture and Fixtures
Depreciation Allowance	Depreciation, Sales of Furniture and Fixtures, Machinery, Building
Machinery	Depreciation, Sales of Furniture and Fixtures, Repairs, Insurance, Interest Expense
Building	Depreciation, Repairs, Property Taxes, Insurance Expense, Sale of Building, Interest Expense

Current Liabilities

Notes Payable	Interest Expense
Accounts Payable	Various expenses and purchases
Accrued Expenses	Payroll Expense, Payroll Tax Expense

Long-Term Liabilities

Mortgage Payable	Interest Expense, Property Taxes

Capital

Net Profit and Loss

Cash Disbursements Journal						
		Check	Cash	Inven.	Accts. Pay.	Misc. Exp.
Date	Payee	#	(CR)	(DR)	(DR)	(DR)
1930				(101)	(102)	(201)
9-12	Moran Brewing	202	500.00		500.00	
9-12	Lexington Hotel	203	125.00			125.00
9-13	Jack McGurn	204	2000.00		2000.00	
9-14	Bob's Beer	205	55.00	55.00		
			2680.00	55.00	2500.00	125.00

1. On September 12, Capone pays Bugs Moran $500 for some beer previously delivered.
2. On September 12, Capone pays the Lexington Hotel $125 for some broken chairs.
3. On September 13, Capone pays Jack McGurn $2,000 on account.
4. On September 14, Capone buys a barrel of beer for $55 from Bob's Beer.

Note the following with regard to these entries:

- Al is happy to see that the credits to the Cash account exactly equal the debits to all the others.
- For this journal, the Asset account for Cash is the only one being credited.
- Each account is assigned a number. Asset accounts start with 100, Liabilities with 200, Equity with 300, Income with 400, and Expenses with 500. Cash is 101.
- "CR" stands for credit and "DR" for debit. (I don't know why.)

The journals most often found in a business are:

- Cash Receipts Journal
- Cash Disbursements Journal
- Sales Journal (Accounts Receivable)
- Purchases Journal (Accounts Payable)
- General Journal
- Voucher Register

Ledgers, the next books up the ladder, are consolidation points for the information in the journals. This information is posted periodically to the *General Ledger,* the book that contains total figures from all the accounts. A subpoena for accounting records should certainly include this item. *Subsidiary ledgers* contain more information about specific transactions by categories, such as accounts receivable.

Other ledgers include the corporate minute books and the corporate stock book. These should also be listed in a subpoena for corporate records, because they will give you the information about who owns stock and who is calling the shots at the company.

USING BOOKS AND RECORDS IN A FINANCIAL CASE

Now that you have an understanding of how these things work, the next question is, how can books and records be used in a financial or money laundering case? Start by assuming that the answer to your questions lies somewhere within the stack of paper now piled on your desk; it usually does. In Al Capone's tax case, investigators reviewed more than *2 million* separate records, looking for the documents they would use to convict him. The agents began to find the answers in some ledgers maintained by a Capone gambling operation, exactly the type of books and records we're talking about here.

Acting on your assumption, you have to *audit* the records, just as an accountant would do, examining the individual pieces until the big picture becomes visible. An audit requires that the records be analyzed, scrutinized, and compared, as follows:

- *Analysis:* the dissection of the ledger balance into its component parts, checking to see if the amounts charged are compatible with the account to which they were charged
- *Scrutiny:* a review of all of the source documents used to arrive at the ledger balances, as well as any leads that might be identified through omission of information, alteration, absence of business purpose, or notations on documents
- *Comparison:* comparing the source documents against the book entries and your analysis to discover anomalies or leads

Certain indicators in the audit process may lead to a conclusion that some form of financial manipulation (fraud, embezzlement, money laundering) may be going on. The following indicators should be red flags that there is more here than meets the eye:

- Maintaining two sets of books and records
- Concealment of assets
- Destruction of books and records
- Large or frequent currency transactions
- Payments to fictitious companies or persons
- False or altered entries and documents
- False invoices or billings
- Purchase or sale of under- or overvalued assets
- Use of nominees
- Large company loans to employees or other persons
- Frequent cashing of checks received
- Frequent use of cashier's checks
- Using photocopies of invoices or receipts instead of originals
- Personal expenses paid with corporate funds
- Payee names on checks left blank and inserted at a later date
- Excessive billing discounts
- Excessive spoilage or defects
- Double payment on billings
- Unnecessary use of collection accounts
- An individual's negotiating checks made payable to the corporation
- Second- or third-party endorsements on corporate checks

CONCLUSION

The books and records of any business, legal or illegal, may be critical parts in your money laundering case. The importance of this evidence cannot be overstated. Nothing obtained from banks or other third parties will be as complete as the records prepared by your subject. You must make every effort to (*a*) obtain the subject's records and (*b*) understand them. You are not likely to get an annual report like Al Capone's in your money laundering investigation, but you may get the books and records you need to create one of your own. Then it's just a question of whether you know what to do and how:

- All of the figures on the annual report are, of course, speculative, but most have been taken from estimates made at the time or actual accounting records obtained from the Capone organization over the years between 1925 and 1932. The figures in some of the journals and ledgers are taken directly from those same books kept by Capone's bookkeepers.
- All of the names used are those of real people who occupied the positions described. They're all dead now, so I don't think they'll be complaining.
- All of the statements attributed to Mr. Capone, including his entire Message to Shareholders, were actually made by him and published somewhere. Many of the quotes are taken from press conferences given by Al, in which he said some pretty astonishing things, given his occupation.
- The only business cover Al Capone ever used officially was that of a second hand furniture dealer. He had business cards printed up to prove it.
- Al Capone was making some serious money. In a time when you could get a full meal for a quarter and see a movie for a nickel, his organization was grossing over $100 million a year. That would be something like $10 *billion* today. It wasn't all profit, but it is still sobering to think of the kind of corruption and assorted evil that kind of money could buy.

CHAPTER 10

INDIRECT METHODS OF PROVING INCOME

"There's more than one way to skin a cat."
Anonymous

"Income tax has made more liars out of the American people than golf."
Will Rogers

There was a time, a hundred years ago, a kinder, gentler time, when Americans didn't have to worry about the income tax. The idea that the government wanted a piece of whatever you earned wasn't a wildly popular concept, even though the tax rate for most people was as low as 1% initially.

Ah, progress. The government wants a lot more than 1% now, and it didn't take long before the rates were high enough that people started to feel like cheating. Some of these people were already breaking other laws and weren't inclined to pay *any* tax. This group included bootleggers, gamblers, and criminals of all stripes. Some things haven't changed much over the years (although those tax rates sure have), and people with illegal incomes are still cheating on their taxes.

As you might guess, the government doesn't care to lose the revenue this cheating represents and has taken steps to recover it. One of these steps was the passage of laws against tax evasion. The Treasury Department set up mechanisms to investigate violations of the statute, but the investigators quickly encountered a serious problem: Tax cheats didn't go around advertising this fact. Instead, they concealed their activity by not filing returns, filing false returns, and hiding evidence of their (often illegal) income.

In response, the Bureau of Internal Revenue developed several methods of proving a taxpayer had received income — even though the bureau might have no direct evidence of this income. These techniques, several of which were perfected over the years, became known as *indirect methods* of establishing income.

These methods worked quite well with any sort of income — legal or illegal — because they didn't rely heavily on the books and records of the taxpayer, records that were likely to be unavailable. As the investigators got more sophisticated, they perfected the techniques, eventually creating the ability to reconstruct income under almost any circumstances.

Because the indirect methods were used so often against criminals, investigators outside Internal Revenue also applied the techniques to proving that criminals had received income, and the courts permitted this evidence to be used at trials of individuals who were not charged with tax crimes. Investigators and prosecutors discovered that this type of evidence, when presented effectively to a jury, could be extremely powerful. It is, for example, one thing to say that a drug trafficker made a lot of money selling drugs, and quite another to demonstrate that, without being employed, he purchased a house, a Ferrari, and a yacht, and had a million dollars in the bank. Not only does this type of evidence convince jurors that maybe the defendant really *is* a drug dealer, it might sell them on the idea that all of those goodies ought to be taken away from him.

INDIRECT METHODS

The first step in convicting a defendant and forfeiting those assets is proving the income. Your witnesses, informants, and undercover agents will establish the likely source of the money — drug trafficking, gambling, extortion, or whatever. Although this will be important information for the jury, it is of no concern to the financial investigator, who is only seeking to prove that the defendant received *some* income from *some* unknown source.

In a sense, the money laundering or financial investigator has an advantage over those who work the tax evasion cases that date back to Al Capone. In tax cases, the investigators have to prove that the income came from some taxable source, and that taxes were not paid on it. The calculations are slightly different for those types of cases, and we're going to ignore them for purposes of this book.

Over the years, several different indirect methods have been applied to proving income from criminal sources. The most common of these methods are:

- Net worth
- Source and application of funds
- Bank deposits
- Unit and volume

Of these, the net worth method is the most widely known, and it adapts readily to nontax investigations of illegal income.

Before we detail the indirect methods, it should be emphasized once again that *the direct route is better* if you can use it. The direct method of proving income relies on the subject's books and records, or those of third parties, documenting sales, expenses, and other financial transactions. This method is sometimes known as the *specific items* approach, because it relies on proof of particular transactions to show income.

Let's say that drug dealer Alex Bell keeps very good records of his sales, and that you seize these in a search at his residence. Further, you have witnesses who can verify many of the sales recorded in the books and confirm that they were drug transactions. By adding up all of the sales described by your available sources (books and witnesses), you will know exactly what Bell made from his drug business (or at least exactly how much you can prove).

Again, the direct approach is always preferable to the indirect variety. Whenever possible, you should try to obtain the books and records of the subject and use these to make the most direct case possible. Even if you ultimately decide to go with an indirect approach, the subject's records can be invaluable in supporting the conclusions reached in your net worth or bank deposits calculation.

NET WORTH

The net worth method is devastatingly effective, though it is not always easy to perform. It also cannot be used in all situations, so it's a good idea to take a little time profiling the subject before you start in with a net worth calculation.

As we saw earlier, net worth is simply the difference between a person's assets and his or her liabilities. You will recall from the chapter on books and records that the formula for calculating net worth was:

$$\text{Assets} - \text{Liabilities} = \text{Equity}$$

Equity is the same thing as net worth. So, you take what the person owns, subtract what the person owes, and you know exactly what he or she is worth.

Under the net worth theory of proof, an increase (or decrease) in net worth from year to year *must* be the result of some income (or loss). If I know what you are worth this year, and it's more than you were worth last year, you must have had some income during the year. Simple.

The net worth method should be used when the subject's books and records are unavailable (or the subject did not keep any) *and* several of the subject's assets or liabilities have changed over the period under investigation. If he or she does not have any assets, you will want to try some other approach (or some other crook).

The formula for calculating net worth is elegantly simple:

	Assets
	Assets
Less:	Liabilities
Equals:	Net worth
Less:	Prior year's net worth
Equals:	Net worth increase (decrease)
Plus:	Living expenses
Equals:	Income (or expenditures)
Less:	Funds from known sources
Equals:	Funds from unknown sources

Notice the resemblance of this statement to the balance sheet used in businesses. A net worth assessment is not much more than two (or more) balance sheets, side by side. Also, check the bottom line — funds from unknown sources. Your corroborative witnesses and cooperating defendants provide the information that identifies those "unknown" sources. The calculation does not concern itself with the source of the money, only cold, hard figures (see Figure 10.1).

A net worth investigation has several stages, the first of which is the identification of the subject's assets, liabilities, and living expenses. You need to find out what the subject has and what he or she is spending before you go further through the calculation.

Where will you find out about the assets, liabilities, and expenses? The same places you'll get all of the financial information in your case:

- The subject, and his or her records (first choice)
- Informants — cooperating individuals
- Real estate records
- Court records, judgments, and liens
- Bankruptcy records
- Motor vehicle ownership records
- Loan applications

"I don't care what your analysis of my net worth shows, you're not getting a raise in your allowance."

- Financial statements
- Tax returns
- Credit card information
- Child support records
- Divorce records (one of my favorites)
- Employment records
- Bank records
- Physical surveillance
- Securities records

Use your imagination. People leave tremendous paper trails behind them — trails that get wider every day in the age of computers and cell phones — and there are clues to assets, liabilities, and expenses in many of these records. These clues lead to other documents until the picture emerges clearly.

Some sources are particularly good for a net worth case. I like divorce records, because both parties have to file income statements and asset/liability statements *under penalty of perjury*. These let you know exactly where the subject was financially at a given point in time, or at least what he or she claimed. In addition, you now know of at least one other person who (*a*) has knowledge of your subject's finances and (*b*) disliked him or her enough to get a divorce. Bankruptcy records are good, too.

Don't overlook traditional methods of criminal investigation. Physical surveillance can lead

	12-31-02 (base year)	12-31-03	12-31-04
Assets			
Cash on hand	$100	—	—
Bank account balance	2,200	7,000	10,000
Jewelry	1,000	9,000	15,000
Art collection	—	—	25,000
Jaguar automobile	—	45,000	45,000
Real estate	—	—	250,000
Total assets	$4,300	$61,000	$345,000
Liabilities			
Note payable — Finance company	500	500	500
Auto loan	—	15,000	12,000
Real estate mortgage	—	—	125,000
Total liabilities	500	15,500	137,500
Net worth	$3,800	$45,500	$207,500
Less:			
Prior year's net worth		3,800	45,500
Net worth increase		$41,700	$162,000
Add:			
Personal living expenses			
Credit card payments		—	14,000
Other personal living expenses		7,300	10,000
Income		$49,000	$186,000
Less:			
Funds from known sources:			
Interest on bank account		300	600
Wages		4,700	1,400
Total funds from known sources		5,000	2,000
Funds from unknown/illegal sources		$44,000	$184,000

Figure 10.1 Net worth calculation: Alex Bell.

you to assets and informants, or undercover agents can establish ownership of property that the crook might have concealed in someone else's name or otherwise tried to hide. This is the type of investigation in which your imagination and resourcefulness can be used to the fullest extent — the type of challenge good investigators relish.

Once the assets are catalogued and the liabilities and expenses accounted for, the calculation can begin. Figure 10.1 gives a sample net worth calculation.

The rules in applying the net worth method have to be followed, or you risk losing the court's permission to use it as evidence at trial. They are as follows:

- Assets are valued at cost. No adjustment is made for depreciation or appreciation.
- Accounting techniques should be the same ones used by the subject.
- All items relating to the calculation should be included, even if they don't change from year to year.
- Consistency is important. If you class an item one way one year, it needs to be carried over that way to all subsequent years. If something changes, as

did Bell's cash on hand, it needs to be included and explained.

Problem areas in the net worth calculation usually involve either cash on hand or living expenses. These are the hardest for the investigator to identify, but they are critical to the calculation. Cash on hand is most difficult to calculate, because, as we know, cash leaves no trail, especially in an illegal business like drugs. We have to establish this figure, though, because if we don't, Mr. Bell's going to claim that in 2001 he had $500,000 cash on hand. He'll say he's been living on that money ever since and that every one of his purchases was made with money from the five hundred grand he kept under his mattress. This is the so-called cash hoard defense, which, although it's almost always bogus, must be taken seriously.

A solid starting point is essential to the entire net worth calculation, and establishing cash on hand is the key to that starting point. Cash on hand refers to coin and currency that are in the subject's possession, such as in his or her house, in a safe deposit box, or in the hands of a nominee. It refers *only* to cash — not to money in bank accounts or other places where a record of it is kept.

Because it's difficult to prove exactly how much cash on hand a person has (How much do you have on hand at this moment?), the courts let us prove cash on hand by circumstantial evidence. Here are some of the ways we can do this, in order from strongest to weakest:

- A written or oral admission to investigators concerning net worth and cash on hand
- A financial statement, preferably made under penalty of perjury, made in connection with an attempt to get credit or in some court proceeding
- Bankruptcy in the period before your calculation
- Net worth or cash on hand established by the subject's own books and records
- Prior year activity, including unemployment or low wage employment, or indebtedness, foreclosure, checks returned for nonsufficient funds, repossessions, and so forth
- Low income reported on tax returns

The cash on hand calculation is so significant that you may be required to extend the entire financial investigation back a few years just to eliminate the possibility of a cash hoard. In Bell's case, we're only interested in 2003 and 2004, when our informants tell us he was in the dope business. He clearly didn't have much going for him as of the end of 2002. Our financial investigation would use several methods to try to prove that he couldn't have had a large cash hoard as of that date.

Proving a negative like that is pretty difficult, but it can be done. In Bell's case, he may have made a statement on a loan application when he bought his Jaguar, or he may have made a statement about his cash on hand to investigators. This raises an important point: If the subject doesn't know you're doing a net worth calculation on him, you don't want to mention this when you interview him. He probably won't be aware of the cash hoard defense until his lawyer tells him he needs it, and most crooks, knowing we're out to seize their ill-gotten gains, will deny ever having a large amount of cash on hand.

Living expenses can also be difficult to calculate, especially if the individual is using cash for his or her purchases. These living expenses exclude anything that can be classified as either an asset or a liability. They include such things as:

- Household expenses
- Automobile service and repairs (and gas)
- Medical expenses
- Entertainment expenses
- Taxes paid
- Net gambling losses
- Gifts to others and contributions
- Losses on the sale of personal assets

In some cases, you can make an estimate of living expenses, but the court may not allow it at trial. If not, you'll have to limit your list to what you are able to prove. Sources for this information include the subject's own records, especially receipts and the like, that you seize from his or her residence with a financial search warrant. Bank records, checking account records, and the records of businesses frequented by the subject can also be used to document expenses. The investigators in the Capone case got big mileage at trial out of detailing his purchase of silk underwear and other items of expensive clothing at various stores in Chicago and Miami. Witnesses from the stores documented the transactions.

Another area that might cause some problems is *funds from known sources.* These include salaries, wages, profits from a business, insurance or lawsuit proceeds, public assistance, interest, dividends, tax refunds, and gifts. The investigator must make an effort to identify as many known sources as possible, because this amount comes off the all-important bottom line — funds from unknown sources — that we really care about.

Defenses to Net Worth

Over the years, many creative and sometimes even effective defenses have been raised against the net worth method. Because IRS has been using the technique for decades, criminals and their attorneys have gotten plenty of practice in court. The financial investigator has to anticipate the defenses that will be raised and prepare in advance to refute them. Some of the more common defenses are described below.

Cash on Hand

Alex Bell claimed that he had a large amount of cash in a safe deposit box before the period of your investigation. We already looked at some of the ways this defense could be refuted with circumstantial evidence, but it's important to note that if he's going to use this defense, Bell will have to actually make the claim. This means that you or the government attorney may get to question him on this issue. If so, you should ask very pointed questions, such as:

- Where did this money come from?
- When was it received and from whom?
- Where was it kept?
- Who else saw or knew about it?
- Why wasn't it kept in the bank?
- Where is it right now?
- How and when was the cash spent, and what was purchased with the money?

Loans, Gifts, or Inheritances

These sources of cash are claimed in some cases. This kind of claim can be difficult to overcome, especially if the source of the "loan" or "inheritance" is overseas. At any rate, your investigation needs to cover the possibility that this claim will be made.

Again, when the defendant makes the claim, he or she will have to identify some source, often a friend or family member. At the end of this chapter, in a study of the Lindbergh kidnapping case, we'll see that this defense was raised by Bruno Hauptmann, who said a friend loaned the money before going back to Germany.

Your investigation may have to be extended to the source of the "loan," to prove that this person didn't have the funds to make any such transfer. In one of my cases, a claim was made that the money involved in large cash transactions had come as a gift from the defendant's mother, who sold a piece of real estate in a foreign country. This claim was refuted when the real estate records were examined and the sale was found to have occurred *after* the large cash transactions were conducted.

Another possible counterpoint to this defense is to question the form of the loan, gift, or inheritance. Was it in cash? If so, why? This is not, after all, the way most loans or inheritances are made. Why wasn't a check used? What documentation exists to support the transaction? What about Currency Transaction Reports (CTRs) or Currency and Monetary Instruments Reports (CMIRs) — do any exist? This is an especially effective approach to take in cases involving assertions that the money came in from overseas. If it came as a check or wire transfer, where is the piece of paper? If it came in cash, where's the CMIR? Why didn't you report it to Customs?

Holding Funds or Assets as a Nominee

"It's not my money, I'm just holding it for Joe." This defense depends on Joe agreeing to go along, which he may not, especially if IRS is involved. It usually works with a specific asset, the claim being for example that the car you included in your calculation *really* belongs to somebody else; it's just in the subject's name for insurance purposes.

You may have to interview Joe, but records relating to the asset might help by proving a connection with the subject. Who's paying for the gas or repairs on the car? Who's driving it? Who's paying for the insurance? The whole point of money laundering is to conceal the source, ownership, or control of the dirty money, so your investigation could involve going behind this concealment to find out the true source or ownership of the asset.

Jointly Held Assets of Subject and Spouse

If assets included in the computation are jointly held by the subject and his or her spouse, the subject could say that the asset was acquired by the spouse using that person's own funds: "Yeah, it's in our names, but she bought it."

You can deal with this by tracing the funds used to acquire the asset back to the subject, or by proving that the spouse did not have the means to conduct the transaction independently. In some cases, the funds of husband and wife will be so commingled that no tracing is possible. If so, the asset gets added into the calculation, and the spouse's legitimate sources of income get subtracted.

Failure to Account for Other Sources of Funds

Under case law established 50 years ago, the government is obligated to investigate all leads provided by the subject and anything that can be reasonably checked. In *Holland v. United States*, 348 U.S. 121 (1954), the Supreme Court ruled that "Where the taxpayer offers no relevant explanation of the increases in his net worth, however, the Government is not required to negate every possible source of nontaxable income — a matter peculiarly within the knowledge of the taxpayer."

So, we've got to be thorough, and this means viewing all of the records with an eye toward any income or transaction that might relate to another source of funds. This includes pensions and annuities, accident settlements, public assistance, and the like.

Conclusion

The net worth method can be a valuable part of your criminal investigation. You don't want to use it in all situations, such as when the subject has few assets, or when you have direct evidence of illegal income. Properly presented to a jury, the net worth calculation will lead them to an inescapable conclusion about the defendant's income.

SOURCE AND APPLICATION OF FUNDS

A close cousin to the net worth method, the source and application of funds technique is easy for investigators to use and easy for jurors to understand. It's based on the concept that if a subject's spending in a given period is greater than the money he or she earned from a known source, the difference is income from some unknown source. You can then trot out any information you might have about the subject's illegal business to make the clear inference that the "unknown source" isn't really much of a mystery.

Courts have accepted the source and application of funds method, also known as the expenditures method, commenting on its similarity to the net worth technique from which it is derived. "The two computations are merely accounting variations of the same basic method, the expenditures theory being an outgrowth of the net worth method"; see *McFee v. United States,* 206 F.2d 872, 874 (9th Cir. 1953), vacated and remanded, 348 U.S. 905, aff'd upon reconsideration *per curiam,* 221 F.2d 807 (9th Cir. 1955).

The same items or accounts are considered in both methods, but in the source and application of funds technique, only increases and decreases in assets and liabilities are considered, along with living expenses. Assets and liabilities that do not change in the period are not included in the calculation.

The formula for the calculation is:

	Application of funds (expenditures)
Less:	Known sources of funds
Equals:	Funds from unknown or illegal sources

You'd want to use this method of proof when your subject is living high but not acquiring a lot of assets. He or she doesn't have much net worth because it's all been spent. This profile fits quite a few drug dealers and many other criminals as well, who frequently take an "easy come, easy go" attitude toward their money and don't plan well for retirement.

Also, if the crook has assets and liabilities, but they don't change much during the period, this would be another reason for using the expenditures method. It can also be used in calculating the starting point in a net worth computation or as a check against reported income.

Doing the calculation isn't too tough. (It's finding all the items to add and subtract that takes time.) First, you consider the *application* of funds or expenditures. Included in these are:

- Increase in cash on hand or in banks
- Increase in personal or business assets
- Decreases in liability balances
- Personal living expenses

Next, you identify known sources of funds, such as:

- Decreases in cash on hand or in banks
- Sale or exchange of assets
- Wages, salaries, or the profits from business
- Interest, dividends, and other investment income
- Tax refunds

	2004	2005
Application of funds		
Increase in bank balance	$5,000	$25,000
Purchase of jewelry	8,000	6,000
Automobile purchase	30,000	—
Art collection		25,000
Credit card payment	—	14,000
Other living expenses	55,000	90,000
Total application of funds	$98,000	160,000
Less: Known sources of funds		
Cash on hand	—	—
Interest on bank accounts	300	600
Wages	4,700	1,400
Total known sources	5,000	2,000
Funds from unknown sources	$93,000	158,000

Figure 10.2 *Source and application of funds calculation.*

- Loans, gifts, or inheritances received
- Unemployment, public assistance, and other income

Subtract the second batch from the first, and voilà, you've got the subject's income from unknown or illegal sources. Figure 10.2 provides a sample calculation.

BANK DEPOSITS

Another well-established indirect method for establishing income is the bank deposits analysis. As with the other methods, we are looking for funds from known and unknown sources. In this technique, though, we're studying the subject's banking activity rather than assets and expenditures.

The idea behind this method is that if you take all of the subject's bank deposits for a given period, subtract any transfers between accounts, and then add any expenditures made in cash, you'll know how much total income the subject must have had during the period.

The bank deposits method can be used only when the subject (*a*) has bank accounts and (*b*) makes lots of deposits into them. The nice part about the bank deposits calculation is that the whole thing relies on third-party records —

those from a bank — which are very complete and all concentrated in one place. If the subject's books and records are unavailable or incomplete, or if he or she is not turning them over, this method will still work.

The bank deposits calculation is as follows:

	Total deposits to all accounts
Less:	Transfers and redeposits
Equals:	Net deposits to all accounts
Plus:	Cash Expenditures
Equals:	Total receipts from all sources
Less:	Funds from known sources
Equals:	Funds from unknown sources

Note that transfers between accounts and the money that is taken out and redeposited are subtracted, because this type of churning doesn't represent income. Also, only expenditures made in cash are considered, because this was money that *wasn't* deposited — it was spent instead. Expenditures made by check are ignored. A good example of a bank deposits analysis appears in the case study on the Lindbergh kidnapping.

A bank deposits case works best if the subject really does have a steady source of income and deposits this money into various bank accounts. It doesn't matter whether the deposits are in cash or some other form; a periodic pattern of deposits creates the inference that the monies came from a regular income-producing activity.

Cash expenditures are established using the following formula:

	Total outlay of funds
Less:	Net bank disbursements (checks)
Equals:	Cash expenditures

Defenses to a bank deposits case include some of the standbys we saw for the other methods:

- Deposits were loans, gifts, or inheritances.
- Deposits were not current income (money hoard).
- Deposits were the spouse's or from some other person or entity.

Another defense to a bank deposits case is the claim that the deposits represent a duplication of current income. All of these defenses should be anticipated and leads followed up to negate them.

UNIT AND VOLUME

If you know how much an item sells for, and you know how many items are sold, you can determine the total sales figure for that item. That's the principle behind the unit and volume method of determining income. It works well for any type of income, including the illegal sort, whether the sales are in cash or otherwise.

The classic case involving the unit and volume method involved a brothel operation in Atlantic City, New Jersey. The investigators knew that each customer was given a towel as part of the service, and they knew what the "service" cost. By going to the laundry, they were able to determine the exact number of towels used by the brothel. The calculation in this case was:

Unit (towel) × Volume (# towels) = Total sales

To come up with a net income figure it would be necessary to account for expenses, such as the prostitutes' wages (and the laundry costs), but the gross income was established. The case agent was IRS Special Agent William Frank, who also did the net worth and bank deposits calculations in the Lindbergh kidnapping case.

This method works quite well in drug cases, too. If you know what the dealer's sales prices are, and you can somehow establish the volume of sales, either through witnesses or the dealer's own records, you can arrive at a gross income figure for the dealer.

This method is best used in situations where the business deals in a limited number of products. (Only one product is even better.) It can also be used as a check against the books and records of the subject or against another method, such as the net worth.

APPLICATION IN MONEY LAUNDERING CASES

Indirect methods of proving income work well in money laundering cases. The direct method, though always preferable, may not be as effective when laundering techniques are used to conceal income or assets. The whole point of a good money laundering scheme is to prevent direct tracing of (dirty) income back to the criminal who made it. Because indirect methods focus on things like assets, purchases, and spending, they're better suited for situations in which secondary sources and circumstantial evidence are needed to put the money in the criminal's hands.

The purpose of all of these indirect methods is to arrive at a bottom line — funds from unknown sources. Once the methods have proved that there are funds from some unknown source and given you an idea about how much money is involved, it's up to the investigator to prove the rest of the money laundering case — that these funds came from a Specified Unlawful Activity.

CRIME OF THE CENTURY — LAUNDERING THE HOTTEST MONEY IN AMERICA

Before the white Bronco and the bloody glove, the details of another "Crime of the Century" captivated the American public. On March 1, 1932, somebody snatched the young son of aviator Charles A. Lindbergh from his nursery in the family's Hopewell, New Jersey, home.

Kidnapping was a more common crime in this era, with great media interest, but the theft of the Lindbergh baby exploded on the American consciousness like a bomb. Indeed, the attention of the entire world was focused on the agony of the Lindbergh family and on the efforts of law enforcement to recover the child and bring the kidnappers to justice.

Although there were a number of leads and substantial physical evidence left at the scene, including a note and a homemade wooden ladder, police initially had little to go on. A ransom demand was made, followed by a lengthy, almost bizarre series of communications with

Bruno Richard Hauptmann.

the self-proclaimed kidnapper. A procession of do-gooders, frauds, intermediaries, and would-be sleuths complicated the payment of the $50,000 ransom, which was finally delivered at a cemetery in New York City on April 2, 1932, a full month after the child's disappearance. Hopes for the baby's safe return were dashed on May 12, when the child's body was found a short distance from the Lindbergh home. The world's attention and outrage immediately turned to finding and punishing the killer.

One wouldn't ordinarily associate financial investigative techniques with a crime like kidnapping. Like most extortionists, kidnappers are caught most often at the ransom drop or at some other point where they are in contact with the victim or the authorities. In fact, as one law enforcement officer noted at the time, the Lindbergh kidnapping was the only one of the period in which the spending of the ransom money led to the suspect's capture.

The police were under overwhelming pressure to solve the case, but the supply of viable leads dwindled quickly, although the media attention did not. Tips were received from around the world, but the investigation centered in New Jersey, where the crime occurred, and New York City, where the ransom was paid. Interagency disputes and jealousies arose, with the result that communications between the New Jersey police, who had all the physical evidence

Figure 10.3 *Gold Certificate, Series 1928. The Lindbergh ransom included more than 3,000 of these distinctive notes, each bearing a gold seal and declaring that the face amount was "in gold coin payable to the bearer on demand." After the May 1, 1933, recall of these notes, they became increasingly conspicuous.*

Figure 10.4 *Searchers at Bruno Richard Hauptmann's garage. Two and a half years after the Lindbergh kidnapping, agents and police finally arrest a suspect and search his Bronx garage, recovering $14,600 in cash, all from the ransom.*

at the crime scene, and authorities in New York broke down.

Although they were fairly certain that the kidnapper lived in their jurisdiction, all the New York officers had to go on was the physical description of the suspect who had collected the ransom, and the ransom money itself. Working with the New York Police Department were agents of the Treasury Department, who had assembled the ransom package, and the Department of Justice, who were about to be given federal jurisdiction over kidnapping cases.

These officers had a significant edge, one that would eventually lead straight to the kidnapper. Before the ransom was paid, Elmer Irey, chief of the Intelligence Unit of the Bureau of Internal Revenue, had insisted that a number of gold certificates be included among the bills given to the kidnapper. Irey knew that gold certificates would be more conspicuous than ordinary Federal Reserve or United States Notes. As a result, two-thirds of the ransom's 4750 bills were gold certificates (see Figure 10.3). Further, over the initial objections of Colonel Lindbergh, and contrary to the instructions of the kidnapper, the serial number of every bill in the ransom package was recorded. Lists of the numbers were distributed to every bank in New York, and Treasury agents visited each branch regularly to remind tellers to check the bills they received against their lists.

The kidnapper wasn't making things easy for those following the money trail. As the bills began to trickle in, beginning shortly after the April 2 ransom payment, it became apparent that the money was being exchanged in small amounts — an average of only $40 per week. The kidnapper was also using the smaller-denomination bills, and not the gold certificates, so that many of the early exchanges were not detected at all. It later became clear that the kidnapper was making small purchases, sometimes as small as six cents, paying with a $10 bill from the ransom, and receiving the "clean" money as change.

The kidnapper was also being extremely careful in where he spent the money. On a pin map, agents recorded the location of every bill recovered. The pins were concentrated in Manhattan and in the Bronx, where the kidnapper was suspected to live. But the person passing the bills avoided exchanging the bills more than once in the same place, or anywhere he was known, and the case dragged on. (See Figure 10.4.)

President Franklin Delano Roosevelt gave the investigators an important break a year later, on April 5, 1933, when he effectively took the country off the gold standard. Roosevelt made it illegal for any American to possess gold bullion, gold coins, or gold certificates. All these items had to be exchanged prior to the May 1 deadline. The investigators knew that the kidnapper still had over $30,000 in gold certificates; hence, an intensive surveillance of New York banks was undertaken by Treasury agents in the days leading up to May 1.

At first, this surveillance appeared to pay off. In the period leading up to the deadline, $15,000 in gold certificates from the ransom money was exchanged. In the largest transaction, a "J. J. Faulkner" of 537 W. 149th Street in New York exchanged $2,980 in gold certificates from the ransom for an equivalent amount of Federal Reserve Notes. After an intense investigation, "J. J. Faulkner" proved to be nonexistent. Because so many people were exchanging gold certificates, the bank employees who handled the transaction were unable to identify the person who had brought in the ransom money. After May 1, the trickle of gold certificates dried up.

A full year later, the notes started reappearing, and the investigators watching the pin map finally got their big break. On September 15, 1934, two and a half years after the kidnapping, a gas station attendant took a $10 gold certificate in payment for 98 cents' worth of gas. As a precaution, he wrote the license number of the customer's car on the bill. The serial number was on the ransom list. Investigators quickly traced the bill back from the bank to the gas station, and then to the customer, Bruno Richard Hauptmann, a German immigrant and carpenter who lived in the Bronx.

Four days later, the police closed in, nabbing Hauptmann as he drove away from his house. On his person was a $20 gold certificate. It, too, was found to be from the ransom money. Back at Hauptmann's house, investigators found more gold certificates — first, a couple that Hauptmann had given his landlady, and then a large stash of the notes, concealed in a secret compartment in Hauptmann's garage (see Figure 10.4). Physical evidence was also recovered, and Hauptmann himself closely resembled the description of the man who picked up the ransom. Investigators were convinced that the kidnapper of the Lindbergh baby had finally been caught. Unable to successfully launder the extremely hot and dirty ransom money, Hauptmann was finally identified through the spending of his loot.

Despite the evidence against him, Hauptmann denied he was the kidnapper, a position he maintained until the very minute New Jersey electrocuted him. The $14,600 in ransom money found in his garage posed a major problem for his lawyers, though; some explanation would have to be found to account for this direct link to the crime. Hauptmann had a simple explanation, a defense he used throughout his trial: a fellow German immigrant, Isidor Fisch, now conveniently dead, gave him the money before Fisch went back to Germany. Hauptmann said he was only holding the money for Fisch and didn't have any idea how his late friend had gotten it.

Investigators decided to do the same type of analysis of Hauptmann's finances that had recently put Al Capone in prison. Two separate indirect methods were used to prove Hauptmann's income: a net worth analysis and the bank deposits method, both developed by the Treasury's Intelligence Unit for use in income tax investigations. You'll recall the simple formula for a net worth analysis:

	Assets
Minus:	Liabilities
Equals:	**Net worth**
Minus:	Prior period's net worth
Equals:	**Increase in net worth from previous period**
Plus:	Known expenses
Equals:	**Total increase in net worth**
Minus:	Funds from known sources
Equals:	**Funds from unknown sources**

In Hauptmann's case, the Treasury agents wanted to find out whether the bottom line — funds from unknown sources — was anything close to $50,000.

A net worth analysis relies on a good starting point, and in Hauptmann's case the agents had a couple of choices. They knew, for example, his exact net worth as of 1923, when he emigrated from Germany to the United States. They also recovered his diaries, in which he meticulously recorded even the smallest financial transactions. These extremely precise entries documented Hauptmann's exact net worth, up to the date on which the ransom was paid.

Agents then went about the task of verifying all of Hauptmann's transactions, going all the way back to the day he arrived in America. His work records were examined, establishing all of his legitimate "funds from known sources." In an interesting coincidence, Hauptmann was found to have been completely unemployed for two and a half years — he'd quit his job and hadn't worked since the day the ransom was delivered.

In concluding his testimony at trial, Treasury Special Agent William Frank reported that since coming to America, Richard Hauptmann had spent or owned $49,950.44 over and above his income from "known sources," as demonstrated by the net worth analysis. Hauptmann's net worth increase from unknown sources was just $49.56 less than the Lindbergh ransom.

Hauptmann's lawyers had no effective rebuttal for these figures and no explanation for the unaccounted wealth, although they tried to confuse the jurors about how the calculation was made. But if the net worth assessment was bad news, the bank deposits analysis was even worse. The standard formula for a bank deposits analysis is as follows:

	Total deposits to all accounts
Minus:	Transfers and redeposits
Equals:	**Net deposits to all accounts**
Plus:	Cash expenditures
Equals:	**Total receipts from all sources**
Minus:	Known sources of funds
Equals:	**Funds from unknown sources**

Investigators modified the formula slightly in Hauptmann's case in order to account for the $14,600 in ransom money found in his garage, and in performing the analysis on Hauptmann's expenditures, Special Agent Frank reviewed only the period following the ransom payment. When Frank was finished, he concluded that in the two and a half years after the ransom delivery, Hauptmann had deposited or handled $49,986.00, getting to within $14.00 of the entire ransom amount. The actual calculations performed in the Hauptmann case appear in Figure 10.5 for anyone who might be interested in a practical application of financial investigative techniques in a capital case.

After Hauptmann's trial, the jury foreman commented on the impact of this evidence on the jury's thinking. Equally damaging was the effect of financial evidence on Hauptmann's defense. Simply put, Hauptmann blamed everything on the dead guy. His friend, Isidor Fisch, had returned to Germany in 1933, but before he left he entrusted a package to Hauptmann's care, Hauptmann said. Later, Hauptmann accidentally knocked the package down and found it contained money. These were the bills police found in his garage. He also claimed that he had kept a cash hoard, money he had earned before April 1932. The money for all of his cash purchases had come from this hoard.

The investigators knew in advance about what would become known as "Hauptmann's Fisch story," so they did another financial investigation, this one on the dead Fisch. The probe didn't take long. Fisch had died destitute in Germany, and they found no evidence that he had ever possessed any significant amount of money while in America. In fact, investigators found a letter from Hauptmann to Fisch's family in Germany, in which Hauptmann asked for repayment of $5500 *Hauptmann* had loaned to *Fisch*. This inconvenient disclosure caused the kidnapper considerable discomfort under cross-examination.

In another demonstration of how critical was this evidence, Hauptmann spent 17 hours on the witness stand, 11 under cross-examination. As much as three quarters of his testimony related to the financial evidence against him. In the end, he could not explain away any of the damning testimony of the financial investigators or the presence of all those gold certificates in his garage.

Hauptmann maintained his innocence to the very end. Recent books and a movie have questioned the jury's verdict, but the financial facts remain utterly unchallenged. The money that Bruno Richard Hauptmann was unable to laun-

Total Deposits to All Accounts

September 15, 1932	$170.00	Cash	Steiner Rouse (securities account)
September 19, 1932	582.50	Cash	Steiner Rouse
October 7, 1932	860.00	Cash	Steiner Rouse
February 27, 1933	700.00	Cash	Steiner Rouse
March 1, 1933	850.00	Cash	Steiner Rouse
March 15, 1933	1,250.00	Cash	Central Savings Bank
April 28, 1933	2,500.00	Cash	Steiner Rouse
May 3, 1933	2,575.00	Cash	Steiner Rouse
June 7, 1933	2,225.00	Cash	Steiner Rouse
July 24, 1933	4,500.00	Cash	Steiner Rouse
January 3, 1934	80.00	Check	Steiner Rouse
February 26, 1934	1,350.00	Cash	Steiner Rouse
Miscellaneous deposits	9,600.00	Cash	Both accounts[1]
Total deposits	$27,242.50		

Transfers and Re-deposits

February 27, 1933	$500.00	Trans.	Central Savings Bank – Steiner Rouse
March 15, 1933	1,250.00	Trans.	Steiner Rouse – Central Savings Bank
February 26, 1934	1,350.00	Redeposit	
Total transfers, redeposits	$3,100.00		

Cash Expenditures

May 1932	$396.00	Radio set
July 1932	126.00	Field glasses
July 1932	706.00	Trip to Europe for wife, Anna
September 1932	150.00	Hunting trip, Maine
October 1932	150.00	Hunting trip, New Jersey
October 1932	56.00	Hunting rifle
February 1933	100.00	Trip to Florida
March 1933	190.00	Investment advice
July 1933	150.00	Vacation
August 1933	109.00	Fishing canoe
July 1934	200.00	Vacation, Long Island
August 1934	5.50	Shoes for wife, Anna
1932–1934	9,185.00	Assorted documented purchases[2]
Total expenditures	$11,323.50	

Ransom Cash on Hand

September 19, 1934	$14,600.00

Figure 10.5 Bank deposits analysis: Bruno Richard Hauptmann.

	Funds from Known Sources	
January 3, 1934	$80.00	Dividend check, securities account

	Bank Deposits Calculation	
	Total deposits to all accounts:	$27,242.50
Minus:	Transfers and redeposits	3,100.00
Equals:	**Net deposits to all accounts**	**24,142.50**
Plus:	Cash expenditures[3]	25,923.50
Equals:	**Total receipts from all sources**	**50,066.00**
Minus:	Funds from known sources	80.00
Equals:	**Funds from unknown sources**	**$49,986.00**

[1] Hauptmann made numerous small deposits, often in silver coins, which he apparently received in change for his many exchanges of ransom bills.

[2] A number of small purchases were noted in Hauptmann's diaries. Receipts documented others, and the expenses of raising the couple's young son, Mannfried, were also recorded.

[3] Includes the $14,600 in Lindbergh ransom money found on Hauptmann's person, in his home, and in the garage hiding place.

Figure 10.5 Continued.

der tripped him up and ultimately sent him to the electric chair.

The Lindbergh kidnapping case provides graphic evidence of the power of the financial investigative technique. Several key points are especially worth remembering: First, Hauptmann initially got away with the crime, successfully taking the baby and eluding authorities at the ransom drop. Second, Hauptmann was well aware of the need to successfully launder the very distinct proceeds of his crime. He developed a placement scheme, one that worked well for over two years, but ultimately he could not distance himself from the tainted funds. Third, although other investigative techniques failed, the financial investigation tied Hauptmann inextricably to the ransom — not just the $14,600 found in his garage, but also the bills that were placed into circulation. In a case in which eyewitness identifications and even physical evidence were shaky, the reliability of the financial evidence was absolute.

Finally, the financial investigation severely limited Hauptmann's defense options and ultimately impeached the only defense he had. He was never able to offer any plausible explanation for his possession and use of those "funds from unknown sources," and this failure cost Bruno Richard Hauptmann his life.

Perhaps the most telling comment on the quality of the financial evidence was made by the New Jersey Court of Errors and Appeals, which voted unanimously to reject Hauptmann's appeal. Justice Charles W. Parker wrote:

> Our conclusion is that the verdict is not only not contrary to the weight of the evidence, but one to which the evidence inescapably led. From three different and, in the main, unrelated sources the proofs point unerringly to guilt *viz:* (*a*) *possession and use of the ransom money;* (*b*) *handwriting of the ransom notes;* and (*c*) *wood used in the construction of the ladder.* (Emphasis added)

Bruno Richard Hauptmann was executed at the New Jersey State Prison at Trenton on April

3, 1936, four years and a day after the delivery of the ransom money that would ultimately condemn him.

For anyone who might be interested in following in Special Agent Frank's footsteps, the original Hauptmann analysis appears in Figure 10.5. Keep two key dates in mind: April 2, 1932, when the $50,000 ransom was paid, and April 5, 1933, when it was announced that all gold certificates were being called in by the federal government. Figures are taken from the original case, with some consolidation and editing for brevity's sake. Steiner Rouse & Company was Hauptmann's stockbroker, where he maintained an account and did as much as $50,000 per month in trades. Central Savings Bank was the Bronx institution where Hauptmann had a joint savings account with his wife, Anna, for about eight years.

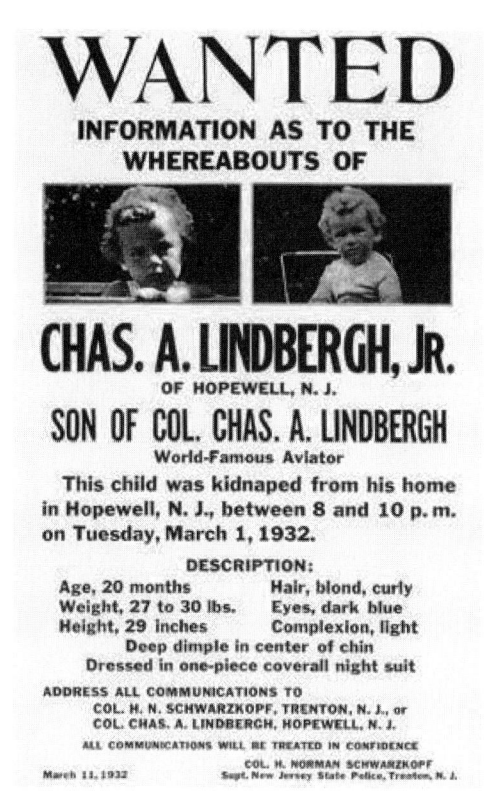

"Wanted" poster for the Lindbergh kidnapper.

CHAPTER 11

BUSINESS OPERATIONS

"He's a businessman. I'll make him an offer he can't refuse."
Mario Puzo, *The Godfather*

"A corporation is just like any natural person, except that it has no pants to kick or soul to damn, and by God, it ought to have both."
Anonymous

There are millions of businesses operating in America today. Some are fronts for criminals or money launderers, needing some pants to kick. Others are fine, upstanding organizations, chock full of useful information for the financial investigator. Some businesses are owned by one person, whereas others have literally hundreds of thousands of owners.

Why do we need to know about business organization and operation? Because businesses generate the records that allow us to do a financial investigation. We have to know where to go for these records, what they look like, and how we can pry them loose from their makers. The other reason is that one of the only two real money laundering scams that exist in the world today is based upon a business front or cover.

Law enforcement people (and the rest of the population generally) often don't have a very clear conception of how businesses work. We know they exist by selling things, of course, but how they function internally and what legal constraints they operate under is something most people don't know or care to know.

And why should we? After all, as long as the store's open, do we care if its parent company is some corporation in Delaware or Hong Kong? It may not be important to Joe or Jane Customer, but in a money laundering case, the answer may be critical. The answer may dictate whether you get the records you need, or whether the whole business entity can be charged with some substantive crime.

There are three basic types of business organization that are recognized in the American legal system. These are:

- Proprietorship
- Partnership
- Corporation

PROPRIETORSHIPS

Proprietorships, also known as sole or single proprietorships, are established, owned, and operated by one person. Responsibility for the legal and business decisions of the business rest with the proprietor, who answers only to him- or herself.

Although no laws specify the size or scope of a sole proprietorship, they tend to be small, localized, and less complex than partnerships or corporations. Seventy percent of businesses in America today are small and operate as sole proprietorships. For that matter, most criminal operations fit this profile as well — very few criminals run down to the Secretary of State's office and incorporate their auto theft ring or cat burglary enterprise.

For income tax purposes, the law recognizes a sole proprietorship as the individual taxpayer him- or herself. There is no tax on the business entity, only on the proprietor. After all, in this type of organization, all of the business profits are owned by the proprietor. That is one of the advantages of being a sole proprietor: anything that comes in is yours.

The flip side, of course, is that you have unlimited personal liability for all of the business debts. This fact alone leads many sole proprietors to incorporate, putting a little distance between themselves and unlimited debt.

Other advantages include the freedom you have — not having to ask a bunch of shareholders or a board of directors for permission to do something. The business is very easily formed, a process that may be as simple as registering a trade name, and it is as easily dissolved. The proprietor just quits. Also, when the proprietor dies, so does the business.

Business entities are often associated with abbreviations characterizing their type, such as Inc. for "Incorporated." The abbreviation that designates a proprietorship is "dba" or "doing business as." For example, "John Madinger, dba ML Services."

From an investigative standpoint, these businesses present some problems. For one thing, if the business *is* the owner, he or she probably has some Fifth Amendment rights with regard to disclosing records. At the very least, the owner can claim this privilege as to the records he or she maintains that tend to incriminate him or her. We'll look at some court decisions that address this claim; it can come up in your case.

The freedom sole proprietors have can cause other problems. Because they aren't answerable to partners or shareholders, they can be more flexible in their accounting methods. Their books and records need only be good enough to satisfy themselves and IRS.

Anyone who enters into a business and doesn't designate the type of organization is automatically considered a sole proprietor.

PARTNERSHIPS

Partnerships are the next step up in terms of complexity. As the name implies, two or more people agree to go into business together. Partnerships are usually formed because two heads — and two wallets — are better than one. Whereas a sole proprietor has only his or her own resources on which to draw, partners each bring capital, skills, or other resources to the business.

Like proprietorships, partnerships are easy to set up, although there is a legal framework in place, designed mostly to protect the partners from each other. An important part of this framework is the Uniform Partnership Act (UPA), which has been adopted by all of the states except Louisiana. The UPA defines a partnership as "an association of two or more persons to carry on as co-owners of a business for profit." The UPA is the controlling authority for the establishment and operation of partnerships, and it sets the broad rules partnerships will follow.

The rules governing a specific partnership are set by the articles of partnership, also known as the partnership agreement. This agreement is significant because it gives the partnership life, describes how it will be operated, and provides for the expiration or termination of the business (see Figure 11.1).

All of this is designed to prevent the disagreements that often accompany human relationships. The UPA is based on English common law, which in turn is based on Roman law, in which the concept of partnerships was understood. The Romans also understood the need to regulate their operations.

A partnership agreement establishes the relationship between the partners and their business. Each partner is a co-owner of the business, with a right to share in the profits and losses. Each has a voice in the management of the affairs of the partnership and co-owns the business assets. How much of a share and how much voice are specified in the agreement.

The partnership agreement is required to set out clearly what this business is, who is involved, what their responsibilities are, where the money

> **LIMITED PARTNERSHIP AGREEMENT**
>
> Alphonse Capone, referred to as GENERAL PARTNER, and Ralph Capone and Jake Guzik, referred to as LIMITED PARTNERS, agree:
>
> 1. That they herewith form a limited partnership under the laws of the state of Illinois, under the name of **ALPHONSE CAPONE SECOND HAND FURNITURE, LTD.**
> 2. The purpose of the partnership is to engage in the business of Beverage Sales and to have all powers necessary or useful to engage in business described. Without limitation this shall include the power to own, sell, or lease property.
> 3. The principal place of business shall be Lexington Hotel, Michigan Avenue at 22nd Street, Chicago, Illinois.
> 4. The partnership term begins on the date of this Agreement and shall continue until December 31, 1940, when it shall dissolve under the terms of this Agreement.
> 5. Each partner has contributed, or will contribute by October 14, 1929, the amount shown next to their signature to this Agreement.
> 6. Limited partners shall not be required to contribute additional capital.
> 7. Each partner shall have a capital account that includes invested capital plus that partner's allocations of net income, minus that partner's allocations of net loss and share of distributions.
>
>   Net income and net loss shall be allocated as follows:
>
>   a. 80 percent to the General Partner
>
>   b. 20 percent to the Limited Partners, according to their respective percentage ownership interests
> 8. Except as otherwise expressly stated in this Agreement, the General Partner shall manage the partnership business and have exclusive control over the partnership business, including the power to sign deeds, notes, mortgages, deeds of trust, contracts, and leases, and direction of business operations.
> 9. The limited partners shall have all powers which may lawfully be granted to limited partners under the laws of the State of Illinois.
>
> **Accounting**
>
> 10. The partnership's tax or fiscal year shall be a calendar year. The General Partner shall make any tax election necessary for completion of the partnership tax return.
> 11. A limited partner may assign his or her rights to receive distributions, net income, and net loss to any person without causing a dissolution of this partnership. No assignment will be effective until the general partner is notified in writing of the same.
> 12. This agreement may only be amended by the written agreement of all Partners.
> 13. This instrument contains the entire Agreement of the parties and any modifications shall be required to be in writing and signed by the parties affected by the modification, or who have the right to cause the change.
>
> Dated: February 14, 1929
>
> | Name & Address | Capital Contribution | Percentage Interest |
> |---|---|---|
> | Alphonse Capone | $ — | 80 |
> | Ralph Capone | 10,000 | 10 |
> | Jake Guzik | 10,000 | 10 |

Figure 11.1 Partnership agreement.

comes from, and where it goes. In the agreement, an example of which follows, you will find:

- Name of the partnership
- Names of the partners
- Location and type of business the partnership will be conducting
- Effective date of formation and a termination date
- Agreement as to the assets initially contributed by the partners to start the business
- Duties and responsibilities of the partners with respect to operation of the business
- Provisions for compensation and the distribution of profits, losses, and liabilities

In each of these areas there is flexibility, and the agreement can be broadened or narrowed to provide for the needs of one partner or another. For example, in a situation where one partner has a lot of money but no interest in making day-to-day decisions about the company, the agreement could allow for the income to be divided on a 50–50 basis, even though the other partner's contribution was less. The agreement puts everything out front, so the partners know where they stand with each other.

Like proprietorships, partnerships are not taxed separately. The income distributed to the partners is reported by them and taxed according to their share of the profits. Partnerships, unlike proprietorships, do file returns with IRS, however, these only provide information about the distributions.

Partnerships fall into one of two legal categories recognized by statute:

- General partnerships
- Limited partnerships

General partnerships are the more common type. They are less complicated, with the characteristics of the old common law partnership entities. In a general partnership, the partners have unlimited liability for any debts or legal obligations. Each partner also has a fiduciary duty, like a trustee in a trust, to act in the best interests of the partnership and his or her partners. This implies some other restrictions on partners' conduct. For example, partners cannot self-deal or profit at the partnership's expense, operate in competition with it, or use partnership assets or resources for a personal, nonpartnership purpose.

All of these restrictions serve to establish the partnership as a legal entity, separate and apart from the individuals who agreed to form it. Those people get some rights, along with the responsibilities, such as the right to a share of the profits and repayment of their initial contributions. General partners also have an equal say in business decisions, unless the agreement says otherwise.

Depending on what the agreement says, decisions are made by voting, either on a majority or unanimous basis. By statute, some decisions, such as whether to admit a new partner, amend the agreement, or assign partnership property to a third party, require a unanimous vote.

Partnerships can be dissolved by agreement, or they may terminate automatically upon completion of the business purpose (e.g., sale of a piece of property) or upon the withdrawal or death of a partner.

Limited partnerships were created to limit the liability found in a general partnership. This type of partnership has two kinds of partners: limited and general. The limited partners come into the business with capital. In return for their money, they receive a share of the profits, their *distribution*. If the business loses money, the limited partners can lose their entire investment, but that's it.

A limited partnership can have as many limited partners as the agreement (or state law) permits, but it has to have at least one general partner, who actually runs the business. This person still has potential for unlimited personal liability.

States pass laws governing these arrangements and outlining how much or little the partners can do. If a limited partner starts getting too involved in the business, he or she could lose limited status and become liable for any debts.

This comes up when a partnership loses a lot of money and goes out of business, and creditors go looking for a general partner, who can't be found. Then the creditors go looking for a limited partner who was making decisions or acting beyond his or her role.

For investigators, the partnership is a little like a proprietorship and a little like a corporation. The business records of a partnership belong to the business, not the partners. Partnerships do not have Fifth Amendment rights like an individual, but the partners themselves can assert those rights. In most cases, production of records will probably be compelled over the objection. In fact, one partner can be compelled to testify about the others.

If you are looking for the records of a third party, someone with whom the partnership has done business, the subpoena needs to be served on a general partner, because the limited partners are not supposed to be involved in operations to the extent of handing over records. Partnerships may have appointed officers or employees who are responsible for the preparation and custody of records. These people can also be served.

Partnership records are more complex than those for a proprietorship. Not only do the partners have to account for their actions to each other, they've got IRS to report to as well.

When you are looking at a partnership from the outside, as when you suspect it might be a front for money laundering, you will need to start with the partnership agreement. This will list all of the partners and their roles. It will also provide some idea about their contributions and outline the plan for distributions. Because limited partners are supposed to contribute the capital, and general partners the management, if the agreement shows a limited partner contributing little or no capital but exercising a decision-making function or even a disproportionate voting share, something could be wrong with the picture.

General Record Information

Annual reports for the partnership may be on file with the state. Records of distributions made by the partnership are technically tax returns and can be obtained from IRS via an *ex parte* court order.

Some partnerships keep minutes of meetings and votes taken. The larger a partnership is, the more likely there will be some written record of this decision-making process. Also, larger partnerships may have their business audited independently every so often. The accounting firm conducting these audits could be a good source of information.

One of the big advantages for a partnership over a proprietorship is that getting credit is easier. The credit rating of a partnership is established by ratings services, such as Standard and Poor and Dun & Bradstreet. Even if you've subpoenaed one of the credit bureaus that rates individuals, you may have missed the partnership's credit information.

Terms Used in Connection with Partnerships

Partnerships are permitted to use several terms in their business name to denote their status as a partnership. The most common of these is "Ltd.," as in *Pacific Laundering Ltd.* "Partners" is also used, as in *Pacific Laundering Partners.*

Other initials you'll see are "L.P.," which denotes a limited partnership. One of the most common of these is a Real Estate Limited Partnership, or RELP, which is formed to take advantage of some real estate transaction or property.

CORPORATIONS

Unlike proprietorships and partnerships, corporations are legal entities, recognized by law as fictional "persons" sanctioned by the state. The word "corporation" comes from "corpus" or body. And so it is — a completely separate legal body, distinct from its owners.

A relatively recent development in business, corporations have several advantages over the other forms of business. The biggest is that the owners of the company have no personal responsibility for the corporation's debts — their liability is limited.

The first step in the creation of a corporation is the filing of *articles of incorporation* with the state in which the corporation is to be domiciled. These articles are filed with the Secretary of State or Registrar of Corporations for the state, who will then approve the creation of the new business. The state agencies registering corporations have various names, although most are found in the Secretary of State's office. You can obtain a list of these offices or find out where corporations register in various states at the Web site of the National Association of Secretaries of State, http://www.nass.org.

The states that allow the creation of this new "person" have varying rules regarding liability and operation. Some states are more restrictive, while others, notably Delaware, have very favorable conditions for business. A large number of American corporations are formed in Delaware, even though they may do little or no business in that state.

The articles of incorporation set out how the company will be formed, what business it will do, where its headquarters will be, and who will own and run it. The articles also contain a phrase stating that the corporation will have perpetual existence, something that neither persons nor proprietorships or partnerships can enjoy. All of this information, when accepted by the state, becomes public record and is available for review and inspection by anyone who cares to check it out. A document known as a *corporate charter* is issued, and the corporation officially exists.

The articles of incorporation are only the first of many documents the corporation will be required to keep. This is one of the disadvantages to incorporating — it is far more complicated a proposition than a sole proprietorship.

The corporation, as a legal entity comprised of its owners, is mandated to behave independently of those owners. If a business decision is made, it is the decision or action of the corporation, not the individual owners. Each of those owners has a share in the outcome, but it's the corporation that reaps the benefits or takes the loss.

Owners of a corporation are known as *shareholders*, and they are given evidence of their share of the ownership in the form of stock certificates. Each of these certificates represents a piece of the corporation, with the owner's total representing his or her share of the whole pie. The articles of incorporation specify how many shares are to be issued initially and the value of these certificates. If more shares are to be issued, a decision will have to be taken by the Board of Directors or the shareholders themselves, who meet to vote on this kind of move.

These features are unique to corporations. Shareholders have whatever voting rights are established for them in the articles of incorporation and another document of public record, the *corporate bylaws*. When the corporation is first created, the creators can appoint officers and directors. Directors can later appoint officers to run the corporation, but only the shareholders get to pick the directors. This may be done in an annual meeting, another requirement of state law.

Summing up, a corporation:

- Is a legal entity, separate and distinct from its owners
- Has continuous or perpetual existence, again, apart from its owners
- Is owned by its shareholders, operated by the directors they appoint, and managed by the officers selected by the directors

Figure 11.2 shows a corporate organizational chart, and Figure 11.3 shows an organizational chart of a corporate accounting department.

Corporate Advantages and Disadvantages

The big advantage enjoyed by corporations is the limit to the owners' liability for debts incurred by the business. Their liability is limited to the amount of money they invested. If I bought $100 in stock in a corporation, and that business went bankrupt the next day, owing billions, I'd be out my $100, but somebody else — the corporation itself — would be responsible for paying the creditors.

Other advantages include:

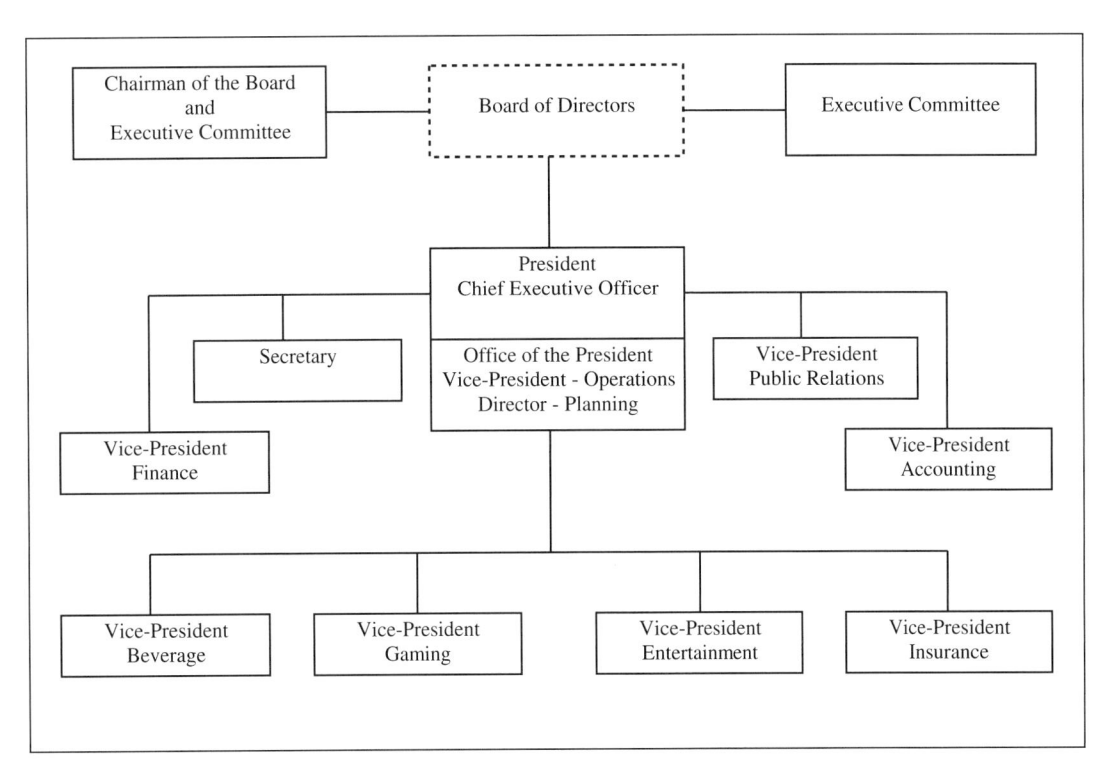

Figure 11.2 A corporate organizational chart.

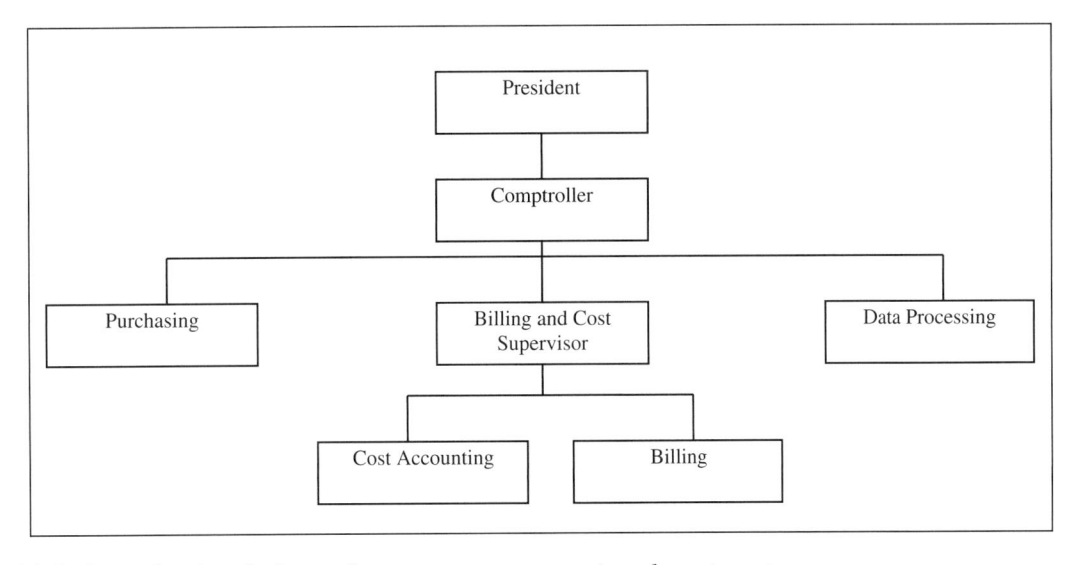

Figure 11.3 Organizational chart of a corporate accounting department.

- Corporations have a broader financial base and are more attractive to lenders than other types of businesses.
- Ownership is easily transferred.
- The business outlives the owners.

However, the corporate structure also has disadvantages. As a separate legal person, a corporation gets taxed like one — and maybe at a higher rate than its owners would pay. Although corporations can take advantage of all sorts of pension, profit-sharing, and stock option plans to lower their taxes, not only must they file an annual corporate income tax return, they also pay as much as 46% in taxes on their income. This has something to do with the fact that, unlike people, corporations don't vote, but it's also recognition that the state is giving the corporation a special status and expects something in return.

Those who might be considering forming a corporation face another concern. The government regulates corporations closely and imposes other legal restrictions on corporate operations. These have always been quite extensive, and after the Enron, WorldCom, and other corporate scandals of recent years, they have become even more restrictive. This is, once again, recognition that the corporation enjoys special legal status, so it has special legal responsibilities.

For the Investigator

A corporation gets to enjoy some of the rights of a real person, but not all of them. This is good news for a financial investigator, because a corporation has no privilege against self-incrimination; corporate records are not protected by the Fifth Amendment. Corporations large and small have challenged court rulings on this point to no avail. If you subpoena their records, they're probably going to have to cough them up.

This applies even to small corporations established by individuals under Subchapter S of Section 1362 of the Internal Revenue Code. These so-called S corporations are small, and the law allows them to be taxed as partnerships would be. In many cases, an S corporation has only one or two stockholders.

In these corporations, the distinction between the owners and the corporation is very fine. The courts have ruled, however, that even if only one person owns all of the stock, the corporate records must be produced. In *Braswell v. United States*, 487 U.S. 99, 108 S.Ct. 2284 (1984), the court held that the collective entry doctrine prevented Braswell from claiming Fifth Amendment protection for his corporate records. Braswell was the sole shareholder of the corporation, as well as the custodian of records.

This is very significant, because corporations, just like people, can be held criminally liable for their conduct. And remember, corporations are frequently used in money laundering schemes, as fronts or instruments of the launderer, which means you may be able to compel the corporation to produce records and then use them to indict the same business.

Corporate Criminal Liability

The question of corporate liability in criminal cases is really several questions, because all corporations involve several persons or entities. You have to answer these questions because, while you can't put a corporation in jail, a big fine or a multimillion-dollar forfeiture may be at stake.

Another very significant point for an investigator in a money laundering case is that although the corporation cannot take any actions on its own, the acts of its agents, executives, officers, or employees may be imputed or carried over to the corporation itself. The general rule is that if any of these people are acting on behalf of the corporation, the corporation may be liable. The higher the degree of control the corporate agent has, the more likely the corporation will be liable for his or her acts.

For example, say a car dealership, Cars Inc., is suspected of laundering money by selling cars to drug dealers for cash and not reporting the transactions. If an undercover investigation established that this was true, the actions of the employees could be imputed to the corporation itself. This would be less likely to happen if a lot-boy or salesman were committing the crime on behalf of the corporation, but more likely if a manager, director, or officer of the corporation were doing so.

In deciding whether the corporation — as opposed to its employees — is criminally liable, the courts will look at whether the employees:

- Were acting within the scope of their authority
- Had the purpose of benefiting the corporation
- Had the capacity to involve the corporation in the conduct, regardless of the employee's status in the corporate hierarchy

If you don't think this scares some corporate executives, think again. This is precisely why car dealerships and other cash businesses have set up training programs for their employees, and why banks have established extensive compliance programs to make sure that their employees understand and follow Bank Secrecy Act requirements. None of them want to follow in the footsteps of the Bank of New England, which was convicted for failing to file Currency Transaction Reports (CTRs) on cash withdrawals by certain customers. In this case, the jury found that the individual employees were acting within the scope of their employment for the bank in failing to properly report the transactions, and that they did so to benefit the bank. It also ruled that the corporation could still be criminally liable, even though higher-level employees or executives didn't know what their subordinates were up to.

In this decision, the appeals court wrote:

> The acts of a corporation are, after all, simply the acts of all of its employees operating within the scope of their employment. The law on corporate criminal liability reflects this. Similarly, the knowledge obtained by corporate employees acting within the scope of their employment is imputed to the corporation. Corporations compartmentalize knowledge, subdividing the elements of specific duties and operations into smaller components. The aggregate of those components constitutes the corporation's knowledge of a particular operation. It is irrelevant whether employees administering one component of an operation know the specific activities of employees administering another aspect of the operation. *(United States of America v. Bank of New England,* 821 F.2d 844 (1st Cir. 1987))

In the example of the car dealership, let's say that a salesman agreed to sell a car for cash and not report the transaction. He's acting on behalf of the corporation and has the purpose of selling a car, which definitely benefits the business. He's also acting within the scope of his employment. Already, Cars Inc. has problems.

These problems will be compounded if the next management level up either ratifies or acquiesces in the conduct. In this case, even if the salesman were acting outside the scope of his duties, the management, by not filing the required report, could be ratifying the salesman's actions, making the corporation liable. See *Continental Baking Co. v. United States,* 281 F.2d 137 (6th Cir. 1960).

At this point, Cars Inc. had better have a pretty effective compliance program in place, and it should be taking it seriously, because the courts have ruled against corporations that were "indifferent to the illegal practices of (their) employees" despite the existence of a criminal compliance program. See *United States v. Beusch,* 596 F.2d 871 (9th Cir. 1979).

You can see that this liability could extend to any number of criminal enterprises in which a corporation is involved. The use of a building or business as a drug distribution center could implicate the corporation if its agents are involved in the activity. Because corporations are used so often in money laundering schemes, they, too, are vulnerable to the filing of criminal charges and to forfeiture of corporate assets and even its corporate charter.

See Table 11.1 for a comparison of business organizations.

OTHER BUSINESS ENTITIES

Most of the other business types or entities you'll encounter will be variations of the Big Three. Still, it's nice to know what people are talking about when they mention some sort of business or other.

Holding corporation — A holding corporation is established to hold or own another business. This is a very common practice in the banking business, where bank holding corporations are allowed to do some things banks — even the one they own — are not. Holding corporations can be used in money laundering schemes to control other companies in a series of interlocking or networked entities. Tracing these sorts of connections can be difficult and time consuming, especially if some are …

TABLE 11.1
Comparison of Business Organizations

Sole Proprietorship	General Partnership	Corporation
Advantages		
Ownership of all profits	Larger capital resources than sole proprietorship	Limited liability of stockholders
Ease of organization	Better credit standing than single individual	Very large capital resources
Freedom of action	More managerial talent than single individual	Ease of transfer of ownership
Minimum of legal restrictions	Few legal restrictions	Long or perpetual life
Maximum personal incentive	High degree of personal incentive	Ease of expansion
No tax on the business entity	No tax on the business entity	Some federal tax incentives
Ease of dissolution	Ease of dissolution	
Disadvantages		
Unlimited liability for business debts	Unlimited liability for business debts	Tax on business income
Limited capital resources	Existence ends with death or withdrawal of partner	Expenses of incorporation
Business ends with death of the proprietor	Restricted transfer of organization ownership	Extensive legal restrictions and regulations

Source: Financial Investigations, Internal Revenue Service

Foreign corporation — In the corporate world, "foreign" doesn't always mean offshore. A foreign corporation is one with a headquarters outside the state in which it is operating. A domestic corporation is one that has its charter in the state where it operates. If I incorporate in Delaware, I am a domestic corporation in that state; I would register as a foreign corporation in Hawaii. Foreign corporations have to establish a registered agent and presence in the state, and many businesses, especially in Delaware, are set up to provide this service. You get an address, an agent, and a periodic reminder that your annual report is due. Some states actively solicit businesses to incorporate there, offering special deals, easy registration, and even some privacy or freedom from the sort of scrutiny other states might insist upon. Delaware is a good example, as are Nevada and Wyoming.

Offshore corporation — Anything outside the United States is offshore. Foreign countries have completely different laws with regard to company formation, and some have extensive provisions for secrecy in corporate formation. These may include nondisclosure of company officers, shareholders, or owners. In some cases, offshore corporations may be "bearer share," meaning that whoever has possession of the shares is the owner. The registered agent for a bearer share corporation — an attorney or some other person — may not even know who the bearer is, making the tracing of this type of business very difficult. Certain jurisdictions are noted for the ease with which offshore corporations can be set up; these include the Isle of Man, Panama, Gibraltar, Bermuda, the Bahamas, the Netherlands Antilles, Hong Kong, Luxembourg, and Switzerland. Now that the Internet is here, much of this process can be handled from your home computer for a few hundred dollars.

Shell corporation — Shell corporations are a mainstay of money laundering schemes everywhere. The shell corporation has no assets and no liabilities, just a charter to operate. It is easy to set up, can be interlocked all over the place with other shells, and, if established someplace with secrecy laws, can make it almost impossible to identify the owners or directors. Being a shell isn't always a bad thing; these corporations are sometimes established by big companies in order to do a specific business deal in a foreign location or to enable them to move quickly in a jurisdiction.

Nonprofit corporation — Nonprofits get special tax breaks because they are not in business to make money. Their employees are still taxed, but these charitable businesses are not. They undergo a lot of regulatory scrutiny, just in case they are treading too close to the "for-profit" line. If so, they jeopardize losing their status. These entities have gotten a lot more scrutiny after 9/11, as the government has looked at, and in some cases even indicted, charitable foundations and other nonprofits that were alleged to be fronts for terrorist financing. You can't use a for-profit corporation for an illegal purpose, such as money laundering or terror financing, and you can't use a nonprofit that way either.

Cooperative — Cooperatives are based on shares, like a corporation, but the shares do not represent ownership. In a cooperative, a share of the profits is distributed based on the amount of business the shareholder does with the cooperative. Co-ops are set up to pool resources, and they typically exist in connection with farming communities, apartment buildings, and small businesses.

Syndicate — Yes, there is *that* kind of syndicate, but legitimate people form them, too, creating an investment group to involve themselves in a specific venture or development. Very similar to a partnership, a syndicate often has a lifespan limited to the completion of the investment purpose. Often unregistered and unregulated, syndicates have to be closely held. If they offer the investment opportunity to the public, they may be required to register as securities dealers and to register the investment as well.

Joint venture — A joint venture is a partnership created for a limited venture or enterprise. Corporations can get involved in these, too, so you might see a joint venture comprised of perhaps two corporations and a couple of individuals to develop a property or a computer program.

Mutual company — Used in the insurance industry, the mutual company is like a corporation, but it does not have stockholders. Rather, it is owned by its policyholders (or depositors, in the case of a mutual savings bank). Heard of *Mutual of Omaha's Wild Kingdom?* Profits of mutual companies are distributed based on the size of the policy or deposit.

Franchise — A franchise is a business arrangement in which a big company, A, establishes a continuing relationship with another business, B, to sell A's products or services. A, the franchisor, owns the product, service, or method and licenses B, the franchisee, to market it, in exchange for various considerations. These may include a franchising fee, a monthly royalty, and an advertising fee. In exchange, the franchisor provides training, equipment, expertise, supplies, and, most important, its name. It may also guarantee the franchisee exclusive rights to a certain territory or area. McDonald's Corporation, king of the franchises and one of the world's best-known brands, charges a minimum initial franchise fee of $12,500, monthly royalties of 12%, and an advertising fee of 4%. This is a fraction of the cost of starting a McDonald's restaurant, however, which is estimated at $500,000 to $1 million. An amazing number of businesses are franchises, many of which are exactly the type of cash-intensive enterprises perfectly suited for the placement of currency. A money laundering scheme could make good use of a franchise fast-food outlet, service business, or even chain hotel property. The trick is to remember that the owner of a Pizza Hut may own everything in the building, but he or she is leasing the right to use the name from Pizza Hut. (Which is, in turn, owned by Pepsi Corporation.) Any franchisor will have plenty of information about its franchisees and will be none too happy to hear that one is suspected in some criminal scheme.

Société anonyme — You would expect that other countries, with other legal systems, would have different business forms. The differences are mostly in name. One of these is the *société anonyme,* abbreviated S.A. Originally, this entity was a partnership in which all of the partners were anonymous but one, and their liability was limited. In England it was the equivalent of a chartered company or corporation. The "S.A." suffix can be found after the names of many foreign corporations. It's essentially the French equivalent of "Inc." The Spanish equivalent is *sociedad anónima,* which in Spanish and Mexican law means simply a business corporation.

SUMMING UP

Businesses are tremendous sources of records of value to a financial investigation. Not only do businesses keep records relating to their own affairs, they also have all sorts of information about third parties, one of whom might be the subject of your investigation.

Getting these records is the subject of another chapter, but for now, understand that no business today can function without generating massive amounts of data, on paper, and, increasingly, in computerized form. The business may, in fact, have so much data that it will have a difficult time locating whatever it is you need. (Try asking for a copy of an airline ticket when all you have is the passenger's name.)

Businesses are also used in money laundering schemes, and, indeed, in all manner of frauds and criminal activity. A business provides a perfect cover to explain illegal income — businesses exist to make money, after all. They are useful in the placement stage of a money laundering operation, to infiltrate the criminal proceeds from the cash transaction system to the business or financial system.

Various business forms, such as corporations and S.A.s, can be used to layer laundered funds, concealing the ownership and control of the money via a series of difficult-to-trace financial transactions.

Finally, the laundered funds can be integrated back into the economy through a business controlled by the launderer, completing the money laundering cycle.

CHAPTER 12

DOMESTIC BANKING

"It's where the money is."
Bank robber Willie Sutton, when asked why he robbed banks.
(He later claimed that a reporter made this quote up.)

*"When Cato was asked what was most profitable in the way of property, he replied,
'Good pasture.' And when the man who asked the question said, 'What about lending at
interest?' Cato answered, 'What about manslaughter?'"*
Cicero, *De Officiis*, 44 B.C.

Every day, a vast river of money flows throughout the United States, the world's largest economy. Well over a trillion dollars in assets change hands in this country each business day. Many of these transactions are conducted in or facilitated by a bank, the cornerstone of civilization's economy for centuries.

It is easy to take banks for granted. It sometimes seems like there's one on every corner. They provide so many services that it is difficult to imagine what life would be like without banks. Surprisingly few people, even those who visit the automatic teller or use a charge card daily, have any idea how the banking system works or how critical the bank's role is in our lives.

When a person writes a check, one small drop enters the river of money. The check passes through several banks for processing and payment before it is returned to the writer with the monthly statement. Whether the check is for a $10 grocery bill or a billion-dollar corporate buyout, banks act as the locks on the river that let the check and the entire money supply flow in a constant, regulated manner.

A thorough understanding of the domestic financial system and the role banks and other financial institutions play is essential to the financial investigator. Knowing how banks, savings companies, credit unions, and other institutions work will help the investigator find information stored in the files of these businesses. Because banks are extremely conscious of their role as repository of other people's money (and their own), the records kept by financial institutions are among the most complete and accurate of any on the face of the earth. The efficient use by law enforcement of these records has, can, and will in the future put untold numbers of criminals behind bars.

MONEY AND BANKING

As Willie Sutton's quote reveals, he had a clear if somewhat narrow view of the functions of a modern bank. Being a repository for money is, of course, only one of many services performed by a "full-service" bank. Nevertheless, the concept that money is at the heart of the banking business is so fundamental that we don't need Willie to point it out.

But how does the money get into a bank? Why is a bank, rather than some other institution, the object of Sutton's affection? And how did we come to a point where banks control such a large part of our lives, our economy, and our civilization itself? A short history of banking will answer some of these intriguing questions.

At an earlier point in this book, we discussed the background and concept of money. Remember that money evolved from the barter system, in which goods and services were traded for other goods and services. Money was developed to simplify the barter process, eventually maturing into a system all its own — one that was, coincidentally, ready-made for banks.

In a barter system, there is no real need for a bank; everyone acts as his or her own. You bring your goods to the marketplace and trade directly with someone else. Several modern groups have established barter exchanges to organize trades among members, but especially in our complex society, where our needs are so diverse, it is impractical to have all the things needed for trade under one roof. (Although Wal-Mart comes pretty close.)

One of the first issues to arise in one of those ancient markets must have been the question of *credit*. Perhaps some prehistoric farmer needed some tool or farm implement but had nothing to trade until his crop came in. The flint-hearted loan officer not yet having evolved, perhaps the farmer's trading partners were willing to advance the needed item in return for a promise to pay later. It probably didn't take too long for those trading partners to figure out that they could ask for a little more wheat in the fall in exchange for that plow today. The concept of *interest* was born.

Your attitude toward interest is probably dictated by which side of the transaction you are standing on. While you would expect a banker to be an enthusiastic supporter, moralists and theologians didn't care for the idea at all. *Usury,* defined as the practice of lending money at excessively high interest rates, was never popular in early Christianity or Islam. Regarded as the antithesis of charity, lending at interest is still proscribed in the Muslim faith. Christianity has been slightly more accommodating; only those interest rates considered excessive are now proscribed. With interest rates on some charge cards over 20%, this flexibility is no doubt welcomed by Christian bankers.

Francis Bacon described usury as the "certainest way to wealth ... and one of the worst." Nevertheless, credit and interest are the bedrock in the foundation of a bank. The concept of money meshes perfectly with the operation of a bank, ancient or modern. The first bank probably didn't look like much; it may have just been a man in the marketplace, keeping track of transactions on a clay tablet. Whatever language was used, the basic concepts would be familiar to the president of Chase Manhattan, Bank of America, or any other financial institution today.

One cardinal principle was that financial transactions are written, inscribed, or in some other way recorded. Whether on a clay tablet or a computer disk, some permanent record is maintained of all the business of the bank. These records serve to protect the interests of both the bank and its customers. Even a banker's vocabulary hints at the close link to records. Loans are documented as "notes," payments are "recorded" with satisfaction, bad debts are (grudgingly) "written off." If a question arises, the record can be examined for the correct answer. (This process must have been much more interesting, and probably more profitable to the bank, when only priests and money lenders could read.)

At a time when almost everyone owes somebody something and our government is running close to an $8 trillion debt, we should all have a fairly clear idea of how credit works. For those who might have been in suspended animation since 1930, credit can be defined as a system of doing business in which a person is trusted to pay at a later time for goods or services that are supplied now. Credit forms the core of any advanced economy, whether modern or ancient. It is the basis for commerce of all kinds, from agriculture to shipping, from frippery to money itself.

Credit is a temporary transfer of wealth from one who has to one who needs. Although it will occasionally work in a barter economy, credit works much better with money. Credit enables the business person to purchase stock, the sale of which generates the money to repay the loan. Credit enables the farmer to put in a crop, which can be sold months later to repay the banker. In both cases, with luck, the borrower will survive to make the loan payment and perhaps to make a profit as well. Credit is civilization. It is so ubiquitous that it may be what sets people apart from other animal species. Credit is so important that almost everyone on earth, including business and governments, is now engaged in both borrowing and lending.

Why is credit so important to the banks? Because it's profitable. And it's profitable because those loans to the farmer and the business person are not free. The lender is always going to charge a fee, large or small, for the use of its money. That fee — interest — is the main way banks make money. By charging some amount, usually a percentage of the total loan, the lender not only obtains repayment of the *principal*, but also receives an additional amount for providing the service. As we will see, all of the many other services in a full-service bank are small potatoes compared to the interest received on loans. In fact, interest on commercial, personal, mortgage, and charge card loans provides the means for banks to furnish their other services, such as savings and checking accounts for individuals or businesses.

Incidentally, interest works both ways. The bank needs money too. After all, it has to have something to lend, so the bank borrows money, some of which comes from you. It pays interest on that loan as well, although you have probably noticed that the amount the bank pays you is always somewhat less than what it would charge you to borrow the same amount. The banks can get away with this because they are so deeply entrenched in our lives and our economy, and because they know that someday you're going to need a loan. And where would you go to get it if there were no banks?

But there weren't always banks. In fact, banks are a fairly recent development in human history, dating back only 500 to 1000 years, although the Romans had bank-like institutions that issued letters of credit, made loans, and took deposits. How did people get by for so long without banks? Mostly because commerce had not developed to the point where banks could play an essential role.

In Europe's Dark Ages, commerce was extremely limited. The Renaissance brought not only new interest in the arts but also an increase in international trade. One of the first innovations in this trade was private banking, which developed in the Lombard region of 16th-century Italy specifically for the purpose of facilitating international commerce. Banks expanded rapidly along European trade routes; traders recognized the need to have a bank at each end of the credit transaction. They controlled both ends by placing trusted relatives in what might be called branches of the main house. The Italians dominated European banking for centuries, and even today traces of this preeminence exist. In Germany, for example, a secured loan is still known as a "Lombard loan." (See Figure 12.1.)

Figure 12.1 Medieval guild members settling accounts, c. 1465, a process that still takes place in banking today.

These private banks were the first elements of what was gradually becoming an interconnected financial system. The individual elements were linked by communication, which, with the increase in literacy brought by the Renaissance, became written. *Paper* joined credit and interest as important parts of the bank's existence. Paper generally refers to documents, but the term carries additional significance in a bank. There, paper represents recorded credit transactions. In its simplest form, each paper is an I.O.U., a promise to pay that loan back, usually with the terms, interest rate, and schedule included. Whether on a bank's books, a computer disk, or a clay tablet, paper is an asset, just like the gold, coins, or bank notes in the vault.

There are many types of paper at a bank. One of the first invented was "four name paper," now referred to as a *banker's acceptance*. As the original name implies, the paper bears the signatures of four persons: the importer, the importer's banker, the exporter, and the exporter's banker. The Italians were using this type of paper as early as the 13th century. We will talk more about this type of paper in the section on international banking.

Another type of paper is commercial paper, debts owed to businesses that banks buy at a discount. Commercial paper works like this: Let's say you are a barrel maker, and you need enough hoops for 500 barrels. Mr. Hooper, of the local "Hoops 'R' Us," offers you 1000 hoops for $1000 cash or $1100 in 60 days. (These are his terms.) You don't have the cash right now, so you sign a promissory note for $1100, (paper), which Mr. Hooper takes to the bank. The banker buys the note for $1000 (a discount on its face value), and you now owe the banker $1100. You have gotten the things you need now to stay in business, Hoops 'R' Us has $1000 to pay its workers and make more hoops, and the bank — well, time and money really are their business. You can see how it would be possible for businesses to perform the bank's role, making and holding their own notes, but everything is so much easier with a bank involved, which is why they're everywhere.

Early banks were mostly concerned with business and commerce. They did absorb some of the more public functions previously performed by business or tradespeople. Goldsmiths accepted deposits of coins, and pawnbrokers made personal loans secured by property. Many individuals were involved in the money exchange business. Banks evolved rapidly, eventually performing many of these services for the general public. One important service was the issuance of "bank money," notes redeemable at the bank and representing deposits already in the bank. A customer could make a deposit of gold or currency (usually coins) into the bank and receive an equivalent amount in bank money. Merchants in town knew and accepted this money as a standard currency, guaranteed by the bank. (Sound familiar? It should — this is the basic principle of the traveler's check, as well as the debit card, for that matter.)

This was critical because when coins were made of precious metal, few countries used a standard currency. Counterfeiting of coins was common, as was the practice of clipping or shaving the coins to remove some of the gold, silver, or copper. These were capital offenses, by the way. Once again, banks had taken steps to become more entwined in the economic life of their communities.

As banks grew in both size and influence, European rulers were coming to the uncomfortable realization that the other Golden Rule ("He who has the gold makes the rules") might apply to them as well. On occasion, these "all powerful" monarchs found themselves a little short of the cash needed for wars, mistresses, or other essential government services. As one might expect, grubbing for a loan from a mere banker did not sit well with the high and mighty. One government response was the creation of central banks, which acted as bankers for the government. The Bank of Sweden and the Bank of England were among the first such central or national banks. They issue bank notes, arrange government borrowing, and manage the national debt.

The United States operates a somewhat different system of 12 regional banks that form part of the Federal Reserve System. Each of the Federal Reserve Banks is actually comprised of a network of private banks and government institutions, with the entire system functioning in the same way a central bank would. Established by the Federal Reserve Act of 1913, the Federal Reserve controls money, credit, and interest rates, all of which are interrelated. The Federal Reserve is the bank of the United States Treasury, performing a number of functions for the Treasury, including the issuance of Federal Reserve Notes (paper money), issuing and redeeming government securities, and acting as a foreign exchange bank of the United States.

One of the most important functions of the Federal Reserve, known familiarly as "the Fed," is to act as a bank for other bankers. In this capacity, the Federal Reserve produces money and lends it to banks, which in turn place the money in circulation. The supply of money is not fixed; the Fed can order more printed at any time, which, if you think about it, would be a really fun power to have. Increasing the money supply has the effect of lowering the value of the money, causing inflation. By tightening the money supply, through increases in interest rates or the printing of less money, the Fed can reduce inflation.

The Federal Reserve monitors the supply of money through a measurement of funds known as M1, or Money Supply 1. M1 includes the total amount of money that is readily available, either in currency, in coins, or in the form of so-called demand deposits at banks. These deposits are those that customers can access quickly for cash or the equivalent of cash — usually checking accounts. M1 is a rough guess by the Federal Reserve at the size of the river of money on a given date. As of March 2005, the M1 was around $1.372 trillion.

A second measurement, M2 or Money Supply 2, includes all of the elements of M1 but also includes time deposits, the money kept by depositors in banks that they are not as likely to "demand" quickly. Time deposits include savings accounts, passbook savings, and certificates of deposit, all of which are placed in the care of

TABLE 12.1
Fund Measurements

Monetary aggregates (daily average in billions) for the week ended March 31, 2005

Money supply (M1) sa	1371.9
Money supply (M2) nsa	1375.7
Money supply (M2) sa	6474.8
Money supply (M2) nsa	6469.8
Money supply (M3) sa	9526.6
Money supply (M3) nsa	9545.4

Commercial paper outstanding (in billions of dollars)

All issuers	1435.9
Financial companies	1302.2

the bank by depositors and upon which interest is paid. In October 1997, the M2 was $3.980 trillion — almost $4 trillion, serious money in anybody's book.

The Federal Reserve supervises the M1 closely and also watches for anomalies in the money supplies within the 12 regions of the system. Investigators have used this monitoring process to observe the large excesses in cash that are handled by certain drug trafficking and money laundering centers such as Miami. In theory, the M1 should be relatively easy to keep track of, since the Fed knows how much money it has printed and it can ask its member institutions how much is on hand in the form of demand deposits. In fact, the river is so big, and money changes hands so quickly, that the M1 is hard to measure accurately. (See Table 12.1.)

BORROWING AND LENDING

As mentioned above, the Fed controls interest rates by charging interest to the banks that borrow money from the Fed. The rate of interest charged by the Fed to commercial and member banks is known as the *discount rate*. Those banks will then loan money out to their customers, adding a bit to the interest rate to assure their profit. The banks' best corporate or business customers are generally able to borrow at a special, preferred rate, known as the *prime rate*. The rest of us pay more for our mortgage, home improvement, or business loans. Obviously, when the discount rate is low, the prime and other rates will also be low. The prime rate is usually around two percentage points higher than the discount rate.

The control by the Fed over interest rates is only one way in which government regulation affects the overall supply of money. Another tool used by the Fed is a reserve requirement for its member banks. The reserve requirement mandates that the banks maintain a certain amount of their demand and time deposits as a reserve, either in the form of cash in the vault or as a deposit with their branch of the Federal Reserve Bank. The reserve requirement is expressed in terms of a ratio, and the Fed can alter the ratio to either increase or decrease the supply of money. If the ratio is increased, the supply of money decreases because the banks have to keep the money in the vault rather than lending it out. Bankers don't like this.

BANK REGULATION AND CONTROL

In theory, it is pretty easy to become a banker in the United States. In order to call yourself a bank, you must meet certain conditions established by state or federal law, but these conditions are not especially harsh. A certain amount of capital is required to start a bank, but this may be as little as $50,000, depending on the state where the bank is located and the size of the community the bank is to serve. The bank is also required to have a certain number of directors, and the directors must each put up some of their own capital to found the bank. With these in place, other than some other supervisory controls, most of the major legal hurdles have been overcome.

That's the theory. In practice, domestic banking is largely a closed community. To protect the banks that are already functioning and to prevent fraud or losses to consumers, state and federal regulators are extremely conservative about letting newcomers into the field.

Once in, banks are subject to many regulatory controls and are overseen by several governmen-

TABLE 12.2
Agencies with Oversight and with Enforcement Responsibilities over Financial Institutions

Oversight
Federal Reserve Board
Federal Deposit Insurance Corporation
Comptroller of the Currency
Financial Crimes Enforcement Network
Internal Revenue Service
Office of Thrift Supervision
National Credit Union Administration

Enforcement
Federal Bureau of Investigation
Internal Revenue Service
U.S. Secret Service

tal agencies. Federally chartered or "national" banks are members of the Federal Reserve System, but their charters are actually issued by the Comptroller of the Currency, an agency of the Treasury Department. The Comptroller of the Currency maintains a staff responsible for examining federally chartered banks. State chartered banks that do not belong to the Federal Reserve System are examined by agencies of the state governments and often are not as strenuously regulated. Table 12.2 lists agencies with oversight responsibilities and those with enforcement responsibilities relative to financial institutions, including banks.

The Federal Deposit Insurance Corporation (FDIC) is an independent agency of the Federal government that, as its name implies, insures the deposits of bank customers. For many years, all accounts were insured by the FDIC up to $20,000. Recently this amount increased to $100,000. Since the inception of the FDIC, no depositor has ever lost money in the failure of an FDIC-insured bank. Although it is a government agency, FDIC works like an insurance company, collecting premiums from the banks it insures. If there were a wholesale failure of banks in this country, these premiums would be consumed quickly, and taxpayers would be liable for the remaining amount, as was the case in the recent savings and loan debacle.

All banks are subject to regular examination, conducted at the bank's expense. Both the FDIC and the Federal Reserve Bank accept the reports of the Comptroller of the Currency's examiners. Contrary to popular belief, a bank examination is not an audit. The primary purpose of the examination is to establish what percentage of the outstanding loans is likely to become "bad." When a bank has too many problem loans, it may be subject to more frequent examination. If the situation becomes too serious, the governing authority may replace the management of the bank. This alone is a powerful incentive for bankers to monitor their loan practices closely. (Federal law requires that the directors of banks have direct personal involvement in decisions about loans made by their banks. If they are later found not to have had this involvement, they may be personally liable for losses. This helps explain why bank loan officers have an unsympathetic reputation in some quarters.)

BANK MANAGEMENT AND OPERATION

Banking in the 21st century has evolved into a "full-service" financial operation. Most banks provide a wide variety of services to their customers, far more than in the past. Most individuals conduct their business with full-service commercial banks, which differ substantially from other financial institutions such as savings and loans, finance companies, or credit unions.

There are, incidentally, a few things full-service banks cannot do. They are prohibited by law from selling insurance or dealing in securities such as stocks and bonds. They are also not supposed to operate a travel agency, one prohibition that probably doesn't distress most bankers too greatly. These prohibitions are designed to keep banks from getting involved with higher-risk activities. Since higher risk usually means larger returns, the banks are aching for the chance to move into some of these markets, and they lobby Congress intensely for the opportunity to do so.

The operation of these banks has become more complex as the number of services has grown, but most commercial banks are organized similarly. Typically they center on two management areas, sometimes known as the floor and the platform. Each of these areas is supervised by a bank officer, often an assistant vice president. The bank manager may also hold the title of vice president or assistant vice president. (You'll discover that there are a lot of vice presidents in your average bank.) Figure 12.2 shows the organization of a commercial bank.

Operations of the floor are the responsibility of a senior bank officer, often a vice president

Organization of a Commercial Bank

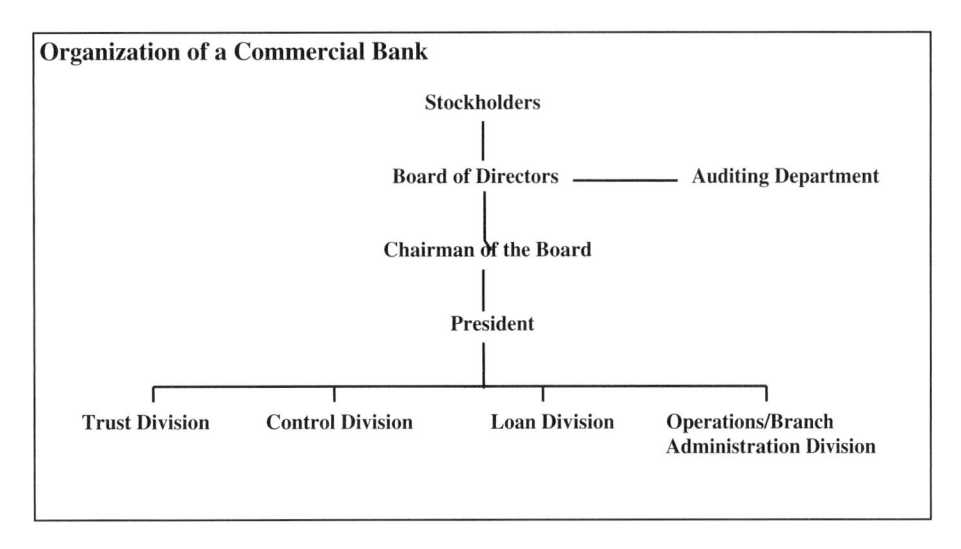

Stockholders
|
Board of Directors ———— Auditing Department
|
Chairman of the Board
|
President
|
┌──────────────┬──────────────┬──────────────┬──────────────┐
Trust Division   Control Division   Loan Division   Operations/Branch
                                                         Administration Division

Figure 12.2 Organization of a commercial bank.

TABLE 12.3
Commercial Bank: Operations/Branch Administration Division

Customer Service Department	Opens checking and savings accounts, answers customer questions about accounts
Tellers Department	Performs teller operations, accepts deposits, pays out withdrawals from checking and savings accounts
Bookkeeping Department	Maintains records and responds to inquiries about accounts
Proof and Transit Department	Proofs and sorts deposits and cashed checks, delivers to drawee banks
Savings Department	Maintains records of savings accounts, NOW accounts, Super NOW accounts, and CDs
Safe Deposit Department	Rents safe deposit boxes to bank customers
Data Processing Department	Posts transactions daily for all bank departments
Personnel Department	Hires employees and maintains employee benefit programs
Miscellaneous Operations	Purchasing, security, maintenance, and mail

who also has the title of operations officer. Floor operations include teller functions, safe deposit boxes, and notes and collections. A more complete description of the operations or branch administration function appears in Table 12.3.

The bank manager may be responsible for the platform, which may include loans and new accounts. If the bank offers more services, such as a trust department; an escrow department; or international, brokerage, or insurance services, each of these departments will be supervised by a separate management official.

In major banks with smaller branches, the head office maintains a large staff to support branch operations. Many of the functions conducted by smaller banks are consolidated in the larger institutions; this may make some records or documents harder to locate.

Financial institutions other than banks have a similar management structure, with supervisors overseeing different functions within the operation. Differences are largely a product of the unique characteristics of the institution. For example, a credit union is an association of its members, and those approving the loans are selected by those members. Credit unions and savings and loan associations offer fewer financial services than full-service banks do, but they have gradually expanded into territories formerly held exclusively by banks. Lending is still the key element of all of these businesses.

BANK FUNCTIONS

Almost all of a bank's services, however extensive, are basically collateral to the main business of lending money and collecting interest. Banks do profit from their other services, but the other things banks do are mostly there to keep customers at the bank until they need a loan. If you are a financial investigator, you are almost always more interested in these other service areas, so knowing what a bank does, how it functions, and what records are generated is important.

The basic functions of a bank, in addition to making loans, are to receive deposits, pay checks, transfer funds, hold property for others, and collect financial instruments. Each of these functions or services will be addressed separately. The most important (to the bank) — that of making loans — is addressed first, with two of the most important to investigators — transferring funds and paying checks — covered in detail later.

MAKING LOANS

Loans are the lifeblood and reason for existence of any financial institution, be it a bank, savings and loan, or credit union. As Mr. Sutton noted, banks are "where the money is," and potential borrowers come daily to seek funds from their bank. Lending may take place in a commercial setting, in which the bank loans to a business, or it may involve personal loans, mortgages for real estate, auto loans for car purchases, or personal or signature loans to pay for college or for smaller purchases.

Banks have also developed a number of special loans with catchy titles, such as the "bill consolidation loan," and loans that don't sound like loans, such as "overdraft protection," but the principle behind all of this lending is the same: buy low and sell high.

Banks obtain the money for their loans from the Fed or some other banking source. (Actually, most bankers do not like to borrow directly from the Fed, preferring to deal with each other when it comes to borrowing.) Very little of the money loaned out by a bank is actually offset by deposits in the bank. This is why bank examiners watch the percentage of "bad" or "problem" loans at each bank, since a sudden increase can cause the bank itself to become a "problem."

The banks pay a fee for the money they obtain, in the form of interest. Of course, the rate paid by the bank is lower, generally by around two percentage points, than the rate it charges its customers. Those two percentage points represent the bank's profit on the loan, after bank operating expenses are subtracted. Incidentally, the difference can be much more than two percentage points. Bank credit card interest rates are often in excess of 18 or 20 percent, while the banks may be borrowing the money to support those loans at a rate of as low as 3 or 4 percent. This type of lending is obviously very profitable for banks, which is why you get a zillion credit card applications in the mail every month.

The lending process is probably familiar to you. Virtually everyone over 18 in the United States has obtained credit at some point, and many have dealt directly with a bank officer in acquiring a loan for a home, car, or other purchase. The first step is usually the completion of a loan application, in which the prospective borrower provides financial information about himself or herself. Some loans are approved or rejected based upon the application alone, whereas others, such as a mortgage loan, require additional work by the lending institution.

Most loans are *collateralized;* that is, they are secured by some piece of property with a value equal to or sometimes greater than the value of the note. In the case of a mortgage loan, the bank will hold the title to the property, which cannot be transferred without satisfying the mortgage. Auto loans are almost always secured by the car itself. The bank will mail you the title right after you make your final payment. If for any reason you fail to make your payments on a home or auto loan, the bank may foreclose on the note, take possession of its property, and sell it to satisfy the debt. This action is unpopular, not to mention expensive, and banks try to avoid it as much as possible. They, like the IRS, are much happier when everyone is paying on time and in the correct amount. The borrower, of course, wants to keep the bank happy, because he or she may need a loan again sometime in the future.

The records kept by a bank in connection with its loans are extensive, and they begin with the loan application. If credit checks are performed, the results and other documents relating to the loan will all be kept in a loan file. For big loans such as mortgages, banks often ask for copies of two or three years' worth of tax returns. The loan file will also include the complete record of payments made by the customer. These records are the ones reviewed by the bank examiners to determine whether the loan is bad or likely to go bad.

RECEIVING DEPOSITS

Taking in depositor money is another honored tradition of banks. People have always needed a safe place to hold their wealth. Most (though not all) people understand that banks are safer than their mattress or a can buried in the backyard. And there's always the possibility that the bank will pay you interest on your deposit. Demand, time, and safe deposits are the main types.

Safe deposits probably should fall under the category of holding property for others, because the bank is really just renting you some space in its vault. The bank has no way of knowing what you have put in the safe deposit box, and it isn't interested as long as you pay the rent each year and the box contents don't start to smell up the vault. Although the bank keeps no records of what is in the box, it does keep very strict records on access to the box. These begin with the box rental application and the signature card. The signatures of all the persons who will have access to the box must appear on the signature card, which is hauled out and checked each time someone signs in to enter the box.

Each of those entries is also noted, either on a separate card for each box, with entries for the date, person signing in, and the times in and out, or on separate cards, filed by date. The latter are much more difficult for investigators to use, since you will probably already know who has the box. What you want to know is when somebody accessed it. If the cards are filed by date, the bank is going to have to go through a year's worth of cards, looking for your box number.

Time deposits are basically savings accounts. As the name implies, the customer is placing money on deposit with the bank for some time. In the case of passbook savings accounts, the time is open ended. The customer can leave it there forever, and the bank will be quite happy, since it can use the money, either as part of its reserve or by lending it to some other deserving person. Because there is no fixed term and the customer can ask for his or her money at any time, these are known as "demand deposits." Since the bank never knows how long it will be able to use the customer's money before he or she demands it back, banks don't like these deposits as much as the ones that have fixed terms, and they pay lower interest on them.

Other time deposits may be limited to a fixed period, such as a six-month certificate of deposit. When the six months are up, the bank returns the principal, along with some interest. These fixed-period deposits generally pay slightly more in interest than open-ended deposits, since the bank has the knowledge that it will have the money for a set amount of time. Certificates of deposit (CDs) can come in varying lengths, several years usually being the longest. The expression "substantial penalty for early withdrawal" was designed for this type of deposit.

The records associated with time deposits vary slightly according to the type of deposit. Passbook savings accounts, as the name implies, involve a small book listing deposits to and withdrawals from the account. This is usually kept in the possession of the account holder. The bank, of course, will have some similar record, probably computerized, so someone can't just walk in with a forged passbook and ask for a million dollars. There may also be deposit slips generated by the customer, deposit tickets generated by the teller, and copies of savings withdrawal slips. Entries relating to the account will also be noted on the paper tapes that are produced by the machines used by each teller.

CD customers who place their money on deposit with the bank receive a certificate documenting the transaction.

HOLD AND ADMINISTER PROPERTY FOR OTHERS

This function is commonly known as *trust services*, which are operated by the bank's Trust Department. As the name implies, customers or clients of the bank are entrusting their property to the bank, usually through some legal arrangement. The bank may be nominated in a will to settle an estate or to administer a trust or guardianship. These functions can also be performed by an attorney, but bankers are often chosen by people who have used the bank for other services. You have probably heard of situations where trust funds are set up for minor children, paying them a small amount until they reach a certain age, when they get access to the whole fund. People know they can rely on the bank to follow the terms of the trust, keeping the money safe until it's time to pay it out.

Another type of service involves the bank's acting as the agent for a customer in a variety of financial transactions. Again, while others, including attorneys, brokers, real estate agents, and escrow companies, can also act as agents, it's nice to have everything all in one place (although not all banks may perform all of these services). Acting as an agent, the bank may become involved in:

- Safekeeping property
- Managing property
- Keeping legal custody of property
- Performing escrow services
- Acting as transfer agent in securities transactions

These areas are not especially profitable for the bank, but they all serve to keep the customer satisfied, hopefully long enough that he or she will come back for a loan. We don't need to get into the services in depth, but it should be noted that each generates paperwork of interest to the financial investigator.

There are a number of other departments or divisions in a commercial bank, including places of interest to the investigator, such as the Legal Department and the Security Department. In this respect, banks are like most other large businesses, and important information may be found in these various locations.

NOT ALL BANKS ARE CREATED ALIKE

The institution we have been talking about so far has been the commercial bank, the one handling most transactions involving business and the public generally. There are quite a few other types of banks out there as well, which we don't have the time or the space to cover in the same depth. Still, you will want to know what these are.

Offshore bank — This is any institution that operates outside the United States. Lots of American banks have offshore branches, taking advantage of various tax and banking laws in foreign jurisdictions. Going "offshore" isn't necessarily a sinister thing, though it certainly complicates the investigator's job. Many businesses maintain offshore banking connections to facilitate their international operations. Some countries, such as Switzerland and the Cayman Islands, do have strict bank secrecy laws, which protect their banks' customers from investigative scrutiny. They may also permit numbered bank accounts or accounts held under pseudonyms. Some offshore banks have branches in the United States, in which case their records and practices must follow American law.

Investment bank — Not really a "bank" in the usual sense of the word, an investment banker exists primarily to underwrite the issuance of securities. There are big bucks in these operations, as well as some considerable degree of risk, which is why regular commercial banks are not allowed to engage in this type of activity. Basically, an investment banking firm bankrolls an initial public offering (IPO) or other new offering of securities. When a company decides to issue shares, it works through an investment banker to prepare all of the materials necessary to float the issue. A price for the shares is decided upon, and the investment banker buys all of the stock to be issued. Usually more than one firm gets involved, creating a syndicate and spreading the risk around a bit. The initial price is fixed, and everybody in the syndicate sells at that price initially. Afterward, the price floats with supply and demand. The company now has the money it needs to expand, and the banker has a lot of shares it can sell, hopefully at a substantial profit.

Federal savings bank — The line between commercial banks and federal savings banks (FSBs; also known as thrifts, savings and loans, or building and loans) has become much thinner lately, as federal regulations have changed. These institutions started out to finance the purchase of real property by would-be homeowners, to take deposits from small investors, and to make loans to small business. Now FSBs offer a wider variety of services, which resemble closely those at a full-service bank. FSBs are regulated by the Federal Home Loan Bank Board. Deposits used to be insured by the Federal Savings and Loan Insurance Corporation (FSLIC). A large number of these institutions got into serious trouble in the late 1970s and early 1980s, primarily because they were heavily into commercial real estate loans when real estate values were tumbling. Quite a few FSBs went under, and some folks even went to jail for abuses and mismanagement. Afterward, the FSLIC, which didn't have enough money to cover all the failures, was merged with the FDIC, and most eligible FSBs are now members of FDIC. Changing all those initials cost the U.S. taxpayer billions. Because FSBs operate like regular banks, their structure is usually quite similar to that of a commercial bank, as are the records maintained.

Private bank — Private banks are exactly what the name implies: private. This privacy relates to both ownership and operation. Established by individuals or businesses to provide their operations with some of the benefits of a bank, private banks generally cannot serve the general public or take deposits, although some jurisdictions permit this. Most are established in jurisdictions where banking laws are somewhat more relaxed than in the United States, although many American banks offer "private banking" to special customers. How special? You've probably got to have at least a million, and sometimes 10 million bucks, to go through that door marked "Private." Switzerland has a number of private banks, some of which are so private we can't even be sure they *are* a bank. In most cases, the funds in a private bank are those of the owner.

Central bank — This is the big enchilada of banking in any given country. The central bank sets, or is at least at the forefront of, the nation's monetary policy and is responsible for protecting the currency from threats like inflation. In the United States, the Federal Reserve System acts as the country's central bank, but in most countries this role is performed by a single institution, such as the Bank of England or Japan Central Bank. As you might expect, the head of the central bank is a fairly important person. For the most part, central bankers are going to be somewhat aloof from the issues facing the financial investigator or ordinary folks generally, though they are probably going to have all sorts of information about the commercial banks they govern.

Correspondent bank — Big banks always need more branches and need them in more places, but no bank is so big that it can be everywhere. Small banks may have only one location or a couple of small branches. In either case, a bank is going to need some help doing business in places where it doesn't have its own branch. When this happens, bankers turn to correspondent banks, which will handle transactions on a sort of mutual aid basis. In the case of a small bank, possibly one in a rural area, it would secure a relationship with a correspondent, say a large bank in a city, by placing a substantial amount of money on deposit with the larger bank. This same arrangement works well for banks in international markets and foreign countries. Business people whose domestic bank has no overseas branch will be able to work through their bank's correspondent, which aids the letter of credit/banker's acceptance process, as well as other functions. One of the most important of these functions, as we'll see in the next chapter, is check clearing, which can be, and often is, handled through correspondent banks.

Cyber bank — A new development with unsettling possibilities is the cyber bank or Internet bank. These institutions take advantage of the global reach of the Internet and World Wide Web to provide certain banking services. Although many regular banks have established themselves on the Net, the cyber bank exists *only* in that medium. As we have seen, the concept of money lends itself quite well to computerized transactions. People are becoming accustomed to dealing with computerized ATMs and even banking by telephone, so the idea that all of your banking business could be done from your home PC with a bank you've never seen before isn't so far-fetched. These banks can be anywhere, and they are extremely difficult to regulate, since their geographical reach far exceeds their physical presence. The possibility of fraud is very real, as are the security problems involved with the transfer and storage of financial data in this medium. There are indications that cyber banks have already been used for money laundering, a trend that will likely continue in the future.

Credit union — Like FSBs, credit unions have become a lot more like "real" banks in their operations over the past few years. Prohibited by law from serving the general public, credit unions have members, usually individuals who work in the same business or industry. Established primarily to take savings deposits and make loans to their members, credit unions offer security, stability, and a level of personal service that may be lacking at a larger institution.

Auto finance corporation — Auto finance corporations are not banks, but they do lend money, extending credit to purchasers of automobiles and other big-ticket items. The General Motors Acceptance Corporation (GMAC) bankrolls dealerships that sell General Motors products, enabling them to offer favorable terms to customers on the spot. The states regulate these businesses. Although auto finance corporations do not accept deposits, individual investors can buy corporate bonds issued by these companies.

Bank holding company — Most banks are themselves owned by a bank holding company, a corporation that maintains the bank as a subsidiary. As we have noted, banks are prohibited by law from doing certain things, such as engaging in ordinary commerce — "nonbank" functions of any kind. The theory is that these other activities distract from the primary purpose of the bank and may weaken it financially. Another concern is that banks, which have all that money, might be able to use those funds to gain an unfair competitive advantage. Bank holding companies have similar restrictions and are regulated by the Fed, which tries to determine where the line between banking and commerce will be drawn. Typically, the bankers find some business they would like to get into, and the Fed decides whether or not the bank holding companies should be allowed to do it.

Securities brokerages — Another nonbank financial institution, the brokerage has a primary interest in the buying and selling of stocks, bonds, and other securities. Over time, brokerage activities have expanded into traditional banking functions. Not only are clients able to maintain funds on deposit in money market accounts, but the brokerage may also allow credit trading on margin. In this situation, the brokerage is effectively lending its money to an investor to make a purchase. The Fed keeps an eye on this activity and limits margin loans to one half of the total investment. The client pays interest to the brokerage for the life of the loan, usually at a point or two above the prime rate. Brokerages make traditional commercial banks nervous, because they usually loan at lower rates than banks offer, and the stock market has traditionally been a better performer than savings accounts. There is more risk involved at a brokerage, something the bankers like to point out, but those same bankers are constantly trying to add these activities to their list of the services provided by a full-service bank. Meanwhile, some brokerages offer credit cards and provide for check writing.

RESOURCES ON BANKING

Suppose you want to know something about a particular bank and its operations. Maybe an officer or employee is suspected of some wrongdoing, or maybe you'd just like to know if your money would be safe there. The agencies that regulate banks are good sources of this information, much of which is available to the general public as well as the financial investigator. Three federal agencies have detailed information on bank operations. These are:

Comptroller of the Currency
Administrator of National Banks
490 L'Enfant Plaza East, S.W.
Washington, D.C. 20219
Phone (202) 447-1810

Federal Reserve Bank
Board of Governors of the Federal Reserve
  System
Federal Reserve Building
20th and C Streets, N.W.
Washington, D.C. 20551
Phone (202) 452-3000

Federal Deposit Insurance Corporation
550 Seventeenth Street, N.W.

Washington, D.C. 20429
Phone (202) 389-4221

For a "Report of Condition" for a given bank, with a description of its assets, liabilities, and nonperforming loans, write or call the FDIC:

Federal Deposit Insurance Corporation
C.S.B. Disclosure Group
Room F-518
550 Seventeenth Street, N.W.
Washington, D.C. 20429
Phone (202) 393-8400

Several reference books provide information about domestic and international banks. One valuable work is the *Guide to Routing Codes*, put out by the American Bankers Association. If you are looking at the back of a check and trying to figure out where it was cashed or deposited, the routing code may provide the answer.

Another good source is the **Thomson Bank Directory**, published in June and December each year. According to the publisher, "this premier 5-volume bank reference directory provides information on banks worldwide. Data includes national bank codes, industry statistics and rankings, standard settlement instructions (SSI), credit ratings and a Resource Guide." For many banks, this directory also lists their routing codes, MICR numbers, and SWIFT address, all of which will be of interest to us in the next chapter.

A companion to Thomson is the **World Bank Directory**, which comes out every September and, according to the publisher, "contains detailed listings for 10,000 international banks and their branches worldwide plus the Top 1,000 U.S. banks. Information includes world and country rankings, international and correspondent contact information, principal correspondent institutions and standard settlement instructions (SSI)." This book is particularly important for investigators who need contact information in order to obtain records from offshore institutions.

Finally, current news about banking and finance may be found in *Moody's Bank and Finance,* published every Tuesday by Moody's Investor Service, a company of the Dun and Bradstreet Corporation. These reports contain very up-to-date financial statements, histories, and transaction information, such as name changes and mergers. The Internet address for Moody's is http://www.moody's.com/fisonline.

CHAPTER **13**

BANKING OPERATIONS

"Let us all be happy, and live within our means, even if we have to borrow the money to do it with."
Artemus Ward, Science and Natural History

"Money: An article which may be used as a universal passport to everywhere except heaven, and as a universal provider of everything except happiness."
The Wall Street Journal

By now, we have a pretty good idea of how important banks are to society and why. Just as banks are good at facilitating the everyday business of honest folks, so are they important to criminals and money launderers, and for the same reasons. As financial investigators, an understanding of how banks operate will give us a good perspective on the types of records they keep and how those records can be used in a money laundering or other investigation.

For starters, we can be certain that absolutely everything relating to the money that passes through the bank will be written down, often several times. The objective of the banker is to create a complete documented history of every penny that passes through the doors of the institution. This objective has been held by every bank and business dealing with money since the Babylonians began making their accounting records on clay tablets, 5000 years ago. (See Figure 13.1.)

This record of all those transactions is the product of a grinding routine, one strictly adhered to by every bank employee. The routine extends to the bank's branches, correspondents, the check clearinghouse, and on to every bank in the system. There may be small variations based on a bank's size or location, but for the most part, a banker plucked from her desk at the smallest bank in Hawaii would fit in quickly at the biggest bank in New York. This routine also means that once a financial investigator has an understanding of the routine, that knowledge can be applied quite nicely to just about every financial institution he or she encounters.

Figure 13.1 Medieval bankers. Note that you do not see any actual money in this picture — only people and accounting records. The bench or table is the "banque." (Source: British Library)

Let's go through the various functions of the bank and examine the records accompanying each.

MAKING LOANS

The extension of credit is the profit center of the commercial bank. Over the years, banks have devised a large, even bewildering array of loans tailored to meet the needs of almost every customer. In all of their various guises, loans consist of the *principal* (the amount actually borrowed), the *interest,* and the *terms,* which describe the method and time frame for the payback. For example, a mortgage loan for $100,000 might be made at a 7.5% annual percentage rate and might be payable monthly over 30 years. This loan would be secured with the property itself as collateral. Other loans might have shorter or longer terms, higher or lower interest, and, of course, principal ranging from a few dollars to a few billion. Most domestic financial institutions (not just banks, but credit unions and savings and loans as well) offer their customers a menu of loan choices.

Incidentally, most consumer loans are based on an *installment plan,* in which the borrower agrees to pay the loan back on a regular schedule, with the interest included in each payment. Some loans require repayment in one lump sum, with the interest included, but these are more common in business transactions. Some of the more common consumer loans are described here.

CONSUMER LOAN TYPES

Mortgage Loans

Designed to finance the purchase of real property, a mortgage loan may be made by a bank or by another entity using a bank as the middleman. Mortgage loans are typically for relatively large amounts of money and for long terms, 15 years and 30 years being common. Although Federal savings banks are frequent mortgage lenders, credit unions are not, because their federal charters limit loan periods to 11 years.

Interest rates on mortgage loans are often lower than on others, because the bank knows it will be getting paid more over a longer period of time. These interest rates will either be fixed for the entire length of the loan or adjustable, going up or down with the market. Adjustable rate mortgages (ARMs) may have shorter periods, such as one year or three years, after which time they are renegotiated.

The banks are also players in a secondary market for mortgages. A bank may offer the loan and then sell it to a mortgage company or an association, such as the Federal National Mortgage Association, also known as Fannie Mae, or the Government National Mortgage Association, also known as GNMA or Ginnie Mae. As is the case with commercial paper, the bank may sell the mortgage, getting its loan amount back. The bank might even continue to collect the loan payments, forwarding these to the secondary buyer.

Secured Property Loans

Secured property loans differ from mortgage loans in that they are made for big-ticket items other than real property. Cars, furniture, appliances, boats, RVs, and the like are good examples of the property purchased. As is the case with a mortgage, the loan is secured with the title to the property. Also, the bank requires a hefty down payment, so that the borrower has some equity in the property. An interest rate is set, usually a few points above the prime interest rate, and a payment schedule over a period of one to five years is established.

In the case of both mortgage and secured property loans, the loan payments almost always include the interest and a portion of the principal. At the beginning of the loan, nearly all of the payment is interest — the bank is making sure its fees are paid. Toward the end of the loan, most of the monthly payment is principal.

NOTE FOR FINANCIAL INVESTIGATORS

Where did the borrower get the item being used for collateral or to secure a loan? How did the borrower pay for *that* item? Once you've learned what assets are being used for security, you'll want to trace the history of those assets, even though they might not be an obvious part of your case. This is especially true in money laundering cases.

Secured Cash Loans

Banks will loan cash, although this type of loan is more common at a credit union, where the loan is made against the member's shares. Most secured cash loans use the customer's deposited funds as collateral. While the loan is in effect, those funds cannot be removed. The bank will pay interest on that money, though, at a rate a few points less than the loan, so it's not a complete loss.

Because secured cash loans require bank resources to establish and maintain, most banks have minimum amounts they will loan under this arrangement. If all you need is a couple of hundred dollars, the bank would prefer that you borrow it as a cash advance on another one of its loan services, the credit card.

Credit Card Loans

Unlike the secured cash loan, credit cards generate significant income for the issuing bank. No wonder, with interest on credit card balances at up to 25% APR. Credit cards are a form of *revolving credit,* a type of loan you can use as many times as you want, up to a preset limit. Payment may be made in full each month, or the bank will accept partial payment with a finance charge (the interest) on the outstanding balance.

Although there are "secured" credit cards backed by a Certificate of Deposit as security, most credit cards are based on an application and the establishment of a set line of credit. These applications are the forms you get in the mail saying, "Your pre-approved VISA card with a $5,000 limit is waiting for you." People with bad credit histories or other problems don't get these letters. Because of widespread fraud in this market, banks have to be somewhat cautious about offering credit cards, but the very high interest rates mean they can absorb some losses from fraud or default.

Incidentally, VISA and MasterCard are not banks, and they don't issue credit cards. The card is issued by a bank that has an affiliation with one or both of these organizations. Currently, more than 300 million credit cards are on issue, and a quite astonishing $560 billion in credit card debt is outstanding — $11,000 per American household — much of which is owed to banks at interest rates above 20%.

Personal Lines of Credit

Similar to a credit card, the personal line of credit (PLC) offers an approved customer the ability to obtain cash quickly, just by writing a check. Customers usually apply for the PLC and, when approved, can then use it at any time thereafter should the need arise. The advantages are that this is a quick and easy way to get into debt, and the borrower is not required to post any security. The disadvantages are that PLCs can be quite costly, including an annual fee, high finance charges (which approach credit card rates), and often a fee just for making the application.

Overdraft Protection

Overdraft protection doesn't sound like a loan, which might be the point. Overdraft protection is a lot like a PLC, although it is related to your checking account. The customer applies for overdraft protection, receiving approval for a certain amount of credit. The customer can then write checks for more money than is in the account, with the knowledge that the bank will cover the overdraft.

Student Loans

Designed to address the increasing cost of a college education, student loans have relatively long terms, with the payback coming after the student has left college and (presumably) gotten a job. Some college loan programs are backed by the federal government, which pays the interest while the student is still in school. Interest rates on these loans are generally lower than other types of consumer loans.

Home Equity Loans

A home equity loan (HEL) is secured by a second mortgage on a property (or, in some cases, a deed of trust). HELs are quite popular because, like mortgages, the interest paid is for the most part tax deductible, a side benefit other loans can no longer claim. Banks like them because, again like a mortgage, they are secured by the property or at least the equity therein. In this case, the equity is the difference between the appraised value of the property and the amount of the first mortgage. The loan period for a HEL is usually 10 or 15 years.

Miscellaneous Loans

Banks have come up with some special-purpose loans with catchy titles, all part of being a full-service financial institution. An example of these loans is the bill consolidation loan, which lets you catch up on all your past-due bills at once and maybe restructure your debt at a lower interest rate. Home improvement loans provide money for additions, remodeling, landscaping, or redecorating a residence. Your bank may offer others, but they are likely to be personal lines of credit or some type of secured loan under another name.

THE LOAN PROCESS

Since bank lending usually involves the handing of money to a total stranger, bankers can be fairly conservative about this process. Loans begin with two simple questions: "How much do you want?" and "How can we be sure you're going to pay us back?"

All loans begin with an application. The would-be borrower tells the bank in writing that a loan is desired. Loan applications may be filled out either at the time the loan is sought or in advance and kept on file by the bank. The application may be quite simple, as in the case of a small secured loan, or very detailed and lengthy, as with a mortgage application.

All loan applications are judged by the bank on four main factors: capacity, character, collateral, and conditions. *Capacity* refers to the source and amount of income the borrower has to apply to the loan. Work history and stability are important, as is the amount of money available to address this particular loan. *Character* relates to the ability and willingness to repay the loan, generally evidenced by the borrower's credit history. *Collateral* refers to whatever asset or property might be used to secure the loan. If the borrower's capacity disappears (e.g., gets fired) or his or her character turns out to be less than sterling (he or she skips out), is there something tangible the bank can seize, such as the car or the house? Finally, *conditions* such as the overall economy or perhaps the borrower's employer's condition might be a factor. The loan application will address all of these factors, seeking enough information to answer these questions to the banker's satisfaction.

NOTE TO FINANCIAL INVESTIGATORS

It's a common practice for banks to request a copy of one or more years of income tax returns to support various loan applications, especially home mortgages. No matter what the applicant turns in, these are *not* tax returns. Only IRS has the original and "real" tax return, and IRS doesn't make copies available to banks. So it's possible for people to make up whatever they want that *looks* like a tax return and attach it to a loan application. Frequently they do just that, fiddling with the income figures to accomplish whatever little scheme they've concocted. The figures can be fudged in either direction — to qualify for a mortgage loan, they would want to show a higher income level, but for a student loan the applicant might qualify only if the income level was lower. In either case, this constitutes making a material false statement on a loan application, a violation of Title 18 U.S.C. Section 1014, and carries an attention-getting 30-year penalty. This is a handy charge to keep in mind in any financial case, by the way. Under federal forfeiture provisions, the proceeds of the loan might be subject to forfeiture as well.

The loan application form is only the first entry in the file the bank opens for each loan. This file will bulk up quickly. In the case of larger loans, especially home mortgages, the bank will request a credit check. The report, obtained from one of the major credit bureaus, will be included in the file. The bank may also request verification of the income amounts reported on the application. The borrower may have to supply one or more pay stubs, as well as copies of two or three years' worth of income tax returns. The bank may ask for references and check with these people or businesses. They may also request that a cosigner accept responsibility for the loan should the borrower default.

Once the bank is as confident as it can be under the circumstances, it will enter into an agreement to hand over the money. This agreement is documented in the form of a promissory note, a loan agreement, or, in the case of a home loan, a mortgage. All parties sign the note, the borrower agreeing to pay back the principal and interest within the agreed-upon time period and under the conditions specified (the terms).

Loan agreements have become much simpler and easier to read in recent years, with some of the legalese replaced with plainer language. Still, some agreements, including mortgage documents, can be fairly complex. Even more complicated are the documents for corporate or business loans, which require a good going-over by the lawyers for both sides. The signed loan papers go into the file.

The money is invariably provided in the form of a check, often a cashier's check, which is drawn on the bank's own funds. A copy of the check or at least the stub will go into the loan file. Also in the file will be the title to any collateral that is being used to secure the loan. In the case of a car loan, the title to the motor vehicle, which is registered in the borrower's name, with the bank as the legal owner, will be included. For real property loans, the original deed will be in the file.

Now the borrower has to start making payments, and a record of these is included in the file. This record may take the form of a liability ledger. There will be other references to these payments in the bank's records as well: microfilmed copies of checks, deposit tickets, coupons from loan payment books, and so forth. As the loan is paid down, the bank keeps track of any late or missed payments. These may be reported to the credit bureaus, affecting the borrower's future loan applications.

When the loan is paid off, the loan file is closed, and it may be moved to another part of the bank for storage. It is important for investigators to request both open and closed loan files in their subpoenas, since open files may be kept at a branch, while closed files may be stored in a records center and no longer tracked on the bank's computer.

A subpoena for bank loan records (and this includes savings banks and credit unions) should be comprehensive enough to describe all of the documents that relate to the loan and its repayment, as well as providing leads to other accounts or financial activity. Money laundering schemes that involve financial transactions disguised as loans are quite common, and it is most important that these be examined very carefully.

Records relating to loans include:

- Loan application and supporting documents
- Collateral registers
- Loan or liability ledgers
- Loan disbursement documents
- Teller tapes
- Bank or cashier's checks
- Credit memos
- Loan repayment documents
- Copies of checks
- Cash-in tickets
- Debit memos

Receiving Deposits

Taking deposits is a starting point for much of a bank's activity. After all, no checks get written unless the writer has funds on deposit to cover the face amount. No interest can be paid to savings account holders, and, most important from the profit perspective, no deposits received means there's nothing to loan out.

Even before a deposit can be made, the depositor has to establish a relationship with the bank. Nothing can happen unless the customer first has an account with the bank. These accounts are opened with a signature card and an initial deposit.

The signature card bears the names, social security numbers, and signatures of every person who is giving the bank the authority to withdraw funds from the account. Although the bank will accept a deposit from anybody who has the correct account number, only those persons whose signatures appear on the signature card can authorize any transfer or withdrawal of funds. Establishing who has signature authority over an account is critical to a financial investigation. For one thing, these are the people who control the money you're looking for. In a money laundering case, these are the people who are moving it around or causing it to be moved. And a whole conspiracy might be found on one signature card.

NOTE TO FINANCIAL INVESTIGATORS

Under the Federal Right to Financial Privacy Act, certain financial and account information is confidential and cannot be released by the bank, except pursuant to a subpoena. This isn't the case for "relationship information," however. The bank *can* voluntarily disclose whether or not an individual has a relationship — holds an account or exercises signature authority. Although many banks might still prefer to get some official process for this information, a subpoena is not required by law.

In addition to personal information about the account holder, other information of importance on the signature card includes the account number, the date the account was opened, the identification used, and the opening balance. If the account was closed, that date and the closing balance will be listed.

In the case of corporations or partnerships, the articles of incorporation, corporate resolution, or partnership agreement is provided to the bank to authorize the signatories to access the account.

The signature card becomes an active part of the bank's file for each account. If there is a question about a large check, the teller may check the signature against the card. (In some branches, probably not the very busy ones, *every* signature is verified against the card.) The cards are maintained in a file at the branch where the account was opened, but cards for closed accounts will be kept elsewhere, and a subpoena for bank records should always specify open or closed accounts, or both.

From the bank's perspective, there are two kinds of deposits, classified based upon the withdrawal terms of each.

Demand deposits — Demand deposits are any deposits made to a checking account. These are subject to withdrawal at any time, because the customer has a checkbook and is making use of these funds on a regular basis. Because banks never know how long they are going to have these funds, they usually do not pay interest on these accounts. (An exception may be made when a specified minimum balance is kept in the account.) Banks also levy all sorts of charges for these accounts, mostly because, as we will see, processing the checks is a complicated and labor-intensive operation.

Time deposits — Time deposits are essentially savings accounts in which the funds are left on deposit for a relatively long period of time. Some savings accounts have a notification requirement — the funds cannot be withdrawn without penalty for a set number of days. Other accounts, such as certificates of deposit (CDs), are left on deposit for a specified period. The longer the period, the higher the interest rate, but in all cases a CD will earn more than a checking account simply because the bank has your promise to leave the funds there long enough for the bank to loan them out to somebody else and make some real money.

"So, that's what they mean by 'substantial penalty for early withdrawal.'"

NOTE TO FINANCIAL INVESTIGATORS

The phrase "Substantial penalty for early withdrawal" was coined for investments like CDs. When funds are withdrawn before the maturation date, federal regulations require the depositor to provide some statement of hardship. This statement can be used in a financial investigation to rebut a later claim of a cash hoard or to establish a figure for cash on hand.

Banks won't accept just anything for deposit — deposits are limited to cash or cash equivalents. These *cash items* include currency, checks, and bond coupons. Each of these items is handled differently, and the documentation supporting the deposit varies as well.

Cash, consisting of currency and coins, is received and transferred to the vault. The documents supporting the deposit of cash will consist of a deposit ticket, the teller's tape, and possibly an entry on the teller's daily proof sheet. There may also be a separate ticket showing the transfer to the vault. In the case of large cash transactions — those over $10,000 — the bank will also prepare a Currency Transaction Report (CTR) for submission to IRS. Incidentally, although the deposit ticket won't show the denominations of the bills received, the teller's tape will, so if this is an issue in your case, ask for the teller's tapes in your subpoena.

Historically, checks were treated differently based on where they originate. There was a good (meaning profit-related) reason for the differences. The checks were accepted in four categories:

1. Checks drawn "on us" — checks drawn on the bank where they are being deposited
2. Local checks — checks drawn on banks within the local clearinghouse area
3. Transit items — checks drawn on out-of-town banks
4. Special items — things like cashier's checks that require special handling

These checks were treated differently because of the time they are given to "clear" through the banking system. Checks drawn "on us" were credited immediately to the depositor's account. Local checks may have been credited immediately or held for a day or so until the drawing bank provided verification that the funds were there. Transit items might have been held for several (as many as nine) business days, time in which the bank did not have to pay interest to the depositor. The time that it takes for checks to clear is known in the business as the *float*. When you're talking about millions of dollars, the interest saved on a few days' float can be quite substantial, and, where it still exists, the bankers take full advantage.

However, big changes have taken place in the banking industry in recent years, modifications that have basically eliminated the float, along with much of the entire check-clearing process. We'll look at some of these changes in a bit. Investigators should keep in mind that as banks get deeper into the digital age, the types of records available will also change.

The supporting documents accompanying a check deposit include the deposit ticket, the teller tape, and a microfilmed copy of the deposited item. We'll cover the check-clearing and -tracing process in detail in a moment.

Bond coupons are small potatoes compared to checks and cash — and getting smaller as zero-coupon bonds become more popular. The bond coupon represents the interest accumulated to the date printed on the coupon; on that date, the bondholder can clip the coupon and take it to the bank. After being deposited, the coupons are sent to the bank's collection department, because the issuer of the coupon now owes the bank, which already paid the bondholder.

Cash items — cash, checks, and coupons — will be credited to the depositor's account when they are received from one of five sources:

1. Regular teller transactions. These include both the walk-up and the drive-through variety — the old-fashioned way of doing banking business.
2. Armored car service, messenger service, mail, and express services.
3. Wire transfers. We will cover these in a separate chapter. As money becomes more and more electronic, more types of wire transfers are taking place. In addition to the traditional bank-to-bank wires, customers may be able to perform a variety of electronic banking services over the telephone or via computer programs such as Quicken and Microsoft Money. Wire transfers are documented with credit memos, and the actual confirmation record of the wire transfer is kept in a separate file.
4. Night and lobby depositories and automatic teller machines (ATMs). Businesses can be given key access to the night depository, usually a locked box on the outside of the bank. The business's receipts, in the form of cash, checks, and credit card slips, are deposited in envelopes or bank bags and retrieved the next morning by the bank staff. Lobby boxes perform the same function in the daytime, for customers who don't want to wait in line for a receipt. ATMs will also accept deposits, but the envelope has to be fairly small to get through the slot.
5. Other departments of the bank may credit a depositor's account when funds are collected by the bank on behalf of the customer. Loan proceeds would be one example.

All deposits are accompanied by a deposit ticket of some type, usually the one you fill out at the counter or take from the back of your checkbook. The deposit ticket lists the items separately: currency, coin, and checks. Typically, each check is listed separately, and a space is provided for the depositor to note the ABA number of the drawing bank or the name of the maker. There's no requirement that these listings be accurate, except in the amount, and the bank won't turn a deposit away if the deposit ticket shows the amount under the "checks" heading, when in fact it was cash. This is why the other records supporting the deposit have to be examined as well.

Deposit tickets can provide a number of leads for a financial investigation. Checks deposited can identify other bank accounts controlled by the subject or people doing business with the subject. Cash deposits can reflect patterns of activity or evidence of attempts to avoid cash-reporting requirements.

The documents supporting a deposit ticket are, obviously, the deposited items themselves, such as the checks, as well as internal bank documents, such as the teller's tape and credit memos. The transaction will also be recorded in the bank's journal for that day. Another source of deposit information is the customer, who is provided with a receipt or copy of the deposit ticket. A notation will be made on the customer's monthly statement, or, in the case of a savings account, the customer's passbook. These are obviously good leads for a financial investigator and should be examined closely if recovered in a search or pursuant to subpoena.

Deposits may be a key part of a money laundering investigation, and the investigator cannot assume that just because no "cash" is being deposited, laundered funds aren't involved. Cashier's checks, money orders, and financial instruments of all sorts have been and are being used in various money laundering schemes. Many of these are ultimately deposited into some bank account. For this reason, every deposited item needs to be examined, and many of them will have to be traced back through the banking system. This procedure is best covered in an explanation of the check-paying and -clearing process.

PAYING CHECKS

Of all the functions performed by a commercial bank, this one is likely to be most valuable in a financial investigation. This is so because checks play such an enormous role in the American economy. Other countries, such as Japan, do not rely so heavily on personal checks, but in this country, trillions of dollars in checks are passed each year. Interestingly, checks are gradually being replaced by debit cards; according to a study by the Federal Reserve, electronic payment methods, including credit and debit cards, surpassed checks in the United States for the first time in 2003. The total number of electronic transactions — 44.5 billion — easily topped the 36.7 billion checks written that year. We'll look at some of the ramifications of this trend later on.

The banks have established an elaborate system to handle each one of these billions of items. This system is depicted in brief in Figure 13.2, but some additional description will aid in our appreciation of the value of checks in a financial case.

Once upon a time, some bright person, probably a banker, got the idea that instead of carrying all that money around, a piece of paper might do just as well. The check, or cheque, had been invented. The check is a promise by the bank to pay some money to the person who takes or receives the check, money that will be coming from an account in the bank. Usually this account belongs to the customer who's writing the check, but sometimes, as is the case with a cashier's check, the bank's own funds are used to guarantee payment.

A check has many nice features, such as portability, security, and fairly wide acceptance, but as money it isn't perfect. For one thing, as anyone knows who's tried to cash an out-of-state check, or any check at a bank other than their own, checks aren't as well accepted as cash. Wherever they are received, checks still have to be converted into a form more like the money they represent.

Let's say I decide to buy a book at the local bookstore, and, rather than paying in cash or by credit card, I elect to write a check for the purchase. Let's follow this check through the "clearing" process. As we know, I have to first establish an account with a bank, which I have done. I've also made deposits, so I have enough in there to cover this particular check, which looks like Figure 13.3.

Each check has certain elements, most of which you are probably already familiar with. The following elements may require additional explanation:

1. 101 is the number of this particular check. There should be no duplicate numbers in a checking account, and banks are now able to note checks out of the number sequence. This number will also be the same as (9).
2. These are the codes that identify the issuing bank, in this case, the fictional First National Bank of Honolulu. The numbers above the line, 59-202, are known as the ABA Transit Number. 59 is the number for the state of Hawaii, and 202 would be the code for First National Bank, if it existed. The numbers below the line, 1213, are the Federal Reserve Routing Code. In this case, the first two digits, 12, denote the 12th Federal Reserve District. The third digit indicates that the check is to be routed through the district's head office in San Francisco, California. The fourth digit, 3, indicates that the check is available for deferred rather than "immediate" credit, and it originates in the state of Hawaii.

Flow of Transactions Within a Bank

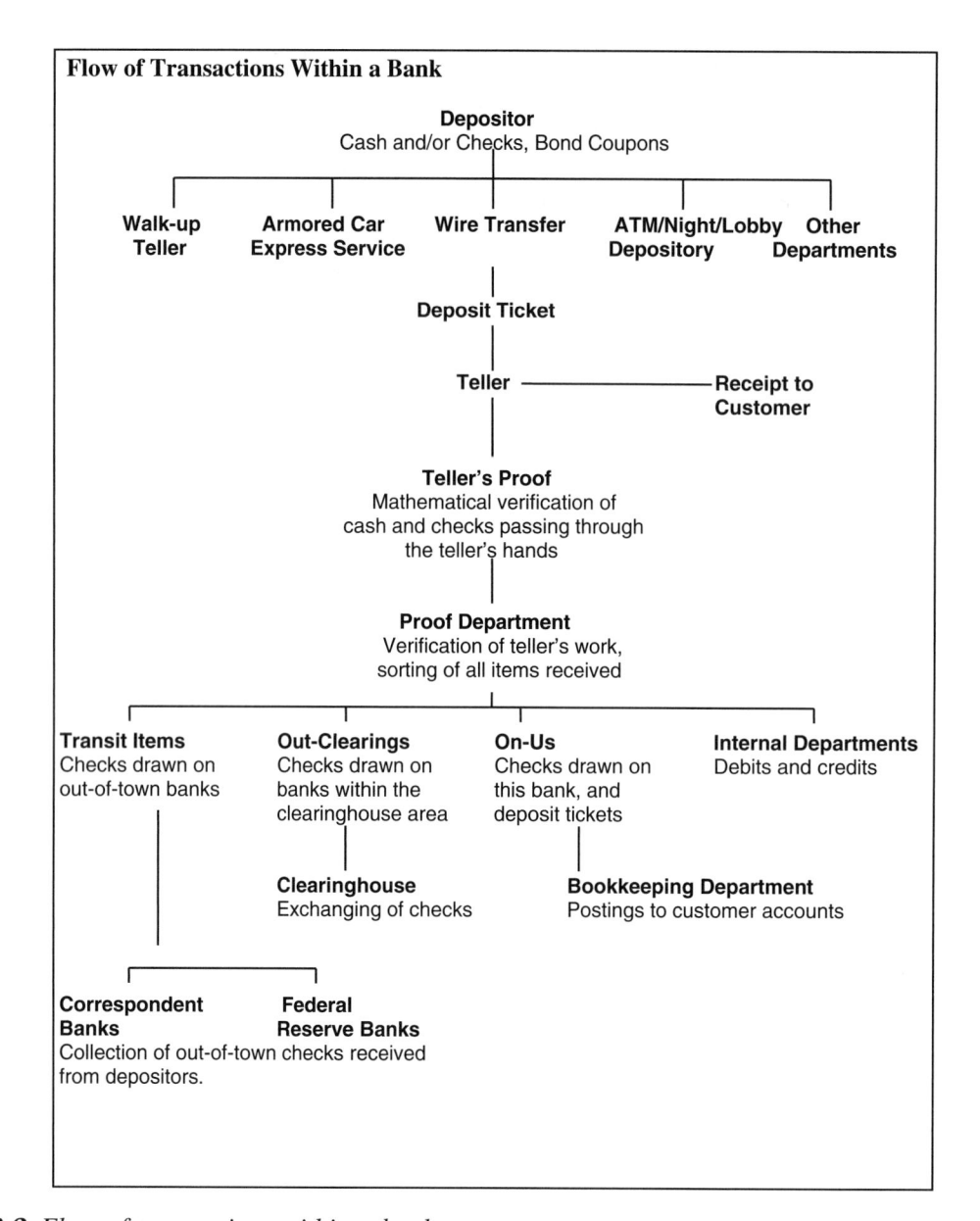

```
                            Depositor
                  Cash and/or Checks, Bond Coupons
        ┌─────────────┬──────────┬──────────────┬──────────┐
    Walk-up      Armored Car   Wire Transfer  ATM/Night/Lobby  Other
    Teller       Express Service              Depository       Departments
                                  │
                            Deposit Ticket
                                  │
                              Teller ─────────── Receipt to
                                  │              Customer
                             Teller's Proof
                         Mathematical verification of
                         cash and checks passing through
                             the teller's hands
                                  │
                           Proof Department
                         Verification of teller's work,
                         sorting of all items received
        ┌─────────────┬──────────────┬──────────────┐
    Transit Items   Out-Clearings   On-Us         Internal Departments
    Checks drawn on Checks drawn on Checks drawn on  Debits and credits
    out-of-town     banks within    this bank, and
    banks           the             deposit tickets
                    clearinghouse area
                         │               │
                    Clearinghouse     Bookkeeping Department
                    Exchanging of     Postings to customer accounts
                    checks
        ┌─────────────┐
    Correspondent  Federal
    Banks          Reserve Banks
    Collection of out-of-town checks received
    from depositors.
```

Figure 13.2 *Flow of transactions within a bank.*

3. The payee — the name of the business I'm paying with this check — is the name that will also appear on the endorsement on the reverse of the check.

4. Here the check-writer enters the amount or face value of the check. This is how much money I'm telling the bank to turn over to Borders. This number must always match (10).

5. The bank that is going to pay this check with my money is printed here. This is also the branch where my account file and signature card are actually located. This check will eventually be routed back to this branch and possibly matched against the signature card.

6. This number, along with (7.) and (8.), is a prequalification code, printed in magnetic ink character recognition or MICR (pronounced "Mike-er") numbers. Special bank equipment can read these characters, automatically routing and processing the checks. The prequalification codes are put on the blank check at the time it is printed to aid in the routing process later.

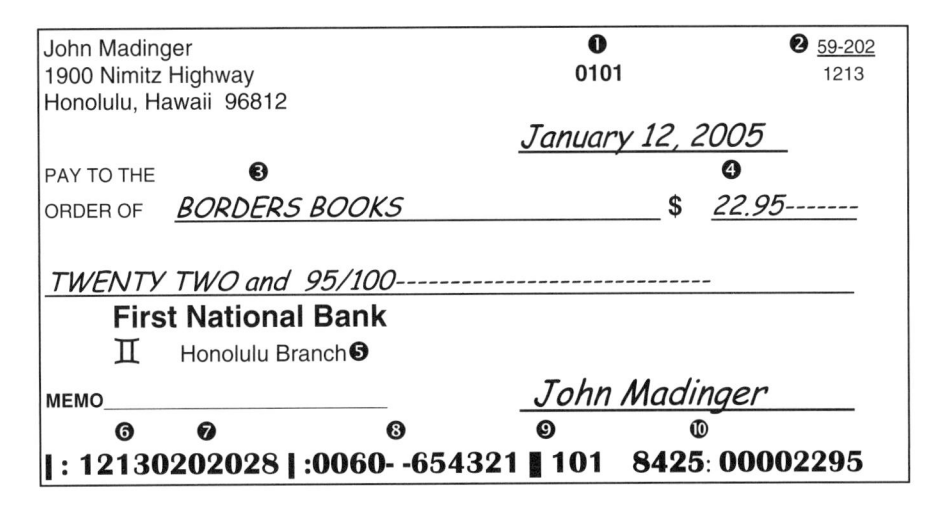

```
John Madinger                    ❶              ❷ 59-202
1900 Nimitz Highway             0101               1213
Honolulu, Hawaii  96812
                                January 12, 2005
PAY TO THE      ❸                      ❹
ORDER OF   BORDERS BOOKS          $  22.95-------

TWENTY TWO and  95/100----------------------------
     First National Bank
     II    Honolulu Branch ❺
MEMO_____          John Madinger
     ❻        ❼        ❽         ❾      ❿
  I: 12130202028 I:0060- -654321 I 101   8425: 00002295
```

Figure 13.3 *A check.*

```
   ❻              ❼              ❽
I: 12130202028  I: 0060- -654321  II
  Check         ABA           Account Number
  Routing       Transit
  Symbol        Number
```

9. and (10.) are postqualification codes, again printed in MICR characters, but this time after the check is deposited at the receiving bank. This printing is done on the proof machine, which also sorts the checks and makes a ledger of the various transactions occurring during the day. The MICR characters are machine readable, enabling the check to be processed almost automatically by receiving banks and the Federal Reserve.

```
    ❾              ❿
   101         8425:  00002295
  -Check      Process  Transaction Amount
   Number     Code    (face value of the check)
```

I sign the check and hand it over, receiving my book in exchange. Although many merchants participate in some form of check verification system, such as TeleCheck or UniCheck, these only confirm that I have an account and that there's some amount of money in it. The bookstore does not gain immediate possession of that money. The transfer of funds occurs only after the check has gone through the clearance process.

```
FOR DEPOSIT ONLY

BORDERS BOOKS AND MUSIC

Acct:  0060-123456

DO NOT WRITE, STAMP, OR SIGN BELOW LINE
```

Figure 13.4 *The reverse of the check.*

In order for the bank to cash or pay a check, first the payee must endorse it. In this case, Borders includes the check in its deposit, which might be picked up by an armored car or just taken to the bank by an employee. For the sake of this example, we'll assume that Borders does its banking at another fictional bank, Second National.

Borders' endorsement goes at the top of the reverse side of the check. It includes the account number at Second National where the bookstore wants the check deposited. The reverse side of my check now looks something like Figure 13.4.

At Second National Bank, the check is received in the Borders deposit and routed through a proof machine. This device performs several functions at once, including, in some cases, taking a microfilm photograph of the front and back of the check. (Even if it isn't done here, every item going through the bank is microfilmed.)

The proof machine puts the postqualification codes on the check, makes the appropriate entries on the transaction ledger, and then automatically routes the check into one of several slots. The slots are set up based upon the type of item received (on-us, out-clearings, transit items, and internal or special). The objective is to get payment from the issuing bank as quickly as possible, so some proof machines have slots to route items to another local bank. My check is an out-clearing, which will be routed to the slot for the local clearinghouse. If my check had been drawn on Second National, it would have been credited immediately to Borders' account, since it would be considered an "on-us" and therefore immediately available.

The proof machine prints a transaction number and the date on the check, and it stamps Second National's routing codes on the check as well.

At the end of Second National Bank's business day, the checks are gathered up from the various slots of the proof machine and bundled together according to where they are going. My check is going back to First National, which still doesn't know that it needs to pay Second National and Borders.

The bundle of out-clearings goes to a local clearinghouse, where after settlement they are routed to the drawing bank, in this case First National. Here they go through another proof machine, which reads the information and makes some new entries, welcoming the check home. See Figure 13.5.

The individual check will be sent to the branch where my account file is physically located and placed in the file folder until it's time for my monthly statement to go out. In the meantime, First National is finally aware that it needs to pay the check I wrote, so it debits my account and credits the amount for Second National Bank. The process is complete (assuming that I have the money in my account and the check isn't returned for nonsufficient funds).

If my check had been written in Los Angeles, the proof operator at the receiving bank would have routed it as a transit item to the

```
FOR DEPOSIT ONLY
BORDERS BOOKS AND MUSIC
Acct: 0060-123456
DO NOT WRITE, STAMP, OR SIGN BELOW LINE


1227    86512

    →121301098←
2ND NATIONAL BANK
Central Proof Dept.
Honolulu, HI, U.S.A.
    →121301098←

JAN 13 98



0110016932  19980115  FNB
```

Figure 13.5 *The reverse of the check after processing.*

```
PAY ANY BANK P.E.G.
12FRC SAN FRANCISCO
   0520 00578 8
```

Figure 13.6 *An endorsement by the Federal Reserve Bank in San Francisco.*

Federal Reserve Bank in San Francisco. There, it would have received an additional endorsement, which might look like Figure 13.6. "P.E.G." stands for "prior endorsement guaranteed," confirmation from the Fed that this check has been processed correctly.

A bank cashing an out-of-town check could alternatively go through a correspondent bank in the city where the account is located. In that case, the check would be shipped to the correspondent bank, which would clear the item through the local clearinghouse. The banks will use whichever option is quicker and more convenient, in the hope of reducing the clearance time and thus the float.

At the end of the month, the check will be pulled from my file at the branch and mailed with the monthly account statement back to me. (Some banks store the checks and mail a microfilm copy or just a summary of the month's activity.) The monthly statement lists all of the transactions, checks written, deposits, interest paid, ATM transactions, and other debits and credits.

Check 21 — Big Changes for Banks (Almost) Everywhere

On October 28, 2004, the Check Clearing for the 21st Century Act went into effect. Popularly known as Check 21, this law changes almost everything about check clearing that you just read. Banks hated the inefficiency of the clearing process, the shipping of all that paper hither and yon, and the need to microfilm the checks and keep them filed away somewhere for years on end. They also weren't pleased that you and I could take advantage of the float by writing a check we knew wouldn't clear for as much as nine days.

Why, those bankers said, if computers let us process transactions instantly through a network of debit cards and ATMs worldwide, can't we process checks just as quickly? Why not? Congress responded (the bankers have a swell lobby), and they created this new statute to take advantage of modern technology.

The first thing that Check 21 did was to accelerate the clearance process to the speed of light. Using my example above, when my check comes into Second National Bank with Borders' deposit, it immediately gets "imaged" — fed through a scanner that digitizes both sides. The information is entered into a computer and sent very quickly — usually the same day — to my bank, which pays — also digitally — immediately. The float is now history. So is the need to ship all that paper and store it, because the check is shredded right after the imaging is complete at the first bank it touches.

But what if I need a copy of my check to prove I made a payment? Or what if a financial investigator needs copies of all of a subject's checks to help prove a case? Check 21 also provides that the digitized image can function as a "substitute check," legally valid as evidence. The substitute check has to contain a statement that "This is a legal copy of your check. You can use it the same way you would use the original check," but that's all that's needed to make the digital version "real" enough for a court.

Paper checks will probably be around for a while longer, but they're going to get scarcer and scarcer. As people increasingly turn to online and digital payment systems, the need for paper declines. Merchants now have the capability of scanning your check at the cash register, just as they would a debit card. In this case, the merchant takes the check, scans it into the reader, enters the transaction amount, and then hands you back your check. It won't be long before businesses everywhere will be doing something similar, eliminating the need for paper checks.

Monthly Account Statements

The monthly account statement is an excellent jumping-off point for a financial investigation. The signature card will tell you that an individual or business holds an account with the bank. The monthly account statement will provide a fairly detailed picture of the activity in this account, activity that can then be further documented by obtaining the actual items listed in the account statement (checks written, deposits made).

In a monthly account statement, transactions are listed as either debits or credits to the account. A debit in this instance means any withdrawal or subtraction of funds; a credit indicates a deposit or addition to the account. On some statements, such as those for savings accounts, these items are listed simply as "withdrawals" and "deposits."

Monthly account statements are designed to be simple enough for the lay person to read and understand. Some codes are used to denote different transactions, but these are usually explained somewhere on the statement. If not, the investigator will have to contact the bank for an explanation, since these may affect calculations in the investigation.

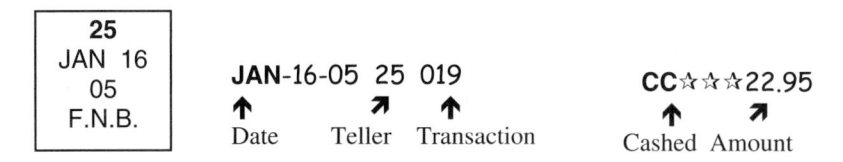

```
    ┌─────┐
    │ 25  │
    │JAN 16│   JAN-16-05  25  019              CC✭✭✭22.95
    │ 05  │      ↑        ↗   ↑                  ↑      ↗
    │F.N.B.│    Date    Teller Transaction    Cashed  Amount
    └─────┘
```

Figure 13.7 *Examples of machine stamps.*

NOTE FOR FINANCIAL INVESTIGATORS

A subpoena for bank records usually includes both the monthly statements and the items making up the deposits and withdrawals. It is often possible and sometimes desirable to specify that the account statements be turned over first, at which time the investigator can make a decision about which items should be obtained next (e.g., all deposit tickets and checks over $1000). Many bank records custodians are familiar with this drill and will ask whether you want to wait for everything or start with certain items.

There is another way that a bank pays checks, and this is by cashing them. Remember that my check to Borders was never actually "cashed" or converted to currency. I gave it to Borders, and the merchant deposited it directly into its bank account. If Borders had been unwilling to accept my check, I could have gone to the bank and written a check to cash, obtaining the money for my book in this more roundabout fashion.

Many banks use a different set of stamps for a check that is cashed as opposed to one that is deposited. Sometimes a code, such as "CC," indicates that the check was cashed. These stamps are often applied to the face of the check at the teller window while you're standing there — watch the next time you go to the bank. If so, the teller's stamp will identify which teller handled the transaction, as well as the date. A symbol or shape, such as a square, may also denote a cashed check, while a diamond shape might identify a deposited check. A few examples of machine stamps are shown in Figure 13.7.

In addition to monthly account statements, records relating to deposits include:

- Teller tapes
- Deposit tickets
- Copies of items deposited
- Cash-in tickets
- Credit memos
- Currency Transaction Reports, if applicable

Records relating to withdrawals, in addition to the monthly account statement, include:

- Teller tapes
- Copies of checks
- Cash-out tickets
- Debit memos
- Currency Transaction Reports, if applicable

TRANSFERRING FUNDS

The transfer of funds is another traditional function of banks. In addition to wire transfers, something we're going to cover in detail elsewhere, several instruments are used for funds transfer. These are known as exchange instruments, or bank checks, and include the following:

- Cashier's checks, also known as treasurer's checks
- Bank money orders
- Bank drafts
- Traveler's checks
- Certified checks

All of these instruments have one thing in common: They are not backed directly by a depositor's money; instead, they are backed by a bank's.

Cashier's Checks

Cashier's checks have been the key element in many money laundering schemes. This is because they are extremely portable, are widely accepted (almost universally accepted in the banking community), have an indefinite shelf life, and, best of all from the launderer's point of view, can be written in any amount. The only drawback, again from the launderer's viewpoint, is that, unlike cash, cashier's checks do leave a paper trail.

As its name implies, the cashier's check is issued by a bank employee who is acting as a cashier of the bank's own funds. This official will issue the check upon receipt of some payment from the customer. This transaction is really a purchase, because the customer is providing funds to buy the paper. Cash is frequently used to purchase cashier's checks, and the bank is required by federal law to log all cash purchases of cashier checks over $3000, solely because money launderers like these checks so much. (This log may contain good leads, since the banks are supposed to view the customer's ID and record identifying information.) Funds can also be withdrawn from a customer's account to pay for the cashier's check.

Cashier's checks provide fabulous leads in a financial investigation, first because they are so often used for the acquisition of big-ticket assets such as houses, cars, boats, and businesses. Cash is nice, but legitimate individuals and businesses do not want the problems connected with accepting several hundred thousand dollars in small bills for a large purchase. Similarly, they may want more security than they can get from a personal check. The cashier's check provides a perfect balance.

Cashier's checks are traceable, the other reason they make good leads. The tracing process is more complicated than with personal checks, because the investigator must find a starting point. This may not be easy, because cashier's checks can be purchased at any branch of any bank and are not matched with the customer's account records.

When a cashier's check is purchased, at least four records are generated. First, the customer gets the original check. When this is cashed or deposited, it eventually returns to the branch where it was purchased, routed exactly as a personal check would be. Second, the bank gets a copy of the check or a receipt showing the purchase. Third, the customer gets a "flimsy" or carbon copy of the check, which he or she can use for personal records. Fourth, the bank makes an entry about the purchase on a log or ledger. If the purchase is made with cash over $3,000, that fact is noted on a log, and if the amount is over $10,000 in cash, a CTR is supposed to be prepared.

If the money for the purchase was withdrawn from the customer's account, this will make your job much easier, because there will be a debit memo noting this fact, which will also appear on the customer's monthly account statement. It will be a rather simple matter to go to the bank and find out whom the check was written to and where it went after it was purchased.

The big problem with investigating cashier's checks is that they may represent a break in the paper trail, especially if they are purchased or redeemed for cash. These items can be investigated in several ways, depending on where you cut the trail. If a name is all you have as a starting point, you can ask for copies of all cashier's checks purchased by your suspect. This request is not going to make you any friends at the bank, because cashier's checks are never filed by the customer's name, nor are they centrally filed. At the very least you will be asked to provide a date and the branch where the checks were purchased.

It may also be possible to examine the suspect's account and look for indications that checks are being purchased — large withdrawals, debit memos, possibly a redeposit of a cashier's check. Surveillance of the suspect or the execution of a search warrant that includes the flimsies or cashier's check receipts might also be productive. At the other end, deposits to checking or savings accounts, or the purchases of assets may lead to cashier's checks used for those purchases or deposits.

Bank Money Orders

Bank money orders work exactly like cashier's checks, but most banks limit the face value of bank money orders. They usually say something on the face like "Not valid over $300." As instruments in a money laundering scheme, these aren't bad, but they aren't as popular as cashier's checks. Incidentally, many nonbank financial institutions also issue money orders, notably the United States Postal Service, whose money orders are limited to $700, and the Western Union Corporation.

Bank Drafts

Bank drafts are also similar to cashier's checks, except that they are drawn on an account the issuing bank is holding in another bank. Let's say I want to buy some real estate in Vancouver, B.C. I don't want to take cash up there, and the seller doesn't want to take a check from the United States. My bank has an account with a correspondent bank in B.C., so I buy a bank draft just as I would a cashier's check and take the draft to Canada. The tracing procedures for bank drafts and bank money orders are similar to those for cashier's checks.

Traveler's Checks

Traveler's checks are also backed by someone else's money, giving them wider acceptance, especially abroad. The traveler's checks are purchased at a bank that operates in connection with a major issuing company. Your local bank buys the checks from American Express Corp., First National City Bank, or another source. The checks are issued in preset denominations, ($10, $20, $50, $100, $500, and $1000) and are purchased by your bank for resale. The customer must sign the checks at the time of purchase, and a sales order or purchase agreement is prepared.

Because traveler's checks don't come back to the bank where they were bought — they go back to the issuing company — they have to be traced by serial number. The bank should have a record of the numbers on the checks it has sold, and these can then be used to obtain the original checks from the issuer.

Traveler's checks are popular items in some money laundering schemes because they can be purchased with cash or funds withdrawn from one account and then deposited into another account, leaving a break in the trail. Example: Withdraw cash from account at Bank A, take to Bank B, buy traveler's checks, deposit checks into account at Bank C. This would be a pretty difficult scheme to trace. Traveler's checks are also easily transportable and cheerfully accepted overseas, and, if purchased in small amounts, they don't even require identification to obtain.

Certified Checks

Certified checks are a slightly different category in that the check is drawn on the customer's account and looks just like a personal or business check. For a fee, the bank will certify or guarantee payment of the check from its own funds. The bank does this by printing "Certified" on the face of the check and immediately taking the money out of the customer's account. Because the check is now a liability of the bank, just as a cashier's check would be, the bank keeps the original after it is paid. A debit memorandum is issued when the funds are withdrawn, and this memo is sent to the customer with the monthly statement.

Exchange Instruments

Because the transfer of funds is such a critical element in any money laundering scheme, these exchange instruments must be clearly understood by investigators. Their use in a scheme will cloud the paper trail and complicate the investigation. Investigators must be alert to signs that exchange instruments are being used and seek to develop any information concerning that use, because these instruments will almost invariably lead to other banks, new accounts, or assets acquired with laundered funds.

Records relating to transfer of funds include:

- Copies of exchange instruments (bank checks, cashier's checks, bank drafts, money orders, traveler's checks, certified checks)
- Copies of application form
- Purchase documents
- Teller tapes (for purchase)
- Copies of items used to purchase instruments (checks)
- Cash-in tickets
- Memos debiting account
- Redemption documents
- Teller tapes (for redemption)
- Copies of items acquired at redemption (new bank checks)
- Cash-out tickets
- Memos crediting account

HOLDING AND ADMINISTERING PROPERTY FOR OTHERS

Banks have always been storehouses for other people's money. Those big vault doors aren't just functional — they're a graphic illustration of the security offered by a bank to its customers. The renting of vault space isn't a particularly profitable enterprise for the bank, just another service, but it is something banks do well.

This holding of property usually takes the form of the rental of a safe deposit box. These boxes are located in a special part of the bank's vault, the only part the general public will have access to. Safe deposit boxes are rented in periods of six months to one year, and they come in a variety of sizes.

The bank has utterly no interest in the contents of a safe deposit box, and in fact cannot even access the box, which requires two keys, one of which belongs to the customer. People with a grudge against the bank have been known to store fish or some other noxious item in their boxes, with the predictable result.

It would be pointless for an investigator to ask the banker about the contents of a particular box, since the banker would have no way of knowing. What the banker *does* know is of serious interest to the financial investigator. When a box is rented, the customer is required to complete a safe deposit box rental contract, containing a signature and identifying information. Any corenters are also listed, and their signatures are on the contract as well. This contract will be kept on file at the branch where the box is located, and most banks have centralized safe deposit rental records on computer.

The other information of interest relates to access. Investigators need to know not only *who* has access to the box, but also *when* the box was opened or accessed. Banks keep this information in two forms, either on a ledger card, maintained for each box, or on separate cards, filed by date. The former is much easier for the investigator to use, since all of the entries relating to a particular box are on one piece of paper. Naturally, few banks seem to use this system. Most keep a stack of small cards at the desk near the vault entrance. The box holder signs this card and writes the box number on the card. A teller then checks the signature against that on the rental contract before opening the box. The teller may also check the customer's ID. These cards are filed by date. This means that if subpoenaed, some bank employee is going to have to go through all of the cards for all the boxes to pull the ones relevant to the box in question — much more cumbersome and time consuming than if the records are all on one card. See Figure 13.8.

This information is of importance in a financial investigation because the dates on which the box was accessed can be matched against other key dates, such as known drug transactions, cash deposits into savings or checking accounts, purchases of cashier's checks, and the like. This is

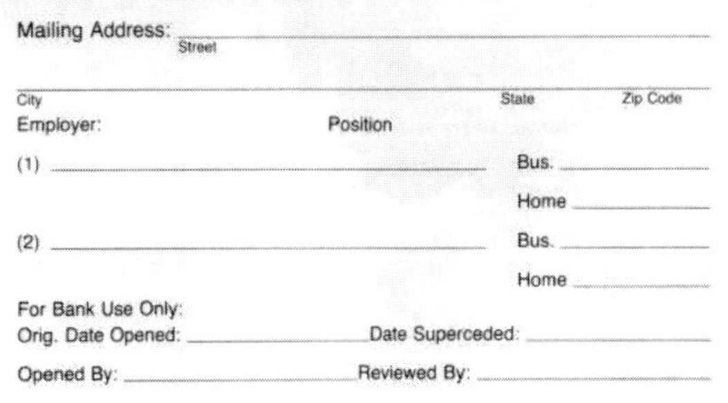

Mailing Address: ______ Street

______ City State Zip Code

Employer: Position

(1) ______ Bus. ______

Home ______

(2) ______ Bus. ______

Home ______

For Bank Use Only:

Orig. Date Opened: ______ Date Superceded: ______

Opened By: ______ Reviewed By: ______

Figure 13.8 *Safe deposit box access card.*

the type of information required to get a search warrant for the safe deposit box, which is what you're going to need to get into it. A subpoena will get you the signature card, the contract, and the access records, but only a court order or a search warrant will compel the bank to drill the lock on the box for you.

NOTE FOR FINANCIAL INVESTIGATORS

Bank tellers, especially those who service the safe deposit box customers, can be good witnesses in your case. They frequently know their regular customers by name and face, and they may be able to identify associates or other accounts or boxes controlled by your suspect. There is also the possibility that the teller may disclose the existence of your inquiry, or that a bank employee might be involved in the money laundering scheme, so precautions should be taken to prevent that type of damage to your case.

Records relating to safe deposit boxes include:

- Safe deposit box rental contracts
- Access cards
- Access ledgers

In addition to safe deposit boxes, banks will rent vault space for the storage of larger items, such as art collections or furs. These rentals are usually handled by the same people who rent the boxes, so a subpoena for safe deposit records should turn up information about this type of rental as well.

COLLECTING AND PROCESSING FINANCIAL INSTRUMENTS

So far, we've mostly been talking about the cash-like items that a bank accepts in deposits and stores in accounts. As we know, money can be almost anything, and banks know this better than anybody. Rather than get left out, banks have devised ways of handling those other items that don't fit into everyday bank business. Again, this is all a part of being a full-service financial institution.

What else finds its way through a bank? Any item that needs "collection." (Technically, checks are "collected" too, but a different process is used.) These are instruments or documents that are, in effect, promises by the issuer to pay someone else. Credit card slips are a good example. A merchant in Hawaii will accept a credit card issued on a Maine bank because the merchant can be pretty sure the bank will pay for the charge. It's impractical for the Hawaiian to take the slip up to Bangor for payment, so banks handle this collection.

Other instruments that banks will collect and process include:

- Bonds and coupons (remember, we did say these would be routed to the bank's collection department)
- Stock certificates
- Drafts, bills of lading, warehouse receipts, and other documents
- Mortgages and real estate contracts
- Notes and acceptances

All of these items are just pieces of paper until they are actually "collected." Only when the bank's collection department gets an advice that the funds for the item have been received will the bank issue the credit memo that credits the customer's account with those funds.

The operations of bank collection departments vary more widely than do some of the other functions. Some records typically generated by the collection department include:

- Correspondence
- Requests for payment
- Copies of the item to be collected
- Credit memos
- Copies of the check or item used for payment

OTHER SERVICES

As if all of the above weren't enough services to keep a banker busy, a few other operations serve special customer needs. These include currency exchange, services for business, and trust department services.

CURRENCY EXCHANGE

A centuries-old tradition for banks, foreign currency exchange operations flourish in banks near international borders and in major tourist centers. Large banks have international operations divisions that deal in matters relating to foreign countries and currency, and most banks monitor the exchange rates for various currencies. Although the bank will take a small percentage of each currency exchange as its commission, these aren't big earners for all but the largest banks.

Banks may restrict the number of currencies they will exchange, finding the hassle of dealing in a few Swedish kroner every year or two to be too burdensome. Similarly, some banks will take the foreign currency and exchange it for American money but will not store baskets of foreign money on the off chance somebody wants some kroner this month.

Money launderers may use *casas de cambio,* or "houses of exchange," small, nonbank financial institutions, to exchange currency. These *casas* frequently operate near a border, and they may also transmit funds by wire out of the country. Because the *casas* aren't regulated like banks, concealing large cash transactions may be easier for the launderer. Other independent businesses, notably American Express–Thomas Cook, also operate in the foreign exchange business.

Banks will also exchange various denominations of American money for their customers, and money launderers, especially drug traffickers who take large quantities of small bills, may want to exchange these for larger denomination notes.

SERVICES FOR BUSINESS

Banks recognize that a good part of their business depends on other area businesses, so, in addition to providing special windows in their branches for business transactions, the banks may assist with the collection of accounts and even maintain accounting records for businesses. A bank may also provide "lock box" banking, where creditors may make their payments to the bank instead of directly to the business.

The types of records kept in these situations vary widely. In some cases, banks may actually maintain all of the accounting, billing, and payment records of professionals such as doctors or lawyers. In other cases, the bank may only perform some of the collection activity and return all of the records to the customer. A subpoena should obtain this information.

TRUST DEPARTMENT SERVICES

Tax evaders and money launderers may use trusts to conceal income and assets from the government. In these cases, the trust department of the bank, whose responsibility is the management of trust assets, may perform an important role in the laundering scheme.

A bank's trust department performs three main services:

- Settling estates
- Administration of trusts and guardianships
- Acting as an agent or performing agency services

A trust is a legal concept that creates a fiduciary relationship in which one person, the trustee, holds title to property (known as the trust estate or trust property) for the benefit of another person, the beneficiary. Trusts are used extensively throughout society and, like everything else involving money or property, can be illegally employed in a money laundering scheme.

The settling of an estate need not involve an actual trust, just a deceased person. The bank may be appointed by the court or heirs or executors of the person's estate to inventory the assets, pay debts and taxes, and distribute the remaining assets according to the will.

Administering trusts and guardianships does involve an established trust. In this case, the bank may be appointed to manage assets or make payments on behalf of the trustee or the beneficiary. In some cases, the bank may be named as the trustee, in which case its actions are based upon instructions in the trust agreement, living trust, will, or other legal document establishing the trust.

Agency services are a broad category in which the bank acts as an agent on behalf of an individual or corporation. Agent services include:

- Safekeeping — holding, receiving, and delivering property on the order of the principal
- Custodian — collecting and distributing income, as well as buying, selling, receiving, and delivering securities
- Managing — actively managing property (including securities or real property), to the extent specified in the agency agreement
- Escrow — acting as escrow agent in the transfer of property (or delegating this function to another company constituted for that purpose)
- Transfer agent — serving as an agent of a corporation in transferring shares of stock and registered bonds
- Registrar — maintaining records of the number of shares of stock issued and transferred, to prevent overissuance
- Paying agent — paying the dividends on stock or the interest on bonds, on behalf of a corporation, for example (This activity is one of the more common agency services that the financial investigator is likely to encounter.)

The records of the trust department are highly individualized, because the terms of each trust are different, as are the requirements for the bank in its trustee or agency capacity.

The use of trusts to conceal assets, income, or the source of that income is not uncommon; these tactics are very common in tax avoidance/evasion schemes, and money launderers like them, too. Our problems increase when the trust is not held in the principal or beneficiary name and when the trust is formed offshore. Tracing assets under these conditions may be difficult.

Many years ago, I investigated a narcotics case in which five parcels of real property were placed in the names of three different trusts, all with catchy names not connected in any way with the drug trafficker, who was also the trustee. There was no legal requirement that trusts be registered, and since the trustee's name didn't appear as the owner on the title records, neither property tax nor land ownership records disclosed his interest. We only found out about the property when we searched his residence and found the trust documents.

BANK RECORD-KEEPING AND REPORTING

As (rather heavily) regulated industries, the banks are required to keep certain records. They would probably do it anyway, but two federal laws and the banks' charters make sure that enough records are made and retained to reconstruct everything that goes on. The Bank Secrecy Act (BSA) and the federal Right to Financial Privacy Act (RTFPA) are two statutes that provide guidelines for what must be kept.

Prior to Check 21, all banks were required to microfilm all checks over $100, as well as deposit tickets and account statements. The banks found it was actually easier and cheaper for them to microfilm everything that goes through the proof and microfilm machines, so they copy it all, front and back.

Records retention is for a minimum of five years, but most of these records are going to be kept somewhere for a lot longer, especially now that everything is being digitized and stored on disk. You will probably have statute of limitations problems before the bank sends the records to the "shredder." Some items, such as loan files, will be active for more than seven years; a mortgage loan file, for example, may be active for 30 years.

Items that are required under the Bank Secrecy Act to be kept for five years include:

- Signature cards
- Any records that record all deposits and withdrawals, including account statements and ledger cards or sheets
- Copies of customers' checks (both sides), cashier's checks, bank drafts, and money orders
- Records of extensions of credit over $5,000
- Records of any transfer of more than $10,000 outside the United States
- Records of any cash transaction over $10,000, including deposits, withdrawals, cashier's check purchases, and currency exchanges

Additionally, banks are required to retain for two years all of the records needed to reconstruct a customer's checking account, including deposit tickets, credit memos, and similar items. The information needed to trace every check deposited into the customer's account must also be retained for two years. Again, most of these records will be retained for longer periods of time.

While the BSA and RTFPA restrict the information financial institutions can give out except pursuant to a subpoena, they also provide for certain voluntary disclosures. Banks are required, for example, to report any violation of statutes or regulations, whether that violation involves a bank employee or a customer. Formerly, these violations were reported on one of several forms, known as Criminal Referrals or Suspicious Transaction Reports, which were routed to various agencies, ranging from the Comptroller of the Currency to the FBI. All of these forms have been combined into one Suspicious Activity Report, FinCEN Form TDF90-22.47, with a more centralized distribution.

If the bank is not reporting a potential violation, it is not permitted to disclose account information, except pursuant to legal process, such as a subpoena, summons, court order, or search warrant. Warning! Federal law also provides that the bank must notify the customer that information from the account was disclosed and to whom, unless the bank is legally instructed not to do so. This can have serious implications for your case. In money laundering investigations, a protective order can and should be obtained preventing disclosure to the customer by the financial institution. Obtaining such an order should be considered a priority.

CHAPTER 14

INTERNATIONAL BANKING

"In France, 'rue' is street, and 'chapeau' means hat. I mean, it's like the French have got a different word for everything!"
Steve Martin, American comic

"All these financiers, all the little gnomes of Zurich and the other financial centers, about whom we keep hearing."
Harold Wilson, British Prime Minister

"International banking." It even sounds intimidating. You get a picture of people with MBAs from Harvard and Oxford, doing all sorts of unusual, even unnatural things with money that normal people can't begin to understand, let alone duplicate. There are people like that, a couple of whom provided insights for this chapter, but most international bankers are no different from, well, regular bankers.

Steve Martin's right, the French *have* got a different word for everything, but the language of banking is not English, French, or Japanese — it's money. "Money spoken here" is the rule at banks all around the world, and as we've seen in earlier chapters, the rules about money are very rigid. One of those rules, probably Rule #1, is that once in the financial system, money doesn't just get lost. This rule is strictly adhered to by banks everywhere, and in following it they all use pretty much the same procedures.

If you think about it, this is a fairly logical approach, particularly in an international economy. The accounting procedures in a Swiss bank are going to be identical for all of its branches, whether they are located in Zurich or in New York City. The people at Chase Manhattan's Hong Kong branch are using the same procedures as their colleagues in Chase's New York operation. And the smaller banks, local operations in Togo or Turkey or Thailand, all deal with the larger banks, so they follow the same procedures, too.

The first international banks were Italian, branches of family-owned businesses. The idea was that you put a trusted family member in the distant location and then did business with him via correspondence. For example, "Guido, give Signor Minetti 100 florins by March 15, signed Luigi." Since Guido and Luigi were cousins, working at different branches of the same family banking business, there was a high degree of assurance involved in these transactions.

It didn't take long before people either ran out of trusted relatives or just decided that maybe banking could be even simpler. By the 14th century, four-name paper was in use. Now known as a bankers' acceptance, this method of international payment is still a mainstay of modern commerce.

The principle behind these transactions was the same in 1400 as it is today — collection with confidence. Every party to the deal (and, as the name "four-name paper" implies, there are usually four parties) needs to be assured that it will

TABLE 14.1
Some Terms Used in International Payments

Advice	The forwarding of a letter of credit or an amendment to a letter of credit to the seller or beneficiary of the L/C by the advising (seller's) bank
Amendment	A change in the terms of an L/C, usually to meet the needs of the seller. The seller requests the amendment from the buyer. If agreed, the buyer instructs the issuing bank to issue the amendment; the original L/C is not altered, but a separate document is created with the new terms, and all parties are advised of the change.
Discrepancy	Some noncompliance with the terms of an L/C. This could be something little, like a misspelling, or something major, like a missing document or a failure to perform. The little things can be fixed easily, but the major ones could cause the invalidation of the L/C.
Forward foreign exchange	One of the things the parties agree to in the L/C is the method of payment and the currency to be used. But currency prices fluctuate, which could cause the profits to be affected. As a hedge, buyers of merchandise may purchase foreign exchange contracts, essentially buying or selling currency on the future or "forward forex" market.
Validity	The time period for which a letter of credit is valid. After receiving notice of a letter of credit opened on his or her behalf, the seller must act within the period of validity to meet all the requirements of the L/C.

be able to collect its end of the transaction. Over the years, the bankers have devised several different forms of payment to fit certain situations, but the general theme is that everyone involved (*a*) understands the entire process and (*b*) has a high degree of confidence that the transaction will be carried out as understood. There are differences in the payment methods, each of which involves at least one bank.

INTERNATIONAL TRANSACTIONS

It doesn't matter where in the world you're doing business, if you're selling something, you want to know first and foremost if and when you're going to be paid. If you're buying something, you want to know when the goods are going to be delivered. All sorts of factors contribute to increased risk in international transactions, from something as traumatic as a revolution, to something as mundane as a misunderstanding of local terminology. The objective of the various forms of international payments is to minimize the risk to both parties. Note that the risk isn't eliminated, only reduced.

There are four common methods of international payment, each of which provides the parties with some degree of protection — for getting paid or for receiving the shipment. Ranking the methods in order of security for the *seller*, these are:

- Cash in advance
- Documentary letters of credit (L/C)
- Documentary collections
- Open account

Note that while banks play a role in all of these transactions, they are most heavily involved in documentary letters of credit and documentary collection, which are the most secure from both parties' standpoint. It is the banks that provide this added measure of security, which in turn paves the path of international trade. Let's examine each of these payment methods. We will discuss documentary letters of credit and documentary collections at more length later. Table 14.1 defines some terms used in international payments.

CASH IN ADVANCE

As you can well imagine, this method is the one most preferred by sellers everywhere. If you've bought or sold anything on eBay, you're familiar with the concept. It certainly provides the most security for the seller, but it puts the buyer at greatest risk. Needless to say, a very high degree of trust is required in the relationship, at least on the buyer's end.

Some sellers can insist on cash in advance for smaller transactions and in initial transactions, where confidence is being established. ("Fronting the money" isn't exactly a foreign concept in the drug business, either.)

A bank's involvement in these types of transactions is limited to the foreign exchange and issuance of bank drafts or checks. ("Cash" doesn't mean cash, although the payment will have to be in a form that the seller will accept, such as a local check.)

Documentary Letters of Credit

Letters of credit are the most common form of international payment, offering the highest degree of security for both seller and buyer. This security is provided by the involvement of the bank that is making a promise to pay a supplier on behalf of the buyer so long as the supplier meets the terms and conditions stated in the credit. The bank has nothing to do with the goods themselves.

Documents are the key to letter of credit transactions. The buyer specifies the documentation required from the seller before the bank makes the payment, and the seller has a solid assurance that he or she will be paid as long as the documentation is in order. We'll look at this type of transaction, along with the banker's acceptance, in some detail later.

Documentary Collection

Think "C.O.D.," with an international wrinkle. The seller gets the order and ships the goods to the buyer. But the seller sends the documents on the transaction, including the title, to his or her bank. The bank sends the documents on to the buyer's bank, along with payment instructions. The buyer's bank will be told not to deliver the documents to the buyer until payment is made (known as Documents Against Payment) or until a guarantee is given that payment will be made within a certain period (Documents Against Acceptance). The buyer has to have the documents in hand before he or she can take possession of the goods.

If buyer and seller have an ongoing relationship, this method affords quite a bit of security. The transaction could still go bad from either end, however, if the seller ships unacceptable goods, or if the buyer doesn't pay for the documents.

Open Account

This alternative presents the most risk for the seller. The buyer agrees to pay for the goods within a designated time period after shipment; 30 days, 60 days, and 90 days are common terms. Again, maximum trust is required, this time on the part of the seller, who has to have a whole lot of faith in the buyer's ability and willingness to pay. The seller had also better hope the ship doesn't sink, rebels don't take the capital, and the value of the local currency doesn't plunge in the meantime.

BASIC DOCUMENTS USED IN INTERNATIONAL TRADE

The documents used in international trade have been standardized so that all the parties understand what they're dealing with. When we talk about the documents that accompany the L/C and other payment forms, they include:

- Bill of lading — the document issued by the transporter or shipper acknowledging receipt of the specified goods for transportation to a specified place (The bill of lading is a title document; it can be issued to the order of a specific party, or "in blank," in which case the bearer of the bill of lading has the right to the goods.)
- Certificate of inspection — a written statement providing evidence of the characteristics of the goods, prepared by the seller or an independent inspector designated by the buyer

- Certificate of manufacture — a document in which the producer of the goods certifies that the production is complete and the goods are at the buyer's disposal
- Certificate of origin — a signed statement providing evidence of the origin of the goods (e.g., "Made in the USA")
- Commercial invoice — a written account of the goods being sold, issued by the seller and charging the buyer for the purchase
- Draft — also known as a bill of exchange, a written order by one party, called the drawer, instructing another party, the drawee (such as a bank), to pay a specified amount of money to a third party, the payee (Drafts are essential elements in most methods of payment and may be either *sight drafts,* which are payable on presentation or demand, or *time drafts,* which are payable a certain number of days after sight or after presentation for acceptance. The number of days is specified.)
- Export license — a document issued by a government agency authorizing the export of certain commodities to specified countries
- Import license — a document issued by a government agency authorizing import of certain commodities into the buyer's country
- Insurance document — a document certifying that the goods are insured for shipment

You can see that a buyer or seller might want any or all of these documents included in the package. Each adds its measure of security to a long-distance transaction.

LETTERS OF CREDIT

Letters of credit, also known as documentary letters of credit, commercial letters of credit, and international letters of credit, are the most common method of making international payments. The basic form of a letter of credit is established by the International Chamber of Commerce under a set of rules called the Uniform Customs and Practices for Documentary Credits, which assures that the form of the credit will be standard around the world.

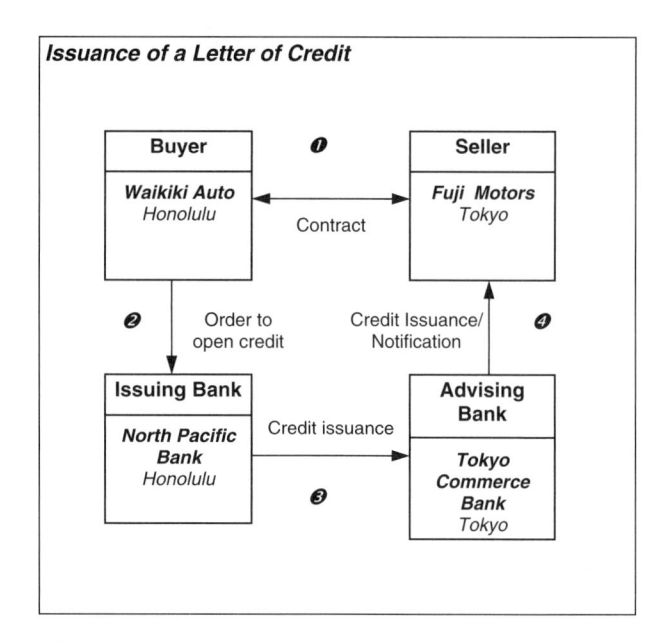

Figure 14.1 *Issuance of a letter of credit.*

There are a number of specific types of letters of credit, and, of course, each transaction is different, but the general terms of each credit must be standard so that the four parties to the letter recognize them. We'll use an example of a car shipment to describe how an L/C works. See Figure 14.1.

Here, Waikiki Auto of Honolulu (buyer) and Fuji Motors of Tokyo (seller) agree on a purchase contract for 200 new Fujis (1). Waikiki applies for and opens a letter of credit with North Pacific Bank (buyer's bank). North Pacific is the "issuing bank" (2). North Pacific, the issuing bank, issues the letter of credit, forwarding it to the "advising bank," Tokyo Commerce Bank (seller's bank, 3). The advising bank notifies Fuji Motors of the letter of credit (4).

A key part of the deal is now done, but nothing has been shipped and no payment made. In order for these things to happen, the letter of credit has to be "utilized." How this is done depends on whether the credit is revocable or irrevocable. *Revocable credits* can be changed by the buyer

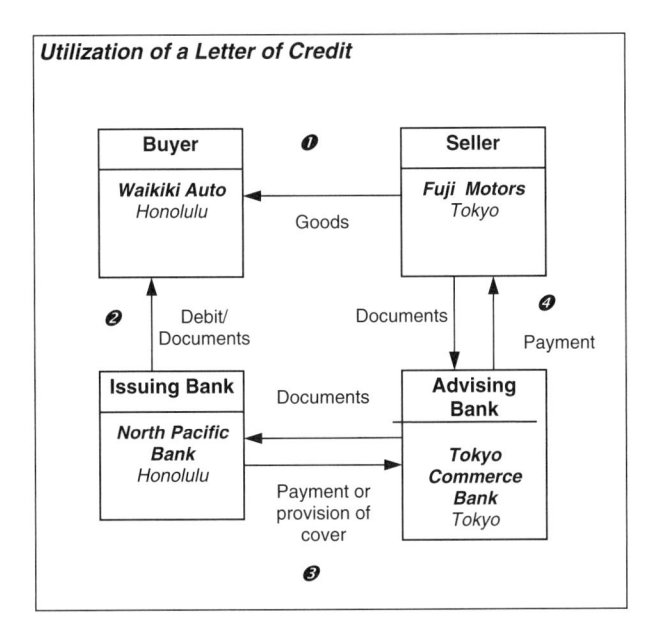

Figure 14.2 *Utilization of a letter of credit.*

without notice to the seller. Because this makes things riskier for the seller — who usually calls the shots — this form is rarely used. *Irrevocable credits* are preferred because the issuing bank commits itself to honor irrevocably the provisions of the credit as long as the beneficiary complies with the terms. Preferred for its security, this credit cannot be changed without the consent of both buyer and seller. Irrevocable credits can be either confirmed or unconfirmed. They're confirmed if the advising bank adds its own guarantee to that of the issuer. The unconfirmed sort put the entire responsibility on the issuing bank.

Now it's time to utilize the credit. See Figure 14.2. Fuji Motors, having notification that the

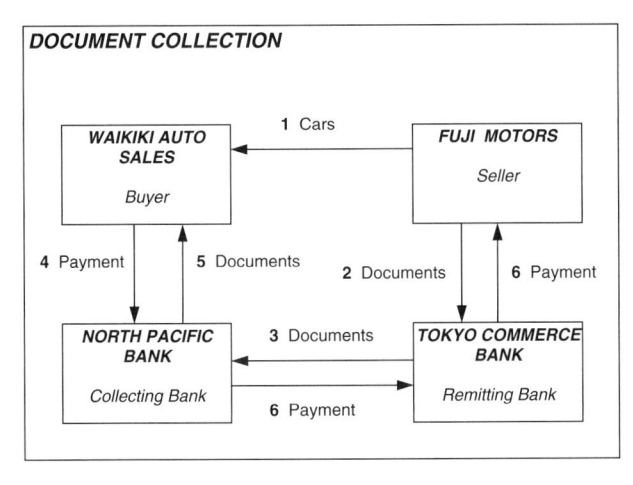

Figure 14.3 *Document collection.*

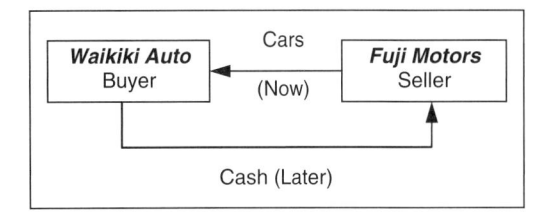

Figure 14.4 *Credit purchase (no bank).*

money is there for payment, ships the cars to Waikiki Motors (1). Fuji also sends all of the documents, as stipulated in the letter of credit, to Tokyo Commerce Bank. Tokyo Commerce Bank, after reviewing the documents, pays Fuji Motors for the cars (2). Tokyo Commerce Bank sends the documents on to North Pacific Bank, which reviews and accepts them. North Pacific then pays Tokyo Commerce Bank (3). North Pacific Bank forwards the documents, including title to the vehicles, to Waikiki Motors, and debits the letter of credit or account (4).

Again, the key in a transaction involving a letter of credit is the document, an example of which is reproduced at the end of the chapter. Note that neither of the issuing or advising banks has anything to do with the actual goods. As long as the documents are in order, they fulfill their obligations with regard to the transaction. This makes the letter of credit vulnerable to at least one type of money laundering operation. See Table 14.2 for descriptions of various types of letters of credit.

A MONEY LAUNDERING SCHEME INVOLVING A LETTER OF CREDIT

Two factors make letters of credit useful in money laundering schemes. First, all actions are taken on the basis of documents negotiated by the buyer and seller. Second, the bank-to-bank transactions that take place are capable of moving millions of dollars instantly between any two countries on the globe.

Put yourself in the money launderer's position. Suppose he's got $10 million he'd like to move from the United States to Hong Kong. If he can get Bank A to issue a letter of credit for that amount, then he's just got to cook up some legitimate-appearing documents to satisfy the bankers, and he's home free.

TABLE 14.2
Types of Letters of Credit

Revocable	Can be changed without the seller's agreement
Irrevocable	Cannot be changed without the agreement of both parties
Straight	The beneficiary must present documents to the advising bank for payment
Negotiation L/C	The beneficiary may present documents to the bank of his choice for payment
Advised	The advising bank is not obligated to pay under the L/C
Confirmed	The advising bank is obligated to pay under the L/C
Revolving L/C	Shipments and payments are made on a recurring basis
Transferable L/C	First beneficiary may transfer the L/C to another beneficiary
Red clause L/C	Advances under the L/C are allowed prior to shipment, allowing purchase of goods
Stand-by or performance L/C	A bank guarantee for payment involving no commercial documents
Back-to-back L/C	A new L/C opened in favor of another beneficiary on the basis of an already existing, nontransferable L/C

Why would Bank A issue the letter of credit? The key word is "credit." Any type of letter of credit is essentially a loan by the bank. The bank will issue this credit just like it would for any other type of loan — if it thinks the money is going to be paid back.

If the launderer already has $10 million on deposit at the bank, the chances that the L/C would be issued are pretty good. And if the buyer and seller in the transaction are in collusion, as one would suspect in a money laundering scheme, the chances that the documents will meet with everyone's approval are pretty good, too.

The launderer could set up a Hong Kong shell corporation and then use this corporation in an "overinvoice" scam or a paper shuffle. (See Chapter 22 for a description of fiendishly complex money laundering schemes.) The odds against detection of a scheme involving letters of credit are high.

DOCUMENTARY COLLECTIONS

Another form of international payment that requires banks, the documentary collection (DC) also has four parties. (See Figure 14.3.) There are three types of documentary collection, all of which focus on the transfer of documents such as bills of lading rather than the actual goods themselves. DCs are easier to use than letters of credit, and they are cheaper as well, since the banks don't charge so much for their services.

The risk is greater for the seller, because payment won't be made until the goods are actually shipped. The banks do not guarantee payment, as with an L/C, so the seller is at risk while the goods are in transit and storage. (See Figure 14.4.) For this reason, DCs are used in transactions with established customers and when the goods are easily marketable.

The three different types of collections are:

- Documents against payment (D/P): In this situation, the buyer only gets the title and other documents after making payment.
- Documents against acceptance (D/A): In this situation, the buyer gets the title after signing a time draft, agreeing to pay at a later date.
- Collection with acceptance (acceptance D/P): The buyer signs a time draft, agreeing to pay at a later date, but the documents are placed in escrow until payment is actually made.

The supplier's protection in this situation is that the buyer can't take physical possession of the goods unless he presents the bill of lading to Customs or the shipping company. And deliv-

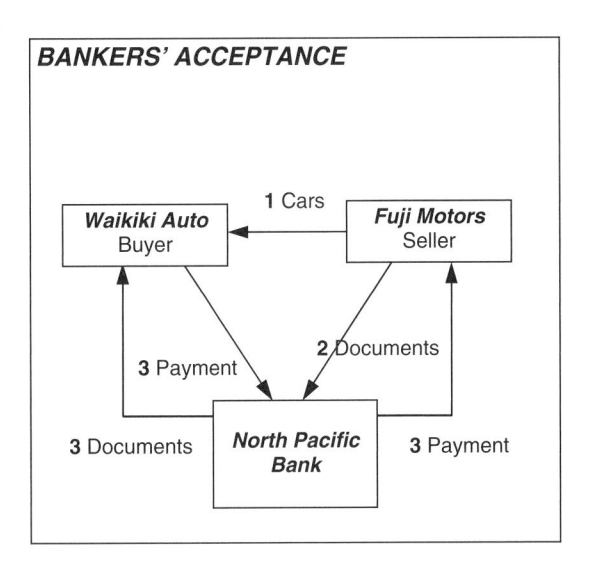

Figure 14.5 *Banker's acceptance.*

ery of the bill of lading won't take place until the document collection process is complete.

DOCUMENT COLLECTION PROCESS

As with the L/C, there are four parties to this transaction, although the banks are referred to by different names. We'll use the same characters as in the previous example to illustrate the process. See Figure 14.5.

Waikiki Auto Sales enters into an agreement to purchase 150 new cars from Fuji Motors. Fuji ships the 150 cars, invoicing Waikiki Auto Sales for $1.5 million (1). Fuji forwards the agreed-upon documents to its bank, Tokyo Commerce Bank, which in this transaction is known as the "remitting bank" (2).

Tokyo Commerce Bank forwards the documents to North Pacific Bank, which represents the buyer, Waikiki Auto, as the "collection bank" (3). North Pacific notifies Waikiki Auto and advises them of the conditions under which it can obtain the documents, which include the titles to the cars. To take possession of the documents, Waikiki Auto either pays cash or signs a time deposit to North Pacific (4).

Since this is a "documents against payment" deal, the collecting bank, North Pacific, with money in hand, gives the documents to Waikiki Auto (5). North Pacific then sends the payment along to Tokyo Commerce Bank, which pays Fuji Motors (6). The transaction is complete.

This process evens out the odds for all parties, spreading the risk around, thanks to the involvement of the banks, who charge for their services. The buyer is in a secure position because he or she doesn't get actual ownership or responsibility for the cars until payment is made to the collecting bank.

Even though the goods have been shipped, the buyer will not be allowed to inspect or sample them before paying for the documents. This is protection for the seller, who has shipped the goods with no legal obligation on the buyer's part to actually pay for them. The seller's position in this transaction would be very shaky if it were not for the participation of the banks in the transaction.

BANKER'S ACCEPTANCE

A banker's acceptance is a time draft (also known as a time bill of exchange) drawn on and accepted by a financial institution. By accepting the draft, the bank commits itself to pay the face amount at maturity to anyone who presents it. Banker's acceptances are extremely big in international commerce and investment.

Here's how a banker's acceptance works. Suppose the buyer, Waikiki Auto Sales, arranges the purchase of 150 new Fujis from Fuji Motors *and* arranges for payment of $1.5 million to be delayed for 90 days. Fuji gets a note, basically an I.O.U. for the amount of the purchase from Waikiki Auto. While this is certainly a swell deal for Waikiki Auto, which has 90 days to sell the cars and make some cash, it's a much riskier proposition for Fuji, which might like a little more security. See Figure 14.6.

In steps a bank. The bank guarantees payment of $1.5 million to Fuji, transferring the risk from Fuji to the bank. *However,* the bank does not make payment right away, issuing a time draft payable in 90 days. The involvement of the bank creates some new stages in the process. See Figure 14.7.

Waikiki Auto contracts to buy 150 cars and the cars are shipped by Fuji (1). Fuji sends the documents, including the bill of lading, to North Pacific Bank (2). The bank accepts the docu-

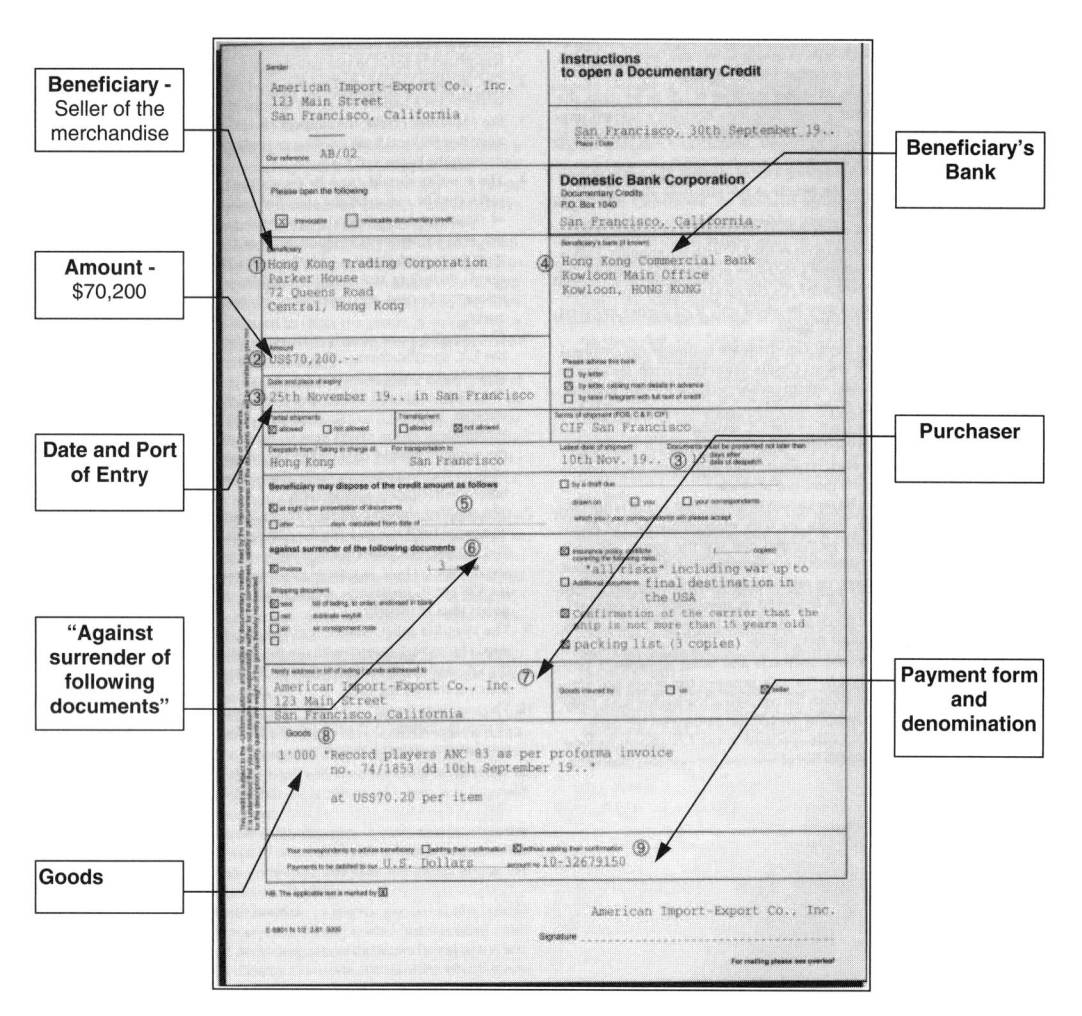

Figure 14.6 *Documentary credit.*

ments and sends an accepted time draft to Fuji (3). Ninety days later, Fuji cashes the draft, Waikiki Auto sends payment for the cars to the bank (3), and the transaction is complete.

At this point, everybody's happy, but what if Fuji needed the cash right away or couldn't wait to cash the time draft? No problem — it's a valuable piece of paper, worth $1.5 million to whoever holds it in 90 days. Fuji could borrow cash against the draft, or it can cut a deal with North Pacific Bank. North Pacific and other banks will generally offer to discount the acceptance, paying less cash now as opposed to the whole $1.5 million later.

Suppose North Pacific discounts the acceptance for $1.4 million. Fuji has that amount on the day the cars are shipped. But where's that valuable piece of paper now? The bank's got it. North Pacific can hold onto it for 90 days, or rediscount it and sell it on the secondary market for bankers' acceptances. There, investors purchase acceptances in an investment opportunity comparable to a certificate of deposit. Banker's acceptances are considered extremely safe, and the yield on a 90-day acceptance is similar to that of a 90-day CD.

These acceptances can be used in money laundering schemes as an investment of integrated funds or as a means of moving money internationally.

FOREIGN EXCHANGE

Welcome to the incredibly strange world where people buy and sell money. Lots and lots of money — over a trillion dollars every day. This is an arcane and sometimes scary place with its own language, its own rules, and the possibility

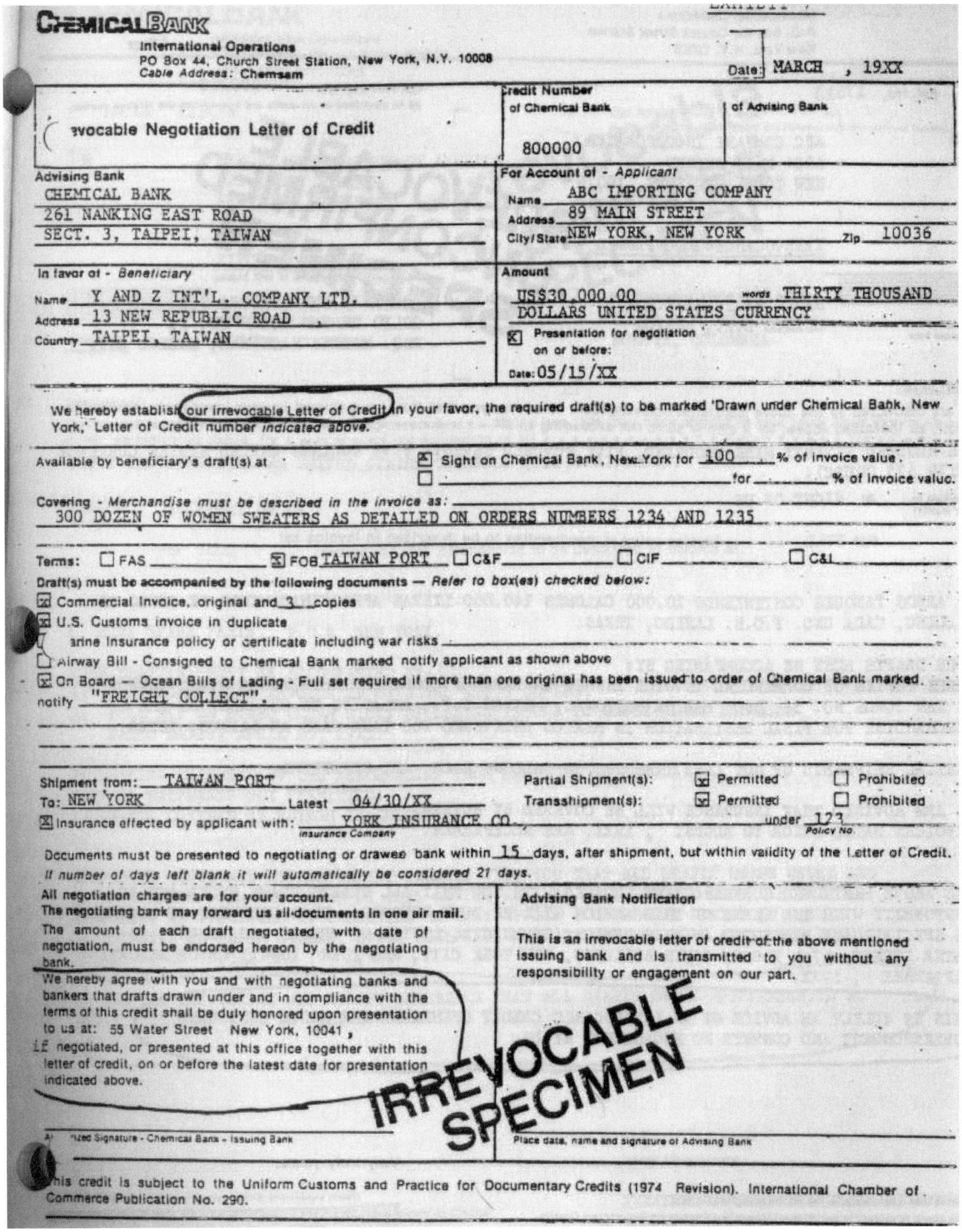

CHEMICAL BANK
International Operations
PO Box 44, Church Street Station, New York, N.Y. 10008
Cable Address: Chemsam

Date: MARCH , 19XX

(...vocable Negotiation Letter of Credit

Credit Number of Chemical Bank: 800000 | of Advising Bank

Advising Bank
CHEMICAL BANK
261 NANKING EAST ROAD
SECT. 3, TAIPEI, TAIWAN

For Account of - Applicant
Name ABC IMPORTING COMPANY
Address 89 MAIN STREET
City/State NEW YORK, NEW YORK Zip 10036

In favor of - Beneficiary
Name Y AND Z INT'L. COMPANY LTD.
Address 13 NEW REPUBLIC ROAD
Country TAIPEI, TAIWAN

Amount
US$30,000.00 words THIRTY THOUSAND DOLLARS UNITED STATES CURRENCY
[X] Presentation for negotiation on or before:
Date: 05/15/XX

We hereby establish our irrevocable Letter of Credit in your favor, the required draft(s) to be marked "Drawn under Chemical Bank, New York," Letter of Credit number indicated above.

Available by beneficiary's draft(s) at
[X] Sight on Chemical Bank, New York for 100 % of invoice value.
[ ] ______ for ______ % of invoice value.

Covering - Merchandise must be described in the invoice as:
300 DOZEN OF WOMEN SWEATERS AS DETAILED ON ORDERS NUMBERS 1234 AND 1235

Terms: [ ] FAS ______ [X] FOB TAIWAN PORT [ ] C&F ______ [ ] CIF ______ [ ] C&I ______

Draft(s) must be accompanied by the following documents — Refer to box(es) checked below:
[X] Commercial Invoice, original and 3 copies
[X] U.S. Customs invoice in duplicate
[ ] ...arine Insurance policy or certificate including war risks
[ ] Airway Bill - Consigned to Chemical Bank marked notify applicant as shown above
[X] On Board — Ocean Bills of Lading - Full set required if more than one original has been issued to order of Chemical Bank marked notify "FREIGHT COLLECT".

Shipment from: TAIWAN PORT
To: NEW YORK Latest 04/30/XX
Partial Shipment(s): [X] Permitted [ ] Prohibited
Transshipment(s): [X] Permitted [ ] Prohibited
[X] Insurance effected by applicant with: YORK INSURANCE CO. (Insurance Company) under 123 (Policy No.)

Documents must be presented to negotiating or drawee bank within 15 days, after shipment, but within validity of the Letter of Credit.
If number of days left blank it will automatically be considered 21 days.

All negotiation charges are for your account.
The negotiating bank may forward us all documents in one air mail.
The amount of each draft negotiated, with date of negotiation, must be endorsed hereon by the negotiating bank.
We hereby agree with you and with negotiating banks and bankers that drafts drawn under and in compliance with the terms of this credit shall be duly honored upon presentation to us at: 55 Water Street New York, 10041, if negotiated, or presented at this office together with this letter of credit, on or before the latest date for presentation indicated above.

Advising Bank Notification
This is an irrevocable letter of credit of the above mentioned issuing bank and is transmitted to you without any responsibility or engagement on our part.

IRREVOCABLE SPECIMEN

A...ized Signature - Chemical Bank - Issuing Bank

Place date, name and signature of Advising Bank

This credit is subject to the Uniform Customs and Practice for Documentary Credits (1974 Revision). International Chamber of Commerce Publication No. 290.

Figure 14.7 *Specimen — Irrevocable letter of credit.*

that your actions could lose your boss a billion dollars, destroy a 200-year-old bank, or even cause a run on a nation's currency. We won't be staying long.

Money, like everything else, has the value that people are willing to pay for it. Some money is worth more than others. As of June 2005, a unit of American money is worth exactly 0.7933 in European money and 107.45 units of Japanese money. That's as of this morning; both of those numbers will have changed many times since then. This is because the values of the major currencies "float," climbing or falling with demand.

All of the world's currencies are benchmarked or referenced against the U.S. dollar, and they trade on either the *spot* or the *forward* market. The spot price is what the currency is selling for, in dollars, as of that moment. Don't come back 10 minutes from now and expect to get the same price, because things change quickly in the foreign exchange business. In the forward market, currencies are exchanged on an "outright" basis — units of currency are bought and sold based on the anticipated value sometime in the future, or as options or swaps.

The most important currencies in the foreign exchange market, besides the U.S. dollar, are the British pound, the euro, the Swiss franc, the Canadian dollar, and the Japanese yen. The Chinese yuan is becoming fairly important, but it isn't traded like the others, although it may be in the near future.

Some countries have restrictions on the exchange of their currencies. These are nonconvertible into the currencies of other countries and don't trade in the major foreign exchange markets. These countries may also have currency controls, restricting how much of their money can leave the country. Both of these restrictions are usually due to the weakness of the local economy and the possibility that trading in the currency would devalue it.

Foreign exchange plays a major part in many money laundering schemes. American money, generated in illegal businesses in this country, can be moved offshore in the form of dollars, whether by being physically moved out of the country or by being banked and wired out. Once offshore, most launderers try to get the money into banks and businesses; this means that it must either be converted to the local currency, something that is a factor in a number of laundering schemes, or deposited into dollar accounts in foreign banks.

These offshore dollar holdings are called *Eurodollars,* even though most of them aren't in Europe. In fact, more dollars are held offshore than in the United States, according to the Federal Reserve. This is particularly true of $100 bills, which are kept offshore in great quantities, often in the vaults of foreign banks.

Why don't people just change their money for the local stuff? Because of the security that U.S. dollars, backed by the "full faith and credit" of the U.S. government, bring. Like VISA and MasterCard, dollars are accepted anywhere you want to be.

An advantage to drug traffickers and other criminals is that their suppliers don't mind taking dollars either, and for the same reasons. This raises some interesting possibilities for money launderers, who are regularly moving dollars offshore. One option is moving the dollars into a black market in the foreign country — blue jeans in Paraguay or gold in India. The dollars are in big demand in these markets and may create a favorable exchange situation for the launderer. Another option is to take the money someplace like Panama, where, by law, U.S. dollars are legal tender.

There have been some interesting proposals in recent years to create two distinct forms of U.S. currency, "red seal" and "green seal." In this system, money with a green Treasury seal could be used only in domestic transactions, and money with a red Treasury seal could be used only overseas. Because the green seal money would essentially be worthless in Colombia or elsewhere, this plan would definitely put the brakes on bulk currency smuggling. It probably won't happen, however, because the government doesn't like the idea of its money being "worthless" anywhere.

INTERNATIONAL BANKING

You have to admit, there's a certain air about having a foreign bank account, especially one of those Swiss versions. The whole process is redolent of mystery, sophistication, and above all money. The reality is a little more mundane.

If your subject has a foreign bank account, this should be a yellow light for the investigator, but we have to keep in mind that individuals and businesses may have perfectly legitimate reasons for holding an account in a foreign bank. In the vast majority of cases, the reasons for

"Can I put you on hold? He's busy shoveling money into his secret Swiss bank account at the moment."

holding such an account *are* completely legal and proper. In some instances, such as the ones we're learning about here, the motivation may be more sinister.

Why do people bank offshore? Whether they are money launderers or legitimate business people, offshore banking is popular for the same reasons:

- *Privacy:* Banking in a foreign jurisdiction can provide a measure of privacy that might not be attained at home. This is especially true if the offshore location is a bank secrecy or tax haven.
- *Security:* Keeping your money in a bank in Switzerland might be preferable, from a security standpoint, to keeping it in Sierra Leone. Some offshore banking centers are extremely stable, economically and politically, offering a safe place to store your wealth.
- *Convenience:* If you or your business is active in international trade, you may want to have accounts in the places where you do business. Even frequent travelers to Paris or Rome might find it convenient to have accounts in those cities.
- *Financial benefits:* You may be able to make more by taking the money offshore. Interest rates on savings deposits in Japan are very low. An investor there might move his or her money to the United States, where an account would yield more in interest.

Where do people bank offshore? All around the world, but certain places are favored over others. Offshore investors are looking for certain things in their banks, including those we just talked about. Another factor is service, something else an offshore bank may be able to provide that the local bank can't or won't. Certain areas of the world are known as offshore banking centers because they provide the benefits that customers are seeking. These are usually places with one or more of the following:

- Laws regarding bank secrecy or requiring confidentiality in the banker–customer relationship
- Low or no taxes on foreign investment or deposits (This is not always the case — some countries have fairly high taxes.)
- Banking regulation or money laundering controls that are weak

Which countries fit this bill? Places like Switzerland, Austria, the Cayman Islands, Panama, Hong Kong, Vanuatu, the Cook Islands, and the Bahamas, although money laundering controls have been beefed up in some of these places.

What kind of banks are in the international arena? From an American perspective, the field shapes up like this:

- Commercial banks operating in the same country in which they are chartered, e.g., Credit Suisse, Zurich, Switzerland
- Foreign banks operating in a country other than where they are chartered, e.g., Credit Suisse, (Switzerland) in Nassau, Bahamas, or Sumitomo Bank (Japan) in Los Angeles
- American banks operating offshore, e.g., Citibank, Cayman Islands
- Private banks, brass plate banks, exempt banks, Class II banks, and so forth (different names for, generally, the same animal) — banks organized for the benefit of an individual or corporation, which do not take deposits from the general public, a type of oper-

ation that certain countries permit, issuing licenses and regulating the licensees, though not always with great efficiency or enthusiasm

INTERNATIONAL BANKING SERVICES OFFERED BY U.S. BANKS

Many American banks provide international services for their customers. This is a logical extension for larger banks, which are, as always, trying to furnish the widest possible services to existing and potential customers. If they did not do so, Americans wanting to do business overseas would be forced to turn to foreign banks licensed to operate in the United States. But service isn't the sole reason. There is money in foreign exchange transactions, payments and collections like those we just discussed, loan syndication, and offshore lending.

American banks provide a number of services to their international customers. Among these are:

- Letters of credit
- Banker's acceptances
- Collections, both paying and receiving
- Acceptance financing

In the lending field, U.S. banks may make loans for international projects, or direct and syndicated loans. Although American bank deposits are kept in dollars, banks may handle foreign exchange transactions for customers and may manage international investment opportunities, including Eurodollar holdings, and securities accounts.

The international operations of a U.S. bank are carried out through one or more divisions within the bank. There may be some overlap among the activities of divisions, but many international operations are conducted by or through the bank's International Banking Department. Generally located in the headquarters or main branch of a major bank, the international banking group maintains accounts for foreign customers and deposits in other institutions on behalf of the bank's customers. International loans will be handled through this department.

International payments involving letters of credit, document collections, or banker's acceptances will be handled by a commercial section, which will have credit information on international customers. Quite a bit of handy information will be available in this department.

One type of international banking is correspondent banking. Remember that correspondent banking involves a relationship between two banks in different locations. If a bank is big enough to have a branch in that distant city, it won't need a correspondent bank there. Smaller banks rely on correspondents in order to deliver international services to their customers without actually having to be a full-service international bank.

The key to correspondent banking is deposits, which the banks keep with each other. Because these funds are on deposit, each bank can be confident that the money will be available to provide the services requested by its correspondent. The two types of demand accounts into which the deposits are made are known as vostro and nostro accounts.

Vostro accounts, also known as "due to" accounts, are the funds, in U.S. dollars, deposited by a foreign bank into a demand account in the U.S. bank. It's called "due to" because the funds are payable to the foreign bank on demand.

Nostro accounts are also known as "due from" accounts: the U.S. bank has deposited those monies with the foreign bank, and they are "due from" that bank on demand by the U.S. bank. These deposits are usually in the foreign currency.

These deposit accounts provide the security for many international banking transactions, including the international payments we discussed.

Another international operation is the *shell branch office.* A shell, as we know, isn't much more than a name and a bank account, which is how banks use them. Operation of the shell branch is conducted from the main office, and all of the books and records are maintained there, even though the shell is ostensibly located in some tax or secrecy haven such as the Cayman Islands. Banks like shells because they can say to a customer, "We'll deposit these funds with our Cayman Islands branch," which sounds good to the customer, and the bank has the added benefit of not having to meet reserve or insurance requirements on the foreign deposits.

A *foreign branch* of an American bank operates like a domestic branch, only under the laws and regulations of the foreign country in which it operates. Businesses prefer to deal with banks that have foreign branches, because they are all part of the same (usually very large) entity. Depending on the location, the foreign branch may be able to compete with its local counterparts for domestic business, or it may just deal in international trade. Major American banks contrive to have a branch in most of the important banking centers of the world.

Under American law, the records of these foreign branches are subject to the same disclosure provisions as their domestic counterparts, so a subpoena for account information for John Doe's Hong Kong account at Citibank–Hong Kong would have to be honored by the bank. After all, Citibank was an American bank first.

FOREIGN BANK ACCOUNTS

Americans can hold accounts in foreign banks. There is no restriction on the amount of funds that can be held offshore by Americans, but individuals are supposed to fill out the Foreign Bank Account Report (FBAR) if they control more than $10,000 in a foreign account during the year. They also have to answer a question on their income tax form each year about whether they have a foreign account. Because the Swiss accounts are the most famous and the most established, we'll use these as an example of what types of services are available from a foreign bank and how you can go about setting up an account.

Banking has a long history in Switzerland, a country known for its neutrality. Switzerland's international banking got a big and ironic boost from the remittances that Swiss mercenaries sent home from their overseas employment. Banking took off, to the point where Switzerland is now one of the most heavily banked countries in the world. This is because Switzerland is stable, secure, and legally very protective of its banks. Confidentiality of banking transactions is mandated by law; however, Swiss secrecy is not nearly as impenetrable as it was in years past.

Several different kinds of banks operate in Switzerland today. Those of interest to offshore investors are:

- Cantonal banks
- Foreign-controlled banks
- Private banks
- Major Swiss banks

Other banks handle mostly local customers, getting little or no business from outside the country. These include regional, savings, and mortgage banks; finance companies; and two mutual credit associations.

Cantonal banks are the equivalent of savings banks in the United States. Switzerland is a federation of cantons, as the United States is made up of states. The 29 cantonal banks are chartered by the individual cantons, and they have a heavy emphasis on savings activity. Some are quite large — among the world's 500 largest banks.

Foreign-controlled banks include a number of American banks that operate in Switzerland. At least 20 foreign banks have branches in Switzerland, and more than 100 other Swiss banks are controlled by foreign interests. Among the American banks that operate in Switzerland are:

American Express Bank AG
Bank of America NT & SA*
Bankers Trust AG
Chase Manhattan Bank (Suisse) SA
Chemical Bank (Suisse) SA*
Citibank N.A.*
Citicorp Investment Bank
First National Bank of Boston*

---
* Branches in Switzerland.

First National Bank of Chicago*
J.P. Morgan (Suisse) SA
Manufacturers Hanover Trust Co.*
Morgan Guaranty Trust Co.*
Security Pacific Bank SA
State Street Bank (Switzerland)
Trade Development Bank

Private banks possess banking licenses and can operate as full-service banks, but they restrict their operations to select customers or activities. Private means *extremely* private; if the banks do not advertise for deposits, they aren't required to file any financial reports or disclose their books. All of the 23 private banks are run as partnerships, with the partners equally liable for all debts of the firm. Thus, the depositors are "insured" by the private fortunes of the individual partners.

Major Swiss banks include the "Big Three" and a few others. The Big Three in Swiss banking are:

- Credit Suisse, headquartered in Zurich
- Swiss Bank Corporation, headquartered in Basle
- Union Bank of Switzerland, headquartered in Zurich

These are three of the biggest banks in the world, with operations spanning the globe. All three have branches in the United States (you'll see UBS ads on television) and in other banking centers. Although some of the cantonal banks are quite large, as are the other major banks, most foreign deposits go to the Big Three.

TYPES OF ACCOUNTS

There are several forms of accounts in Swiss banks. As in the United States, the banks attempt to provide whatever services the customer desires.

Current accounts are the equivalent of demand or checking accounts in the United States. Checkbooks may be issued, and funds can be withdrawn at any time. One wrinkle is that the Swiss will set up this account in one or more currencies other than the Swiss franc, including U.S. dollars. Only Swiss residents can receive interest on these accounts, and they don't get much — between 0.25% and 0.5%. Maintenance of an account costs about 100 Swiss francs per year.

Savings accounts can be of the passbook type, an investment savings account, or one of a "private" type. Withdrawal of funds from these accounts is restricted. A certain amount can be withdrawn each month without notification, but larger amounts require 30 days' notice to the bank. Fees are low, but so is the interest paid, and taxes are withheld from the interest paid. Most of these accounts are held in Swiss francs.

In addition to the above, Swiss banks will set up securities accounts consisting of a portfolio of stocks, bonds, or other investment types; precious metals accounts, which invest in and store precious metals designated by the customer; and fiduciary savings accounts, which allow the banker to function as an investment broker on behalf of the customer. There are lots of options for the customer.

OPENING A SWISS ACCOUNT

The potential customer is required to fill out an application form, which is subject to the bank's approval and acceptance. The Swiss are now requiring personal contact with a banker in order to open an account. They also like to receive banking references or letters of recommendation from other bankers.

Depending on the bank, you may need to bring some serious money to the table. Minimum deposits at some banks could be 200,000 Swiss francs. Cantonal banks require less, 10 to 100 Swiss francs at some, well within the average money launderer's reach.

The banks ask for a power of attorney form giving the bank the power to make decisions and take action on behalf of the account holder. The customer may also want to appoint an *avocat* or representative to deal with the bank. This is

---
* Branches in Switzerland.

expensive and would probably be done only on large accounts.

If the customer is accepted, statements and correspondence will be handled according to the instructions of the customer. Swiss statements are mailed out two or four times each year, not monthly as are the American versions. If the customer asks for it, the statements will be mailed in plain envelopes without bank markings, mailed to the *avocat,* sent to a post office box under a pseudonym, or mailed from a country other than Switzerland. The bank will also hold the forms for pickup on your next trip to Zurich.

ACCOUNT IDENTIFICATION

The Swiss still have those famous "numbered" accounts. A number–letter combination is used to designate the account, with the identity of the holder known only to a few employees in the bank. Although personal identification is required to open an account, deposits can be made without a verification of ID. Withdrawals may be a different story, since, as we've seen, there are restrictions on large withdrawals from savings accounts.

The number–letter code, rather than a signature, is used in all transactions, with most orders made in writing, using the code. If an *avocat* has been appointed, the transactions will be arranged through this person, who may be known to the banker.

Confidentiality is the byword of these relationships, extending even to having the bank issue its own checks on request, so that the customer doesn't have to put his or her name on one of his or her own. (Swiss law requires true signatures on all checks, and you wouldn't want to put your secret number on something like this, anyway.)

DOCUMENTS AVAILABLE FROM FOREIGN BANKS

If your MLAT request is approved, and you have the ability to look into a Swiss bank (or any other foreign bank, for that matter), you could ask for the following documents:

- Letter of inquiry to establish account
- Application to open account
- Power of attorney
- Contract between bank and customer
- Instructions concerning operation of the account
- Instructions concerning the handling of correspondence by the bank
- Correspondence
- Account statements
- Signature cards of account holders
- Copy of acknowledgment by customer of the rules, conditions, and regulations pertaining to the account
- Instructions concerning *avocat* designation
- Deposited items
- Checks drawn on account
- Wire transfer information

Now that you know how to open a Swiss account, you should know that other places offer more or at least comparable secrecy, including Austria, Hungary, Panama, and the Cayman Islands. Still, "he's got a Swiss account" does have a certain ring to it. See Figure 14.8 for an example of an application for a Swiss bank account.

Application for the opening of an account

with SWISS BANK CORPORATION in

Please complete form using typewriter or block capitals

CSITE	NKTO	Rubr.

Account-holder(s) Name and first names (Married women please indicate maiden name)	Legal Domicile (exact address)	Nationality Date of Birth	Profession

References / Identity Papers

Correspondence (Language   )

except in the case of special circumstances left at the bank's discretion –
To be sent to the following address:

To be retained, against remuneration, by the Bank which is hereby discharged of any liability for possible consequences, and if not claimed by me/us can be destroyed after a period of 5 years.

Power of Attorney in favour of: (Please indicate name, first name and domicile)
(as per separate document)

Account / Securities deposit
- ☐ Account in Swiss francs
- ☐ Current account in foreign currency
- ☐ Securities deposit

Remittances received in a currency for which there is no corresponding account are to be credited at the Bank's discretion to an already existing account or to be maintained in the currency received.
If a Joint Account is opened, remittances received in the sole favour of one account holder only shall automatically be credited to the joint account, unless a separate account exists in the exclusive favour of the beneficiary or unless the Bank is in possession of instructions to the contrary.

Capital Increases
- ☐ Please ask for instructions
- ☐ Exercise the rights
- ☐ Sell the rights
- ☐ The bank is authorized to act at its discretion in the customer's interest.

Special Instructions

The bank is discharged of all liability for decisions left to its discretion.
I/We acknowledge having taken note of the translation of the General Conditions reproduced on the reverse side and consider myself/ourselves bound by the official text in French and furthermore accept jurisdiction of the Courts in_____
Precious metals are subject to the separate regulation concerning the custody of precious metals and coins.
As far as a married woman is by law required to obtain her husband's consent to maintain this account, the Bank may consider this consent as having been given.

Signature(s)

Figure 14.8 Application for a Swiss bank account.

CHAPTER 15

MONEY TRANSFERS

"Hello my honey, hello my baby, hello my ragtime gal. Send me your love by wire."
Popular song of the early 1900s

"A billion here, a billion there — pretty soon it adds up to real money."
Everett Dirksen, U.S. senator

Senator Dirksen was talking about the federal budget, but he could have been marveling about wire transfers. In today's global economy, the transfer of wealth by wire dwarfs any other means. Trillions of dollars are moved every day on the strength of little more than some electronic impulses.

Although the amounts involved are quite mind-boggling, equally astonishing is the variety of means used to send money by wire. Not only are banks shipping electronic money to each other, but stock exchanges, brokerages, commodities dealers, businesses of all types, credit card companies, money remitters, arbitrageurs, governments, telegraph companies, and even private individuals are also on the wires, busily sending money here and there.

The three major electronic funds transfer (EFT) systems, CHIPS, SWIFT, and Fedwire, handle around $2 trillion in transfers *daily,* raising the questions like, "Where is all this money going?" and "Why doesn't any of it ever stop in my account?"

Actually some of it does (though I'm sure it's not nearly enough), if you have direct deposit. Twice each month, your employer tells its bank to send your salary to your account at a local bank. Just like magic, your account is credited with some money, and everybody's happy. Your paycheck becomes another blip in the electronic flood of EFT transactions conducted every day.

As the world becomes more wired, this system of electronic transfers is only going to grow. Even now, bankers are figuring out new ways to use this technology. Cyberbanking and smart cards are only two of the new techniques that are coming on fast. It is quite possible that cash as we know it may well become obsolete. Don't think so? Consider the possibilities of the smart card, on which any amount of money can be deposited onto a chip embedded in a piece of plastic. I could deposit $200 onto my smart card and then go out and buy some clothes and a hot meal or two before I had to go back and reload the card. Or I could deposit $2 million onto my card, get on an airplane, and fly to Colombia or Hong Kong and unload the card there. Farfetched? The technology is here now, and if you've made long distance calls using a phone card that you bought at 7-11 or bought merchandise with a gift card from a merchant, you've already used it. Tomorrow, in EFT terms, is here today.

Phone cards and even smart cards are the small potatoes in EFT right now. We'll look at how the system works today, as operated by the big players, the really big players, and the

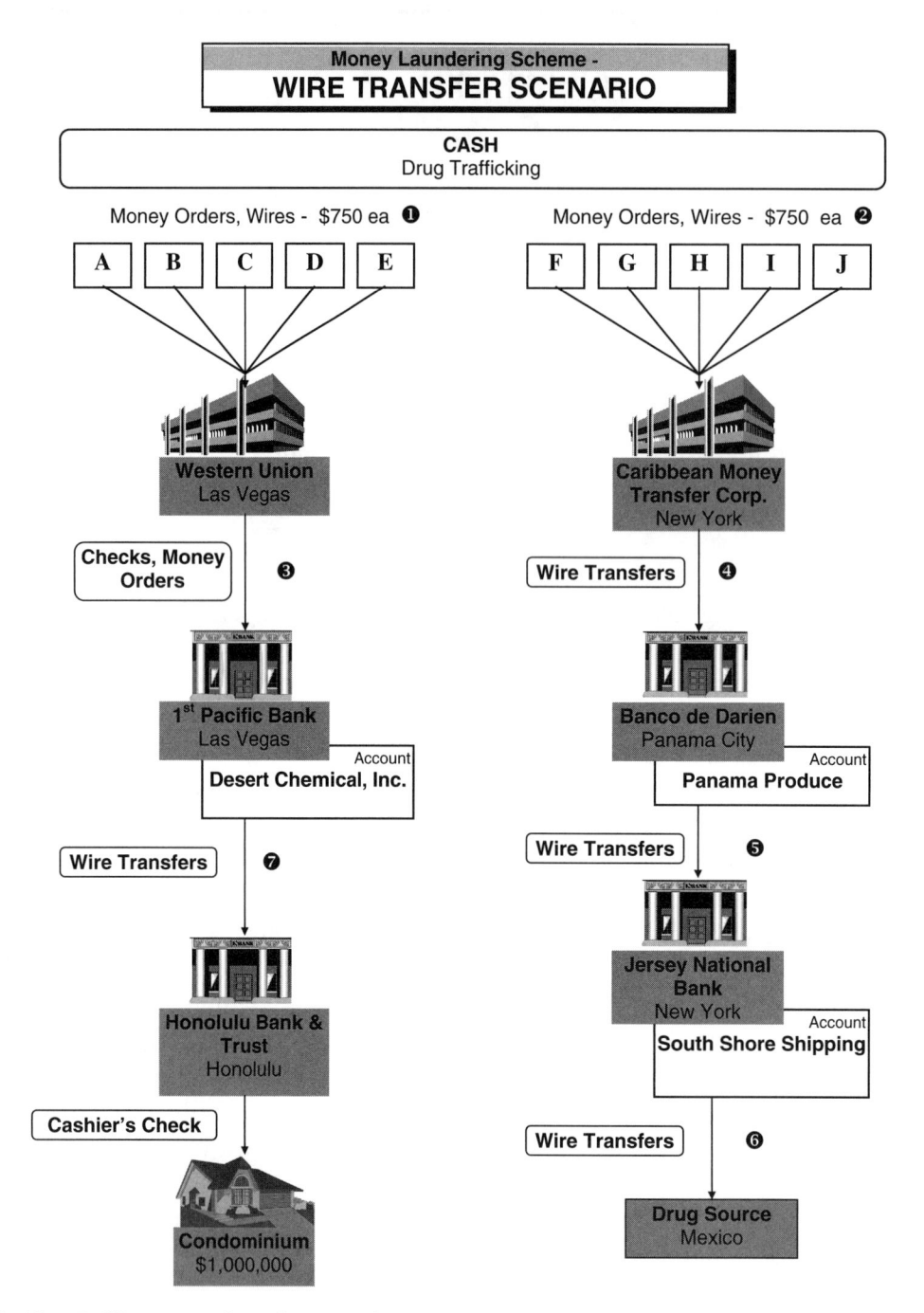

Figure 15.1 *Alex Bell's money laundering scheme.*

megaplayers, and we'll look at the backroom folks using new technology to transfer money the same way their ancestors did a thousand years ago.

Senator Dirksen was right; at this point, it all adds up to *real* money. To find out just how much and how it (almost) unerringly gets where it's going, we'll use another money laundering case example. (This one is fictional, though it uses components from several real cases.) Figure 15.1 provides the schematic of this scheme.

Case Example

Drug trafficker Alex Bell had perfected a sweet little money laundering scheme he figured would see him into retirement. Bell had a firm rule: No cash, no dope. His distributors dealt in both, of course, but Bell no longer handled either. He had arranged, through much planning and at great expense, to run his entire operation by remote control.

His secret was wires. Bell moved all of his money by electronic funds transfers. In fact, he used EFT in the placement, layering, and integration stages of his operation. The scam started with the cash his distributors took in. Rather than accepting it in that form, Bell insisted that all of the cash be converted to either Western Union money orders (1) or a wire transfer from another licensed transmitter. In Bell's area of operations, Caribbean Money Transfer Corp. (CMTC) had numerous agents operating out of stores in the neighborhoods served by Bell's organization (2).

Bell's dealers spread their money around, never making any transfers larger than $750. At Western Union, you can obtain a money order that can be cashed anywhere on the system using only a code phrase. The Western Union money orders can be picked up at various outlets in Las Vegas, Nevada, which is close to Bell's source of supply for methamphetamine. There, these transfers could be cashed or deposited as checks into the bank account of Bell's Nevada corporation, Desert Chemistry, at First Pacific Bank (3). At CMTC outlets, the dealers wired the money to the account of a front company, Panama Produce, at the Banco de Darien in Panama City (4).

In the next phase, Panama Produce wired the collected transfers from Banco de Darien to the account of South Shore Shipping, at Jersey National Bank (5). (In real life, Bell would probably layer it a little before this.) Bell now had all of his money back home in the USA. If he decided to buy some asset or transfer the funds abroad, he could do so from the Jersey National Bank account (6), or from the other banks.

When Bell decided to buy a condominium in Honolulu, the full purchase price of $1 million was transferred from First Pacific Bank to Honolulu Bank and Trust Company for payment to the escrow company (7).

All of this activity involves wire transfers in a variety of forms. Each transfer uses a different system, each transaction joining millions of others in a constant flow of money transfers occurring every day. The sheer volume of transactions makes it highly unlikely that Bell's scheme is going to be detected through the transfers. There are nevertheless some weak points, and the government has gone to some lengths to make Alex Bell's life a little more difficult.

STARTING SMALL*: LICENSED MONEY TRANSMITTERS

In the placement phase of Bell's operation, his distributors are making numerous wire transfers from two different licensed money transmitters. Federal law requires that all transmitters of money by wire be licensed. They must also register with FinCEN as money services businesses (MSB) and provide FinCEN with information about their agents. To find out whether a transmitter is registered with FinCEN, go to http://www.msb.gov/guidance/msbstateselector.php, where you'll find a complete listing of the current MSBs; 23,481 MSBs were registered as of April 2005.

Some of these money transmitters operate in a limited geographic area and have only a few outlets, while others, such as the giant Western Union Corporation, operate all over the place and have thousands of outlets and agents.

Some pretty big names are in this business, including American Express, Deak International, Citicorp, and Bank of America. How many transactions do these transmitters conduct? Millions upon millions, and many of these involve laundered funds, though it's hard to know the full extent of the illegal activity. Drug dealers and others do like them, though, for the same reason the general public uses them —

---
* Of course, it's all relative.

speed and convenience. Your funds are here today and there ... today. Also, the agents of the transmitters are everywhere, in supermarkets, convenience stores, hotels, travel agencies, foreign exchange outlets, and a variety of other locations. As long as the transmitter has a representative at both ends of the transaction, the money can flow. Western Union, still the biggest player in this field, has 18,000 agents in the United States and 6,000 more overseas.

OPERATION

Licensed transmitters use a messaging system, one that hasn't changed a whole lot from the days when everything was done on a telegraph using Morse code. A customer walks in to an agent, plunks down some cash, and fills out a message form with the information about the transfer. The customer can designate a recipient and a specific location where the money is to be sent, or, in the case of Western Union, the message is posted on the system and the money can be picked up anywhere by the recipient. The customer is charged for the transaction, usually on a percentage basis, depending on the amount being transmitted. These fees can run as high as 10 to 20% of the total, so sending money this way can get expensive.

The funds to be transferred are not actually wired by the agent who's doing the transaction. The money is deposited into a bank account maintained by the licensed transmitter, and the agent sends a message by telex, fax, or even telephone, describing the transaction amount and the person designated to receive the money. As you can see, it wouldn't take much equipment to become an agent for one of these companies.

In money laundering operations, any transmitter's system can be used, but the launderer will be looking for a few attributes. The transmitter should have a convenient location (or multiple locations) for sending the transmission. Discretion, if large amounts of cash are involved, and security are also pluses.

The transmitter should have the ability to move the funds to the desired location. This may be close to the supplier or to some location where the money can be discreetly passed further along. Major drug trafficking syndicates may arrange for a money broker or other business in a foreign country to receive wire transfers from the United States, but smaller operations rely on wire transfers directly to the source of supply.

Speed is often a factor. Money launderers like to move quickly, but they have to convert their cash into wire transfers, and this usually means many wire transfers. This requires the launderer to go to more than one outlet or send his employees around to multiple outlets.

A high comfort level is also nice. Many of the licensed transmitters have roots in certain ethnic communities — Haitian Transfer Express Company or Remesa Universal Corp., for example. Many people in the ethnic communities of the United States remit money back to their homeland or to family members back home. Some of these people are more comfortable with the agents of the transmitters who speak their language and deal extensively within their neighborhood or community. Those remitters will likely have more outlets back home, too.

At Western Union, hundreds of thousands of messages are sent over their system each day. Many of these are traditional telegram-type messages — people "sending their love by wire." Others are EFTs. Once the cash is received at the sending location, a message to this effect is posted to Western Union's system. The designated recipient can be at a certain location — Las Vegas, for instance — or anywhere in the world. How will the system know the right person is picking up the money at the other end? The recipient has to either present identification or know the specifics of the transaction, including a code word or phrase. For transactions under $1000, neither the sender nor the recipient is required to give their real names, provide identification, or do anything else to help figure out who conducted the transfer. If "Mickey Mouse" wants to send $750 by Western Union to "Daffy Duck," Daffy can pick up that money anywhere in the world as long as he or she knows the answer to the test question, "What's up, doc?" Western Union will provide the funds to the recipient in the form of a check or in cash. Cash received will be available for remittance within a day on the Western Union system.

RECORDS

As is the case with any business dealing with large amounts of cash, certain records are kept by the transmitters. Some of these records are maintained because there needs to be a proper accounting for the funds passing through the system, while others are required by the government. These records start with a copy of the customer's message form and the actual record of the wire. The former can come in handy, because for smaller cash transactions (under $3000), the transmitter isn't required to obtain any identification from the sender, who can give any name he or she wants. The handwriting on the message form might be the only clue to the sender's identity. As a matter of company policy, Western Union is now requiring identification for smaller cash transactions ($1000 and up).

In the case of larger cash transactions, those over $10,000 in cash, the transmitter is required to file a Currency Transaction Report (CTR) with IRS. The IRS Examination Division, by the way, is the regulatory agency for these MSBs and will conduct examinations to check on compliance.

Licensed transmitters and remittance corporations generate thousands of CTRs, most of which are prepared by the banks who receive the deposits from the company agents. If an agent in a busy location receives 30 orders for money transfers, each averaging $500, a total of $15,000 in cash will be deposited into the remittance corporation's account at the end of the day. Although the bank will prepare a CTR identifying the agent, this will not provide us with any information about the individual wires.

A record of each transaction is also preserved somewhere in the transmitter's computer system, which maintains a chronological log of everything that transpires. At Western Union, a Money Transfer Control Number is assigned to each transaction to assist in tracking the funds. In practical terms, finding one of these transactions among all those conducted is going to be difficult unless the requesting agency has more information, such as the sending or receiving location, date, sender's name, or recipient's name. Figure 15.2 is a Western Union money transfer slip.

Subpoenas for information about Western Union wire transfers can be mailed to:

Western Union Financial Services, Inc.
Central Accounting Office
13022A Hollenberg Drive
Bridgeton, Missouri 63044
Attn: Chief Compliance Officer

USE OF REMITTANCE CORPORATIONS IN MONEY LAUNDERING SCHEMES

In a scheme like Bell's, the individual agents of the money transmitter or remittance corporation serve as the collection points for the funds to be laundered. These agents, whether they are clerks at a grocery store Western Union counter or the operators of a travel agency representing CMTC, are under no obligation to know anything more about their customer than the fact that he or she has the money to send and the fee to pay for it.

In our example involving Mr. Bell, cash from methamphetamine sales is converted to wire transfers at Western Union and CMTC in a series of small, anonymous transactions. See Figure 15.3 for a schematic. In the case of Western Union, the money transfers bought in New York at locations A–E are picked up in Las Vegas (1). At CMTC, the recipient is designated as Panama Produce. CMTC agents F–J deposit the amounts into CMTC's account at a local bank (2) and then let CMTC know by fax that the money is supposed to go to Panama Produce (3).

The next round of wire transfers involves movement of funds via an entirely different and much bigger system — that of the world's banks.

Figure 15.2 A Western Union money transfer slip.

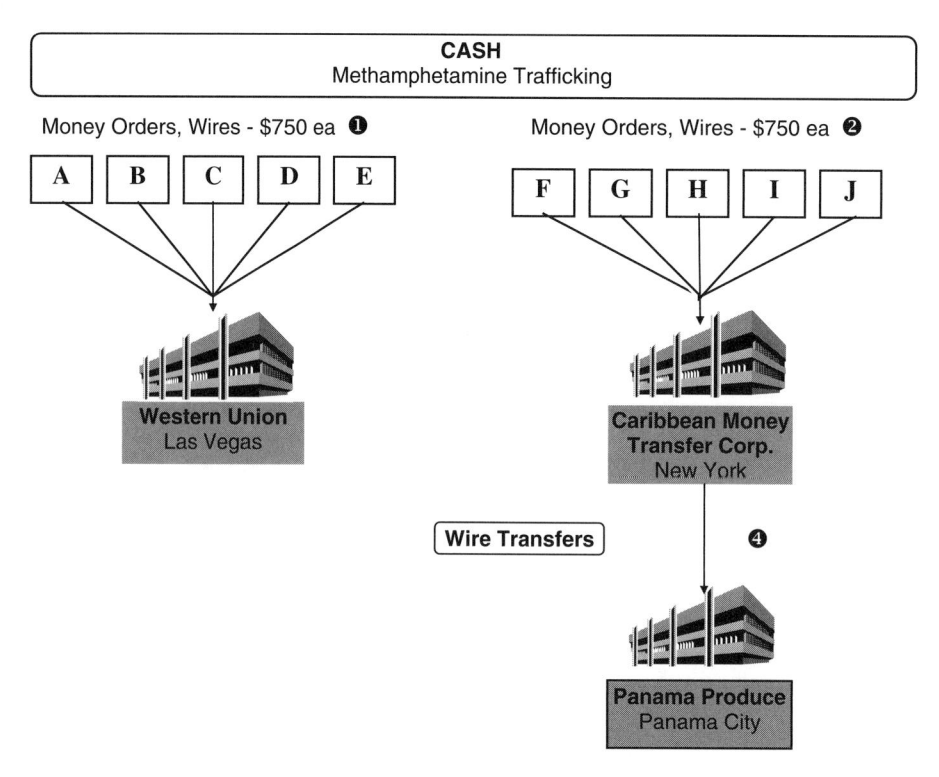

Figure 15.3 Alex Bell's system for handling cash proceeds of drug sales.

TABLE 15.1
The Major EFT Systems

EFT System	Operated By	Primary Function	Daily Wires	Daily Dollar Volume
CHIPS	New York Clearinghouse	International transfers	150,000	$900 billion
SWIFT	S.W.I.F.T.	Initiating messages	1 million	—
Fedwire	Federal Reserve System	Domestic transfers	277,000	$824 billion
Telex	Telex	Initiating messages	—	—

MAJOR ELECTRONIC FUNDS TRANSFER SYSTEMS: FEDWIRE, CHIPS, AND SWIFT

In the world of EFT, the megaplayers number three. These are the largest and most complex of all the systems, and they move the most money. The Clearing House Interbank Payments System (CHIPS) is operated by the New York Clearinghouse System and serves as this country's main EFT system for processing international transfers of dollars among international banks. CHIPS handles $900 billion in transactions among its 132 banks in 33 countries every day. Of all international interbank transfers, 95% go by CHIPS wires, at a rate of 150,000 each day.

The Society for Worldwide Interbank Financial Telecommunications (SWIFT) is an international message service by which banks and other financial institutions worldwide send the messages that initiate funds transfers. Over 80% of CHIPS transfers are initiated with a SWIFT message. Securities brokers, securities exchanges, and clearing institutions can also belong to SWIFT, which is a cooperative society located in Belgium. SWIFT has more than 2600 member institutions, including almost all of the world's major banks, and they send a million messages a day through the system.

Where CHIPS and SWIFT are international in scope, the main domestic EFT system is Fedwire, operated by the Federal Reserve System. Fedwire links all of the Federal Reserve Banks and almost 12,000 domestic financial institutions that participate in the system. In 1993, Fedwire handled an average of 277,000 wire transfers every day, with a monetary value of $824 billion. At the domestic level, Fedwire combines both the actual movement of the funds (CHIPS' function) and the electronic message traffic that initiates those movements (SWIFT's function).

In addition to these three systems, Telex, an international communications network, also can be used as a means of initiating financial transfers. Telex differs from SWIFT in that businesses as well as banks worldwide can subscribe, and Telex messages are not as rigidly structured as SWIFT's. The precision of SWIFT's messages allows for maximum speed and accuracy in the execution of transactions, which is why banks use it more frequently than Telex.

Table 15.1 summarizes the major EFT systems, giving a quick view of a major problem confronting investigators — the sheer volume of traffic. Finding a few "dirty" wires among the 1.5 million or so zipping around the world every day is going to be a little difficult. And this is just the banks.

All wire transfers begin with a request by the customer to transfer the funds. This may look like Western Union's Money Transfer form and will contain similar information. Banks thoroughly document wire transfers, because the amounts of money involved can be quite large and the banks don't want to misplace any of it. Actually, when you consider that there are an estimated 700,000 wire transfers and millions of messages sent every day, remarkably little money goes astray.

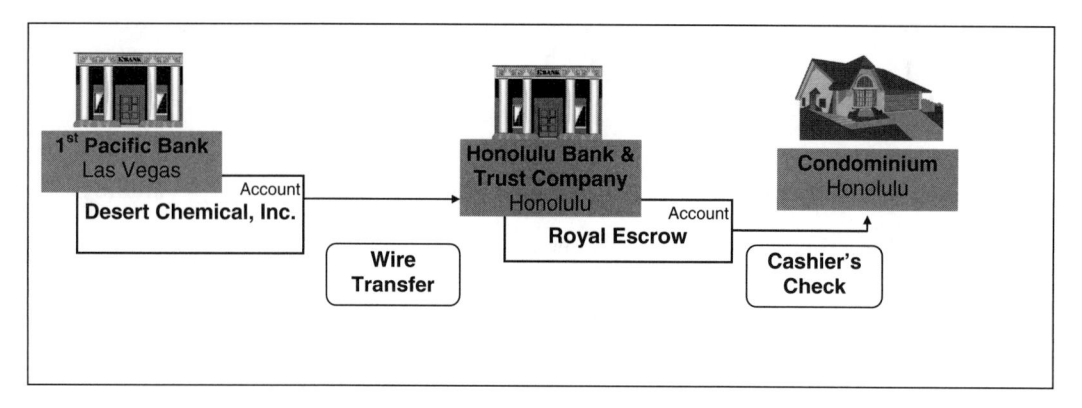

Figure 15.4 *Wiring money domestically.*

FOLLOWING THE MONEY

For the purposes of this exercise, we'll follow a couple of specific transactions relating to Mr. Bell's operation. The first of these is the movement of $1 million from Nevada to Honolulu, where Bell wants to buy a condominium. Since this is strictly a domestic transfer, the appropriate system for his banker to use is Fedwire. Both First Pacific Bank, where Bell has $1 million on deposit, and Honolulu Bank and Trust, which will be paying the escrow company, are members of the Fedwire system. See Figure 15.4.

Bell could get a cashier's check from First Pacific, but he decides he wants the money there more quickly, so he makes a request for a transfer of funds from First Pacific. His first step is to fill out a funds transfer request at the Las Vegas branch of First Pacific Bank. The form authorizes the bank to transfer $1 million by wire to payee bank Honolulu Bank and Trust. The other information on the form identifies Bell and his account. He did this transaction in person, but it could have been done by mail or by fax.

Because the account is held in the name of a corporation, proper authorization in the form of a resolution is required. Bell provides this as well. When everything is verified and double-checked, the bank prepares a message to the Federal Reserve Bank in San Francisco to be sent via Fedwire. This message is pretty brief, and it contains all the information needed by the Federal Reserve to route the money properly.

A copy of this data is maintained at the sending or originating bank, and the transaction is logged a total of three times, once at First Pacific upon sending, once by the Federal Reserve Bank, and once by Honolulu Bank and Trust, the receiving bank.

Back at First Pacific, the bank debits the account of Desert Chemical, Inc., to the tune of $1 million, plus the charge for the wire transfer. This information, in the form of a debit memo, will be included on the statement Desert Chemical will receive at the end of the month. Fedwire transactions are "real time," so the debit takes place immediately.

This particular transaction involves only one Federal Reserve district. Had Bell's bank been in New York, it would have routed the message through the New York branch of the Federal Reserve, which would send the message to San Francisco. At each Federal Reserve Bank, the transaction is indexed and every transfer placed on microfiche. These records are kept for seven years, but they'll be hard to locate unless you can provide information such as the date, names of the sending and receiving banks, and the exact dollar amount of the transfer. All transactions are indexed by these fields and a journal kept, which is in turn supported by the microfiche records.

RECORDS GENERATED IN A FEDWIRE TRANSFER

Numerous records are produced in connection with every Fedwire transfer. Figure 15.5 lists the records and where they can be found.

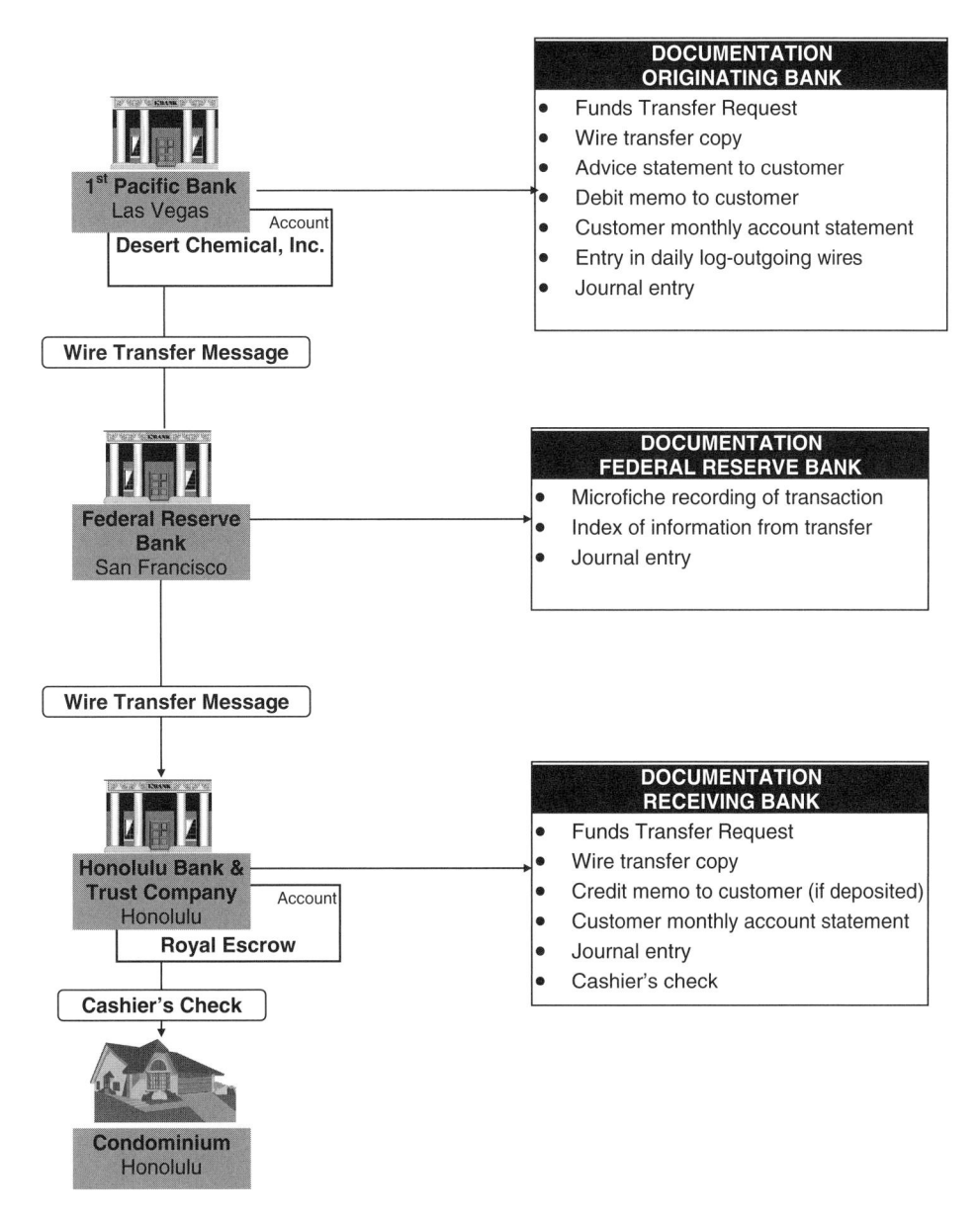

Figure 15.5 *Documents relating to wire transfers.*

FORMS USED IN WIRE TRANSFERS

The forms used by banks and the Federal Reserve include the advice statement or confirmation of wire transfer (Figure 15.6), the debit memo (Figure 15.7), the internal log of outgoing wire transfers (Figure 15.8), and the journal (Figure 15.9).

The advice statement reproduced here would be interpreted as follows: On January 7, 1998, First Pacific Bank sent $1 million on behalf of the ordering customer, Alex Bell of Desert Chemical, to Honolulu Bank and Trust in Honolulu.

The symbols that appear on the advice statement have the following denotations:

- Reference #: number assigned to the wire transfer by the bank
- ORG: the ordering customer
- BNF: the beneficiary of the wire transfer
- AC: the beneficiary's account number
- BBI: bank-to-bank information pertaining to the wire transfer
- SEQ: a particular sequence number assigned by the bank to the wire transfer

```
┌─────────────────────────────────────────────────────────────────┐
│  ❋First Pacific Bank                                            │
│     Advice Statement - Confirmation of Wire Transfer            │
│  Date: 01/07/98   Reference #:  980107003795                    │
│  1st Pacific Bank has debited your account #: 689236 for transfer of funds. │
│  Amount: $ 1,000,000 1st Pacific Bank. (ordering customer's bank) │
│  /ORG=Mr. Alex Bell, Desert Chemical, Inc. LAS VEGAS, NV        │
│  /BNF=Royal Escrow Company- Honolulu Bank and Trust             │
│  /AC—0079876 BBI= Wire Transfer SEQ—980107003795                │
└─────────────────────────────────────────────────────────────────┘
```

Figure 15.6 Advice statement or confirmation of wire transfer.

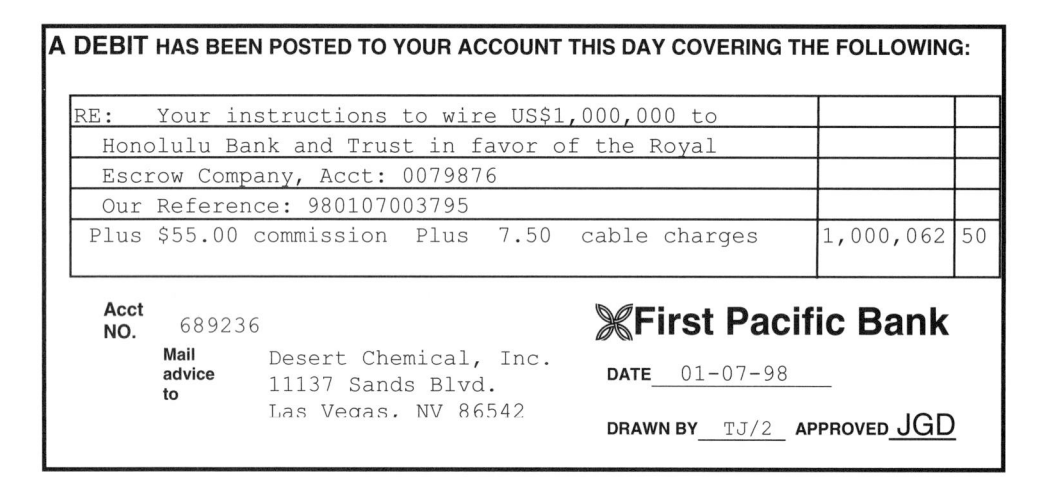

```
┌─────────────────────────────────────────────────────────────────┐
│ A DEBIT HAS BEEN POSTED TO YOUR ACCOUNT THIS DAY COVERING THE FOLLOWING: │
│ ┌──────────────────────────────────────────────────┬──────────┐ │
│ │ RE:   Your instructions to wire US$1,000,000 to  │          │ │
│ │   Honolulu Bank and Trust in favor of the Royal  │          │ │
│ │   Escrow Company, Acct: 0079876                  │          │ │
│ │   Our Reference: 980107003795                    │          │ │
│ │   Plus $55.00 commission  Plus  7.50 cable charges│1,000,062│50│
│ └──────────────────────────────────────────────────┴──────────┘ │
│  Acct                                                           │
│  NO.  689236                      ❋First Pacific Bank           │
│   Mail   Desert Chemical, Inc.                                  │
│  advice  11137 Sands Blvd.        DATE  01-07-98                │
│   to     Las Vegas, NV 86542                                    │
│                                   DRAWN BY  TJ/2  APPROVED JGD  │
└─────────────────────────────────────────────────────────────────┘
```

Figure 15.7 Debit memo.

```
┌─────────────────────────────────────────────────────────────────┐
│ TRANSACTION LOG - WIRE TRANSFER                                 │
│ Sequence Number: 980107003795                                   │
│ ROUTING INFORMATION                                             │
│                 ABA      NAME                    ABA     NAME   │
│ Source Bank:   121501   1st Pacific  Target Bank: 121504 Honolulu B&T │
│ Wire-Key: FWOF                                                  │
│ Tran Type: Outgoing Wire Transfer                               │
│                       Caller Name: Alex Bell                    │
│                                                                 │
│ FINANCIAL INFORMATION                                           │
│ Credit Acct: 0079876       Honolulu Bank and Trust              │
│ Debit Acct:  689236        Desert Chemical, Inc.                │
│ Amount Sent:                                                    │
│                                                                 │
│ FEDWIRE MESSAGE FORMAT                                          │
│ 1st Pacific Bank (Originator)       ORG = Desert Chemical       │
│ Honolulu Bank & Trust (Recipient bank)  BNF = Royal Escrow/   BBI = Escrow payment │
│                                                                 │
│ TRANSACTION HISTORY:  Timestamp       Oper ID  Initials  Term ID│
│    Entry:             01/07/98 10:35  Smith    JS        001    │
│    Review/Release:    01/07/98 10:45  Jones    AJ        002    │
└─────────────────────────────────────────────────────────────────┘
```

Figure 15.8 Internal log of outgoing wire transfers.

For Mr. Bell's transfer, the journal entry might look like this:

1. 12
   (Fed. Res. Bank, SF)
2. 021234989   1000   980107
   (1st Pacific ABA) (Regular Transfer) (Date)
3. 021000021   980107003795   1,000,000
   (Honolulu Bank ABA) (Sender reference #) (Amount)
4. 1st Pacific/ORG-Desert Chemical
   (Originating bank and account name)
5. Honolulu Bank/CTR/BNF-Royal Escrow/AC-0079876/PHN
   (Receiving bank and beneficiary account name and number. 'PHN' signifies phone contact)
6. RFB-ESC3795   OBI - Escrow Payment
   (Contact information)   (Description of the purpose of the payment)

Figure 15.9 *Journal of transfers entry for a wire transfer.*

The debit memo is fairly self-explanatory.

The bank's internal log of outgoing wire transfers will contain the following elements:

- Sequence number: an internal reference or sequence number assigned by the source bank to the wire transfer
- Source bank: the originating bank initiating the wire transfer; i.e., the bank that maintains the internal transaction log on the wire transfer, in this case, First Pacific Bank
- Target bank: the bank that is to receive the wire transfer, either the beneficiary's bank or an intermediary bank; in our example, Honolulu Bank and Trust
- ABA: the particular bank's ABA number
- Wire-key: a code indicating the particular type of wire transfer (e.g., FWOF signifies outgoing Fedwire funds transfer)
- Tran type: the type of transaction
- Caller name: the person calling in the wire transfer request to the bank's wire transfer operations division (for example, the customer him- or herself or an employee from the customer's particular bank branch)
- Credit acct.: a Federal Reserve ledger account, maintained by the source bank, which is to be credited when there is an outgoing wire transfer to be sent through Fedwire
- Debit acct.: the ordering customer's bank account to be debited by the source bank as a result of the wire transfer being sent out of the customer's account
- Originator's bank: the ordering customer's bank
- Recipient bank: the bank receiving the wire transfer
- ORG: the ordering customer requesting the wire transfer
- BNF: the designated beneficiary of the wire transfer
- BBI: bank-to-bank information accompanying the wire transfer

The log also includes the following transaction history information:

- Entry: the exact time the wire transfer request entered the bank's wire transfer operations room
- Review/Release: the exact time the wire transfer was sent out of the bank's wire transfer operations room
- Oper ID, Initials, and Term ID: the identification, initials, and computer terminal of the wire room operators who handled this particular wire transfer

Actual Fedwire transfers contain most of the information in the log, much of it in coded form. If we were to request information from the Federal Reserve on a specific transfer, the entry from the journal of transfers would consist of six lines of coded data, as in Figure 15.9, providing the following information:

1. Information concerning the Federal Reserve Bank
2. Receiving bank ABA number; type code; date
3. Sending bank ABA number; sender reference number; amount
4. Sender information
5. Recipient information
6. Information as to how the receiving bank can be contacted about the transfer, and information about the purpose of the transfer

For a list of the various codes used in Fedwire transfers go to www.frbservices.org/wholesale/pdf/fedwirerefcard.pdf. Two of these codes bear special mention. OBI, or Other Bank Information, is transaction data from the sender to the recipient. It may contain an explanation of the purpose of the transfer, as it does in Bell's case. This information and that in BBI (Bank-to-Bank Information) can provide leads to suspicious or money laundering activity.

To obtain information from Fedwire by subpoena, contact:

Electronic Funds Transfer Product Office
Federal Reserve Bank
Atlanta, Georgia
(404) 521-8384

When requesting information, remember that this system carries almost 300,000 messages each day. In order for them to find the transfer(s) you want, you're going to have to be fairly specific by providing information about the date, amount of the transaction, originator, sending bank, beneficiary, receiving bank, and the account numbers involved. The Federal Reserve Bank retains wire transfer records for 180 days. Requests for information older than this will probably have to be made to the sending and receiving banks.

CHIPS AND SWIFT*

Whereas Fedwire is designed to handle domestic transfers of funds, the CHIPS and SWIFT systems are set up for international transactions. In Bell's case, his transfers to Mexico are going to be processed on the CHIPS and SWIFT networks.

The two systems perform different functions. SWIFT is not a transfer system per se; it resembles a big e-mail network among the world's biggest banks. Twenty-six hundred banks in more than 65 countries participate. Almost all of the world's largest banks participate, sending 1.6 million messages to each other each day.

It was this volume of traffic that led to the creation of SWIFT in 1973. The banks recognized several needs — standardization, accuracy, authentication, and secrecy — which they addressed with this cooperative system. A standard message format, consisting of 10 message categories covering the 120 possible types of messages, was one response to the need for standardization across national, cultural, and language barriers.

The system uses a fixed format with set codes to maximize accuracy, and encryption is used to prevent security breaches during the transmission of the data. Authentication is performed through use of an algorithm that permits detection of any changes in the transmission. Figure 15.10 is a sample SWIFT message using only required fields.

If no funds are actually transferred by these SWIFT messages, how then does the money get moved? Mostly over the other system, CHIPS. Over 80% of the more than 150,000 daily CHIPS transactions — $900 billion worth — are initiated with a SWIFT message.

CHIPS handles 95% of the international interbank dollar transfers. Operated by the New York Clearinghouse Association of 12 New York

---

* Much of the information and all of the examples relating to SWIFT and CHIPS in this text are from two FinCEN publications written by Michael Rosenberg. *Key Electronic Funds Transfer Systems: Fedwire, CHIPS, SWIFT* and *Investigative Guidelines to Wire Transfer* are both excellent resources on this subject and examples of the superb work done by FinCEN in this area.

```
:20PAYREF-TB54302
:321:910103BEF1000000
:50:CUSTOMER NAME
AND ADDRESS
:59:/123-456-789
BENEFICIARY NAME AND ADDRESS
```

Figure 15.10 *Sample text of a SWIFT message containing only required fields. Codes used: 20 – transaction reference number assigned by the sender to identify the transaction; 32A – value date, currency code, and amount of the transaction; 50 – customer ordering the transaction; 59 – party designated to be the ultimate recipient of the funds.*

banks, CHIPS is the system preferred for use in moving U.S. dollars offshore. About 145 banks participate in the CHIPS system, which functions, as its name implies, like one of those clearinghouses used by banks for checks. In the check clearinghouse, all the various checks are brought to a central location, where they are "settled" and cleared for payment. In this settling process, each bank totes up what checks it has that are drawn *on* their accounts and what checks are payable *to* their accounts. The difference is the settlement between the two banks. Don't leave the room just yet, because the banks will continue the settling process with all the other banks present, until everybody has a net settlement, moving as little money as possible.

CHIPS works like this, except that instead of checks, everybody's using electronic funds. Unlike Fedwire, CHIPS is not a real-time system. It takes a while to add up everybody's incomings versus everybody's outgoings and come to a settlement, so all transactions are accumulated during the day and the net settlement occurs at the end of the day. Fedwire transfers are effective immediately upon entry. (Fedwire, incidentally, is the means used to actually settle up the accounts among the banks at the end of the day.)

Michael Rosenberg of FinCEN describes two types of EFTs: "book transfers" and those involving correspondent banks. Both can be used in connection with the CHIPS system. Here's how Mr. Rosenberg outlines the book transfers:

Most funds transferred electronically among banks are paid through "book transfers." Essentially, "book transfers" refer to the accounting process that actually moves the funds from one account at a bank to another account at the same or another bank. For example, if both the ordering party and the beneficiary maintain accounts at the same bank, the ordering party can send funds to the beneficiary by simply instructing the bank to make an internal book transfer of the funds from the ordering party's account to the beneficiary's account. The "book transfer" method can also be employed by banks which have a correspondent relationship (i.e., when one bank maintains an account at another bank for the purpose of clearing transactions). For example, a customer may order its bank, which is located in Chicago, to transfer funds to a beneficiary whose bank is located in New York. If the ordering party's Chicago bank maintains a correspondent account at the New York bank, the Chicago bank, on behalf of its ordering customer, may instruct the New York bank to transfer funds out of the Chicago bank's correspondent account to the account of the beneficiary.

Mr. Rosenberg describes the role of correspondent banks in wire transfers as follows:

A correspondent bank holds deposits owned by other banks and performs banking services (such as wire transfer payments) for these other banks. Banks using correspondent banks maintain an account there for carrying out and clearing transactions. For example, a bank in San Francisco may maintain a correspondent bank account at a particular bank in New York City which is a participant member of the CHIPS system. By maintaining this correspondent banking relationship, the San Francisco bank will be able to enjoy access to CHIPS and therefore effectuate wire transfers on behalf of its customers through the CHIPS system.

CHIPS transactions, like those on Fedwire, begin with an application by the customer to transfer funds. After the transfer request has been checked and the funds are verified, the message transferring the funds is sent via the

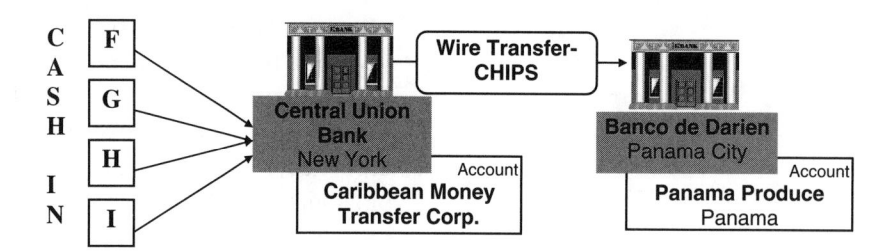

Figure 15.11 *The placement stage of Alex Bell's operation.*

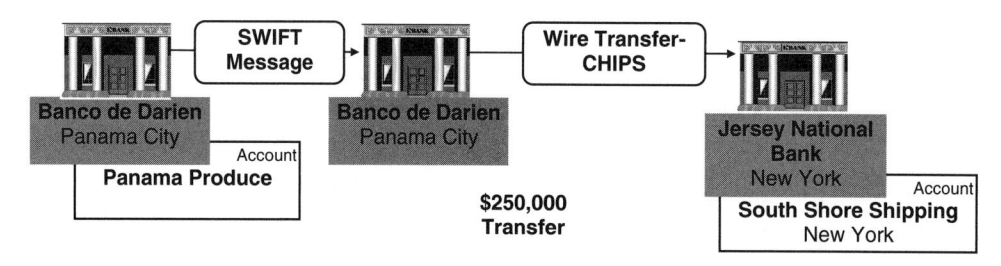

Figure 15.12 *Alex Bell repatriates his ill-gotten wealth.*

CHIPS computer. We will look at an example involving Mr. Bell to follow the system's operation. See Figure 15.11.

In the placement stage of Bell's operation, his dealers were using agents of the Caribbean Money Transfer Corp., buying wire transfers of $750 each, the recipient being a Panamanian company, Panama Produce in Panama City. The money from CMTC's New York account is wired to Panama over CHIPS. Bell did nothing (transfer request, etc.) to initiate this transfer, and he probably doesn't even know how it is taking place. His company, Panama Produce, will get a credit memo and an advice letting them know the funds have been received at Banco de Darien.

Bell repatriates his money directly back from Panama (though again, in real life he would layer the transactions). See Figure 15.12. He instructs Panama Produce to wire $250,000 to South Shore Shipping, a front company he owns in New Jersey. Messages initiating this transfer are sent via SWIFT, and the funds are transferred using the CHIPS settlement process, as both of the banks involved, Banco de Darien and Jersey National Bank, are, for the sake of our example, members of the system. Had they not been, they would have used their correspondent banking relationship with one of the 142 or so banks that are CHIPS members.

In our scenario, Panama Produce instructs its bank, Banco de Darien, to pay South Shore Shipping $250,000 for shipping a load of peppers. (These would be Bell peppers.) Banco de Darien sends a SWIFT message to its New York branch, which initiates the payment via CHIPS. That payment is made to the Jersey National Bank, which credits the account of South Shore Shipping. This transaction generates a number of messages on both SWIFT and CHIPS, including confirmations and instructions. Telex traffic between Panama Produce and its bank or between Panama Produce and South Shore Shipping might also take place. Retrieving these messages will be a lot easier at the participant banks than from SWIFT.

INFORMAL BANKING SYSTEMS AND UNLICENSED TRANSMITTERS

Operating right alongside the big players, but just out of sight, are two other financial systems of interest to the investigator. The first has been around for centuries, long before wires, and the other is a child of electronic funds transfers.

The first system, sometimes referred to as a parallel or underground banking system, is known as *hawala* or *fei chi'en*. Originally part of a support system for immigrant groups, these networks provide financial services for people unable or unwilling to trust the world's banking system. We're going to get into *hawala* operations more extensively in a later chapter.

Although they are unregulated and for the most part undocumented, these networks are efficient, effective, and capable of moving large amounts of money quickly in near total secrecy. Surprisingly little is known about the operation of these networks, as the participants are generally reluctant to discuss their roles. For the most part, the system is based on trusting relationships, almost invariably within a single ethnic group.

To illustrate how this system works, let us assume that an ethnic Chinese merchant in Hong Kong wishes to transfer $50,000 to a relative in San Francisco. He contacts a businessman in Hong Kong who is part of the *fei chi'en* (which means, literally, "flying money") network. The merchant gives the businessman $50,000 plus a commission and the name of the relative to whom the money is to be given. The businessman calls his associate in San Francisco and asks that the money be given to the relative. The associate gets the money from funds already in the United States and provides these to the relative. Later, the associate will be conducting a similar transaction with another client who wants to move money from San Francisco to Hong Kong, so everything will eventually wind up approximately even. No money has actually moved across international boundaries, but transfers have unquestionably occurred.

In a similar arrangement, the customer in Hong Kong is given a piece of paper with an identifying mark or sentence, along with instructions on where to present it for payment. When presented, this paper is honored without question. Though it is not technically a wire transfer, confirmation of the validity of the paper may take place by phone or fax.

The money laundering implications are obvious. Not only are criminals able to move their own funds quickly and in complete secrecy, but this system also allows the *fei chi'en* operator to make use of the criminal's funds for other transactions. Since the entire operation is usually conducted on a cash basis, a paper trail is nonexistent. Law enforcement sources believe that much of the money from the sale of Southeast Asian heroin traffic, long dominated by ethnic Chinese groups, is laundered via this underground banking system.

The *hawala* is a similar operation, which originated in Southwest Asia from the same fundamental distrust of banks and the government. Like its Chinese equivalent, *hawala* is frequently used by expatriates to send money back to India or Pakistan, or by Indians and Pakistanis to send money to their relatives abroad. Although the system is used by legitimate business people, it can also be used to launder money, and, more important, it can be used by terrorists to fund their operations. One method involves exchanges of drug money for gold. The *hawala* system is believed to be very active in Europe, including England, Holland, and parts of the former Soviet Union.

Tracing transactions in this underground banking system is next to impossible without inside information. Penetrating such an operation is always difficult, not least because of the emphasis on trust that permeates the entire scheme. Investigators can watch for telephone and fax transmissions between participants, however, which may indicate illicit transactions. The fact that *hawala* operators, known as *hawaladars*, keep no written records definitely complicates matters.

The other type of transmitter is the unlicensed sort (which technically includes those in the *hawala* and *fei chi'en* networks as well). Under federal law, operation of an unlicensed wire transmission business is a crime, a felony violation of 18 U.S.C. 1960. Despite their illegal status, unlicensed money transmitters have proliferated, largely because the field is easy to enter. All you really need are a place to receive the funds, someone on the other end to receive them, and a telephone. Bank accounts are useful.

Many of these operations are centered on a single ethnic group. The business where the money is taken in is commonly located in one of those "predominantly (fill in ethnic group) neighborhoods." Not coincidentally, the receiving parties are typically from the same ethnic immigrant group. The transmitter may function just like a licensed operation, with a bank account at the local branch of the Bank of "St. Martin." Back in "St. Martin" itself, the transmitter may have a storefront or just a contact person to whom people can go for their money. The bank account will be used to receive the funds, which can then be disbursed in accordance with the wired instructions.

State agencies that attempt to regulate these businesses are aware of many fly-by-night operations, but it is likely that the unlicensed businesses will continue to operate. The USA PATRIOT Act substantially changed 18 U.S.C. 1960, making prosecution of persons engaged in illegal money transmitter businesses somewhat easier, and the charge should be considered whenever you find a situation where a crook is using questionable means to transfer funds or when a seemingly legitimate business person is transferring funds for the crook.

MONEY LAUNDERING AND WIRE TRANSFERS

Wire transfers are an integral part of many money laundering schemes. The benefits are obvious: Your money is where you want it instantly; the cost of this movement is usually low, as is the risk; and the chances of your hot wire being detected in the cascade of messages are remote.

The Congressional Office of Technology Assessment (OTA), trying to come up with some way of detecting some of the dirty money being wired, has estimated that there are about 250,000 transfers of dirty money every year. That is a lot, but then, according to the OTA, there are 700,000 wires per *day* overall. In other words, less than 1% of all wires are potential money laundering violations.

Wire transfers can be used in the placement stage of an operation, to get cash into another form or to move it from one place to another. Licensed money transmitters are frequently used in this fashion, even though their fees are higher than those for interbank transfers.

In the layering stage, few devices used by the launderer are more effective than wires. Funds can be shifted from account to account, bank to bank, and country to country, in a matter of minutes. Tracing such transactions is extremely difficult, and the use of shell corporations in bank secrecy countries complicates the problem even further.

Integration of the illegal funds is easily accomplished with wire transfers from a legitimate-sounding company via a completely legitimate bank. Because all of these activities are simplified with wire transfers, it is essential that the investigator have an understanding of the processes and the means by which information can be retrieved.

INVESTIGATING WIRE TRANSFER SCHEMES

The most logical focal point of an investigation involving wire transfers is at the beginning of the entire process. The originating bank may handle a couple of hundred transfers a day, but those are easier to deal with than 1.6 million. If you get into the scheme at the beginning, you are more likely to be able to get information about the relevant transfers without having to sort through thousands of irrelevant ones. The customer's account statement, which will show all of the incoming and outgoing transfers, is the best source of wire transfer information. An example is shown in Figure 15.13.

As of January 1, 1996, federal rules were put in place to assist with the investigation of wire transfers by law enforcement. The banks didn't like these rules, but they also don't want any more (even more stringent) rules, so they seem to be pretty good about following these. The new rules relate to any transfer over $3000, and they require that the bank obtain and retain original, microfilm, or other copy or electronic record of the following information relating to the payment order:

SOURCES OF INFORMATION ON WIRE TRANSFERS

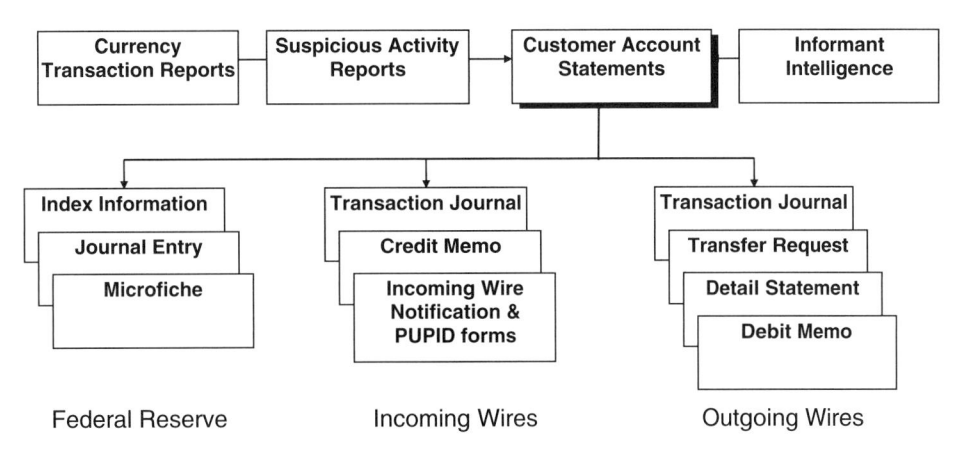

```
Currency            Suspicious Activity    Customer Account      Informant
Transaction Reports    Reports          →   Statements           Intelligence
                                              |
        ┌─────────────────────┼─────────────────────┐
        ↓                     ↓                     ↓
   Index Information    Transaction Journal    Transaction Journal
   Journal Entry        Credit Memo            Transfer Request
   Microfiche           Incoming Wire          Detail Statement
                        Notification &         Debit Memo
                        PUPID forms

   Federal Reserve      Incoming Wires         Outgoing Wires
```

Figure 15.13 *Sources of information on wire transfers.*

- Name and address of originator
- Amount of the payment order
- Execution date
- Any payment instructions
- Identity of the beneficiary's bank
- Name and address of the beneficiary
- Account number of the beneficiary
- Identifiers pertaining to the beneficiary

If the originator and beneficiary are not established customers, then the bank also must record:

- Identification and Taxpayer Identification Number (if the order is made in person)
- Taxpayer Identification Number (if the order is not made in person)

Starting at the beginning, the investigator should be looking for a chain of documents linked to a transaction or set of transactions. See Figure 15.13. The tracing of many wire transfers will begin with the customer's account statement, but some cases may involve surveillance or informant information that reveals that a subject is making wire transfers. It will then be necessary to establish whether that individual has an account at the bank(s) in question. From there, the account statement can be used to determine who is the beneficiary of the transfers and how much money is being sent.

Banks prefer to do wire transfers with established customers, but it is possible to wire money if you're not an account holder. In that case, the transaction would resemble an electronic cashier's check, in which funds from the bank's own account are used — after, of course, the originator "buys" the transfer with some money of his or her own. These are difficult transactions for an investigator to locate.

It is also possible that the beneficiary may not be an account holder and will be collecting the funds in person. In that case, banks use a PUPID (Pick Up with Proper ID) form to verify that the person standing there is really the intended recipient.

Because large transactions — at least those larger than $3000 — are now better documented, the use of wire transfers is a somewhat riskier proposition for the launderer. The crooks respond by reducing the amounts of cash being transferred in a given transaction; if they know the transmitter asks for ID on every transfer over $1000, they'll do their business in multiples of $900.

The government has another option in this case, called a Geographic Targeting Order (GTO). GTOs are directed at transmitters in a certain area and might require that all transactions over a lower amount, say $750, be reported. GTOs are burdensome for the transmitters, so they are supposed to be in place for limited periods of time. The information they yield can be extremely valuable.

The transmitter should not be overlooked as a source of information. Wire transfer data from banks is available by subpoena or search warrant, and the agents of licensed transmitters may also have valuable knowledge of money laundering and structuring activity. Cooperative agents of licensed transmitters have identified individuals engaging in suspicious transactions and trends that led to structuring or money laundering cases.

Informants familiar with the operation of an illegal enterprise should always be questioned about any transfer of funds, by wire or otherwise, and your antenna should immediately go up if you find copies of wire transfers or money orders in a search warrant. In all cases, the investigator should remain alert to the possibility that these methods are being used to move the proceeds of crime out of sight and out of reach.

CHAPTER 16

REAL PROPERTY

"Land is the basis of all wealth."
Anonymous

"The meek shall inherit the earth but not the mineral rights."
J. Paul Getty, American oil man

In 1986, the Statistical Abstract of the United States reported that three fourths of the combined value of all assets in the country was in the form of real estate. When you consider how much of what Americans own is in the form of cash, bank accounts, stocks, bonds and other investments, that's a pretty amazing total.

On the other hand, if you look at the average person's net worth, the largest numbers by far — in both the assets and the liabilities columns — are going to relate to real estate. Real property is the basis of even more wealth, however, because many investments such as stock and bonds are themselves valuable because of the land and buildings the issuer owns.

Even the name "real property" gives you the impression that everything else you can buy, own, hold, or sell is illusory or *un*real. Land is permanent. Land is solid. Land can be acquired for the next generation and passed along with assurance.

Land, along with the buildings on it, represents the hopes and aspirations of countless people around the world, including more than a few criminals and money launderers. Schemes involving real property are hardly uncommon, as the number of forfeiture cases with titles such as "United States of America v. One Parcel of Property Located at ------" demonstrates. Real property is not only an objective in money laundering schemes, it can be the means by which a scheme itself is effected.

As we've seen in several of the case examples, real property was one of the assets acquired with the proceeds of the illegal activity. Aldrich Ames, Russian spy, purchased a $540,000 home in Virginia and three pieces of property in Colombia. Al Capone bought an estate in Miami and at one point was trying to buy an entire island in the Bahamas.

When part of a money laundering scheme, real property offers challenges and opportunities for the investigator. As a very big ticket asset, the real property could well be the heart of your forfeiture case. And nothing, not even bank transactions, creates the type of documentation that accompanies real property transfers. Real estate leaves a paper trail that is in some cases hundreds of years old. Some real estate records in this country go back for over 300 years, still carefully preserved in county courthouses around the country. Knowing who owned the place in 1765 may not help much with your current case, but you can at least be assured that the subject's records relating to that same property are going to be in the same place and in the same complete and accurate condition.

Why are real estate records so comprehensive? The law recognizes that real property is the key to wealth. Meticulous records are kept to avoid disputes that can interfere with the use of this wealth in commerce. Without assurances that the titles to real property are complete, no one would be able to buy, sell, or will a home. No business would be able to borrow money against its property. The security that makes land ownership so appealing would be gone. So, government agencies keep the land records, some dating back to the Louisiana Purchase, Spanish and English land grants, or the founding of the Jamestown Colony. Those records will be there when you need them for your case. Finding them is what this chapter is all about.

REAL ESTATE TRANSACTIONS: BASIC ANATOMY

Every real estate transaction follows a precise pattern, each step along the path creating a set of documents and records. Unlike some transactions relating to personal property, real estate deals almost invariably involve several parties. In fact, a real estate transaction that doesn't need several outsiders to complete is unusual enough that it should get a second look from the financial investigator. We'll work our way through a real estate transaction from beginning to end, introducing some of the terms investigators need to know.

AUTHORIZATION TO SELL

There are always two parties to every real estate transaction, the buyer and the seller. In legal terms, these are the *grantee* and *grantor,* respectively, so known because the seller is granting title to the property being transferred.

The very first step in a real estate transaction is a decision to sell. The property owner decides either to sell the property him- or herself or to introduce the first outsider to the deal, a real estate *broker.* Brokers are licensed by the state to act as agents on behalf of the buyer or the seller.

If the seller decides to appoint a broker, a form is prepared, essentially a contract between the two. The seller agrees to pay a commission to the broker upon sale of the property. The form used is an Authorization to Sell, and it gives the broker the power to advertise the property and take whatever steps are necessary to sell the property at the price and terms authorized.

ADVERTISING

At the broker's office, a file is opened on the property, which will eventually contain records of everything that transpires in the transaction. The broker will also advertise the property. This is known as "listing." Many areas of the country use the Multiple Listing Service (MLS), which gives brokers who subscribe to the service computerized access to information about properties for sale all over the area. If you know a broker, the MLS book or a computer with MLS access can give you some basic information about the property in question.

DEPOSIT RECEIPT OFFER AND ACCEPTANCE

At the time a buyer actually appears and makes an offer on a property, the broker prepares a form that acknowledges the offer and documents the receipt of the deposit. This form is one of the key parts of a transaction, because it brings the two parties together for the first time.

The Deposit Receipt Offer and Acceptance (DROA) is known by other names, such as the Deposit Receipt and Agreement of Sale or the Uniform Agreement of Sale and Deposit Receipt, but the document itself is standardized in a specific area or state.

A DROA is initiated by the buyer, who is representing that he or she can produce the financing to purchase the property, provided that the seller can produce clear title. It establishes the following elements:

- The parties to the contract
- The conditions of the contract
- The form of the payment
- The total price

Although the DROA is preliminary to the main event of the transaction, it contains quite a bit of useful information.

Seller Approval

The ball now goes back to the seller, who has to decide whether or not to accept the offer, one that may be lower than the price he or she originally asked. If the seller likes the offer, an acceptance form is prepared. This creates a binding contract — the buyer has made a good faith offer, and the seller has accepted. Neither can now back out without good cause. The transaction can now "go into escrow," where the title is delivered to the buyer and the money delivered to the seller.

At this point, at least three parties are already involved in the transaction. If the buyer has retained a broker to represent his or her interests, there are four, all of whom have copies of the forms that have been exchanged.

Escrow Papers

The fifth party to the transaction is an impartial agent who acts on behalf of buyer and seller. Practices differ around the country. In some places, an independent escrow company is used in real estate transactions, while in others a title company acts as the agent.

Everything from both sides goes through the *escrow agent,* which creates an escrow file for the transaction. The escrow agent exchanges documents, holds moneys, and acts in accordance with its instructions. It is the clearinghouse of the transaction. The *escrow file* will contain every piece of paper relevant to the real estate transaction; this file must be obtained in a financial investigation.

Two important deposits are made to the escrow company. The seller deposits the title to the property, and the buyer deposits those funds that he or she will be supplying to pay for the property. This is the *down payment.* Both items will be held until the transaction "closes," at which time the escrow agent will deliver them.

While the buyer is arranging to obtain the balance of the purchase price, a title company is doing research to assure that title to the property is unencumbered or "clear." Any liens that are found or any problems arising with respect to prior ownership could cause a delay in the transfer.

At this stage, most buyers are seeking the assistance of yet another outside party, a lending institution that will make a mortgage loan on the property. The process of obtaining a mortgage loan entails even more paperwork, this time at the bank or mortgage company, where the buyer will be preparing financial statements, submitting three years' worth of tax returns, and generally providing a wealth of financial information.

Once the mortgage is approved, the buyer is required to deposit the *note* for the amount of the loan, along with a *trust deed* on the property that secures the note. This trust deed essentially secures the loan for the bank that wrote the mortgage.

If the title search comes up clean, the deal is ready to close. The escrow agent pays the seller the purchase price, usually subtracting the broker's commission, which is paid directly to the broker. The note is sent to the lender. The escrow agent sends the deed and the trust deed to the government agency that records property transfers — in most cases, the *County Recorder.* After recording, the deed is sent to the buyer and the trust deed to the lender. The title company issues a title report and a title insurance policy, which assures the buyer that he or she has a good "clear" title and the lender that it has a good lien.

At this point, the following have taken place:

- The seller has received a check for the purchase price, less commission to the broker.
- The buyer has received a deed, proclaiming him or her to be the owner of the property.
- The lending institution has received a note from the buyer promising to pay back the loan. Just in case he or she doesn't, the lender has a lien on the property, documented by the trust deed.

Everybody's happy, and there is paper on this transaction all over town. What records now exist, and where can we find them?

Seller	Deed, bank records reflecting receipt of the purchase price, contract with broker
Seller's broker	Copies of the major documents in the case, DROA, acceptance, record of payment
Buyer	Deed, copy of note, trust deed, mortgage loan file, mortgage payment records
Buyer's broker	Copies of buyer's records, DROA, counteroffer and acceptance records, commission payment
Escrow company	The full package: broker documents, DROA, acceptance, mortgage loan information, copies of checks used for payment, title information, copies of deeds, a complete chronological recitation of the entire transaction, records of the escrow fees and charges
Title company	Records of the title search, lien information
Lending institution	Mortgage loan application, credit check, title report, mortgage loan information, note, trust deed, copy of cashier's check
Buyer's bank	Bank records, canceled checks, cashier's check for down payment
County Recorder	Recorded and filed copies of deed, trust deed, mortgage, and title information

It's an embarrassment of riches for the investigator. And it could get even more complicated. If the seller has an outstanding mortgage, that has to be released before the title transfers, so that yet another party gets involved in the transaction.

Your best source for information about the transaction is the escrow company. They package everything nicely and keep track of everything that happens and everyone who's involved.

REAL ESTATE OWNERSHIP

As you can see, buying real property is not as easy as going out and picking up some groceries or adopting a dog. It turns out that owning real property isn't simple either. In fact, there are numerous different ways in which an *estate*, which is what an ownership interest in real property is called, can be held.

There are two major types, *freehold* and *non-freehold*. A freehold estate continues for an indeterminate period, with title to real property held for the lifetime of the owner and then passed to an heir. Non-freehold estates, also called *leasehold*, endure for a limited time (the length of the lease). Non-freehold estates are considered personal property, as opposed to real property. If your subject is a leaseholder on some property, that lease may well have a lot of value, but he or she doesn't own the property, only the lease.

The question of whether the ownership is "complete" or not also comes up. A person who owns the property absolutely and without condition is known as a *fee simple* owner. He or she can do anything (legal) that he or she wants with the property, including willing it to someone. The fee can be split, as when an owner sells something like the air or mineral rights to the property.

Qualified fee estates have limits imposed by the owner. One example would be if property were willed to the city with the proviso that it only be used as a public park. If the city later tried to use the property for some other purpose, the grant of the original deed could be revoked by the grantor's heirs and title reclaimed.

In a *life estate,* ownership is limited to the lifetime of a person. The owner of a life estate is a life tenant. Ownership transfers to someone else upon the life tenant's death.

Two or more people can own the same piece of property in fee simple. This fact can play havoc with forfeiture and money laundering cases, because the ownership interest of the criminal may be complicated by other, possibly innocent ownership interests. This type of ownership or *tenancy* falls into several categories:

- *Tenancy in severalty* refers to the case when one person owns all of the interest in a property — sole ownership.
- *Tenancy by the entirety* is the term for when a husband and wife own property as one person. If either one dies, the other becomes the sole owner. This

method of ownership is not recognized in community property states.

- *Community property* applies only to property held by a married couple. Community property states are modeled on old Spanish law that looks at ownership of marital property based on when it was acquired. Property acquired during the marriage is community property, and what was acquired before the marriage is separate property. Community property is held equally by each of the spouses, and each has full ownership of the separate property. The community property states are:
  - Arizona
  - California
  - Idaho
  - Louisiana
  - Nevada
  - New Mexico
  - Texas
  - Washington
- *Joint tenancy* refers to ownership of an undivided interest by two or more people not related by marriage, but with rights of survivorship. This means that if one of the joint owners dies, title passes to the survivor. Some states have banned this type of ownership.
- *Tenancy in common* refers to ownership by two or more people without rights of survivorship. The share of ownership may be equal or unequal, but the survivors don't get the deceased's share. Under this arrangement, each owner is responsible for expenses in proportion to his or her share, and income from the property is divided the same way. If your case involves a property with this type of ownership, and the defendant's interest is forfeited, you may have to force the sale of the entire property and then distribute shares of the sale price to the other owners.
- *Tenancy in partnership* is the name for ownership by a partnership, as established under the Uniform Partnership Act. The property is owned by the partners in proportion to their interest in the partnership.

Another common form of ownership is the *condominium,* in which a fractional interest in a larger property is held by an individual owner. Condominium co-ownership is frequently found in large, multifamily dwellings, but other property can be subdivided in the same way. The arrangements that accompany condominium ownership also provide for a centralized association of owners, to make joint decisions about common interests.

How does this diversity in ownership methods impact a money laundering investigation? If the intent is to conceal ownership or control of an asset, a spouse, relative, or associate may be placed on the title as the owner in one of these various forms. If this person's true role cannot be fully established, the property may not be forfeitable.

Some court decisions have held that merely titling property in the name of a relative may not be sufficient to show intent to conceal or disguise the transaction; see *United States v. Sanders,* 929 F.2d 1466 (10th Cir. 1991). The presence of multiple owners on a title or the holding of property in joint tenancy or tenancy in common is going to complicate your case.

There are two other ways in which property can be owned, both of which frequently come up in money laundering cases. These are corporations and trusts.

CORPORATIONS AND TRUSTS

We'll remember from our earlier discussion of business operations that corporations are fictional persons, created by the state. Corporations can own property just like real people, and the placing of real estate in the name of a corporation is a popular way to conceal the ownership interest of a criminal money launderer.

As we've also mentioned before, trusts are fiduciary arrangements in which property is turned over to a person (or an institution, such as a bank or trust company) to be held and administered for the benefit of a person or organization. The key parties in a trust are the *trustor* or *creator,* who establishes the trust; the *trustee,* who acts for the trust; and the *beneficiary.* Trust agreements set out the identities and roles of these people.

Two types of trusts are common in real estate activity. The *Real Estate Investment Trust* (REIT) functions like a corporation, with investors acquiring shares of the trust, and the corporation then acts on behalf of the investors. An *express private trust* usually involves only a small number of beneficiaries, most often the creator's immediate family. These trusts can be established to operate during a person's lifetime or to take effect after the person's death. This type of trust can be used as a device for concealment in money laundering schemes, because the title at the County Recorder's office will show the name of the trust as the owner of the property, not the beneficiary or the trustee.

In one of the author's cases, six different properties were titled in the name of three different trusts, none of which contained the defendant's name. A check of the land ownership under the defendant's name would have disclosed that he owned nothing.

Researching Real Property Records

Establishing an undisclosed interest in real property or determining true ownership and control of real estate may well be a key to your money laundering investigation. Computers have made this job easier, although the criminals have found new ways of hiding even something as big as a ranch or an apartment complex.

One problem that investigators face is the decentralization of land ownership records. Although these records are public in every state, properly researching ownership means visiting county recorders in every county of every state. Since there are several thousand counties in the United States, this could take a while.

Computer services that consolidate these records make searching public records much simpler. Not everything is in the databases yet, but services like Lexis-Nexis and ChoicePoint are making headway. For example, Lexis-Nexis now has records from county courthouses in more than 40 states. Now, a nationwide property search can be conducted through one of these services in a matter of minutes. You can also find out about property ownership by looking at tax records, since most real estate is subject to some form of property tax. These records are usually kept by another government agency, often the County Assessor, and they will show at least who currently owns the property and is paying the taxes. This can raise some interesting questions if your money launderer is paying the taxes on a piece of property he or she apparently doesn't own.

In Hawaii, real estate records are centralized at the State Bureau of Conveyances. A search of the records here or in any County Recorder's office begins with the Grantee–Grantor Index. Real estate records are filed by the names of the grantee (seller) and the grantor (buyer). Two indexes track these names alphabetically, enabling the researcher to determine in a moment whether the subject of the inquiry has bought or sold property in the area.

Figure 16.1 focuses on one particular transaction, which we will study as an example. Here, John Joe and his wife have purchased a property from Jane Smith. Class of Instrument describes what type of document was recorded. In this case, it was "D" for "Deed." Mortgages, liens, leases, assignments, and other legal documents are also recorded, so you'll need a key to the codes used in the office that holds your records.

The document number is assigned by the Recorder. Having this number will enable you to go look at the copy of the document on file. Date of Record refers to the date on which the document was recorded at the office, and this is the official date on which the event, John Joe's purchase, was legal.

"Description" refers to the legal description of the property involved. Legal descriptions are

Class of Instrument	Grantor	Grantee	Document No.	Date of Record	Description
D	Joe, John &WF	Smith, Jane	97-01234	06/12/97	Lot 160 FP 324

Figure 16.1 One transaction in the Grantor Index.

lengthy and extremely precise, containing information provided by surveyors, going back in some cases a hundred years.

Land in the United States is surveyed based on a grid system of meridians and base lines. Within these grids, the land is sliced up into quadrangles, townships, tiers, ranges, sections, and quarters. This system works fine out in the country, but in town, where hundreds or even thousands of small parcels could fit in a single township, a system of plats was devised. There are plats for subdivisions and plats for condominiums. The subdivision plat map shows the locations of all the properties in that area, along with the owner's name and some data about each lot. A condominium map relates only to condominium properties and describes ownership by apartment number. In Joe's case, he bought lot 160 in a subdivision plat.

With the information from the Grantor–Grantee Index, you can find out whether the subject still owns the property and what other documents are connected with the purchase, ownership, or sale. You must check both of the indexes, though — the Grantor–Grantee and the Grantee–Grantor. If you only look at one, you may be missing important data.

In our example, the grantor's name is the one indexed alphabetically. That's fine if you're looking for information about John Joe. If you want to know about Jane Smith, you'll have to go to the Grantee–Grantor Index. There, her name will be filed alphabetically, and you'll know that on June 12, 1997, she deeded a piece of property to John Joe.

To learn more about a specific real estate transaction or ownership interest, you can go from the Recorder's office to other public records, or to the escrow company, title company, or real estate brokers who handled the transaction.

Building permits are another good source of public information about real property. Plans, permit applications, inspection data, and other records relating to a property will be on file with the county building department, the city building inspector, or the permits branch. These, too, can be useful in establishing true ownership, because the applicant may be different from the owner of record.

Other government services available to property owners include sewer, water, and trash collection. The public records of these services can be checked to establish ownership or at least who is paying the bills.

In the private sector, the escrow and title companies, real estate brokers, and others involved in the transactions will have information about real estate transfers. Condominium owner associations have information about their members, fees paid, and the residents of apartments that aren't occupied by the owners.

FINDING HIDDEN ASSETS

You wouldn't figure something as big as a house would be easy to hide, and, of course, it isn't. What is easy to hide is a connection to the property. People who don't want their interest in an asset to be known can hide it in a number of ways, with nominees, corporations, and trusts being the most popular. (Aliases and false identification can be used, but passing title upon death is a problem under these schemes.)

Assorted investigative techniques can be used to locate hidden assets, no matter what method is being used to conceal them. Because the asset owner wants to retain control over the property, he or she can be counted on to have some information about the property. Finding communications related to this information should be a focus of the financial investigation. Investigative techniques that can be used to locate assets include:

- Mail covers — Look for mail from County Assessors, real estate management companies, escrow companies, brokers, utility companies, insurance companies, or contractors.
- Pen registers — Look for calls to or from real estate management companies, brokers, real estate investment trusts, and utility companies, or periodic calls that might relate to rental property.
- Document search warrants — A warrant at the subject's residence may turn up deeds, title information, escrow records, or other leads to undisclosed assets.
- Bank records — Look for canceled checks to County Assessors, real estate brokers, utility companies, property managers, or contractors. Financial statements provided by the subject for loan applications and so forth may disclose other assets.
- Tax returns — Depreciation on business property can be deducted from income, so the tax return may list assets not disclosed elsewhere.
- Informants — Debriefings should always include questions about real property ownership. Even questions about other locations where the subject might own property could narrow your search of County Recorders' offices.
- Court records — Records of divorce and child custody cases are especially useful. These cases require submission of accurate financial statements, and the other party, who is likely to know about hidden assets, may set forth this information in his or her own affidavit.

Every document you encounter should be viewed as a potential lead to assets acquired by the subject. Does the subject have correspondence from a condominium owner's association? Why? Does she make payments to a County Assessor in another state? Why?

If you become aware that the subject is using a corporation, trust, or nominee in any capacity, you have to assume that this entity is also being used to hold and conceal ownership in real property. All of those checks then need to be reperformed, looking under the new name.

It's a tedious process, but it can be very rewarding, because land is the basis for all wealth — even the dirty kind of wealth.

NOTE TO FINANCIAL INVESTIGATORS

When title to real property is conveyed, the state requires payment of a conveyance tax. This tax is usually based on the dollar amount of the sale. Because the amount of the tax is shown on the recorded deed, the purchase price can be established (roughly) from this figure. For example, in a state where the conveyance tax is $1.00 per $1,000, and the tax was $250, you know the property cost $250,000.

CHAPTER 17

SECURITIES

"May. This is one of the peculiarly dangerous months to speculate in stocks in. The others are July, September, April, November, October, March, June, December, August, and February."
Mark Twain

"Gentlemen prefer bonds."
Andrew Mellon, banker and Treasury Secretary

Investments involve people putting their money to work for them. As one observer said, "How do you make a million? You start with $900,000." And where do you get the $900,000? Some inherit, some invent, some work for a living. Some sell dope. But no matter how they make the money in the first place, if they're smart, they're going to invest the proceeds. If the proceeds are from an illegal activity, they may be laundering money. If they're *really* smart, they're laundering their money in the markets.

Securities are defined as "evidence of debt or of property, as a bond or a certificate of stock." On an average day $700 billion worth of stock is bought and sold on the floor of the New York Stock Exchange. Over at the American Stock Exchange, they might do another $50 billion, and at NASDAQ another $800 billion more. Volume is, as they say on TV, "heavy." Trillions in currency, stocks, bonds, mutual fund shares, commodities and futures contracts, and other securities are changing hands 24 hours each day in markets all around the world — a quite mind-boggling universe of money.

"The markets" are a big part of the world economy. Everything is interconnected; distress in the Hong Kong stock exchange recently reverberated throughout other markets around the globe. What happens to bank stocks in Tokyo can affect wheat prices in Argentina and Treasury Bills in New York, not to mention hotel occupancy in Honolulu.

If it seems like everybody's involved in the investment markets in some form or another, it's because they are, even though they may not be aware of it. Take a humble police officer who keeps all of her money in the bank. No interest in the market? Not if the police department's pension fund invests in stocks or bonds. Many public and private pension plans are heavily involved in securities. What about the bank? Chances are that its stock is listed on an exchange and that some of its investments are in some market or another.

Buying savings bonds for your child's college education? Have some shares in a mutual fund? You're a bit more involved. Others play the game regularly, under rules that make it easier every day. Electronic trading via the Internet now enables investors to make trading decisions from their home computer. The Internet also puts a vast amount of information into the investor's hands, something that would have required expensive subscriptions and volumes of printed material only a few short years ago.

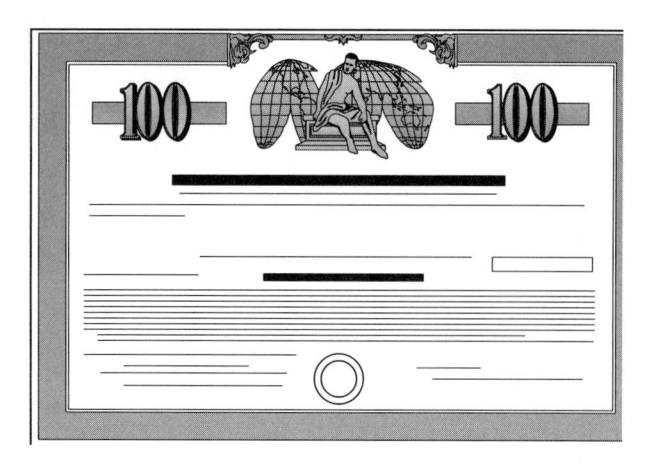

Figure 17.1 *A stock certificate.*

But what are all these people doing, and how are they doing it? In this chapter, we'll examine the world of securities and how they fit into the money launderer's portfolio.

STOCKS: OWNING A PIECE OF THE PIE

Stocks are also known as *shares*, because each one quite literally represents a "share" of a company. See Figure 17.1. A corporation, the only business entity issuing stocks, has as many owners as there are holders of the shares outstanding. In the case of AT&T, it has more than 2.4 million *shareholders*, and the company has 1.34 billion shares outstanding. Each one of those shares is a fractional piece of the entire company. This piece is the shareholders' *equity,* or ownership interest, which you'll find on the corporate balance sheet. (You can go back and look at Al Capone's Annual Report for a look at how some of these terms are used in corporate filings.)

TYPES OF STOCK

There are two types of stock, common and preferred. Common stock represents an ownership share in the company. Common stock is sold by the corporation in an initial public offering (IPO) or in subsequent offerings. After the company sells the shares, they are traded publicly among investors in various markets.

An investor can make money from common stock in two ways. First, the shares pay *dividends,* periodic payments — usually quarterly — made by the corporation to shareholders; they are typically a small percentage of the share's value. The dividend can go up or down each period, depending on how well the company is doing. The second way also depends on how well or poorly the company is doing, as well as what the stock is doing on the market. If the price of the stock goes up, the investor can sell it and make a profit. If it goes down, the stockholder is a loser. Common stock is a total gamble, but the odds are on your side; over long periods of time and on average, stocks consistently outperform other investments. And, like in Las Vegas, you can always get jackpot lucky with a stock like Microsoft that takes you through the roof.

There are two other items of good news on common stock. Unless you're trading on margin, you can only lose everything, but no more. Unlike investments in commodities futures and similar gambles, you can't lose *more* than your investment — shareholders in a corporation aren't responsible for the debts of the company. And, you get a vote in how things are done.

It's not much of a vote. In most cases, you get to vote your shares, so if you're holding one of those shares of AT&T stock, you've got a 1.34-billionth say in where the company should build its next assembly plant. Still, the corporation is giving away some control to its stockholders, in return for which those people give it money to do something useful, like paying exorbitant salaries to its executives and building new factories.

The other type of stock is preferred. Although preferred stock is also considered an ownership share, the owner in this case doesn't get to vote. Why is it called "preferred," then? Mostly because if the worst happens, you'd prefer that you had this stock, rather than the common stuff.

The dividends on preferred stock are guaranteed, but they do not go up when the company is doing better. If the company starts tanking, the dividends will keep getting paid on preferred shares, whereas they will be deferred or postponed on common stock. If things get really bad and the company goes under, the preferred shareholders will recover their investment before the other stockholders.

In addition to the types of stock, there are *classes,* such as "Preferred A," which may be issued by a company for some specific investment purpose or subsidiary. The class is usually designated by a letter suffix.

MAKING MONEY ON STOCK

"Buy low and sell high." Doesn't get any simpler than that. The trick, of course, is knowing when to do what. Once you've got your piece of the corporation, you can do a number of things with it. Some of them might even make you some money in the big Wall Street casino.

One option is to sit back and wait for the money to roll in. Usually, this will take the form of those quarterly dividends. Some investors, those who are in for the long haul, buy stocks that have a high dividend yield over time. The yield is expressed as a percentage of the purchase price and is calculated by dividing the annual dividend amount by the amount you paid for the stock.

In the calculations in Figure 17.2, we bought the stock at $50. If the company pays four quarterly dividends of 50 cents each, the annual yield would be $2, or 4%. If all goes well and you hold this stock for 25 years, at the end of the period, you'll have gotten your purchase price back in dividends and have the share to boot. Stocks that pay dividends regularly are known as *income stocks*, and they are usually issued by established, mature companies.

Dividends don't always have to be made in cash. Sometimes a corporation will issue shares of stock or other property as a dividend.

Cash dividends are paid either by the corporation or by a dividend disbursing agent, usually a bank. If the subject of an investigation had income from cash dividends, the disbursing agents or the corporation itself will have a record of the payments and the checks issued.

Stock dividends are paid in the corporation's own stock. This is a good news, bad news deal. Plus: You did get some more shares in the corporation, so your net worth increased. Minus: Everybody else got some more shares too, so your proportionate share of the ownership of the company didn't increase. The other good news is that a stock dividend, unlike the cash kind, is usually not taxable.

Property dividends are paid in the form of stock from some other company.

Some companies don't pay dividends of any kind. These are usually newer companies that need the cash to expand their operations, so instead of giving it to their shareholders, they reinvest the money in the business. Stocks in such corporations are known as *growth stocks*. Investors in these issues are not counting on the dividend income; instead, they're hoping that as the company grows the stock price will go up.

Investing in income stock is a long-term strategy. There are investors who look for the stocks with the biggest and most consistent yields. The quicker way to big money is in the actual trading of the shares, which is where the "buy low, sell high" maxim comes into play. Predicting a stock's performance is a chancy business, which is why the really good analysts make a lot of money at it.

A number of factors will determine whether a stock's price will go up or down after it is first issued. The biggest factor is whether anybody wants the stock or not. The investor is obviously looking for somebody willing to pay more for the stock than he or she did. Whether there are any such people out there at the moment will depend on what the corporation's profits are like, on whether it is paying dividends or deferring them because it needs the cash for operations, and on factors not necessarily under the company's control. If your company is very big in the snow removal business, but this year's winter was mild with little snow, sales may be affected.

Annual Dividend	÷ Purchase Price	= Annual Yield
$2	$50	4%
$4	$50	8%

Figure 17.2 *Yield calculations.*

The stock price may reflect this problem by going down — fewer people are willing to pay a higher asking price for the stock.

Market prices will drive a stock higher or lower, but where is this "market"? As noted, there are a number of stock markets around the world where traders can buy or sell securities. In fact, there's one open somewhere every minute of the day. The biggest American markets are located in New York, two on Wall Street in Manhattan. The New York Stock Exchange, or NYSE, is the oldest, and most prestigious. The American Stock Exchange, or AMEX, was founded some years later. The exchanges are private associations, and the members or traders buy "seats" on the exchange. A seat on the NYSE has sold for as much as $1.1 million.

In order for a stock to be listed on an exchange, it has to meet certain requirements. On the NYSE, a company has to have pretax earnings of $2.5 million annually, 1.1 million shares outstanding, and a value of at least $18 million. The requirements are lower for the AMEX, which has two different sets of listings or categories of stock.

Another element of the stock market, though technically not an "exchange," is the NASDAQ, an electronic marketplace run by the National Association of Securities Dealers. Almost 5700 companies are listed on the NASDAQ, all of which are required to have $4 million in assets, at least 400 shareholders, and $750,000 in pretax income. Some very big companies, including Microsoft, trade on the NASDAQ, which has two types of listings, its National Market Issues and Small-Cap Issues. The smaller, emerging companies are listed in the Small Caps.

Some lower-priced stocks are traded in the Over the Counter (OTC) market. Most of the 28,000 companies trading over the counter are newer and smaller, and there are no minimum requirements for income or shareholders as at the other exchanges. OTC stocks are not listed in the financial pages because they don't trade as regularly, and there's no exchange like the NYSE or AMEX. Some of the more active issues are summarized on a "pink sheet" for brokers. If you're hot for a Canadian gold mine or some emerging software developer, and it is trading publicly, you can find them here.

There are also several regional stock exchanges, where trading in shares from all of the major markets can take place. These include the Pacific Stock Exchange in Los Angeles and exchanges in Boston, Philadelphia, Chicago, and Cincinnati.

Individuals cannot trade directly with any of these exchanges; they have to go through a licensed broker. What with trading on the Internet and over the phone, the stock market is getting to be less of a closed society, but the restrictions are still there.

The item all of these exchanges are "exchanging" is, of course, a stock certificate. These certificates are unique to the company issuing them, although they all contain some common features. See Figure 17.3.

Stock certificates contain a number of safety features to prevent theft and forgery. The CUSIP number is issued by the Committee on Uniform Securities Identification of the American Bankers Association. Every publicly traded stock or bond will have a CUSIP number, as well as one issued by the Securities and Exchange Commission (SEC) and one by the company or its transfer agent. The number of shares is repeated in several places on the certificate. Note that the owner of the shares is clearly identified. Bearer shares may be legal in some parts of the world, but not in the United States. A record of this owner will be on file with the corporation and its transfer agent, who will mail out the dividends and the ballots according to the information in its records.

Market Operations

A corporation elects to sell shares to the general public in order to raise cash for its operations or expansion. Most businesses and small corporations don't trade publicly; they are closely held by the original owners. In fact, most states have laws regarding how many stockholders a company can have. If a corporation chooses to offer shares to the general public, the securities must

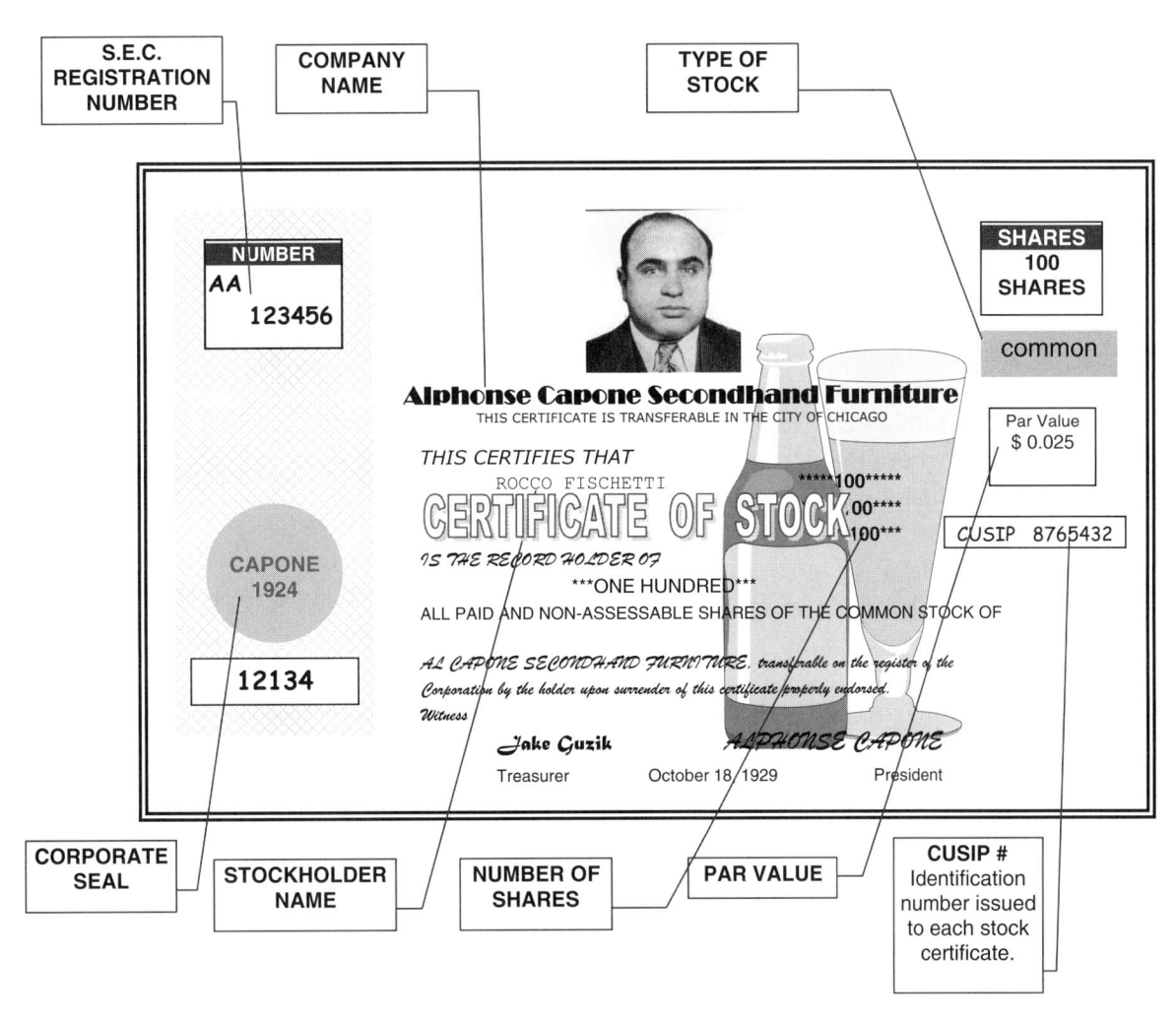

Figure 17.3 *Features of a stock certificate. Photo courtesy of UPI.*

be registered, and special procedures for the offering will be required. This is primarily to prevent fraud and loss of investor confidence.

In the case of major corporations, stock offerings are made through an initial public offering. The IPO is coordinated through an investment banker or group of bankers who agree to buy all of the issued shares for a prearranged price. The shares are then traded on the open market. At this point, the company has all of the capital it wanted to raise, and its shares are now being publicly traded. The price at which the shares are traded will depend on how much people are willing to pay. Some shares go right up on the day of the IPO.

The shares are now listed in one of the three major exchanges (except for OTC stocks), and their activity is tracked in the financial pages of major newspapers such as *The Wall Street Journal*. Most newspapers carry at least some of the listings.

Every stock listed on an exchange is identified by a symbol. On the NYSE and AMEX, these letter combinations have one to three characters. NASDAQ issues have four or five. There may also be an extra character or two to identify special categories, such as preferred shares.

Stocks are traded in lots and priced in *points* or dollars, with fractions in decimals. The standard unit of trading is a *round lot,* consisting of 100 shares of stock. An *odd lot* is anything less than 100 shares. It trades at the same price as the round lot, plus an odd-lot differential.

As orders to buy or sell come into the exchange from brokers, the transactions are posted on an electronic board, which is still

```
QNTM        DOL         Tpf
24.25       4000S63     2S78.5
```

Figure 17.4 *A transaction from a ticker tape.*

known as the "tape." The sales are conducted on an auction basis, with the buyer making a bid for the stock at the price quoted or offered. As demand for the shares rises and falls, the sellers will change their prices.

Each transaction will be reflected on the tape, in a short synopsis that contains the ticker symbol, the number of shares traded, and the price per share. Round lots are reported with a number 2 through 9, sales of 1000 or more shares with the actual number exchanged. In Figure 17.4, the tape reflects three transactions, as follows:

1. 100 shares of Quantum, a NASDAQ stock, sold at $24.25 per share
2. 4000 shares of Dole Foods, a NYSE issue, sold at $63.00 per share
3. 200 shares of AT&T Preferred, an NYSE stock, sold for $78.50 per share

(These are hypothetical examples. In reality, you would not see NASDAQ and NYSE transactions on the same tape.)

The total number of shares exchanged and their dollar values are calculated at the end of the day, a figure that is watched with great interest and reported widely. Also reported are several "averages," such as the Dow Jones Industrial Average (DJIA). These averages are made up of groups of selected stocks, 30 industrial issues in the DJIA, for example. The average used to be computed by dividing the total price of the selected issues by 30, but now a more complex formula is used.

BUYING AND SELLING STOCKS

The corporation got all the money it was going to get in the initial public offering. After that, the shares are being bought and sold by investors on the open market, in a process that only benefits the company indirectly. This trading is conducted through *brokerage houses* licensed to do business with the exchanges. These brokerage firms operate much like banks, in that they offer a form of credit and will hold and invest your money for you. Over the years, real banks have gotten nervous about how closely the operations of brokerage firms resemble banking — generally with higher and more attractive rates of return.

The brokerage house is an exchange member and is subject to extensive regulation by the Securities and Exchange Commission. *Brokers* or *stockbrokers* act as agents to conduct your transactions, executing the buy and sell orders. *Traders* are people who are buying or selling for their own accounts. Some are employed by brokerage houses and others by institutional investors.

The first step in a stock transaction is an order by the customer. Suppose I decide I want to get a piece of Al Capone's publicly traded corporation. I study the financial pages, maybe look at some newsletters, or perhaps just act on the advice of my stockbroker, and then make the decision to purchase some shares.

I have a couple of options in placing my order. First, I could make a *market order*, which instructs the broker to move immediately to get the best price possible now. If I thought that the price of the Capone stock was going to go down, I might place a *limit order*, which would have the broker buy when the stock reached a certain level. If I were selling the stock, I could also place a *stop-loss order*, which would prevent further losses by selling when the stock fell to a specified level. Stop-loss and limit orders can also be time sensitive, automatically canceled at the end of the day (a "day order"), or *Good Till Canceled* (GTC). This is what Martha Stewart claimed she had in the transaction that landed her in trouble over insider-trading allegations. The government said she got inside information that the stock was going to tank and acted on it. She said the trade happened as a result of the stop-loss order. The jury decided she'd lied.

Once the order is placed, the brokerage firm passes the order to a *floor broker*, the person who actually does the buying and selling. In a barter-like process that would probably be familiar to an ancient Egyptian, the floor broker contacts another floor broker who is looking to sell Capone stocks, and the two see if they can come to some agreement. If so, the order is filled and my purchase recorded. If not, the floor broker holds onto the order until he or she gets a deal.

Brokers charge commissions depending on how much work they have to do. Full-service brokers charge substantially more than the discount or deep-discount brokers.

I got lucky and was able to get 100 shares of Alphonse Capone Second Hand Furniture, which was selling for $40 per share. I now owe my broker $4000 plus his commission of $50. The broker can get this money from me in the form of cash or a check, or I could authorize him to take it from the cash management account I maintain at the brokerage house.

Another alternative is buying on *margin,* which is essentially a credit transaction. Once I've established credit at the brokerage, I may be able to use some of its money to buy stocks. I first have to deposit at least $2000 in cash or securities with the brokerage, and then I can conduct all the margin trades through this account.

Margin trading can be very exciting, because it can be very risky. In the case of my Capone stock, I could have done a margin trade by borrowing $4000 from my broker, adding it to my $4000, and using the full $8000 to purchase 200 shares.

The good news is that if the stock went up in value by, say, $20, my investment would now be worth a cool $12,000. If I sold at this point, my broker would get his $4,000 back, and I'd get to keep everything else. (That is $8,000 on my initial $4,000 — a 100% return on investment!)

The bad news is, if the stock went down, the brokerage would be required to make a *margin call* as soon as the stock fell to a certain level — 75% of the investment price. I would then have to pump more money into the investment. If, for whatever reason, I can't meet the margin call, I've got to sell the stock, pay the broker his

"Yes, now that you mention it, the second pig probably should have gotten into stocks instead of real estate."

$4000, and keep the balance. Margin calls are mandated by law; there's no chance to "wait and see" if the stock is going to go back up again. Margin trading complicates a financial investigation because, while you might see big investments in securities, they may not be comprised solely of the subject's money. Some of it may be the broker's.

In addition to straight buying and selling transactions, brokers can handle some other activity for you. Two of these are selling short and issuing stock warrants.

Selling short is another credit-type transaction. This time, you're borrowing the shares from the broker and betting that the price of the stock is going to go *down.* For example, let's say I know Al Capone's going to lose his tax case, and I think his stock is going to slip as a result. I establish an account with my broker and borrow or "sell short" 100 shares of Capone at $40 per share. A month or so later, the guilty verdict comes in and the stock drops to $20 per share. I now buy 100 shares of Capone at $20, give these to the broker to repay the original loan, and pocket the $2000 difference, subtracting the broker's commissions and the interest it charged for the loan.

The risk, of course, is that the stock might go *up,* in which case I'd have to pay back the loan with shares that cost more than I received from the sale.

Stock warrants are bought by people who are guessing that the price of the stock is going to go *up*. For a fee, an investor can buy a "warrant" that guarantees the right to buy a stock at a certain price for a given period. The fee involved is usually a small percentage of the share price. Warrants are issued by the corporation, just like the stock itself, and they are listed on the tape with a "wt" suffix after the stock symbol.

On my Capone stock, I might purchase an available warrant if I believed the Big Guy was going to beat the rap, causing his stock to soar. For $4 a share, I get a warrant that allows me to buy Capone stock for $40 per share for 5 years. If, in that time, the price of the stock doubles to $80, I can exercise my warrant, buy as many shares as the warrant allows at $40, and sell them immediately for a major profit. All of these activities will be described in the brokerage account statements maintained for your subject.

Brokerages may maintain stocks for their customers, usually in margin transactions. In other words, instead of having the certificates actually issued to you and kept in your possession, the brokerage firm can have the stock issued to it and kept in a "street name" in its possession. Your account statement will reflect this fact. Note, though, that an inquiry of the corporation would not disclose your ownership of the shares. Only the brokerage would have that information. Any dividends are paid by the corporation to the brokerage, which passes them along to you.

The accounting term for securities that are held by the brokerage in a street name is *segregation*. Within the brokerage, securities held in this fashion are separated into segregated files. A related service is called *safekeeping*. In this case, the securities are issued in the customer's name, but the actual certificates are held by the brokerage for safekeeping. The dividends are paid directly to the customer.

Information About Stock Transactions

Corporations register their securities and keep records of the people who are holding their shares, but much of this work is done for the company by others, either brokers or *transfer agents*. Also active in stock transactions is the *dividend disbursing agent*, who may or may not be the same entity as the transfer agent.

Information at the Brokerage House

The best source of information is the brokerage house, through which every transaction must flow. Not only will some individual broker or account executive be familiar with the subject and his or her trades, but also quite a bit of financial information will be on file. This is especially true if the subject maintains a margin trading account.

Some of the information available from the brokerage firm includes:

- Account application form/signature card
  - Name
  - Address, telephone number
  - Social security number
  - Financial references
  - Date opened
  - Type of account
  - Initial transaction
  - Special instructions
- Account executive's customer card
  - Name
  - Address, telephone number
  - Business address
  - Investment goal
  - Special instructions
  - Personal knowledge
- Securities receipts, including certificate numbers and amount of securities sent from the customer to the broker
- Cash receipts, including the amount and form of all payments by the customer to the broker and possibly photocopies of checks received by the brokerage
- Confirmation slips
  - Identification of securities bought or sold and the number of shares or bonds
  - Identification of the price per share or bond and the total price to be paid by the customer
  - Trade date (date order was placed)

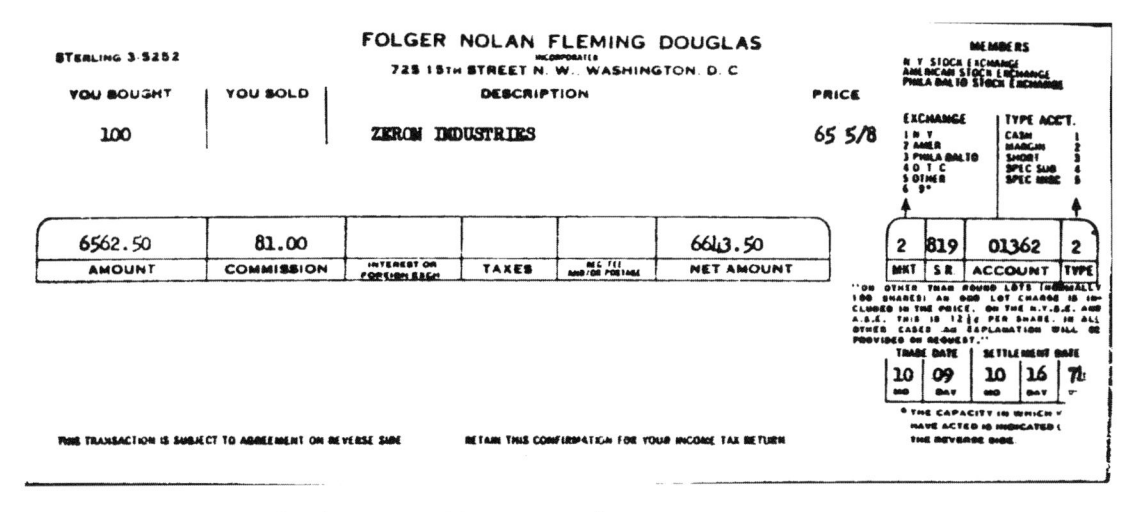

Figure 17.5 Confirmation slip for a securities transaction.

- Settlement date (date on which the purchase amount is due to be paid or the date on which certificates sold must be received by the broker)
- Canceled checks
- Forms 1087, summarizing dividends paid by the broker to the customer for stock held in street name
- Monthly statements
  - All transactions during the month
  - Full description of all trades, including securities purchased, sold, delivered, or received
  - Market price of all securities purchased or sold
  - Amounts debited or credited to the account as a result of trades
  - End-of-month balances, in both money and securities
  - Margin interest charged for the month
- Identification of account executive

The confirmation slip is a key form in the securities business. This is the central billing document, used to record all transactions. It is generally mailed on the same day the securities are bought or sold, and it contains information about the customer's account as well as details of the trade. (See Figure 17.5.)

Another key form is the monthly account statement. Much of the information from the confirmation slip is also contained in this monthly summary. In a financial investigation, such as that involving Bruno Richard Hauptmann, analysis of these documents is required to establish the nature and extent of the activity in the account. Hauptmann had tens of thousands of dollars in trades each month, but his monthly balance might have been only a thousand dollars.

Information at the Transfer Agent

The transfer agent is an individual or entity, often a bank, appointed by a corporation to handle matters relating to its stock. The transfer agent maintains a record of each stockholder, containing the person's name and address and the number of shares owned. If stocks are received from the customer, the transfer agent makes sure they are properly canceled and that new certificates being issued are properly transferred and recorded.

Records of the transfer agent include:

- Stockholder ledger card
- Stock certificates

Information in these cards and certificates will include:

- Stockholder identification
- Stockholder position (what he or she owns)
- Stock certificate numbers

- Number of shares represented by the certificates
- Dates certificates were issued or surrendered
- Evidence of returned certificates
Name of transferees and transferors

Information at the Disbursing Agent

Dividend disbursing agents are, as their name implies, the people who distribute the corporation's dividends. Sometimes the transfer agent acts in this capacity. Dividend disbursing agents are usually banks.

The records kept by dividend disbursing agents include:

- Canceled checks
- IRS Forms 1099

These records will contain information relating to:

- Stockholder identification
- Stockholder position
- Amount of dividends
- Form of dividend (cash, stock, property)
- Dates on which dividends were paid
- Evidence of payment

Each corporation will be able to furnish the names of its transfer agents. The broker may have this information as well. Other sources of information about transfer and disbursing agents include:

- Financial Stock Guide Service (an extremely comprehensive reference on securities)
- Moody's Investor Service
- Standard and Poor's
- Local brokerages

Hundreds of millions of shares of stock are transferred every day, not just in the United States but in markets around the world. Although the volume is immense, stocks are not the only securities to be traded. The markets for bonds, currency, and commodities also provide opportunities for investors.

BONDS: OWNING DEBT

A *bond* is an instrument of debt. You've heard the expression "My word is my bond"? People use it when they're promising to do something. In the case of a bond, the financial instrument issued by governments or corporations, they are promising to pay you something.

There are a number of ways that corporations can obtain the money they need for their operations. One way is to issue stock. This does have the effect of diluting the value of the shares already owned by investors. The corporation could also borrow the money from a bank or another lender. A third option is a bond issue.

When a corporation decides to borrow money for a set period, generally for more than five years, it may sell a bond issue. Each of the bonds is a certificate of the debt; they are usually issued in denominations of $1000. When a bond is sold, the corporation or "issuer" now owes the purchaser a set amount, the *par value,* as of the *maturity date,* the date on which the loan is to be repaid.

Several factors will go into setting the conditions for the bond. First, how long does the company need the money? Short-term bonds are generally issued for a year or less, intermediate-term bonds for 2 to 10 years, and long-term bonds for periods of 30 years or more.

Second, how badly does the company need the money? This will dictate the *yield,* essentially the amount of interest the company will be paying on the loan. The higher the yield, the more attractive the bond is to investors, and, of course, the more it costs the company in interest.

Bonds are known as *fixed-income securities,* because once you buy them, you know exactly what you've got and when you'll get it. With inflation low and interest rates fairly steady, as they are at the moment, bonds do provide reliable income on a regular basis. However, because bond interest rates are fixed, inflation can leave the holder with a security that pays less over time.

Bonds are initially sold by the corporation at par value. The purchaser might get a certificate, just as he or she would in a stock purchase, but these days many bonds are registered and stored electronically as *book entry bonds*. These certificates can be sold on a secondary market, the price depending on the bond's yield as compared to other bonds on the market. If a newer issue comes along that pays a better yield, the older bond is going to be less attractive. Bonds issued when interest rates are high gain in value as interest rates fall, because they are still paying off like clockwork at the higher rate.

As you might have guessed, there are different kinds of bonds out there, each of which is designed to fill a particular need of the issuer. Some of the terms used with bonds are:

- *Asset-backed bond* — This type of bond is secured by specific assets of the corporation.
- *Debenture* — This is the traditional and most common form of corporate bonds. Debentures are backed not by assets but by the credit of the issuer. Ratings services "rate" or evaluate these bonds to establish risk; you might hear about a bond rating being "downgraded."
- *Mortgage-backed bond* — This type of bond is also based upon credit, this time by a pool of mortgage loans.
- *Convertible bond* — This type of bond provides an option allowing the bondholder to exchange or convert the bond to corporate stock.
- *Bearer bond* — Whoever holds it, owns it. Bearer bonds are no longer issued in the United States, but they are still legal elsewhere. Bearer bonds have coupons attached, which are clipped periodically and taken to a bank, where they can be redeemed for the interest due. Since most bonds are no longer issued in certificate form, there are no coupons to clip.
- *Zero-coupon bond* — "Coupon" in bond language means "interest." Zero-coupon bonds pay no interest until maturity, at which time the bond is redeemed at full value. "Zeros" are purchased at *deep discount*. For example, a zero might be sold for $500 and redeemed at maturity for $1000.
- *Municipal bond* — This type of bond is issued not by a corporation but by some governmental agency, though not always a municipality. The big attraction to a "muni" is the fact that the interest paid is free of federal and most state taxes. The bond's yield is usually a little lower than for its corporate cousins.
- *Agency bond* — This type of bond is issued by a government agency, such as the Government National Mortgage Association, for such purposes as financing mortgages or flood control projects. Agency bonds pay better interest rates than other government bonds and are almost as safe.
- *Treasury bond* — Issued by the United States government to fund its operations, treasury bonds are backed by the "full faith and credit of the United States" and are as safe as any investment in the world. All that security comes at a price, expressed in terms of lower yields. The Treasury issues a number of different bonds, including the "benchmark 30-year bond," against which all other bonds are measured. Two others are:
  - *Treasury notes, T-bills, and strips* — Strips are zero-coupon bonds sold at deep discount. T-bills are short-term, zero-coupon bonds with maturity dates of 13 weeks or 26 weeks.
  - *Savings bonds* — Savings bonds are U.S. government bonds, sold at a discount (a fraction of face value) and redeemed at maturity for full value. Savings bonds differ from other bonds in several respects. First, they are bearer bonds, even though they are registered with the Bureau of

Public Debt in the name of the purchaser. Second, unlike other zero-coupon bonds, they are tax exempt until maturity. Finally, they are not marketable. Savings bonds aren't traded as are other bonds.

INFORMATION ABOUT BONDHOLDERS

If your subject has invested in bonds, this information may be available through his or her broker. Although bonds are issued by a corporation or government entity, they are sold, like stocks, through brokerages. The broker will know when the bond was purchased and will have records, such as the monthly account statements and confirmation slips, to document bond holdings.

The interest on bonds is paid through an authorized agent of the issuer, usually a bank, which will have a record of the interest paid. Because this interest has to be properly paid, all bonds other than the coupon or bearer type are registered with the issuer in the name of the bondholder. Interest payments are made by check by the authorized agent.

Records available from the authorized agent include:

- Canceled checks
- IRS Forms 1099

These records will contain information relating to:

- Bondholder identification
- Bondholder position (what he or she owns)
- Amount of interest payments
- Dates on which interest was paid
- Evidence of payment (canceled checks)

MUTUAL FUNDS: POOLING YOUR MONEY

With all sorts of investment choices out there, it makes sense for investors to spread their money — and their risk — around. This often means having a mix of stocks, bonds, or both. In this way, an investor is protected against sudden fluctuations in the price of certain securities.

This investment strategy dilutes the purchasing power of an investor who can't go as deep into a security as he or she might like. The solution for many is the *mutual fund,* which pools the money of many investors to buy large blocks of many investments. The risk is spread, but the purchasing power is still there.

Mutual funds are set up by investment firms, also known as mutual fund companies, as well as brokerage houses and sometimes banks. Currently in the United States there are more than 350 different such companies, offering more than 4000 different mutual funds.

Most mutual funds are *open-end,* meaning that investors can buy as many shares in the fund as they want. This continues until the fund gets too big, and then it is closed to new investors, but not to people already in the fund who want to buy more shares. *Closed-end* or "exchange traded" funds offer a fixed number of shares and, as their alternative name implies, are traded on an exchange or over the counter.

Some mutual funds specialize in stocks, some in corporate bonds, and some in tax-free municipal bonds. Further specialization may involve growth stocks, income stocks, or stocks from certain industries. Very popular now are mutual funds made up of stocks from "environmentally friendly" companies or stocks relating to minority-owned businesses. Along this line, some funds exclude certain stocks, such as tobacco. These are called "green" or "conscience" funds.

Of particular interest to the financial investigator are *money market funds,* which operate very much like a bank account. In fact, investors can even write checks on money market accounts, which might explain why your subject doesn't have a bank checking account.

Money market funds operate on the same principle as a savings account: For every dollar invested, you get a dollar back, plus the interest earned while it's in the hands of the investment firm. These funds are very low risk, they don't pay much interest, and they can be either taxable or tax free, depending on the type of investments made by the funds.

If you are buying shares in a mutual fund, you will either be paying a commission, or *load,* or not. "No-load" mutual funds charge no commission to buy shares, but there may be a "back-end load" to sell the shares. No-loads are an added incentive to invest and are a cheaper way to go.

There are two big questions to ask about a mutual fund: "How is it performing?" and "What are the fees?" Performance is the thing the investment firms want to talk about in their ads. Performance is a factor of time and the success or failure of the securities that make up the fund. If the investment firm picked some winners, the total return for the fund is likely to be good. If not, investors making a comparison with other funds are likely to put their money elsewhere.

Because mutual funds are generally regarded as longer-term investments, performance is rated over relatively long periods, three years and five years being benchmarks. *The Wall Street Journal* publishes performance information for thousands of mutual funds. Investors are obviously looking at this information for the highest yields — but remember that, as the ads say, "prior performance does not guarantee future results."

The second factor, fees, relates to expenses connected with investing in the fund. The fees include the loads or commissions at the front or back end, but there are other periodic charges that the investment firm makes to pay for operating the fund. If these fees are high, the fund may be unattractive for an investor, even though the performance might be solid. The fees are capped by law at 8.5%, and most average between 3% and 5%.

INFORMATION FROM INVESTMENT FIRMS

The investment firm will have up-to-the-minute information on all of its funds, much of which is available via automated telephone systems.

Information available from the investment firm includes:

- Account application form/signature card
  - Name
  - Address, telephone number
  - Social security number
  - Financial references
  - Date opened
  - Type of account
  - Initial transaction
- Cash receipts, including the amount and form of all payments by the customer
- Confirmation slips
- Canceled checks
- Monthly or periodic statements
- Summary of share purchases and sales, balance, interest, and money market fund activity

Some of these statements can take a little getting used to, as they may be written in terms of shares rather than dollar amounts. A key usually appears somewhere to help you figure it all out.

FUTURES AND OPTIONS: BETTING THE RANCH

The last investment category we're going to cover involves *futures* and *options*. These investments are more complex than the others, and at the same time simpler. Unlike stocks, futures and options do not represent ownership, nor do they signify debt, like bonds. They are more like big bets, placed on which way the price of something is going to go.

Futures are traded in *contracts,* basically an agreement to buy or sell something in a given time period. Futures contracts can involve almost anything, from corn and cattle to shares in a Fortune 500 company. Win or lose, there's little chance that on the day the contract is due, somebody's going to deliver a thousand cows to your door, however.

Futures are also *very* risky, and this kind of gambling is something Al Capone would have understood and appreciated — especially since he operated from Chicago, home to three of the eleven largest futures exchanges. As a way of

CASH PRICES			
Grain and Food Products			
	Wed	Tues	Yr. Ago
Barley, top quality Mpls. Bu ½	2.10	2.10	2.20
Beer, Chicago, gal	.50-.52	.51-.53	.57
Bran, wheat mid, KC ton	12-14	13-15	17
Corn, No. 2 yel, Ill, bu	2.50	2.55	6

Figure 17.6 *Newspaper summary of spot prices for commodities on February 1, 1930.*

explaining how these markets work, we'll use beer as an example, although this isn't a commodity actually traded on the exchanges. We'll assume that it's February 1930, and we'll also pretend that beer is one of the items traded on Chicago's Midwest Commodity Exchange.

Most people who are actually in the beer business, such as Al Capone, buy and sell their product on the cash or *spot market,* so called because payment is made in cash on the spot. The spot prices for beer are posted daily in *The Wall Street Journal* and other financial publications, so everyone interested knows the current rates for the commodity. A newspaper summary on February 1, 1930, might look like Figure 17.6.

This table summarizes the commodity, the exchange, and the quantity in which it is measured (bushels, gallons, tons, etc.), along with the current and historical prices. The chart lets you know that beer is currently selling on the spot market for $0.50 to $0.52 per gallon, down from last year's level of $0.57.

You know that beer is subject to seasonal fluctuations in demand; more people like a nice cold brew in those hot summer months, even with Prohibition in full swing. You decide to bet that the price of beer is going to go up substantially in June or July.

Futures contracts are made for set amounts, the size of which varies with the commodity. A wheat contract is 5,000 bushels. Gasoline contracts are 42,000 gallons. Our fictional beer contracts are 5,000 gallons.

You contact your broker and order him to buy 10 July beer contracts. In futures parlance, this is known as "going long in beer." The July contracts are selling on the floor of the exchange for $0.50 per gallon, so each 5,000-gallon contract will cost $2,500, or $25,000 for the lot.

Futures trading is heavily leveraged. This means that, as in margin trading in stocks, the commodities broker puts up some of the money. Your initial investment is only 10% or $2500; the rest is leveraged.

Now you sit back and wait. Futures can be extremely volatile, with large price swings, depending on external events, supply, and demand. By April 1, the price of beer has risen $0.10, to $0.55 per gallon. The value of your contract went up accordingly, and it is now worth $27,500, giving you a cool 100% return on your initial $2,500 investment. At this point you could go "short" and sell, but you decide to hold on at least until June, when you think you'll do even better.

In May, however, beer stocks rise due to new production coming on line and beer-buster Eliot Ness going on his annual vacation. Prices fall, and your profits are wiped out. Not only that, the price drops all the way to $0.40 per gallon, a full 20% decline.

Your investment is now worth only $20,000 and you're $2,500 under your initial margin amount. Your broker makes a margin call, and you've got a decision to make. If you stay in, you'll have to keep pumping in cash to stay above the margin level. If the price keeps going down, you could lose substantially more money. This is how it's possible for commodities investors to lose much more than their initial investment in a big hurry. Not a place for the faint of heart. (See Figure 17.7.)

Estimates are that 75 to 90% of all commodities investors lose money each year — and most investors stay in the market for only 11 months or less.

Anyway, you decide to cut your losses by selling all 10 July beer contracts. This cancels your original promise or contract to buy. (This *offset* is how you keep somebody from delivering 50,000 gallons of beer to your home on the third Friday in July.) Your broker subtracts his commission from whatever money is left, and

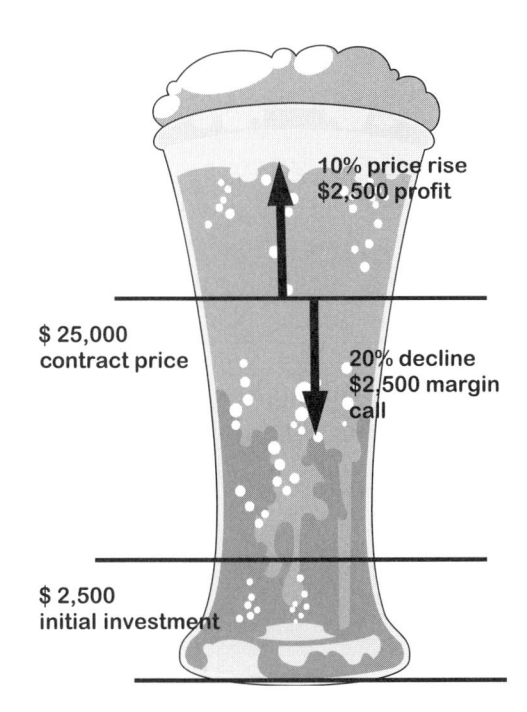

Figure 17.7 *An example of futures trading in beer.*

you flee with the rest to some other, more sedate investment opportunity.

Traders try not to let things get this bad, buying and selling offsetting contracts to balance out the potential losses. Some safety devices, such as "hedges," allow the risk to be spread a bit. This type of investment requires extremely close attention.

SECURITIES AND MONEY LAUNDERING

Securities can be a major part of a money laundering scheme, either as instruments of the money laundering crime or as the fruit or object of that crime. As instruments, securities may be used in the actual manipulation of the dirty money. For example, stock certificates represent ownership of a corporation. If I had 100% of the outstanding shares of a corporation, I would own that company, lock, stock, and barrel. Such corporations, especially the "shell" or bearer-share variety, are used to layer money laundering schemes. The shares used in such schemes are seldom those of publicly traded corporations, the type that are listed on the major exchanges.

There are also money laundering schemes that involve the use of securities to obtain loans.

We'll look at these in another chapter. And because securities are by their nature oriented toward investment, they are expected to produce legitimate-appearing income. This allows securities to be used as integration mechanisms and for other laundering purposes.

For example, let's suppose I am a businessman who wants to influence a politician on some zoning matters, and the politician is open to being influenced. My scheme might have a couple of steps. First, an "investment opportunity" would be created, possibly in something like, say, cattle futures. As we've seen, this type of venture allows for a potentially huge payout on a relatively modest investment.

I have the politician put up a small amount of money, or maybe I put it up for him, and then I manipulate the contract so that the politician gets back the investment plus the big bribe, er, contribution, that I promised in the beginning. (What I'd probably do is invest in several contracts with different positions, short or long, and report the big winner as being the one the politician's money happened to be in.) It looks like he just got lucky in the market, and I've concealed the true source of and nature of the funds.

In the second category, fruits of the crime, securities may be the object of a money laundering operation. The scheme may involve the conversion of dirty cash into clean securities. Securities of all sorts, including those of "blue chip" companies, are ideally suited for this purpose. Because the volume of trading in stocks, bonds, mutual funds, and options is so heavy, suspicious transactions can be difficult to detect. Some brokerage firms are being much more cautious in the handling of currency from their customers, especially after a couple of them got hammered for assisting in money laundering schemes. Recent legislation has compelled securities brokers to report suspicious transactions, just as banks do, and to implement other anti-money laundering controls.

If an investigation discloses that a suspect is involved with securities, it is essential to locate the broker or brokers who are working the trades. This brokerage firm will be the source of much of the information relating to the suspect's activity. Furthermore, the broker may have personal knowledge of the customer. On occasion, the relationship may be extremely close, so use caution in developing these leads.

In conducting the financial investigation, the case agent should be alert for checks to or from brokerage firms, mail from such firms, and the actual records themselves, if encountered in a search warrant.

Because many securities transactions are reported to IRS, an *ex parte* order for tax return information may be useful in identifying brokerage accounts or other activity. Such a request should be written to include "information returns," such as IRS Form 1099.

In the case of securities issued by nonpublicly traded corporations, the companies themselves may be the best source of information. However, the possibility that the subject of the investigation is directly involved in the operation of these corporations is strong. Caution is urged.

CHAPTER 18

OBTAINING FINANCIAL INFORMATION

"We have learned the answers, all the answers. It is the questions we do not know."
Archibald MacLeish

"Knowledge advances by steps, and not by leaps."
Lord Macaulay

In his book *The Anderson Tapes,* the late bestselling author Lawrence Sanders described a crime, every detail of which was recorded somewhere on someone's surveillance tape. Sanders was commenting on the loss of privacy in our modern society and exaggerating the intrusion of surveillance, but he was also describing a situation wherein the investigators had so much data, from so many sources, that they were unable to see the forest for the trees. Not until after the crime had been committed did they realize what they already knew.

As the police officers in the infamous Rodney King beating case discovered, those video cameras are everywhere these days — but the really comprehensive information is financial. People today leave tracks wherever they go, an amazingly detailed trail of paper extending from birth to death. Much of this information is documentation of the things people buy, sell, and own. Other information may provide leads to financial data, and financial data may provide leads to nonfinancial evidence.

In fact, there may be so much information that simply managing the sheer volume of evidence becomes a problem. Before you get to this point, however, the evidence must first be obtained. Since it will be coming from a variety of sources and acquired in a number of different ways, it's a good idea to be flexible in your approach.

One of the themes of this book is that a money laundering or financial case is just a regular investigation that employs some additional analytical techniques. Financial cases provide some opportunities that may not exist in other criminal matters, though. For one thing, there is that wide paper trail out there, just waiting for somebody to get onto it.

The records that make up the evidence in a financial case will ultimately come from two basic sources:

1. Subject records
2. Third-party records

It cannot be stressed strongly enough that every effort must be made to acquire the subject's own records. These are the primary and best source of information on the activities of the subject and his or her organization. *You must try to get the subject's records.*

Whether a person is a small-business person, the president of a Fortune 500 company, or a low-level drug dealer, there will be some records. Leads to the subject's records, or to those kept by a third party, may come from a variety of sources, including many techniques that have been used by criminal investigators for centuries. The investigator must keep in mind that the financial information is critical to a money laundering case and must take pains to develop it.

RISK VS. REWARD

At this point, you should be convinced that financial evidence has value to your case. Before you can exploit the information, you first have to get it, a process that has some bumps. Some of the bumps are legal, placed in the investigator's way to protect the privacy of individuals. Other potential problems are practical, relating to the speed or direction an investigation will take.

One big consideration for investigators of money laundering or financial crimes is premature disclosure. The disclosure might be broad, such as the discovery by the subject that he or she is under investigation, or narrow: that the agents have found a bank account, safe deposit box, or other asset that the subject thought had been successfully laundered. Neither one of these situations is very attractive, and proper planning of the case is necessary to prevent unpleasant surprises. Because so many of the methods used to acquire financial information involve legal processes, such as subpoenas or search warrants, the participation of the United States Attorney or the prosecutor in this part of the case is rather important.

Decisions will have to be made about who will be subpoenaed and when. Will a gag order be required for the subpoena? Would a search warrant be a better tool or a subpoena, or should both be used?

All of these decisions should be thoroughly explored by the agents and the attorneys. They should be weighed or evaluated on a scale measuring the potential risk of disclosure against the value of the information sought. Figure 18.1 provides a graph of this process.

Computer checks, at the very low end of the risk scale, often provide important financial leads. Thorough checks of public and law enforcement databases should always be at the

RISK v. REWARD
Determining when and how to use a source of financial information

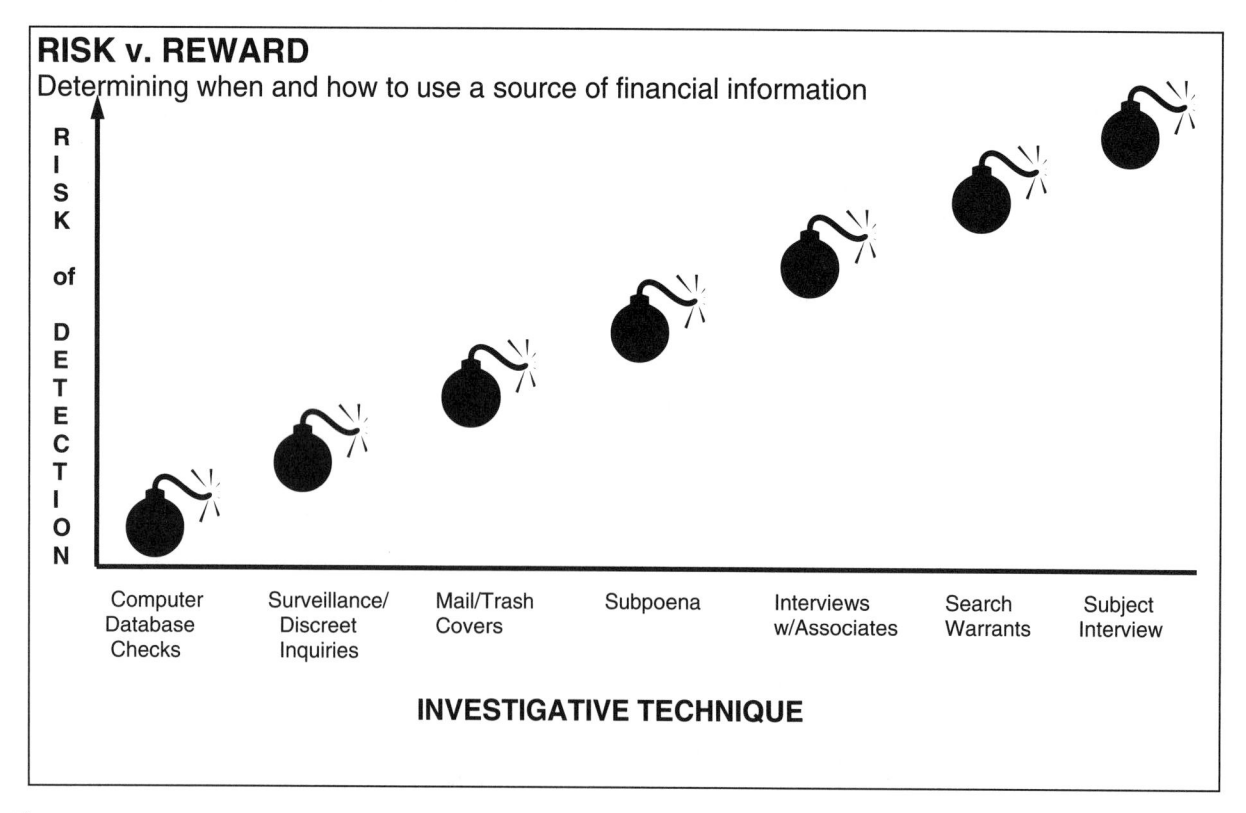

(Graph: RISK of DETECTION vs. INVESTIGATIVE TECHNIQUE, showing increasing risk across: Computer Database Checks, Surveillance/Discreet Inquiries, Mail/Trash Covers, Subpoena, Interviews w/Associates, Search Warrants, Subject Interview)

Figure 18.1 *Risk vs. reward: determining when and how to use a source of financial information.*

foundation of a money laundering investigation. A more complete discussion of some of those databases appears in the next chapter.

TRADITIONAL SOURCES OF INFORMATION

There's really no way to distinguish a financial investigation from any other criminal case, except that you are concentrating on acquiring information of a financial nature. In many cases, the sources of this information will be the same ones who are providing information about the unlawful activity underlying the money laundering transactions.

Informants, cooperating defendants, undercover agents, and surveillance are all key elements of criminal investigations involving financial crimes. Although some caution must be used in employing these techniques in financial cases, the leads produced can substantially advance an investigation.

"Traditional" sources can be used to establish facts or to refute defenses, as well. For example, a confidential informant who has bought drugs from your subject in the past can also be asked about the records kept by the subject, any assets the subject owns, and any banks the subject uses. These leads could save a lot of time and cut the risk of exposure that might accompany some of the other methods.

Similarly, if the subject were to claim that all of his or her wealth came from the operation of a video rental business, the informant could refute this claim by testifying that the subject rented the tapes at a loss to blend the drug money into his or her bank deposits.

Although the traditional sources of information might be valuable in locating and identifying the subject's records, their main value may well be in helping to identify people or businesses with whom the subject is conducting financial transactions — one of the objectives of a money laundering prosecution.

Where is that subject banking? A mail cover should disclose the addresses of the financial institutions, but a pen register on the telephone, a well-placed informant, or physical surveillance might also produce the same information.

INFORMANTS

Informants have been one of law enforcement's most effective tools almost forever. For purposes of this discussion, an informant is someone who is actively cooperating in a law enforcement operation or investigation. In a money laundering case, a well-placed informant may be the only way to penetrate a scheme that has been effectively layered and the proceeds integrated. If the launderer him- or herself turns against his or her employers, the impact on a criminal organization would be massive.

Because the value of this inside information is so high, investigators should always seek to identify and develop potential informants; they can do so in the financial community as well.

Caution: One of those "bumps" we mentioned earlier relates to the use of informants. Federal law covers the type of information financial institutions can provide to law enforcement and the conditions under which it can be provided. Law enforcement officers are not supposed to evade these statutes (the Bank Secrecy Act and the Right to Financial Privacy Act) by using bank tellers or employees as informants.

Another no-no is obtaining an individual's credit report from an informant who is employed at a car dealership or other credit bureau subscriber. If you want the credit report, get a grand jury subpoena.

These cautions aside, confidential sources can come in a couple of categories. They could be criminal informants who also have financial information, or they could be "pure" financial informants, possessing information only about financial transactions, not criminal activity.

In the former category, the informant debriefing must be conducted to develop fully *all* of the information possessed by the informant. He or she will be asked not only about specific illegal activity but also about financial matters within his or her knowledge. Does the informant know of any assets? Can he or she describe the flow of money through the illegal business? How many customers does the subject have, and what is the volume of business? A complete informant debriefing guide, obtained from the Department of Justice's *Financial Investigations Checklist,* is included in Appendix B.

One area that you should emphasize in a debriefing of a criminal informant relates to the subject's records. Fully explore any knowledge the informant may have as to how or where these records are kept. This information will be of significance in the affidavits for document search warrants.

The other type of informant is one who has knowledge only of financial transactions. This person could be an employee at a car dealership, real estate agency, or a brokerage firm. Typically, this informant would know about placement activity by the subject, possibly large cash transactions or suspicious financial dealings. Interestingly, Title 31 U.S.C. §5323 provides for rather substantial awards to persons providing information about violations of these statutes, something that might motivate individuals to come forward with whatever they know.

It's well established in the law that an informant cannot do anything that an agent cannot legally do. This means that if *you* can't go to a foreign country without permission, neither can you send an informant to do so. If you can't use a ruse to get around an attorney–client privilege, neither can an informant.

Something else to remember is that informants cannot conspire with the subject, although they can be used in connection with the "attempt" provisions of Title 18 U.S.C. §1956 (a) (3), the so-called "sting" provision. Even with these restrictions in place, a good informant is one of the best resources possible to penetrate a money laundering scheme.

Undercover Agents

Undercover agents have been used extensively in money laundering investigations, with often astounding results. Some of the largest money laundering cases and seizures have been made in undercover stings. Some of these cases will be discussed in another chapter, but we'll look briefly here at some of the legal implications of using undercover agents to acquire financial information.

First of all, the same restrictions on informants apply to undercover agents. It would be improper to send an agent to work in a bank just to get access to customer account information. Second, the undercover agent can have only restricted contacts with people who are represented by counsel. Still, an undercover agent is often the best witness in a money laundering case and can provide direct testimony, not just about the criminal activity but also about the disposition of funds *and* the statements of the principals.

Interviews

Interviewing is a staple of any criminal investigation; it is no less important in a money laundering case. You may be interviewing a broad spectrum of individuals, from people who are intimately connected with the suspect to business people who conducted financial transactions.

The format of interviews in money laundering cases will vary, but they will generally be directed at either the Specified Unlawful Activity or the financial transaction elements of the money laundering offense. In some cases, the interviewee may have knowledge about both, as would be the case if the person had engaged in multiple drug transactions with the subject. The disposition of the cash, the amount paid, the price of the drugs, the method of payment, and any records kept of the sales would all be of interest to the investigator.

Witness statements must be corroborated, and in financial cases this is often accomplished by documenting financial transactions described by the witness. For example, a drug trafficker arranged for deliveries by taking calls from his supplier at a gas station pay phone. The supplier's phone records documented telephone calls to the pay phone, but how could it be established that the trafficker was the one on the phone? A witness said so, and the trafficker's gas company credit card records showed he had bought gas at that location on the same dates as the phone calls. This type of corroboration involved only one small part of the huge paper trail left by this particular trafficker, but it illustrates how even the smallest financial transaction can help document a money laundering crime.

If an indirect method of proof will be used to show income to the subject, the number of interviews required will probably jump dramatically. In the government's investigation of Al Capone, at least 1500 interviews were conducted, many of which were with business owners or employees who had taken cash from the Big Guy. The statements made were then corroborated by some of the 2 *million* records the investigators reviewed.

There are fewer "bumps" in the interview process. Some witnesses will not provide information unless they receive a subpoena. The *shop book rule* relating to business records is an exception to the general principle that hearsay testimony is inadmissible. Under this rule, the person who is the custodian of records at a business can testify to their authenticity if the books are maintained in the ordinary course of business. One of the functions of the investigative search for financial evidence will be to locate the person at a business establishment who is in charge of the records. An interview of this person has to cover the facts needed to allow the hearsay to come in under the exception.

Similar authentication is required for the subject's records. This can often be done by witnesses who saw the records being prepared or who witnessed their use in the business. In the drug case already mentioned, ledgers were seized in a search of the trafficker's residence. These ledgers contained what appeared to be coded records of drug transactions. A handwriting exemplar proved that the trafficker had written the entries, but one of his customers tied the knot by testifying that the trafficker used the records to document credit or "front" sales of narcotics and that several of the entries referred to purchases made by the witness and payments to the trafficker.

A legal consideration that applies to some financial records is *privilege.* Some records or testimony may be protected by the attorney–client privilege, something you should review with the government's attorneys. No such privilege is enjoyed with respect to the records of accountants or bookkeepers, or employees or agents of the subject, however.

As for the Fifth Amendment privilege against self-incrimination, there are a couple of useful exceptions to that as well.

SURVEILLANCE OPERATIONS

Surveillance is another investigative technique as old as law enforcement. It has caught up with the times, however, and electronic, audio, and video surveillance techniques have made the investigator's job both easier and harder. On the one hand, a video surveillance tape with full audio is certainly devastating evidence to put before a jury. On the other hand, with all the *60 Minutes* type shows on television, jurors come to expect this sort of evidence and may get a bit miffed if they don't get it.

Unfortunately, this type of high-tech surveillance does not play a major role in most financial cases. If it's available, it takes a backseat to the records of financial transactions that may have taken place years before. This isn't to imply that surveillance doesn't have its place, and a very essential one in money laundering cases. Some of the major cases described in this book were advanced and even initiated as a result of surveillance techniques.

Physical Surveillance

Physical surveillance is the method that most people associate with law enforcement: two guys sitting in a car, waiting for something to happen. That's exactly how it works in a money laundering case, too, except that the "something" they're waiting for might not be what people expect.

The agents might be looking for links to financial institutions or to specific transactions. In our drug case example, surveillance was used to follow the subject to two different banks and to an apartment complex where the trafficker owned two apartments under a false name. At the time this was going on, none of this was particularly exciting to the agents, who were looking for drug transactions. The information later became very important when it came time to seize the apartments, however.

Is the suspect going from a drug meet to the bank? Safe deposit box records for that day might show the box being used to hold cash or drugs. Is the suspect visiting a mail drop location? He or she may be receiving monthly statements from bank accounts in another name or from another country. This is some of the seemingly routine or innocuous activity that may be of crucial value to a financial investigator.

Another technique involves "covers" on the subject's mail, trash, or telephone. Because communications are so essential to money laundering activity, all three of these covers will reveal contact between the subject and places where financial transactions are taking place.

Mail Covers

Mail covers are arranged through the Postal Inspection Service and permit the recording of information from the outside (only) of mail being delivered to the subject's address. Mail covers are made for a limited amount of time and need to be carefully justified. Figure 18.2 is a sample request for a mail cover.

You are only getting the information on the envelope, but this can provide links to the banks, brokerages, lenders, and businesses with which the subject is in regular contact. You won't know the contents of the envelope — what's in the bank statement, for example — but you'll sure know which bank is mailing it.

Even if there's no return address, there should be a postmark. Articles postmarked in the Cayman Islands or Zurich might give some helpful hints, as offshore banks may not put their name or address on the outside of the envelope. (Some will even mail correspondence from a third country in order to protect their customers' privacy.)

Even though the information may be limited, the mail cover should be considered in every financial case. This cover should include all of the locations where the subject is known to have mail delivered, especially commercial mail drops and the addresses of associates used as mail drops. The post office should be able to identify any post office boxes held in the subject's name.

Trash Covers

Trash covers are not one of the more pleasant jobs in law enforcement, but they can be among the most productive. People do discard a lot of important stuff, much of which can be used in a financial investigation. Credit card slips, bank statements, canceled checks, repair bills, tax assessment records, correspondence — a person's whole life eventually gets discarded.

Under current federal case law, a person's trash has been officially abandoned once it is put out at the curb for pickup or in some other way discarded. As long as the agent can get the trash from the curb or the Dumpster, anything in the rubbish is fair game.

Having done this a few times, I'll attest to the nastiness involved in being this sort of G-man, but it certainly paid off. Among the items recovered were records of illegal gambling operations, drug records, and clippings from false identification the suspect was manufacturing.

Trash covers provide direct leads to financial institutions, almost all of which mail statements regularly to their customers. Accounts and even specific transactions may be identified in this fashion, if the suspect is discarding checks or deposit tickets.

Another good lead from trash covers is just the information that the subject receives, maintains, and discards financial information at that location. This knowledge will be needed to obtain a document search warrant for the premises. This is especially true if the subject is discarding something incriminating, such as gambling records, or is shredding that type of document.

Great caution must be taken to avoid detection in the pickup of the trash. In the FBI's investigation of Soviet spy Aldrich Ames, a duplicate trash can was purchased, the substitution made in the early morning hours, and the

OBTAINING FINANCIAL INFORMATION

External Law Enforcement Agency
REQUEST FOR MAIL COVER

Complete all sections of the mail cover template below and attach a cover letter on your agency letterhead with an original signature by your immediate supervisor. These should be placed in an envelope endorsed RESTRICTED INFORMATION. Seal the request in the envelope, place it in a second envelope, and mail to the CISC. The mail cover request should be addressed as follows:

CISC Manager
Attn: MC Specialist
222 South Riverside Plaza, Suite 1265
Chicago, IL 60606-6117

For further instructions on mail cover requests submitted by external law enforcement agencies, please see Publication 55, USPS Procedures for Mail Cover Requests. This publication may be requested by contacting our Mail Covers Unit at 312-669-5673.

1. DATE OF REQUEST	2. TYPE OF REQUEST: New Request: ☐ Extension: ☐ *(Complete only Item 13)* Fugitive: ☐ *(Refer to Item 7)* Forfeiture: ☐ *(Refer to Item 8)*	3. NUMBER OF DAYS: Indicate the number of days requested: 30 days ☐ **Fugitive only:** 30 days ☐ 60 days ☐

4. SUBJECT OF MAIL COVER NAME & ADDRESS: **Only one subject address may be requested on each mail cover template.** Identify the individual(s) or business(es) to be covered by indicating full name(s), address, and ZIP+4 Code:

Name(s):

Address:

City:

State & Zip+4:

If coverage of "All Other Names" receiving mail at the subject address listed above is needed, provide justification. Also, indicate any names that should be excluded from this request.

All Names at Subject Address: ☐ Yes (provide justification below)   ☐ No

Justification:

5. INDICTMENT: Has the subject been formally charged, i.e. indictment or information with the offense that is the basis of this mail cover request? ☐ Yes ☐ No

6. ATTORNEY:

   a) Does the subject(s) of the investigation have a known attorney?   ☐ Yes   ☐ No
      If so, state the attorney's name and address.

   b) If this request involves a fugitive, does the fugitive have a known attorney?   ☐ Yes   ☐ No
      If so, state the attorney's name and address.

   c) Is the mail cover subject a judicial officer (e.g. attorney, judge, etc.)?   ☐ Yes   ☐ No

7. FUGITIVE: If the cover involves a fugitive, state the fugitive's name, aliases, and any relationship between the fugitive and the mail cover subject.

August 2005

- 1 -
-RESTRICTED INFORMATION-

Figure 18.2 *A request for a mail cover.*

8.	**FORFEITURE:** If the only purpose of the mail cover is to identify property for forfeiture, state the legal basis for the forfeiture investigation, including the applicable forfeiture statute.
9.	**VIOLATION:** State the applicable violation description, statute number, and penalty. If this involves a fugitive and the statute for the warrant is Unlawful Flight or Failure to Appear, also state the original charge. Violation Description, *e.g. Wire Fraud*: Statute, *e.g. Title 18 USC 1343*: Penalty, *e.g. Ten Years*: Is this violation a felony with imprisonment more than one year? ☐ Yes ☐ No
10.	**REASONABLE GROUNDS:** a) Basis - How has the mail cover subject violated, or is suspected of violating, the criminal statute? Make a definite statement that an official investigation into the possible violation of this criminal statute, fugitive search, or asset forfeiture is being conducted and cite the applicable section(s) of the United States Code or applicable State or Local law. Explain in detail your justification. b) Purpose — What information do you expect to obtain from the mail cover? How will the mail cover facilitate the investigation, including the location of property or assets for forfeiture, or the location of a fugitive, e.g. banking information, co-conspirators, etc.? c) Connection - If the mail cover subject is not the subject of the investigation, describe the affiliation of the mail cover subject to the subject of the investigation.

August 2005

-RESTRICTED INFORMATION-

Figure 18.2 Continued.

11.	CLASS OF MAIL:	Indicate the class of mail requested. Justification must be included for other than First Class.

☐ First-Class Mail (Personal or business correspondence: Includes Priority Mail [generally over 11 oz.] and Express Mail)

☐ Standard Mail (Bulk Business Mail)

Provide further justification for these classes of mail:

☐ Package Services (Parcel Post, bound printed materials, media mail and library mail)

Justification:

☐ Periodicals   (Magazines, newspapers)   ☐ Foreign Mail
Justification: Justification:

---

12. **SPECIAL INSTRUCTIONS**: State any special instructions or concerns about this particular request.

---

13. **REQUEST FOR EXTENSION**: *(For an extension request, complete only the section below.)*

At the expiration of the mail cover period, or prior thereto, the requesting authority may request and be granted additional 30-day periods (60-day periods for fugitives). To ensure there is no gap in the mail cover, the extension request should be submitted a minimum of 10 days prior to the end of the mail cover. The requesting authority must provide a statement of the investigative benefits of the mail cover and the anticipated benefits to be derived from its extension. The request for an extension must state whether the subject has been indicted or an information filed and if the subject is represented by an attorney.

Per Postal Regulations, no mail cover shall remain in force longer than 120 continuous days unless personally approved for further extension by the Chief Postal Inspector.

(a) MAIL COVER REFERENCE NO.:

(b) State, in detail, how the results of the prior mail cover assisted, or did not assist, the investigation.

(c) Describe the anticipated benefits to be derived from this mail cover extension.

(d) Regarding the violation under investigation, has the subject's indictment status changed since the previous mail cover approval?   ☐ Yes   ☐ No

(e) Has the subject's legal representation status changed since the last mail cover approval? If so, state the nature of the change, including attorney's name and address.   ☐ Yes   ☐ No

-RESTRICTED INFORMATION-

Figure 18.2 *Continued.*

==Mail covers are issued only to law enforcement agencies empowered by statute or regulation to conduct criminal investigations and are strictly controlled to assure proper use.==

Mail Covers are an investigative tool, and are not to be used as an initial investigative step.

14. AGENCY NAME, REQUESTOR NAME, ADDRESS WHERE MAIL COVER RESULTS SHOULD BE MAILED (with Zip +4 code), TELEPHONE NUMBER, FAX NUMBER AND E-MAIL ADDRESS:

In order to process this request, all fields below are required to be completed (fax and e-mail are optional fields)

Agency Name:

    Is this a law enforcement agency? ☐ Yes ☐ No

Requestor's First Name:

Requestor's Last Name:

Requestor's Title:

Address:

City/State/Zip+4:

Telephone Number:

Fax Number:

E-Mail Address:

15. NAME, TITLE, AND SIGNATURE OF SUPERVISOR AUTHORIZING MAIL COVER REQUEST:

Supervisor's First Name

Supervisor's Last Name

Supervisor's Title

Supervisor's Address:

Supervisor's City/State/Zip+4:

Supervisor's Telephone Number:

Supervisor's Signature and Date:

AN ELECTRONIC VERSION OF THIS FORM IS AVAILABLE UPON REQUEST BY CONTACTING THE MAIL COVERS UNIT AT 312-669-5673.

AS INFORMATION, ALL COMPLETED MAIL COVER REQUESTS WILL NEED TO BE SENT VIA THE UNITED STATES MAIL TO THE CRIMINAL INVESTIGATIONS SERVICE CENTER PER INSTRUCTIONS AT THE TOP OF THE FIRST PAGE OF THIS TEMPLATE.

(For CISC Internal Use Only)

Reviewer's Initials & Date: _____

August 2005

-RESTRICTED INFORMATION-

Figure 18.2 *Continued.*

original can returned before dawn, with all the uninteresting trash included. This is a pretty good system.

Some crooks know about this technique and take steps to prevent their trash from being examined. They may buy and use a shredder or burn their important papers. They may wait until the trash truck is at their door before putting the trash out. In one instance, the subject had a relative sit outside with the can until the trash was collected.

Anything collected in a trash cover should be treated as evidence, complete with chain of custody. These are the subject's records and will require authentication before being brought into court.

Case law in some states does not allow for trash searches without a search warrant. You'll have to check with your prosecutor to determine the case law in your jurisdiction. If it's legally possible to include trash searches in your money laundering investigation, you should do so. It's a dirty job, but it can be very rewarding.

Pen Registers

Another good source for leads is a pen register on the subject's telephone. Dialed number recorders (DNRs), or pen registers, do not (usually) require a wiretap order, and when placed on the subject's telephone line they will provide details of the numbers dialed for all outgoing calls. Combined with a "trap and trace," the pen register will cover incoming calls as well.

You don't get any voice, but you do know every number the subject is calling, including his or her bank, broker, jeweler, travel agent, and car dealer. This technology has reached the point where a computer does most of the work in organizing the data recovered. Other computer programs can analyze the traffic to permit some fairly sophisticated conclusions about what the subject is doing and why — all without ever hearing anyone's voice on the line.

Pen registers require a court order to install and generally run for 30 to 90 days, although they can be renewed. Most of the newer models allow for the unit to be dialed from the office, downloaded, and the data analyzed, all from the agent's desk. If you are using the phone company to make the installation pursuant to the order, make sure a nondisclosure provision is included. This should be one of the items in your tickler file to stay on top of; renew all the nondisclosure orders until they are no longer needed.

A wiretap or a fax intercept order is much harder to get and way more complicated (and costly) to operate. Of course, the information received is likely to be far better — good enough that this method should be considered.

Money laundering schemes are communication intensive. There's something about having all that money floating around, not closely identified with anyone in particular, that makes money launderers nervous. Like anybody else with lots of cash, they tend to be protective of it and to make at least some effort to keep track of all of it. This requires instructions to the bank, to nominees, and to front people or smurfs. Conversely, these people need to provide notifications to the subject that funds were received or transferred.

Many of these calls may be nothing more than the equivalent of "the check's in the mail," but those calls *are* made. When combined with other investigative techniques, the pen register/trap and trace can be a rather useful tool.

The foregoing are more traditional approaches to obtaining information. What follows are the methods investigators use to acquire the financial evidence they need to complete a money laundering investigation in court.

FROM THE HORSE'S MOUTH: THE SUBJECT'S RECORDS

You must attempt to get the subject's records.

I know I've said it before, and I will again, but the records kept by the subject are the *best* source of information about any money laundering case.

Imagine for a moment the most sophisticated money laundering operation in the world, one with false fronts and numbered bank accounts all over the place. You'll never be able to reconstruct such a scheme from the records kept by third parties or the statements of witnesses. But somewhere the records of the money launderer him- or herself exist, with a complete description of the whole scheme.

The chances of finding those records are admittedly slim, but most money laundering cases don't involve such sophisticated schemes, either. And everybody keeps records. If the subject is operating a business as a front, the business has to keep records. If the subject has any sort of relationship with a financial institution, he or she has some sort of records. You may not get the mother lode describing every detail of the money laundering scheme, but you may be able to get enough of the subject's own records to figure out what's going on and where the money went.

All that said, how can the subject's own records be obtained? In four ways.

JUST ASKING ...

One way would be to just go and ask for them, taking the direct approach. This probably won't work, definitely not if the subject's lawyer has anything to say about it, and you'll definitely alert the subject to the existence of the investigation.

Still, you never know, and if you're at the very end of the string, with no chance to get the records any other way, there may be no harm in asking.

OBTAINING RECORDS THROUGH A SECOND PARTY

On occasion, a second party may provide the records you're looking for. When I first went to work for IRS, I was amazed by the number of people who came in with information about tax crimes, often bringing large amounts of documents with them. I referred to these people as "exes," because they were all ex-wives, ex-husbands, ex-bosses, ex-employees, ex-landlords, ex-tenants, all with two things in common: some access to their ex's business affairs and some motivation to give that person up.

The records provided in this situation are often very valuable. Accepting them poses a couple of legal problems. Remember that an informant cannot do anything the agent couldn't legally do, so you can't tell informants to go steal a bunch of the subject's records. If they've *already* stolen them, however, before they ever came in contact with you, the government is under no obligation to turn the information away.

If the informant still has legitimate access to the subject's records and can obtain a copy or even bring the originals to your office, this is probably going to be upheld as well, although the question will probably turn on what type of legal access the person really had. In this case, it may be better just to get a very thorough description of the records and their location and then to seize them with a warrant, but there is something to be said for keeping the subject in the dark, too.

The informant may be able to get copies of the records by asking for them — "I need a receipt for my records." In this case, the subject would be generating a record and voluntarily providing it to a second party; there's nothing wrong with that.

Caution should be exercised in using a witness to obtain records from the subject, especially if you can't be sure how he or she is going to get them. You may want to speak with counsel or the Assistant U.S. Attorney before proceeding.

SUBPOENAS AND SPECIAL EXCEPTIONS

Can the subject of an investigation be compelled to produce the documents that (you certainly hope) will incriminate him or her? The average citizen and even most experienced criminal investigators would say no, but the answer, surprisingly enough, is maybe.

The Fifth Amendment generally prevents the government from forcing people to give evidence against themselves. Courts have ruled that this protection extends to the documents and records they have prepared or maintained.

Under some circumstances, this protection may not be as broad as the subject might like, and this may be of special interest to investigators in money laundering cases. The doctrine is expressed in two Supreme Court decisions, each regarding a different type of record and the circumstances under which those documents must be produced.

In the first case, *Braswell v. United States,* 487 U.S. 99, 108 S.Ct. 2284 (1984), the Court held that the collective entry doctrine prevented Braswell from claiming Fifth Amendment protection for his corporate records. Braswell was the sole shareholder of the corporation, as well as the custodian of records.

Other Supreme Court decisions have consistently distinguished the records of a corporation from those of the individual officers, employees, or shareholders — and found that corporate records do not enjoy Fifth Amendment protection. In *Braswell,* the distinction between Braswell, the individual, and Braswell, the corporation he owned completely, was narrow, but the Court still found that the records must be produced.

What about a sole proprietorship, a partnership, or another noncorporate entity? Somewhat surprisingly, the Court also found a Fifth Amendment exception for these records as well, albeit a limited one.

In *United States v. Doe,* 465 U.S. 605 (1984), the government issued grand jury subpoenas for production of business records to Doe, a sole proprietor. He refused to produce the records, claiming a Fifth Amendment privilege. The Supreme Court ruled against this claim, saying that in some instances, the privilege might not apply to business records.

Specifically, if the government's request for documents involved (1) business records that (2) were voluntarily prepared in the normal course of business, and (3) there was no testimony by the person producing the records, and (4) no authentication of the records by the producer was required, then the subject could be ordered to produce the records.

For purposes of the production, the subject is granted "use immunity" — the fact of the production cannot be used against him or her. As further protection, the materials are produced to the grand jury under the name "John Doe."

Under this decision, the contents but not the act of production can be used against the subject.

The government would have to find some other means of authenticating the records, such as a witness, handwriting analysis, and so forth, because the subject still cannot be compelled to testify to this information.

The implications in a money laundering case are significant. If you know that your subject kept records relating to offshore investment or transactions, the type of information that would not be available from those offshore locations, you might be able to force disclosure directly from the subject.

Whether the subject would actually produce such incriminating documents is open to question, but the subpoena and production order could be effective in a situation where the subject has employees working within a business who are familiar with the records.

The forms used to compel production under this doctrine are provided in Appendix C. Although this may be a technique of last resort, it is at least a tool that is available to investigators.

Financial and Document Search Warrants

The technique that does not rely on the subject's cooperation is the good old-fashioned search warrant — with a twist. For the purpose of this discussion, we'll break search warrants into two categories, financial search warrants and document search warrants, although both relate to financial records.

The financial search warrant is one directed at the premises of a second or third party. Although this type of warrant may be used to get the records of the subject, it is usually used to get third-party records. We'll cover this more in the next section.

A document warrant is aimed right at the subject. The objective is to obtain relevant records in the subject's possession. Like every other technique, there are advantages and disadvantages to using a search warrant. On the plus side, the subject won't know you're coming and won't have time to conceal or destroy the records. Also, a document warrant allows for a more thorough search, and the agent, as opposed to the subject, third party, or a lawyer, makes the decision about what is covered by the warrant.

On the downside, the execution of the warrant generally lets everybody know you're here and you mean business. If the location is wrong or the documents aren't found in the search, the subject may well be busy destroying them somewhere else.

On balance, a document warrant is such a powerful tool that it should be used whenever the circumstances warrant. (No pun intended.) There are several legal and constitutional questions you have to address in the preparation and execution of the warrant, but, regardless, Congress and the courts have given us a very useful weapon.

The Fourth Amendment to the Constitution specifically states:

> The right of the people to be secure in their persons, houses, papers, and effects, against unreasonable searches and seizures, shall not be violated, and no Warrants shall issue, but upon probable cause, supported by Oath or affirmation, and particularly describing the place to be searched and the persons or things to be seized. (Emphasis added.)

Document warrants are, as their name implies, strictly limited to "papers" (although these may be in electronic form nowadays). Over the years, the courts have defined what the document warrant can do and how it can be applied, again with positive and negative implications from our perspective.

The good news relates to the "probable cause" part of the equation. In a series of appellate decisions, courts have held that a magistrate is entitled to draw reasonable inferences about where evidence is likely to be kept, based on the nature of the evidence and the type of the offense; see *United States v. Angulo-Lopez*, 791 F.2d 1394 (9th Cir. 1986). The courts have held that financial records are the type of item generally kept by individuals and businesses and that they may be kept for long periods of time. This finding has implications as to the timeliness of the probable cause.

For example, in 2005 an informant tells you that Alex Bell has been in the drug business from 2002 through the present. The informant hasn't seen any records in Bell's possession since 2004, but she knows that he kept them in prior years up to that point. When combined with other information, this knowledge may allow the judge to conclude that Bell currently maintains records at the location you want to search.

Another aspect of these warrants is that the expertise and experience of the affiant can be used to help in establishing probable cause. Although an agent's conclusion is never a substitute for the facts and circumstances constituting probable cause, the conclusion *can* be a factor for the reviewing magistrate to consider.

Search warrant affidavits should contain a section describing the affiant's expertise and experience, as well as a clearly labeled section containing the affiant's conclusions about *why* he or she believes the records are relevant and will be found.

One consideration of importance in a document warrant relates to "particularity." As the amendment states, the items sought need to be "particularly described." Courts have ruled in a number of cases on search warrants that the defendants claimed were too broad in their descriptions of the items to be sought. The established principle is that the items must be described as best as they can be, to exclude items irrelevant to the matter at hand.

If a warrant "effectively tells the officers to seize only those records indicating" a specific criminal activity, it will probably not be considered overbroad, but the language should be as particular as the officers can make it. The Ninth Circuit allowed a warrant that authorized seizure of "records, notes, documents indicating the defendant's involvement and control of prostitution activity including *but not limited to* photographs, handwritten notes, ledger books, transportation vouchers and tickets, hotel registrations, receipts, bank documents and records, toll records, bail bondsmen's receipts, and medical billings. See *United States v. Washington*, F.2d 1461 (9th Cir. 1986).

A key feature in a number of court decisions has been the issue of time limits. The courts have ruled in the government's favor when time limits were placed on the documents sought. These limits might be something like "for the period January 1995 through the present" or "for the years 1992, 1993, and 1994." The agent should articulate why these specific time limits are relevant and make it clear that all documents not falling within the time limits are going to be excluded.

If you know the subject didn't get involved in the illegal activity until 2001, don't ask for records going back to World War II. (Exception: If you need to go back farther to establish your net worth starting point, or if you have some other valid financial reason, articulate this clearly. You are showing good faith, and your request will probably be granted.) This isn't all that hard to do, and if it's something the appeals courts look for, we should give it to them.

Another aspect of document warrants deserving of our attention is the scope of the search. Because the warrant is limited to documentary evidence, only those areas in which such evidence could be located can typically be searched. If contraband or other evidence is encountered during the search, it can be seized on the spot or another warrant can be obtained, depending on the circumstances, but a document warrant *cannot* be used as a ruse or device to make a wholesale search of the premises for other evidence.

Document warrants are a good illustration of how other investigative techniques can be employed in a financial case. The objective of a document warrant is to obtain financial records, but in order to obtain the warrant, other, more traditional methods must be employed. Informants, surveillance, trash covers, pen registers, and financial information can all be used to help establish the probable cause needed to obtain a valid document search warrant.

An affidavit for a financial or document search warrant must include a number of elements. These are:

- Affiant's background and experience
- Facts and circumstances relating to probable cause — a description of the criminal activity
- Probable cause that the documents sought will be on the premises searched
- Evidence of financial activity
- Description of the place to be searched
- Description of the items to be seized

The affiant's background and experience distinguish a document or financial warrant from the others. For a document warrant, the judge will be asked to consider the affiant's conclusions in making a decision about probable cause. The affiant should include work experience, education, and training, as well as specific examples that relate to the question — for example: "I have participated in over 100 investigations involving money laundering and narcotics trafficking, and in the execution of search warrants on businesses or residences."

A sometimes overlooked addition to this section is the experience of other investigators or informants as conveyed to the affiant. If you have participated in multiple debriefings in which the subject of drug records was discussed, then mention this fact in the affidavit if it is relevant and would help the judge make a decision.

A relevant case on this issue is *United States v. Fannin,* 817 F.2d 1379 (1987), a Ninth Circuit decision. The court held that in weighing the evidence supporting a request for search warrant, the magistrate may rely on the conclusions of experienced law enforcement officers regarding where evidence of a crime may be found. In the *Fannin* case, the probable cause was somewhat stale, but there was evidence that the criminal activity was ongoing. The affiant concluded, based on his experience and knowledge of drug trafficking operations, that documents of the type normally kept in such operations were still likely to be on the premises. The magistrate and the Ninth Circuit agreed. Your conclusions will not substitute for evidence of probable cause, but the magistrate should at least be able to consider them within the context of the overall showing of probable cause.

The section in the affidavit relating to probable cause is a detailed description of the criminal activity underlying the money laundering offense. The documents sought in the warrant are supposed to relate directly to this activity. This section will generally be the longest in the affidavit. It is the primary focal point for the magistrate's decision, and it should contain sufficient information to allow a conclusion that (*a*) there is evidence that a crime is being or has been committed, (*b*) there is good reason to believe that documentary evidence of this crime exists, and what this evidence would look like, and (*c*) the evidence described is likely to be found at the premises the officers want to search. Probable cause must be established for each.

Probable cause is not an especially hard burden for the government to meet, but there have to be sufficient facts within the "four corners" of the affidavit to make the case for the issuance of the warrant. In a money laundering or financial case, most of these facts will be similar to those you would be using to get a warrant in a drug or firearms case. Statements of informants, corroboration by surveillance, and public and government record information will all be used to establish probable cause. Not only will this be meaningful in showing the Specified Unlawful Activity underlying the money laundering crime, but it also lays the foundation for the contention that records of this activity are likely to be found on the premises to be searched.

Evidence of financial activity is the heart of the document search warrant. This information will take two forms, positive and negative.

On the positive side, you're trying to show that (*a*) the subject has conducted financial transactions, and (*b*) records were kept or are likely to have been kept in connection with these transactions. Some of the financial transactions conducted by the subject may be of the illegal sort, such as drug sales or receipt of income from criminal activity. Perhaps you are able to describe the purchase of goods or the investment of the proceeds of the illegal activity. Other transactions may be completely legal, such as the expenditure of large sums of money or the possession of large amounts of cash.

On the negative side, you may be attempting to show that the subject had no legitimate source of income. This information should always be included when available, as it is deeply relevant to the question of the source of unexplained wealth.

As we've seen, information about financial transactions can come from a number of sources, including informants, witnesses, surveillance, and other financial records. Because you want to particularly describe the records you'll seek to seize, details about the books, papers, documents, or records should be included when they are available.

Any evidence of transactions with third-party record-keepers, such as banks, should also be described. The subject's records of these transactions should be sought, especially if they involve offshore institutions or businesses.

Finally, evidence of large amounts of cash and any unexplained major expenditures has consistently been held by the courts to be indicative of illegal activity. Sudden acquisition of money is admissible, even if it is not traced to an illegal source; see *United States v. Jackskion,* 102 F.2d 683 (2nd Cir. 1939). Evidence of a trip to Las Vegas shortly after a robbery was admissible; see *United States v. Crisp,* 435 F.2d 354 (7th Cir. 1970). "Evidence of the possession of huge amounts of money is highly relevant in an operation ... the profits therefrom are astronomical" — see *United States v. Barnes,* 604 F.2d 121 (2nd Cir. 1979).

On the other side of the equation, evidence that the subject had no legitimate employment or income is equally persuasive, when combined with descriptions of large cash purchases. How *did* that guy come up with the money for that new Porsche? Information on this line can be developed from the subject's own statements, such as those made under oath on a tax return or in financial statements such as loan applications or divorce records.

Tax returns may be a problem, although they can be obtained in a federal investigation through use of an *ex parte* court order. If you are unable to obtain the returns in this manner, you may be able to get them from a state taxing authority or use copies attached to a loan application or provided in connection with a lawsuit, such as a divorce action. The fact that a subject appears to have a lot of unexplained wealth and doesn't file tax returns is also information the magistrate would find interesting. Failure to file tax returns by someone with large expenditures is admissible to support an inference that he had no legitimate source of income; see *United States v. Hinton,* 543 F.2d 1002 (2nd Cir. 1976).

A description of the place to be searched must be accurate and complete, although court decisions have held that it is not necessary to specify the exact location within the premises where the documents are located. This gives the investigator some leeway in searching the location for items the subject might have moved or stored elsewhere.

The description of the items to be seized in a document or financial warrant is one of the elements of the warrant most likely to be challenged. Claims that the warrant was "overbroad" or allowed too much discretion by the searching agents are routine in cases involving documents or papers. For this reason, your description of the items to be seized should be as complete as possible and as limited as you can make it. Numerous court decisions provide guidance on this issue, and we'll look at a few to get an idea about what to expect.

In the Supreme Court decision of *Andresen v. Maryland,* 427 U.S. 463, 96 S.Ct. 2737 (1976), the Court noted that:

> there are grave dangers inherent in executing a warrant authorizing a search and seizure of a person's papers that are not necessarily present in executing a warrant to search for physical objects whose relevance is more easily ascertainable.

Courts are concerned that descriptions may be so broad as to authorize a "general" or "exploratory" warrant, because they recognize that the relevance of documents is difficult to establish. You don't have this problem with other evidence; a sawed-off shotgun or a kilo of cocaine is pretty much going to be relevant every time you run into one. Certainly the language of a subpoena *duces tecum,* "any and all books, papers, documents, and records," should be avoided in a search warrant. (I also try to avoid "including but not limited to," even though at least one court said that was okay. It just *sounds* like I'm going fishing, even though I'm not.)

The affiant should make a determined effort to describe the records sought and their relevance within the affidavit. Restrictions can show a good faith effort on the part of the government to narrow the scope of the warrant. These restrictions might be by time frame: "limited to the years 1996 and 1997"; by subject matter: "records relating to the sale of controlled substances"; or by name: "relating to the below named individuals."

Remember that any language that would convert the warrant into a general or exploratory one will void it, a risk that is greater in document warrants. Language that has been rejected by the courts includes:

- "Any property or devices used or obtained through fraud"
- "Miscellaneous jewelry"
- "Stolen merchandise"
- "Any other illegally maintained drugs or firearms of various descriptions"
- "Any and all other records and paraphernalia" connected with a corporation

In the *Fannin* case, the court held that the description of the items to be seized must be specific enough to enable the officers who are executing the warrant to identify those items that may legitimately be seized. Sweeping language that would allow any items to be seized is forbidden.

In *United States v. Kow,* 58 F.3d 423 (9th Cir. 1995), the court held that the government's descriptions were too broad and that "generic classifications" were not acceptable unless more precise descriptions were unavailable. In this case, the government was seeking the records of a corporation. Almost all of the items described in the warrant were documentary, but the language was generic, as in "Ledgers or other records summarizing financial transactions." The court felt that if these descriptions had been modified with some limiting features, the warrant might not have been overbroad. The descriptions could have been limited by describing the suspected criminal conduct to which the items related, by specifying a time frame, by specifically describing the items, or by advising where within the premises the items might have been located.

In light of *Kow* and other decisions regarding document warrants, officers should be extremely cautious in preparing the list of items to be seized. Whenever possible, this list should be as precise as possible, and it should contain evidence that the officer is acting in good faith to limit the warrant to *only* those items that can legally be seized.

PREPARING A LIST OF THINGS TO BE SEIZED

This is one instance when it's okay to start at the end, rather than the beginning. When you are putting your search warrant together, start with the list of things you are proposing to seize. This is, after all, the bottom line.

1. Make up a working copy of your list, including every item you would *like* to take, and then prioritize the list.
2. Number the items, one through whatever, starting with the most important to your case. (For example, if your case involves a drug operation with credit sales, your "most wanted" records might be owe–pay sheets or records of credit sales.)
3. Next, establish a time period to which that item relates, and specify those dates next to the item description. Be as specific as you can be. If you know the account wasn't opened until June 2003, don't ask for any records before then.
4. If there are any names connected with the item, write those in. If there are known business entities, note those.
5. If you have exact descriptions, such as "ledger book with green cover," include those.
6. If you know of any location within the premises where these items are likely to be found, write that in.
7. If you can *exclude* any records that you know you won't need, write those in too. (This demonstrates a conscious effort to avoid unreasonable or unnecessary searches, and judges appreciate that effort.)

Your list has probably lengthened during this process, and you can now see which items are thoroughly described and which need a little work. If the latter are important, go do the extra work.

Now that the list is done, go back through the affidavit and make sure that somewhere therein is a paragraph or a sentence relating to the probable cause for each item on your list. Write that paragraph number next to each item on your list. Any list items without paragraph numbers from the affidavit need to get one, even if you have to put a new paragraph in the affidavit.

When everything is documented properly, make up a clean copy of your new list (without the paragraph numbers), and attach it to the warrant. *That* ought to do it.

"PERMEATED WITH FRAUD": A USEFUL PHRASE

Courts have held that if you can show that the business you are seeking to search is "permeated with fraud" or tainted with illegality, *all* of the business records can be seized. Meeting this standard can be tough, but this may be something you want to prove in your affidavit. In *United States v. Offices Known as 50 State Distribution, Co.,* 708 F.2d 1371 (9th Cir. 1983), *cert. denied,* 465 U.S. 1021 (1984), the Court upheld a broad search warrant based on a showing that fraud permeated the business and that "it was not possible through more particular description to segregate those business records that would be evidence of fraud from those that would not." See 708 F.2d at 1374.

VALUABLE HEARSAY: THIRD-PARTY RECORDS

Because the subject's records aren't always available, and because those of third parties almost always are, these documents become the lifeblood of a financial investigation. The law recognizes that business records are an inevitable part of modern life and makes provisions for the use of these materials in criminal investigations.

LEGAL CONSIDERATIONS

Production of business records for use in a criminal proceeding is based on a couple of legal principles. First, everybody with evidence of a crime is obligated to come forward with it if called upon. This obligation is fairly universal, with some privileges given to certain witnesses (spouses, attorneys, etc.). In financial crimes, those with evidence are often the banks or businesses that are somehow related to the scheme. The records of these "third parties" often play a major role in the resolution of financial crimes, something the law recognizes, so that provisions are made to compel production *and* to require that the records be kept in the first place. The Bank Secrecy Act is a good example of this kind of requirement.

Second, third-party records are considered hearsay, but they are admissible under the previously discussed shop book rule. Finally, the law tries to obtain some balance between the privacy of the individual and the needs of the government. The Right to Financial Privacy Act and the Bank Secrecy Act are examples of this attempt at balance.

There are several means by which the government can legally obtain access to the private but often valuable financial information of an individual or business. In all likelihood, the records obtained in this process will form the very heart of a money laundering or financial investigation.

REQUEST FOR PRODUCTION

Third-party records come in all shapes, varying as widely as the businesses generating them. Some are protected by federal or state laws, such as the Right to Financial Privacy Act (RTFPA). Others have no legal protection whatsoever, even though the record-keeper may insist on being subpoenaed.

One means of obtaining third-party records is a simple request for production. Contrary to public belief, there is no "Privacy Act" that prevents people from disclosing information about other people. A claim by some business person that "those records are confidential" generally has no legal basis whatsoever.

Practically speaking, this reluctance on the part of your potential witness is probably not going to be overcome by arguing with him or her, so you may have to get a subpoena. It doesn't hurt to ask, however, and if you can get the information informally, assuming that the third party is not going to tell the suspect, so much the better.

Caution: Financial institutions are covered by the Right to Financial Privacy Act of 1978 and cannot legally disclose account holder or customer information, except under certain situations described by the RTFPA. If your "informal" request doesn't fit one of those exceptions, you and the bank employee can be civilly liable and subject to disciplinary action. This is why having a bank teller as an informant isn't as good an idea as it sounds. You can, however, ask for and receive "relationship" information from the financial institution. This includes whether or not the person has an account with the bank and probably the account number.

ADMINISTRATIVE SUBPOENA

Again, in recognition of the need for government agencies to collect financial and other information relevant to their inquiries, Congress has provided for agencies to have administrative subpoena powers.

A *subpoena duces tecum* is an order compelling an individual or business to produce records. Although many subpoenas are issued by courts or grand juries, administrative subpoenas are issued by agencies of the executive branch, such as the Drug Enforcement Administration (DEA) or the FBI.

The subpoena power granted to the DEA is a good example of how this process works. Title 21 U.S.C. Section 876 covers investigations of violations of the controlled substance laws within Title 21. This section authorizes the Attorney General or his or her delegate to subpoena witnesses, compel the attendance and testimony of witnesses, and require the production of any records (including books, papers, documents and other tangible things that constitute or contain evidence) which the Attorney General finds relevant or material to the investigation.

That's a pretty broad charge, and the statute provides for "enforcement" — action to be taken if the person subpoenaed refuses to testify or make the required production.

Administrative subpoenas can generally be employed for any matter that falls under the jurisdiction of the issuing agency, and authority for the issuance of subpoenas gets delegated downward, sometimes all the way to the investigators themselves.

There may be some restrictions on these subpoenas. In some cases, law or agency policy requires that once a matter has been referred to the U.S. Attorney or to a grand jury, the administrative subpoena can no longer be employed. This is the case with subpoenas and summonses issued under Title 31 and Title 26.

Another question relates to disclosure of the existence of the subpoena to the subject. Depending on the statute, federal law may not require disclosure, but some businesses will do so anyway. It may be possible to obtain an order preventing disclosure of the administrative subpoena, but it might be a better idea to get a grand jury subpoena with a nondisclosure order from the court.

One final consideration is the question of payment. Witnesses are entitled to "fees and mileage" for their appearance, and they may be able to bill the issuing agency for the expenses of producing the records requested. Financial institutions are able to obtain reimbursement for the costs of finding and copying records. Because this can be a very costly proposition, you should find out in advance whether (*a*) the subpoenaed party can or will charge for production, and (*b*) you have the money to pay for it. This factor may cause you to limit the scope of your subpoena.

GRAND JURY SUBPOENA

The federal grand jury is the investigative mechanism used to initiate criminal cases in federal court. Grand juries have tremendous power, much of which is based on their ability to issue subpoenas for witnesses and their records. These subpoenas form the backbone of most financial investigations.

The *subpoena duces tecum* requires the production of records to the grand jury and allows for much broader requests for information than would a search warrant. Fourth Amendment claims against overbroad or unreasonable subpoenas have consistently been rejected, mostly because the subpoenas aren't usually classified as a "search and seizure." A subpoena, to be valid, has to (1) be pursuant to a lawful investigation or inquiry, (2) be relevant to the inquiry at hand, and (3) include an adequate but not excessive description of the documents requested. These standards, set forth in the case *Oklahoma Press Publishing Co. v. Walling,* 327 U.S. 186 (1946), leave a lot of leeway in the use of *subpoenas duces tecum.*

In the case of a grand jury subpoena, the best chance the subject has of getting it quashed is in the claim that the request is too broad or too burdensome. A request for all of the corporate records of the General Motors Corporation would definitely fit this category. The court, in studying a motion to quash the subpoena, will consider the relevance of the request, the cost and disruption to the business of compliance, the volume of records requested, and whether production can be staggered or scheduled to minimize the impact on the business.

Important issues related to grand jury subpoenas are the records requested, method of service, time considerations, secrecy, and payment.

Records Requested

The material you're requesting will vary, depending on the type of business. We have included model language for subpoenas for a number of businesses in Appendix C. Your list should be comprehensive but not excessive. Limit the inquiry by time period, if you are able, and by name, if you can. "All records relating to Joe Blow, for the period 1992–1995" is much better than "All records." Your subpoena has less chance of being quashed for being overbroad or burdensome this way.

Specify whether you want originals or copies. This will depend on what the Assistant U.S. Attorney wants, so consult with him or her.

Service

A grand jury subpoena for records can be served on the custodian or any person responsible for keeping records at a business. Officers or designated employees at a corporation, partners in a partnership, or employees of other businesses may be responsible for the production of records. When serving a federal grand jury subpoena, the server should make a note of who will be producing the records and get a phone number.

Time Considerations

You've got to give the recipient time to produce the records. There are some instances when a "forthwith" demand may be made, and the individual will have to produce the materials to you while you stand there or bring them directly to the grand jury. This is relatively rare and used only in cases when you think the records might be in danger of destruction or some other action that would make them unavailable.

In most cases, you'll want to give the person sufficient time to compile the records and bring them to the grand jury all at once. (Banks sometimes like to drag things out, producing subpoenaed records in bite-sized pieces as they get them together. This isn't necessarily a bad thing, but it can confuse your case file.)

Secrecy

Materials subpoenaed before a grand jury are covered by the same secrecy rules that govern testimony — Rule 6 (e) of the Federal Rules of Criminal Procedure. This means extreme caution has to be taken in the protection of these records, once they've been turned over to the grand jury. Usually an agent is appointed as custodian of the records for the grand jury. This person will have to make sure that the records are protected from unauthorized access and that no one who is not on the 6 (e) disclosure list is allowed to view them.

The witness, however, is under no secrecy obligation and can disclose any information if he or she wants to, including to the customer. This disclosure can be a problem, because the government may not want the fact that it has subpoenaed some records to be known to the subject of the investigation. In this case, the government will obtain a court order directing the recipient of the subpoena not to disclose the existence of the subpoena or the production of the material. These orders may cover a limited period, and you may have to renew the order periodically to keep your investigation confidential. This is something you definitely want to keep on top of.

Under the Right to Financial Privacy Act, financial institutions are *required* to notify their customers that information about them has been disclosed to the government in certain instances. If you have a grand jury subpoena, federal law prohibits notification of the customer under certain circumstances. Title 18 U.S.C. § 1510 (a) (2) reads:

Whoever, being an officer of a financial institution, directly or indirectly notifies

(A) a customer of that financial institution whose records are being sought by a grand jury subpoena; or

(B) any other person named in that subpoena;

about the existence or the contents of that subpoena or information that has been furnished to the grand jury in response to that subpoena, shall be fined under this title or imprisoned not more than one year, or both.

So, the banker could be in some misdemeanor trouble for a violation. Under the statute, a "subpoena for records" means a federal grand jury subpoena for customer records relating to a violation of or a conspiracy to violate, among other statutes, Title 18 U.S.C. §1956 and §1957, as well as chapter 53 of Title 31. The U.S. Attorney can advise the financial institution in writing that the subpoena relates to one of these offenses, and the bank is on notice that it is not to notify the customer.

Payment

Federal law allows financial institutions, as well as individuals and small partnerships, to recover some of their costs in complying with subpoenas. This process is handled by the United States Attorney's office, but cost may be a consideration in the scope or breadth of your subpoena.

FINANCIAL SEARCH WARRANTS

We are distinguishing between *document* warrants, for subject records, and *financial* warrants, for third-party records, although the terms are sometimes used interchangeably.

Financial search warrants are those that are used when a grand jury subpoena can't be. Search warrants are very intrusive, though subpoenas can be as well. A search warrant permits investigators to immediately obtain the records sought, preventing their destruction or concealment.

Federal law and rules (28 C.F.R. §59.5) govern this type of search warrant. In determining whether a subpoena or a search warrant should be employed, a number of factors can be considered. The most important of these is whether it appears that the use of the subpoena or another alternative that gives advance notice of the government's interest in obtaining the materials would be likely to result in the destruction, alteration, concealment, or transfer of the materials sought.

To make this determination, you want to consider:

1. Whether a suspect has access to the materials sought
2. Whether there is a close relationship of friendship, loyalty, or sympathy between the possessor of the materials and a suspect
3. Whether the possessor of the materials is under the domination or control of the suspect
4. Whether the possessor of the materials has an interest in preventing the disclosure of the materials to the government
5. Whether the possessor's willingness to comply with a subpoena or request by the government would be likely to subject him or her to intimidation or threats of reprisal
6. Whether the possessor of the materials has previously acted to obstruct a criminal investigation or judicial proceeding or refused to comply with or acted in defiance of court orders
7. Whether the possessor has expressed an intent to destroy, conceal, alter, or transfer the materials

If the answers to any of the above make you nervous, a search warrant, rather than a subpoena, may be your preferred alternative. You also have to factor in the immediacy of the government's need to obtain the materials. Is there some reason you need to have the documents now? Consider:

1. Whether the immediate seizure of the materials is necessary to prevent injury to persons or property
2. Whether the prompt seizure of the materials is necessary to preserve their evidentiary value
3. Whether delay in obtaining the materials would significantly jeopardize an ongoing investigation or prosecution
4. Whether a legally enforceable form of process other than a search warrant is reasonably available as a means of obtaining the materials

As long as you can demonstrate that less intrusive means are not suitable, the use of the financial search warrant will probably be allowed. Current Department of Justice (DOJ) policy, however, requires DOJ approval for the execution of a search warrant on a third party, and state and local prosecutors may have similar policies.

If the financial search warrant for third-party records is your choice, you are still bound by the same considerations regarding scope, particularity, and probable cause that apply to document warrants. This includes sufficient probable cause to demonstrate that a substantive crime has been committed and that evidence of this crime — consisting of financial records — is located at the premises you want to search. Your experience and the fact that business records are normally kept or retained at the place of business can form part of the basis of this probable cause.

One drawback to financial search warrants is that there is no hiding the fact of their execution. Once the warrant is served, no gag or restraining orders will prevent those at the business from telling whomever they want that you were there.

Tax Records

After Richard Nixon misused the IRS for political purposes — keeping an enemies list and the like — Congress tightened up on the rules under which tax returns could be disclosed to law enforcement. The general rule now is that they can't. As with all good rules, there are exceptions.

Title 26 U.S.C. §6103 provides for disclosure of a couple of different types of tax information. One sort, known in typically confusing government fashion as "return information other than taxpayer return information," includes the kind of material gathered in an IRS investigation but *nothing* reported by the taxpayer on his or her returns. This kind of information can be given to federal investigators in written form by the IRS Criminal Investigation Division in nontax cases. For example, in the course of an investigation, IRS-CID develops information about drug trafficking. They aren't doing a separate tax case on the subject, so CID can disclose the drug information to the appropriate federal agency.

You're going to need a court order to get information from IRS about somebody's tax returns. This order will be *ex parte,* so there's no requirement that the taxpayer be involved or even notified of the disclosure, but you'll have to get the court to sign off before IRS gives you a tax return. See *United States v. Barnes,* 604 F.2d 121 (2nd Cir. 1979).

Ex parte orders can be obtained through the Assistant U.S. Attorney who is working with you on your case. Since the courts allow it and there's a relatively simple process for doing it, there's really no reason why an *ex parte* order shouldn't be one of the first things you do in your financial case. Some good reasons for doing this are as follows:

- Income tax returns can provide a foundation or starting point for the admission of other financial information. See *United States v. Falley,* 489 F.2d 33 (2nd Cir. 1973).
- Failure to file returns by a defendant who made large cash expenditures is admissible to support the inference that the defendant had no legitimate source of income. See *United States v. Hinton,* 543 F.2d 1002 (2nd Cir. 1976).
- Unidentified "miscellaneous" and "other" unspecified income listed on a defendant's tax returns was a "warning signal that the money came from a

source which the recipients preferred not to disclose" and was admissible as probative evidence of a drug conspiracy and drug sales in *United States v. Barnes,* 604 F.2d 121 (2nd Cir. 1979).

Practically speaking, tax returns contain a wealth of information about assets, banking relationships, and business associations. Two points to remember: Tax returns only reflect activity from prior years, *not* what the taxpayer is doing right now, and this information is extremely sensitive, requiring special protection from additional disclosure.

Moral of the story: Do yourself a favor, get the returns and see what the subject had to say for him- or herself.

INFORMATION FROM ABROAD

Official and Unofficial Liaison

American law enforcement agencies maintain overseas posts to facilitate the exchange of information between governments. Overseas representatives from FBI, DEA, ICE, IRS, and the Secret Service also assist their own agencies with requests for information from abroad. These liaison officers will be very knowledgeable about the local laws and conditions and able to provide guidance as to how information can be obtained for use in American courts.

The Internet is a remarkably good source of information from foreign countries, many of which make their government Web sites available on the Internet in English. And IRS produces a very comprehensive book for investigators entitled *Sources of Information from Abroad,* containing descriptions of where information may be obtained in various countries around the world.

Currency controls are a potential avenue for exploration. A country with currency controls may require disclosure of currency movement. South Korea, for example, records large cash transactions in its citizens' passports and maintains computerized records of inbound and outbound currency movements. If your subject has no Currency and Monetary Instrument Reports (CMIRs) showing movement of money to Korea, but Korean computer records show that he declared a couple of million dollars in inbound transfers, this information might be useful to your case.

Any informal liaison contacts may be very interested to learn of currency movement to their country, and especially currency movement *from* the country. Since this is a rather common defense to tax and money laundering cases, you should establish what currency controls, if any, are in effect.

Caution needs to be used in disclosing information to foreign contacts, but such informal liaisons are nevertheless sought by law enforcement all over the world and developed through activities such as the International Asian Organized Crime Conference, professional organizations, and, of course, Interpol. Remember, though, that informal contacts are just that — informal. You can't use information acquired from your new buddy in court; you'll have to go the formal route for that, and this means going through the Department of Justice, Office of International Affairs (OIA).

OIA is another good resource, especially with regard to what information may be available by treaty or agreement with a foreign government. Formal legal requests for information are going to be processed through OIA. These things take a lot longer than a phone call to a friend in Hong Kong, but they do the job.

Compelling Production

The Fifth Amendment says people can't be compelled to testify against themselves, but what about being forced to produce their records? Ordinarily, the government cannot make them do this, but an interesting exception appears to exist for *some* records, in some situations. This exception, which has important implications in money laundering cases, relates to the records of a third party that are maintained "offshore."

A Supreme Court case, *John Doe v. United States,* 487 U.S. 201, 108 S.Ct. 2341 (1988), saw the government seeking Cayman Island bank records for a subject. (Note: This case is different from the *Doe* case discussed previously.) The banks refused to turn the records over, citing the secrecy laws of the Cayman Islands, which prohibited disclosure without the customer's permission. The government then went to Doe and asked him to consent to release of the records. Doe refused on Fifth Amendment grounds, but in a case that went all the way to the Supreme Court, his refusal was ultimately rejected.

The Court ruled that the Fifth Amendment privilege could be claimed only to resist compelled or implicit disclosures of incriminating information, and that the execution by Doe of the consent directive that authorized the Cayman bank to disclose his records had no testimonial significance. The Court also ruled that the contents of bank account records maintained by a foreign third party are not privileged and the banks cannot invoke the Fifth Amendment in refusing to turn over the records. As with the other *Doe* case, the act of producing the records can't be used against the subject.

In this case, the investigators were aware of some Cayman Islands activities and knew that information was located at a certain financial institution, but the ruling was fairly sweeping. If you have information that your subject has concealed assets offshore or used foreign bank accounts to conduct financial transactions, this decision strongly suggests that you can insist on a signed consent directive from the subject, authorizing the foreign bank (or any other third party) to disclose the information to you.

Practically speaking, you have to have a pretty good idea where the accounts or information is located, but that's what your money laundering investigation is all about.

TAX AND MUTUAL LEGAL ASSISTANCE TREATIES

The United States has entered into treaties with a growing number of countries around the world regarding the exchange of information in criminal cases. These Mutual Legal Assistance Treaties (MLATs) allow for the release of information under very strict conditions.

Quite often, information pertaining only to certain limited crimes (usually drug trafficking and money laundering) will be subject to the treaty. In the case of America's treaty with the Cayman Islands, information pertaining to drug trafficking can be released. In order to get it, the United States government has to certify that the information sought does relate to a drug case, at which point the Caymans government would presumably arrange for disclosure of the bank or business records sought.

Obtaining information via the MLAT process is time consuming and generally a bigger hassle than just handing a grand jury subpoena to somebody, but at least the information is (supposedly) available. The Department of Justice and the Department of State both get involved in this process, which will be conducted through your U.S. Attorney. A list of the countries with which the United States has MLATs in force and a sample MLAT request appear in Chapter 7.

The United States also has tax treaties with a number of foreign countries, under which information about individuals and their tax status can be exchanged. If you have obtained an *ex parte* order to obtain the subject's federal income tax returns, you may be able to use the tax treaty to obtain any foreign returns or return information that might exist as well.

This type of request will also have to be processed through your U.S. Attorney — there's no way an individual agent or officer can get the information — and through the procedures the Justice and Treasury departments have established for exchanging this information.

Customs Cooperation Agreements also exist between the United States and other countries, which allow for some exchange of information relating to Customs matters on a less formal basis.

LETTERS ROGATORY

A letter rogatory is the traditional means for obtaining information from places, such as Switzerland, that don't like giving it up. A letter rogatory is a formal judicial request for information from abroad. It has to have some legal basis, like a treaty or international agreement, and letters rogatory are technically made from one court to another.

A letter rogatory may be a request for bank information, for records from a business, or to permit the interview of a citizen or resident by American authorities. MLATs bypass this process by skipping the court involvement, keeping the request more on an agency level.

These letters are issued through the Department of Justice, and your U.S. Attorney will have the contacts and the forms. It's not the sort of thing one can just go out and do on his or her own, although you're going to have to be the one to provide the background information.

SUBPOENAS

Most foreign banks and businesses are legally able to laugh at your subpoena, but those who have a business relationship with a customer in the United States *and* have a U.S. branch are supposed to comply with our process. For example, if your subject obtains a letter of credit from the U.S. branch of a Swiss bank, that branch can be subpoenaed to provide details of that transaction.

CHAPTER 19

SOURCES OF INFORMATION

"If a little knowledge is dangerous, where is the man who has so much as to be out of danger?"
T.H. Huxley, "On Elementary Instruction in Physiology"

"I learned just by going around. I know all about Kleenex factories, and all sorts of things."
Princess Anne

Welcome to the Information Age, where you can know too much about Kleenex factories and other things. For an investigator, this is a very challenging time. Never has there been more information available from such a wide variety of sources. The power of computers has revolutionized criminal investigations and will continue to do so in the future.

Nobody can know everything, of course, but as investigators we seek to know the truth of a matter by collecting all of the relevant facts available. There was a time when this involved talking to witnesses and informants, or seizing some evidence. Things have changed. Those techniques are still important to an investigation, but anymore much of the data making up the case file comes from other sources.

There's a story that illustrates the modern investigative process quite nicely, and it may even be true. The story goes that toward the end of his life, when Albert Einstein lived on the campus of Princeton University, he was approached by another faculty member, who engaged Einstein in conversation. After a few minutes, the other instructor asked Einstein for his telephone number to continue the discussion at a later time. To his astonishment, Einstein responded that he did not know his phone number.

"But you're Albert Einstein, the smartest man in the world," he exclaimed.

"My dear sir," Einstein said, "I have no need to know the number when I know how to find it."

This exchange summarizes the nature of the investigative profession. The job of the investigator is not to know all, but to be able to find information when it is needed. Some contemporary investigators may resemble the legendary Sherlock Holmes, able to solve crimes through the process of deduction and an encyclopedic memory. Most, however, will succeed by painstakingly gathering information from a wide assortment of sources.

Knowing where these sources are and what is available from them has become more complex, if only because there are so many more of them out there. Many are open to the public and contain personal information, addresses, telephone numbers, even financial data most people might prefer to keep confidential.

Good luck. Commercial databases have the information, which may also be on the Internet and the World Wide Web. Business computer systems also contain financial, credit, and even health information about individuals. Thousands of government systems hold information on hundreds of millions of people and businesses. And, although the computer is replacing paper files, there are still millions of those "permanent files" we heard about in grade school.

This can all be pretty intimidating if you're trying to hide from the law or a creditor, but, for financial investigators, this wealth of information makes our jobs easier. Some laws have been passed by Congress restricting our ability to just obtain records willy-nilly, the Bank Secrecy Act being one such, but in general the information is there if you know how to find it.

This chapter looks at some sources of information, but we're not going to re-cover the ones already discussed. Bank, real estate, securities, and some business records are discussed elsewhere in this book. In this chapter, we'll examine some of the sources of financial and other information that can provide leads in money laundering cases.

The chapter is divided into sections on the following sources:

- Federal databases and information systems
- Government agencies and records
- Commercial databases and online research
- Credit-related sources
- Business and miscellaneous sources

As much as possible, the sources in this guide relate to money laundering and financial investigation, but they obviously apply to other types of cases as well.

FEDERAL DATABASES AND INFORMATION SYSTEMS

Computers have forever changed the way law enforcement does business. The ability to perform checks; verify identification; and enter, retrieve, and process information has made law enforcement officers more capable of performing their roles. It has also meant that to be effective, today's officer must become familiar with new technology and able to fully exploit its potential.

Federal agencies have been at the forefront of the information explosion, developing a number of computer databases that support law enforcement efforts.

TECS II

The Treasury Enforcement Communications System (TECS) is managed by United States Customs and Border Protection, now a bureau of the Department of Homeland Security. TECS used to contain records of the Customs Service and other Treasury agencies, most of which left for other parts after 9/11. Now, TECS links information from Homeland Security and Treasury, and even from the Bureau of Alcohol, Tobacco, Firearms, and Explosives of the Justice Department.

TECS has several functions, the most important of which for our purposes are communications and data storage and retrieval. TECS terminals are located at all border entry points, where Customs inspectors can use the system to make inquiries about incoming passengers or shipments.

TECS links its sponsoring agencies with other law enforcement systems, including the FBI's National Crime Information Center (NCIC) and the National Law Enforcement Telecommunications System (NLETS). Through these systems, TECS users can make inquires about wanted persons, stolen property, criminal histories, driver's licenses, and motor vehicle registrations. Information about fugitives and alerts for certain persons, vessels, or vehicles are forwarded through TECS to terminal users.

TECS also functions as a data storage and retrieval system, containing millions of records. Many of these records, such as Bank Secrecy Act data, are transferred to TECS by tape from agencies such as IRS that collect the data. Customs information is also included.

An inquiry to TECS can result in important leads in a money laundering case. Is the suspect traveling? Are there large cash transactions? TECS may have the answers.

Among the financial and related data that could be of significance in a money laundering case, TECS has data on a subject's:

- Currency Transaction Reports (CTRs)
- Currency and Monetary Instruments Reports (CMIRs)
- Casino CTRs
- Foreign Bank Account Reports (FBARs)

The system also includes information related to:

- Records of passengers entering the United States by air or sea
- Records of shipments of goods to the United States
- Outbound currency declarations
- Intelligence on smuggling activity
- Open and closed cases by Customs, ATF, IRS CID, and Secret Service
- Private aircraft inspections
- Aircraft, vessels, businesses, and individuals suspected or known to be involved in smuggling activity

Direct access by law enforcement to TECS is restricted, but inquiries can be made through FinCEN or the El Paso Intelligence Center (EPIC), a DEA-sponsored operation that houses representatives from a number of other federal agencies, and through the Bureau of Immigration and Customs Enforcement.

NADDIS

The Narcotics and Dangerous Drugs Information System (NADDIS) is DEA's primary intelligence system. NADDIS contains relevant case data on DEA investigations, as well as identification information for businesses, individuals, telephone numbers, and addresses that are related to DEA cases.

NADDIS contains some information about assets and financial information that is case related. Other DEA systems provide for analysis of events and telephone tolls and contain information about persons registered with DEA to handle controlled substances and to manage DEA cases and seized assets.

Information from NADDIS can be accessed through EPIC.

NCIC

The National Crime Information Center (NCIC) is operated by the FBI and contains information in several indices that can be of use in a financial investigation.

The Interstate Identification Index File contains criminal histories, rap sheets, and fingerprint records. Other files contain information on stolen vehicles, license plates, boats, aircraft, securities, guns, and other property.

NLETS

The National Law Enforcement Telecommunications System holds criminal history, driver's licensing, and motor vehicle registration records. Like NCIC, NLETS is a staple of law enforcement and does not need any additional recommendation or explanation here.

Any money laundering case should begin with checks of these major systems. Remember that a money laundering investigation involves two tracks: proof of the financial transaction or activity *and* proof of the underlying criminal activity. TECS, NADDIS, NCIC, and NLETS provide the background establishing who your subjects are and what they've been doing. You may even get leads to assets from these sources.

GOVERNMENT AGENCIES AND RECORDS

FEDERAL AGENCIES AND RECORDS

One step beyond the federal computer databases is the information maintained by the federal agencies. Some of these agencies are directly involved in law enforcement activities, some with money laundering jurisdictions. Others have regulatory roles, and still others maintain programs such as Social Security, which directly impact the average citizen and generate extensive files on millions of Americans.

Not all of this information will always be useful, but it's out there.

FinCEN

The Treasury Department's Financial Crimes Enforcement Network (FinCEN) was created to support the country's effort against criminal proceeds. FinCEN exists to collect and disseminate information about money laundering and other financial crimes. Here's what FinCEN has to say about its services:

> FinCEN was chartered to provide intelligence and analytical assistance to Federal, state, and local law enforcement agencies nationwide and certain Federal regulatory authorities. This assistance is provided by using law enforcement and financial databases made available to FinCEN through Memoranda of Understanding and by the purchase of commercial database services. Assistance given to law enforcement agencies centers on narcotics/money laundering, financial crimes, fugitives, and information on alleged violators of a wide spectrum of other crimes. We may on occasion return requests to agencies without any work completed if our level of workload is causing a backlog of requests. We will determine which requests to return in such a manner by using our prioritization criteria.
>
> Information we obtain from commercial databases and the Financial Data Base (e.g., Bank Secrecy Act Information) can be disseminated without any further clearance. Information from the law enforcement databases will be cleared with the agency that maintains the database prior to its dissemination. We will also maintain an internal database (FinCEN Database) which will record all requests for information from FinCEN as well as the results of the analytical work performed as a result of the request. The agency responsible for us creating the record will be contacted prior to any dissemination of information from the FinCEN Database. Generally, agencies will not be able to re-disseminate reports received from FinCEN without our approval.
>
> Queries of the various commercial, law enforcement, and financial databases may be based on any of the following identifiers:
>
> Individual name and address;
>
> Nickname/alias;
>
> Social security number/employee identification number;
>
> Driver's license number;
>
> Passport number;
>
> Checking, saving, or other bank account number;
>
> Other identification number (e.g., alien registration number);
>
> Telephone number (residential or business);
>
> Names of officers, directors, or beneficial owners (those owning more than 10% of the stock of a company) of publicly held companies:
>
> Date of arrival/departure and name of airport for passengers on international flights;
>
> Criminal histories maintained in the National Crime Information Center (NCIC) and the National Law Enforcement Telecommunications Network (NLETS);
>
> Subject or associate of current or closed criminal investigation by the United States Customs Service, the USNCB-Interpol, the Bureau of Alcohol, Tobacco and Firearms, the Drug Enforcement Administration, and the United States Postal Inspection Service, the Immigration & Naturalization Service, the United States Secret Service, and the Internal Revenue Service Criminal Investigation Division;
>
> FAA Private Aircraft Enforcement System records;

Records of import/export declarations and related international shipping documents;

Canadian criminal history data and Canadian person, vehicle, driver's license, auto registration, boat, gun, and securities files;

Demographic data on individuals to include: spouse's name; names and dates of birth of other family members; length of residence; dwelling type; names, addresses, and telephone numbers of up to thirty neighbors; forwarding addresses;

Full text of major American newspaper and magazine articles from the past ten years based on a search of a key word or phrase. International newspaper and magazine sources provide coverage of Asia, Canada, Europe, Japan, and the Soviet Union;

Abstracts of Latin American newspaper and magazine articles based on searches of a key word or phrase;

Selected public information, to include judgments, tax liens, bankruptcy actions, notices of default, civil court actions, Uniform Commercial Code filings, corporate records to include registrations with the Secretaries of State, names of officers, directors, and registered agents;

Business financial and narrative information (from domestic and selected international businesses);

Financial database information containing data compiled from the following reports filed with the U.S. Customs Service/Internal Revenue Service:

Currency Transaction Reports

Currency Transaction Reports by Casinos

Currency and Monetary Instrument Reports

Reports of Foreign Bank and Financial Accounts

Suspicious Activity Reports

Index of Nonbank Financial Institutions

Report of Cash Payment Received by Trade or Business;

- Personal history, educational and employment background information on individuals currently or formerly licensed as securities dealers. Information on brokerage firms ownership, management, and any disciplinary action which may have been taken;
- Records of individuals who have purchased United States government securities;
- Records of foreign nationals including companies owning agricultural property in the United States;
- Records reflecting non-immigrant travel to the U.S. and identities of individuals residing in the U.S. on student visas.

This is a wealth of information. A FinCEN request can save a lot of time and trouble. The best news about FinCEN is that it has no independent investigative or enforcement role, so there's no possibility that someone's going to "steal your case." FinCEN does ask that you let them know how the case turns out, which is a small price to pay for the valuable data these folks can provide.

FEDERAL GOVERNMENT DEPARTMENTS

Department of Agriculture

Investigative operations within this agency occur in a number of offices, including the Office of Inspector General (OIG). The *U.S. Forest Service* maintains records on forest, mining, and pasture leasing, and on law enforcement activities in national forests.

The Food and Nutritional Services Agency has records relating to food stamps. These records, which are computerized at the national level and maintained in local offices, include the name, address, and personal histories of persons to whom food stamps are issued. Also of interest, since there have been several money laundering cases involving food stamps and many cases of food stamp fraud, are the department's records relating to businesses that accept food stamps.

Department of the Air Force

The *Office of Special Investigations (OSI)* conducts criminal investigations for the Air Force. This may be a good contact and starting point if one of your subjects is connected with the Air Force, either as a service member or a civilian employee.

Department of the Army

The *Criminal Investigation Division (CID)* is responsible for criminal investigations of Army personnel, with a CID detachment located at major Army bases. Records of criminal investigations are kept at the U.S. Army Counterintelligence Record Facility, Fort Holabird, Maryland.

Department of Commerce

The Commerce Department has some enforcement responsibilities. The *National Marine Fisheries Service* keeps track of vessels fishing in local waters. Also, the Commerce Department tracks import and export prices. This data, along with some provided by shippers to Customs, has been used in the analysis of possible money laundering schemes. Do you need to know the average world price of widgets? The Commerce Department may know or be able to find out.

Department of Defense

Millions of people work for this department, either as civilians or as military personnel. It would not be unusual to encounter DOD personnel in one of your cases.

Records relating to military personnel are kept separately by service, so if you need to know about an individual's military record, you would need to provide a complete name and serial number (Social Security number) to one of the following:

United States Army Finance Center
Indianapolis, IN 46249

Air Force Finance Center
3800 York Street
Denver, CO 80205

Director, Bureau of Supplies and Accounts
Department of the Navy
13th and Euclid Streets
Cleveland, OH 44115
(includes Navy and Marine Corps personnel)

If you need the address of a service member, a DOD Form 2223, Request for Address of Military Personnel, can be prepared and sent to one of the above addresses. These forms take a while to process, so be patient.

If you need information about discharged Army, Navy, or Marine Corps personnel, including their personal and medical histories, a request can be made to:

Military Personnel Records Center, GSA
9700 Page Boulevard
St. Louis, MO 63132

These requests need to include the complete name, service serial number, date and place of birth, dates of service, and branch of service.

The *Defense Investigative Service* conducts the background checks for military and civilian personnel and may have extensive information provided by the individual as part of the security clearance process.

The *Defense Criminal Investigation Service* conducts investigations involving the many contracts that DOD has with private industry.

Department of Health, Education, and Welfare

The *Food and Drug Administration (FDA)* regulates the medical, pharmaceutical, and other health-related industries. FDA also conducts criminal investigations of violations of the food, drug, and cosmetic laws.

The Social Security Administration

The Social Security Administration (SSA) has extensive information about virtually every

American, including his or her work history and contributions to or payments from the Social Security system. Federal law prohibits release of this information, except to IRS for investigation of tax law violations.

One thing that is public is the Social Security Death Index, which contains the names of everyone with a Social Security number whom the SSA knows is dead or for whom death benefits have been paid. If your subject's parents are listed, you may want to check with probate court to see if any inheritances might account for the subject's increase in wealth. If you want to access this information for a case or just check on an ancestor, you can try ssdi.genealogy.rootsweb.com.

Department of Homeland Security

Created after the terrorist attacks in 2001, the Department of Homeland Security (DHS) consolidates the law enforcement, intelligence, and other functions of 22 federal agencies and bureaus. The new agency has broad law enforcement responsibility over many areas of American life, not just those that relate to the war on terror.

U.S. Citizenship and Immigration Services (USCIS) has records relating to all immigrants and aliens legally in the United States, including names, addresses, photographs, relatives, criminal histories, and employment. USCIS also maintains lists of passengers and crews of vessels calling at American ports, including the vessel, date, and point of entry.

Individuals who sponsor an alien for entry into the United States may be required to provide a full financial statement documenting their income and net worth. This information could be helpful in a case involving indirect methods of proving income.

The *U.S. Coast Guard* licenses merchant seamen and officers serving on American registered vessels, as well as the operators of passenger-carrying craft. Commercial fishing boats and larger vessels are also registered with the Coast Guard.

Customs and Border Protection (CBP) consolidated the border inspection and protection functions of the Customs Service and the Immigration and Naturalization Service. CBP records include those items previously mentioned in TECS. CBP issues clearances to individuals who are employed by private businesses in secured areas and will have information about these individuals. A key document in the Customs system is the declaration that airline and shipborne passengers complete before entering the country. Information from these forms is entered into TECS, providing CBP with a record of passenger entries. This form and the CMIR can be useful in a money laundering investigation. The Border Patrol will have information on aliens arrested while attempting to cross the border.

Immigration and Customs Enforcement (ICE) is the largest investigative function in DHS. ICE combined the investigators from the Customs and Immigration services and added officers from the Federal Air Marshals' Service and the Federal Protective Service. ICE is active in money laundering investigations, particularly in cases where international transportation is an element of the scheme. ICE is also interested in cases involving illegal aliens and alien smuggling.

U.S. Secret Service records relate to the agency's role in enforcing federal law relating to counterfeiting, forgery, and access fraud. The Secret Service investigates cases of cellular phone and credit card fraud, both of which come up in financial crimes. The Secret Service also collects intelligence concerning possible threats to those persons it is charged with protecting, including the President, the Vice President, and foreign dignitaries.

Department of the Interior

The *Bureau of Indian Affairs* maintains census records of the Indian tribes, including names, degree of Indian blood, tribe, family background, and current address. Indian gaming casinos are also regulated by the department, which has an *Office of Inspector General* to investigate criminal activity involving Department of the Interior programs.

The *National Park Service* has records on the mining, leasing, pasture, and concessionaire permits that relate to National Park Service properties.

Department of Justice

The *Drug Enforcement Administration (DEA)* has extensive files on criminal activity relating to narcotics and controlled substances. DEA has offices in a number of foreign countries, which can be used to support drug money laundering investigations or financial investigations with international connections. DEA sponsors the El Paso Intelligence Center and participates in the National Drug Intelligence Center (NDIC), both of which have extensive information about drug trafficking activity in the United States and abroad.

All persons and businesses that handle controlled substances, including doctors, pharmacies, wholesalers, manufacturers, and importers, are required to register with DEA.

The *Federal Bureau of Investigation (FBI)* has extensive investigative jurisdiction over federal crimes and an active interest in money laundering matters. In addition to the case-related information that the FBI can bring to a money laundering investigation, the Crime Laboratory, Records Analysis Unit can analyze criminal records, including coded drug or gambling records. This service can be very helpful in tracing funds. FBI legal attaches are stationed overseas in various countries to support FBI operations abroad.

Bureau of Alcohol, Tobacco, Firearms and Explosives keeps records of persons registered as dealers in firearms, as well as those persons possessing certain weapons.

Department of the Navy

Investigations of criminal activity by Navy personnel are conducted by the *Naval Criminal Investigative Service,* which maintains offices at major naval installations.

U.S. Postal Service

The Postal Service can provide information about post office box holders, including their address. This information can be obtained through the local office of the *Postal Inspection Service,* which investigates mail fraud and other postal-related crimes. Mail covers can also be requested through the postal inspectors.

Department of State

The Department of State maintains passport information on anyone with a U.S. passport. In requesting this information, you should provide the name and the date and place of birth of the passport holder. The department also has records of import and export licenses.

Department of the Treasury

The *Alcohol and Tobacco Trade Bureau* has programs relating to the production of alcoholic beverages and tobacco products, and it may have information about persons licensed or registered in these industries (winemaking, for example, or brewing).

The *Office of Foreign Assets Control* maintains lists of persons, businesses, enterprises, and countries that are suspected of involvement in terrorism or narcotics trafficking.

Federal Aviation Administration

The Federal Aviation Administration (FAA) maintains records of ownership of all civil aircraft registered in the United States. These records include information about manufacture, sale, inspection, and maintenance of the aircraft. The sales records include contracts, bills of sale, mortgages, liens, transfers, and modifications.

Information can be obtained directly from the FAA, but certified copies of the documents must be requested in writing from:

Aircraft Registration Branch AC 350
Federal Aviation Administration
Field Box 1082
Oklahoma City, OK 73101

Federal Maritime Commission

The *Division of Investigation* conducts background investigations of persons who apply to the Federal Maritime Commission (FMC) for licenses to engage in the overseas freight forwarding business. Applicants complete a Form FMC-18, which contains the names, addresses, dates and places of birth, and citizenship of all officers, directors, partnership members, or individual proprietors of the business.

Securities and Exchange Commission

The Securities and Exchange Commission (SEC) regulates the securities industry and keeps a record of all corporate registrants of securities offered for public sale, as well as of persons who are licensed to sell these securities.

Small Business Administration

Anyone who has applied for a small business loan from the Small Business Administration (SBA) will have been required to fill out SBA Form 4, which contains extensive information on the applicant and his or her business associates.

Department of Veterans Affairs

The Department of Veterans Affairs (DVA) has records of loans, tuition payments, and insurance payments, as well as information about disability payments made to veterans. This information could be important if your subject claimed the VA as a legitimate source of income.

Court Records

Court files can be bonanzas for the financial investigator. Not only do court cases require a lot of paperwork, but much of the business is conducted under oath. A financial statement submitted in connection with a divorce action or a lawsuit carries extra weight if the maker swears to it.

A number of different courts may have financial or other information for your case. These include:

- U.S. District Court
- U.S. Bankruptcy Court
- U.S. Customs Court
- U.S. Tax Court
- State District or Circuit Courts
- Specialized state courts

U.S. District Court

U.S. District Courts exist in every state, the District of Columbia, Guam, Puerto Rico, and the Virgin Islands. District Courts have exclusive jurisdiction over bankruptcy, maritime and admiralty matters, patents, copyright penalties, claims against foreign states, and any matter in which the United States is a party, as well as all federal crimes.

Court files include all the pleadings and other documents submitted as evidence in the case. These are summarized by a docket sheet listing, in chronological order, all of the actions or events connected with the case. The docket sheet is a good place to start to identify the documents you want to get from the file.

U.S. Bankruptcy Court

All bankruptcies are handled in U.S. Bankruptcy Courts, which keep extensive records. Bankruptcy files contain impressive amounts of financial information, submitted by both the person filing for bankruptcy and creditors who are making claims.

These records may be particularly significant if the subject went bankrupt several years before and is now prospering through some illegal activity, because you will have his or her exact financial condition as of the bankruptcy filing date. Bankruptcy fraud is on the rise in this country, as is the number of filings generally.

U.S. Customs Court

U.S. Customs Court handles disputes about the import duties on merchandise brought into the United States. In court files you will find information about the importer and the merchandise, as well as data about prior business activity.

U.S. Tax Court

Not many tax cases get to U.S. Tax Court, but any dispute that cannot be resolved within IRS is taken to Tax Court. The benefit for criminal investigators is that information that would previously have been zealously protected from disclosure by the Internal Revenue Code is now available to the public in Tax Court records. Due to the long lead time in getting this far, the information may be somewhat dated.

State District or Circuit Courts

No matter which state you're in, some state court will have primary jurisdiction over civil and criminal disputes. As with the federal District Courts (only more so), these court files contain very useful information and lots of it.

One defense frequently raised in money laundering or financial cases is a claim that the source of the income was a lawsuit or settlement. This claim can be quickly checked against the court files. You'll have to know the subject's name to get the data, but court files are almost invariably public record material. This includes such things as financial affidavits, statements filed under penalty of perjury, and disclosures of assets that may have been hidden previously.

Information on state court cases may be held with the clerk of the court or the county clerk's office, depending on the jurisdiction. A good place to start looking is with one of the commercial databases — Lexis-Nexis or ChoicePoint, both of which maintain information about court cases and filings. You should also check on the Internet to see if the records of the court you're interested in are online. In many cases they will be.

Specialized State Courts

Many states have set up specialty courts to handle certain matters within their jurisdiction. Two that are especially useful in financial investigations are Family or Divorce Court and Probate Court.

Family or Divorce Court is a very handy source of financial intelligence. The affidavits filed by both parties, listing income and assets, make a perfect starting point for a net worth case. *And* you may get a bonus — the divorced party may be ready, able, and very willing to testify against your subject. These courts may handle child custody and support questions, which also have financial ramifications.

Probate Courts handle matters relating to estates, wills, and death generally, which may become an issue if your subject is saying he got all his money from his dead Uncle Fred. In fact, you may want to check locally at the beginning of your financial case to see whether the subject's close relatives are deceased (check the Social Security Death Index) and whether they left anything to the subject.

STATE, COUNTY, AND MUNICIPAL GOVERNMENTS

Nobody gets through life anymore without extensive contact with government, most of which happens at the local, county, and state levels. From the day you're born (birth certificate) to the day you die (death certificate and probate and estate tax records) the government's making paper on you. It's kept all over the place, but it's all there somewhere.

The problem is that there is so much information, and, depending on the state, it can be kept by almost any agency. You'll just have to familiarize yourself with the local terrain and make a list of who has what. I recommend that you create a three-ring looseleaf binder that contains not only the names, addresses, and telephone numbers of your local information sources but also copies of the forms they require to request information. Index and cross-reference it. This will save a lot of time down the road. You can add to your binder as new sources are developed, or make changes as the need arises.

With regard to individuals and businesses, the state, county, or municipality keeps the following sorts of records:

- Sales and transfers of real property
- Mortgages, liens, encumbrances, and releases
- Judgments, garnishments, chattel mortgages, mechanics liens, and *lis pendens*
- Real estate tax assessments and payments
- Inheritance and gift tax returns

- Wills, living trusts, and other estate planning documents
- Letters of administration
- Inventories of estates
- Excise and sales tax information
- Conditional sales contracts
- Uniform Commercial Code filings (loans, secured property loans)
- Birth certificates
- Marriage licenses
- Death certificates
- Driver's licenses
- Motor vehicle registrations
- Vessel registrations
- Building and occupancy permits, and related material such as inspection records, building plans, and fire inspections
- School and voter registration
- A fictitious name index (register of corporations)
- Corporate records, including annual filings, reports, and lists of officers and directors
- Business registrations and licenses
- Records for licensing and regulatory boards of regulated industries or professions (e.g., Board of Medical Examiners)
- Individual name changes
- Alcoholic beverage sales
- Public assistance payments
- Worker's compensation claims
- Unemployment compensation records
- Police reports
- Regulatory actions
- Records related to environmental protection and permitting
- Records of water, sewage, and trash service

COMMERCIAL AND ONLINE DATABASES

Commercial Databases

Commercial interests have gotten into the information business in a major way. Several large commercial databases exist to serve those who have a need (and the money to pay) for information. Since much of the information in these commercial databases was originally government information that you could get for free by going to the county courthouse, what you're really buying is the convenience of having all of this information in one location.

You absolutely *cannot* do a financial investigation without having access to one of these commercial services. This is a resource you should be using daily.

These services operate by obtaining massive amounts of data from federal, state, county, and city governments, as well as court files, newspapers, magazines, and other public sources. They then package this data so that it can be retrieved in a name query. The result is nothing short of spectacular. They are not omniscient (yet), but they're coming perilously close.

If you don't have access to Lexis-Nexis, ChoicePoint, or Autotrack, you can obtain the same results by going through FinCEN, which subscribes to these and more.

For purposes of our discussion, we're going to use Lexis-Nexis as an example, although ChoicePoint and Autotrack are comparable. This should not be construed as an endorsement of this service or of its parent company. We can get a good idea about how all of them work by looking at this one.

The book listing all of the data in Lexis-Nexis is almost an inch thick, and even summarizing it is impractical here. We'll look at just a few of the libraries and group files. Here is a sample:

ALLOWN — county real estate records from 40 states plus Washington D.C. and the Virgin Islands

ALLBKT — bankruptcy petitions, discharges, and dismissals from all 50 states

ALLBIZ — state and county business filings from most states, including d/b/a files and a franchise index

ALLDBA — county d/b/a filings from 47 states

ALLJGT — judgments and liens from 38 states

ALLSOS — business filings with Secretaries of State for 45 states

ALLUCC — UCC lien data from all 50 states

ALLVER — 15 state and national verdict reports

B-FIND — business locator listing 11 million U.S. and Canadian public and private companies

DCEASE — Social Security death benefits master list for 48 million individuals

P-FIND — nationwide white pages directory covering 3400 ZIP codes

P-TRAK — nationwide person locator of over 300 million records

The "Assets" library can locate real estate assessment records from 669 counties in 40 states, current deed transfers from another 30 states, FAA aircraft registration records, vessel ownership data from the Coast Guard and Florida, and motor vehicle registration information from Florida and Texas.

Also of extreme interest to financial investigators are the following:

- Real estate ownership information
- Dun & Bradstreet records for 43 million U.S. and overseas companies
- Court dockets in 14 states
- A nationwide telephone number cross-reference directory
- B-FIND, a file that can tell you every business in the system in which your subject has an interest

With half an hour of computer time, nationwide asset searches, business connections, prior addresses, and some financial data can be obtained about virtually anyone in the country. This information may not be completely accurate, but it's a great source for leads.

Does your subject have interests in corporations or real property in another state? Even if you don't know which state, you soon will. When combined with the other databases run by the government, the information in these public sources is even more effective.

In case you were wondering, you're probably in the databases, too.

ONLINE RESEARCH

The Internet is more than just a place to play games and chat with strangers. Nowadays, it seems like everybody's "on the Web." Many businesses and individuals are online, including a growing number of cyberbanks, which have the ability to launder money.

Some of these "banks" actually advertise the ability to convert cash without reports being filed. Since they operate from offshore locations, they are not subject to American regulation and in fact may not be banks at all, in the conventional sense of the word.

Apart from its ability to foster criminal communications, the Web offers research opportunities as well. A company's Web site may contain biographical information about its officers, employees, products, services, and operations. Individuals sometimes post an astounding array of personal material on their Web sites. A number of search engines allow the user to check the entire Web for information about an individual, business, or product.

As a research tool for financial investigators, the Web is only fair. Unlike government or public records, most of the material is self-generated, so the accuracy is not always outstanding. Also, there is so much data on the system that if your subject or business has a common name, your inquiry might receive 100,000 hits, and there may be no way to narrow the search down. Again, I'm not endorsing a particular service or search engine, but Google, Alta Vista, Infoseek, and Yahoo have interesting features. The Internet addresses for these search engines are:

Google	http://www.google.com
Alta Vista	http://www.altavista.com
Infoseek	http://www.infoseek.com
Yahoo	http://www.yahoo.com

There are many others, but these will provide a good start.

One thing to remember when doing research on the Web is that your research may not be confidential. Other computers have the ability to recognize the signature of your computer and to make a record of the inquiry. If you check out a certain business you think may be laundering money, and they see that it's the law calling their Web site, your case may be weakened.

CREDIT-RELATED SOURCES

Credit is the lifeblood of commerce, and it's hard to believe we ever got along without it. Credit is everywhere, and it has become so vital that an entire industry has sprung up to help potential creditors decide whether or not they should give credit to certain people or businesses.

Aside from medical information, there probably isn't any more personal data about people than their credit history. The law recognizes this and has placed restrictions on the availability of this information to law enforcement.

CREDIT AGENCIES OR BUREAUS

Credit bureaus are in the business of collecting financial information, and they've got a lot of it. There are three nationwide credit bureaus that deal with individual credit. These are:

- Equifax
- Trans-Union
- Experian

These agencies collect consumer credit information on individuals, which they provide to their subscribers for a fee. Let's say I'm a car dealer, and I need to know whether a customer is a good credit risk for a $10,000 car. I subscribe to one of the Big Three, which allows me to call the bureau with the information the customer provides on a credit application. I will receive, within a matter of minutes, a credit report describing the customer's history for several years, including payments made, loans, foreclosures, liens, and income and employment data. I'll also get an address, and maybe a rating. All for a couple of bucks.

And the files are enormous. The Big Three have hundreds of millions of files, on virtually everybody in this country who has ever borrowed money, held a credit card, or used credit in any way. They are not supposed to have banking information such as checking or savings account balances, but they may have bank references, and they'll definitely have a record of bank loans.

This information can provide leads to all sorts of assets and financial transactions, but caution is advised. The Fair Credit Reporting Act of 1971 (FCRA) provides for criminal penalties for anyone — including law enforcement officers — who obtains information from a credit agency under false pretenses, as well as for unauthorized disclosure.

This applies to consumer credit reports. These reports can be furnished to law enforcement in response to a court order; a grand jury subpoena or a search warrant will do. Consumers can get their own credit reports, and businesses that subscribe can get the credit reports they're paying for.

Note that the FCRA provides that the credit reporting agency *can* provide limited information to law enforcement without a court order. This data, consisting of *identification information only*, includes the consumer's name, address, places of employment, and former places of employment. (A credit bureau may still ask for a subpoena, even for this limited disclosure.)

OTHER CREDIT REPORTING AGENCIES

Several nationwide businesses offer credit reporting information similar to that of the Big Three, only for business, rather than individuals. The largest of these "rate" businesses as credit risks, evaluating their performance and creditworthiness. The best known is Dun & Bradstreet (D&B).

Is your subject operating from a business front? Is this a shell corporation? If Dun & Bradstreet hasn't heard of it, the company has never applied for credit or been reviewed by D&B.

Remember that D&B is one of the services available on Lexis-Nexis. The rules about disclosure of this type of commercial credit information are less stringent than for the consumer kind.

INTERNATIONAL BUSINESS RATINGS

In checking out a foreign business, it may be possible to check with an international credit reporting agency, the biggest of which is Dun and Bradstreet. The Treasury Department identifies some regional reports/agencies:

- International Credit Reports (Division of Dun & Bradstreet)
- International Market Guides (Central and South America)
- Continental Europe (European businesses in 39 countries)
- Guide to Key British Enterprises
- Synopsis of Dun — Mexico
- Synopsis of Dun — Brazil
- Reference Book — Argentina
- Bradstreet Register
- International Mercantile Claims Division

SPECIALIZED COMMERCIAL CREDIT ORGANIZATIONS

Businesses within certain industries have set up their own commercial credit reporting agencies to service their members. Some of these are:

- United Beverage Bureau (brewers and bottlers of carbonated beverages)
- National Fuel Credit Association (gasoline and oil company credit)
- Jewelers Board of Trade
- Lumberman's Credit Association
- Produce Reporter Company (wholesale and retail growers and processors of perishable fruits and vegetables)
- Packer Produce Mercantile Agency (also fruits and vegetables)
- Paper and Allied Trade Mercantile Agency
- Lyon Furniture Mercantile Agency (dealers in carpet, furniture, floor coverings, upholstery, major home appliances, radios, and televisions, and suppliers to department and general stores)
- American Monument Association (funeral home services, etc.)

The Hooper-Holmes Bureau, Inc., of Morristown, New Jersey, offers several credit-related services to its clients, including a record of credit card abusers and an index of individuals who have filed insurance claims. This "Casualty Index" also has data on anyone who has applied for insurance, as well as a history of prior accidents or sickness claims.

Within a given metropolitan area, smaller credit bureaus or agencies may serve local clients. The files kept by these agencies may include more data on area businesses and individuals than the nationwide services, though obviously not on so many people. You should check in the yellow pages for the names of any such local agencies, or with the National Association of Retail Credit Bureaus.

Trade or professional associations don't have much to do with credit, but they are familiar with their members and the sources of credit within the industry. They could be a good starting point.

OTHER CREDIT ISSUERS

Those who actually issue credit, such as banks, finance companies, credit unions, department stores, and oil companies, maintain files on their credit customers, including applications for credit and payment records.

CREDIT CARD ISSUERS

Now, here's an idea whose time has come. The first credit card was issued in the 1950s for air travel, and the concept sort of "took off" after that. Almost everybody's got at least one card now, and some people have 10, 20, or more.

There's big money in the retail credit business, which is why you get two or three letters a week from banks offering you "preapproved" VISAs or MasterCards. With credit card interest rates as high as 24% per year, the profits are high and the competition for customers is fierce.

There are several different kinds of credit cards, and several names for plastic money. One type of card is the *Travel and Entertainment Card (T&E),* which is how the whole idea got started. T&E cards, such as Diner's Club, Carte Blanche, and American Express, are not as widely accepted as some other cards, and they may not be credit cards in the true sense of the word at all. American Express requires you to pay off your balance each month, something the bank card issuers would prefer you didn't do. These T&E card programs are run independently of each other and have their own administration. You would subpoena the security or legal division of the card issuer for information about a cardholder.

Bank cards are true credit cards in that they really are an extension of credit by a financial institution. Although most banks participate in one or both of the major credit card systems — VISA and MasterCard — the bank, not the system, will be left holding the bag if the cardholder skips out on the payments. For this reason, banks charge a high interest rate for credit balances on their cards, and they obtain extensive credit information from customers. If you get one of those "preapproved" applications in the mail, you can bet the bank has already checked your credit thoroughly.

Credit card records can be a gold mine of information, especially if the subject uses the card extensively. Not only will you know what he or she is spending, but exactly where and when. Patterns of use can be significant in a financial case, especially with respect to defenses in indirect methods cases.

Finding out where your subject has credit cards isn't very difficult. The credit bureau will know, as will everyone else who has credit with the subject. A mail cover will reveal monthly statements mailed by the issuer, and it will also turn up all those unsolicited preapproved credit card offers.

Note that some cards may look like credit cards, even carrying the VISA or MasterCard logo, but they are actually secured or debit cards. A secured card is backed up by funds on deposit with the issuing bank, usually in the form of a certificate of deposit. The cardholder can't withdraw these funds or charge beyond a certain limit, usually 100 to 150% of the deposit.

As almost everybody knows by now, a debit card takes the money directly out of an account at the bank. Debit cards are hugely popular and have already surpassed written checks in terms of the number of transactions conducted each year. Some may have a credit feature, something like overdraft protection on a checking account. This allows the cardholder to charge beyond what's in the bank account. Most are affiliated with one of the credit card issuers — VISA or MasterCard — as well as with the networks linking automatic teller machines, such as Star, Cirrus, and Maestro. These networks allow debit cards to be used worldwide, and the whole concept provides a lot of potential information for an investigator.

Because debit cards are linked directly to a bank account, you can, by getting the bank records, track the subject's purchases, ATM activity, and even whereabouts, often down to the minute. This can lead you to all sorts of assets and spending activity that might be useful in a net worth calculation.

Smart cards are the next step. These cards can be "loaded" with a certain amount of money and then charged down to nothing. Prepaid phone cards are a good example of the principle. The loading takes place at a bank or other location, even an ATM, where you give the bank some real money for the electronic version that goes on the card. Smart cards represent a big money laundering headache, because, in theory at least, you could load up a smart card with an unlimited amount of money and then take it wherever you wanted and unload it. Even better from the money launderer's perspective, someone can load the smart card with cash at multiple ATMs without ever coming into contact with a real person who might ask tough questions.

Credit applications contain good leads to bank accounts and other assets, and credit use and payment histories provide revealing clues in your financial case. Let's say you get 5 years' worth of bank and credit records for your subject. During the first 2 years, the patterns of spending involved extensive use of checks, withdrawal of cash from ATMs, and credit card charges. Then this all stops. Suddenly, your subject isn't doing any of the above. This is a very strong indication that some other source of (untraceable cash) income is now fueling her spending. You may not have direct evidence of this cash spending, but logic tells us (and the jury) that *something* had to have replaced the previous activity.

This type of analysis can also be used in destroying defenses to the net worth, expenditures, and bank deposits methods of proving income. If a person was running a credit balance on his charge cards or maxing them out, this is a fairly good indication that he didn't have some secret cash hoard that explains all of his extravagant cash expenditures or deposits. Jurors understand that if people have that kind of resource, they don't miss a payment or two on their VISA card.

Finally, your subject may have little or no credit background, because she doesn't use it — paying for everything in cash. This, too, can cause inferences to be drawn, because very few people in society today can exist without a credit history.

BUSINESS AND MISCELLANEOUS SOURCES

When you get right down to it, the only reason for being in business is to make money. And as we've already seen, the process of making money automatically generates all sorts of documentation. This documentation is going to be kept in different places and in different forms wherever you go, so it would do no good to try to describe them all here.

Generally speaking, though, certain industries have to keep certain types of records. Sometimes this is the nature of the business, and sometimes government requires it. Federal tax law requires that businesses keep all records for at least 5 years. In regulated industries, where the business needs a special license or permit to operate, the record-keeping requirements may be even more stringent.

Businesses also tend to keep a lot of information about their customers, and this practice has increased recently with the proliferation of "price clubs" and "frequent flyer/buyer/renter/customer" programs. Not only will a business with such a program have each customer's initial application, but the computer will track every purchase by each customer, whether it be airline tickets or groceries. These programs can lay a person's life bare, something that probably wasn't fully considered when they started multiplying like rabbits. Once you know a little about your subject, you will have a better idea about where to go for business information about that person.

Business and Industry

Every business with which your subject comes in contact is a potential source of documentary evidence. This contact may be direct or peripheral, but every single instance represents a chance to break into the paper trail the subject has left behind.

Each segment discussed in this section will be rated on the risk involved in subpoenaing records from that source and the potential value of the records in a financial or money laundering case. Each case is different, as will be your needs in each instance, but some businesses do have more financial data on file.

Travel and Transportation

Hotels have always been good sources of information for investigators. Not only can you get the registration information, but you can also usually get the records of telephone calls made from the room and any services provided to the guests. This is good stuff to have in a conspiracy case or in proving that your subject was somewhere when a financial transaction or an unlawful act took place. Because hotels require credit cards for deposits and reservations, they may be a source for financial information, even if the customer pays in cash. **Subpoena risk:** Low. **Potential:** Medium.

Airlines are another good source, although the information is sometimes difficult to obtain, due to the way it is stored. Frequent flier programs have eased this situation, because the details on each customer are available in one place. You should be able to get information such as the dates of travel, the class, how the ticket was paid for, where the ticket was bought, and whether the passenger was traveling alone or in a group. **Subpoena risk:** Low. **Potential:** Medium.

Travel agencies can be used in money laundering schemes, and they should be approached with caution, as many people who deal with travel agencies have a special relationship with an agent. If the subject uses a travel agency regularly, getting information about his or her travels will be much easier, because almost all agencies keep files on their customers, with all the details about their activity. **Subpoena risk:** High. **Potential:** Medium.

Automobile rental records may be decentralized. Many outlets are franchise operations, although they are connected to a central reservations computer. The larger car rental companies have established frequent renter programs that are linked to various airline programs. All car rental agencies require production of a credit card, which can provide some financial leads. **Subpoena risk:** Low. **Potential:** Low.

Automobile sales records are comprehensive, and since this is a type of business that criminals like to frequent, they can be the source of good leads. Each sale creates a "deal file" that is kept at the dealership. The customer's credit application and usually a credit report will be in this file, along with the records relating to that specific automobile. The service records for the vehicle will also be kept, though not in the deal file.

Caution: If the dealership helped structure the cash purchase of a car, something that isn't exactly unheard of, the personnel there may be implicated, and they may have a relationship with the purchaser. If cash was involved, the receipts and perhaps a Form 8300 will be in the deal file. If it was a cash purchase and no 8300 was filed, you may have a case against someone at the dealership, which could be helpful in getting a cooperative witness against the subject. **Subpoena risk:** Low. **Potential:** High.

Aircraft sales and leasing are big-ticket transactions, documented to the max. As with car dealerships, the risk of collusion between the business and the customer is present. Much of the information you want may be available from the FAA, which should be your first stop. If your subject has an airplane, the records that are at the dealership and at the maintenance facility should be very interesting. **Subpoena risk:** Low. **Potential:** High.

Boat dealers, like aircraft dealers, have information about big-ticket transactions. The bigger the boat, the more money is involved, and boat ownership generates quite a bit of paperwork that can lead to assets. **Subpoena risk:** Low. **Potential:** High.

Communications

Telephone companies have been a source used in criminal investigations since phones had cranks. As phone networks increasingly go digital, the data kept in their computers gets ever more comprehensive. Already records of the long-distance calls your subject makes can be retrieved, but a dialed number recorder (pen register) may be required to get information about local calls. This may be especially true if your subject is using a prepaid phone card and hence no long-distance charges are going onto his or her bill.

Calls to banks may be local, so a pen register might be the ticket if you're looking for leads to assets. Phone records are also useful in identifying associates, business connections, and leads to assets. Because the phone company wants to protect itself from toll fraud, it collects credit information from customers. This type of data is also kept if the customer has a phone card. **Subpoena risk:** Low. **Potential:** Medium.

Cellular telephone companies are better sources than the phone company because their records contain more data about numbers called, numbers calling, and credit information. One problem is that there are so many different companies, identifying which one the subject is using can be a problem. This is especially true since telephone number portability went into effect, letting customers keep the same number when they change service providers. Once you've figured out who the provider is and gotten the records, you may have a lot of calls to go through. Any to real estate agents, stockbrokers, banks, marinas, or the like may be leads to assets. Investigators may have ignored such calls in the past, when they were only worried about calls to associates setting up drug deals. In a money laundering case, such calls may now be the focus. **Subpoena risk:** Low. **Potential:** High.

Long-distance communications providers may be another good source of leads. Life used to be easy before phone company deregulation: You took your subpoena for toll records to one place, and a couple of weeks later, presto — you've got reams of long-distance records. Today, there are any number of long-distance service providers, most of whom call you during dinnertime to get you to switch over to their service. Getting toll call information is much more complicated these days and getting harder all the time. As noted, prepaid phone cards make documenting long-distance calls even more difficult.

One lead you may have is the dialing of long-distance access numbers from the subject's home or cellular telephone. Once these toll-free access numbers are identified, you can subpoena the providers for information about the calls. Toll-free cross-reference directories can provide this information, and several are on the Internet. **Subpoena risk:** Low. **Potential:** Medium.

Public Utilities

Electricity and water customers don't have to undergo the kind of credit checks you'll see at the phone company, but the utility companies will have information about the subject's residence, who's paying the bills, when service began and ended, phone numbers, and possibly prior addresses for the customer. Information from these sources can be useful in rebutting a "cash hoard" defense.

The other way these utility records can be useful is in identifying the residents at a given location, or at least who's paying the utility bills. A subject who is paying the bills on a house he or she ostensibly doesn't own may have tried to conceal an interest in the property. **Subpoena risk:** Low. **Potential:** Low.

Insurance Companies

Life insurance companies can be used in money laundering schemes, especially those operating offshore. Most insurance companies are legitimate, and they keep plenty of records relating to their customers. There's more than one kind of insurance company, remember, and most people deal with more than one. Your subject could have a life insurance policy with one company, homeowner's with another, and car insurance with a third. All can be good sources of information.

A homeowner's policy may provide you with a complete inventory of all personal property in the house. If the subject has a million dollars in jewelry insured, this would be handy to know, and it would turn up on a fur and jewelry floater policy, complete with appraised value and description.

On a historical basis, the insurance company may have descriptions of all the vehicles it has insured for the customer in the past. If your informant says she was driving a Mercedes in 1995, you may not be able to confirm that with DMV, but the insurance company might remember.

Insurance applications contain quite a bit of financial information along with the personal stuff. Most ask the applicant to identify insurance carried with other companies, a good way to find out what other assets are insured elsewhere. Some insurance information is centralized, but much of it will be with the individual agent or office. This could be a problem if that person is very cozy with the subject. **Subpoena risk:** Low. **Potential:** Medium.

Entertainment

Wine, women, and song are the long-term goals of many criminal enterprises. You'll discover, if you haven't already, that most crooks with hot money in their pockets can't spend it fast enough. These are the people who *won't* be the subjects of your money laundering case, because they didn't keep any long enough to launder.

This type of expenditure is hard to document, but it can form a large part of the "lifestyle expenses" in a net worth, bank deposits, or, especially, expenditures method case. Getting the information from the bars, nightclubs, restaurants, and resorts where the money was spent isn't a snap. Informants could be useful in that regard, as well as employees familiar with the subject's spending habits.

Wagering is another activity that has boomed in the last 30 years. Where previously gambling activity was limited to Las Vegas and Atlantic City, casinos are now just about everywhere you look. Some form of gambling is now legal in every state except Utah and Hawaii.

Casinos, and any other wagering operation, for that matter, are money intensive, generating the usual mass of paperwork to track that money. Large cash transactions — the kind most admired by casino operators — are supposed to be reported to IRS on a Currency Transaction Report for Casino (CTRC). Any transaction over $10,000 is required to be reported, including the purchase of chips, cashing in of chips, and accumulated cash wagers.

Smaller casinos report these transactions on Form 8300. All of them are also supposed to report gaming payouts or winnings to IRS on a Form 1099W, once the winnings reach a certain level. The CTRCs are available to investigators in the FinCEN, TECS, or IRS databases, but the 1099s are tax information and cannot be disclosed without a court order.

The casinos have very good records, which they will provide if subpoenaed. They have credit applications and reports; records of "comps" (the perks given to high-rolling gamblers); the totals won, lost, and bet by these people; and records of any collection efforts made on the casino's behalf.

Casinos are very useful as money laundering devices. With a little planning, a casino can provide a perfect integration mechanism for the launderer. "I won it in Las Vegas" is a perfect explanation for a large sum of cash or the possession of a valuable asset. If the casino backs up that story, the launderer is halfway home. One very simple scheme involves depositing cash with a casino cashier and then withdrawing the money in the form of a check. Casinos will even write the checks on accounts they have in innocuous-sounding names, in case you *don't* want it to look like the money came from gambling.

In this type of scheme, you'll have to go deeper into the casino's records to trace the "winnings" back to the source. More often than not, you'll discover that the subject's winnings are more than offset by losses — which is how Las Vegas got to be so glittery in the first place. **Subpoena risk:** Low. **Potential:** High.

MISCELLANEOUS SOURCES

The Library

Don't overlook the library in your search for information. Not only are libraries full of all sorts of interesting facts, they're specifically organized to get those facts to their customers — for free.

Most drug traffickers are not listed in *Who's Who* or *The Thomas Register of American Manufacturers*. These and other directories that you can find at the library can still be a valuable source of information to the financial investigator. How so, you may ask, if the crook isn't listed?

The really serious money launderer is going to attempt to conceal his or her ill-gotten gains beneath some sort of business facade, either foreign or domestic. Perhaps the crook will create a "front" corporation or even buy an existing business concern. To make the front look more real, the launderer may have the business engage in actual commerce with others in the industry.

Whenever business is done, competitors, suppliers, and customers take an active interest.

Word travels quickly, and executives in the same industry or area can often furnish timely, accurate intelligence about a new entrant in their field. "Yeah, I know them. All new trucks, lots of traffic from the warehouse. Funny thing, nobody I know buys his stuff." Or: "I made a sales call on the place right after they opened up. Place was deserted, just a secretary and the guy in charge. He didn't seem to know what I was talking about." The directories can help the investigator find this kind of witness.

There are several types of business publications, each with a different purpose. They include the following:

- *Annual reports* are produced by the companies themselves and are the primary sources of public information on a corporation or business.
- *Directories* are publications that list companies, products, and other information, classified by industry, name, product, or area of operation.
- *Investment material* is compiled by services and provides comprehensive information on the historical background and performance of companies, including their financial status, profitability, and other data of interest to an investor.
- *Business periodicals* are publications with a primary focus on business and economics. These may be general and widely known, such as *The Wall Street Journal;* limited in scope, such as *Aviation Week and Space Technology;* or local, such as the *Bay Area Investor.*
- *Miscellaneous publications* include indexes, rate and data services, audit guides, law reporters, and guidebooks.

All of these publications can be found in the library, and they can prove to be good sources of leads. Larger libraries will also have foreign and out-of-state directories or publications. These can be useful if your subject has a presence overseas or in another state.

Newspapers

Local newspapers keep copies of back issues and clippings on certain topics on file in the newspaper morgue. Quite a few will also sell you a copy of an original photograph that has run in the paper. The newspaper may have an index to its articles, cross-referenced by the names of individuals who appear in the stories, and this index should also be available at a public library, which will also have copies of the newspaper on file, usually in microform.

Many papers are publishing on the Internet now, and the names of people who are mentioned in the articles can be retrieved in a search of the Web. As noted, however, if your subject has a common name, there may be tens or even hundreds of thousands of "hits," which could take a little time to review.

One way of narrowing this search down is to see if your paper's Web site has a search engine and use it to search only that site for the name you're checking. You may wind up with the interesting information that your subject shot a hole in one or wrote a letter to the editor, but there may be more relevant news as well.

PUTTING YOUR RESOURCE GUIDE TOGETHER

An investigator is as good as his or her sources. The more you have, and the better you're able to mine them, the tighter your cases will be. We talked earlier about developing a resource guide for your area. Ideally, this book should contain the name of every source you could possibly encounter, with indexes and cross-referencing. In fact, you're always going to be finding out about some new source of information or encountering some new problem, which is part of what makes criminal investigation so interesting: different day, new challenge.

Divide your three-ring binder into sections by type of information you're cataloguing (banks, real estate, state government, credit, education, etc.). You can get contact information from the phone book, but *always* get a business card when you serve a subpoena or otherwise contact someone for information. Leave one of yours, too, because you never know.

Put the business card in the book, or at least make sure the information about that business is included. You'll also want to know more about the business and how to get information from it, so take the opportunity to ask:

- What types of information does the agency maintain on individuals? Businesses? Others?
- Is the information centralized in town? Is it maintained at other sites?
- How is the information kept? In files? On a computer?
- Is there a central index to information? How is information indexed (name, address, Social Security number, agency identifier)?
- Who is the principal point of contact for information requests (name and position, phone number, address)?
- If we obtained a subpoena for information from your agency concerning an individual or business, what information would be available, and how should the subpoena be worded to (*a*) get the right information and (*b*) minimize the impact on your agency?
- What information is available to the public? To law enforcement? Upon subpoena?
- Bottom line: What information do you have that I might be able to use, and how do I get it?

In financial investigations, you'll wind up contacting the same people often, because, for example, they are records custodians at large banks. For these folks, you'll also want to include a note about how their institutions like to fill subpoena requests. Some banks want to do all the research before responding, while others like to break it up and send it out as they get it. If you can accommodate their needs and still get the job done, it's a good idea to keep these people happy.

If you have a special contact, such as a credit bureau employee who will give you the identification information she can legally provide without a subpoena, make sure that name is in the book. Otherwise you'll be talking to the guy who says, "We have to have a court order."

Financial information can be found in some unusual places, so it pays to keep an open mind about your contacts with potential sources. Whatever you can do to make it easier for them to provide the information should be done. If they are entitled to payment for the records, make sure they get paid promptly. If you can reduce the size of your request without compromising the need for the information, make it so. In the long run, this consideration will pay off in information dividends.

In sum, if you can't know everything, it's best to know where to find out. Financial information is everywhere, in overwhelming quantities, but you have to be looking for it. Developing sources should involve the same sort of effort you would use to develop informants, because the information they provide is equally important to a money laundering case.

CHAPTER 20

BASIC MONEY LAUNDERING SCHEMES

"The finest plans have always been spoiled by the littleness of those that should carry them out."
Bertolt Brecht, *Mother Courage*

Well, we've already seen that money can assume any form, limited only by the imagination. We've examined the enormous complexity of the world's financial system and can now appreciate how easy it would be to make a few billion dollars here and there disappear. Given these incredible parameters, how are we ever going to be able to catalogue all of the various money laundering schemes and operations?

We probably can't. Not in this space, anyway. The best we're going to be able to do is describe some of the more popular, explain why they are preferred, and outline some of their weaknesses. Many of the operations have common elements or characteristics that make them more easily identifiable as money laundering schemes. The simpler schemes are also building blocks for the more complex operations. The most convoluted, detailed scam in history can still be broken down into its component parts.

The concept of components is a good one. Money laundering schemes are a lot like computer systems, made with many individual parts and pieces, all designed to work together to process information. The most complicated money laundering schemes in history are ones that the organizers loaded up with all sorts of fancy component elements, like Swiss bank accounts, letters of credit, shell corporations, nominees, or front businesses. Just looking at the big picture, we've got little chance of unraveling such a rat's nest, but if we isolate these components, addressing them as separate parts of the whole system, investigators may be able to reduce the problem to a manageable size.

Two items of good news: The vast majority of money laundering schemes are neither very complex nor particularly well run. After all, the vast majority of criminals don't have an MBA from Harvard or, for that matter, an MBA from anywhere else. True, the really rich crooks (most of whom also don't have a Harvard degree, but do have enough money to hire somebody with one) can afford good advice and fiendishly complicated plans. We'll show you how these people are vulnerable, too, because although you don't run into many like them, they are the pot of gold at the end of the money laundering rainbow.

Also, although the good money launderers are fully capable of throwing all sorts of smoke and mirrors at us, they've really only got one complete scam. Once we understand that one, we've just got to get a handle on whichever little tricks are being used this week to complete the illusion. You'll recall from our stage magician analogy that the performer uses a number of different props to achieve an illusion, but once the audience understands how those props work, there's precious little mystery left, and no magic at all. This is how the various money laundering schemes should be viewed.

We'll look at three schemes in this chapter, including a description of each scheme, using an actual case as an example, and a chart that

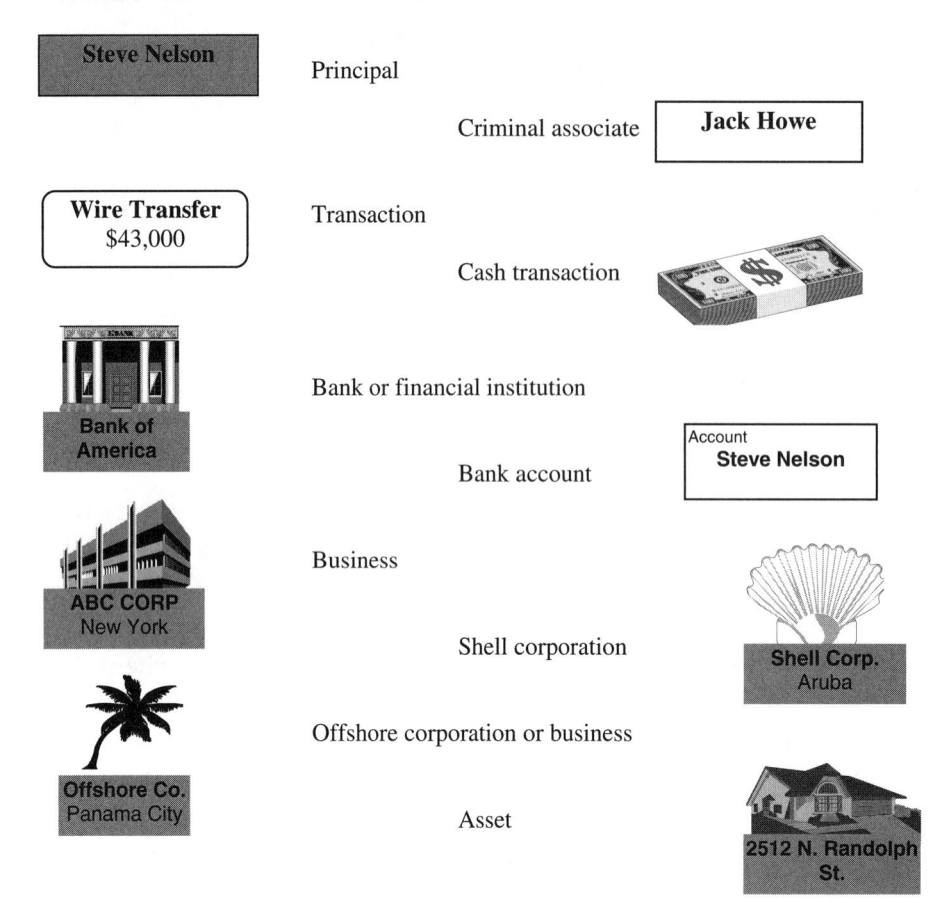

Figure 20.1 *Key to graphics.*

hopefully clarifies the operation. We will also note the vulnerabilities or weaknesses of each scheme and list some tip-offs that might help in either identifying or investigating each scheme. Figure 20.1 provides a key to the graphics used in the charts.

USE OF A NOMINEE

If the use of a nominee is the extent of the money laundering scheme, you should be finished with the case by lunch. Seriously, there's not much to most nominee schemes, yet they are very popular with crooks. (Nominees are elements in more complex scams.)

A *nominee* is anyone appointed to fill a particular post or designated to perform certain acts or functions. In the case of a money laundering operation, assets such as cars, bank accounts, or even real property may be placed in the name of a nominee.

Nominees almost invariably have several common characteristics. Nominees are:

- Almost always real, as opposed to just being an alias or a name on a document
- Usually witting; that is, aware that they are being used in this capacity
- Generally trusted by the person nominating them, something you'd expect since they're essentially being given control over the money or asset
- Close enough in proximity that they can communicate — receive instructions and execute tasks
- Often relatives, close friends, or associates in the illegal activity

OBJECTIVES

The main objective in the use of a nominee is concealment, so this subterfuge mostly applies to the layering stage of the money laundering cycle. Although nominees can be used to conduct transactions, their chief value is in holding assets in such a way that the true ownership is concealed.

ADVANTAGES AND DISADVANTAGES

From the launderer's point of view, the principal advantage to a nominee-based scheme is that a cursory check of the subject reveals that he or she has no assets under his or her name. Without any further information, such as the names of the nominees, the investigator won't be able to connect assets to a specific individual.

The primary disadvantage of the scheme is that it is superficial. Once penetrated, nominee schemes tend to fall apart fairly quickly. Since the principal often uses the assets, he or she can usually be connected with them, and the nominees identified. Also, these schemes don't really get rid of heat so much as they transfer it. Now it is the nominee who has the explaining to do.

SPECIAL SITUATIONS

In some situations, the use of a nominee can be a case stopper. This is especially true when the nominee is an attorney in a country where secrecy in this type of relationship is mandated by law. For example, your investigation discloses that the owner of an asset is a Panamanian attorney. You may contact this person for information, but he or she is not going to tell you who the client is, if anyone.

Another type of nominee is a person selected to serve as an officer or director of a corporation, especially in an offshore location such as the Bahamas. These people are selected by a management company or attorney and may not be aware of the money laundering purpose behind the corporation they now serve.

Case Example

Steve Nelson, a cocaine trafficker, had a not uncommon desire to enjoy the fruits of his illegal labors. His business accumulated considerable profits, over and above the amount needed to pay his supplier for the next shipment. He decided to spend some of the money on a luxury automobile, specifically a Porsche 911. (Coincidentally, one that previously belonged to a rather famous and very attractive television actress.)

At the dealership, Nelson produced the asking amount for the car, $43,000 in cash, in a duffel bag. The finance manager told Nelson that large cash transactions had to be reported to IRS. This was certainly attention Steve didn't need, so he instructed the manager to title the vehicle in the name of his associate, Jack Howe. All of the paperwork for the transaction, including the IRS Form 8300 and the registration, was prepared in Howe's name. If anyone ran a computer check on the Porsche, Howe's name would appear as the registered and legal owner of the car.

Nelson used this same scheme to purchase at least four other vehicles, although Howe was not the nominee for all of those cars. (In this example, Nelson could also have used nominees to hold bank accounts or to conduct financial transactions for him.) See Figure 20.2.

DOCUMENTATION

Several records accompany the transaction described in the case example. The Form 8300, Report of Currency Received in a Trade or Business, will contain a lot of information, especially if it is properly prepared. Note that Section III of this document describes the person on whose behalf the transaction was conducted. If Nelson's name doesn't appear in this section, the dealership could be guilty of filing a false report.

The other documents that always accompany a nominee scheme are the ownership and title documents, registrations, and perhaps tax records. If real property is involved, the documentation will be extensive, and much of it will be notarized. Nominees often have to literally

Money Laundering Scheme - USE OF A NOMINEE

Steve Nelson

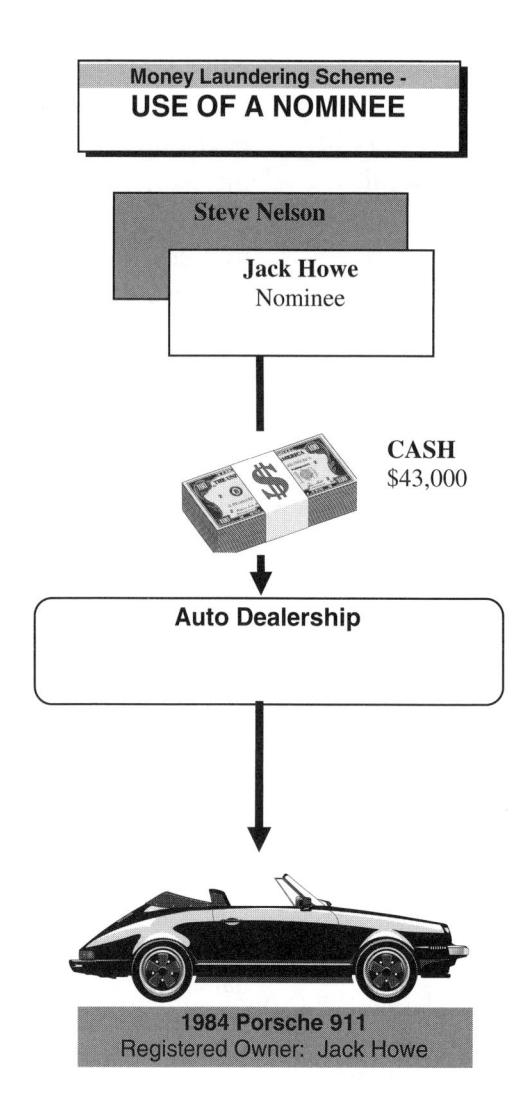

Jack Howe
Nominee

CASH
$43,000

Auto Dealership

1984 Porsche 911
Registered Owner: Jack Howe

Note: All of the names used in this example are completely fictitious. Any resemblance to any person, living or dead, is entirely coincidental.

Figure 20.2 Use of a nominee.

sign their lives away to get the job, and their footprints are all over every transaction.

The secondary documentation is equally critical. Okay, Howe is the registered owner of the car, but who buys the gas? Who pays the insurance premiums? Who takes it to the Porsche dealership for servicing or has the windows tinted? If Nelson lives in an apartment complex, is the car registered there under his name?

INVESTIGATION OF A NOMINEE SCHEME

The vulnerability in a scheme involving a nominee *is* the nominee. This person has been selected on the basis of trust and affiliation and may be a criminal associate of the principal. In any case, it is virtually impossible to be a nominee in a money laundering operation without knowing about the object of the scheme (concealment). Because so many records are made in connection with the purchase and use of an asset, it is also difficult for a nominee to act without falsifying some of these records, often another offense.

SOURCES OF INFORMATION

The nominee is a good potential source of information. Often this person has been poked way out front by the principal, creating all sorts of tax and other criminal liabilities. Only the flimsiest of covers protects many nominees, who find themselves completely at a loss to explain just how they came by such a valuable asset.

Documents, especially secondary documents, are also important. All assets require maintenance or support, activities that generate more paper. Investigators who have done forfeiture cases may already be familiar with the process of establishing true ownership. Some of the documents that might prove useful are the following:

- Bank records: Who is making payments for the asset? Has anyone borrowed against the asset? Does the principal list the asset on loan applications?
- Tax records: Who pays the taxes owing on the property?
- Business records: In the case of a vehicle, who performs the maintenance, and how is it paid for? For real property, who pays the utility bills?

Another set of questions can be asked about the nominee. Why, for example, if Mr. Howe owns a Porsche, is he driving around in an old Toyota? Demonstrating that the nominee does not have the resources to acquire an asset on his or her own can be effective evidence of nominee status. Income tax records may be valuable in this regard, as well as loan applications and other financial statements.

Physical surveillance is useful in establishing nominee status. If surveillance verifies that Howe always drives the old Toyota and never drives the Porsche, but Nelson does just the reverse, this is fairly indicative of who owns what.

SPECIAL SITUATIONS

When the nominee is one of those Panamanian attorneys or somebody equally difficult to deal with, your main focus will be indirectly showing the connection between the principal and the asset or transaction. Since you won't be getting much cooperation from the nominee, you'll need some evidence that will allow the jury to reach a conclusion. You might also be looking for evidence of payments by the principal to the nominee for services rendered.

Note: The terms, "straw," "straw owner," and "straw man" are sometimes used to describe nominees and their transactions. A "straw purchase" is one in which the true purchaser is not known or publicly identified.

POTENTIAL VIOLATIONS

- 18 USC 1956 — Money laundering
- 18 USC 1956 (h) — Money laundering conspiracy
- 26 USC 6050I — Causing the car dealership to file a false Form 8300
- 31 USC 5331 — Causing the car dealership to file a false Form 8300
- 18 USC 371 — Conspiracy
- 18 USC 1001 — False statement

SIMPLE BUSINESS COVER

One step beyond a nominee, in terms of effort and expense, is the creation of a business "front." As is the case with a nominee, the principal is attempting to remove him- or herself one step from the activity generating the dirty money. A business has several advantages over an individual or a nominee.

First, a business is expected to generate revenue; this might allow illegally acquired money to blend in with ordinary-appearing bank deposits. Second, the principal can establish the business in such a way that he or she still controls it; in the case of a corporation, the principal could be the sole or majority stockholder. Third, as with the nominee, assets can be held in the business name, not the principal's, so a cursory asset check (real estate or motor vehicles, for example) would not disclose the principal's interest.

The business cover might be a corporation, a partnership, or even a sole proprietorship. In some cases, the principal doesn't even go through the motions of establishing a bona fide business entity, just uses a name. As an added benefit, the business "front" may also be used as a headquarters or a place where the illegal activities can be conducted. (For example, prostitution, gambling, narcotics, and receiving stolen property can all be conducted from a bar owned by the principal.) For additional layering or insulation, the principal could use a nominee as the owner, president, or general partner in the business, making identification more difficult.

To be useful in the placement stage of a money laundering scheme, the business should have a couple of attributes. It is usually an enterprise that by its nature deals in cash; illegal funds can better be concealed in the cash flow. Given a choice between dealing in goods or services, a service business would be preferable, because who's to say how many DVDs or parking spaces you *really* rented? Also, most business fronts tend to employ few people; there's no point in having a lot of employees hanging around watching you launder money, after all.

Some types of businesses launderers have found useful as business fronts include:

- Bars and nightclubs
- Restaurants
- Fast food sales
- Convenience stores
- Videocassette rentals
- Pawn shops
- Parking lots
- Theaters, adult movie/video stores
- Car washes
- Small grocery stores
- Used car lots
- Bail bond companies
- Laundries, laundromats, dry cleaners
- Travel agencies
- Currency exchanges
- Money transmitters
- Motels and hotels
- Equipment rentals

Note that all of these businesses generally deal in cash and can be operated with a few people. Some are regulated or require a license, which may be a drawback from the money launderer's perspective.

Businesses are obviously used in the layering and integration stages of money laundering operations as well, although these entities will probably have other characteristics. There is not so great a need to deal with cash, for one thing, and concealment of the operators may be more important to those setting up the scam.

Some businesses are better than others. Import–export companies are popular, as are shipping companies and manufacturers.

Case Example

Jan and Nadia Brown were very happily married and quite successful in their joint career as methamphetamine traffickers. Working together, they had accumulated over $750,000 in cash before they decided that some steps should be taken to invest this money against the time they might have to get out of the drug business.

Nadia, who was the brains of this particular outfit, knew that sooner or later, someone was going to wonder how they had gotten so wealthy without having been employed. Furthermore, she realized that nothing good lasts forever, and she wanted to make provisions for life after crank. In short, this money should be laundered.

Nadia's scheme was very simple. She started by establishing a business, JNB Equipment Leasing, Inc., a domestic corporation. The attorney who had handled Jan's last possession case drew up all the papers. Jan, who in the distant past had been employed in construction, contacted some contractors he remembered and purchased a number of items of equipment, including two dump trucks, two dump trailers, two flatbed trailers, two backhoes, two small bulldozers, some compressors, welding machines, and some fairly expensive specialty tools. Many of the larger items were bought used, and only the two trucks and four trailers were

**Money Laundering Scheme -
BUSINESS COVER or
"FRONT"**

Jan and Nadia Brown
Drug Trafficking

CASH
$160,000

JNB EQUIPMENT LEASING, INC.

Purchase Assets
$160,000

Construction Equipment
Owner: JNB Equipment Leasing, Inc.

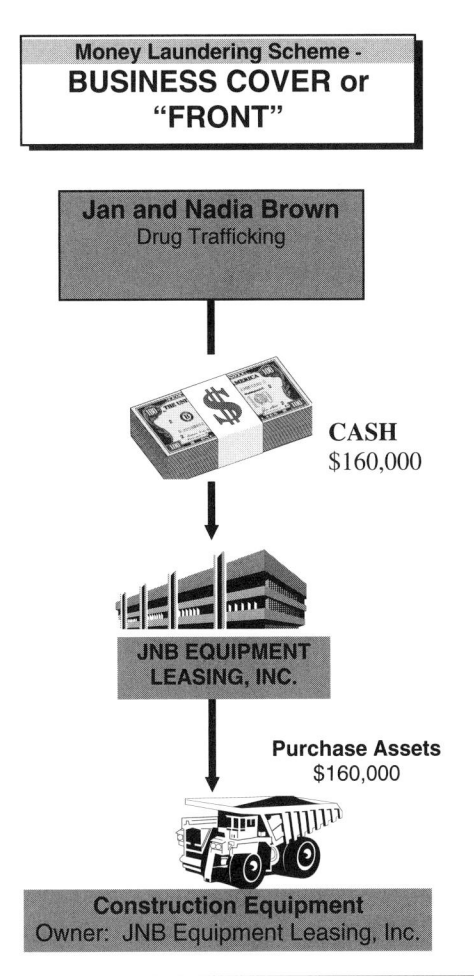

Note: All of the names used in this example are completely fictitious. Any resemblance to any business, bank, or person, living or dead, is entirely coincidental.

Figure 20.3 Business cover or "front."

required to be registered as motor vehicles. These were titled in the company name. Jan spent $160,000 on all the equipment.

There was quite a bit of construction going on in the area, so the equipment was in demand with contractors, especially since it was rented out at rates below the industry average. Cash is frequently used in the construction business, with "under the table" payments for wages and rentals not uncommon. On the books of the corporation, Nadia recorded many cash rentals, and she even cooked up an invoice scam with a couple of customers in which they pretended to rent equipment and she pretended to charge them. (We'll look at invoice scams later.)

At the end of the year, Nadia filed a corporate tax return for JNB Equipment Leasing. She and her husband were also able to file their own return (for a change), reporting their salaries from JNB as income. See Figure 20.3.

DOCUMENTATION

The scheme described in the case example generated a lot of business records, many of which were maintained on a personal computer. Just as a completely legitimate business would have to keep records for tax and business purposes, so does a business front for money laundering. In addition to those records maintained by JNB,

> **Example:** A hot dog stand suspected of being a front for money laundering is depositing $3,000 daily into an account at a local bank.
>
> | Transaction | Documentation |
> |---|---|
> | -Hot dog stand buys 300 hot dogs per day | -Purchase orders, invoices, checks, journal and ledger entries |
> | -Hot dogs are sold daily for $3.00 each | -Cash register tape, sales journal |
> | -Sales receipts are deposited in bank | -Deposit tickets, bank statements |
>
> Internal controls and documents can account for bank deposits of around $900 per day on hot dog sales. There is no way that this process will support deposits of $3,000 daily.

Figure 20.4 *Audit of a business front.*

there are also records of the customers who are renting the equipment.

Other records on file include the corporate filings at the Secretary of State's office, as well as corporate tax returns.

SPECIAL SITUATIONS

As with nominees, businesses located in offshore jurisdictions can be used as fronts. Access to information about a company incorporated in the Bahamas, Panama, Liechtenstein, and a number of other countries can be very difficult to obtain. Some countries provide for secrecy for corporate officers, directors, and shareholders. Domestic corporations, partnerships, and sole proprietorships will be easier nuts to crack.

INVESTIGATION OF A BUSINESS FRONT

Is this business a going concern or is it a front for something else? Even a business that is legally constituted, properly registered, and compliant with tax and business laws can be a cover for money laundering. How are we going to find out what's really going on?

The best way is to audit the business exactly as a tax examiner or accountant would do. Audits are structured to look for certain things and then measure those things against accounting standards. The auditor is looking for specific items, one of which is whether transactions reported actually occurred. Many business fronts report sales that never really took place in order to infiltrate the dirty money in with the regular deposits.

An audit easily uncovers this type of deception. All businesses conduct their operations via a *process*. While the process may contain some features unique to the business or industry, much of the process is supposed to be controlled by certain standard procedures. Sales, for example, are handled and documented in a consistent pattern that creates a uniform accounting path. The auditor looks at this process and the *internal controls* ruling it, quickly establishing which transactions took place off the path. See Figure 20.4.

SOURCES OF INFORMATION

Business records from the suspect company may provide important clues. Depending on the type of business (corporation, partnership, sole proprietorship), these records may be available by subpoena. A search warrant might be a better approach, with better assurance that the records are going to be there when you look for them. Also valuable are the records of vendors, suppliers, customers, and others doing business with the subject organization.

Government records, such as corporate filings, business license or registration files, and tax records (sales or income), can be significant.

Bank records contain all sorts of information about the business, especially if the business checking account is active or the business has applied for a loan.

Others in the industry keep track of their competition. These people may know whether something fishy is going on long before the smell reaches our noses. If the business was acquired from someone else, the former owner will know all about the market, customers, suppliers, overhead, and cash flow.

POTENTIAL VIOLATIONS

- 18 USC 1956
- 18 USC 1957

SIMPLE BANKING OPERATION

Along with the first two operations we've examined, the simple banking operation is one of the building blocks of many more complicated money laundering schemes. Banks are one of the best ways to change the form of the dirty money in the placement stage of the money laundering cycle. If the launderer can find a way to move the currency into or through a bank, one step has been taken toward the ultimate goal of cleaning the cash.

As we've noted previously, this movement from the cash transaction system to the financial or business transaction system is an extremely vulnerable moment for the criminal. Cash reporting requirements and federal scrutiny of cash transactions increase the exposure.

The simpler banking operations are placement oriented. Get the money on deposit. Buy cashier's checks. Change the money from cash to something else. It gets more complicated later on, and banks can certainly help with some of the launderer's layering or integration problems, but at this level, we just want to use a bank the way most honest people do.

The first step is to open an account. It's not illegal to have a bank account, so it may be opened in the principal's name, or perhaps in the name of a nominee or a business front. The next step is to actually conduct transactions. Money launderers like to make these look as normal as possible, but this may not be practical, depending on how much cash is involved. If we're talking gunny sacks, the launderer may have to use other measures to avoid the cash reporting requirements that accompany large transactions. (See Figure 20.5.)

Some of these measures could include buying the cooperation of a bank employee, spreading the deposits around to multiple branches, using associates to make numerous smaller deposits (known as "smurfing") or perhaps opening multiple accounts using different names, nominees, or businesses.

The primary objective is always to conduct the cash transactions with the least amount of official attention. Once this goal is achieved, the money in its new form can be used in a variety of ways to suit the principal.

Banks got to be the cornerstone of the financial system by providing a wide array of services. Once the launderer has opted to use banks in the scheme, all of those services become available, just as they would for the regular customer.

SPECIAL SITUATIONS

Most of the common wrinkles on bank-related scams involve some effort to get the cash into the bank without generating one of those Currency Transaction Reports (CTRs). To this end, the money may be "smurfed" or structured into smaller transactions, spread out among a number of associates.

Other variations on this line include somehow gaining the cooperation of a bank employee, getting on the exempt transactions list, or concealing deposits among those of a business. Nominees or businesses can be used to conduct transactions or hold accounts.

To process more money, the launderer would only have to add more accounts and/or more banks. The use of nominees complicates the process of identifying accounts and connecting them to the principal. Another complication involves the transfer of funds back and forth within the various accounts. This process, known as "churning," can greatly confuse a bank deposits analysis. Finally, the purchase of instruments such as cashier's checks are separate transactions from the cash deposits. You can buy these and the transactions won't show up in bank correspondence or in the customer's account records.

Case Example

When last we saw her, Nadia was taking an organized approach to laundering the family

Money Laundering Scheme - SIMPLE BANKING SCHEME

Jan and Nadia Brown — Drug Trafficking

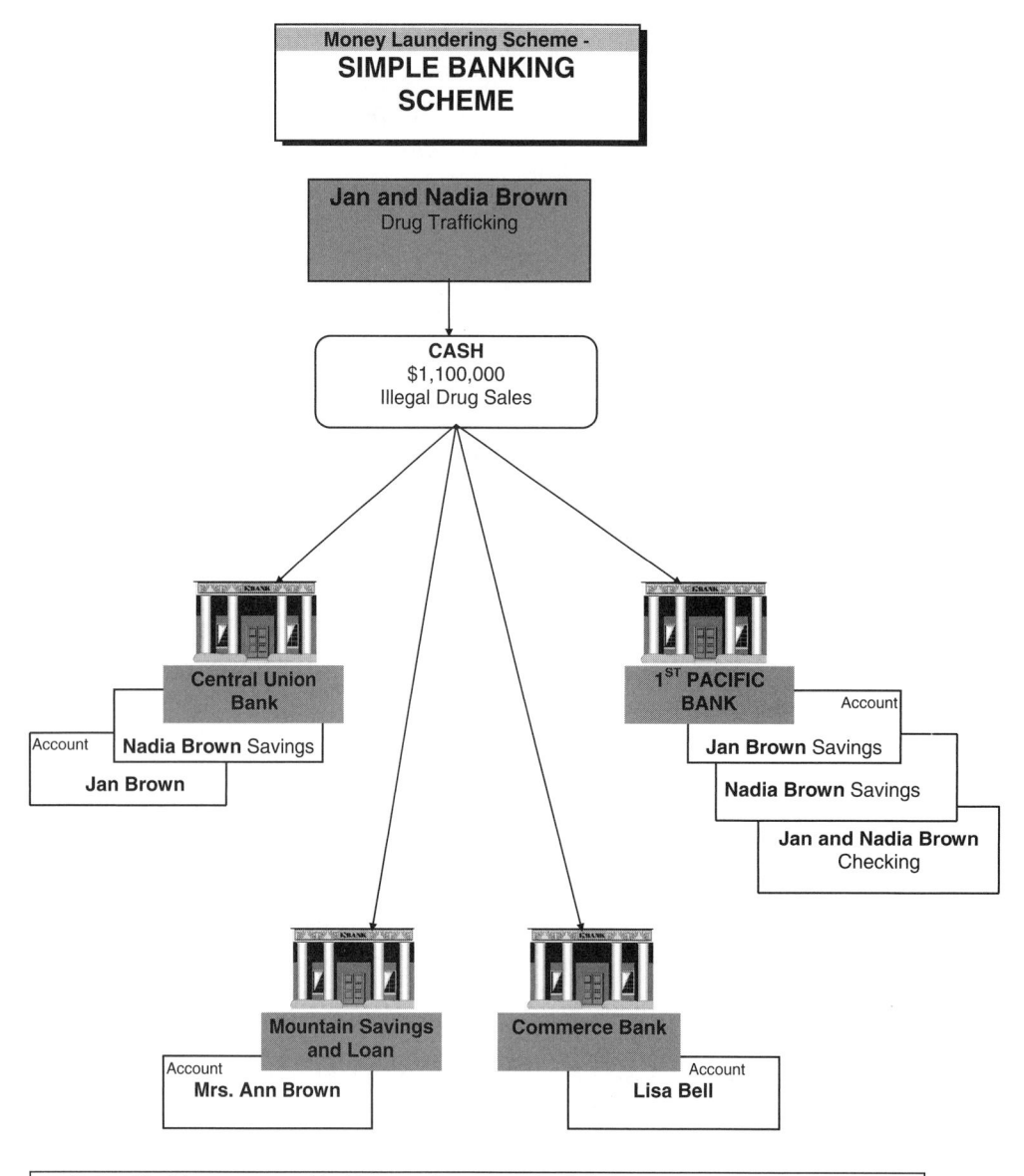

CASH $1,100,000 Illegal Drug Sales

- **Central Union Bank**
  - Account: Nadia Brown Savings
  - Jan Brown
- **1ST PACIFIC BANK**
  - Account: Jan Brown Savings
  - Nadia Brown Savings
  - Jan and Nadia Brown Checking
- **Mountain Savings and Loan**
  - Account: Mrs. Ann Brown
- **Commerce Bank**
  - Account: Lisa Bell

Note: All of the names used in this example are completely fictitious. Any resemblance to any business, bank, or person, living or dead, is entirely coincidental.

Figure 20.5 Placement problem.

fortune. She had already set up a profitable business front, but she knew that it would be necessary to use the services of a bank to really get the money clean. There are a lot of businesses that simply don't take cash, and there are others who will, but look funny at you when you walk in with a stack of hundreds. Nadia wanted to write checks. The only time people look funny at you when you write a check is if there isn't enough money in the account. Nadia knew this wasn't going to be a problem.

She started off small, opening a joint checking account at a nearby branch of a large bank, First Pacific. A savings account for herself, and another for Jan, both at First Pacific, followed. She went to another bank, Central Union Bank, to open a checking account under her name. Eventually, a second checking account was opened at Central Union under Jan's name.

Fearing to keep all of the accounts in names that could be traced directly back to her, Nadia opened accounts in the names of two trusted relatives, her sister and Jan's mother. These were opened at Commerce Bank and Mountain Savings and Loan. Correspondence from these banks was mailed to a post office box rented by Nadia, but the correspondence for all the other accounts went directly to Jan and Nadia's house.

At this point, Nadia had seven different bank accounts at four different banks. By making deposits of $3,000 to $4,000 daily to each account, Nadia could convert almost $30,000 every day without ever getting close to the $10,000 CTR threshold. The size of their drug trafficking operation wasn't that great; $6,000 a day for short periods of time was the maximum the banks really had to handle.

These deposits were made by Nadia, her sister, and Jan's mother. (Jan was a bit unreliable; Nadia didn't let him handle the money.) The deposits were spread out among a number of branches; Nadia chose banks with more than one branch for precisely that reason. She also wrote out all of the deposit tickets and even printed up her own currency straps to hold the cash. Over one million dollars was laundered using this very organized method. See Figure 20.6.

DOCUMENTATION

The scheme described in the case example creates a paper trail several yards wide, and the banks hold onto that paper for years. In fact, that's one of the objectives of the scheme — to create the illusion that Nadia's financial affairs were just like anybody else's, with paper to prove it.

The cash still posed a problem for Nadia, drawing attention to her activities every time she went to the bank. Also a problem, just as the law intended, were those pesky IRS forms. These had to be avoided by conducting more transactions in smaller amounts, thereby creating even more paper for the trail.

PLACEMENT PROBLEM

An illegal drug enterprise has sales of ten pounds of cocaine per week at $12,000 per pound. This generates a total of $120,000 per week.

Assuming that the currency taken in is equally divided into denominations of $5, 10, 20, 50, and 100, at the end of the week, the organization would have:

$24,000 in $ 5 bills	10 lbs
$24,000 in 10 bills	5 lbs
$24,000 in 20 bills	2.5 lbs
$24,000 in 50 bills	1 lb
$24,000 in 100 bills	.5 lbs
Total	19 lbs of money

Stacked in one pile, this money would be 37" high.

Figure 20.6 *Placement problem.*

INVESTIGATION OF A SIMPLE BANKING SCHEME

This is a very straightforward investigation using bank records. The focus of the investigation is *cash* coming in and *anything* going out. We first want to establish who controls the accounts. Signature cards and checks written will identify most of the players. Deposit tickets, on the other hand, won't tell you much more than the amount of the deposit and the location, because no signature is required.

Checks provide good leads to other assets, and since the objective of this scheme is to convert the cash to some other usable form, the investigator has to find out the use to which the money has been put. A check written to the county assessor's office may be a lead to a piece of property held in a nominee's name. A wire transfer to Colombia might be a clue about some other activity of interest.

How cash is handled in the various accounts is important because these transactions may be criminal acts in and of themselves. If they can be linked to the Specified Unlawful Activity, money laundering violations may have been committed. If the deposits are structured to avoid cash reporting requirements, this may be a violation *and* an element of the more serious money laundering offense.

In all cases, the investigator must attempt to obtain the records of the subject in addition those made by the bank. A document search warrant can be employed for this purpose. If a corporation is used in the scheme, the corporate records are unprotected by the privilege against self-incrimination.

Finally, any clues about others who are involved in the financial transactions must also be followed up. Smurfs and anyone acting on behalf of the principal are potential defendants and witnesses.

Sources of Information

Bank records are likely to be the source that is most complete, most accurate, and least subject to fudging by the subject. At minimum, you'll need the statements, copies of deposit tickets, deposit items, large checks, and information about withdrawals (wire transfers or cashier's check purchases).

Subjects' records should also be sought. Until you get them, you won't be sure you've found all the bank accounts, and you may also find evidence of special relationships with the bank or transactions not reflected in the account records (cashier's check or traveler's check purchases with cash, for example). Being very thorough and organized, Nadia had very good records, which she kept handy in her little home-office.

Witnesses, including associates of the subject, can establish the M.O. for the scheme. Bank tellers also make good witnesses.

Government records, especially CTRs, may provide leads to money laundering schemes that are using banks. Suspicious Activity Reports should also be checked.

Potential Violations

- 18 USC 1956
- 18 USC 1957
- 31 USC 5324

BANKING–BUSINESS COMBINATION

This is the last of the (relatively) easy scams and the first that moves further through the full money laundering cycle. As the name implies, this scheme uses elements of two we have seen previously. In this case, the launderer is trying to take advantage of the best features of each to place, layer, and even integrate the dirty money.

These schemes can get extremely complicated (though we'll stick with the basics here), especially if the launderer is smart enough to use offshore banks and offshore business entities as part of the scheme. In many ways, this could be considered the *only* money laundering scheme, with everything else being a variation or elaboration.

Remember that the goal of the money launderer is to make it *appear* that the money came from some legitimate source. Most of everybody else's money came from a business by way of a bank, exactly the effect the launderer is trying to create. By incorporating banks and businesses into the scheme, the launderer can go a long way toward achieving the full effect — further, in any event, than can be done with a simple banking scheme where the money just magically appears. How far he or she gets depends on the complexity of the scheme, how many lights and mirrors are used to create the effect.

The first thing we need to remember is that, by going this route, the money launderer gives up all of the flexibility that goes with dealing in cash. Now he or she is forced to play by someone else's rules — those governing the operation of the world's financial system. This system is precisely organized and rigidly run to do exactly the opposite of what a launderer seeks. *Every* transaction is recorded, always. *Every* asset is accounted for. *Nothing* just "appears" or "disappears" from this system; permitting such a thing to happen threatens everyone else in the system.

The launderer, confronted with this unwelcome inflexibility, has two choices. He or she can look for places where laws provide for secrecy that conceals at least some of the actions the launderer would like to hide. ("Yes officer, there is a trail, but you can't follow it past this point.") Second, the launderer can use the system and its enormous capacity for documentation to advantage. ("You want a trail; I'll give you a *trail*.") There are various mechanisms for doing either of these, and a good launderer will use both approaches. ("Sorry, our law won't allow you to follow that million-dollar wire transfer *from* your subject, but these documents will verify this million-dollar loan *to* your subject.")

Domestic versions of this scheme abound, though not all complete the full money laundering cycle. The Bank Secrecy Act permits the type of investigation that should open up a domestic banking–business scheme in short order.

Special Situations

Rather too numerous to explore at this point. Most of what follows in the chapters on diabolically clever and fiendishly complicated money laundering schemes are variations on the banking–business combination. Get this one down and you're on your way.

Case Example

Richard Lee was a businessman. He had been before he got into the drug business, and he understood the value of both businesses and banks in processing large amounts of money. Richard didn't wait until the big money from the heroin sales arrived to open a company as a front.

With the assistance of an attorney, Lee and his partner established Kam Ling Trading Company, Inc., the name coming from the two partners' middle names. The purpose of this company, according to the corporate filing, was to import general merchandise from Asia. (And how true this was!) A bank account for Kam Ling Trading was opened at First Pacific Bank.

A second business, RKL Enterprises, Inc., was set up some months later, after Lee found the volume of currency too great for Kam Ling to handle alone. RKL Enterprises acquired a lease on a retail shop and began selling merchandise imported from Taiwan. Receipts from this store, Formosa Gifts, were deposited into a bank account opened at Liberty National Bank.

Lee knew that large amounts of cash attracted attention he didn't need, so he made attempts to reduce cash deposits in several ways. First, all payments for heroin were made in cash, delivered by courier or international mail to the source of supply in Hong Kong. Second, Lee required several of his distributors to bring him a portion of their receipts in cashier's checks or travelers checks. Third, Lee dispatched his partner to purchase postal money orders at various area post offices. All of these items were then deposited in the business accounts of the two front businesses.

The money accumulated quickly, and Lee started looking for ways to invest some of the excess. A cashier's check for $350,000 from the Formosa Gifts account went to Western Commerce Bank in Los Angeles, where Lee used this money to purchase a liquor store. Another $520,000 from this account was used to purchase a home in Honolulu.

Having connections in Asia, and understanding the value of banking offshore, Lee opened another bank account at the Taiwan Straits Bank in Hong Kong. Although Lee's account was established at the Hong Kong branch, the bank was headquartered in Taipei, the location where Lee wanted most of his money to end up.

To this end, Lee eventually transferred over $3 million from First Pacific Bank to the Taiwan Straits Bank, money he then used to purchase a hotel in Taipei. See Figure 20.7.

Documentation

You'll note that the domestic end of Lee's assorted enterprises is all well documented. Many of the individual transactions, including the cashier's check and money order purchases, contribute to a paper trail, in addition to being evidence of money laundering transactions. In fact, it was a cashier's check receipt, found in a search of one of Lee's distributors, that led to the bank accounts

Money Laundering Scheme - BANKING/BUSINESS COMBINATION

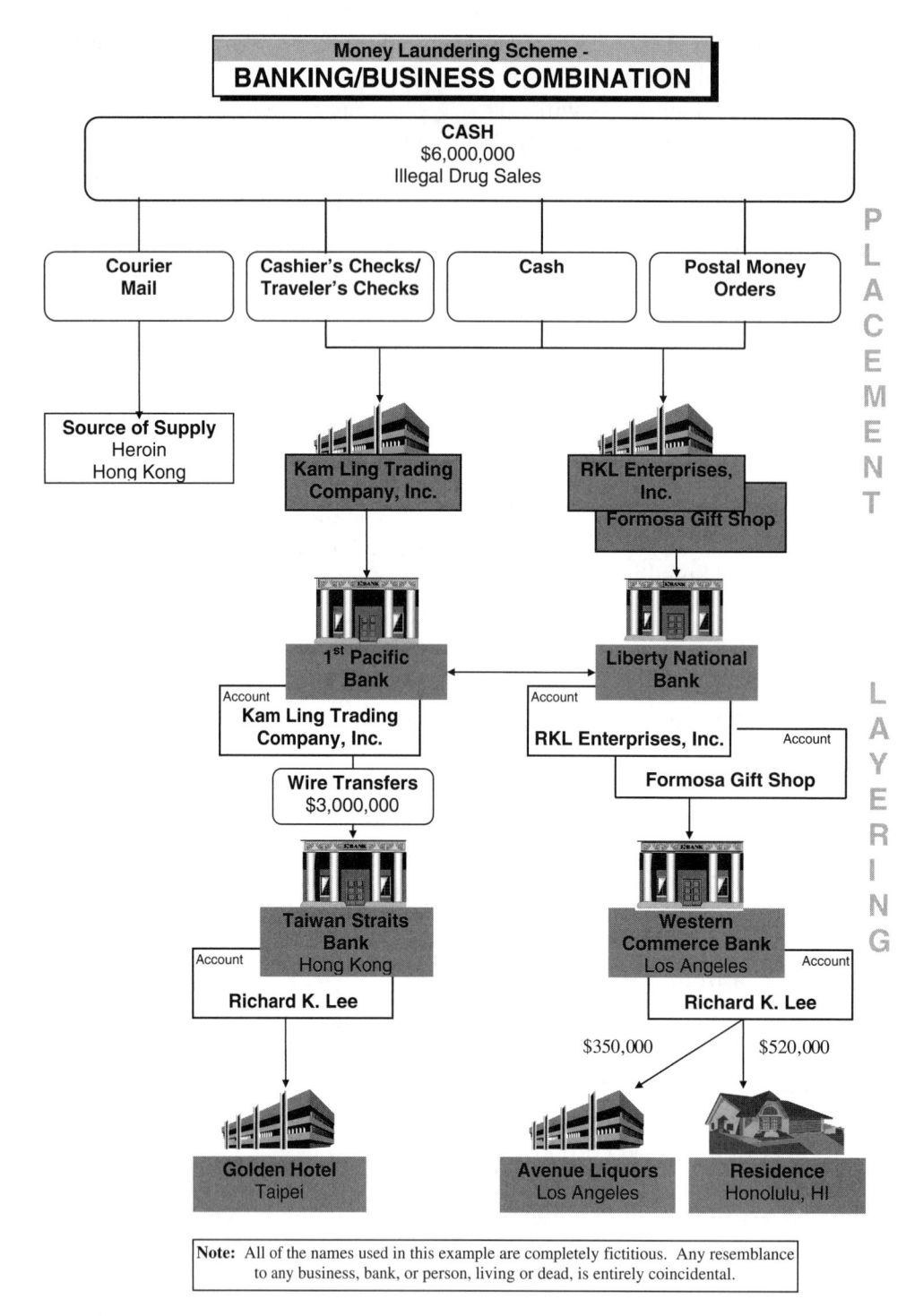

```
                         CASH
                      $6,000,000
                    Illegal Drug Sales

    Courier      Cashier's Checks/       Cash        Postal Money
     Mail        Traveler's Checks                      Orders

 Source of Supply
     Heroin          Kam Ling Trading         RKL Enterprises, Inc.
   Hong Kong         Company, Inc.            Formosa Gift Shop

                     1st Pacific              Liberty National
                        Bank                       Bank
           Account                    Account              Account
        Kam Ling Trading          RKL Enterprises, Inc.   Formosa Gift Shop
         Company, Inc.

          Wire Transfers
           $3,000,000

         Taiwan Straits                Western Commerce Bank
             Bank                         Los Angeles
           Hong Kong
   Account                                                Account
        Richard K. Lee                   Richard K. Lee

                              $350,000       $520,000

          Golden Hotel        Avenue Liquors      Residence
             Taipei            Los Angeles       Honolulu, HI
```

PLACEMENT

LAYERING

Note: All of the names used in this example are completely fictitious. Any resemblance to any business, bank, or person, living or dead, is entirely coincidental.

Figure 20.7 *Banking–business combination.*

and the liquor store purchase. The movement of funds by wire from First Pacific to Taiwan Straits Bank was also documented, though harder to find among First Pacific's records.

One interesting aspect to this case was the fact that although several CTRs were filed in connection with transactions conducted by Lee and his associates, none of these were linked to the operation until after the fact. When investigators went looking for information about known Lee associates, they discovered the CTRs and some Suspicious Activity Reports as well.

This should be a caution for financial investigators. Criminals aren't always stupid, and once they've discovered that the reports are being submitted, they may change their M.O. to avoid those filings. Thus, your subject may have only one or two CTRs on file, because he or she figured out some other way of handling the large cash transactions. (This is exactly what happened in the Steve Nelson example, related earlier.)

INVESTIGATION OF A SCHEME INVOLVING A BANKING–BUSINESS COMBINATION

In our example, Mr. Lee has just about completed the money laundering cycle. He has the full enjoyment of quite a bit of money in Taiwan, where, so far as anyone knows, he was a successful businessman in the United States. If anyone in America wants to check, he is also able to claim a legitimate-appearing source of funds from offshore — that Taipei hotel.

This scheme isn't particularly complex, and it can be investigated from two directions. One way would be to begin with the Specified Unlawful Activity — drugs — and try to trace the money this activity generates. With this approach, informants and witnesses will identify transactions, cash flow patterns, entities used for money laundering, and assets acquired with the funds. If these witnesses are available, the investigator can enter the money trail at some point and work in either direction from that spot.

The second alternative is to approach the case from a financial perspective, looking at the financial transactions known to have been conducted by Lee. By obtaining bank records and the records of the various corporations established as fronts, the investigator will eventually turn up large amounts of unexplained cash. The assets acquired may be identified, and even assets or accounts offshore may be located.

These two approaches are not mutually exclusive, but your approach may depend on the source of your information and the quality of your informants. The financial information exists, especially in domestic banks and businesses.

In this investigation, a cashier's check receipt was found in the apartment of one of the principal's distributors. This receipt led to an account in a Los Angeles bank into which other cashier's checks had been deposited. Following the money forward, investigators found assets in California that were purchased from this account. Tracing the money back, the investigators found bank accounts, people who were smurfing money into those accounts, more assets, and transfers offshore.

Mr. Lee's money laundering case began as an offshoot of a drug investigation. Using only financial information acquired from banks and businesses, the matter was initially pursued without the assistance of any cooperating witnesses from inside the organization. At the same time, efforts were made to "turn" those insiders, several of whom ultimately pleaded guilty to money laundering or Title 31 charges. Not only were these cooperating defendants able to document the Specified Unlawful Activity needed to make the money laundering charge, they were also able to identify more assets, including the offshore property, and to help in tracking the cash transactions.

This is the type of integrated approach that is required to resolve more sophisticated money laundering operations. When a launderer begins using a combination of banks and business entities, the complexity of the scheme increases rather dramatically — and this is *before* all the customized smoke and mirrors are thrown in.

SOURCES OF INFORMATION

In a word, *abundant,* at least on the financial end of things. We can again note the irony that the crook, in attempting to hide his or her actions with this scheme, actually generates *more* evidence of money laundering. Our problem is finding this evidence and properly applying it.

Business records, of course, are a significant source of information. Once again, it is always good to get the records of the businesses themselves. These often contain evidence of fraud, attempts to conceal transactions, or efforts to evade taxes. They provide leads to other bank accounts and transactions, such as cashier's check purchases. Consider using a document search warrant, if possible.

Bank records are readily available via subpoena, reliable, and relatively inexpensive. (You do have to pay for the research and copying costs incurred by the bank.)

Criminal records can be extremely significant, especially the type of records maintained by drug traffickers to record credit sales and cash receipts. These records may document cash transactions or movement that is not reflected in bank records, and they are invaluable in corroborating the statements of associates or other witnesses. In the Lee case, records detailing hundreds of thousands of dollars in drug sales were seized from the distributor's apartment. The records showed deliveries of cash by the distributor to Lee, and some of these dates corresponded closely with deposits into Lee's bank accounts.

Business witnesses frequently have little or nothing to do with the illegal activity or the laundering. They may rent space to or do some legitimate business with the front companies. Unless there's some personal relationship, they don't have much incentive to lie for the criminal.

Criminal informants, particularly those who have been involved in specific financial transactions, may have important information *and* a motivation to give it up. The penalties for laundering money are pretty severe, and, as is often the case, much of the evidence in a financial case implicates criminal associates at first. This is especially true in any money laundering scheme that uses layering techniques. All those layers are comprised of little people who may well resent the fact that they are going to jail while the person who used them is sipping champagne on a yacht somewhere. Informants and cooperating defendants will be critical in any money laundering case that involves couriers and transportation of dirty money offshore. This activity doesn't leave a clear paper trail, so old-fashioned testimony will be needed to bridge the gaps.

Records relating to communications between the participants provide important leads, as well as corroboration of transactions. These schemes cannot function without extensive communications. Name me one bank or business in America that doesn't have a telephone. They've *all* got phones because communications are essential to their business. A money laundering enterprise is no different, and it uses faxes, cellular phones, computer e-mail, digital phones, and pagers to communicate. These records can be quite helpful.

POTENTIAL VIOLATIONS

- 18 USC 1956   Money laundering
- 18 USC 1957   Financial institution money laundering
- 18 USC 1956 (h) Money laundering conspiracy
- 31 USC 5324   Structuring

SUMMING UP

Virtually every money laundering case you can name will have a business or a banking element, or both. Due to more intensive scrutiny by federal regulators over financial institutions, launderers today are increasingly turning to direct movement of funds offshore, as well as the use of nonbank financial institutions in the United States.

Once the money gets offshore, however, businesses and banks are once again involved. The need for launderers to move from the cash transaction system to a business transaction system of exchange means that they must use the same mechanisms that are employed by legitimate business people to handle their income.

In the modern world, these mechanisms are banks and businesses. Although the schemes we've looked at were fairly simple, these three form the foundation of most of the other, more complex scams.

If you go back and look at some of the historical examples in this book, such as the Hauptmann or Ames cases, you'll see how and why the banks and businesses were employed by the criminal. Or, the next time you see money laundering mentioned in the newspaper, check out the role of the bank or business entity.

CHAPTER 21

DIABOLICALLY CLEVER LAUNDERING SCHEMES

"I can't say I was ever lost, but I was bewildered once for three days."
Daniel Boone, pioneer

"Our life is frittered away by detail. ... Simplify, simplify."
Henry David Thoreau, *Walden*

As we approach some of the more complicated of the money laundering schemes, it's good to remind ourselves of some reassuring facts:

1. No matter what scheme the criminal employs, he or she will be forced to live by certain rules that are beyond his or her ability to change.
2. Once the launderer opts for a scheme involving a bank or business, records of transactions are automatically generated. This is evidence we can use, if only we can find it.
3. A laundering scheme depends on the movement of money, not once, but many times. Each of these movements creates an opportunity for detection.

In the previous chapter, we looked at some of the schemes that form a foundation for more complex variations. Those basic schemes are also the ones most criminals employ, mostly because it's what they understand. Some, however, will jazz things up with some special modifications — the smoke and mirrors of the money laundering illusion.

These diversionary tactics may be employed in any stage of the money laundering cycle. Some, such as smurfing, are designed specifically as placement mechanisms to avoid known detection devices, in this case, the Currency Transaction Report (CTR). The use of smurfs to avoid the $10,000 threshold for CTR filings is a variation of the banking scheme discussed in Chapter 20.

Another tactic, the shell corporation, is a variation of the business cover or front technique. The other two schemes, known as loan-backs, are derived directly from the banking–business combination. As we look at all of these variants, keep in mind that other devices are available to the launderer as well, such as the use of nominees to further cloud ownership. Another tactic, pyramiding of corporations, uses companies, owned by other companies, owned by other companies, and so on, until the true ownership is almost impossible to establish. These techniques can be used in either the placement or layering stage, and even to integrate or repatriate the now clean-appearing money.

SMURFS AND STRUCTURED TRANSACTIONS

Smurfs are those little blue guys from the children's cartoon program. They are also a money launderer's tool. The term was first used in the laundering context in the early 1980s, after investigators in Florida noticed that launderers were using numerous associates to go to banks and conduct multiple cash transactions, all under the $10,000 amount that would cause the bank to file a CTR.

There was a time when banks were less careful about filing CTRs, but that changed with a couple of major criminal cases and some actions against the nonfiling banks. At the same time, law enforcement was starting to use these CTRs as the intelligence tools they were intended to be, which meant that the launderers had to come up with some way to conceal detection of their placement of money into banks.

Smurfing was one solution. It's actually fairly simple, although it certainly can be wearing on the individuals doing all the work. (It's also expensive for the principal.) You just give a very large amount of cash to a trusted but low-level (expendable) associate and instruct this person either to deposit the money directly into bank accounts or to buy some financial instrument with the money. You may use a number of accounts, at a number of banks, information that is also given to the smurf. The other key instruction is the amount to be transacted. In all cases this will be below, often far below, $10,000. This will mean more transactions by the smurf, but the person is getting paid for the effort.

Smurfing became very popular, so much so, in fact, that Congress passed a law against the structuring of cash transactions to avoid a reporting requirement. Still, the practice continues, aided by the fact that unless the transaction is over a certain amount or considered suspicious, the financial institution is not required even to identify the customer depositing cash or buying cashier's checks.

In the simplest of smurfing operations, a launderer can move hundreds of thousands of dollars daily, in individual transactions of only $2000 to $3000 each. The only limit on the launderer is the number of banks and accounts used. This is not a major problem in a large city, where there's a bank on every corner. And these operations aren't limited to one city. The smurfs may be given large amounts of money and routed to several different cities, where they buy cashier's checks to be returned to the principal.

In whatever form it takes, structuring or smurfing is a common technique to avoid the now well-publicized CTR filing, and it is something to look for in any laundering investigation.

Incidentally, movement of funds offshore can also be done by couriers, each carrying amounts under the $10,000 amount that would cause a Currency and Monetary Instrument Report (CMIR) to be filed with U.S. Customs. This is a less common form of structuring, however.

Major smurfing organizations aren't the problems they were in the early 1980s. Revisions in federal law and banking procedures have forced the big groups into other methods of moving the currency, but structuring of large cash transactions continues to be a significant part of many money laundering schemes. Structuring may take place as deposits, cashier's check, or money order purchases, or even in the exchange of small-denomination bills for larger, more easily transported fifties and hundreds.

Another change has been the increased use of nonbank financial institutions, such as currency exchanges, money transmitters, casinos, and *casas de cambio.*

SMURFING IN THE 1990S

Smurfing isn't a money laundering scheme in and of itself. Smurfs are elements in more complete schemes, enabling launderers to place cash. We'll look at a couple of ways smurfs can be used, one of which we touched on briefly earlier.

Case Example

Alberto Barrera became known in law enforcement circles as "Papa Smurf," for his role in a money laundering scheme that was detected in 1983. A tip from a Phoenix, Arizona, bank first led agents to Jorge Obando, who was apparently going from bank to bank in the Phoenix area, purchasing cashier's checks for $5000 each.

When Obando moved on to Denver, Colorado, agents searched the trash left behind in Obando's Phoenix hotel room, discovering the names of others who were buying checks. Some of these people were also found in Denver, along with a surprise: Alberto Barrera and his mistress, Margarita Mejia. Papa Smurf, already suspected of money laundering, had flown out from Miami, possibly to issue instructions or maybe to deliver a new supply of the money his crew was using to buy cashier's checks and money orders.

The smurfs, whom agents referred to as Barrera's Traveling Circus, were followed to numerous Denver-area banks, where they purchased cashier's checks for $5000 each. After several days, the group decamped, moving to Omaha, Nebraska.

Operating out of a hotel in Omaha, Obando et al. began buying cashier's checks in large numbers at banks in Omaha and Lincoln. Finally, after a side trip to Portland, Oregon, the group returned to Miami, where more checks were purchased.

At every city where the Traveling Circus stopped, agents visited banks with photographs and questions about people buying cashier's checks with cash. Many of the tellers recalled conducting transactions with members of Barrera's group and were able to make identifications from photographs.

Agents now turned to the bank records, first identifying cashier's checks that had been purchased and then tracing those checks back through the banks where they were deposited. They discovered that many of the checks had been deposited into accounts at two Miami banks. The records of these banks were obtained, and the shape of the operation to place this drug money now emerged.

Irving Trust Bank, Miami, Account of Banco Santander (Colombian Bank)

September 14	Deposit $190,000	Instruments bought in Phoenix September 6–10
September 19	Deposit $513,000	Instruments bought in Phoenix September 13–17
September 23	Deposit $158,000	Instruments bought in Phoenix September 20–22
September 23	Deposit $129,000	Instruments bought in Phoenix September 20–22

Bank Leumi Le-Israel, B.M., Account of Banco Leumi Le-Israel in Panama City

September 20	Deposit $104,880	Instruments bought in Phoenix September 13–17
September 23	Deposit $505,700	Instruments bought in Denver/Miami September 20–22
October 5	Deposit $765,000	Instruments bought in Omaha/Denver September 27–30
October 16	Deposit $299,580	Instruments bought in Portland October 10–13

Altogether, in 32 days, $2,665,160 was deposited into the two bank accounts.

Following their arrests, some of the smurfs discussed their roles with law enforcement. They disclosed that they generally moved $50,000 to $100,000 each per day, purchasing cashier's checks, travelers checks, and money orders. The pay wasn't bad — each smurf received 0.5 to 1.5% of the cash he or she converted, an average of $500 to $1,000 per day for every day they were on the road. Airline tickets, rental cars, food, and clothing were also paid for by the organization. See Figure 21.1.

INVESTIGATION OF A SMURFING OPERATION

The Barrera case is a good example of how financial investigation can be used in conjunction with other, more traditional techniques. The case started with a physical surveillance. Investigators recovered evidence from the participants' trash. Later, the communications of the group were monitored via a pen register and telephone toll analysis. Searches of suspect premises also recovered evidence. When combined

Money Laundering Scheme - SMURFING OPERATION

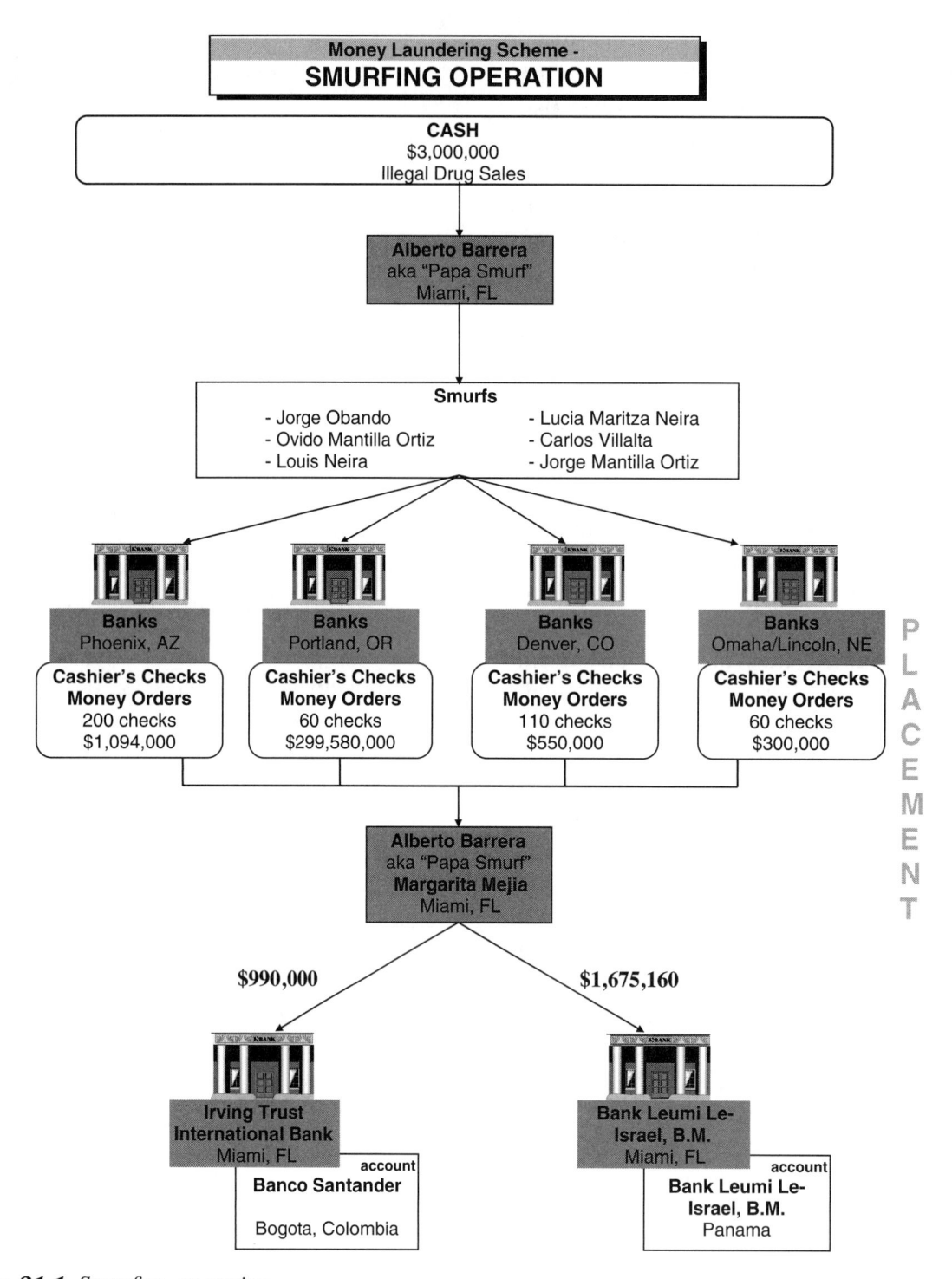

CASH
$3,000,000
Illegal Drug Sales

Alberto Barrera
aka "Papa Smurf"
Miami, FL

Smurfs
- Jorge Obando
- Ovido Mantilla Ortiz
- Louis Neira
- Lucia Maritza Neira
- Carlos Villalta
- Jorge Mantilla Ortiz

Banks Phoenix, AZ	Banks Portland, OR	Banks Denver, CO	Banks Omaha/Lincoln, NE
Cashier's Checks Money Orders 200 checks $1,094,000	Cashier's Checks Money Orders 60 checks $299,580,000	Cashier's Checks Money Orders 110 checks $550,000	Cashier's Checks Money Orders 60 checks $300,000

PLACEMENT

Alberto Barrera
aka "Papa Smurf"
Margarita Mejia
Miami, FL

$990,000 → **Irving Trust International Bank** Miami, FL — account **Banco Santander** Bogota, Colombia

$1,675,160 → **Bank Leumi Le-Israel, B.M.** Miami, FL — account **Bank Leumi Le-Israel, B.M.** Panama

Figure 21.1 Smurfing operation.

with financial evidence in the case, the full picture of the operation came into clear focus.

These schemes require extensive communication between the smurfs and their bosses. Telephone toll, cellular phone, and cloned pager records can identify smurfs and their contacts. Patterns of activity can be discerned from this information. If sufficient evidence is developed, a court order permitting interception of the voice or data communications can be obtained. Addressing the communication links between the parties is a good approach in this multiparty conspiracy.

The value of the financial records cannot be overlooked. Deposits will lead to bank accounts that need to be examined. Leads to other accounts or assets can be obtained by tracing checks or other items deposited into or transferred from any identified account. In the Barrera case, investigators were very pleased to discover the bank accounts where the cashier's checks were being deposited. This discovery enabled them to begin the process of tracing the cash produced by this cocaine trafficking organization.

Finally, the smurfs themselves are potential sources of information. By structuring transactions to avoid the reporting requirement, they become the most accessible felons. They may also be most susceptible to an approach soliciting their cooperation against those organizing the operation.

Sources of Information

Smurfing operations generate piles of documents, even if they aren't conducted on the scale of Barrera's organization.

Bank records will extensively document transactions, even if no CTR was generated. Bank surveillance camera tapes should be requested, although these may not be available after a few weeks. (Banks record over the tapes to save money.)

Criminal records are often maintained to keep track of the operation. All that money has to be accounted for, so there may be lists, addresses, the account numbers written down, or other data of interest.

Government records, especially CTRs or Suspicious Activity Reports (SARs), may be filed despite the best efforts of the launderers to avoid this. Banks are getting better at detecting structuring, using computer and Know Your Customer (KYC) programs.

You might also find some trace of the activity in other government records, including the following:

- Cash Transaction Reports by Casino (CTRC)
- Suspicious CTR by Casino (SCTRC)
- Foreign Bank Account Report (FBAR)
- Currency and Monetary Instrument Report (CMIR)

Potential Violations

- 18 U.S.C. 1956   Money laundering
- 18 U.S.C. 1957   Money laundering
- 31 U.S.C. 5324   Structuring

Note that 31 U.S.C. §5313 was enacted to deal with exactly this type of activity, as were the rules requiring banks to obtain identification and log all purchases of monetary instruments paid for with cash between $3,000 and $10,000. These provisions have cut back on the type of smurfing practiced by Barrera, but structured transactions are still common.

Black Market Peso Exchange Schemes

Smurfs play key roles in one of the more popular money laundering schemes supporting the U.S.–Latin American drug trade. This is the black market peso exchange (BMPE), an efficient and difficult-to-detect operation that typically involves Colombian traffickers and legitimate business people in Colombia and the United States. The BMPE is a variation of the business–banking combination, and smurfs are used to get the cash into the banks without attracting government attention.

There are four main players in this script:

1. Colombian drug cartel, with operations in the United States and Colombia
2. Colombian peso broker, with representatives in the United States and Colombia
3. Colombian business (sort of legitimate)
4. American business (legitimate)

The smurfs work for #2, the peso broker.

Case Example

Jose, a world-class cocaine trafficker based in Bogota, has an extensive network of distributors in the United States, and sales of his product generate millions of dollars on American streets. Jose has no need of this cash in America, however. He wants the money back home, where he can buy more cocaine and all of the other goodies that accrue to wealthy dope dealers. He can use dollars for the coke, but he needs pesos for the rest of the things.

Maria is a legitimate (sort of) businesswoman, also living in Bogota. She knows a lot of people, including some on the shadier side of the street, one of whom is Jose. Maria goes to Jose and makes him an attractive offer: She'll buy U.S. dollars from him, paying in Colombian pesos. Where will she get these pesos? From another acquaintance, Robert, who runs a business selling personal computers and software in Bogota.

Robert's suppliers are all legitimate computer manufacturers in the United States, and he's a good customer who always pays promptly. His problem is that his customers in Colombia all pay him in pesos and the Americans want dollars for their merchandise. Maria has a solution that will make everyone happy.

She tells Robert she has a million dollars in the United States that she will make available to him to pay his suppliers. Robert just needs to give her a million dollars' worth of pesos in Bogota. Robert agrees and places a million-dollar order with his supplier, Orange Computers in California.

Maria tells Jose they've got a deal, and Jose gives her title to 1 million American dollars, held at various secret locations in Florida. Maria gets this money for a 10 to 20% discount, her fee for doing the transaction. She arranges for her associates in Florida to get the cash from Jose's people and smurf it into various bank accounts she has set up, being careful to avoid large transactions that might be reported on a CTR or SAR. They also buy money orders and cashier's checks, busily spreading the bread around South Florida until it has all changed form. The cash has now been placed.

Maria then has all these instruments sent to Orange Computer, which is expecting Señor Robert's payment. Upon receipt, they ship the computers off to Bogota. Meanwhile, Maria has collected the pesos from Robert and delivered them to Jose.

The beauty of the BMPE is that none of the pesos ever leave Colombia, and none of the dollars ever leave the United States. The main players are never actually in contact with all that dirty money, and everybody winds up with what they wanted in the first place. Jose's happy, because although he had to pay Maria for her services, she safely laundered a bunch of money for him. Robert's happy, because not only did he get the merchandise he needed, he saved money by avoiding Colombian taxes and costs connected with the official exchange rate. (This "parallel exchange rate" is the reason why they're called "black market" pesos.) See Figure 21.2.

INVESTIGATION OF A BLACK MARKET PESO EXCHANGE OPERATION

The principals in this scam may or may not ever come to the United States, but even if they do, they're never going anywhere near all that drug cash. Cutting into one of these operations isn't easy, and proving that Maria or Robert had knowledge of the source of the dirty dollars is also going to be tough. Maria is our target, though, because she's the one who knows it all. The smurfs in Florida work for her; she knows where they went to collect the cash and who got it after it changed form.

These schemes, like Barrera's, are communications-intensive. As you can imagine, having a million or more dollars floating around, changing hands or sitting in a closet waiting for a pickup, makes everybody nervous. There will be a lot of phoning back and forth to confirm pickups, deliveries, and amounts. Robert's dealing

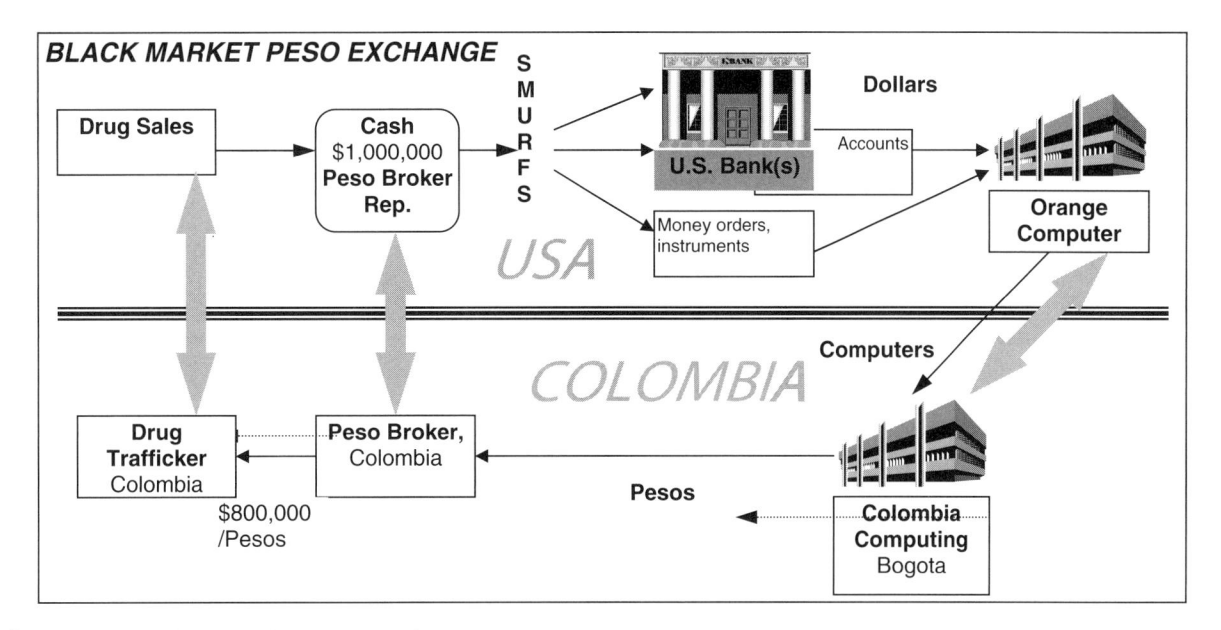

Figure 21.2 Black market peso exchange.

with his supplier and Maria, Jose is making sure his people get with Maria's people, and Maria's talking to everybody. A pen register or, better yet, a wire or cell phone intercept will yield excellent results if you can figure out which phone (or phones) is being used.

The financial end also has some possibilities. We've got a lot of financial transactions taking place; Maria's smurfs are going around buying money orders and cashier's checks, making deposits and generally keeping busy down in Florida. Banks and money service businesses may catch on and report some of these transactions on Suspicious Activity Reports. The SAR review teams in various districts should be looking for patterns of activity linked to BMPE.

Another lead is at Orange Computer. Getting a pile of money orders and cashier's checks has got to raise at least one eyebrow in the accounting department. This payment method is definitely out of the ordinary, and some American businesses will report suspicious transactions to a law enforcement contact.

The other possibility is on the drug side of the operation, where informants and cooperating defendants can be interviewed concerning their knowledge of cash exchanges and BMPE-type activity. This may put investigators onto the trail at another point. Undercover operations may also be valuable, and any piece of paper seized in a search warrant should be thoroughly investigated and analyzed. This is particularly critical if there are phone or account numbers, as these may lead to smurfs, financial transactions, or people like Maria.

Sources of Information

Bank records and the records of money service businesses used by the smurfs will document transactions, most of which will involve amounts far less than $10,000. Orange Computer and Robert's business will also have some records, although neither of them will know much more than their own narrow end of the operation.

Communication records, particularly of the cell phone and other communications between Maria and her people, are very useful. As the gray arrows in Figure 21.2 show, there is communication between all of the players, although Maria is the centerpiece.

Criminal records include those maintained by Maria, as well as those of her people and Jose's. This is a sizable chunk of money we're talking about, and nobody wants to lose any of it; bad things can happen. There will be notes and records kept, account numbers written down, phone contacts listed. Getting your hands on these can unravel big parts of the scheme.

Maria and the others probably won't hold onto the records of this deal any longer than necessary, though; no point keeping a lot of incriminating evidence around. Trash covers could be a good source, assuming you have the right can.

Government records, especially CTRs or SARs, may be filed despite the best efforts of the launderers to avoid this. Banks are getting better at detecting structuring, using computer and KYC programs.

Potential Charges

- 18 U.S.C. 1956   Money laundering
- 18 U.S.C. 1956 (h)   Money laundering conspiracy
- 18 U.S.C. 1957   Financial institution money laundering
- 18 U.S.C. 1960   Operating illegal money transmitter business
- 31 U.S.C. 5324   Structuring
- 31 U.S.C. 5332   Bulk cash smuggling

Financial Action Task Force Description

Here's another description of the operation of the black market peso exchange, this from the Financial Action Task Force (FATF)'s *1997–1998 Report on Money Laundering Typologies:*

> Drug traffickers in the U.S. collect and stockpile cash from illegal drug sales in "stash houses" located throughout the U.S. and this creates a logistical problem for the traffickers. The solution is as follows:
>
> 1. Black market money brokers in Colombia direct Colombians visiting or residing in the U.S. to open personal cheque accounts at U.S. banks, and deposit minimal amounts.
>
> 2. Cheques on these accounts are signed in blank by the customers and given to the brokers who pay them US$200–400 for each account. The brokers keep a stock of signed cheques on these "shell" U.S. accounts.
>
> 3. Colombian drug cartels sell their stockpiled cash at a parallel or "discounted" exchange rate to the Colombian money brokers in exchange for pesos which are paid in Colombia.
>
> 4. The brokers purchase the dollars at the discounted rate and the cartels lose a percentage of their profits but avoid the risks of laundering their own drug money.
>
> 5. Once the drug money is purchased, the broker directs his network smurfs to pick up the cash, and structure deposits into the various "shell" cheque accounts.
>
> 6. The broker then offers to sell cheques drawn on these accounts to legitimate Colombian businessmen (who need U.S. dollars to conduct international trade) at a "parallel" exchange rate.
>
> 7. The broker fills in the dollar amount on the signed cheque, but leaves the name of the payee blank. The broker also stamps his symbol on the cheque as a means to guarantee his payment on the cheque in the event there are ever insufficient funds in the "shell" checking account.
>
> 8. The businessman can then fill in the payees' name when he uses the signed cheque as a U.S. dollar instrument to purchase goods (perfume, gold, etc.) in international markets such as Free Trade Zones.
>
> 9. The businessman then ships or smuggles the goods into Colombia.
>
> 10. The Free Trade Zone distributor, who is often a knowing participant in the black market exchange process, forwards the cheque to his U.S. bank account or it may even clear through his local bank account.
>
> 11. Once cleared, the cheque account is debited, and the distributor's U.S. account is credited.
>
> Through this scheme:
>
> Drug cartels in Colombia receive their profits from the U.S. drug trade in Colombia, without having the normal expenses of money launder-

ing. The brokers make a profit on the "discounted" purchase of U.S. dollars from the drug cartels and a second profit on the subsequent sale of the dollars to Colombian businessmen at the "parallel exchange rate." The businessmen save money by exchanging their pesos for U.S. dollars on the "parallel" exchange market, and avoiding government scrutiny and taxes.

SHELL CORPORATIONS

Barrera's smurfing operation was a placement mechanism, using multiple individuals to quickly change the form of the money received from drug sales. The equivalent layering scheme might be one that uses shell or pyramided corporations. These operations use multiple corporate entities to conceal the true ownership of assets or the identity of those conducting financial transactions. Shell corporations can also be used for placement of funds, and we'll look at an illustration of this as well.

There's usually not much to a shell corporation, which is how it got the name in the first place. Shells look good from the outside, but, as the name implies, they're hollow inside. Shells are designed to perform some functions, but they don't conduct the normal business of a corporation. Mostly what they do is move things, using their names to conceal control over the transaction.

Shells can be pyramided — one linked to the next, and the next, and so on — creating a very confusing path for the investigator to follow. If the shells are incorporated in some jurisdiction where the law permits secrecy in business relationships, the identity of the true owners of some of the shells may never be established. This is, of course, precisely the effect the launderer is seeking, and why shells are effective as layering devices.

Many shell corporations consist of little more than a name, an address (often that of the lawyer doing the incorporation), a couple of officers (nominees?), some stock, and shareholders. Oh yes, and a bank account or two. These accounts play very important roles in money laundering schemes, because they can be used to receive deposits and as transfer points to the accounts of other shells, businesses, or individuals.

Operation of these simple shells consists of little more than the activity in the bank accounts, but some of the more sophisticated operators will make their shell corporations look like real businesses, complete with transactions, assets, and even financial statements.

As placement mechanisms, shell corporations have the outward appearance of legitimate businesses, and their bank accounts can be used to receive cash deposits structured in exactly the same way a smurfing operation would function. In the illustration below, cash deposits of $1 million per month can be handled using only four shells and nine bank accounts. The daily deposit into each account is only $5000. See Figure 21.3.

Case Example

Nobody visiting Ferris Alexander's string of adult entertainment stores in Minneapolis–St. Paul would have been able to connect the owner with the business. Granted, this probably wouldn't be the primary purpose of the visit, but the question of ownership was important to some people — like Ferris Alexander and IRS.

For 30 years, Alexander had dealt in what some might call "obscene materials." He began selling magazines and showing movies, later moving on to videocassette sales and rentals. His businesses were very profitable — IRS estimated that he underreported his gross receipts for 1982 and 1983 by over $2.7 million. What made Alexander stand out was that for the most part, he didn't exist.

Beginning as early as 1959, Alexander was using nominees to hold his assets. Ten years later, he began using shell corporations as fronts for the same purpose. The first nominee was Kenneth LaLonde, an employee, whose name appeared on the licenses, own-

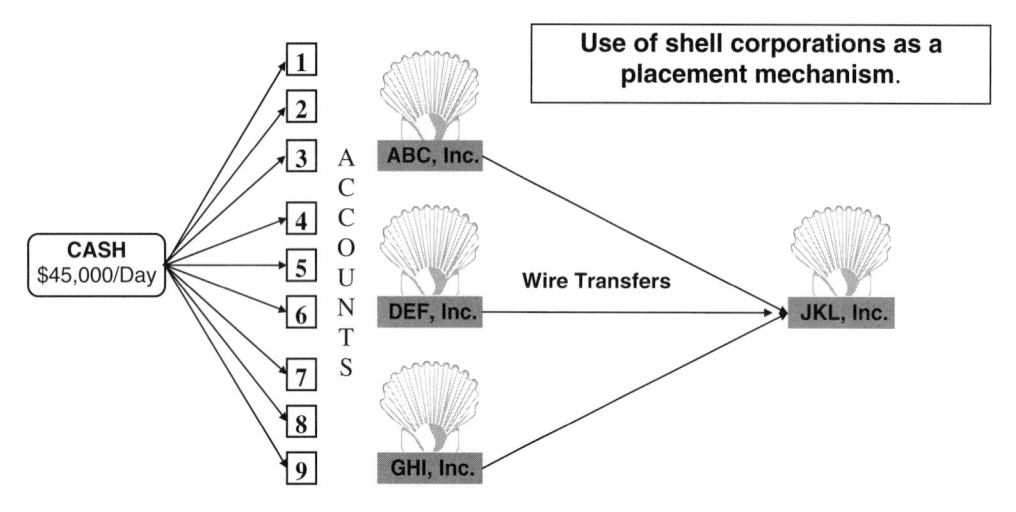

Figure 21.3 *Use of shell corporations as a placement mechanism.*

ership papers, and bank accounts for Alexander's businesses, now known as Kenneth LaLonde Enterprises. In 1969, with the help of an attorney, Alexander formed several corporations, using the name Kenneth LaLonde Enterprises, Inc.

Bank accounts were acquired in the corporate name and used to conduct operations. In 1977, two more corporations were formed to hold all of the theaters controlled by Alexander. The name of LeRoy Wendling, another employee, was substituted for LaLonde's on all the corporate and bank records, but this only lasted until 1980, when Wendling was fired and "John Thomas," an Alexander alias, was substituted.

In 1984, Alexander employee In Sok Na, a Korean immigrant, was used to incorporate 10 more corporations. (In an apparent demonstration that Alexander had a sense of humor, six of the corporate names were in Finnish and four in a Philippine dialect. All were obscene, but nobody at the Secretary of State's office caught on.) Two of the corporations were used to buy real estate and a bookstore, and all of the corporations had bank accounts that Alexander used to move money.

Alexander carried this scheme to an extreme. The receipts of the various businesses were reported (some of them, at least) as income to the corporation, which paid the corporate taxes due. Alexander's nominees claimed the income on their personal returns, keeping Alexander completely off the government's radar screen. See Figure 21.4.

Documentation

Ferris Alexander's scheme, though strictly domestic and not particularly elaborate, illustrates the use of nominees and shell corporations to hold assets and operate a business. Alexander maintained a warehouse, used for packing, storing, and shipping materials, and a couple of primary bank accounts to service all of the retail outlets. The other corporations were used to conceal Alexander's interest and to spread cash deposits around.

Extensive records were created in establishing and operating the shell corporations, but few if any of these records referred to Ferris Alexander, which was, after all, the whole point.

Note: All of the information for this example was taken from the appellate decision in *Alexander v. Thornburgh*, 943 F.2d 825 (1991).

Investigation of a Shell Corporation

His network of shell corporations served Ferris Alexander quite well. But, at the time of his conviction, he was ordered to forfeit his interest in 10 pieces of commercial real estate, his interest in a wholesale business and 13 retail

DIABOLICALLY CLEVER LAUNDERING SCHEMES

Money Laundering Scheme - SHELL CORPORATIONS

CASH, CHECKS, CREDIT CARD SLIPS
Tax Evasion, R.I.C.O., Sale of Obscene Material

SHELL 1, Inc. / SHELL 2, Inc.
SHELL 3, Inc. / SHELL 4, Inc. / SHELL 5, Inc.
SHELL 6, Inc. / SHELL 7, Inc. / SHELL 8, Inc.
SHELL 9, Inc. / SHELL 10, Inc.

LAYERING

In Sok Na, Incorporator, Director, Nominee

Warehouse — St. Paul, MN
Banks — St. Paul, MN (Account Shell 1 Corp., Account Shell 2 Corp.) — Primary Bank Accounts
Adult Bookstores — St. Paul, MN
Real Estate — St. Paul, MN

Ferris Alexander, Sr. — St. Paul, MN

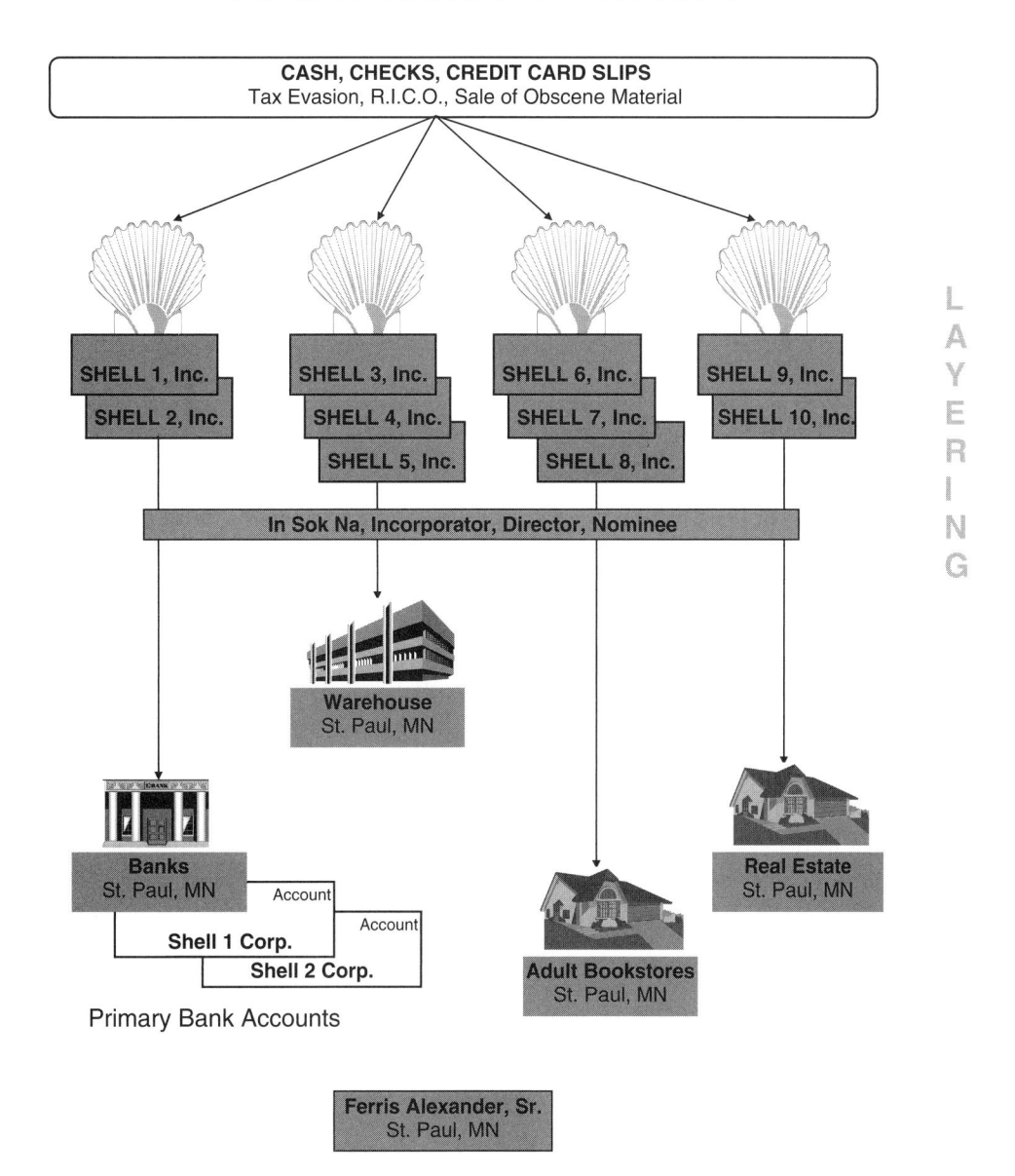

Figure 21.4 Shell corporations.

businesses (adult bookstores and video stores), and $8,910,548.10 derived from the racketeering enterprise.

What went wrong? On paper, Alexander had nothing. The corporations he had established were the owners of record of all the assets forfeited. In Sok Na, Alexander's employee and nominee, was the incorporator and director of the 10 corporations. Alexander had layered himself pretty effectively, or so he thought.

One of the problems lay with the nature of shell corporations themselves. They don't actually *do* much of anything. In this case, Alexander operated the business from a central location using a couple of bank accounts to pay for merchandise and operating expenses. What possible legitimate business purpose did all of those other corporate entities have? The best Alexander could come up with at trial was that he wanted to "limit civil liability."

Shell corporations are different, much as a money launderer may try to make them appear like any other corporate entity. Some clues may be present to allow an investigator to recognize a shell when it's encountered.

What does the corporation do?

If the corporation exists only to hold other corporations or to hold bank accounts, this may be an indication that it is a shell or is being used for some manipulative purpose. If the corporation functions solely as a transfer point for funds moving from one account or business to another, this may be another indication.

What is the capital structure of the corporation?

The stock issued in shell corporations may be of the bearer variety, meaning that whoever has possession of the stock owns the company. This is a very popular arrangement in places like Panama, where not even those who set up the corporation will know who holds the stock. Registering the stock and listing the principal as a shareholder completely defeats the layering purpose of the shell corporation — to conceal.

What do the financial statements look like?

Corporations are required to file annual reports, and the legitimate variety file financial reports as well, because they're doing real business, obtaining credit, making sales, and so forth. Shell corporations don't have much to report, unless the launderer is working hard to make the company appear to be legitimate. In that case, the financial reports will often contain clues to their fraudulent nature. On a balance sheet, these clues might include:

- Unverifiable interests in nonpublicly traded corporations or corporations that cannot be authenticated
- Cash in offshore or unidentifiable banks
- Ownership of oil, gas, or mining properties
- Overvaluation of goodwill
- Ownership of real estate that is inadequately described
- Letters of credit as assets
- Large unspecified "reserves"
- Accounts payable and notes payable liabilities
- Income that is unrelated to the stated business purpose

Another clue could be in the review or lack thereof of the financial statements by an independent CPA. Also, Dun & Bradstreet evaluates the creditworthiness of corporations; if there's a D&B report for the corporation, it's probably not a shell.

Who are the owners of the corporation?

Use of bearer shares or unregistered stock is a common practice in offshore jurisdictions. If a company creates a shell for a legitimate purpose, it will have no problem identifying the ownership of the shell.

Who's in charge here?

Every corporation has to have at least one officer and at least one director. Some jurisdictions require more. The identities of these individuals are normally public record. If the officers and directors are nominees, such as attorneys or offshore management companies, this may be an indication that the shell is being used for financial manipulation or some other fraudulent purpose.

SOURCES OF INFORMATION

The information we're looking for here is truth — who *really* owns the corporation behind those transactions. The best source for this information is inside the operation — exactly the type of source that's hardest to get. But it happens occasionally, as we'll see in the following example. In lieu of an inside source, analysis of financial records can provide some insights.

Bank records from domestic and sometimes foreign banks will identify the people with signature authority over accounts, as well as whoever is actually signing the checks. As we know, banks will take most deposits from just about anybody, but they are real touchy about who can *withdraw* money from an account.

Corporate officers and directors are identified on the corporate documents. In domestic corporations, the stockholders are also supposed to be identified. Bearer share corporations are a different matter — anybody can own those shares. The officers and directors of an offshore shell corporation are likely to be attorneys, corporate management companies, and nominees of some sort. Still, it's a clue.

Government records, particularly the Foreign Bank Account Report, filed annually with the Treasury Department, can provide leads if filed by the account holder. If that person didn't file, he or she is liable to some civil and criminal penalties. (You first have to show he or she actually *had* the account, sort of a Catch-22.)

Records of communications, especially phone toll records, can be invaluable in establishing relationships between individuals and their shell corporations. Don't overlook such techniques as mail and trash covers to obtain this type of information.

OFFSHORE SHELL CORPORATIONS

Whereas Alexander's operation was strictly domestic, other, wiser money launderers have perfected the use of offshore shell and dummy corporations. Taking advantage of bank secrecy laws in offshore tax havens is nothing new, and some of those jurisdictions go even further, providing for secrecy in corporate relationships as well.

The principle behind the use of an offshore shell corporation is the same as for the domestic type: Provide the operators with a layer of secrecy to hide behind. One aspect of offshore shells that is especially useful for launderers is the lack of a requirement that shareholders (who are the owners of a corporation) be identified. In places like Panama, anyone who holds the shares of these companies is an owner, and transfers of the shares needn't be reported

It's not difficult to establish an offshore corporation, nor is it very expensive. Off-the-shelf

In the computer age, your shell corporation is anywhere you want it to be.

companies are available from a number of company registration agencies operating around the world. Several of these operate on the Internet, where a corporation in any of 30 or 40 countries can be established from your home computer in a matter of days.

These ready-mix corporations have everything needed to function as shells, including the ability to open bank accounts all over the world (the agency will help you do this, too). Attorneys in tax haven and bank secrecy countries will assist with formation of corporations, giving added protection via the attorney–client privilege.

Case Example

Using only three shell corporations, Billy Bell was able to accommodate all of his client's needs. Mostly what the client needed was secrecy, but the corporations also allowed the client to move funds to and from bank accounts controlled by the companies. This would be useful in buying assets or conducting large financial transactions.

Bell used three different jurisdictions to domicile the corporations, knowing that secrecy laws in two of the countries would effectively prevent any inquiry by law enforcement. In America, Bell incorporated Pacific Import–Export, Inc., in Delaware, and he opened an account for the company at a major U.S. bank with overseas branches.

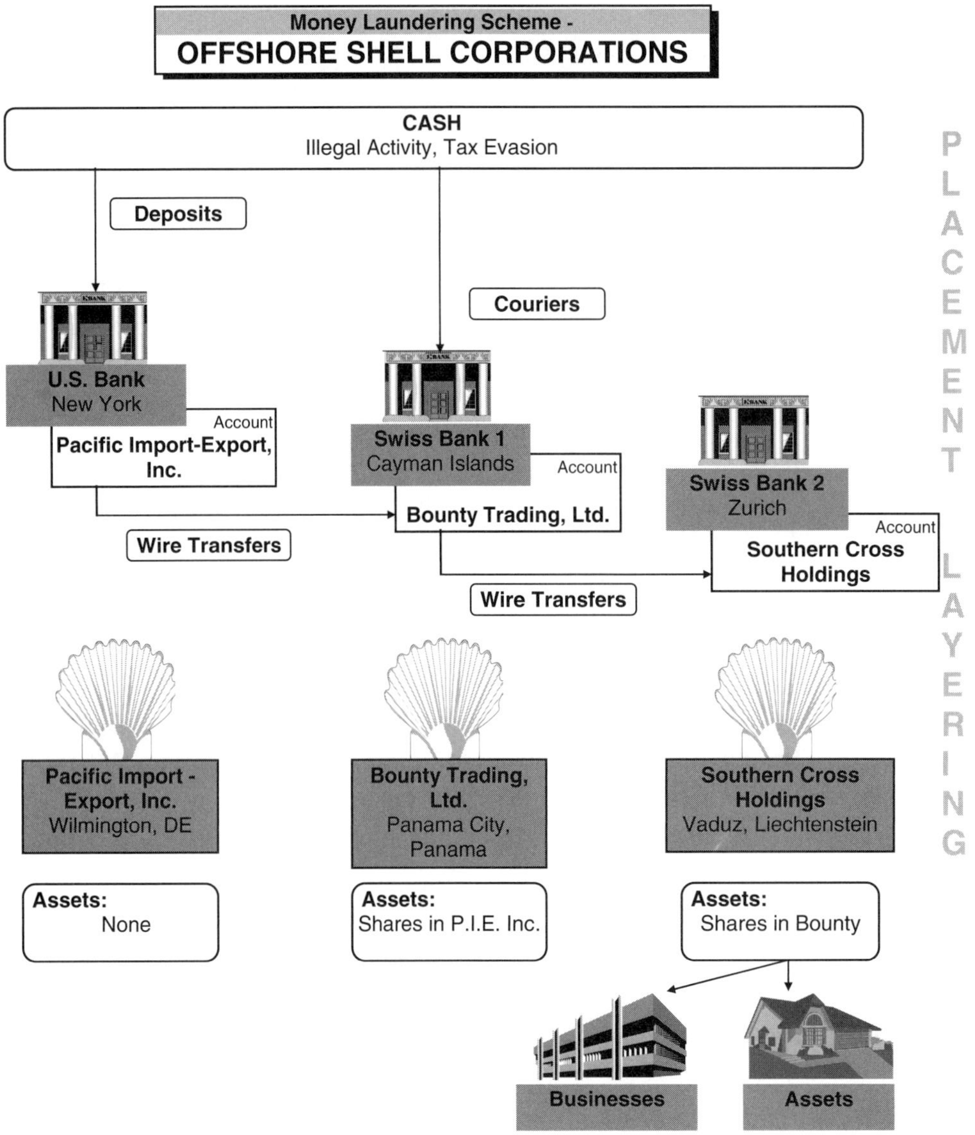

Figure 21.5 *Offshore shell corporations.*

All of the shares of this corporation were owned by the second shell corporation, Bounty Trading, Ltd. Bell used a Panama City attorney to establish this company in Panama. It was a bearer shares company, and the corporate papers did not show the name of the original shareholder. Not even the Panamanian attorney, who was also the president and director, knew who had possession of the shares. Bell opened a bank account for Bounty Trading with a major Swiss bank in the Cayman Islands.

The last shell was established in Liechtenstein as Southern Cross Holdings, Inc. It, too, was a bearer shares corporation, with a bank account at a second Swiss bank.

Cash from the client's illegal activity was deposited into the account for Pacific Import–Export or flown offshore to the Cayman Islands for deposit at the Swiss bank. Funds from this account were wired later to the second account and used by Southern Cross Holdings to buy assets. See Figure 21.5.

OFFSHORE CORPORATIONS AND THE INTERNET

The Internet is making the creation of offshore corporations and businesses easier than ever. For a few hundred dollars, you can buy an already existing business or set one up from scratch.

At least 10 different businesses offer incorporation services on the Internet, with access to countries around the world. And the number of countries that are offering special advantages to businesses wanting to incorporate in their jurisdiction is growing. It's a great deal for the countries involved. After all, they don't have to do much more than file some papers and collect the licensing and registration fees. Since most countries require a registered agent to reside within the jurisdiction, employment is provided for local attorneys and others.

It is even possible to obtain licenses as a banking or insurance business, both of which provide special opportunities for money laundering. These cost a little more, and fewer jurisdictions offer them.

Some of the online incorporation agents can also obtain offshore bank accounts and identification, and at least one has offered passports. Not much more than access to a home computer and a credit card is needed to establish a presence offshore. If you're in a real hurry, the agents already have a number of companies "on the shelf," waiting for a buyer.

Offshore Jurisdictions

The following countries offer relatively easy incorporation by foreigners, along with some other benefits, such as corporate secrecy, bank secrecy, tax-free business, and so forth. (*Note:* This list is by no means complete.)

Anguilla	Cayman Islands	Isle of Man
Antigua		Liechtenstein
Aruba	Channel Islands	Luxembourg
Austria		Malta
Bahamas	Cook Islands	Monaco
Belize	Cyprus	Nauru
Bermuda	Hong Kong	
Netherlands Antilles	Niue	Seychelles
	Panama	Switzerland
Nevis	Samoa	Vanuatu

The fact that a business is incorporated in one of these countries does not mean it is involved in money laundering or any other criminal activity. However, if your subject is involved with a business domiciled in one of these places, you should be alert to all possibilities.

LOAN-BACK SCHEMES

In the hit movie *Lethal Weapon 2*, actor Joe Pesci, playing a money launderer, boasts about the scheme he invented to launder millions of dollars in drug money. The scheme he describes is known as a loan-back, and Joe's character didn't invent it. Loan-backs have been a tax scam for as long as there have been taxes on income and deductions for interest payments. Money launderers found that this scheme worked quite nicely for illegal incomes as well.

The loan-back concept is a variation on the banking–business combination scheme. It is based on two simple precepts: Loans are a source of money that can explain wealth, and loans have certain important tax benefits.

Remember that in the integration phase of the laundering process, the criminal is hoping to make the ill-gotten gains come from some legitimate-appearing source. Having successfully placed and layered the money, he or she is looking for some explanation for where it all came from. "Where did I get the million dollars? I borrowed it from (fill in the blank). Here are all the loan documents, and here are the canceled checks showing I'm current on my loan payments." This *is* a pretty good explanation.

A loan has benefits relating to taxes as well. First of all, a loan is nontaxable as income, since it isn't really your money as long as you're planning to pay it back. Second, under certain circumstances, the interest paid on loans is tax deductible, something Pesci gloatingly described in the movie.

So, if I had $100,000 in illegal income that I wanted to integrate, and I had a choice between reporting the money as ordinary income from some offshore business or reporting it as a non-taxable "loan" from some offshore business, going the loan route would save me 30% or so in federal taxes alone.

But what about having to pay all that money back? So long as it's my money I'm paying back, *and* I'm paying it back to myself, this is a very nice proposition. It's illegal, of course, but nice. This is very much an integration tactic; we assume I've already changed the form of my dirty money and moved it to some safe place. Now all I need to do is arrange for a loan of that same money. This loan can be from an individual, a business (and we just looked at shell corporations), or a financial institution. The only other qualification the lender needs is the money to lend. Someone with lots of illegally earned cash has the solution to that little problem.

Once the lender is lined up, appropriate documentation can be prepared to record the existence and terms of the loan. The loan principal is transferred to the borrower, who must begin making payments on the note. At this point, the borrower has full access to the entire amount of the laundered funds and doesn't have to pay taxes on any of it. The money can be invested in an income-producing (legal) enterprise, which can in turn be used to service the loan. If anyone asks, the trail of the loan can be laid out for examination. This is a win–win proposition for everybody except the government.

Our first example of a loan-back scheme is an embellishment on the one described in *Lethal Weapon 2*. This particular scheme as described wouldn't work, so we've made a couple of minor changes to make it more feasible.

Case Example

The story line in *Lethal Weapon 2* has money launderer Leo Goetz servicing a half-billion-dollar account on behalf of some bad guys operating out of the South African consulate in Los Angeles. They catch Leo stealing, try at least once to kill him, and now he's under police protection, telling his story to our two detective heroes.

Leo (sort of) describes a money laundering scheme known as the loan-back, in which the launderer essentially loans himself some of his own money. As Leo points out, not only is the money "now laundered," but the interest payments are tax deductible.

Because we didn't get the full story in the movie, and because, in true Hollywood fashion, this particular scheme wouldn't work, we'll have to fill in a little of Leo's scheme. It begins with the dirty money, proceeds of millions of dollars in drug transactions. Leo is required to get the money offshore, which he does by employing couriers to move the currency itself to Panama. (In the movie, the money was being shipped in a container by sea, something real-life launderers have done.)

Once the money is in a place like Panama, where the dollar is by treaty legal tender, no questions are asked about large, container-sized deposits. Leo arranges for the money, US$1 million, to be placed in an account in the name of Goetz S.A. at Banco de Darien. The placement stage is now complete.

To layer the money, Goetz could move it from bank to bank and shell corporation to dummy company, but we'll keep this simple. He moves the million dollars, less his commission of 2%, or $20,000, to a second account at First Pacific Bank. This is an account held by a dummy finance company, GGG Finance, Inc. Both Goetz S.A. and GGG Finance, Inc., are bearer share corporations, the bearer being one of those South Africans in Los Angeles who gave Leo the money in the first place.

Goetz draws up some loan documents purporting to show that GGG Finance loaned $980,000 to Frontline, Inc., a company set up in California to front for the bad guys. Frontline begins making payments on this loan by sending checks to the First Pacific Bank account of the lender, GGG Finance. The interest portion of these payments is tax deductible as a business expense, although GGG is supposed to report it.

At the end of the cycle, Frontline has $980,000 in "clean" money (which they're going to need after Mel gets finished with their pole house). If anyone asks about the source of the money, Frontline can point to the loan documents and refer the questioner to GGG, whose Panamanian attorney probably won't have much to say.

Leo: "All I did was, I laundered a half a billion dollars in drug money, okay? Give or take a few. Who can count with that much money?" See Figure 21.6.

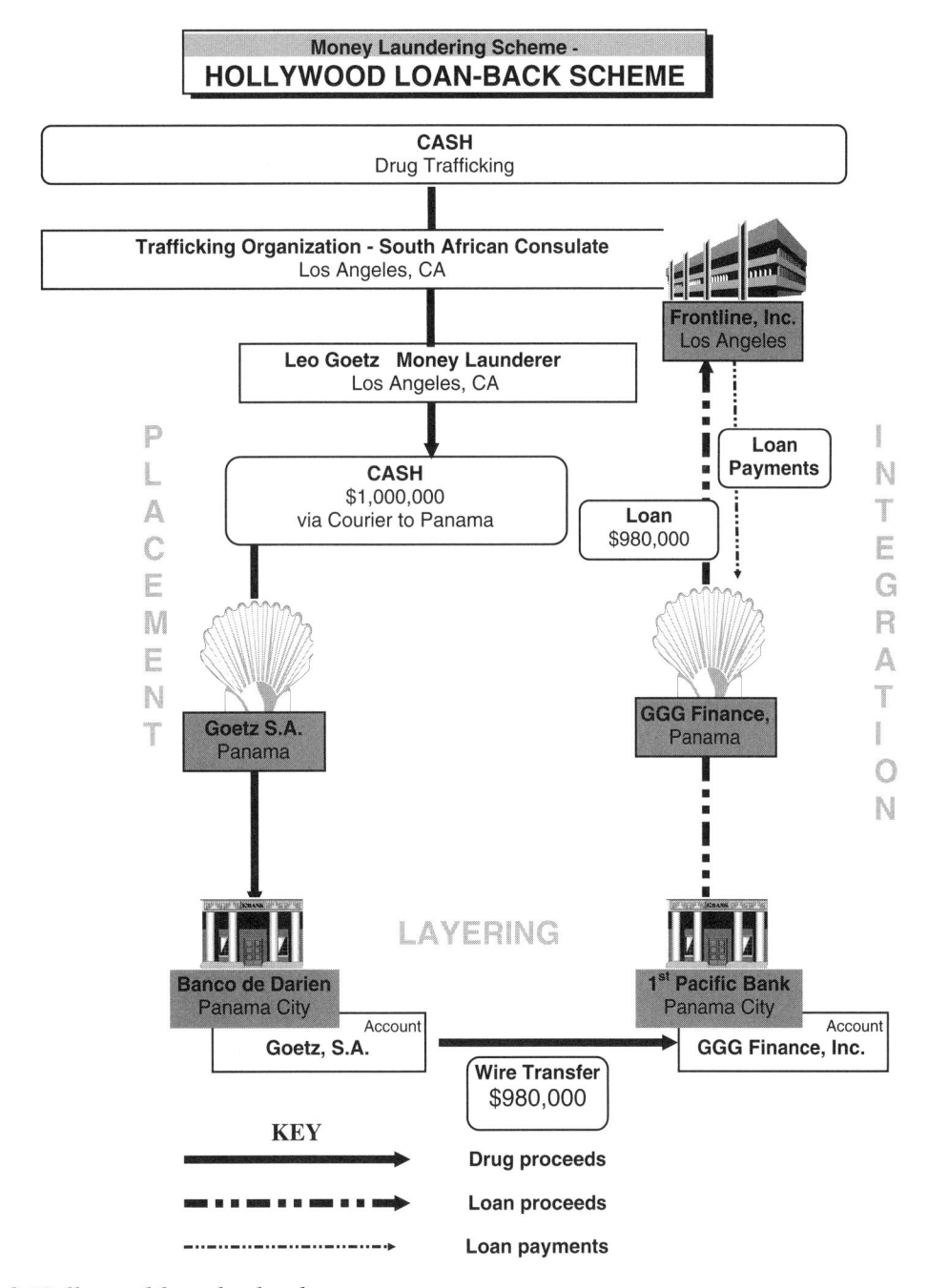

Figure 21.6 Hollywood loan-back scheme.

Documentation

Most of the documentation in this particular scheme is generated by the participants — not a good start for our case. There will be records of the wire transfers between the accounts, but tracing the funds back from GGG, Inc., will be difficult. This will be especially true if co-conspirator GGG, Inc., doesn't want to discuss the matter. Under Panamanian law, they don't have to.

Having Goetz available to describe the entire scenario is a big help, but not something you can count on in most cases.

Investigation of a Loan-Back Scheme

In the movie, the police had the advantage of inside information from the man who set up the entire operation. It doesn't get much better than this. Short of this, you're going to need some luck, especially if the launderer takes the money offshore and brings it back from there.

IRS has been dealing with this particular scheme for decades, and it has an advantage over other law enforcement agencies in that it can force an individual to completely document all aspects of an item such as a loan. If the nature of the loan is questioned in the examination of a tax return, the auditor can ask for all sorts of records — anything necessary to prove the genuineness of the loan. Even if that money is coming back from an offshore secrecy haven, if the taxpayer wants to exclude the income or claim the deduction, he or she will have to produce the documents.

If the loan is domestic, our burden is a little easier. We should be able to obtain bank records to document the movement of money and loan repayment. We can get information about the companies involved and determine whether they are legitimately engaged in business or not.

Whether the transaction is "arm's length" or not is important, at least as far as the tax consequences are concerned. Are these two parties closely related? Is the loan really between two separate parties, or is it a sham for tax purposes?

Sources of Information

Criminal sources may be most valuable, since they can point to specific operational details. Having the launderer him- or herself is extremely desirable, though a difficult task to accomplish. Having subordinates who may possess pieces of the overall picture, especially couriers, is an alternative.

Bank records of wire transfers could document transfers between the "lender" (GGG Finance) and some other source for the funds (Goetz, S.A.). The records relating to the loan payment are instructive.

Business records at the borrower and lender are important, as these may reveal the special relationship that secretly exists. If the loan is not a truly "arm's length" transaction, it could be considered fraudulent, and at the very least it would cause suspicions to be raised.

Tax records might be useful if the lender is reporting the interest payments. If the lender isn't, it has tax problems, and the borrower might as well.

Potential Violations

- 18 U.S.C. 1956   Money laundering
- 18 U.S.C. 1965 (h) Money laundering conspiracy
- 18 U.S.C. 1957   Financial institution money laundering
- 31 U.S.C. 5332   Bulk cash smuggling

Loan-Back 2

A variation of the *Lethal Weapon* loan-back involves a legitimate financial institution as the lender. You'll recall that Leo Goetz relied on a dummy finance company of his own creation to make the loan. In a version of the scheme known as the "Loan Sandwich" or the "Dutch Sandwich," an established bank is prevailed upon to do the lending.

Under what circumstances would a legitimate bank do this? Three conditions would need to be present. First, the bank wouldn't know the money was dirty, it having already passed through the placement and layering stages at this point. Second, the bank would need to have sufficient confidence in repayment. This means the borrower has good credit or collateral or some other security for the loan. (From the bank's perspective, the best scenario would be if the borrower already had the full amount of the loan or more on deposit in the bank.) Third, there has to be something in it for the bank, which there usually is, since lending at interest is a bank's business.

The advantage to using a bank is that if you ask, it will quickly verify the existence of the loan. It also provides a very legitimate-appearing source. There usually wouldn't be any question about the source of these funds, though there might be about the security or collateral posted.

Case Example

Drug trafficker Billy Bell has a seemingly legitimate business, BB Video, Inc., a California corporation. BBV was chartered to operate a video rental and entertainment business in San Francisco. (See Figure 21.7)

Wishing to expand, BBV approaches its banker, Central Union Bank for a $1.8 million loan to be used for the purchase of a four-screen theater complex, SouthCity Cineplex in nearby Burlingame. The theaters are appraised at $2.1 million and appear to be profitable. The asking price for the cineplex is $2 million even.

After an investigation, Central Union Bank approves the loan, on condition that BBV pays a $200,000 down payment and obtains additional security for the loan.

Using various placement methods, Bell has succeeded in moving $2 million to an account he maintains at a Panamanian bank, Banco de Darien (1). When he receives word of the loan's approval, Bell orders Banco de Darien to transfer $2 million to the account of Pacific Action, S.A. (PASA), a shell corporation Bell established in the British Virgin Islands (2). (In this stage, you can add as many layers using as many shells and accounts as you want, but we'll keep it simple and only do it once.)

PASA transfers the $2 million by wire to the Central Union Bank account of BP Trading, a Hong Kong company (3). Within a day, BP Trading moves the $2 million by wire to its account at Central Union's San Francisco branch.

BP Trading's Hong Kong attorney provides Central Union Bank with papers agreeing to guarantee BBV's note. The $2 million is used to buy a CD at Central Union for the duration of the loan (4). (The bank pays interest on this CD — an added benefit for Bell.) If Bell is asked, he can represent that he had done some business with the Hong Kong company in the past, and they were looking for an opportunity to get into the American market. Who's going to know the difference?

BBV puts up the $200,000 down payment from its funds, and the bank loans the balance of the $2 million purchase price (5, 6). BBV now makes the payments (7) on its theater, which looks very clean, as well as a $2 million CD that looks pretty good as well.

INVESTIGATION OF THE LOAN-BACK SCHEME

The loan-back is a magician's delight. Presto! A million (or 10 million) rabbits magically appear to do the conjurer's bidding. And best of all, these bunnies are tax deductible!

Tax cheats have employed this dodge for years, giving examiners some experience in detecting fraudulent loans. After you understand the theory, you can ask the right questions to deconstruct the operation.

- Is the loan being repaid? (If not, you can be pretty sure there's a problem here.)
- How is the loan being repaid?

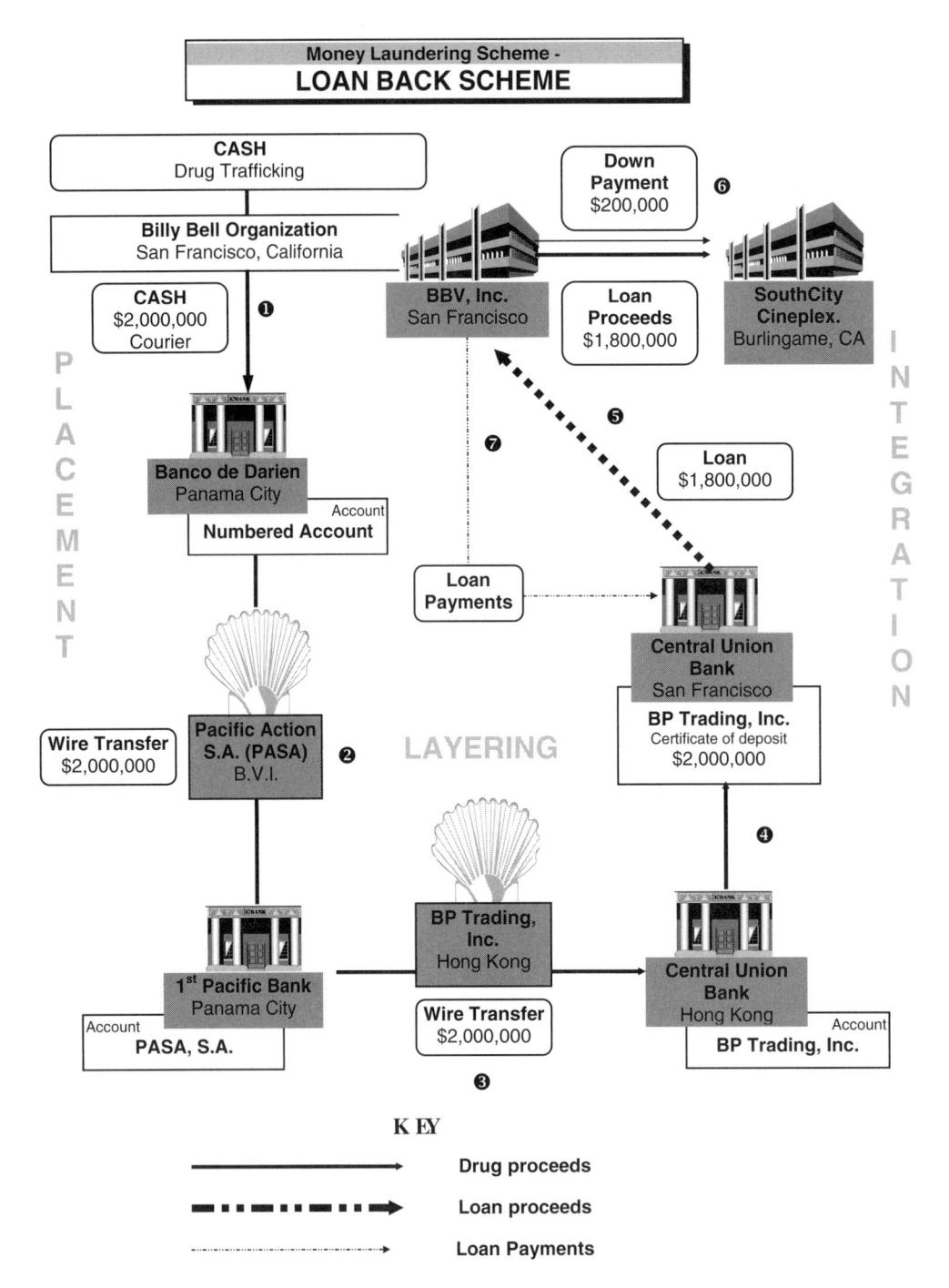

Figure 21.7 Loan-back scheme.

- Are all of the payments regular and in concordance with the note?
- Are there balloon payments or big drawdowns?
- Who is signing the checks? (This is useful information in any event.)
- Who is receiving the payments?
- Are the checks always deposited into the same account?
- Who are the other players?
- Who is the guarantor, and what's his relationship to the borrower?
- Who's putting up security, and why?
- Who is the lender, and is this loan reasonable from his point of view? (A video store lending money to finance the purchase of an oil tanker might not be.)
- What are the terms of the loan?
- Are the terms reasonable given the conditions?
- Is there any connection between the borrower and lender (e.g., the same lawyer represents both parties)?
- What is the security, and where did *it* come from?

CHAPTER 22

FIENDISHLY COMPLEX MONEY LAUNDERING SCHEMES

"Anyone who isn't confused here doesn't really understand what's going on."
Anonymous, with reference to the sectarian conflict in Northern Ireland

"But evil men and seducers shall wax worse and worse, deceiving, and being deceived."
Bible II: Timothy 3:13

Before we get any deeper into even more complicated money laundering schemes, let's review what we already know about the process:

1. Money laundering is a cycle, in which dirty cash is eventually made to resemble clean funds.
2. The cycle consists of three phases: placement, layering, and integration.
3. Despite the seeming complexity of the schemes employed, when broken down into their components, most money laundering schemes have common elements and vulnerabilities.
4. The money launderer is forced to operate under a number of restrictions.
5. Despite their reputations, most money laundering schemes aren't that complicated.

When you read about money laundering in the newspapers or hear about it on TV, the most complex schemes seem to employ convoluted mechanisms for moving the funds. Confusing systems of banks, businesses, and nominees function to conceal the background or source of the money. While it is true that most money laundering cases do not involve such complexity, the ones that do can be assumed to handle a very great deal of money. After all, why go to the trouble (and considerable expense) of establishing some Gordian knot of entities and bank accounts to conceal a few thousand dollars in burglary proceeds?

COMPONENTS OF MONEY LAUNDERING SCHEMES

We've looked at some schemes and seen how the components work, either individually or together as elements in a larger scheme. Each of these components works best in a particular segment of the money laundering cycle.

MECHANISMS FOR PLACEMENT

Placement of the laundered funds — that initial transformation of the bulk cash proceeds of crime into some other form — is the stage at which the launderer is most vulnerable. A variety of placement mechanisms can be used and almost all of them involve at least one of the following:

- Stashing the money (buried treasure)
- Transporting the money (smuggling it offshore à la *Lethal Weapon*)

- Commingling the money with the receipts of a legitimate business
- Placing the money with some sort of financial institution, whether a bank, currency exchange, *casa de cambio,* or other nonbank financial institution

All of these options pose problems for the money launderer. How he or she decides to solve these problems will dictate the type of case you have. In any event, whether the launderer decides to buy the cooperation of a bank official or set up a dog grooming business as a front, the choices are limited. He or she can:

- Act on his or her own or with accomplices (smurfing or transporting the funds)
- Use nominees to conceal his or her interest in the transaction(s)
- Set up businesses to be used as fronts, to commingle funds, or to hold bank accounts
- Establish one or more bank accounts to receive deposits

Any number of variations or combinations of the above are possible, but the point remains, this activity represents the most danger to the launderer.

Mechanisms for Layering

Layering of the proceeds, once the initial placement is accomplished, is much more difficult to detect. As we've seen, once the money gets into the financial system, it is just another drop in the trillions of dollars in wealth that are moved around the world every day. In the layering stage, the criminal is likely to use nominees, businesses, shell corporations, and bank accounts as the "layers" in the scheme. Movement of the funds through these layers is likely to involve a number of financial instruments or transactions, including:

- Wire transfers
- Cashier's checks
- Bank drafts
- Money orders
- Traveler's checks
- Letters of credit
- Bearer securities
- Cash transportation

The objective of the layering phase is to put as much distance as possible between the money and its source. Good layering schemes use offshore tax haven and bank secrecy jurisdictions.

Mechanisms for Integration

Integration of the laundered funds is the bottom line. Once the money has been cleaned, it can be returned to its source in a form that can be used for any purpose, legal or illegal. We looked at a couple of schemes that are used to integrate laundered funds, notably the loan-back schemes. The really complex schemes all provide for integration of the funds. They are the most difficult to detect or investigate. These schemes are the well-protected payoff for the criminal.

The schemes covered in this chapter involve the integration of laundered funds. Don't be intimidated by the chapter title; none of these schemes are so complex that you can't follow the thread. The big problem for law enforcement is not that the integration scheme is so complex, it is that by the time the launderer has reached this stage, the money already appears to be clean. It is very easy to bring these funds back into the economy once they've been through the soak and lather cycles. It is very hard for investigators to detect this activity at this late point in the process. There are a few hints, but some luck would be very useful at this stage. (An insider witness would also be helpful.)

INVOICE SCAMS

An *invoice* is a bill for goods delivered or services rendered, usually containing an itemization of the charges and terms. There are *purchase invoices* and *sales invoices,* depending on where you are in the transaction. Money launderers can have all sorts of fun with invoices. Let's examine these precious bits of paper to find out why.

First of all, think back on our books and records discussion, and remember that when an item is ordered or delivered, accounting entries are generated, along with supporting documentation. These actions take place at two locations — on the books of the buyer and of the seller. In credit transactions, *invoices* are generated by the seller and delivered to the purchaser, who is expected to remit payment according to the terms described on the invoice.

On the books of the purchaser, this transaction might be debited to Inventory and credited to Accounts Payable. On the books of the seller, Accounts Receivable would be debited, with another account — Sales, maybe — credited. More entries will follow when payment is actually made, of course, but in the meantime, that invoice documents a transaction involving assets to both ends of the deal: merchandise (buyer) and a receivable (seller).

Another thing to keep in mind is that as an asset, this document has value as *commercial paper;* it's now an item that can be sold or transferred to another party. The most wonderful thing about invoices, as far as a money launderer is concerned, is that the amount shown as owing on this unique asset can be whatever the two parties agree upon. This is most definitely not the case with other financial instruments (such as cash), most of which have set values on their face or are subject to market conditions. The amount on an invoice is subject only to what the seller decides to charge and the buyer agrees to pay.

The potential for manipulation of this tool is substantial, especially if the two parties to the transaction are in cahoots with each other. If so, those on either end can realize major benefits from either of the two invoice scams. If a money launderer controlled both ends of a transaction, great quantities of dirty money could be integrated into the economy, and probably without anybody noticing. Everything would look very much like the normal operation of a legitimate business. As with loan-backs, invoice scams have long been used as tax dodges. Figure 22.1 is a letter of credit application showing the invoice description and amount.

Underinvoicing

Let's suppose that in a moment of supreme lunacy I decide to (*a*) take a mistress and (*b*) buy her a big diamond ring. I've got $5000, and I know a jeweler with a good selection. There are a couple of reasons why that jeweler might be willing to invoice that ring below the amount I agree to really pay him.

And I've got a couple of really good reasons for concealing the true amount paid, too. I don't want to come to anybody's attention as a big spender, and I certainly don't want my wife to know I'm spending that kind of money. So, I approach the jeweler to see whether we can work something out. I offer to pay the jeweler the full asking price of $5000 (very generous, considering the markup on retail jewelry), but only if he will make out the invoice for $10 over his cost — $2510.

I pay the $2510 by check and then pay the balance of $2490 in cash, and everybody's happy. How happy? Well, the jeweler shows a sale on his books for $2510; his net profit on the deal, as far as an IRS auditor is concerned, is $10. That auditor, if she were to trace the check back to me, would find it in my records. The seller in this case now has $2490 in cash that he doesn't have to pay any taxes on.

The money laundering implications are obvious. Take the example a step further, and assume that I was a drug dealer, operating through a front business. The cash is drug money. At the end of this deal, I've got a $5000 asset — the diamond. I've also placed or concealed $2490 in cash, and my girlfriend is very pleased. But, suppose she wasn't, and I had to sell this jewel, getting $4000 from another jeweler. Although I'm distressed that my girlfriend didn't like her gift, I'm somewhat consoled by the fact that I now have almost $1500 in "income" from a nondrug source.

In an invoice scam, the bottom line is manipulated to the benefit of one end of the transaction or the other. In an underinvoicing scam, the true value of the goods sold is *greater* than the stated price. In my example, I actually made up the

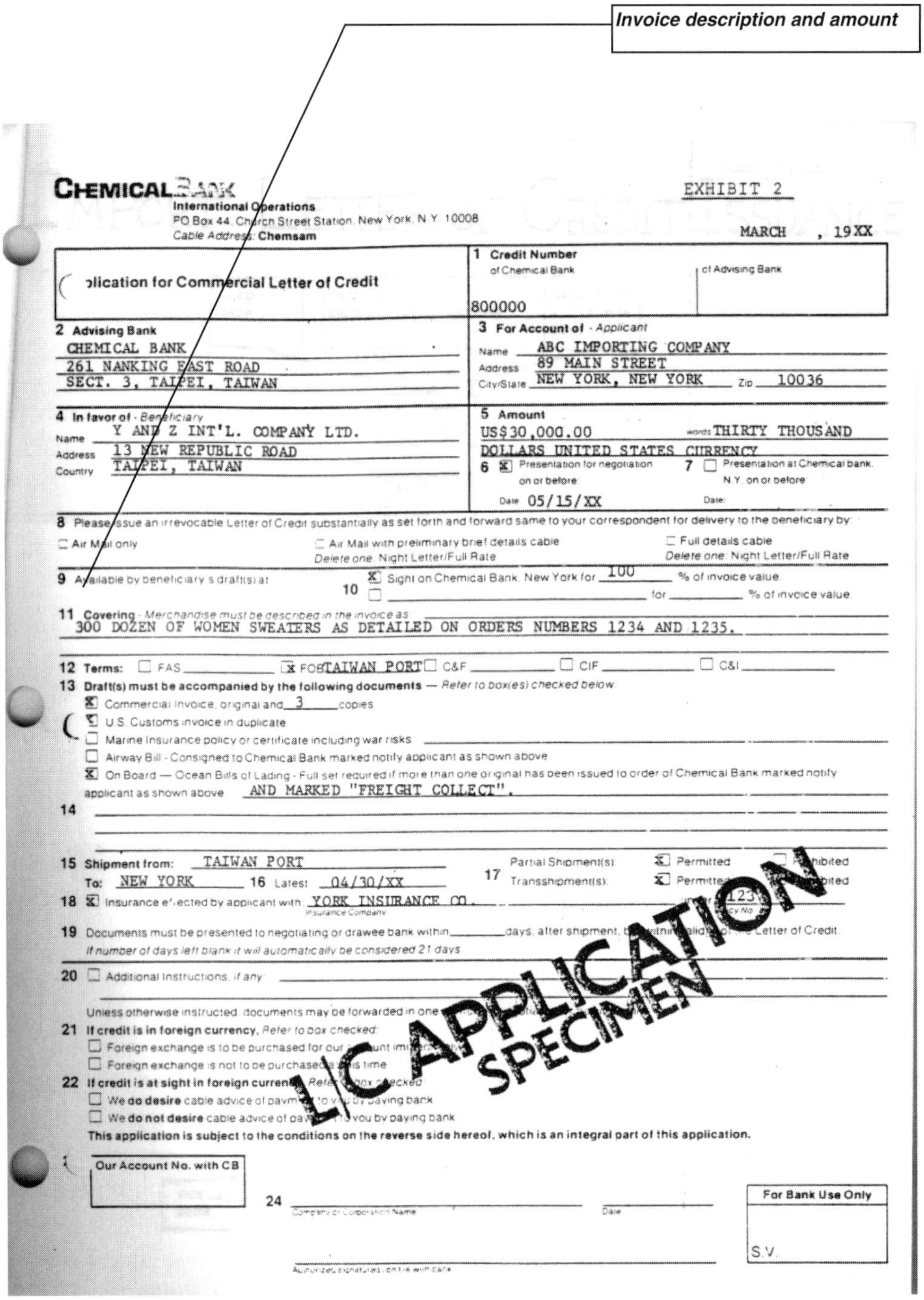

Figure 22.1 Commercial letter of credit application showing invoice amount.

difference between the true value of the item and the purchase price. In a money laundering scheme, the extra money may change hands only on paper. This is because in a well-planned invoice scam, the money launderer controls *both* ends of the transaction.

How common is this type of scheme? Nobody really knows, because trillions of dollars in business deals happen every day, and invoices are flying around the world like some sort of paper blizzard at a rate greatly exceeding the ability of any government agency to track.

These schemes can work with any purchase — including real estate, by the way, yet another avenue for the launderer to explore. In one case, a drug dealer wanted to buy a home

Laundering Scheme -
UNDERINVOICING

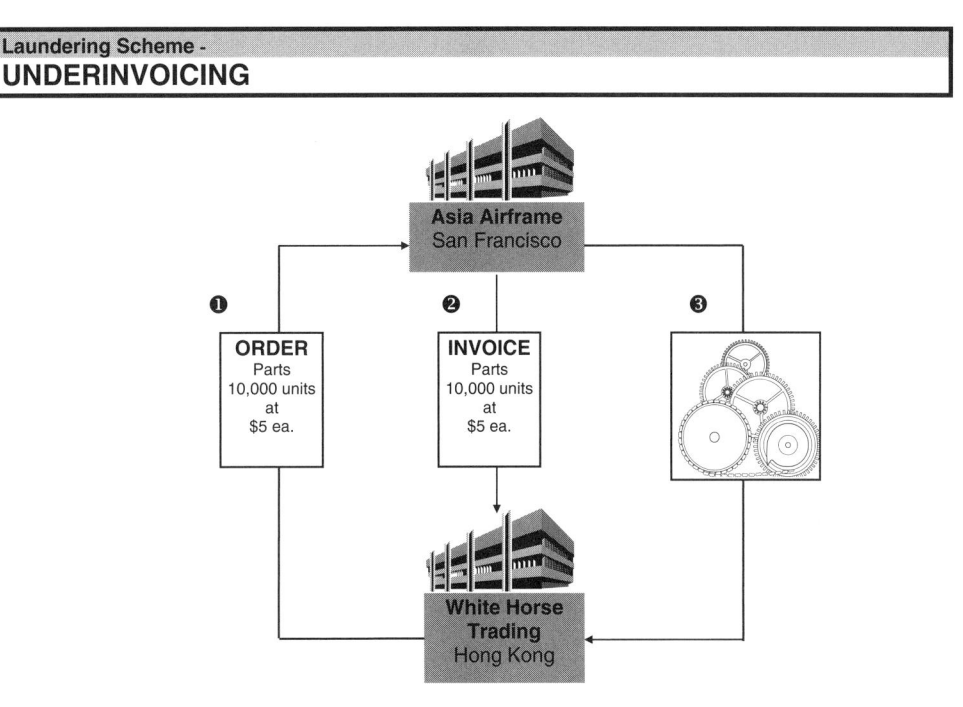

Figure 22.2 Underinvoicing scheme.

but didn't have enough income from legitimate sources to justify spending more than $200,000. The house he wanted was listed at $400,000. He cut a deal with the owners to buy the property for $375,000, paying $175,000 of the amount "under the table" if they would show the sale price as $200,000. The sellers were happy to do this, since they were saving the taxes owed on the $175,000. (They did have the problem of dealing with all that cash, however.) The drug dealer had successfully hidden $175,000. Note also that this transaction could have been done with the connivance of the real estate agent or without, as a sort of side deal with the owner — although the agent wouldn't be too happy about losing the commission on the $175,000 that was paid under the table.

Case Example

What's needed in an invoicing scheme are a buyer and a seller who are very comfortable with each other. This was the case with George Lee and John Kong. Not only were they closely associated through their heroin business, they had seemingly legitimate ties as well.

Lee operated an import–export business in Hong Kong known as White Horse Trading. Kong had a business, Asia Airframe, specializing in aircraft parts in San Francisco, California. Kong needed another shipment of heroin, which he could acquire from Lee, and they agreed that payment was to be in the form of substantially undervalued merchandise. See Figure 22.2.

Lee began the process by ordering $50,000 in aircraft parts (1). The actual value of these parts was significantly higher — around $500,000. The difference was the amount of drug money Kong needed to move to Hong Kong. There was a contract specifying the actual amount, but this was kept in a safe place in a third country, Taiwan perhaps.

Asia Airframe shipped the parts and sent a bill to White Horse for $50,000 (2). After the parts were received (3), White Horse paid the invoice amount of $50,000, even though they were able to sell the parts for almost $500,000 more. Lee shipped the heroin to Kong after the parts were sold.

If this had been purely a money laundering device, Kong would have shipped the undervalued parts and then arranged for the proceeds of the sale to be deposited offshore. By this means, he would then have moved $450,000 offshore, with significant tax and Customs benefits.

Research on Invoice Schemes

Money Laundering Alert, a very useful publication put out monthly by a Miami corporation, has reported several times on invoice schemes that have been or may be part of money laundering operations. Two of the articles focused on a study performed by two researchers at Florida International University.

Professors Simon Pak and John Zdanowicz reviewed import and export figures maintained by the U.S. Customs Service and discovered that traders were declaring invoice amounts that were grossly distorted when compared to the average world prices.

For example, the study detected instant cameras that were invoiced at $3127 each, smoke detectors for $653, sleeping bags for $1500, and bottles of salad dressing at $720 each. The professors commented that they had expected to find some differences in prices, but not to the extent they discovered. Dr. Zdanowicz commented, "From the standpoint of an economist, there is no reason why the difference should be this large. In a normal market, these deviations are a lot smaller. The preliminary statistics imply that something must be going on."

What that "something" is could be one of several possibilities. It could be that the traders are seeking to evade taxes through favorable transfer pricing. Some form of capital flight might be taking place, or the distorted invoice prices could be an indication of money laundering.

A look at some of the countries where the disparities were noticeable could point toward the possibility of money laundering. The research showed that underinvoicing involving the transfer of capital from the United States to Colombia occurred in several startling cases. Safety headgear that normally sells for $38.01 was sold for $2.28 per dozen, 6% of the usual invoice amount. Cooking stoves normally invoiced at $425.65 each were shipped at $76.62.

On the overinvoice side, razors were shipped from Colombia to the United States at an invoice price of $34.81 each. The average world price for this item is $0.09. (Perhaps they were selling to the Pentagon.) Memo pads that usually transfer at $0.28 each were shipped at an invoice rate of $4.05. It would seem, based upon these figures, that some form of financial manipulation is taking place.

Overinvoicing Case Example

Paul Gavin is the successful owner of a Los Angeles appliance business, JPG Wholesale Appliance, Inc. His close friend is Peter Van Zandt, a businessman in Cape Town, South Africa. Van Zandt is planning on relocating his business, Cape Products, to the United States, but due to legal restrictions designed to prevent the flight of capital from his country, he is unable to just sell out and leave with the money.

Gavin agrees to help his friend with his problem, and the two men decide on an invoice scheme that takes advantage of their business ties. See Figure 22.3. The first step in the scheme is Van Zandt's order for 1,000 refrigerators, to be shipped by JPG to Cape Town (1). The invoice price for these items is $1 million, or $1,000 per unit. Both Gavin and Van Zandt know full well that the true value of this shipment is more like $400,000, or $400 per unit, and in fact the two men have a secret contract documenting the correct amount, which is kept in a safe deposit box in a Swiss bank.

JPG sends its bill for $1 million to Cape Products (2) and ships the refrigerators (3). Upon receipt of the shipment, Cape Products wires $1 million to JPG (4). As specified in their secret contract, Gavin immediately wires $600,000 to Van Zandt's

Laundering Scheme -
OVERINVOICING

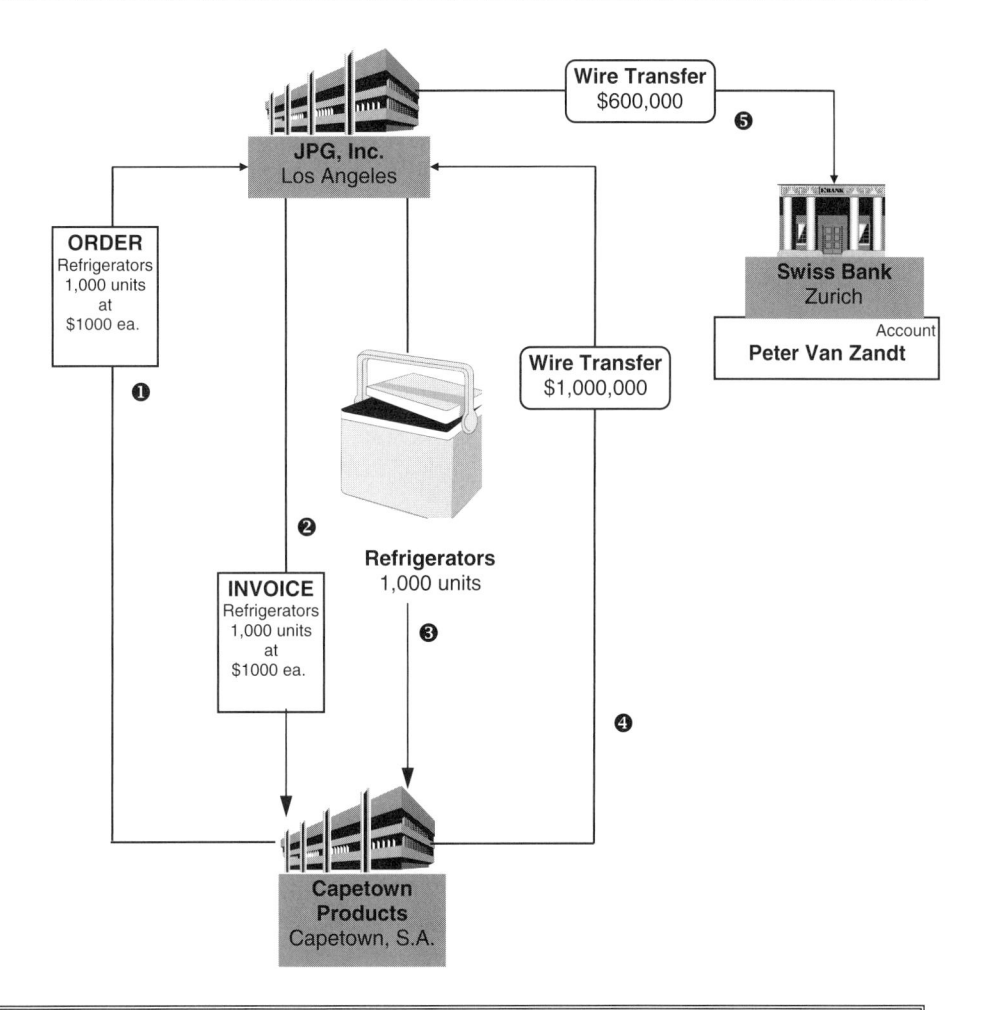

Figure 22.3 Overinvoicing laundering scheme.

Swiss bank account, completing the transaction (5).

Van Zandt still has the overpriced refrigerators for sale. Proceeds from these sales, along with other money he wants to move out of the country, will form the basis for his next transaction with Gavin.

This example relates to capital flight, something that most governments would prefer to avoid, and those with shaky national economies need to prevent. The transfer of wealth offshore can be very harmful to a weakened economy that needs all the domestic investment it can get. For this reason, many countries have instituted laws governing how much currency can be removed from the country and what types of overseas investments its citizens can have.

Some of the strictest of these controls were in the former Soviet bloc; nobody was allowed to remove a single ruble from the country. Korea and the Philippines, to name only two Pacific Rim countries, still have restrictions regarding the export of currency and capital flight. Korea, for example, has a restriction on the value of real

Laundering Scheme - OVERINVOICING - II

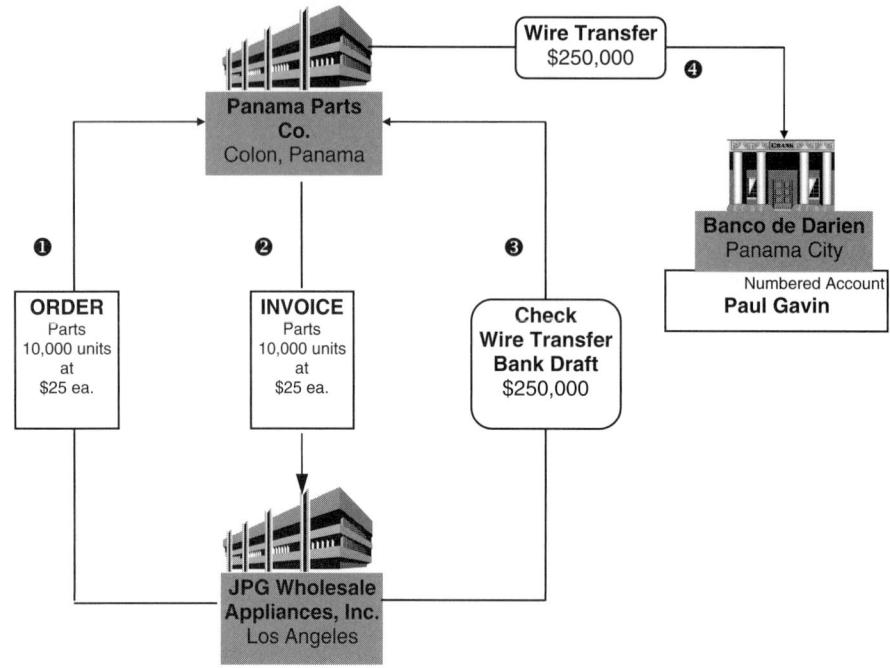

Figure 22.4 Overinvoicing laundering scheme.

estate that individuals can own abroad. Countries that have these types of restrictions are often very interested to hear about one of their citizens' being caught in some scheme involving large amounts of currency or assets.

These are situations that need to be considered when looking at invoice or other money laundering schemes. Suspicious transactions do not always involve money from drugs or some other illegal source. Sometimes they may be intended to make an investment that is perfectly legal everywhere except in the country where it is taking place.

The other concern to keep in mind is that this activity comprises a whole other underground economy, which a money launderer may be able to exploit in concealing the profits of crimes such as drug trafficking.

Case Example

The following over-invoicing scam is essentially nothing more than a paper shuffle. No goods or services actually change hands. Again, this is possible only because the players control both ends of the transaction; it could never happen in legitimate commerce. But then, there's nothing legitimate about money laundering.

See Figure 22.4. In this scheme, Paul Gavin of JPG Wholesale Appliances, Inc., places an order for $250,000 in appliance parts from Panama Parts Company of Colon, Panama (1). All of the appropriate entries are made on JPG's books. Little does anyone suspect that Panama Parts is really a shell corporation, set up by Gavin to launder drug money.

Upon receipt of the order, Panama Parts issues an invoice for the parts, in the amount of $250,000 (2). When he gets this invoice, Gavin orders payment to be made, via check, bank draft, wire transfer, or letter of credit, to Panama Parts (3).

When payment is received in Colon, the attorney for Panama Parts causes the funds to be transferred to Gavin's numbered account at the Banco de Darien (4). Gavin can now use these funds in some other integration scheme.

INVESTIGATING INVOICE SCAMS

"Something's not right here" could summarize an outsider's view of an invoice scam. Certainly none of us would agree that razors ordinarily imported for nine cents should be invoiced to a buyer for almost $35 each.

An investigation of invoice schemes should have two objectives: detection and investigation. Detection is difficult because the kinky transactions are concealed in the vast tide of international commerce taking place every day. Detection of the few extraordinary invoices among all the hundreds of thousands of shipments occurring every day was difficult, even for the two professors using advanced computer modeling techniques. Even if an alarm bell rings, the invoice is only one piece of paper in a complex set of contracts, bills, orders, shipping documents, certificates, Customs forms, and assorted other records. It's important to be able to examine all of these documents. For example, in the case example illustrated in Figure 22.4, no goods actually changed hands. Even though the sale was documented on an order and an invoice, there would be no bill of lading, shipping record, or any of the accounting records relating to inventory (unless the launderer went to the trouble to forge these). Lack of such supporting documentation would be an additional indication of manipulation.

Qui bono? (Who benefits?) The biggest questions should be asked of the party that benefits most from the transaction as it appears on paper. In the case of those $35 razors, the seller certainly gained the most from that transaction, at least on paper. This gain should be examined from a tax and Customs perspective. In the case of the diamond ring for my mistress, some questions should be asked about how I got such a great deal on the jewelry.

Save a few questions for the loser in the deal — the guy who supposedly paid the $35 for those nine-cent razors should have a very interesting explanation for his seemingly incredible stupidity. If this were a completely legitimate transaction, you'll probably find this executive on the unemployment line. If he's still at his desk, your first question might be, "Why are you still here?"

Analysis of a financial transaction involving invoices requires a good bit of tracing. Computer programs designed for invoice analysis can assist in this process. IRS-CID issues this type of program to its agents, and other law enforcement agencies may be able to obtain assistance from CID in performing this work.

SOURCES OF INFORMATION

Customs records document international shipments by and to American businesses. If your subject is doing business internationally, some record of the shipments will exist.

The *Commerce Department* also keeps import and export records, as well as statistics on the normal or customary world prices of items in international trade. These are useful for comparison purposes.

Subject records, especially the books and records of the domestic party in the transaction, should be a wealth of information. Because it's so important that the transaction be completely traced, these records are critical.

Bank records are also useful. Most international transactions involve four parties: the buyer, seller, buyer's bank, and seller's bank. The two banks will keep records on each deal.

At least one criminal prosecution has been undertaken in which invoice schemes formed the Specified Unlawful Activity, this being a case involving Falcon Instruments Inc. in the Eastern District of Virginia. In this case, Pakistani importers used inflated invoices to move capital to Pakistan. This case was reported in *Money Laundering Alert,* November 1994.

BUY-BACKS

We talked about the loan-back, a scam that involved the crook "loaning" him- or herself laundered funds. It's no great strain to pay this loan back, since the borrower *is* the lender. A variation of this scheme is the buy-back, in which the criminal uses laundered funds to buy something that he or she already owns. This type of operation doesn't always have the tax benefits enjoyed by a loan-back scam, but it does provide the criminal with a ready supply of clean-looking money from an unimpeachable (or at least seemingly so) source.

Even though this is definitely an integration mechanism, the magic in a buy-back is in the layering. The trick is to have the buyer appear to be someone totally removed from the seller, an extension of what is sometimes referred to as an "arm's length transaction." In the launderer's case, it needs to be a very long arm indeed.

A buy-back will work with any type of asset, big or small, depending on how much money you want to launder. Businesses are good, as is real estate, jewelry, or even intangibles, such as rights to a song or a trademark. Finding a buyer willing to pay the asking price isn't going to be a problem, so the deal is almost done.

This scheme, like the loan-back, relies on documentation to make everything look legitimate. Let's say I have successfully placed $1 million in dirty money offshore in my Swiss bank account. I'd like to have use of this money back in the United States. I decide on a buy-back scheme involving this book. I start by having a lawyer in Switzerland set up a publishing company, ML Books, Inc. The lawyer gets somebody to serve as a nominee director/officer, but I hold all the shares. Through my lawyer, I direct ML Books, Inc., to make me an offer for the worldwide publishing rights for this book. I get a letter from the president of ML Books with an initially insulting offer. I hold out for a million bucks, and after some intense negotiations, he agrees to my price. All of this is well documented, of course, except the parts where I'm telling the lawyer what to say.

I transfer my million dollars in dirty money to an account in ML Books' name, and ML Books transfers the money to me in the form of a nice clean cashier's check. I take this to my bank here in town, brag a little on my success, and head back to the typewriter for my next effort. I have to pay taxes on this income, of course, which is why it isn't as good a scheme as the loan-back. It's less complex, however, and I think you'll agree that the explanation for the money is pretty ironclad. My money has been successfully integrated.

The tax consequences are a big factor. The purchaser may have none, since this person may be located offshore and isn't earning any income on the deal anyway. The seller is going to be taxed at least at the capital gains rate, on the full amount, though some tax planning might shift some of the load.

As an element in a larger money laundering scheme, the buy-back is a very useful tool. You'll note that it may contain some of the elements we've talked about previously, such as shell corporations and nominees, as well as the cover of a business. As was the case with those elements, the buy-back can itself be used in a more complicated money laundering scheme. Obviously, a well-prepared scam would have absolutely no detectable connection between buyer and seller, other than this transaction. Extensive layering would be designed to conceal any such connection.

Case Example

Drug trafficker George Rice set up a Bay Area corporation to assist in the laundering of his drug proceeds. This business, Berkeley Services, Inc., was little more than Rice and a couple of relatives on file as the officers and directors. See Figure 22.5.

Over the years, Rice had been able to move a good deal of money offshore to Panama, where it now resides safely in Banco de Darien (1). Rice had, aside from his connection to Berkeley Services, no legitimate source of income, and he wanted to change this sad situation before anyone started asking difficult questions.

FIENDISHLY COMPLEX MONEY LAUNDERING SCHEMES

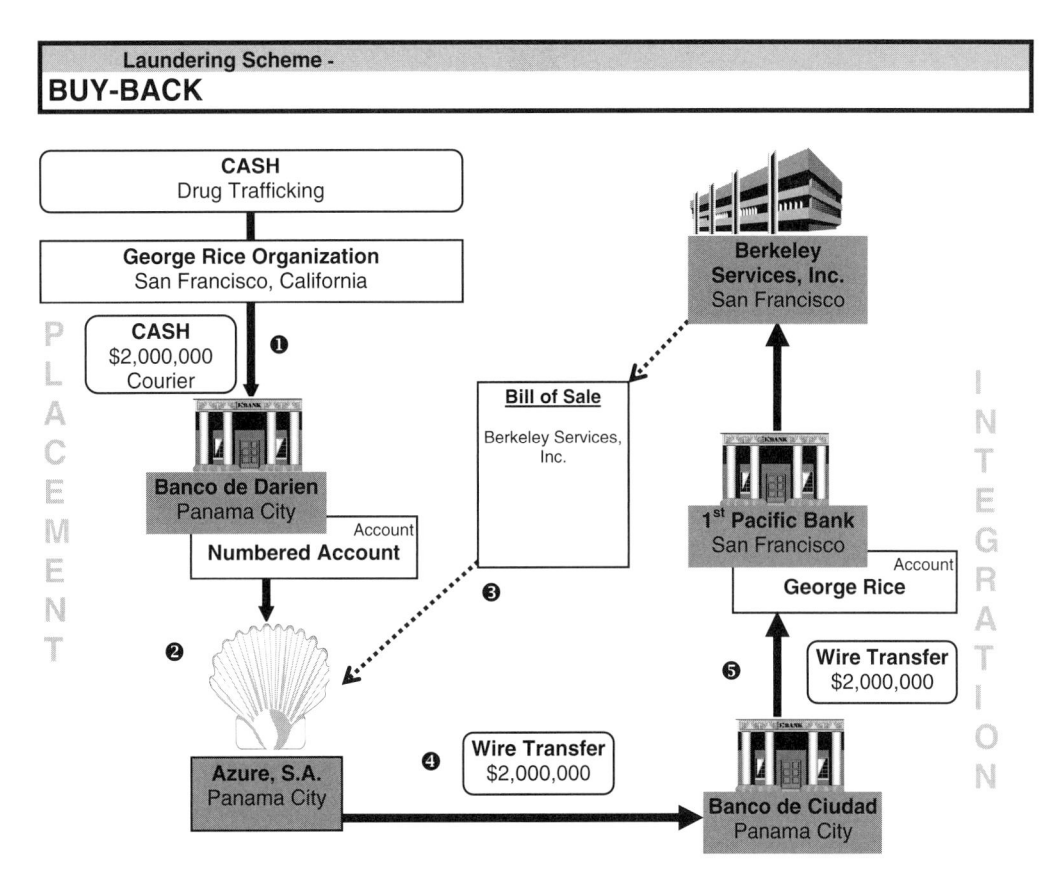

Figure 22.5 *Buy-back scheme.*

Rice flew down to Panama and arranged with an attorney to set up a new company, Azure, S.A., a bearer share corporation (2). The Panamanian attorney obtained a nominee to act as president of Azure, S.A., and set up another account for the business at a different bank, Banco de Ciudad.

A week or two later, Rice, acting as president of Berkeley Services, Inc., entered into negotiations with a Panamanian company, Azure, S.A., for the sale of Berkeley Services. After some haggling, the price of US$2 million was agreed upon, and attorneys in San Francisco prepared the paperwork documenting the sale (3).

Rice secretly directed his attorney to transfer the money from Banco de Darien to the Azure account at Banco de Ciudad (4). When the paperwork was completed, these funds were wired to Rice's account at First Pacific Bank in San Francisco (5).

VARIATION ON THE BUY-BACK THEME

A variation on the buy-back theme is the buy-back at a loss. This remedies some of the tax problems inherent in a straight buy-back scheme. Simply put, the seller of the property is forced to sell an asset at a substantial loss, most of which is tax deductible. In fact, some of the loss may well carry over into subsequent tax years, protecting future income.

Using the case example involving Mr. Rice's company, we add that his business, Berkeley Services, was a going concern, into which, over the years, Rice had invested $3 million. Now Rice moves to sell his company, but buyers are scarce. He arranges with a Panamanian company to buy the business for $2 million, creating a loss on paper of $1 million. Rice has repatriated the $2 million he had previously smuggled offshore, and he has a nice tax break for the current year.

In order to accomplish this goal, Rice would have to establish a *basis* — which is essentially his financial interest in the company, or what he has put into the business. (I'm not going to get into the various ways in which such a basis could be established, but it would only take some time, some money, and some legal and accounting assistance — all of which Rice has.) If the business is sold for a price less than the basis, a loss would result for tax purposes.

INVESTIGATING A BUY-BACK SCHEME

The key link in this whole scheme is that between the ostensible seller and the purported buyer. We know in our example that the two are one and the same, and this is what you'll be trying to prove in any buy-back scheme investigation. But how are you going to find out?

This won't be easy, especially if the deal has been properly layered. If the scheme is purely domestic, the perpetrator will probably use nominees, friends or relatives, or possibly an attorney to conceal his or her interest in the buying end. His or her interest in the selling end is very open; that's the point of the buy-back scheme — to have an obvious explanation for the funds.

There will be communications back and forth between the parties, but these aren't much help, since there would be such communications in any event. Every aspect of the transaction, especially the history of the asset being sold, needs to be thoroughly investigated, as should the buyer and the buyer's business.

SOURCES OF INFORMATION

The scheme is going to be well documented, especially at the seller's end. The really crucial documentation — those papers showing the secret link between the seller and the buyer — are going to be concealed. Consider the use of:

- *Wire intercepts,* including fax and oral communications, which may provide information about instructions
- *Financial search warrants,* at the seller's place of business, residence, or another location where records are kept, which may recover materials documenting the seller's connection to the other end of the deal (the bearer securities, for example)
- *Informants* from within the organization (Individuals who devise these schemes often feel the need to boast about how clever they are, or they may just entrust too much information to the wrong people.)

SECURITIES MANIPULATION

Securities are a fertile field for assorted schemes, many of which have been perfected by those in the industry. Because stocks, bonds, and other securities so closely resemble currency in their characteristics, they make excellent money laundering instruments. A billion-dollar corporation, with factories, offices, ships, trucks, and resources, can all fit in my briefcase if I've got the stock certificates.

It would be impossible to describe all the ways that securities could be manipulated for money laundering purposes, and pointless, since people are thinking up new ways daily. Old-time confidence men, inside traders, and white-collar criminals have devised a wealth of scams that use securities as a means to some fraudulent end.

Stolen securities are a feature in some of these schemes. Although there aren't any bearer stocks in the United States anymore, stolen securities can still be used in schemes to acquire loans, especially if the lender isn't too picky about the unfamiliar name on the certificates.

A variation on this scheme caused problems for Richard Nixon's best friend, Charles G. "Bebe" Rebozo, a Miami banker. Rebozo took 900 shares of IBM stock that had been stolen in New York by organized crime, and he made a large loan using the stocks as collateral. He then arranged to sell the stock, getting rid of it right before the investigators showed up. The benefit for the criminals was getting nice clean cash, in the form of the loan from the Key Biscayne Bank, in exchange for the hot securities.

Another securities manipulation is the purchase of securities with dirty money and the use of these instruments as collateral for a bank loan.

This scheme has the benefit of not using visibly "hot" paper. The banker making a loan based on the securities would have no way of knowing they were purchased with drug money (or whatever), and the loan proceeds would provide the launderer with a "clean"-appearing source of wealth. This type of scheme could be expanded to allow the launderer to pay back the loan with more dirty money or with the profits of investments made with the loan funds.

If the criminal has access to an offshore shell corporation, this can be used to purchase and hold securities. Brokerage firms operate offshore, too, and are happy to get the business. Once money is moved to an offshore account, it can be applied to securities purchases with little difficulty. The criminal can then place the orders from anywhere, hold the certificates anywhere, and use these for such things as securing loans anywhere.

As an integration mechanism, securities manipulations can be effective, blending right in with all the hundreds of millions of shares, bonds, notes, and other instruments changing hands every day.

DOCUMENTATION

Securities schemes leave a wide trail. American securities are all numbered and registered in somebody's name, with transfers being recorded on the corporation's books, on the broker's books, and in the purchaser's records. If someone obtains a bank loan by using securities as collateral, the certificates will be on file at the bank. Brokerage companies keep good records and actually hold many of the securities for their customers. If the deal has been layered properly, however, all those documents aren't going to do much good in identifying the people behind the transactions.

Case Example

In this scenario, the criminal uses several scams, all involving securities. For purposes of the example, we'll use stock certificates, but bonds would work as well, or mutual fund shares, or whatever. See Figure 22.6.

Jay Gould prospered in the alien smuggling business, organizing the shipment of hundreds of would-be immigrants into the United States by land, sea, and air. His profits from this activity were substantial, and, being a big believer in capitalism, Gould is investing these profits in the stock market. He devised several schemes to do this in a way that prevented the transactions from being traced directly to him. After all, he did not want to lose his investment to the government.

Gould's first scam was the most direct. He opened a brokerage account at the firm of Jarrell Finch and began moving cash from his alien smuggling operation directly into this account, always in amounts under $10,000 (1). Gould churned this account unmercifully, an investment strategy designed to delight his broker, who was inclined to overlook the nature of the cash deposits in light of the commissions generated by all that churning activity.

The second scheme took advantage of Gould's underworld connections. Through a friend, Gould was able to obtain a large number of stock certificates that had been stolen in the daylight robbery of a Wall Street courier. The numbers on the shares were all registered, and the shares could not be sold on the open market, which is why Gould was able to use some of the cash from his smuggling operation to buy the shares at only 20% of face value.

Gould had $1 million in stock for an initial outlay of only $200,000 (2). Gould took the shares to his contact at First Pacific Bank and used them as collateral for a $500,000 loan (3). With these funds, Gould was able to invest in some clean securities at his own brokerage, Jarrell Finch (4).

The last scheme required Gould to use his offshore corporation, Atlas Shipping, to buy and hold clean securities. Gould had estab-

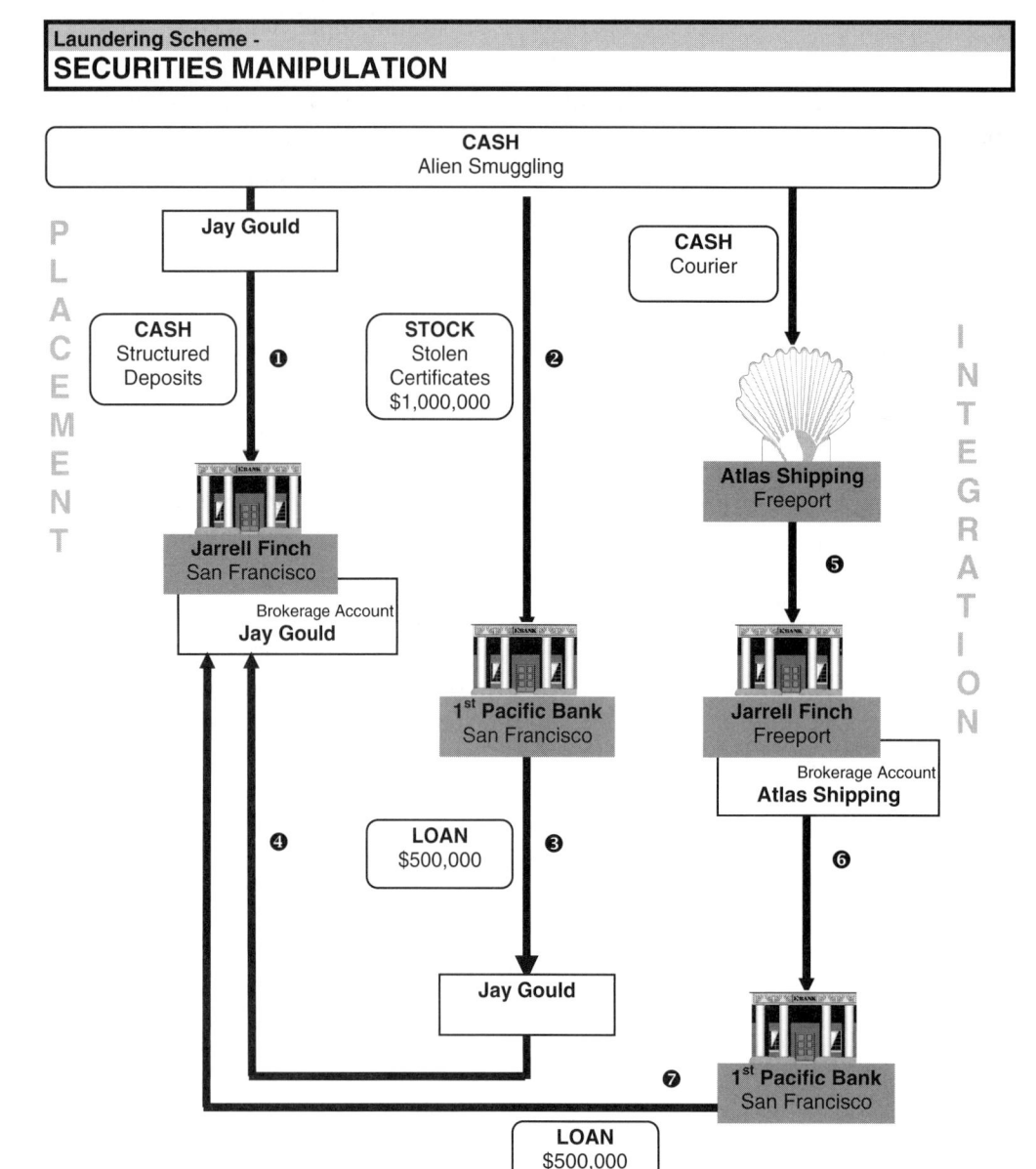

Figure 22.6 *Securities manipulation.*

lished offshore bank accounts and a couple of shell corporations to facilitate his smuggling business, and it appeared these would come in handy for the laundering of the profits. Atlas opened a brokerage account at the Jarrell Finch office in Freeport, Bahamas (5). From his residence in California, Gould was able to make telephone orders for securities purchases by Atlas Shipping, accumulating a portfolio of about $1 million in assorted NYSE blue-chip issues (6). Using these certificates as collateral, Gould obtained a loan from a California bank for $500,000 (7). (In real life, Gould would have layered this deal a little better, hiding a direct connection between himself and Atlas Shipping.)

There were some significant costs involved in this operation, including broker commissions, interest on the various loans, and other expenses. The benefits were substantial, however. For one thing, Gould had a solid portfolio of investment grade stocks, as well as those assets he bought with the loan proceeds. He was still holding the stolen certificates, but he rolled these over into a long-term CD and didn't have to worry about them for a while.

Best of all, everything he owned looked pretty legitimate from a money launderer's point of view.

INVESTIGATING A SECURITIES MANIPULATION

Lots of tracks are left in one of these deals. In places like Panama, bearer securities are permitted, but the days when a criminal could steal $10 million in "negotiable bearer bonds" in the United States are gone. Now, everything is tracked through the numbers and owner's name on the securities. There are an awful lot of these pieces of paper out there, though, which is how they can still be used in scams to obtain loans.

Let's look at Gould's three schemes separately. The first scheme, simply placing the bulk cash with the brokerage firm, is very direct. Gould is changing the form of his dirty drug money and getting into some investments that yield income from a legitimate-appearing source. Several brokerage firms have been busted for this type of activity in the past, and, like other financial institutions, they're required to report large cash transactions, as well as structured and suspicious ones, to the government. If Gould has a connection at the firm, he may be able to get around these requirements, or he may be able to avoid them, as he did in this instance, by breaking the deposits up into smaller amounts. Even a superficial analysis of the brokerage records would disclose the cash nature of the deposits.

The second scheme, using stolen securities to secure a loan, is hardly a new idea. Bankers are supposed to be familiar with this little ploy and take steps to protect themselves from getting stuck with a vault full of hot collateral. Bank examiners are supposed to check out the property used as collateral for loans. Again, if Gould has a contact in the bank, someone flexible in his or her definition of "diligence," Gould may succeed in getting the loan. The records of the loan will be extensive, and the securities themselves will be kept by the bank for security.

The third scheme, using offshore shell companies to make purchases, will generate communication between the manipulator (Gould) and the brokerage firms carrying out the instructions. If it's layered better than we've done here, this scheme can be difficult to detect. One thing to look for is connections (trades, transfers, deposits, etc.) between the subject's brokerage accounts and those of other entities.

SOURCES OF INFORMATION

Brokerage accounts are extensively documented. Social Security numbers or, in the case of a business, Taxpayer Identification Numbers are required to open these accounts. All transactions are thoroughly recorded, with reports being issued to IRS about large cash transactions and gains on the sale of securities.

Communication records, such as telephone toll records showing calls to brokerages or others involved in securities sales (banks), may provide leads to accounts. Brokerages also mail an incredible amount of stuff to their clients, so a mail cover on the right address will quickly turn up information about brokerage contacts.

Bank records, including loan files and the collateral used in securing loans, are useful. If the subject of the investigation has loans to him- or herself or to his or her businesses, these can be traced back through the lender. The objective of this tracing is to verify the legitimacy of the loans and their sources. A loan could be a loan-back scheme, after all, or it may be a legitimate loan secured by hot securities.

Subject records, such as those recovered in a financial search warrant, a trash cover, or perhaps through use of a John Doe subpoena, might prove very informative.

CHAPTER 23

TERRORISM FINANCING

"What's the sense of sending $2 million missiles to hit a $10 tent that's empty?"
George W. Bush, private Oval Office meeting, September 13, 2001

"We've got to go after the guts of this. This could be like a planaria. If you just cut off its head and it regenerates another head, that's not going to be very helpful. So, while, of course, Osama bin Laden and his lieutenants are part of the story, the real part of the story is to choke off the bloodline of this network."
Condoleezza Rice, *Fox News Sunday,* September 23, 2001

The bloodline of terrorist networks is money. You can have all the fanaticism and motivation in the world, but it's no good unless you can get out of that $10 tent and put it to some bad use. In the case of Osama bin Laden and his 9/11 plotters, they had plenty of money; they had enough to get all the way from Kabul to New York and Boston, where their fanaticism could play itself out in a spasm of horror that shook the world.

There's a tendency to think of people like bin Laden as leaders of a sort of ragtag, irregular version of armed forces, and there are some similarities. Al Qaeda, like most terrorist groups, has organization; a command structure; military, political, and other wings; and, of course, lots of armed men. (Though not as many as they used to.)

Certainly a terrorist network, however extensive, is far less costly to operate than a "conventional" military force. The American juggernaut that overwhelmed Afghanistan's Taliban regime and then toppled Saddam Hussein spends more money in five minutes than Osama's bunch had in its entire existence. The British, in their seemingly endless war against the Irish Republican Army and its fellows, outspent their rivals probably by a factor of thousands, if not millions.

Still, terrorists can get a lot of bang for their buck, as Mohammed Atta and his crew demonstrated on September 11, 2001. And achieving maximum impact at the lowest possible cost has always been the goal of terrorist groups, which are, after all, microscopically small organisms on the body politic. They will always be forced to economize, but this doesn't stop them from attempting to raise enough money to pay for all the mayhem they want.

What does terrorist financing have to do with money laundering? Why is this chapter even in the book? The two best reasons are that there are an awful lot of similarities between terrorist financing and money laundering, *and* we can use the same investigative techniques and procedures against this criminal activity.

After 9/11, Congress and governments all over the world made a startling discovery: It walked like a duck, quacked like a duck, and did a few other things like a duck, but terrorist financing wasn't a duck. At least, not the money laundering duck everybody was used to. The most important difference related to the source of the money. Money launderers, as we know, can only be convicted of laundering money that comes from some illegal source — a Specified Unlawful Activity (SUA). But terrorists don't always finance their operations with money earned in some illegal activity. In fact, terrorists traditionally have obtained their funding from four main sources, three of which, though not exactly legitimate, don't fit the definition of an SUA by a long shot.

In this chapter we will look at a couple of groups involved in terrorism, examining their funding needs, sources, and methods of operation. It will be useful to compare the two groups — the Provisional Irish Republican Army (PIRA) and Osama bin Laden's Al Qaeda — to see whether there are any common characteristics or vulnerabilities.

As noted, terrorist financing comes from four main sources:

- Criminal activity
- Charitable contributions or donations
- Legitimate or semilegitimate business
- Government or state sponsorship

Keep in mind that only the first could constitute an SUA under federal money laundering law, and then only if the offender had one of the four "intents" prescribed by 18 U.S.C. §1956 (a) (1).

See Figure 23.1 and Figure 23.2 for two important documents relating to international efforts to suppress the financing of terrorism: the United Nations International Convention for the Suppression of the Financing of Terrorism and the FATF 8 Special Recommendations on Terrorist Financing, respectively.

FINANCING THE PIRA

It seems sometimes that the Irish have been fighting the British for approximately forever, which is why the financing activities of one of the leading Irish groups, the Provisional Irish Republican Army (PIRA), make a good case study for us. Born in 1969 as a descendant of the original Irish Republican Army, itself founded in 1919, PIRA is best known for its paramilitary campaign in Northern Ireland in the 1970s and 1980s. Closely coupled with a "political wing," Sinn Fein, PIRA provided the armed combatants, the "provos," in the long conflict with Great Britain in the North.

Some in Ireland and elsewhere would dispute the British characterization of PIRA as a terrorist organization (certainly IRA and Sinn Fein would object), but it cannot be denied that some of the group's tactics, notably car bombings and attacks on civilian targets such as subways and department stores, fit the definition. PIRA argues that most of its actions are directed at military, police, or government targets, though it admits to causing some collateral damage. At any rate, the organization has been legally banned, which is why you hear about the "outlawed IRA," and there's currently a truce under way that has stopped most of the killing.

PIRA's lengthy history and extensive experience make it a good example of how terrorist (or, as they prefer, "paramilitary") groups operate, and an especially good illustration of how they are financed and supported. In PIRA's case, it has obtained funding over the years from all four of the sources listed earlier. Before we look at these sources, we should see what exactly all that money gets spent on and why terrorist groups need money in the first place.

NEEDS OF TERRORIST GROUPS

In the grand scheme of things, terrorism comes pretty cheap, certainly compared with maintaining a fleet of nuclear submarines or even a big school district. One PIRA sniper with a rifle and a few bullets or a roadside bomb made out of fertilizer and diesel fuel isn't going to break the bank. Still, there are a number of hidden costs, and these things do add up, especially when the organization itself isn't anywhere near the size of its competition.

Weapons are a major expense, even in the smaller numbers that terrorist groups require. Rifles, explosives, mortars, and similar low-tech equipment still cost money, especially when they must be purchased on the black market and

Article 1

For the purposes of this Convention:

1. *Funds* means assets of every kind, whether tangible or intangible, movable or immovable, however acquired, and legal documents or instruments in any form, including electronic or digital, evidencing title to, or interest in, such assets, including, but not limited to, bank credits, travellers cheques, bank cheques, money orders, shares, securities, bonds, drafts, letters of credit.

2. *State or governmental facility* means any permanent or temporary facility or conveyance that is used or occupied by representatives of a State, members of Government, the legislature or the judiciary or by officials or employees of a State or any other public authority or entity or by employees or officials of an intergovernmental organization in connection with their official duties.

3. *Proceeds* means any funds derived from or obtained, directly or indirectly, through the commission of an offence set forth in article 2.

Article 2

1. Any person commits an offence within the meaning of this Convention if that person by any means, directly or indirectly, unlawfully and willfully, provides or collects funds with the intention that they should be used or in the knowledge that they are to be used, in full or in part, in order to carry out:

(a) An act which constitutes an offence within the scope of and as defined in one of the treaties listed in the annex; or

(b) Any other act intended to cause death or serious bodily injury to a civilian, or to any other person not taking an active part in the hostilities in a situation of armed conflict, when the purpose of such act, by its nature or context, is to intimidate a population, or to compel a government or an international organization to do or to abstain from doing any act.

2. (a) On depositing its instrument of ratification, acceptance, approval or accession, a State Party which is not a party to a treaty listed in the annex may declare that, in the application of this Convention to the State Party, the treaty shall be deemed not to be included in the annex referred to in paragraph 1, subparagraph (a). The declaration shall cease to have effect as soon as the treaty enters into force for the State Party, which shall notify the depositary of this fact;

(b) When a State Party ceases to be a party to a treaty listed in the annex, it may make a declaration as provided for in this article, with respect to that treaty.

3. For an act to constitute an offence set forth in paragraph 1, it shall not be necessary that the funds were actually used to carry out an offence referred to in paragraph 1, subparagraphs (a) or (b).

4. Any person also commits an offence if that person attempts to commit an offence as set forth in paragraph 1 of this article.

5. Any person also commits an offence if that person:

(a) Participates as an accomplice in an offence as set forth in paragraph 1 or 4 of this article;

(b) Organizes or directs others to commit an offence as set forth in paragraph 1 or 4 of this article;

(c) Contributes to the commission of one or more offences as set forth in paragraphs 1 or 4 of this article by a group of persons acting with a common purpose. Such contribution shall be intentional and shall either:

(i) Be made with the aim of furthering the criminal activity or criminal purpose of the group, where such activity or purpose involves the commission of an offence as set forth in paragraph 1 of this article; or

(ii) Be made in the knowledge of the intention of the group to commit an offence as set forth in paragraph 1 of this article.

Figure 23.1 *United Nations International Convention for the Suppression of the Financing of Terrorism, adopted by the General Assembly of the United Nations in resolution 54/109 of December 9, 1999. (Source: Financial Crimes Enforcement Network)*

I. Ratification and implementation of UN instruments

Each country should take immediate steps to ratify and to implement fully the 1999 United Nations International Convention for the Suppression of the Financing of Terrorism.

Countries should also immediately implement the United Nations resolutions relating to the prevention and suppression of the financing of terrorist acts, particularly United Nations Security Council Resolution 1373.

II. Criminalising the financing of terrorism and associated money laundering

Each country should criminalise the financing of terrorism, terrorist acts and terrorist organisations. Countries should ensure that such offences are designated as money laundering predicate offences.

III. Freezing and confiscating terrorist assets

Each country should implement measures to freeze without delay funds or other assets of terrorists, those who finance terrorism and terrorist organisations in accordance with the United Nations resolutions relating to the prevention and suppression of the financing of terrorist acts.

Each country should also adopt and implement measures, including legislative ones, which would enable the competent authorities to seize and confiscate property that is the proceeds of, or used in, or intended or allocated for use in, the financing of terrorism, terrorist acts or terrorist organisations.

IV. Reporting suspicious transactions related to terrorism

If financial institutions, or other businesses or entities subject to anti–money laundering obligations, suspect or have reasonable grounds to suspect that funds are linked or related to, or are to be used for terrorism, terrorist acts or by terrorist organisations, they should be required to report promptly their suspicions to the competent authorities.

V. International co-operation

Each country should afford another country, on the basis of a treaty, arrangement or other mechanism for mutual legal assistance or information exchange, the greatest possible measure of assistance in connection with criminal, civil enforcement, and administrative investigations, inquiries and proceedings relating to the financing of terrorism, terrorist acts and terrorist organisations.

Countries should also take all possible measures to ensure that they do not provide safe havens for individuals charged with the financing of terrorism, terrorist acts or terrorist organisations, and should have procedures in place to extradite, where possible, such individuals.

VI. Alternative remittance

Each country should take measures to ensure that persons or legal entities, including agents, that provide a service for the transmission of money or value, including transmission through an informal money or value transfer system or network, should be licensed or registered and subject to all the FATF Recommendations that apply to banks and non-bank financial institutions. Each country should ensure that persons or legal entities that carry out this service illegally are subject to administrative, civil or criminal sanctions.

Countries should take measures to require financial institutions, including money remitters, to include accurate and meaningful originator information (name, address and account number) on funds transfers and related messages that are sent, and the information should remain with the transfer or related message through the payment chain.

Countries should take measures to ensure that financial institutions, including money remitters, conduct enhanced scrutiny of and monitor for suspicious activity funds transfers which do not contain complete originator information (name, address and account number).

VIII. Non-profit organisations

Countries should review the adequacy of laws and regulations that relate to entities that can be abused for the financing of terrorism. Non-profit organisations are particularly vulnerable, and countries should ensure that they cannot be misused:

i. by terrorist organisations posing as legitimate entities;

Figure 23.2 FATF 8 Special Recommendations on Terrorist Financing.   *Continued.*

ii. to exploit legitimate entities as conduits for terrorist financing, including for the purpose of escaping asset freezing measures; and

iii. to conceal or obscure the clandestine diversion of funds intended for legitimate purposes to terrorist organisations.

IX. Cash couriers

Countries should have measures in place to detect the physical cross-border transportation of currency and bearer negotiable instruments, including a declaration system or other disclosure obligation.

Countries should ensure that their competent authorities have the legal authority to stop or restrain currency or bearer negotiable instruments that are suspected to be related to terrorist financing or money laundering, or that are falsely declared or disclosed.

Countries should ensure that effective, proportionate and dissuasive sanctions are available to deal with persons who make false declaration(s) or disclosure(s). In cases where the currency or bearer negotiable instruments are related to terrorist financing or money laundering, countries should also adopt measures, including legislative ones consistent with Recommendation 3 and Special Recommendation III, which would enable the confiscation of such currency or instruments.

Figure 23.2 *Continued.*

smuggled into the area of operations. Munitions are expendable, and the more active the group, the more it is expending, so replacement or resupply is an issue. There is also the likelihood that the opposition will capture some of the weaponry, which means buying more than you need. And when you start going high-tech, buying shoulder-fired missiles or other big-ticket items, costs rise sharply.

Security costs can be substantial. Weapons and personnel need to be kept secure in "safe houses" that are free from prying eyes or government interest. Arms may be cached, as the PIRA has, in secret bunkers built in Ireland and Northern Ireland. Costs may also be incurred in securely transporting the weapons (or personnel) to other safe houses or to an operational area.

PIRA and other groups rely on supporters within the community to provide some of these services, but they also buy or rent property, and they reimburse those who allow them use of homes or businesses. Al Qaeda, when it had access to the entire country of Afghanistan, was able to set up large, semipermanent camps or even take over small towns to train and support its personnel. PIRA doesn't have this luxury; it gets by with more limited and more transient accommodations.

Security costs also include such things as false identification and other concealment mechanisms. You'll note the similarity here to more conventional criminals, who incur expenses relating to hiding their assets or laundering their money. Terrorist groups may have access to false identification documents such as passports from friendly governments, but they might not want the attention that comes with a passport from some country on the U.S. State Department's list of countries sponsoring terrorism.

Communications also cost money. Al Qaeda is known to use satellite telephones and the Internet, but much communication is still done the old-fashioned (and expensive) way — by courier and messenger. This has the advantage of being difficult to intercept, but it means paying for transportation and for the courier. Prior to the 9/11 attacks, some of the communication took place by e-mail, but many of the plotters traveled extensively to meetings where they could communicate directly. In Iraq, American forces captured valuable information, including a letter to Osama bin Laden, contained on a CD-ROM. The disk was being transported by an Al Qaeda courier, a graphic illustration of the melding of old and new technology in communications.

Modern organizations do use more up-to-date methods; radios, cellular phones, and the computer are used by the legitimate and illegitimate alike. The cost of cellular service is relatively low, but it still contributes to budget concerns.

Personnel costs are generally the largest in any organization, legitimate or illegitimate. PIRA and other groups tout their use of "volunteers," people willingly serving a cause without compensation. Mohammed Atta, lead hijacker of the 9/11 plot, would have scorned the idea that he should be paid for his role in the attacks, an attitude common to fanatics everywhere.

Still, there are many personnel expenses, all of which add up, and not all of the PIRA personnel went unpaid. After all, they needed to support themselves and their families while they were on "active service," often for extended periods. British antiterrorism experts estimated that payments to PIRA personnel could have amounted to £12,000 per week or more, serious money, and only the tip of the iceberg.

A similar situation existed in the Middle East, where the Palestinians seemed to have an endless supply of volunteers wishing to "martyr" themselves by packing a suicide bomb into an Israeli pizza parlor. These folks might have been true volunteers, but the Israelis have thoroughly documented the support payments made to their families by governments such as those in Saudi Arabia and Saddam Hussein's Iraq, as well as by terrorist organizations such as HAMAS or Islamic Jihad.

You've also got to take care of the relatives of jailed PIRA men, those who supported the organization with services such as housing and transportation, and the "widows and orphans" who were at the center of IRA fundraising campaigns in years past. I don't know if many Al Qaeda or PIRA men live to retirement age, but one would suppose there would be a need for some form of pension benefits for those too old to pull a trigger. (An IRA IRA, perhaps....)

Costs may even be incurred to pay members to stop making mischief or going "off the reservation." Idle terrorists (or "paramilitary operatives") are the devil's workshop, you might say, and British and Irish intelligence have described situations when the organization paid off PIRA men who might have caused trouble by breaking a truce or attacking an unapproved target.

Some of the most expensive personnel costs relate to training. Setting up and maintaining those terrorist training camps that President Clinton tried to hit with cruise missiles is a major endeavor. Sometimes a friendly government will pick up the tab; Libya and Saddam Hussein's Iraq had a reputation for generosity in this area. In other hot spots, notably Colombia, Indonesia, the Philippines, and various African locations, the camps have to be established somewhere in relatively safe territory controlled by the terrorist group or a friendly warlord. You then have to transport your trainees to the camp; feed, clothe, house, and equip them; and then send them off when they've completed the course. Even on an ad hoc basis, this can get quite expensive.

Related activities also cost a terrorist organization. Sinn Fein, the legitimate side of the IRA, incurs all of the normal costs associated with running a political party. It, too, needs to raise money, and the British long suspected that contributions to Sinn Fein were being channeled to its darker side. Many groups, Hezbollah and HAMAS in the Middle East being prime examples, operate charitable, social, and public service sides, providing medical care, social services, and related benefits to the populace from which they draw their support. It's great PR, and these related activities make it possible for donors to give to the cause without directly supporting the terrorist side of the house. "Sure, I give to HAMAS, because they run medical clinics in the Palestinian community," goes the rationalization.

Sources of Funding

Various estimates have been made over the years of the total amount of funds raised by PIRA to support its operations. Since it's not a publicly traded company, there's no annual report detailing the source and application of funds, but the best guesses range from $8 million to $15 million annually. Ironically, now that the cease-fire is in effect and Sinn Fein's political profile is much higher, the costs are probably much greater. At any rate, keeping this money stream flowing becomes a high priority for the organization.

For decades, PIRA has relied on all four means of funding, one very overt, one very covert, and two that everybody knows about but the IRA doesn't advertise. On the overt side, PIRA actively solicits *donations and contributions,* both in Ireland and abroad, particularly in North America. The Northern Aid Committee (NORAID) and Friends of Sinn Fein (FOSF) present a very high public profile, actively going out into Irish communities to solicit contributions from individuals and businesses.

The funds raised not only serve to support the activities of Sinn Fein and the IRA, but they also serve as a cover for money laundering and a placement mechanism for the money that comes from less reputable sources. PIRA would have everyone believe that the vast majority, if not all of their funding comes from little people putting something in the jar on the bar at the pub or writing out a small check to Sinn Fein. This is a good public image, and one that played well for decades in Irish-American communities, where NORAID cans were stuffed with "something for the widows and orphans." Irish fundraisers would travel regularly to New York and Boston to solicit funds, and these trips have gotten an even higher profile now that Sinn Fein is a recognized political party in the North and a partner in the ongoing peace process.

The fund-raising profile is also high; NORAID and the Irish Northern Aid Committee, Inc. (INAC) maintain slick Web sites and very open points of contact. INAC claims recognition by IRS as a 501 (c) (3) nonprofit organization. Is there any evidence that funds donated to these groups are used to support terrorist (or paramilitary) operations? Cases in the past have linked NORAID money to weapons shipments, and there is no doubt that all of the funds raised by or on behalf of PIRA are commingled and spent on operations legal or illegal without regard to the source. What is clear is that there is no evidence that any of the contributed money comes from an illegal source or SUA, and tracing it from the NORAID, FOSF, INAC, or Sinn Fein account into a weapons purchase or other illegal use is going to be tough.

At the opposite and *very* covert end of the spectrum are the monies and other items of value PIRA gets from state sponsors. PIRA is never going to admit it got a penny from the likes of Libya's Muammar Khadafi, but that's what British intelligence seems to think.

State sponsorship is sort of like the pot of gold at the end of the rainbow, to borrow an appropriate Irish expression. After all, nobody's got more money than the government, with the possible exceptions of Sam Walton or Bill Gates, neither of whom is in the terrorism-supporting business. Having a whole country's support, particularly one like Libya that pumps money out of the ground, is too good to be true.

It's also too sensitive to be admitted, because most governments that are inclined in this direction fear the consequences of getting caught at it. This is going to be even more true after the Taliban got thoroughly kicked to the curb (and out of power) when they tried it in Afghanistan. Some governments — and the United States maintains a list of the ones that qualify — are known or suspected of "repeatedly providing support" for terrorism and subject to sanctions. According to the State Department:

> Countries determined by the Secretary of State to have repeatedly provided support for acts of international terrorism are designated pursuant to three laws: section 6(j) of the Export Administration Act, section 40 of the Arms Export Control Act, and section 620A of the Foreign Assistance Act. Taken together, the four main categories of sanctions resulting from designation under these authorities include restrictions on U.S. foreign assistance; a ban on defense exports and sales; certain controls over exports of dual use items; and miscellaneous financial and other restrictions. Designation under the above-referenced authorities also implicates other sanctions laws that penalize persons and countries engaging in certain trade with state sponsors. Currently there are six countries des-

ignated under these authorities: Cuba, Iran, Libya, North Korea, Sudan and Syria.

This list is important because it emphasizes the inherent danger in having countries in the terrorism business. This danger extends to the financial realm, because governments can launder money very efficiently themselves, or they can simply turn a blind eye to things like terrorist financing and money laundering taking place in their banks or on their soil.

Governments also buy a lot of weapons; they've got armies and navies, after all, which may be armed to the teeth but go for years without having anybody handy to shoot. A government such as Libya, for example, that held a grudge against another, much more powerful government, such as Great Britain, for instance, might slide a few of those weapons under the table to some paramilitary operatives who were willing to put them to productive use somewhere like Northern Ireland.

Libya wouldn't want to get caught at this, no doubt fearing the appearance of F-111s over Tripoli or sharing the fate of the Taliban in Afghanistan, so it would make its PIRA buddies promise never to tell where the Kalashnikovs or plastic explosives came from. PIRA wants to keep that little secret, too, hoping to get more goodies in the future. PIRA is also extremely wary of the bad publicity sure to follow the disclosure of a link to the man whose agents blew up Pan Am 103 over Scotland. Both sides will work hard to layer these transactions.

Al Qaeda was the king of government sponsorship, holing up first in the Sudan, one of the countries on the State Department's list, before moving to very accommodating Afghanistan. Here, Al Qaeda had the ability to set up large training camps, recruit followers, and engage in fundraising activities unimpeded by any government restrictions.

Most terrorist groups aren't that lucky, and after 9/11 most countries are going to be very reluctant to allow terrorist groups to operate so openly; the consequences are too severe, and the United States demonstrated in Iraq and Afghanistan that if we can't take it out directly on the terrorists themselves, we'll hammer their sponsors. (The list used to include Iraq and Afghanistan, but they were removed after we took them out of that business.) Sponsors in the rogue states on the list and elsewhere are going to be a lot more circumspect, making our ability to track the money flow more important.

Terrorist groups are also into *legitimate business,* for many of the same reasons that money launderers use businesses. According to John Horgan and Max Taylor, who studied PIRA financing:

> Legitimately-owned businesses have included private security firms, the "black" taxi cabs in Belfast ... at least two known hackney cab services in Dublin, construction firms, shops, restaurants, courier services, guest houses, cars and machinery, pubs which at one time or another have included at least one in Boston in the United States, two small pubs in Finglas, two in Coolock, also in Dublin with several more in the city centre, three in Letterkenny, three in Cork (including one Cork hotel), and more small pubs "scattered about" the country.

That's a pretty diversified mix of business interests, but they are sensible choices for the organization. The cab companies generate income in cash and have the added benefit of being available to transport personnel or materiel. Pubs also bring in cash, make good meeting places, and are vehicles for raising money through contributions. All of the businesses can be used for the placement of laundered funds, and most can be used to integrate money as well.

Income from legitimate business, some of which may actually be reported to the taxing authorities, can be funneled directly into PIRA coffers or routed through banks or shell corporations, just as a money launderer would do. There is substantial intelligence that Al Qaeda, too, relies on legitimate business as part of its financial schemes; that aspirin factory in Sudan that President Clinton ordered bombed was supposed to have been connected with Osama bin Laden's outfit. Osama himself is supposed to be the scion of a wealthy family and was alleged to have invested his money in his terrorist enterprise.

Another possibility involves the manipulation of financial markets, something that can generate profits for an organization or individual. Groups in the Middle East are known to be involved in the gold trade, and they may traffic in other legitimate commodities. These activities, particularly those on the fringes of (or all the way inside) the black market, can be very profitable. Groups in South America have been observed moving and selling blue jeans, electronic goods, and other products.

Finally, terrorist groups have always relied on *money from illegal sources,* money they not only have to make, but they have to launder as well. Some of the more popular methods are the ones you might expect: kidnapping for ransom, extortion, and armed robbery. These are exactly the sorts of crimes a large group of heavily armed, well-trained, and very organized individuals might lean toward.

In December 2004, such a group raided Northern Bank in Ulster, grabbing £22 million in bank notes. It was one of the largest robberies ever, and the IRA was immediately suspected. Although the IRA and Sinn Fein denied involvement, it is generally thought that only the IRA had the ability to (*a*) pull off the heist in the first place and (*b*) launder the incredibly large number of £20 and £100 notes. (The bank, in response to the theft, is recalling all notes in these denominations and issuing new ones that are substantially different in color and design. This action may make most of the stolen money worthless.)

PIRA and its fellows have been associated for so long with fundraising through bank robbery and other crime that their involvement in a heist is now assumed by many in Ireland and Northern Ireland. Even some of their supporters now question the need, with a cease-fire in place and political discussions under way, for a heavily armed cadre of trained fighters to continue to raise money by ripping off banks. In his book *Revolution in the Revolution,* Regis Debray notes that as a terrorist organization loses a clearly defined focus or political objective, the group continues to exist but members may drift into activities they have been trained to do well. This would certainly seem to apply to the IRA and its involvement in bank robbery.

People have also noticed other PIRA fundraising activities in the illegal sphere, including extortion of legitimate business and the always lucrative drug trade. Both of these are perfect fits. It's not a long step, after all, from asking a pub owner to put a contribution jar on the bar to telling the owner he or she had better put one out, or else. And pretty soon there's a quota that had better be met. Or maybe some of the "hard men" come in and just make a naked threat.

As the IRA has gotten into legitimate business, the extortion racket has become more sophisticated. Now, a PIRA rep can approach a businessperson and suggest that it would be a good idea to hire an IRA-controlled or -owned security company. The reluctant businessperson might get a graphic, even forceful, demonstration of why this would be so. There are currently dozens of security firms in Belfast, many of which are connected to the movement. These companies provide employment opportunities for PIRA personnel and fundraising opportunities as well.

Another lucrative extortion possibility involves shaking down people in illegal businesses, notably drug traffickers. Imposing a "tax" on somebody unable to complain about it has all sorts of advantages. A drug dealer has little choice but to pay up; the terrorists are always going to be better armed and more organized, and they get a cut of the drug profits without having to actually dirty their hands by dealing heroin or marijuana.

The question of whether PIRA is actively involved in the drug trade itself is hotly disputed. There's no doubt that Al Qaeda is a player. With the majority of the world's opium supply in its backyard, with established routes of clandestine communication and a network of contacts and safe houses, the terrorist group is perfectly positioned to reap some of the huge profits from the heroin business.

Narcotrafficker–terrorist connections are well established all over the world. In Colombia,

Figure 23.3 DEA "wanted" poster connecting Colombian cocaine traffickers to terrorist activity. (Source: DEA)

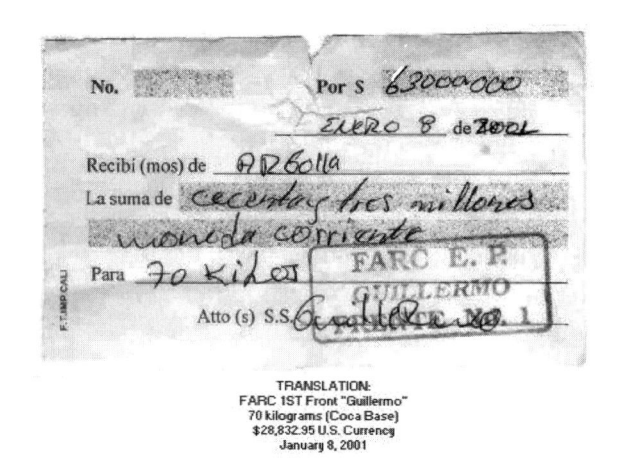

Figure 23.4 Receipt for 70 kg of cocaine base from "Guillermo" of FARC, the Revolutionary Armed Forces of Colombia, a designated terrorist organization. (Source: DEA)

Southeast Asia, Europe, and Afghanistan, ties between drug traffickers and terrorist groups are quite close, and money flows both ways. Terrorist groups are well armed and well positioned to provide services (or make trouble) for drug trafficking groups. There are numerous reports of terrorist groups' extorting money from narcotraffickers, "taxing" drug shipments, and collecting protection money for allowing shipments through the terrorist group's area of operations. These groups have also been known to actually provide protection or security for drug shipments, something the IRA has been accused of in the past. It's a logical connection; for a dope dealer or a "paramilitary operative," the government is the enemy. And the money is huge, so siphoning some off to the terrorist group makes very good business sense for the drug trafficker. After all, he or she doesn't need any additional problems with heavily armed and highly motivated individuals operating in the same patch. (See Figure 23.3 and Figure 23.4.)

In the United States, at least one major drug investigation, DEA's Operation Mountain Express II, detected links between traffickers in pseudoephedrine, a precursor for methamphetamine, and Middle East terrorist groups Hezbollah and HAMAS.

Some illegal activities are closer to the line between legitimate commerce and crime, such as the smuggling of cigarettes from low-tax states to high-tax jurisdictions and trafficking in counterfeit merchandise. In a recent California case, the *Los Angeles Times* (May 26, 2005) reported that federal agents and prosecutors suspected Hezbollah operatives in the U.S. and other groups accused of terrorist activity were raising as much as $30 million a year in America through the sale of counterfeit merchandise and other criminal enterprises, and sending unknown but substantial sums back home.

INVESTIGATION OF TERRORIST FINANCING

LEGAL MEASURES

The September 11, 2001, terrorist attacks jolted the American government (and, to some extent, governments around the world) into action. Although some measures taken to counter the terrorist threat involved the use of military force and intelligence assets, Congress acted quickly to pass provisions such as the USA PATRIOT Act and other measures, closing loopholes in the federal laws dealing with terrorism. One area of specific concern was the problem of terrorist financing. The primary statutes in this area are found in 18 U.S.C. §2339A, §2339B, and §2339C.

Section 2339A prohibits providing material support for terrorists or "concealing the nature, location, source, or ownership of material support or resources." This language should be very familiar to us, as it closely resembles that in the money laundering statutes. The astute investigator would suppose, therefore, that the techniques involved in investigating and proving this crime would be very similar, as indeed they are.

We immediately see the financial component, although "material support" is not necessarily limited by the statute to money or other financial resources. In fact, the statute states:

> "Material support or resources" means currency or monetary instruments or financial securities, financial services, lodging, training, expert advice or assistance, safehouses, false documentation or identification, communications equipment, facilities, weapons, lethal substances, explosives, personnel, transportation, and other physical assets, except medicine or religious materials.

The law also has a rough equivalent to money laundering's SUA, in that those providing the material support must *know or intend* that it is to be used in preparation for or in carrying out a violation named in a list of federal offenses that broadly relate to terrorism or acts of violence.

This second element will probably be a greater sticking point in most 2339A investigations. As noted earlier, many terrorist organizations maintain legitimate fronts, political wings, or public service components that ostensibly do not engage in terrorist activity. Contributors or others providing material support to HAMAS could claim that they never had any intent to finance the nastier aspects of HAMAS' program, perhaps noting that the organization runs medical clinics and other social services in Gaza and the West Bank. Someone shipping weapons or explosives to the same address would be less successful in this argument.

In the case of the IRA, someone making a contribution to the "widows and orphans" fund or to one of the NORAID, FOSF, or INAC Web sites would have no knowledge of the ultimate destination of the funds or the uses to which they might be put. Because this intent requirement is more difficult to prove, a second provision, 2339B, addresses the question more directly. It reads as follows:

§2339B. Providing material support or resources to designated foreign terrorist organizations

(a) Prohibited Activities.—

(1) Unlawful conduct.— Whoever, within the United States or subject to the jurisdiction of the United States, knowingly provides material support or resources to a foreign terrorist organization, or attempts or conspires to do so, shall be fined under this title or imprisoned not more than 15 years, or both, and, if the death of any person results, shall be imprisoned for any term of years or for life.

This statute simplifies matters for the government. Once a foreign terrorist organization has been identified or designated, anyone who provides material support or resources to that organization is guilty of a 2339B violation and subject to the 15-year penalty. We do not have to show that the money was intended to be used for some bad purpose — only that it went to a bad group, one the government designated as a terrorist organization under section 219 of the Immigration and Nationality Act. See Figure 23.5 for a list of designated foreign terrorist organizations.

This law is aimed directly at the money and at cutting the flow to groups the government deems terrorist risks. Other provisions in the statute require financial institutions that have "possession of, or control over, any funds in which a foreign terrorist organization, or its agent, has an interest" to maintain control of the funds and notify the Treasury Secretary of the money.

The final section addresses the providing and collecting of funds to be used to carry out terrorist acts. It reads as follows:

§2339C. Prohibitions against the financing of terrorism

(a) Offenses.—

(1) In general.— Whoever, in a circumstance described in subsection (b), by any means, directly or indirectly, unlawfully and willfully provides or collects funds with the intention that such funds be used, or with the knowledge that such funds are to be used, in full or in part, in order to carry out—

(A) an act which constitutes an offense within the scope of a treaty specified in subsection (e) (7), as implemented by the United States, or

(B) any other act intended to cause death or serious bodily injury to a civilian, or to any other person not taking an active part in the hostilities in a situation of armed conflict, when the purpose of such act, by its nature or context, is to intimidate a population, or to compel a government or an international organization to do or to abstain from doing any act, shall be punished as prescribed in subsection (d) (1).

Since the devil (quite literally in this case) is in the details, the law defines "provides" as including "giving, donating, and transmitting" and defines "collects" as including "raising and receiving."

The penalties of this provision apply, therefore, not just to those who are out collecting money on behalf of HAMAS, Islamic Jihad, or Al Qaeda, but also to those who are donating or transmitting the money. The days when representatives of designated terrorist organizations (DTOs) could openly fundraise in the United States — formerly a major source for some groups — are over. If they're smart (and they are), fundraisers for the DTOs will rely more heavily on front groups, "charitable organizations," and other entities to layer the monies collected.

This will mean additional work for the investigators, who will be required to trace funds from the source, through domestic and international financial institutions, and on to accounts, companies, or individuals known to be associated

- Abu Nidal Organization (ANO)
- Abu Sayyaf Group
- Al-Aqsa Martyrs Brigade
- Ansar al-Islam
- Armed Islamic Group (GIA)
- Asbat al-Ansar
- Aum Shinrikyo
- Basque Fatherland and Liberty (ETA)
- Communist Party of the Philippines/New People's Army (CPP/NPA)
- Continuity Irish Republican Army
- Gama'a al-Islamiyya (Islamic Group)
- HAMAS (Islamic Resistance Movement)
- Harakat μl-Mujahidin (HUM)
- Hizballah (Party of God)
- Islamic Movement of Uzbekistan (IMU)
- Jaish-e-Mohammed (JEM; Army of Mohammed)
- Jemaah Islamiya organization (JI)
- al-Jihad (Egyptian Islamic Jihad)
- Kahane Chai (Kach)
- Kongra-Gel (KGK, formerly Kurdistan Workers' Party, PKK, KADEK)
- Lashkar-e Tayyiba (LT; Army of the Righteous)
- Lashkar i Jhangvi
- Liberation Tigers of Tamil Eelam (LTTE)
- Libyan Islamic Fighting Group (LIFG)
- Mujahedin-e Khalq Organization (MEK)
- National Liberation Army (ELN)
- Palestine Liberation Front (PLF)
- Palestinian Islamic Jihad (PIJ)
- Popular Front for the Liberation of Palestine (PFLF)
- PFLP-General Command (PFLP-GC)
- al-Qa'ida
- Real IRA
- Revolutionary Armed Forces of Colombia (FARC)
- Revolutionary Nuclei (formerly ELA)
- Revolutionary Organization 17 November
- Revolutionary People's Liberation Party/Front (DHKP/C)
- Salafist Group for Call and Combat (GSPC)
- Shining Path (Sendero Luminoso, SL)
- Tanzim Qa'idat al-Jihad fi Bilad al-Rafidayn (QJBR; al-Qa'ida in Iraq; formerly Jama'at al-Tawhid wa'al-Jihad, JTJ, al-Zarqawi Network)
- United Self-Defense Forces of Colombia (AUC)

Figure 23.5 *Designated foreign terrorist organizations (FTOs).*

with the DTOs. In this sense, a terrorism financing investigation becomes more like a money laundering case, with investigators working to overcome the smoke and mirrors thrown up by the criminals to conceal or disguise the movement of money or the source, ownership, or control of assets. The high stakes — 10- to 20-year penalties — and the international character of terrorist groups mean that DTOs will rely on increasingly sophisticated means of conducting their business.

As if to illustrate this point, the statute also addresses those in the United States (or who are U.S. nationals outside the country) who knowingly "conceal or disguise" the:

> nature, location, source, ownership, or control of any material support, resources, or funds, knowing or intending that the support or resources were provided in violation of section 2339B of this title; or knowing or intending that any such funds or any proceeds of such funds were provided or collected in violation of subsection (a).

Once again, note the similarity to the wording of the money laundering statutes, particularly the parts about concealing and disguising and about the "nature, location, source, ownership, or control" of funds. The means used to prove this element — all of the financial investigative techniques discussed so far — will be very familiar to anyone who's worked money laundering cases.

Finally, a word about the law's definition of "funds." It's pretty encompassing, and it takes us back to the first chapter, in which we looked at the nature of money itself. According to the statute:

> the term "funds" means assets of every kind, whether tangible or intangible, movable or immovable, however acquired, and legal documents or instruments in any form, including electronic or digital, evidencing title to, or interest in, such assets, including coin, currency, bank credits, travelers checks, bank checks, money orders, shares, securities, bonds, drafts, and letters of credit.

That's painting with a broad brush indeed, and an excellent description of the concept of money. It is certainly recognition by Congress that terrorism may be financed in a myriad of ways and by any type of scheme — legal or illegal. By enacting these three statutes, lawmakers sought to provide law enforcement with tools to fill holes in the money laundering and other measures that left the nation vulnerable to a new and frightening peril. Fortunately for the financial investigator, enforcement of the new laws will require use of the same techniques employed in solving other, more familiar crimes.

MONEY LAUNDERING AND TERRORISM FINANCING

Is it possible to use the money laundering statutes in a terrorism prosecution? Yes. Many terrorist offenses are SUAs, and if we've got an SUA and a financial transaction, we've got a money laundering violation. One SUA that has been employed in the prosecution of terrorist financing cases is the little-known Section 206 (relating to penalties) of the International Emergency Economic Powers Act. Found in Title 50 United States Code, Chapter 35, Sections 1701 to 1708, this statute permits the president to take steps in emergencies against money transfers and other transactions.

Under this section, the President can:

> Investigate, regulate, or prohibit any transactions in foreign exchange, transfers of credit or payments between, by, through, or to any banking institution, to the extent that such transfers or payments involve any interest of any foreign country or a national thereof, or the importing or exporting of currency or securities.

Once these transactions have been regulated or prohibited, further activity may be a financial transaction involving funds derived from an SUA — a possible money laundering violation.

Money laundering charges — specifically 1956 (h) conspiracy charges and 1956 (a) (1) (A) charges — have been brought under this theory, including one case we are going to examine in a moment.

INVESTIGATIVE RESOURCES

In his testimony "Progress Since 9/11: The Effectiveness of U.S. Anti-Terrorist Financing Efforts," before the House Committee on Financial Services Subcommittee on Oversight and Investigations, Steven Emerson stated:

> The manner in which terrorists have raised money for their operations has ranged from a variety of sources including, but not limited to, the use of charitable organizations, corporate "front" entities, tax fraud, coupon redemption programs, and cigarette smuggling, as well as deliberately concealing their activities behind the cover of academic, religious and civil rights veneers. A common thread among these methods is the utilization of U.S. financial institutions to support jihad.

Financial institutions are useful to terrorists groups for the same reasons that money launderers need them: because they are in the business of holding and moving money. They are, as we have described, integral parts of the placement, layering, and integration process.

Suspicious Activity Reports

Suspicious Activity Reports (SARs) are a great resource for investigators. Bank employees read the newspapers, too, and are conscious of what's normal and what's not in their financial institution. When it became widely known that some of the 9/11 hijackers had attended flight schools and received money from abroad, customers with similar characteristics or backgrounds received extra scrutiny. As the chart below shows, SAR filings relating to terrorism peaked right after 9/11, with a gradual decline thereafter. Quite a few of these transactions involved individuals or organizations on government watch lists.

SARs are some of those little "dots" we're all supposed to be connecting better. Financial institutions and their employees should be encouraged to report activities they find questionable, especially in the area of terror financing. Because banks and other financial institutions play key roles in so many money laundering and terrorist financing schemes, SARs can give us early warning of activity that otherwise might not be detected until too late.

Figure 23.6, a document prepared by FinCEN, describes SAR activity in the period following the September 11 terrorist attacks.

Tax Returns and Tax Information

You wouldn't normally think terrorist groups would take much interest in complying with the tax laws, but they do; like those in legitimate society, they take advantage of those laws to conduct their business. Many of the front groups raising money for terrorist organizations are registered with IRS as 501 (c) (3) nonprofit organizations. This status provides the groups with certain tax advantages and may make some or all of the contributions to the group's "charity" tax deductible to the donors.

With this status comes certain responsibilities, such as the requirement to regularly file tax returns with IRS, returns that must accurately reflect how much money came in and the uses to which the money was put. Since the organizations know that the federal government doesn't recognize transfers to HAMAS or Al Qaeda as legitimate uses of the "charitable" or nonprofit status, they are compelled to lie about where the funds ended up. Filing a false tax return is a felony.

Investigators can still get valuable information from tax returns, even those that are false or fraudulent. Background information on the organization's officers and operations, references to banks, and transfers to overseas entities that may be fronts for terrorist groups are all likely to be contained in the organization's tax filings. And because the law requires accurate record-keeping to support the returns, additional information may be available at the offices of the organization.

There are numerous examples of groups that have used section 501 (c) (3) as part of their fundraising appeal, notably the Holy Land Foun-

SARs filed relating to terrorism for the 18-month period (by calendar year quarters)

October 1, 2001 thru March 31, 2003

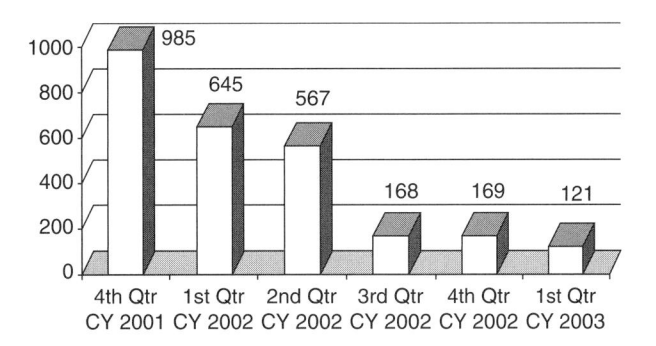

Quarter	SARs
4th Qtr CY 2001	985
1st Qtr CY 2002	645
2nd Qtr CY 2002	567
3rd Qtr CY 2002	168
4th Qtr CY 2002	169
1st Qtr CY 2003	121

As the above chart demonstrates, the number of filings began to steadily decline after the 4th quarter of calendar year 2001, the three-month period directly following the September 11th terrorist attacks.

Following is additional information about the 290 SARs filed between October 1, 2002 and March 31, 2003 (the last six months of the study) that reference terrorism and/or terrorist financing:

- Sixty-nine financial institutions, including five foreign banks licensed to conduct business in the United States, filed SARs (three banks filed 155 of the 290 SARs or 53.4 percent of the SARs filed).
- The suspicious activity reported in the SARs occurred in 35 states and the District of Columbia.
- Alleged suspicious activity amounts ranged up to $193 million.

Eighty-four SARs (29 percent) filed were the result of apparent matches of names on OFAC's list of Specially Designated Nationals and Blocked Persons, from the USA PATRIOT Act's Section 314 (a) Information Requests from law enforcement, names gleaned from media reports, or as a result of subpoenas issued by law enforcement.

The activity described in the SARs remained consistent with the activity described in previously issued SAR Review Reports. The activity included wire transfers predominantly to and from Middle Eastern countries; frequent use of domestic and foreign Automated Teller Machines (ATMs); and large currency transactions. The majority of the SARs filed (206 SARs or 71 percent) were a result of depository institutions' discoveries during the due diligence process. This denotes the first time since the events of September 11, 2001, that a marked increase in independent depository institution filings occurred, i.e., without the aid of government published lists. It is also worth noting that, previously, the filings were reversed in that 75 percent to 80 percent were filed based on government watch lists, while 20 percent to 25 percent were filed at the depository institutions' initiative.

The above-mentioned SARs were filed based on one or more of the following criteria, which the financial institution believed might be associated with terrorist activity:

- Even dollar deposits followed by like-amount wire transfers;
- Frequent domestic and international ATM activity;
- No known source of income;
- Use of wire transfers and the Internet to move funds to and from high risk countries and geographic locations;
- Frequent address changes;
- Occupation "student"—primarily flight schools;
- Purchases of military items or technology; and
- Media reports on suspected/arrested terrorists or groups.

Figure 23.6 FinCEN document describing SAR activity following the September 11, 2001, terrorist attacks. (Source: Financial Crimes Enforcement Network)

Figure 23.7 *Osama bin Laden.*

dation and the IRA's supporters. Since 9/11, IRS has monitored these groups more closely, and indictments, such as that of the Holy Land Foundation's officers, have included counts relating to the filing of false tax returns.

TERRORIST FUNDRAISING AND FINANCING: THE AL QAEDA TERRORISM MONEY TRAIL

Since 9/11/2001, Al Qaeda and its leadership have been at the center of America's war on terror. The story is well known, but it bears repeating, since the group has demonstrated rather graphically its willingness and ability to commit mass murder in the United States.

Osama bin Laden (see Figure 23.7), son of a wealthy Saudi businessman, was widely reported to have inherited a large fortune that he used to indulge his main interest — destroying the United States. Bin Laden had fought with Afghans in their war against Soviet occupation in the 1980s and held the belief that if he and his fellow Islamic warriors could defeat one global superpower, the second (and sole remaining) superpower couldn't be too much tougher.

He had some evidence in support of this hypothesis: The United States had absorbed a series of terrorist attacks around the globe spanning over 20 years, and the response hadn't amounted to much — some criminal investigations and a few cruise missiles fired at some of those empty tents President Bush mentioned in the quote at the head of the chapter.

Figure 23.8 *Ayman al Zawahiri, Egyptian physician and lieutenant to Osama bin Laden. (Source: FBI)*

These measures didn't intimidate bin Laden too greatly, and he and his like-minded companions (see Figure 23.8) created an organization they hoped would be the centerpiece of their effort to establish an Islamic caliphate across the entire globe — Al Qaeda, or "The Base." Established in the mid-1980s, Al Qaeda expanded to form a junction of terror groups from the Middle East, Asia, and Africa. Operating in safe areas in the Sudan and Afghanistan, bin Laden's Base established camps that may have trained as many as 10,000 people from countries all over the world. Al Qaeda also served as a model for and supporter of groups active in the Philippines, Indonesia, Thailand, Pakistan, India/Kashmir, China, Uzbekistan, Russia/Chechnya, Egypt, Saudi Arabia, Iraq, Kuwait, Yemen, Somalia, Ethiopia, Kenya, Tanzania, and Algeria, to mention only a few of the hotter spots. As we now know, Al Qaeda also had terror cells in Europe and the United States.

An organization of this size, complexity, and ambition needs money, and bin Laden took advantage of all four of the primary means by which terrorist groups are funded. He had some government sponsorship; certainly the Taliban government of Afghanistan provided the sort of material support that would be illegal under American law. Bin Laden was also known to have interests in a number of income-producing businesses in Africa and the Middle East, particularly in the Sudan. The big moneymaker for Al Qaeda, however, was donations and contributions. See Figure 23.9.

Terrorist Financing Scheme -
World Islamic Front for Jihad Against the Jews and Crusaders

Zakat Donations
- Individuals
- Companies
- Banks

Bank Transfers

Charities and Relief Organizations
- Domestic
- Overseas

Government sponsorship

Hawala Transfers

Terrorist Organization
Al Qaeda

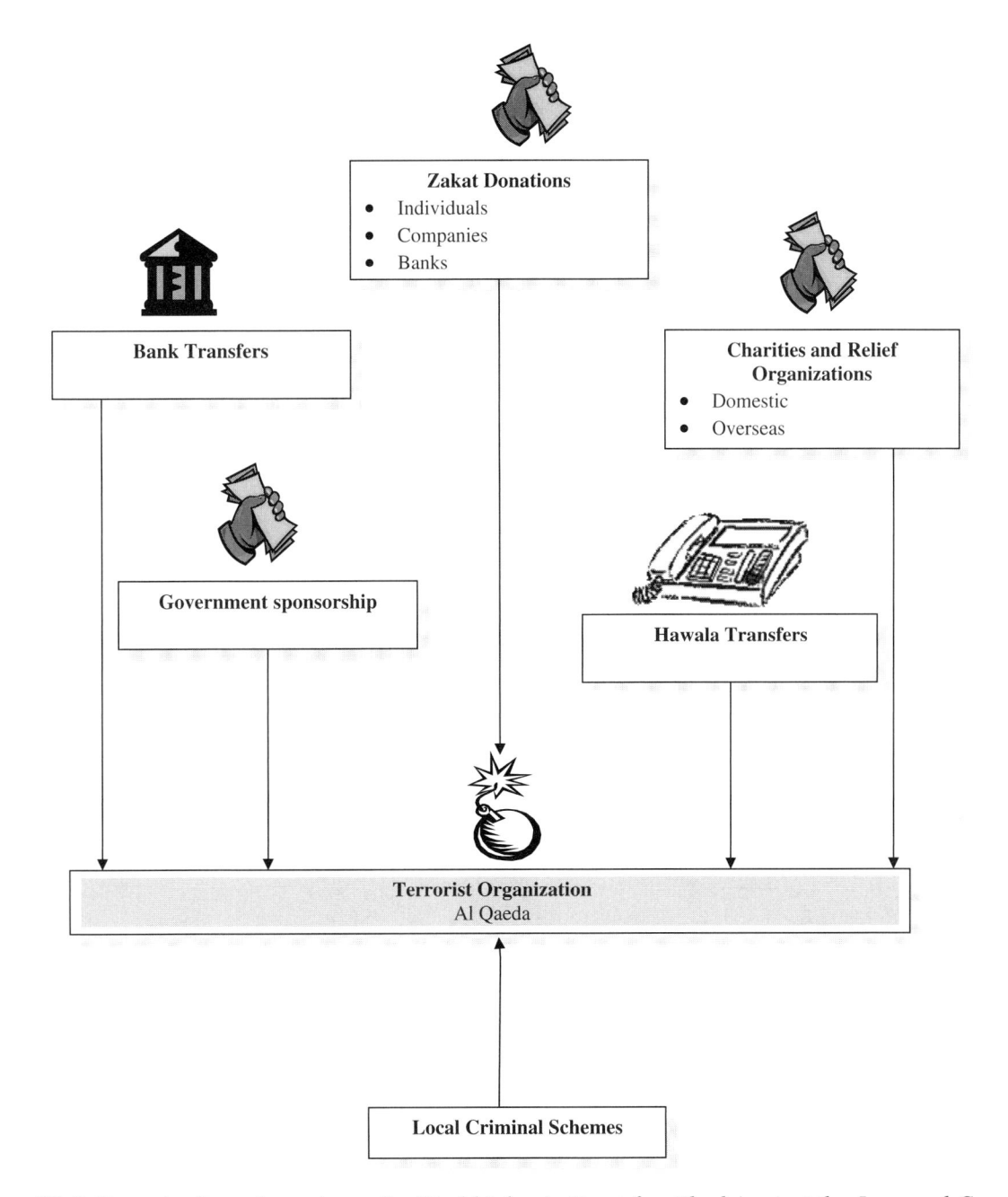

Local Criminal Schemes

Figure 23.9 Terrorist financing scheme for World Islamic Front for Jihad Against the Jews and Crusaders.

Osama bin Laden, with his Yemeni origins, wealthy Saudi family ties, Wahhabi Muslim philosophy, and sustaining hatred of America, is more than just a figurehead leader; he is an ideal fundraiser as well. And past operations in Africa and the Middle East, not to mention the carnage on 9/11/2001, give bin Laden and Al Qaeda a proven track record. Contributors know exactly what they're getting for their money.

Bin Laden raked in piles of money, often in very large amounts, from Saudi, Yemeni, and other sources in the Persian Gulf — like-minded individuals who backed up their beliefs with cash. Some of the donations took the form from *zakat,* the charitable contributions required of believers by Islam. Other funds were unquestionably provided with the clear understanding that they supported bin Laden's "jihad" against the West in general and the United States in particular.

Intelligence agencies believe that substantial sums were provided by prominent Sunni Muslims of the Wahhabi sect, which dominates politics and government in the Kingdom of Saudi Arabia, including people close to, if not within the Saudi royal family. After 9/11 the United States made strenuous efforts to shut down this portion of bin Laden's money pipeline. The Saudi government, chagrined to learn that 15 of the 19 9/11 hijackers were Saudi (as is bin Laden himself), has reportedly been much more cooperative in addressing terrorist funding issues involving its citizens.

Al Qaeda also profits from Afghanistan's lucrative opium and heroin trade. Intelligence reports have linked Al Qaeda to opium and heroin trafficking; Afghanistan is the world's largest producer of opium for the illegal drug trade. Al Qaeda, with cells in Europe and established communications channels between Afghanistan's production area and European markets, is perfectly positioned to take advantage of a very lucrative black market. As government and Saudi funding declined, Al Qaeda undoubtedly turned to these darker alternatives for cash.

Investigating Al Qaeda's Funding

Jihad is an expensive proposition, especially when you have global ambitions, as does Al Qaeda. With terror cells in North and South America, Africa, Europe, and Asia, Al Qaeda's far-flung operations cost money to create and sustain.

Because Al Qaeda's funding comes from all four of the terrorist financing sources — contributions, government sponsorship, legitimate business, and crime — an investigation of the funding is going to follow multiple tracks. By this time, American investigators have turned over every rock at least once in their quest for Osama's money. This investigation started long before 9/11, though it became more important on that day.

One line led backward from the hijacker cells in the United States, a money trail that led to Germany and the Middle East. Another line went from other known Al Qaeda operations in Yemen, Saudi Arabia, and Africa backward along those money trails. Investigators also looked at known funding sources in Saudi Arabia and the Gulf states, some of which had been identified in previous cases, and they went to bin Laden's home turf in Afghanistan and Pakistan to look for traces of the money flow.

All of these efforts created a very accurate picture of Al Qaeda's funding. It also gives us a good idea about how the organization moves its money around and spends it, important clues for preventing the next terror attack. Investigators were particularly interested in the roles played by banks and financial institutions, and that of the *hawala* networks used to move money around the world. Because all of these institutions make and keep records (though *hawala* records aren't as extensive), they may contain important leads to past and future terrorist operations.

Sources of Information

Once again, the importance of the *subject's records* cannot be overemphasized. Investigators must always try to get their hands on the books, papers, records, and documents kept by the subject. Al Qaeda is no different from any other organization, legal or illegal, in that it creates records to track its own activities, and some of these are financial. When American troops captured the Al Qaeda training camps in Afghanistan, they didn't just pick up the propaganda tapes showing hooded terrorists doing the obstacle course. They also looked hard for any financial records, hoping to trace money from Afghanistan to terror cells in Europe or America.

The capture of top Al Qaeda operative Khalid Sheikh Mohammed in Pakistan also netted his computer and a wealth of information in digital form. Investigators can't afford to overlook computer evidence today, particularly since terrorists and money launderers have taken to using computers so routinely in their operations. The use of document warrants should always include language to seize digital or computer evidence, and these search warrants should be one of the goals of any investigation of terrorist financing.

Suspicious Activity Reports and other cash transaction reports may also provide good leads, especially when combined with other evidence of terrorist activity. In the past, SARs were not always linked to terrorist plots before the action took place. Only afterward were investigators able to follow the trail backward, sometimes using bank reports or third-party records to see how monies were received, spent, and distributed. In the future, federal law enforcement is going to be more aggressive in analyzing any SARs or transaction reports that are even remotely linked to terrorism.

Witnesses and informants from within the organization are obviously extremely valuable, one reason there's a $25 million bounty on the Al Qaeda leadership figures. We would spend that money gladly for a lead to Osama's current whereabouts, and probably just for an idea about where his records are kept.

ZAKAT SCHEMES

UNITED STATES OF AMERICA V. HOLY LAND FOUNDATION FOR RELIEF AND DEVELOPMENT

The indictment of the Holy Land Foundation for Relief and Development, filed on July 26, 2004, in the Northern District of Texas, provides a perfect roadmap of how this type of organization funds terrorist activity, in this case that of HAMAS, a specially designated terrorist organization. See Figure 23.10.

According to the indictment, the Holy Land Foundation for Relief and Development (HLF) was created for the purpose of providing financial and material support to HAMAS. Created in California in 1989, it relocated to Richardson, Texas, in 1992, where it was incorporated and "represented itself to be a non-profit, tax exempt, charitable organization designed primarily to assist needy individuals in the West Bank and Gaza." HLF also maintained offices in New Jersey, California, Illinois, Jerusalem, the West Bank, and Gaza. Some of the officers, directors, or representatives of HLF were associates of HAMAS members back in the West Bank and Gaza, and some were related by blood or marriage.

The indictment documents numerous transfers from HLF to HAMAS and top HAMAS leaders. Some of the transfers were to these individuals, and others were made to accounts of entities controlled by HAMAS, such as the Islamic Center of Gaza, the headquarters of HAMAS spiritual leader and founder Sheikh Ahmed Yassin. As shown in Figure 23.10, the HAMAS-controlled zakat organizations served as conduits for the money sent by HLF, forwarding it through the HAMAS political bureau to its military and "calling" wings.

HLF raised funds in the United States by sponsoring conventions, seminars, and rallies, the purpose of which was ostensibly to support Palestinian causes. On many occasions, radical Islamic clerics and HAMAS officials were brought to the United States to speak and to encourage contributors. On occasion, HLF paid for this travel.

HLF's scheme was simple and direct, although things got a little complicated after HAMAS became a specially designated terrorist organization in January 1995. HLF actively solicited contributions and zakat donations from American Muslims and immigrants from the Middle East. Prior to 1995, it was no secret that at least some of these funds were going directly to HAMAS. Nor was it any big surprise to the contributors that the money was going to be used for HAMAS' stated goal of eliminating the state of Israel, by violent means if necessary.

Funds were raised in seminars and rallies that featured skits of Jews being killed and of terrorist actions. Speeches by radical Islamic clerics employed fiery rhetoric to encourage donations, and, even after 1995, donors were made aware that some of the funds were going to support the same causes — and the same group — as before.

Terrorist Financing Scheme - HOLY LAND FOUNDATION

- Fundraising events
- Mosque services
- Seminars

Holy Land Foundation for Relief and Development
- Shukri Abu-Baker
- Mohammed El-Mezain
- Ghassan Elashi

Richardson, Texas

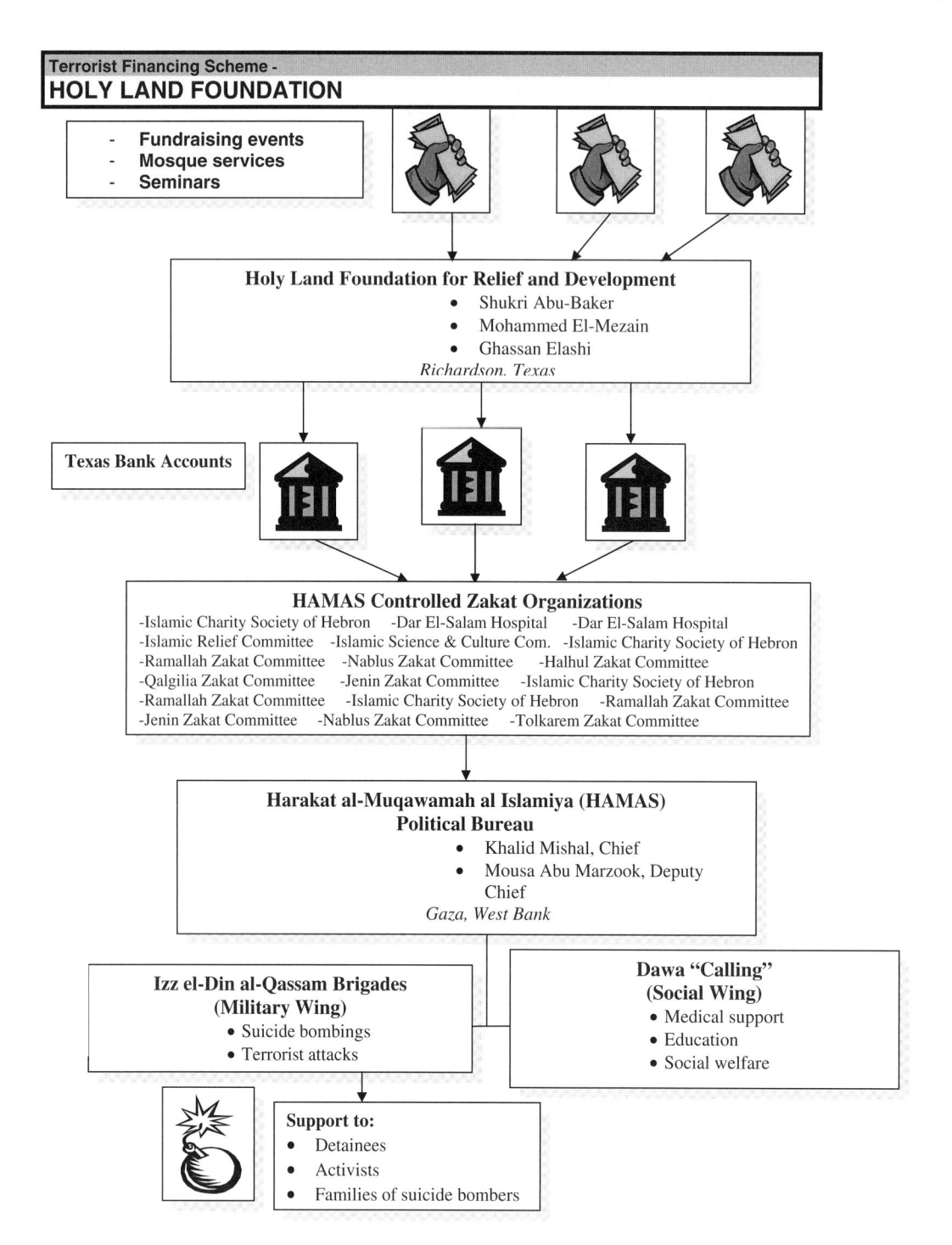

Texas Bank Accounts

HAMAS Controlled Zakat Organizations
-Islamic Charity Society of Hebron   -Dar El-Salam Hospital   -Dar El-Salam Hospital
-Islamic Relief Committee   -Islamic Science & Culture Com.   -Islamic Charity Society of Hebron
-Ramallah Zakat Committee   -Nablus Zakat Committee   -Halhul Zakat Committee
-Qalgilia Zakat Committee   -Jenin Zakat Committee   -Islamic Charity Society of Hebron
-Ramallah Zakat Committee   -Islamic Charity Society of Hebron   -Ramallah Zakat Committee
-Jenin Zakat Committee   -Nablus Zakat Committee   -Tolkarem Zakat Committee

Harakat al-Muqawamah al Islamiya (HAMAS) Political Bureau
- Khalid Mishal, Chief
- Mousa Abu Marzook, Deputy Chief

Gaza, West Bank

Izz el-Din al-Qassam Brigades (Military Wing)
- Suicide bombings
- Terrorist attacks

Dawa "Calling" (Social Wing)
- Medical support
- Education
- Social welfare

Support to:
- Detainees
- Activists
- Families of suicide bombers

Figure 23.10 *Terrorist financing scheme for Holy Land Foundation.*

When monies came in, these were deposited into banks in the Richardson area and then wire-transferred to the accounts of HAMAS-controlled zakat organizations in the West Bank and Gaza. The indictment documents numerous transfers, and the sums were substantial. The indictment charges that "between 1992 and 2001, the defendants ... reported approximately $36,230,891 on Line 13 of the HLF's 'Returns of Organization Exempt from Income Tax.'" This was money HLF claimed it sent to the Middle East for such things as "assistance to non-profit medical/dental clinics, orphanages, schools, refugee camps, and community centers." In fact, these monies were distributed to individuals associated with and organizations controlled by HAMAS.

INVESTIGATING A ZAKAT SCHEME

Fundraising organizations aren't very covert, although they may try to hide some aspects of their operation, such as a direct link to a DTO. Fundraising events are widely publicized or advertised, and appeals in mosques and other public settings are intended to garner lots of attention (hopefully followed by lots of money).

Once the money arrives, it must be moved elsewhere to the beneficiary, whether it is a DTO on the West Bank or a terrorist cell in Hamburg. This means transferring funds, which, as we've seen previously, involves wire transmission and the creation of tracking records.

Following the money will be one of the most important parts of this type of case, because it has to be proved that the funds were raised and transferred with the intent to support a terrorist organization. This is where financial investigative techniques will be most helpful.

SOURCES OF INFORMATION

There should be a wealth of information in the organization's records — if you can find them. These enterprises, especially the ones with tax-exempt status, maintain extensive books and records, usually in a visible location. The group may have multiple offices in different states, and it may communicate frequently between offices. The connections to beneficiaries in the Middle East will also be documented, although the threat of prosecution under American terrorist financing legislation now requires additional layers to protect parties on both ends. Some organizations have deliberately situated their offices in places where records are more difficult to acquire, such as Switzerland and the Gulf States in the Middle East.

Tax returns may be valuable, particularly those of the organizations themselves. Individuals may claim deductions for charitable contributions, and these can be matched against those of the 501 (c) (3) organization.

Suspicious Activity Reports may be filed by financial institutions or money transfer businesses. These may name individuals, the organization, or both. SARs will provide leads to bank accounts and to the origin and destination of funds being transferred. Of particular importance is the destination of wired monies. Having the cash wired directly to an account held in the name of HAMAS or Osama bin Laden certainly makes your case much easier for the jury to follow.

Document search warrants at the organization's offices, the residences of officers or directors, and other locations where financial records are likely to be found have been key parts of terrorism financing cases to date. These warrants will not only uncover evidence of financial transactions and money transfers — crucial elements in the criminal case — but they also uncover evidence of links to the designated terrorist organization and to individuals also on the government's list. Evidence that the charity knows the illegal uses to which the money will be put is also helpful.

Informants from within the organization can direct investigators to important events, individuals, or transactions. Informants may also be able to penetrate some of the layers that the fundraisers try to place between themselves and the DTO.

HAWALA SCHEMES AND INFORMAL VALUE TRANSFER SYSTEMS

Nobody's ever lost money in a *hawala;* that's the claim of the people who run this ancient form of transferring value — it probably predates banks.

Case Example

Ahmed and Omar are big believers in the *hawala* system, which has worked well for people in their region for centuries. People in Pakistan didn't always need to send money to New York or vice versa, but in the

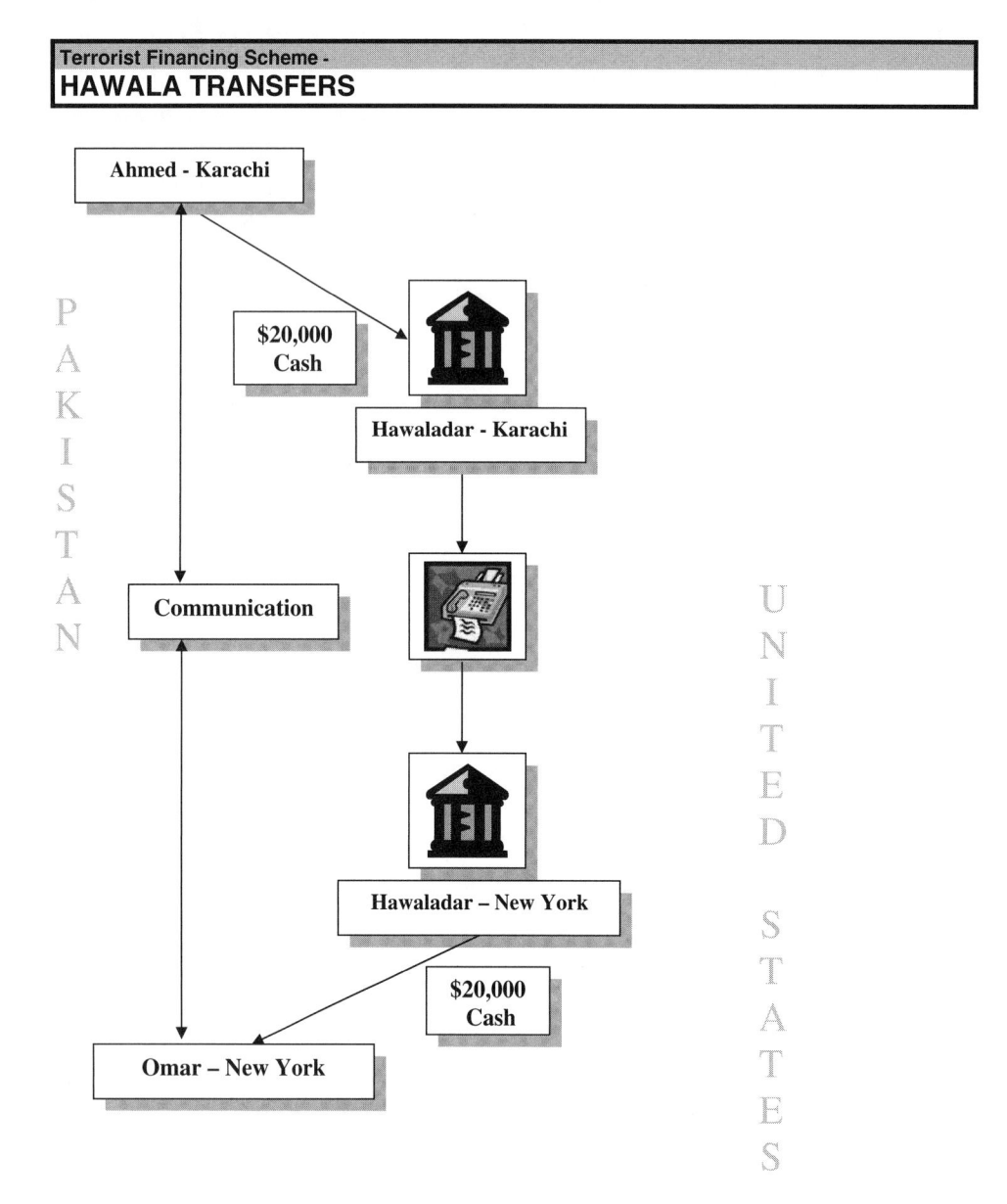

Figure 23.11 *Terrorist financing scheme using hawala transfers.*

modern world you have to change with the times. See Figure 23.11.

Today, Ahmed, an Al Qaeda operative in Karachi, wants to send $20,000 to Omar, a member of a terror cell in New York City. Ahmed has a couple of problems with using banks or Western Union for this transaction. First, both are likely to ask questions about the cash deal, especially in America, where the law requires large cash transactions to be reported. You also have to present identification in most situations, something Omar might not want to do.

Second, the cost of sending the money by wire may be a factor. Western Union charges big fees, and even bank fees might be substantial. Finally, there's the convenience factor; Western Union isn't everywhere, although it is in Karachi, and banks are more limited.

The solution is easy. Ahmed goes to a *hawaladar,* the broker for the local *hawala* money transfer network. Khalid has been in business a while and has a number of contacts in places Pakistanis frequently want to send money to or receive money from. Khalid isn't everywhere, either, but if he didn't have someone in New York, Ahmed could go to another *hawaladar* who did.

Ahmed gives Khalid the $20,000 in cash and a commission, along with the name of the person who's going to be collecting the money on the other end. They work out a password to secure the transaction, but there's little risk to the money.

Khalid sends a fax to Ayman, his partner in New York City, instructing him to pay $20,000 to Omar when he shows up with the password. Omar comes in, gives the word, and walks out with $20,000 in cash, to be used for some future terrorist action. Ayman is now out $20,000, but he knows there will be other Pakistanis in New York who will want to send money to Karachi, so he makes an entry on his books and waits for the money to come in to make them balance.

This informal value transfer system (IVTS) is simple, fast, safe, and effective, which is why it is popular in immigrant communities whose access to banks may be limited. The *hawala* gets things done, as it has for centuries. One thing that doesn't get done is extensive record-keeping. Neither Khalid nor Ayman is likely to have any identification information on their clients. They also aren't going to have any record that this transaction ever took place, at least not after it's been concluded. Once the account has been settled, the *hawaladars* are probably going to shred the faxes and other records of the transaction, partly for privacy, but mostly because there's no need to keep the unnecessary documentation. This complicates an investigation of the deal, which suits Ahmed and Omar just fine.

INVESTIGATING A *HAWALA* SCHEME

Good luck. This is like catching smoke, or maybe catching electronic blips as they fly through the atmosphere. That might be one way to go about it. Using a wiretap or a fax intercept on the *hawaladar* could be useful if the business line can be identified. This presumes that you know about him or her in the first place. Since *hawaladars* don't advertise in the yellow pages under "hawala," you may not know he or she exists, although you can be assured that there is a *hawaladar* in any major city with a Middle Eastern or South Asian population.

SOURCES OF INFORMATION

Suspicious Activity Reports could be a good lead to the American end of the *hawala* transaction. Sooner or later, the *hawaladar* does have to go to the bank, and this person may be making cash deposits that generate either an SAR or a CTR. It isn't likely, but Ayman may actually have obtained a license from the state of New York to act as a wire remitter, and he might be filing SARs and CTRs for his own large cash transactions. Most *hawaladars* don't bother, even though the provisions of Title 18 U.S.C. §1960 relating to the operation of an illegal wire transmitter business make prosecution easier and more likely.

The records of the *hawala* business are obviously the best lead to Omar, the terrorist in New York City we most want to nab. These aren't going to amount to much: contact information, phone and fax records, and probably a ledger (maybe computerized) detailing past transactions. Investigators have found that these ledgers often don't contain much more than the date, the amount, and the name of the *hawaladar* on the other end. They're mostly kept as a means to settle accounts and make sure the books balance. Still, there could be some identifying information for the person who picked up the cash.

Document search warrants at Omar's place may lead back to the *hawaladar,* which might mean leads to other transactions or other cell members. Officers searching terrorist suspects, particularly those from the Middle East and Southwest Asia, should be on the lookout for *hawaladar* contacts and look for phone numbers and notes referencing the sending or receiving of money.

Informants from within the community should be asked about *hawala* activities.

Because these operations rely on word-of-mouth advertising, only people from within the particular ethnic group or immigrant community are likely to know about them. It doesn't hurt to ask an informant if he or she knows who is sending money back to the old country and how they're sending it. The answer will often be some local business person, a travel agency, or some other respected and established member of the community.

Investigating a *hawala* operation requires patience, rapport with witnesses and informants, and good intelligence. Federal agencies have had some success in using informants or undercover agents to send money internationally via *hawala* and other informal value transfer systems. This technique implicates the people at both ends of the transaction and makes a prosecution under 18 U.S.C. §1960 more viable, but it needs a lot of coordination and usually a very good informant. It also requires the government to give a large amount of money to some man in a bazaar or strip mall and then wait while it's delivered to a similar person halfway around the world. That takes some faith, but the *hawaladars* will tell you that nobody's ever lost money in a *hawala*.

CHAPTER 24

INVESTIGATING MONEY LAUNDERING CASES

"Before turning to those moral and mental aspects of the matter which present the greatest difficulties, let the enquirer begin by mastering more elementary problems."
Sherlock Holmes, in Sir Arthur Conan Doyle's *A Study in Scarlet*

"I am afraid, my dear Watson, that most of your conclusions were erroneous. When I said that you stimulated me I meant, to be frank, that in noting your fallacies I was occasionally guided towards the truth."
Sherlock Holmes, in Sir Arthur Conan Doyle's *The Hound of the Baskervilles*

Money laundering has been described as the "crime of the 1990s" and even the "crime of the 21st century." While I'd guess somebody will come up with some other crime du jour to grab the headlines, I'd also be willing to bet that money laundering will increasingly be a part of all sorts of other crimes. One of the things this book has tried to do is emphasize how essential money laundering is to a successful criminal enterprise.

Now that we've spent 20 or so chapters talking about financial investigation, it's time to ditch that term. Why? Because there is no such thing. A financial investigation is really just an investigation using some added financial techniques. The late Richard Nossen, a former IRS special agent and administrator, developed and wrote extensively on what he called the "Seventh Basic Investigative Technique." Mr. Nossen was of the opinion that financial analysis is just one of the tools that can be effectively used in a criminal investigation.

Although he's not talking specifically about money laundering, financial analysis is part of this integrated approach, which must be a part of money laundering investigations. Mr. Nossen writes in his handbook, *The Seventh Basic Investigative Technique*:

For countless years, criminal investigators have relied on six basic investigative techniques to solve crimes:

1. the development of informants,
2. use of undercover agents,
3. laboratory evidence of physical evidence,
4. physical and electronic surveillance,
5. interrogation, and
6. where permitted by law, wiretapping.

Each of these techniques has its uses and results in varying degrees of success.

The purpose of this handbook is to introduce criminal investigators, on a broad scale, to an investigative tool, a seventh basic investigative technique, used primarily in the investigation of violations of the Federal income tax laws. This tool, if properly applied, can greatly enhance the success of the investigation of cases where illegal profits and a greed for wealth are the principle [sic] motives of the violators (p. 12).

If Mr. Nossen is right (and I think he is), the financial investigative technique is not only effective, it's essential to a case involving money laundering. In these cases especially, the financial investigative technique cannot stand alone. It will be a major part of an investigation, but it cannot do the whole job.

Here's a challenge: Take any one of the case examples in this book, or look at the very next money laundering case you see in the newspaper. Analyze the case by what types of investigative techniques were used to reach the conclusion. You'll find that, in almost every instance, at least three and occasionally all seven of the techniques described by Mr. Nossen were employed. This is especially true in money laundering cases, because the investigator must always prove two things under federal law — financial transaction and a Specified Unlawful Activity (SUA).

Now, you can try real hard, but I still haven't figured out how to prove a person was in the drug business using *only* financial investigative techniques. This means at least half of any money laundering case is going to involve some of the other six methods. In fact, half of the case is going to rely very heavily on exactly the same type of investigative activity that a drug case would. How can the SUA be proved, absent the testimony of witnesses, informants, or undercover agents? Physical surveillance is a critical part of many criminal investigations, and, as we'll see, it is pretty important here, too. So is the seizure and analysis of physical evidence. So don't worry. You won't have to give up your day job if you decide to dabble in financial investigations.

What I'm urging is the adoption of an integrated approach to money laundering cases. Recognize that the case has two main parts, both of which have to be proved beyond a reasonable doubt. Recognize that you won't get from here to there without using a blend of investigative techniques. One of these, financial analysis, is not only going to prove one part of the case, but it's also going to provide some pretty compelling evidence of the SUA.

DECISIONS, DECISIONS ...

Every money laundering investigation is going to be different from the last. One of the attractions of criminal investigation as a profession is the challenge provided by the new people, facts, and circumstances associated with each case. Even though every case is different, the same rules apply to each investigation.

The investigative process in any case is really a series of decisions, made by the investigator after weighing the evidence. Who will be the next witness interviewed? When should I get a warrant? Should I try to flip this guy or that one? In a complex case, literally dozens of such decisions will have to be made over the course of the investigation.

It's no different for money laundering cases; it's just that some of the decisions will relate to the financial evidence. Because the money launderer has such limitless choices in filling out his or her scheme, our options in investigating the matter may be confusing. But the launderer is operating under constraints as well, which makes our choices a little easier. Other options will be dictated by the law.

One of these is the question of whether to investigate the SUA or the financial activity. Since you have to prove *both* to get a money laundering conviction, this decision is easy. And the way to this end is also clear. Take a two-track approach. One track is the proving of the SUA. The second is the linkage of the SUA to the financial activity. These investigations should not be conducted separately but integrated with each other, so that the information developed on one track will support and enhance that developed on the other. By integrating the case in this fashion, you double your chances of getting viable criminal charges. Figure 24.1 illustrates the process.

CASE DEVELOPMENT PROCESS

As Figure 24.1 shows, the case development process follows a two-track strategy, beginning with the initiating information and ending with a (hopefully) successful criminal prosecution.

MONEY LAUNDERING CASE DEVELOPMENT PROCESS

Initial Information

Financial Sources
- BSA Forms
- Informants
- Other Financial

SUA Sources
- Informant
- Witnesses
- Case Offshoot

Basis for the Investigation

Tracing Assets or Transactions to SUA

Linking SUA to Assets or Transactions

Case Organization

General Administration and Organization

Developing an Investigative Plan

Evidence Collection

Financial
- Informants   - Undercover
- Subpoenas   - Interviews
- Document SW   - Other

SUA
- Informants   - Undercover
- Interviews   - Searches
- Surveillance   - ELSUR

Evidence Analysis

Financial
- Financial Analysis
- Indirect Methods Case

SUA
- Application to SUA Cases
- Application to Financial Case

Presentation

Criminal Prosecution
- Money Laundering
- Underlying Criminal Activity

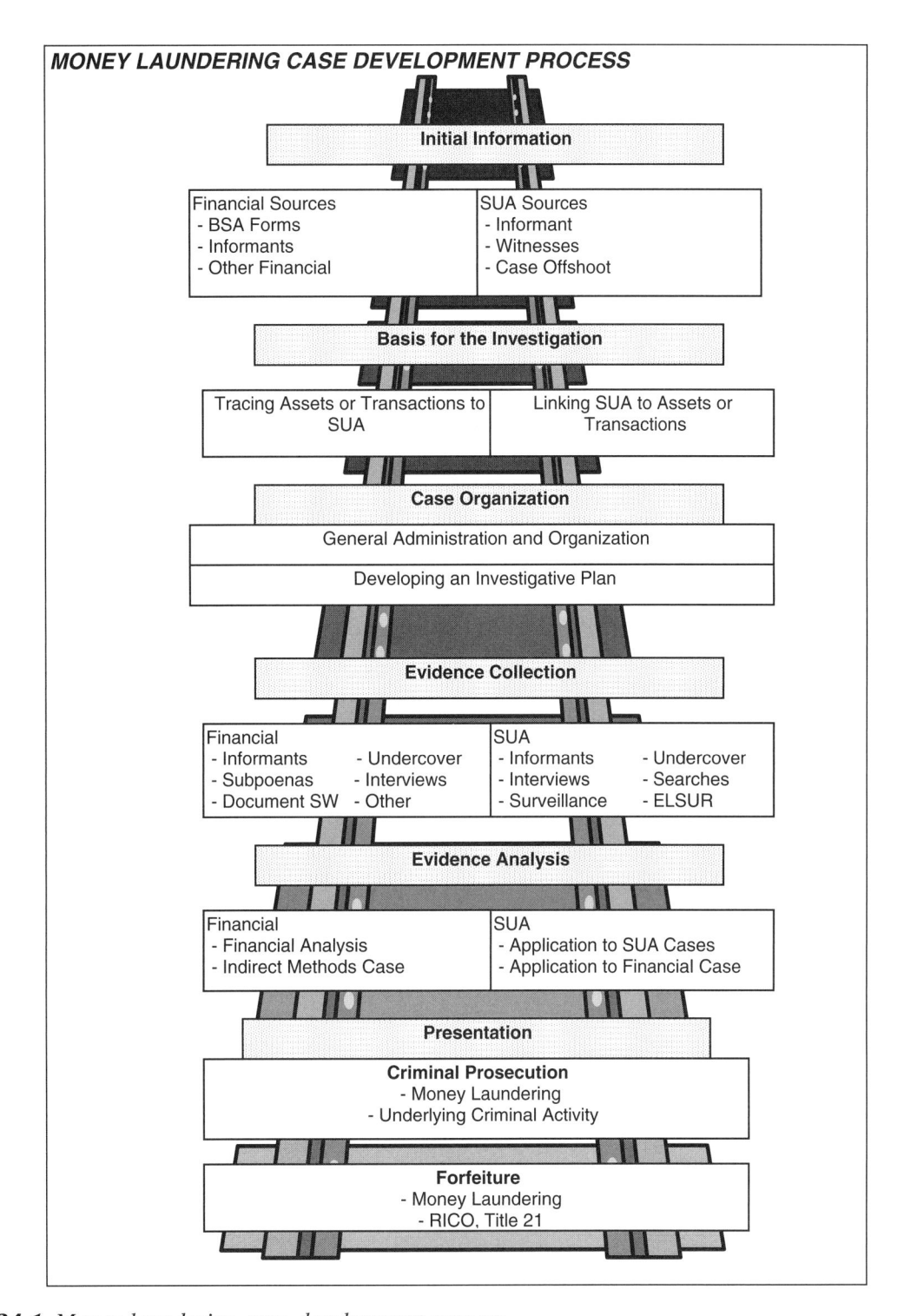

Forfeiture
- Money Laundering
- RICO, Title 21

Figure 24.1 Money laundering case development process.

Note that although the middle stages of the case may be distinct in terms of the financial and SUA tracks, the ending phase merges both.

In examining the case development process, I'm going to use an actual case from the early 1980s. Although the Money Laundering Control Act would not be passed for several more years, the facts are easily adaptable to a money laundering charge. While you're reading the facts of the case, look for (*a*) what schemes were being used to place, layer, and integrate the dirty money and (*b*) what decisions the agents made at various points in the investigation. *Note:* All of the names have been changed to protect the innocent.

Case Example

Lieutenant Colonel Wallace J. Daley, U.S.A.F. (Retired), had come a long way from flying nuclear-armed FB-111 strike aircraft for the Air Force. He'd been poor, and he'd gotten rich, and rich was better.

Upon leaving the Cold War, Daley drifted for a while, eventually meeting up with a couple of guys who were already in the dope business. When he saw the kind of money that could be made, Daley enlisted in the drug war — on the wrong side. Like most dealers, Daley started small, although he had a bit of an edge; one of his contacts, Harry, had the connection to Florida. Daley didn't stay small, however, and by the time Harry died, Daley had taken over the business, becoming the largest distributor in the state. According to an informant, Daley was buying Quaalude tablets in large quantities, which he sold in 10,000-dose lots.

"The Colonel," as he was known, had two things going for him that most drug dealers don't. First, he knew how to save his money, so that when he quit, he was going to quit ahead. Second, he knew when to quit. Quitting time was the day after his main runner got arrested delivering 10,000 'ludes to an undercover agent. Fortunately, the runner didn't talk, but Daley took the money and ran.

Gone, but not forgotten, at least in the minds of the agents who had never quit wondering who was behind that load of Quaaludes. A year later, they found out. Another undercover buy, this one for only 100 tablets, resulted in the arrest of a man suspected of being in the Quaalude business for years. This guy, John Able, rolled over. He said that although the drugs he'd sold had come from a different source, the one the agents *really* wanted was Wallace Daley, aka "The Colonel." And he was right.

Agents began looking at Daley, knowing that he'd apparently been out of the business for some time. He had a nice house in a good neighborhood. He drove a Buick, and his wife, a Toyota. He jogged and cycled and generally lived the genteel life of a retired military officer. There were no major assets in his name; even the house was in the name of some sort of a trust. Although he lived exactly like a retired Air Force colonel, Daley had, Able assured the agents, made and saved at least $2 million by the time he quit the business.

No matter which way the agents decided to move, it was clear that this was going to be a historical case. Daley was inactive. There was no record of large cash transactions. Able's statements were the only leads, and Able knew nothing about where the money might have gone — only that The Colonel was smart enough to have kept it all.

CASE INITIATION

Like any other case, a money laundering investigation has to get initiated at some point. How you get *there* from *here* will depend a lot on (*a*) where you start and (*b*) the decisions you make along the way. See Table 24.1.

With the initial information, you'll be presented with your first choices. The source alone may dictate your approach. The first question you'll want to ask is:

What is the source of this information?

Specifically, does the information come from the SUA or the financial side of the house? For example, a confidential informant reports that the subject is making large amounts of money in the cocaine business. Logic tells us that the subject must be doing *something* with the money, so a money laundering investigation might be in order to find out where the money is going.

TABLE 24.1
Initial Information

Financial Sources	SUA Sources
BSA Forms	Informants
Informants	Witnesses
Other Financial	Case Offshoot

The initial source of this information is from the SUA part of the picture. Your approach to the money laundering case would probably be to track the criminal activity to determine what's happening to the money the subject is making. You could also try to locate some evidence of assets and financial activity and then trace these back to the SUA.

On the other side of the coin, many money laundering cases are developed through Bank Secrecy Act (BSA) forms, Suspicious Activity Reports (SARs), or straight financial intelligence. For example, a bank files several Currency Transaction Reports (CTRs) and SARs reporting that an individual is making multiple structured cash deposits. There is no information at all on any SUA, but the best approach in this case would be to document the financial transactions while moving on a parallel track to prove up some illegal source for the structured deposits.

The source of the information — what you originally have to work with — will dictate your approach to the case, specifically whether you will trace the money back to the SUA, or trace the SUA to the assets or transactions.

The next question relates to the status of the criminal activity — either the SUA or the financial transactions.

Is the activity ongoing or historical?

Again, the answer to this question will dictate your approach to the case. If, according to the informant, the SUA is ongoing, you should start with the investigative techniques you would use to detect that SUA. These might include physical surveillance, undercover contacts, pen registers, wiretaps, and search warrants.

If your informant says the group is no longer active, the more proactive investigative techniques won't do any good. If the subject is now enjoying his or her ill-gotten gains on the beach, surveillance would only be a frustration. In this (historical) setting, you would want to get right on with collecting the financial data and start trying to locate some witnesses who can put the subject in the SUA in the past.

Note that, in either situation, the agent has the flexibility to employ the most effective investigative package. Also note that neither situation precludes a two-track approach — it only describes how each track should initially be followed. There are variations on this theme, as when the financial activity is ongoing even though the SUA has ceased. In any event, this guide will help you make decisions about how the case should be approached initially.

BASIS FOR THE INVESTIGATION

Now that you've decided to do something, you need to figure out the basis of your case. This can be somewhat difficult in the earliest stages, because, after all, you haven't even started to collect any evidence or information in the case. Lots can change before the hammer finally falls, but you need to act on what you know now. See Table 24.2.

You have two alternatives in pursuing this type of case:

- Tracing the assets or financial transactions to an SUA
- Linking the SUA to assets or transactions

Let's look back at a couple of our case examples for guidance. In the case of Bruno Richard Hauptmann, the Lindbergh kidnapper (Chapter

TABLE 24.2
Basis for the Investigation

Tracing assets or transactions to the SUA	Linking the SUA to assets or transactions

10), investigators began with the SUA, which was kidnapping. They believed that Hauptmann had received the ransom, and they set out to find any assets or financial transactions that Hauptmann could have conducted with the SUA proceeds. The investigation ultimately uncovered quite a few money laundering transactions, as well as the evidence that Hauptmann was trying to conceal or disguise his ownership and control of the ransom money. This, clearly, was a question of linking the SUA to assets or transactions.

In Al Capone's case, the investigators knew full well that Capone was involved in all sorts of SUAs, but their case began from a financial standpoint — with the many transactions he was known to have conducted. In this instance, the approach was first to link Capone with the financial transactions (not an easy job, given all of his efforts to avoid this connection) and then to find witnesses to attribute a likely source to the funds. Here we have an example of tracing assets or transactions to the SUA.

A better example would be the Alberto Barrera smurfing organization in the early 1980s (Chapter 21). Agents became aware of Barrera's activities through information about structured transactions at an Arizona bank. They then followed the smurfs to other banks in other cities, documenting dozens more money laundering transactions. In the meantime, the agents, who strongly suspected that the underlying SUA was narcotics trafficking, were working hard to prove some link to the SUA. Ultimately they were successful.

In initiating the case, the agents determined that it would be historical, since Daley was out of the business. The absence of financial leads made it likely that the investigation would initially focus on linking Daley to the illegal activity and then attempt to link the SUA to assets or transactions.

CASE ORGANIZATION

Once the broader concepts are understood, it's time to get organized. Some general issues need to be resolved right up front, and this is a good time to formulate an investigative plan. See Table 24.3.

On the administrative and organizational side, a few questions need to be answered.

QUESTIONS ABOUT PARTICIPANTS

Who's invited to the party? Relatively few money laundering cases are done by one agency anymore. Most cases involve personnel from two or more investigative agencies in addition to the prosecutor. Considerations in this area revolve around what each participant is bringing to the table. These considerations include:

- *Agency jurisdiction* — jurisdiction over the underlying SUA or the money laundering offense (In some cases, the jurisdiction may be geographic, as when crimes are being committed in the jurisdiction of a local or state police agency.)
- *Agency resources* — personnel, money, undercover agents, surveillance equipment, and so forth
- *Agency expertise* — specifically the accounting or financial background needed to complete the case (In addi-

---

Daley Case Example (continued)

Routine checks disclosed no major assets in Daley's name, no large cash transactions, and no intelligence in law enforcement databases. One intriguing note: Daley's phone number was found in the address book of the trafficker arrested with the 10,000 Quaaludes the year before.

He had taken his 10 years in silence, however. Besides Able, no other participants in the operation were clamoring to tell their stories.

TABLE 24.3
Case Organization

General administration and organization
Developing an investigative plan

tion, expertise such as DEA's knowledge of drug trafficking patterns could come in very handy.)
- *Information* — financial information or intelligence about the underlying criminal activity (This is frequently where state and local agencies can be major contributors to a money laundering case.)

Participation is an issue that needs to be decided up front, because whoever joins in late will have to play catch-up. Also, the question of equitable sharing of forfeited assets is going to arise if the case is successful. Since sharing is contingent on actual participation in the case, the agencies want to be in on the ground floor.

When you are organizing the team that will work on the case, make sure that you have the expertise you need to get the job done. Some of the specialists who can be put to good use are:

- Agents with a financial background
- Auditors
- Intelligence analysts
- Investigative aides or accounting techs
- Forfeiture coordinators or asset management people

Determine whether and when you'll need the Marshals Service forfeiture resources or the personnel who will handle the seized property. They all like a lot of lead time, too.

Questions About Prosecutor Involvement

This is actually a nondecision, because the United States Attorney or state prosecutor is going to have to be a participant in the case at a very early stage. You'll require the input of the prosecutor on a number of issues, including pen register and wiretap authorizations, search warrants, assistance with defendant witnesses, and, above all, grand jury subpoenas.

Money laundering cases don't get done without financial records, many of which are in the custody of banks or other third-party recordkeepers. Since the prosecutor has the power, through the grand jury, to compel production of the records *and* the means and procedures to pay for that production, it's a good idea to harness this power early.

One question that will probably be resolved by the prosecutor will be the role of any civil forfeiture attorney in the case. In some offices, the civil and criminal aspects of a case are all handled by one prosecutor, while in others a forfeiture attorney handles that side of the case. This won't be the investigator's call, but once it's made, be sure to mark your scorecard appropriately.

Questions About the Case File

Believe it or not, the case file can be a problem, one that would be good to sort out as soon as possible. These cases generate a lot of paper, and it all needs to be in one place. Some of the paper will be covered by Rule 6 (e) as grand jury material, requiring additional protection, or tax records, which can be even more sensitive.

The case file should be accessible to everyone on the case who needs (and is authorized) to see it. It should also be secured for chain of custody purposes. Depending on the size and complexity of the case, you may need several filing cabinets. Some cases are so big that the investigators are forced to rent space to store their documents.

Legal Considerations

Among the legal considerations that need to be addressed are venue and statutes of limitations.

Bear in mind that venue for the money laundering crime or the financial transactions may be different from that for the SUAs.

If some of the SUAs or the financial transactions occurred more than 5 years ago, the statute of limitations may have already expired on those acts. The money laundering may have continued forward, however. After all, dirty money *never* gets clean, it only looks that way.

THE INVESTIGATIVE PLAN

Some general said once that even the best of plans didn't survive the first contact with the enemy. This is probably true, but it's no reason not to have one anyway. In fact, a good plan will be a big help in organizing your case and prioritizing your needs. And in financial cases, there actually are some things you can plan on and reasonably expect them to succeed.

The plan will be driven by the type of case you are hoping to make or the charges you ultimately hope to bring. You don't want to plan out a drug conspiracy case if your subject is making all his money from mail fraud, but in a money laundering case you may not know which SUA is the source of the funds. Therefore, each money laundering case is planned with its two tracks in mind: proving the SUA and proving the financial activity.

The order in which you do things is probably the most important part of the plan. Some investigative actions can be put off until later, whereas others need to be done right away. Criminal investigations are evidence driven. If the evidence is there, providing leads and direction, the case can move forward. If nothing much is happening, the case may stall.

Most money laundering cases have several phases of evidence collection. Your investigative plan should account for all of these phases. Each relates to the others, in terms of the types of leads it develops and the impact of disclosure on the subject. For purposes of planning, the evidence collection phases in a money laundering case can be categorized as:

- Profiling
- Covert evidence gathering
- Semiovert evidence gathering
- Overt evidence gathering

We'll get into these categories in detail in the next section, but for purposes of planning your case, you generally work from the top of the list down.

Daley Case Example (continued)

Since Daley was out of the business, there was no hope of getting a buy from him or making a seizure from his house. It also seemed likely that any records of the business had long since been destroyed.

Still, the agents wanted to try some covert options before they took more overt steps against The Colonel. An investigative plan was prepared in which these covert measures would be taken first, before the agents went after the financial and other records that would prove, the agents hoped, that Daley had headed a conspiracy to distribute controlled substances.

As it turned out, the final case looked nothing like the original plan.

EVIDENCE COLLECTION

The options for collecting evidence in a case are as wide as the agents' imagination, narrowed somewhat by things like circumstances and the Constitution. I'll assume that as a criminal investigator, you already know how to employ the more traditional investigative techniques in your cases, so we won't get into how to execute a search warrant or interview an informant. We will speak briefly about how and when these techniques can be used in your financial case.

If you look at Table 24.4, you will see overlap in several of the categories. You should expect that a financial witness, such as a bank teller, can provide information about cash deposits, but don't rule out the possibility that he or she may also be able to identify criminal associates who accompanied the subject into the bank. And informants who participate in the illegal activity must also be questioned about the financial affairs of the subject. The pen register on the subject's phone will identify criminal associates, but it may also give you the name of the subject's bank. The same holds true for each of the other "traditional" techniques. Use them on both of your investigative tracks.

As stated above, money laundering cases usually follow a pattern, moving from the more discreet investigative techniques to the glaringly obvious. Almost all cases begin with the preliminary

TABLE 24.4
Evidence Collection

Financial	SUA
Informants	Informants
Undercover	Undercover
Subpoenas	Surveillance
Interviews	Interviews
Document Search Warrants	Search Warrants
Other	Electronic Surveillance

collection of intelligence about the subject and his or her associates. Quite an amazing amount of information is available about people from open sources and from government records systems.

PROFILING

Profiling is not the radioactive racial sort that gives the concept a very bad name. It's the process of gathering basic information about a subject from openly available sources. Profiling is done to establish a basic understanding of the individual, his or her relationship to the case, personal history, and associations with others under investigation.

Profiling is something done initially on the main players, but *every new name that comes into the case in a significant way must also be profiled.* Why bother? When the objective of the criminal enterprise is to conceal the ownership or control of dirty money, we can have no way of knowing whether the new name is someone who is critical to the laundering scheme or just a bystander.

The profiling technique you develop must be systematic, although it will change a little as the case develops and more information is obtained. At the very least, your profile should consist of:

- Law enforcement database checks
- Public records inquiries
- Commercial database checks

Make up a profile sheet before you get started, listing all of the sources that will be used for the profile. As new names are uncovered, use the profile sheet as a checklist to make sure the new person is fully identified and his or her role understood. Figure 24.2 provides a profile sheet. The Department of Justice Investigative Checklist, which appears in Appendix B, is also a good model. Profiling every name is a hassle, but it will pay off later on in your investigation.

All of the profile information for each person should be kept in an individual file, until his or her role in the scheme has been fully established. If the person turns out to be important, you can use the profile as a starting point for a more in-depth inquiry.

A note about FinCEN. Profiling is one service that FinCEN offers. This can be a major timesaver, especially the BSA data. For this reason, you may want to put FinCEN on your profile sheet, unless you're capable of duplicating their work (and you want to). A response from FinCEN may take longer than doing it yourself, but they do a good job.

COVERT EVIDENCE GATHERING

Covert evidence gathering is one step above profiling. The techniques involve little or no risk of disclosure to the subject. Surveillance, both physical and electronic; the use of informants or undercover operations; and such techniques as mail and trash covers fit into this category.

You go this route in money laundering cases to prove both sides of the equation. Surveillance can link the subject to an illegal activity, to associates, and to specific illegal transactions. Surveillance can also detect financial activity or at least links to assets.

You'll do your covert gathering before you do the more in-your-face search warrants and other techniques, because once the investigation is disclosed, the subject will likely change his or her methods of doing business.

Daley Case Example (continued)

Although the covert options were limited, Able and Daley were still on good terms. To

SUBJECT PROFILE	Name

Law Enforcement Databases
- TECS
- NADDIS
- CBRS - BSA
- NLETS
- NCIC
- Police - Criminal History
- Police - Police Reports
- Police - Warrants
- Other LE

Government Records Systems
- Driver's license
- Motor vehicle registration
- Boat registration
- Firearms ownership
- Professional licensing
- Corporate affiliations
- Business registration
- Land ownership
- Grantee - Grantor Index
- Grantor - Grantee Index
- UCC Filings
- ABC/Liquor Commission
- Real Property Tax Assessment
- General Excise/Use Tax License
- State Labor/Employment Data
- Court records - Circuit
- Court records - District
- Court records - Traffic
- Court records - Bankruptcy

Commercial Databases
- LEXIS-NEXIS - Real Property
- LEXIS-NEXIS - Corporate Affiliation
- LEXIS-NEXIS - UCC Filings
- LEXIS-NEXIS - Aircraft
- LEXIS-NEXIS - Licenses
- LEXIS-NEXIS - P-Trak

Figure 24.2 Subject profile form.

corroborate some of Able's statements, it was decided that he would call Daley and offer him a discount on some merchandise at Able's shop. In the recorded conversation that followed, agents hoped that Daley might confirm some of the things Able had said about the activities of the year before.

The conversation went well, even though nothing really incriminating was said. Daley did discuss some of the other players in the organization and referred obliquely to some property he had purchased in the past.

Now another set of decisions needed to be made. The case could go in a couple of directions. Subpoenas could be issued for third-party records, with the hope that these would provide evidence of unexplained wealth. This would further corroborate Able's statements.

Another possibility was to make conspiracy cases against some of those people identified by Able as having been within Daley's organization. If these people, some of whom had been arrested before, could be turned against Daley, the case would be much stronger.

Both of these options carried the risk that Daley would learn of the investigation. If so, he might take further steps to hide his money. After some discussion, a third option was chosen. This decision, which took place very early in the investigation, turned out to be one of the most pivotal.

Semiovert Evidence Gathering

Semiovert evidence gathering involves outsiders in your case, specifically, third-party records custodians. This is the subpoena or grand jury phase, in which information is being gathered by use of official process. Even though the subpoenas may be accompanied by nondisclosure orders, there's no guarantee that word won't get back to the subject.

The grand jury subpoena is a powerful tool for collecting financial evidence. We've discussed it in more depth in other chapters, but now is a good time to remember that subpoenas generate massive amounts of information. Dozens of new leads can come from a single bank account. Interviews that accompany the service of grand jury subpoenas can also be useful, especially in identifying nominees or other facets of the money laundering schemes.

Overt Evidence Gathering

Overt evidence gathering includes document search warrants and interviews of the subject or his or her associates. In this stage, subtlety is probably going to be lost on the subject. You no longer care whether the subject hears footsteps. In fact, some interviews or enforcement actions can be conducted with the intent of gauging the subject's reaction. An interview of a key associate about hidden money might prompt the subject to head for a previously unknown safe deposit box.

The investigator may be prompted to take more overt steps by developments in the case. For example, information could be received that the subject is planning to move the bulk of his or her money out of the bank accounts. If seizure of those funds is a priority, the case may need to be accelerated.

Daley Case Example (continued)

Only a month into an investigation that would ultimately last another year and a half, the prosecutor approved a search warrant for documents at Daley's residence. The focus of the warrant was any documentation of income from any source other than his Air Force pension. Able said that Daley had been a meticulous keeper of drug records, and the ledger books in which he recorded his sales were also named in the warrant.

Daley was surprised to see the agents, but he didn't seem especially concerned. No drugs were recovered, nor was any other contraband. Several boxes of financial records were recovered, including legal papers and one ledger book, from which most of the pages had been removed.

The records were reviewed to identify all bank accounts and financial transactions that could lead to Daley's ownership of large assets. Several records were most promising. Among these were three documents establishing trusts, for which Daley was the trustee. Each trust had a Hawaiian name, and Daley's own name did not appear in the names of any of the trusts.

When real property records were checked for each of the trusts, a total of six different properties were found, including two apartments, raw land, Daley's personal residence, and two other expensive homes. All of the major goodies had been found.

Two other types of documents were also significant. The general financial records in Daley's possession — his check registers, credit card statements, bills, and canceled checks — provided leads to thousands of dollars in expenditures, including over $80,000 in art. These papers ultimately led to other bank accounts, safe deposit boxes, and expenditures.

The ledger book filled in another blank. Although Daley had removed most of the pages from the book that had contained the records of drug sales, two pages had been overlooked. Incredibly, those two pages had a detailed account of Quaalude sales to John Able and two other people. Not only had Able described those exact pages before the ledger was seized, but the other two dealers would ultimately be able to do the same. Sometimes you just get lucky.

EVIDENCE ANALYSIS

As the evidence piles up, put it to some good use. For starters, use it to get more evidence, and spend some time to figure out what it all means. Analysis of the records should take several forms. One could be doing a net worth, bank deposits, or source and applications of funds calculation to locate or identify unexplained income. See Table 24.5.

TABLE 24.5
Evidence Analysis

Financial	SUA
Financial Analysis	Application to Substantive Cases
Indirect Methods Case	Application to Financial Cases

As the financial evidence comes in, the investigator will get a better idea of which method is likely to be the most applicable in this particular case. If the subject has a tremendous number of bank deposits but not many visible assets, the net worth case might not be as good as one that analyzes the bank deposits. Picking a method isn't an urgent priority; it can be done as the facts come in.

The financial records also should be analyzed for leads to more accounts, additional transactions, and links to the SUA. Remember, court decisions obligate us to follow up every reasonable lead in calculating income by indirect methods. This means that all bank accounts have to be reviewed and every readily identifiable source of income examined.

Several techniques, long used in the intelligence business, work well in financial cases. Link analysis is very useful for diagramming the organizational structure and associations of the subject's group. A link chart outlining references to the subject's financial associations should be a part of the case file and should be updated frequently.

You should also prepare a timeline for the case, listing all of the major events and important financial transactions. These two analytical aids are invaluable in witness interviews and in making sense of the evidence in its various forms, and they should be updated throughout the investigation as information comes in. Money laundering cases may involve hundreds of events or transactions, all of which need to be placed in context with the SUA or with other people or events. Several computer programs are available to assist with the preparation of link charts and timelines. It's money well spent.

Leads coming out of the SUA part of the investigation must also be linked with the financial evidence, and vice versa. We're also trying to prove the underlying criminal offenses, something the financial evidence can support.

Another useful tool in this part of the case is a lead chart, with the leads identified for further investigation. There should only be one such chart, not separate ones for each track; this way, you're reminded that each lead can apply to either side of the case.

Evidence analysis is an ongoing process. Each item generates more leads. Each new name needs to be profiled and, if called for, investigated more thoroughly. The intent of a money laundering scheme is to conceal and disguise. The purpose of the evidence analysis is to unravel this scheme — destroying the cover carefully built up by the perpetrator. If we're more organized and systematic than the launderer was, our chances for success go up.

Daley Case Example (continued)

At this point, a detailed financial analysis was undertaken of both the seized records and the records that were being subpoenaed from banks and other sources. A complete net worth calculation was conducted, using the services of the FBI, who provided an accounting technician to do the schedules and a special agent CPA to testify to the records in court.

The bank records showed that Daley had made numerous cash deposits into his bank accounts over the period during and after he was in the Quaalude business. All of these were well below the $10,000 amount that would have triggered a CTR. From there, the cash (in its changed form) was traced out to other bank accounts and used for real estate purchases and lifestyle expenses.

At the conclusion of the net worth assessment, Daley was found to have increased his net worth by more than $1.6 million over and above his Air Force pension checks and his wife's salary.

The analysis of the financial records also yielded solid leads in proving the allegations concerning the SUA. Daley had traveled repeatedly to Florida to collect shipments of Quaaludes. The documents contained airline, hotel, and telephone records pinpointing these trips. Credit card receipts documented Daley's presence in Florida and California when shipments were supposed to have occurred.

By proceeding along both tracks and using the financial evidence to support both sides, the investigators strengthened each aspect of the case. On the SUA side, additional witnesses were developed from among Daley's former subordinates. They gave evidence about specific deals and firmed up the connection of the unexplained wealth to the SUA.

The laundering scheme that Daley used was simple but effective. The cash from the Quaalude sales was deposited in amounts well under $10,000 into Daley's personal bank accounts (placement). Daley then opened additional accounts in the names of his three trusts and shifted money for the real estate purchases to these accounts (layering). The money from the rental of the four income properties was also deposited into these accounts, providing Daley with a seemingly clean source of funds (integration). Without access to the trust agreements, no one would know of Daley's control of the assets, but the layering phase of the scheme was ultimately the weak spot.

PRESENTATION

Presentation of the money laundering case is not the *fait accompli* handed the prosecutor in other criminal cases. After all, he or she has probably

**TABLE 24.6
Presentation**

Money Laundering
Underlying Criminal Activity

---

been consulted at every stage of the game so far anyway. Even so, the case needs to be presented in a professional package that answers all of the relevant questions.

There are usually two sides to the presentation, one relating to the criminal case and the other to the forfeiture of assets uncovered in the investigation. (See Table 24.6.) Sometimes this will require dealing with more than one Assistant U.S. Attorney or prosecutor. With regard to the criminal case, yet again, there are two issues to address. First, there is the question of the money laundering charges. Have all of the elements been met? Have all of the transactions been identified? How much money are we talking about? (This affects the sentencing guidelines.) Has the SUA been proven? Are all of the linkages complete?

The second issue relates to the underlying SUA. If these crimes are also to be charged in the indictment (and whenever possible they should be), the prosecutor should be assured in your presentation that the evidence will support those charges as well.

Is money laundering the "big gun" or "top count" in the indictment? This is sometimes the case when the SUA is other than drugs. This fact will be an issue in plea bargaining; the defendant never wants to plead to the count with the heaviest penalty. At 20 years, this could be the money laundering count.

On the forfeiture side of the presentation (see Table 24.7), there are several questions to be answered. Is the case to proceed as a civil forfeiture, a criminal one, or both? Where is the property, and will substitution of assets be an issue? If so, the criminal forfeiture alternative will be preferable. Do we want to seek forfeiture of the assets under some other statute as well? The same property could be subject to seizure for RICO violations, drug offenses, or tax violations. The Assistant U.S. Attorney may want to charge the property under multiple theories in that case.

Thanks to the Civil Asset Forfeiture Reform Act (CAFRA), time limits and filing deadlines are a major consideration in planning the forfeiture case. Proceeding too quickly on the civil side may mean disclosing way too much of the case before you're ready.

Preseizure planning should be a part of every case, and it should begin at case initiation — definitely as soon as it appears that assets may be seized. Give the Assistant U.S. Attorney and the asset forfeiture specialists as much lead time as possible in developing their parts of the case. This will pay off later when your seizures go smoothly and take less time to go through the forfeiture process.

A big part of the presentation of the case is your case file, which we'll discuss in the next chapter. If you've been keeping up with the evidence, the package should be neat and tidy, though probably bulky. The jury won't be seeing the case file, but you'll need to produce some graphics of the financial schedules and of the indirect methods calculations. Prosecutors today are very keen on these high-tech methods of displaying evidence. Juries not only appreciate them but, after watching all that Court TV, expect to see them. It's a good idea to have these made up well before trial, so your expert witness can familiarize him- or herself with the details.

**TABLE 24.7
Forfeiture**

Money Laundering
RICO Title 21 or Title 26

Daley Case Example (continued)

Daley was indicted for operating a Continuing Criminal Enterprise (CCE). All of his assets, including the six properties, his art collection, and his vehicles, were named in the same indictment as property to be forfeited. Also named in the indictment were six of Daley's associates, including his wife.

Ultimately Daley was convicted of the CCE charge and sentenced to 15 years imprisonment. The jury forfeited everything but his wife's Toyota. Interviewed after the verdict, the jury described the financial evidence as being the deciding factor in the case. See Figure 24.3.

MONEY LAUNDERING UNDERCOVER OPERATIONS

Money laundering is an activity that is very vulnerable to an undercover approach. Many successful undercover operations have been conducted in the past, resulting in hundreds of millions in forfeitures, as well as hundreds of defendants. Indeed, with catchy code names like "Swordfish" and "Dinero," these types of cases enjoy the highest profile for their success.

There are a couple of ways to conduct a money laundering undercover operation. How you go about this will ultimately dictate the final charge in the case, as well as many of the operational decisions. The key question at this stage is, "Are we laundering their money or ours?"

LAUNDERING THEIR MONEY

In some investigations, the undercover agents act on behalf of the criminals in placing or layering the dirty cash. Many of these cases involve "pickups," in which the agents collect the cash from the suspects and move it through the undercover channels to the bank account or other destination designated by the criminal. In these cases, we're actually laundering *their* money, or at least appearing to do so. One nice aspect of this is that the criminals actually pay a fee for this service, something they'll no doubt feel pretty stupid about later on.

The objectives of this type of operation are to (*a*) identify the bank accounts or other destination of the funds and (*b*) identify as many of the participants in the criminal operation as possible. Identification of the bank accounts, whether in the United States or offshore, is very valuable, because the records of these accounts can be obtained to trace additional money being deposited by other launderers, as well as to follow the money forward to individuals and assets at the very top of the criminal enterprise. The bank accounts represent a break in the money trail that, once entered, can be followed to all kinds of interesting places.

Also of interest are the other players in these schemes. We can identify not only smurfs or low-level employees but also those at the top, to whom the profits of crime are supposed to flow, through their receipt of the funds.

Examples of successful operations in this vein are many. Current policy is that they be of limited scope and duration. We don't want to actually launder *too* much of the crooks' money, no matter how well they're paying us.

An example of a more ambitious investigation is Operation Dinero, in which the government obtained an actual "brass plate" private offshore bank. This was a highly successful operation that had tremendous potential for developing an understanding of how these banks function in real money laundering schemes.

The criminal charges in these undercover operations are likely to be under Title 18 U.S.C. Section 1956 (a) (1) (A), (a) (1) (B), or (a) (2). The money being laundered is the proceeds of an SUA, the undercover agent is being asked to conduct a financial transaction (or transportation), and the intent is to avoid a reporting requirement, evade taxes, promote the SUA, or conceal the ownership of the funds.

Numerous problems can arise in these cases. We are probably talking about lots of money, so there are serious security concerns. The financial records of the operation need to be impeccable, because they'll be questioned at trial. This is also true in the event that the operation is allowed to "churn" the commissions from the operation.

In some cases, authority will be received to use the commissions received from the criminals to pay for operational expenses. This certainly helps the taxpayer, but it's a big hassle for the people who have to account for every penny of

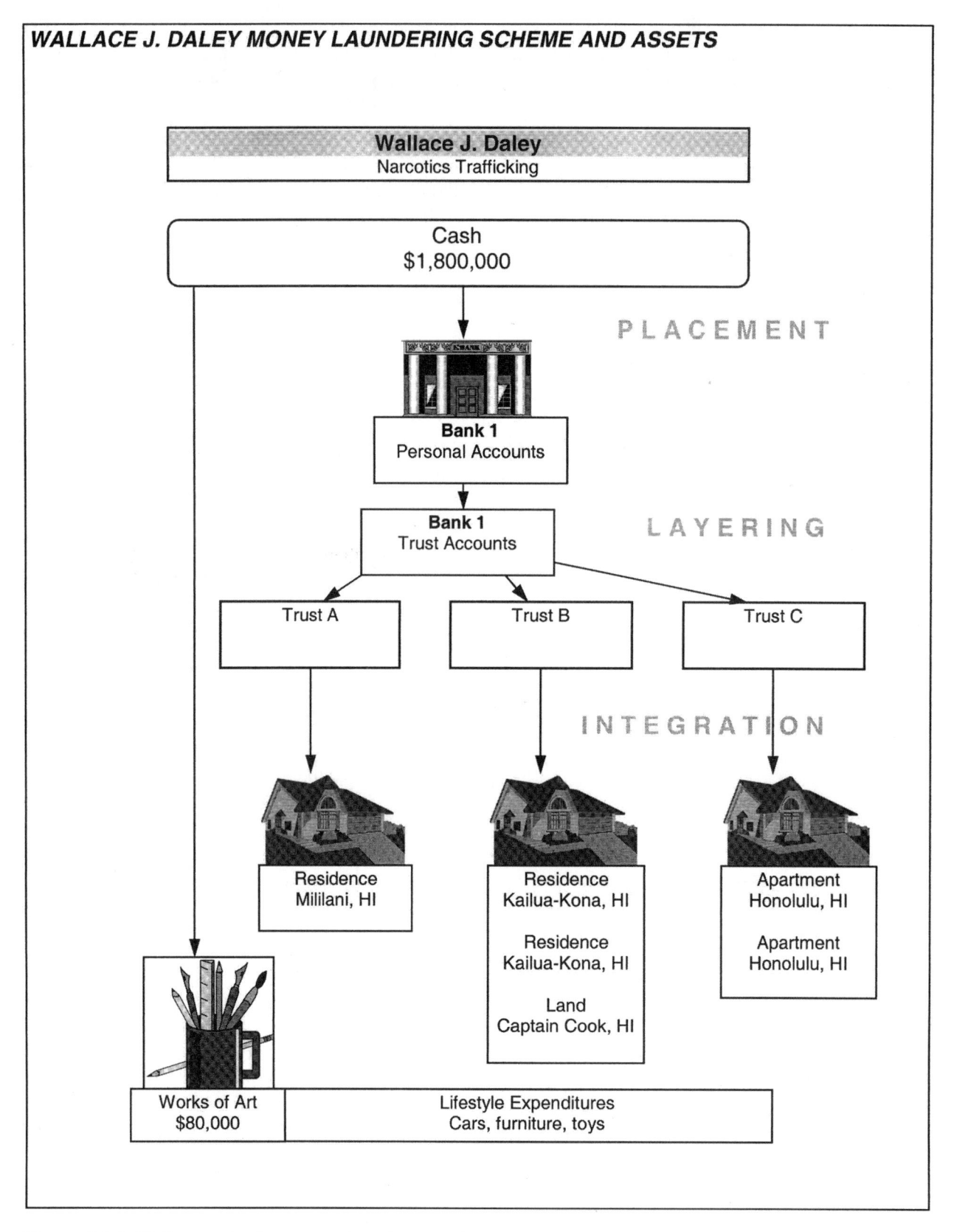

Figure 24.3 Wallace J. Daley money laundering scheme and assets.

the money. IRS-CID cases are audited every month or two by an independent auditor to detect problem situations early and correct them before they get out of hand.

All of the extra work that goes into one of these cases will pay off if the objectives are met. The extensive corroboration of every detail makes these cases very difficult to beat in court.

STINGS: LAUNDERING OUR MONEY

The other kind of undercover operation is one in which the subjects are laundering *our* money. This type of case may involve a professional money launderer who is taking on the undercover agents as another client or some business person who thinks he or she is handling dirty money and profiting from it.

These types of "sting" operations are charged under Title 18 U.S.C. §1956 (a) (3). This provision was written specifically to deal with cases in which the money being laundered is not *really* the proceeds of an SUA but is *represented* by the undercover agent to be such.

One big question in these cases is whether the money being laundered will be recovered or not. The government generally frowns on its agents giving away large sums of the taxpayers' money, so considerable confidence is required that we'll be seeing those funds again at the other end of the laundering pipeline. If so, the intelligence gained from such an operation can be extensive. If the subject is a professional money launderer, not only will you know what he or she did with your money, but you'll also get some good ideas about what he or she is doing with other clients'.

Another possibility is that a business person is laundering money in a less systematic fashion. A number of undercover "sting" operations have related to car dealerships and other "big ticket" merchants who believed they were taking drug money in exchange for their products.

In these stings, the undercover agent must represent that the funds are the proceeds of a Specified Unlawful Activity and that the agent would like to avoid a reporting requirement, conceal the ownership or control of the money, or further the illegal activity. As a tool for promoting compliance with cash reporting regulations, these undercover operations are pretty effective at getting the attention of area merchants in the same industry as the arrested parties.

All of the rules that apply to undercover operations in other criminal cases apply to money laundering crimes as well. The undercover agent should have the background and training to be able to carry off the role successfully. In Operation Dinero, the government actually contracted with experts in the field of private banking to gain the benefit of their experience.

This illustrates the complexity of some of these money laundering schemes. Successful criminals, like successful people everywhere, are prosperous because they have mastered the techniques of their profession. They've probably got a fairly good laundering scheme already, but they are always on the lookout for something better. The undercover agent is going to have to enter this environment equipped with the knowledge that will enable him or her to sell the better mousetrap — without letting on that it really *is* a mousetrap.

This is not a particularly easy job, but it's one that can advance an investigation by months or even years at one jump. Careful consideration must be given to the risks, as well as to the potential for rewards, all before the undercover agent makes the first contact.

One final note for investigators who've never done one of these cases. Due to the compulsive need for the government to cover itself in every possible eventuality, the paperwork involved in completing one of these cases can be staggering. The volume of evidence in such forms as tape-recorded conversations can also reach an overwhelming level. Still, there is all that money out there, and what better way to find it?

CHAPTER 25

THE CASE FILE

"'Where shall I begin, please your Majesty?' he asked. 'Begin at the beginning,' the King said gravely, 'and go on till you come to the end: then stop.'"
Lewis Carroll, *Alice's Adventures in Wonderland*

"When you're up to your neck in alligators, it's hard to remember your original objective was to clear the swamp."
Anonymous

Nothing in law enforcement will get you deeper in alligators more quickly than a financial investigation that's humming along. Financial cases can produce huge quantities of evidence, and each new batch that comes in generates more leads. Many criminal investigations may suffer for lack of evidence, but financial investigators are often overwhelmed by the sheer volume of material that comes their way. Just managing all this material becomes a major priority. To help us appreciate the importance of effective evidence management, let's return to the Capone investigation, a prime example of how massive such a project can be.

The case against mob boss Capone used a number of investigative techniques, but its center was a financial analysis of Capone's illegal income. The lessons learned in 1930 still apply today.

United States of America v. Alphonse Capone

In the summer of 1930, the investigators of Al Capone's finances were coming to the depressing conclusion that, after two years, they weren't any closer to putting the Big Guy in jail. They had reviewed over a million records, including many seized from Capone's organization. They had succeeded in identifying many expenditures by Capone, but they still could not show any income to the man, who openly boasted of having nothing in his own name.

The financial investigation wasn't the only thing not working; other investigative techniques, notably surveillance and informants, were not doing any better in linking Capone directly to illegal income. Frank Wilson, the lead investigator, had succeeded in placing two undercover agents in the Capone camp, but neither was close enough to the action to be able to do more than just pass along gangster talk that came their way.

Wilson did have one informant who was well connected in the Chicago underworld: Eddie O'Hare, a lawyer and businessman who held the rights to the mechanical rabbit used at greyhound racing tracks. O'Hare had joined forces with Capone in the operation of a dog track in Cicero and had some other questionable connections with local bootleggers. O'Hare provided valuable inside information for an unusual reason: his son Edward O'Hare, Jr., known as "Butch," wanted to go to the U.S. Naval Academy. His father wanted to help him fulfill that dream.

Even O'Hare's access was limited; he dealt mostly with the ranks of frontmen Capone had established to insulate himself from his crimes and their profits. Other witnesses were too afraid of Capone to talk, and Wilson was getting frustrated. Despite some limited success in prosecuting Capone underlings on tax charges, Capone's grip on Chicago was as strong as ever.

This was the situation when word came from one of the undercover agents that a Capone associate had dropped a nugget of information. Years before, the government had seized some records in a raid on a Capone operation. The hoodlum said that although the records implicated the boss, the Internal Revenue agents "didn't know what they had."

Wilson wasn't enthusiastic. Over the years, local police and Prohibition agents had made numerous raids on Capone's breweries, brothels, and gambling joints, often seizing records. Many of these had found their way to Wilson's tiny office, where they filled filing cabinets that now spilled into the hallway. Wilson and his men had already gone through the records, hundreds of thousands of them, but he recalled nothing like the materials his agent was describing.

The records were supposed to be in a ledger seized in a 1926 raid at the Hawthorne Smoke Shop, a gambling joint across the street from Capone's headquarters at the time, the Hawthorne Inn. (See Figure 25.1.) After a particularly notorious murder, police and vigilantes had raided a number of Capone's establishments, and many records had been taken from the places raided. Wilson started looking for the files.

Days later, ready to give up, while looking for a place to store some documents, Wilson came across a bundle of papers in a disused file cabinet. Opening the package, he found

Figure 25.1 Hawthorne Smoke Shop, circa 1925. *This Capone front for gambling and prostitution was located directly across the street from the Hawthorne Inn, which can be seen in the background. Records seized from the Smoke Shop would prove to be extremely valuable in the prosecution of Al Capone. (Source: Chicago Historical Society)*

a ledger, and in the ledger he found notations describing a gambling operation that had net profits of over a half-million dollars in 18 months. He also found references to payments to "Al" and to "town." The former, he hoped, referred to Alphonse Capone, and the latter to payoffs to local government. Wilson's case was back on track.

TYPES OF DOCUMENTARY EVIDENCE

Financial cases usually involve two types of evidence, *documentary evidence* and *testimonial evidence*. Under the first are two categories: the subject's own books and records, and those records prepared or maintained by a third party. Each of these types of documents has its place in a financial case, and each brings its own set of problems to the investigation. See Table 25.1.

Subject records consist of anything maintained by the subject or the business entities under his or her control. The ledger seized from the Hawthorne Smoke Shop was such a record, even though Al Capone probably never set eyes on it. In many cases, the subject may indeed have

TABLE 25.1
Sources of Financial Records

Subject's Records	Third-Party Records
Financial Search Warrant	Grand Jury Subpoena
Other Searches and Seizures	Administrative Subpoena or Summons
John Doe Subpoena	Government Documents
Subpoena for Corporate Records	Informants and Witnesses
Trash Cover	
Informants and Witnesses	

prepared the records — for example, his or her own check register or the owe–pay sheets in a drug ring. *These records are the primary source of information and best evidence of the crime you are trying to prove.* Every effort must be made to obtain these documents.

Third-party records are those that have some relevance to the case and are maintained by others. The records kept by your bank about your checking account are a good example. Third-party records are also critical to most financial cases, because they will aid in the reconstruction of activity when the subject's records are unavailable.

Privileges apply to the subject's records. In most cases, he or she cannot be compelled to produce the documents that might be incriminating. As we saw earlier, there are a couple of notable exceptions. One has to do with corporations. Corporate records must be produced pursuant to a subpoena, even though the subject may be the only officer, director, and shareholder.

Another exception has been created in court decisions involving use of a "John Doe subpoena." In this case, production of the records can be compelled from the subject when his or her identity as the producer has been concealed and when the records are those that would normally be available from a third party. See Chapter 18 for details.

No such privileges apply to third-party records, but laws such as the Right to Financial Privacy Act and the Bank Secrecy Act will govern the disclosure of information about the subject. A grand jury subpoena is frequently used to acquire these materials. Administrative subpoenae or summonses, search warrants, and mail and trash covers may also yield valuable documentary evidence of financial crimes.

These things tend to pile up rather quickly, so it's essential that a system of document control be in place *before* the situation gets critical. The agents created such a system for the Capone case, enabling them to identify the materials most important in their investigation and to trace Capone's income from the initial transaction to his pocket. This tracing function is an element in money laundering cases as well.

United States of America v. Alphonse Capone (continued)

Frank Wilson knew that Al Capone was extremely cautious in the operation of his various enterprises, and nowhere was this more true than in Al's receipt of income from the bootlegging, gambling, prostitution, and racketeering that brought in over $100 million annually. Capone almost never signed anything. He had no bank accounts, and not a single piece of property, real or personal, was titled in his name. He paid cash for almost everything. He used aliases, including the name of his brother, to conceal his interest in specific transactions. (See Figure 25.2.)

Figure 25.2 Al Capone. (Source: FBI)

Capone's scheme for money laundering was deceptively simple. He used nominees — trusted associates and family members — to handle financial transactions such as the acquisition of property. His mansion in Miami was titled in his wife's name, as was their Chicago home. Many other properties, such as the businesses used as speakeasies and fronts for gambling or prostitution — there were 161 in the Chicago suburb of Cicero alone — were purchased in the names of his associates or their relatives. The Treasury Department investigators assigned to the Capone case knew when they signed on that proving income to "Big Al" was going to be difficult; it took two years to find out just how difficult it would be.

The investigators had two problems, both relating to evidence. On one hand, Capone's bribes had successfully reached many potential witnesses in the net worth case the investigators were trying to make. Capone bullets had silenced, directly or indirectly, many others. Information from inside the outfit was hard to come by.

On the other hand, the investigators had too much evidence. They had file cabinets, boxes, entire rooms full of documents, books, and records of all description. What they needed was something linking Capone directly to the millions of dollars these records described. The Hawthorne Smoke Shop ledger might be the first.

In order to get this evidence admitted, Wilson was going to have to authenticate it and hopefully get someone to testify as to the meaning of the entries. Someone must always testify in court about the preparation of documents submitted as evidence. In this case, the best witness would obviously be the man who prepared them — the bookkeeper at the Hawthorne Smoke Shop.

The identity of this person was not known, and none of the informants could provide it. Wilson began collecting handwriting exemplars of every known Capone associate and comparing these against the writing in the ledger. After months of searching through thousands more documents, Wilson finally put a name together with the neat, precise handwriting in the ledger: Leslie Shumway.

Shumway took some finding. He had left Chicago, moving to Miami, where, ironically enough, he frequented the same racetracks as his former boss, Mr. Capone. Wilson used this against Shumway when they finally met, pointing out that Capone wouldn't be too happy to hear that Shumway had been subpoenaed before a grand jury and wouldn't wait to find out whether Shumway had talked. Shumway agreed to cooperate.

The little bookkeeper was able to identify the ledger he had prepared years before, as well as 33 others that he kept for the Smoke Shop. Shumway had used two different writing styles in preparing the records, but he could still describe all of the transactions, as well as the inner workings of the gambling operation at the Hawthorne Smoke Shop. See Figure 25.3.

Wilson knew that Shumway did not have the full picture; Capone was too smart to entrust any one person, especially someone at Shumway's level, with such dangerous information. Still, the arrows were starting to point in the Big Guy's direction. Wilson now needed additional records to corroborate his witnesses and additional witnesses to testify about the records.

INTRODUCING DOCUMENTARY EVIDENCE IN A FINANCIAL CASE

Documentary evidence is generally circumstantial, and it can be introduced in a criminal proceeding only if accompanied by the testimony of a witness who can describe the document's existence and authenticity.

Subject records may be authenticated by the maker of the records, which is exactly what Wilson planned to do with Shumway. The person making the record can identify it and explain its

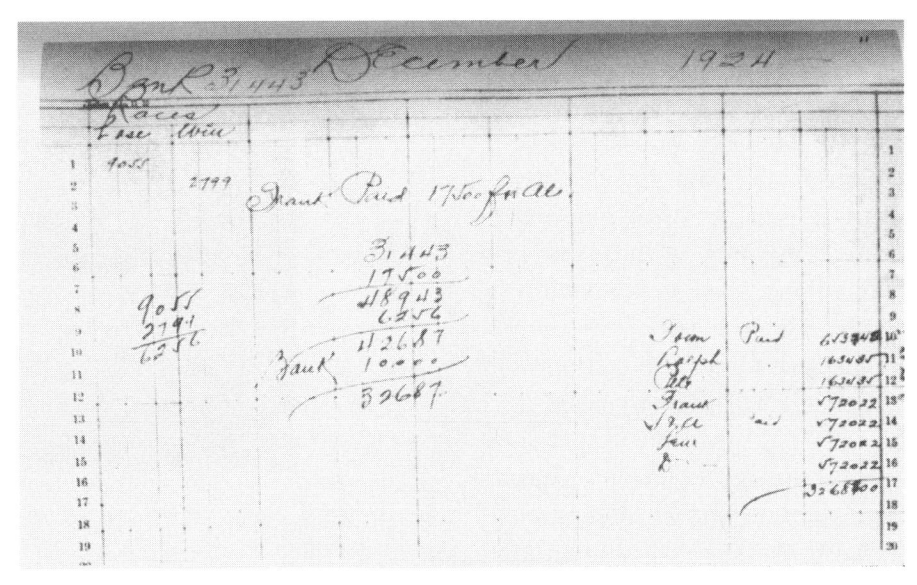

Figure 25.3 Ledger page from the Hawthorne Smoke Shop ledgers. Bookkeeper Leslie Shumway was able to explain all of these entries and to describe their relationship to Al Capone. Of special interest to the investigators was the notation "Frank Paid 17,500 for Al," a reference to the percentage of the profits allocated for the boss.

relevance to the case. These records can also be authenticated and described by a third party, such as a customer who had been shown the records by the maker. An example of this situation might be an owe–pay (or "pay and owe") sheet, shown by a drug dealer to his or her customer and later seized by police. The customer could testify that the entries on this particular sheet related to his or her transactions and that the trafficker had displayed it to him or her to record debts and payments.

Third-party records, such as those made by a business or a bank, can be introduced by the maker or by a custodian, who can testify under an exception to the hearsay rule known as the *shop book rule*. Under this rule, books of original entry that are kept in the ordinary course of business can be introduced by someone other than the maker. You can appreciate how useful this exception is by considering what would happen if you were forced to bring in *every* bank teller who ever did a transaction with your subject. The shop book rule is also known as the business records hearsay exception.

Another rule of evidence relates to chain of custody. The government, in order to authenticate an exhibit, must be able to show a continuous chain of custody from the time it was seized to the time it is introduced in court, and the government must also show that the evidence has not been altered in the interim. There were all sorts of problems with Wilson's chain of custody of the Hawthorne Smoke Shop ledgers, but in the end it didn't matter. Today's investigator would be wise to establish and maintain a strict chain of custody, tightly controlling access to evidence and preventing the type of difficult questions that would have embarrassed the Capone investigators.

United States of America v. Alphonse Capone (continued)

The objective of Wilson's investigation was to prove that Al Capone had income during the years 1924 through 1929 and that he hadn't paid any income taxes on it. Every one of Chicago's 3 million inhabitants who could read the newspaper knew this was true. Wilson's problem was proving it to a jury. Capone's use of nominees was a simple but effective laundering scheme, but with Shumway and another insider witness, Fred Ries,

Capone's shield of nominees was beginning to weaken.

Having linked Capone to the illegal gambling operation, Wilson began tracing the proceeds of this activity. Shumway stated that checks received from out-of-town bookies were endorsed by one of three men: Frank Pope, Ben Pope, or Pete Penovich, Shumway's boss. The checks were then deposited into an account in Frank Pope's name at the Pinkert State Bank or cashed at that bank.

Wilson sent some agents to the bank, and, after overcoming some initial reluctance (indecision on the bankers' part as to whom they feared most, Capone or the feds), the agents gained access to the bank's files. In addition to the Pope account, they also discovered that $750,000 in cashier's checks had been purchased for cash at the bank, all in the name of "J. C. Dunbar." Dunbar appeared to be an alias, but the most interesting connection was that the endorser of many of these cashier's checks was Jake "Greasy Thumb" Guzik, Capone's primary financial advisor. (See Figure 25.4.) Guzik had already received a five-year sentence on tax evasion charges, but he had refused to cooperate against Capone.

It now became imperative to locate "Dunbar," and informant Eddie O'Hare provided the answer. "Dunbar" was Fred Ries, another bookkeeper in the Capone operation, also hiding from Wilson's investigation.

Ries was located and persuaded to testify against Capone. His evidence was significant. Ries said he had been the cashier at the Ship, an outfit resort in Cicero, and that Al Capone had been his boss. He also said that the cashier's checks to J. C. Dunbar had represented Capone's net profits from the gambling operation. Pete Penovich had given Ries the instructions to obtain cashier's checks, and the "Frank" in the notation "Frank Paid Al 17,500" referred to Frank Pope.

This testimony, combined with that of Shumway and other financial witnesses, was enough to get an indictment of Capone on tax evasion charges. It didn't matter that the amount of income he was charged with receiving was only a small fraction of what he had really made; Al Capone's empire was starting to crumble.

Figure 25.4 *Jake "Greasy Thumb" Guzik. A one-time pimp, Guzik kept Capone's books and his secrets. Guzik was responsible for keeping track of the Capone empire's finances and for making the payoffs to politicians and police. (Source: Chicago Historical Society)*

DOCUMENT CONTROL

The sheer volume of Wilson's files threatened to crowd the investigators out of their own already cramped office space. Equally breathtaking was the diversity of this evidence, which ranged from witness affidavits to bank records, gambling records to receipts for silk pajamas. Eventually, someone was going to have to make some sense out of all this material, not to mention presenting it to a jury in federal court.

The first order of business in a complex financial investigation is to get on top of the alligators before they get on top of you. This means having an organized system in place before the first subpoena goes out.

IRS often claims its Special Agents are "the best financial investigators in the world." (Maybe so, although the outstanding graduate in my training class was an exchange student from

Hong Kong.) If they are, their success is partly a result of the fact that their system of handing evidence is designed specifically for processing financial data.

The system you devise will, of course, be governed by the evidence-handling procedures of your agency, but many of the techniques can be employed no matter what agency rules are in place.

PLAN AHEAD

Plan ahead for the following features:

- Acquisition
- Storage and retrieval
- Security
- Analysis
- Presentation

ACQUISITION

Acquisition of evidence would seem to be one of those taken-for-granted sorts of things. After all, without evidence, you've got no case. We talked about this in the chapter on sources of information. With respect to the case file, documentation of the acquisition of evidence is important.

Creating a couple of logs will save a lot of time and trouble later on. One log should record all acquisition of evidence pursuant to grand jury subpoena. The log itself should be stamped with a 6 (e) stamp and access controlled. The best format for the log would include a summary sheet in this format:

Provider Name	Date Served	Record Received	Records Returned	Fully Satisfied	Exhibit Number
Pinkert Bank	10-12-30	11-5-30	11-5-30	11-5-30	30I-12

A copy of the subpoena itself should be included in the file with the log. The subpoena should always have the name of the person who provided the records to the government, as well as who will be testifying about the records in court. (It's a good idea to staple this person's business card to the subpoena.) The exhibit number in this example is that assigned by the grand jury, and it differs from the DCN or exhibit number assigned by the investigators.

Storage and Retrieval

Storage and retrieval of the different types of evidence is another problem. What's important and what's not? How can you find what you need quickly?

What you've got are files, and what you need is a filing system. Start with an agreed-upon numbering system, whether it involves exhibit numbers, document control numbers, or some other identification scheme. If you decide on document control numbers, get one of those sequential number stamps and keep it handy. Stamp the documents as they are received, and log the numbers in your evidence log. Decide whether you are going to number individual pages or by document, and then stick with the plan. Any deviation from your scheme will open you up for questions at trial.

I'd strongly suggest that you use a computer to log your evidence. IRS-CID and other federal agencies have programs to catalogue materials. Spreadsheet and database programs will also work, but they need to be tailored to your specific needs.

Once the evidence is numbered and logged, it should be stored in appropriate containers. It's a good idea to try for uniformity, but documentary evidence tends to come in so many different sizes and shapes that this goal often gets misplaced. Don't misplace the evidence, however. File it in some order that will enable you to retrieve it quickly. Even in a case with relatively few records, if you toss everything in one drawer, you'll eventually find yourself pawing through folders, looking for the one piece of paper you really need. You'll save time and energy if you label everything for easy retrieval.

One really exciting possibility is the use of scanners, optical character recognition, and recordable CD-ROMs or DVDs. These disks can store huge quantities of data, including copies of thousands of documents scanned into the computer. This system is already revolutionizing the storage and retrieval of documentary evidence. As banks go forward under Check 21, more and more records will exist only in digital form. It won't be long before you can ask for everything in digital form and input it directly into a completely electronic case file. Retrieval of this information is smooth and almost instantaneous, and it plays very nicely in court, too.

Security

Security involves a couple of issues beyond just having a locked file cabinet. One of the most important of these is the requirements of Federal Rule 6 (e), relating to the secrecy of grand jury proceedings and information. Another is the requirement that all material that must be disclosed to the defense under the *Brady, Giglio,* or *Jencks* doctrines must receive special handling. Certain information may contain references to confidential informants, and other material may require extensive redaction. Tax returns are also sensitive.

Grand Jury Material

Grand jury material must be separated and access restricted to those persons who are listed on the 6 (e) disclosure order. *Only* those persons who are so listed may view grand jury exhibits or transcripts. Abuse or misuse of this material can lead to extremely severe consequences, including the abandonment of the case and contempt citations by the court.

It is highly recommended that two special measures be taken with grand jury material. First, every document, *and* all copies should be marked with a stamp identifying them as being covered by Rule 6 (e). Second, each document should be labeled in such a way that it is immediately identifiable as a grand jury exhibit. A red file folder label or an exhibit sticker could be employed — anything to distinguish the materials from others less sensitive.

Grand jury materials should also be filed with a copy of the subpoena causing them to be produced. This lets you quickly associate documents with their provider.

Some experts recommend that two copies be made of grand jury exhibits, one kept with the exhibits in a locked container and the other used as a work copy. It is probably wise to work from copies rather than the documents actually furnished to the grand jury. If so, all copies *must* be marked with the 6 (e) stamp and care used in numbering the copies to correspond with the originals.

If possible, a custodian should be appointed to receive all of the grand jury exhibits and to maintain the security of the documents after they are received. Whoever this custodian is, his or her initials should appear on the container and on the subpoena that accompanies the records in storage.

Discovery Material

Other materials may be discoverable under Rule 16 of the F.R.Cr.P., given to the defense under various doctrines, notably *Jencks, Brady,* and *Giglio.* Some notation will have to be made to this effect and a copy made for defense counsel. You've got two choices in making this discovery copy — now or later. If you make the copy when the records are first obtained, you'll have it later, but in the meantime it takes up space, and it may be a waste of time and copying paper (if the defendant dies or pleads guilty before discovery).

If you make the copy later, when it's finally needed for discovery, you may be in a situation where you are forced to copy a room full of records in a short period — not a happy time. This is especially true if the documents have to be redacted to remove nondiscoverable information. I'll leave it up to you, with a reminder that those alligators can get mighty deep at discovery time.

Analysis

Once you've got all these records, some sense has to be made of them. The financial analysis of the records is going to resemble the type of audit that accountants perform, in which individual transactions are verified, monies traced, and leads developed. We talked about this earlier; the process will be easier if your files are well organized.

Presentation

Presentation of the evidence is the ultimate goal of the investigation. First the evidence is presented to a prosecutor, who will make a decision to go forward or not, based on what he or she sees. Second, the evidence is presented to a grand jury, which will decide whether to indict or not. Finally, the ultimate end of the entire process is reached: presentation of the case to a judge or jury.

Assumptions are frowned upon, but this one should be taken as gospel: *always* assume that your money laundering case, and every action you take in it, will end up in front of a jury. If you start with this assumption, your actions in collecting the evidence in the case will bear up well, especially if you have a set procedure for handling the evidence (and you follow it). This assumption means that the evidence has to be in a form that *can* be presented to a jury. The jurors have to be able to understand it and make the logical connections you obviously believe are there. They have to be able to understand the relevant material and not be distracted by the irrelevant. They have to understand *why* this or that piece of evidence is important.

This is where the organization of your case file can help. Again, every agency has a different way of reporting the results of investigations, but if you have some flexibility, try to report financial materials in a "flow-down" fashion. In a way, this is a lot like accounting itself, in which all of the information flows from the original source documents, through journals and ledgers, to the financial reports.

In your case file, everything should flow from individual exhibits, through the schedules analyzing those exhibits, to the report, which links the information to other evidence and explains its importance. Every reference in the report to either a schedule or an exhibit must be annotated or footnoted. Anyone reading the report should be able to turn quickly to the schedule cited, locating the figures, and from the schedule be able to see how the figures are supported by exhibits.

EXHIBITS AND THE EXHIBIT LIST

For an example of how this system might work, we'll consider the receipt by Al Capone of $110,000 in Western Union money orders. An actual exhibit (see Figure 25.5) is assigned a number, W16-3. On your comprehensive exhibit list, the reference to this document would look like Figure 25.6. Note that Henderson's statement, in which he describes his activities and the exhibits to follow, is the lead item on the list.

Schedules and Summaries

In the analysis of these wire transfers so critical to Capone's tax case, the investigators prepared a schedule showing the key points about each transaction, as well as the bottom line: $110,000 in income to Alphonse Capone. A case file may use a number of schedules, each documenting some aspect of the crime. Each schedule should be numbered so that it can be referenced in the body of the report. We'll call this one "S-1, Schedule of Wire Transfers, 1928." (See Figure 25.7.)

Schedules may be consolidated into a table or appendix that summarizes information from a number of accounts or periods. For example, Appendix A might consolidate the data from Schedules S-1, 1928; S-2, 1929; and S-3, 1930, into one "Schedule of Wire Transfers." The point is that each of the schedules documents all of its figures, allowing the reviewer to quickly verify every exhibit against the total.

Case Report

The case report is supposed to explain everything. It should be written for the nonaccountant, since that's who's going to be reviewing it. Because the success or failure of a money laundering or financial case depends on the accuracy of the figures, the case report must present these in a complete and understandable way. Each exhibit and schedule referred to in the report should be footnoted or annotated. If the reviewer is so inclined, he or she can stop and check things out right then and there. You can bet the defense attorney would do just this.

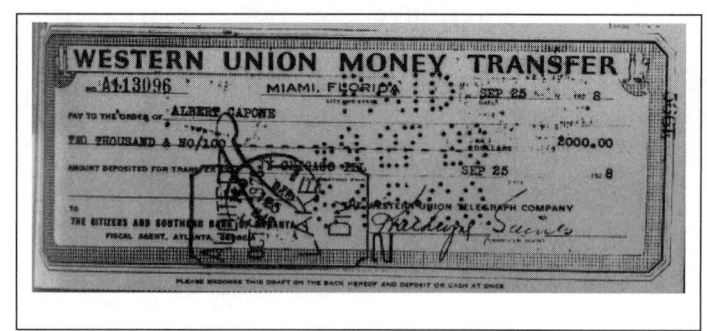

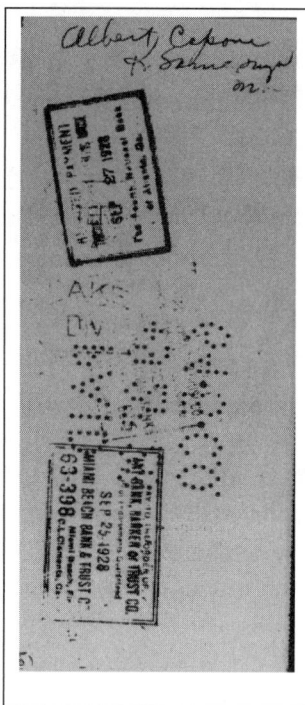

Figure 25.5 *Western Union money transfer dated September 25, 1928, in the amount of $2000, made out to Albert Capone.*

Exhibit List		
W16	Parker Henderson, Jr. Ponce de Leon Hotel Miami Beach, Florida Phone: 555-356	
	Affidavit of Parker Henderson October 12, 1931	1
	Western Union Money Order August 2, 1928	2
	$1,000	
	Western Union Money Transfer September 25, 1928 $2,000	3

Figure 25.6 *Exhibit list entry for the money order in Figure 25.5.*

I'm not going to get into how to write the case report, since everybody does it differently. Most supervisors won't object if you put in some references to your exhibits, though, and some may appreciate it, since it makes their job a little easier. What you're doing is creating the audit trail, just as an accountant would do.

The portion of the report relating to the wire transfers might read like Figure 25.8.

CONCLUSION

Financial evidence can have an overwhelming impact on a jury — but only if it is properly presented in a way the jurors can understand. These are not CPAs; they're going to have to be brought to an understanding of this complex material. It is the investigator's job to begin that process, a process that includes a well-organized

S-1 SCHEDULE OF WIRE TRANSFERS, 1928				
Date	Payee	Purchaser	Amount	Exhibit #
(Continued) 08-02-28	Albert Capone	Unknown	$1,000	W16-2
09-25-28	Albert Capone	Rocco Fischetti	2,000	W16-3
09-28-28	Albert Capone	Rocco Fischetti	2,000	W16-4
10-05-28	Albert Capone	Unknown	2,000	W16-5
			$ 110,000	

Figure 25.7 Schedule of wire transfers for 1928, part of our Al Capone case file.

case report and extensive documentation of every fact in issue.

Money laundering cases are a challenge, a chance to investigate a crime the old-fashioned way, through legwork and brain power. Patience, persistence, and the desire to reach the bottom line will pay off.

United States of America v. Alphonse Capone (continued)

If Al Capone had been tried 65 years later, money laundering charges would have been among those in his indictment. The law may have changed in the intervening years, but the investigative techniques used to make the case would have been perfectly familiar to Frank Wilson or U.S. Attorney George E. Q. Johnson.

Two years and over 2 million records later, the government succeeded in ending Al Capone's grip on Chicago. Crime went on, of course, though Prohibition was repealed in 1933. The system of documentation developed by IRS for the evidence in the Capone case was used effectively in many other prosecutions, down to the present day.

One absolutely critical point must be made about this and any other so-called financial investigation. These financial investigative techniques are just one more tool available to the investigator. They will enhance almost any investigation of a crime based on greed, and they are essential to a money laundering case, but they cannot work without the other, more traditional investigative techniques.

Capone found this out the hard way. Despite the prosecution's solid documentary case against Capone, it was saved from disaster by an informant. Immediately before the start of the trial, Frank Wilson's ace informant, Eddie O'Hare, contacted him to report that Capone had a list of the entire panel from which the jury would be picked. Every individual on the panel had been either bought or threatened into cooperating with Capone's defense. As proof, O'Hare brought a piece of paper containing 10 names, veniremen 30 through 39.

Not even the U.S. Attorney had this list, but when it was checked against that held by the judge, the 10 names matched exactly. Capone had won his acquittal before the jury was even picked.

Except he didn't. Because of the warning from O'Hare, the judge was able to switch panels with an uncorrupted one and select the jurors from an untainted pool. Capone was finished not only as a result of the financial evidence but also because of some old-fashioned police work. Melding these investigative techniques into a complete package is the goal of a money laundering case.

27. In his affidavit of October 12, 1931, Parker Henderson identified himself as the manager of the Ponce de Leon Hotel in Miami Beach. He said that he was acquainted with Capone, and had assisted him with cashing numerous Western Union Money Orders and Wire Transfers in 1928, 1929, and 1930. **(W16-1, Affidavit of Parker Henderson, p. 1, para. 2)**

28. Henderson stated that these money orders were in amounts from $1,000 to $5,000, and arrived in batches, with "Albert Capone" listed as the payee. **(W16-1, p. 1, para. 3)** Henderson said that Alphonse Capone endorsed the money orders in his presence and gave them to Henderson to be cashed. Henderson took the money orders to the Miami Beach Bank and Trust Company, cashed the checks, then returned the cash to Capone. **(W16-1, p. 1, para. 4)** Henderson was shown a number of money orders listing "Albert Capone" as the payee, all of which were dated in 1928, 1929, and 1930. **(W16-2 through 17, Western Union Money Transfers)** Henderson identified these money orders as being those he had cashed for Capone at the Miami Beach Bank and Trust Company. **(W16-1, p. 2, para. 4)**

29. A review of the money orders recovered from Western Union revealed that 17 of these, totaling $30,000 with Albert Capone as the payee, were cashed by Henderson at the bank as described. **(Schedule S-1, Wire Transfers, 1928)** An additional $80,000 in transfers, all in the name of "Albert Costa," was also recovered. **(W16-18 through 41, Western Union Money Transfers)** Henderson identified these as well, saying that "Albert Costa" was another name used by Capone to conceal his identity. **(W16-1, p. 2, para. 6)**

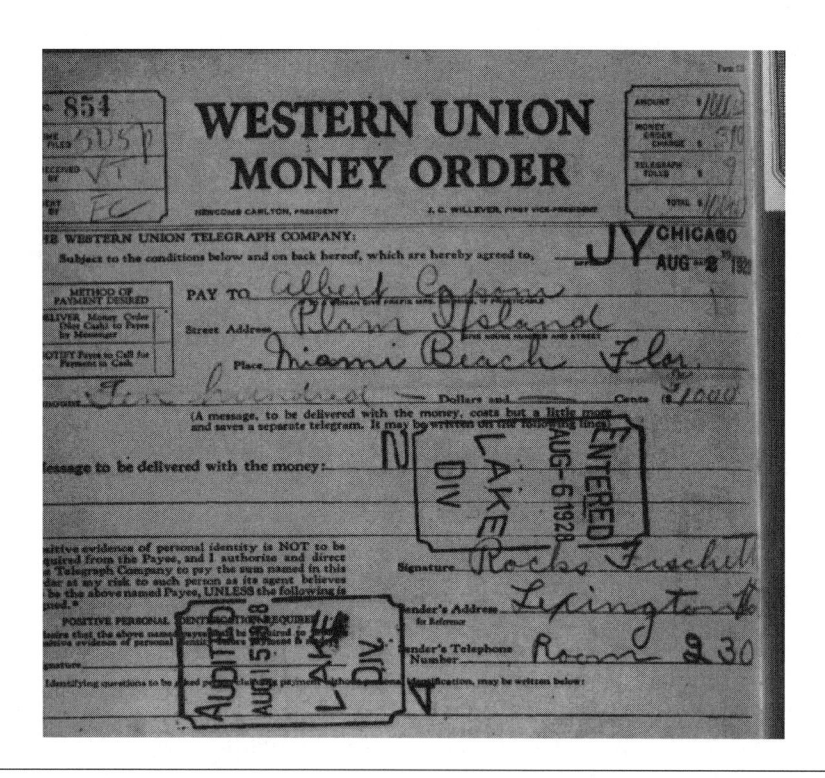

Figure 25.8 *Portion of our Al Capone case report relating to the wire transfers, including one of the real Western Union money orders referenced.*

The Rest of the Story

What happened to the participants in the case?

Al Capone got 11 years for tax evasion. He was released in 1940, after serving about eight years. Capone suffered from the effects of neurosyphilis, contracted in his youth. He never returned to claim the power he once held in Chicago. He died in 1947.

Frank Wilson left Internal Revenue, becoming Chief of the United States Secret Service. The other agents in the Capone investigation went on to compile an impressive record in other organized crime and political corruption cases, including the prosecution of Capone's successor, Frank "The Enforcer" Nitti.

Leslie Shumway and Fred Ries disappeared from view. There is no evidence that the Capone organization ever caught up with them.

No such luck for Eddie O'Hare, who was murdered eight days before Capone's release from prison. The Treasury agents had kept their part of the bargain with O'Hare, who lived to see his son graduate from the Naval Academy, but not long enough to hear the end of that story.

Figure 25.9 *Edward H. "Butch" O'Hare, Jr. (Source: U.S. Navy National Archives)*

Butch O'Hare won the Medal of Honor on February 20, 1942, when he shot down five Japanese bombers and drove off four others attacking his aircraft carrier. He was the first naval aviator to become an ace and the first to win the medal. O'Hare returned to combat and was killed in action on November 26, 1943, an American hero. See Figure 25.9.

In September 1949, Chicago's O'Hare International Airport, now the world's busiest, was named in memory of the Chicago boy whose father helped finish Al Capone.

Bibliography

Balter, Harry Graham, *Tax Fraud and Evasion,* Warren, Gorham & Lamont, Boston, 1983

Barber, Hoyt L., *Tax Havens: How to Bank, Invest, and Do Business — Offshore and Tax Free,* McGraw-Hill, New York, 1993

Beaty, Jonathan and Gwynne, S.C., *The Outlaw Bank: A Wild Ride Into the Secret Heart of the BCCI,* Random House, New York, 1993

Bergereen, Laurence, *Capone: The Man and the Era,* Simon and Schuster, New York, 1994

Berkman, Robert I., *Find It Fast: How to Uncover Information on Any Subject,* Harper & Row, New York, 1990

Blau, Charles W. et al. *Investigation and Prosecution of Illegal Money Laundering: A Guide to the Bank Secrecy Act,* U.S. Department of Justice, Washington, D.C., 1983

Botting, Douglas, *The Pirates,* Time-Life Books, Alexandria, Virginia, 1978

Boyer, Robert P., *Money Laundering and Forfeiture Provisions of the USA PATRIOT Act of 2001,* U.S. Department of Justice, Washington, D.C., 2003

Brissard, Jean-Charles, *Terrorism Financing: Roots and Trends of Saudi Terrorism Financing,* Report prepared for the President of the Security Council, United Nations, December 19, 2002, New York

Browne, Harry, *Complete Guide to Swiss Banks,* McGraw-Hill, New York, 1976

Cassella, Stefan D., *Money Laundering — 18 U.S.C. §§ 1956 and 1957 Case Outline,* Asset Forfeiture and Money Laundering Section, Department of Justice, 2005

Chemical Bank, *Letter of Credit Customer Workshop,* Chemical Bank, New York, September 1981

Clarke, Thurston and Tigue, John J., *Dirty Money: Swiss Banks, the Mafia, Money Laundering and White Collar Crime,* Simon and Schuster, New York, 1975

Cullison, Alan, *Inside Al-Qaeda's Hard Drive,* The Atlantic Magazine, September 2004

Customs Service Breaks Secret of Laundering by Imports, Money Laundering Alert, November 1994, page 1

Dowd, Merle E., *Money, Banking, and Credit Made Simple,* Doubleday, New York, 1994

Doyle, Charles, *The USA PATRIOT Act: A Sketch,* Congressional Research Service, Washington, D.C., 2002

Drug Enforcement Administration, *Drug Money Laundering in India,* Washington, D.C., February 1995

Edelhertz, Herbert; Stotland, Ezra; Walsh, Marilyn; and Weinberg, Milton, *The Investigation of White Collar Crime,* U.S. Government Printing Office, Washington, D.C., 1977

Eid, Mike, *An Overview of How States Are Using Project Gateway,* Financial Crimes Report, National Association of Attorneys General, January/February 1998

Emerson, Steven, *Terrorism Financing and U.S. Financial Institutions: Testimony Before the House Committee on Financial Services Subcommittee on Oversight and Investigations,* Washington, D.C., March 11, 2003

Exports, Imports Cover Flight of U.S. Drug Proceeds, Money Laundering Alert, January 1992, page 1

Financial Action Task Force on Money Laundering, *Report on Money Laundering Typologies 2003–2004,* FATF, Paris, 2004

Financial Action Task Force on Money Laundering, *The Forty Recommendations,* FATF, Paris, 2003

Financial Investigations Checklist, U.S. Department of Justice, Washington, D.C., June 1992

General Accounting Office, *Terrorist Financing: U.S. Agencies Should Systematically Assess Terrorists' Use of Alternative Financing Mechanisms,* General Accounting Office, Washington, D.C., 2003

Green, Edwin, *Banking: An Illustrated History,* Rizzoli, New York, 1989

Greenberg, Maurice R.; Wechsler, William F.; and Wolosky, Lee S., *Terrorist Financing: Report of an Independent Task Force Sponsored by the Council on Foreign Relations,* Council on Foreign Relations, New York, 2002

Harbin, Harry S., *Patriot Act — Asset Forfeiture and Money Laundering Provisions,* Department of Justice, Washington, D.C., 2004

Harbin, Harry S., *Update on Money Laundering Case Law and Legislative Initiatives,* Department of Justice, National Advocacy Center, Columbia, S.C., August 2004

Heady, Christy, *The Complete Idiot's Guide to Making Money on Wall Street,* Alpha Books, Indianapolis, 1994

Hoggson, Noble Foster, *Banking Through the Ages,* Dodd, Mead & Company, New York, 1926

How Money Is Laundered in International Commerce Through Exports and Imports, Money Laundering Alert, July 1992, page 8

Internal Revenue Service, *Financial Investigations: A Financial Approach to Detecting and Resolving Crimes,* Washington, D.C., 1993

Internal Revenue Service, *Indirect Methods of Tracing Funds*

Internal Revenue Service, *Money Laundering and Tax Havens,* January 1982

Internal Revenue Service, *Money Laundering from the Federal Perspective,* Office of Chief Counsel, Criminal Tax Division, Washington, D.C.

Internal Revenue Service, *Securities and Commodities,* Washington, D.C., 1986

Internal Revenue Service, *Sources of Information from Abroad,* Washington, D.C., 1992

The Investigation of White Collar Crime: A Manual for Law Enforcement Agencies, U.S. Government Printing Office, Washington, D.C., 1977

Jacobs, Donald; Farwell, Loring C.; and Neave, Edwin H., *Financial Institutions,* Richard D. Irwin, Homewood, IL, 1972

Jannott, Paul F., *Teller World,* Bank Administration Institute, Rolling Meadow, IL, 1989

Joseph, Lester M., *Title 18 USC §§ 1956 and 1957: The Money Laundering Statutes,* Asset Forfeiture and Money Laundering Section, Department of Justice, Washington, D.C.

Kobler, John, *Capone: The Life and World of Al Capone,* G. P. Putnam's Sons, New York, 1971

Koch, Timothy, *Bank Management,* The Dryden Press, Chicago, 1988

Lernoux, Penny, *In Banks We Trust,* Anchor Press, New York, 1984

Lormel, Dennis, *Terrorism Financing and U.S. Financial Institutions: Testimony Before the House Committee on Financial Services Subcommittee on Oversight and Investigations,* Washington, D.C., March 11, 2003

Mayer, Martin, *The Bankers,* Weybright and Talley, New York, 1974

McClintock, David, *Swordfish: A True Story of Ambition, Savagery, and Betrayal,* Pantheon Books, New York, 1993

Money Laundering: State Efforts to Fight It Are Increasing but More Federal Help Is Needed, General Accounting Office, Washington, D.C., October 1992

Morris, Kenneth M. and Siegel, Alan M., *The Wall Street Guide to Money and Investing,* Lightbulb Press, New York, 1993

Murphy, Harry J., *Where's What: Sources of Information for Federal Investigators,* Quadrangle, New York, 1976

Murphy, T. Gregory, *Uncovering Assets Laundered Through a Business,* Police Executive Research Forum, Washington, D.C., 1992

Naylor, R. T., *Hot Money and the Politics of Debt,* Linden Press/Simon and Schuster, New York, 1987

Nossen, Richard A., *Determination of Undisclosed Financial Interest,* U.S. Government Printing Office, Washington, D.C., 1979

Nossen, Richard A., *The Seventh Basic Investigative Technique,* Law Enforcement Assistance Administration, Washington, D.C., 1975

Official IRS Tax Audit Guide, ARCO Publishing, 1976

Passas, Nikos, *Hawala and Other Informal Value Transfer Systems: How to Regulate Them,* Risk Management, 2003

Passas, Nikos, *Informal Value Transfer Systems and Criminal Organizations*, Presentation to U.S. Department of Justice, 2008

Posner, Gerald, *Warlords of Crime: Chinese Secret Societies — The New Mafia,* McGraw-Hill, New York, 1988

Powis, Robert E., *The Money Launderers,* Probus Publishing, Chicago, 1992

Robinson, Jeffrey, *The Laundrymen: Inside Money Laundering, the World's Third-Largest Business,* Arcade Publishing, New York, 1996

Rosenberg, Michael, *Investigative Guidelines to Wire Transfer,* FinCEN, Washington, D.C., 1993

Rosenberg, Michael, *Key Electronic Funds Transfer Systems: Fedwire, CHIPS, SWIFT,* FinCEN, Washington, D.C., 1992

Rosenberg, Michael, *Remittance Corporations,* FinCEN, Washington, D.C., 1994

Spiering, Frank, *The Man Who Got Capone,* Bobbs Merrill, Indianapolis, 1976

Sussman, Barry, *The Great Coverup: Nixon and the Scandal of Watergate*, Ty Crowell, New York, 1974

Terrorist Financing, United States Attorneys Bulletin, July 2003

Thony, Jean-Francois, *Money Laundering and Terrorism Financing: An Overview,* Paper Delivered May 10, 2000, OCDE

Tomko, Edwin, *Document Control in Complex Litigation,* U.S. Department of Justice

United States Department of Justice, *Federal Money Laundering Cases,* Asset Forfeiture and Money Laundering Section, Washington, D.C., January 2005

United States Department of Justice, *Financial Investigations Check List,* June 1992

United States Department of Justice, *Financial Investigations Guide,* June 1998

United States Department of Justice, *Money Laundering Statutes and Related Materials,* Washington, D.C., January 2005

United States Department of Justice, *Report From the Field: The USA PATRIOT Act at Work,* Washington, D.C., July 2004

United States Department of Justice, *Selected Federal Asset Forfeiture Statutes,* Washington, D.C., January 2005

United States Marshals Service, *Pre-Seizure Planning Guide,* Government Printing Office, Washington, D.C., 2001

United States Treasury Department, *Sources of Information,* Federal Law Enforcement Training Center

Waller, George, *Kidnap: The Shocking Story of the Lindbergh Case,* Dial Press, New York, 1961

Wise, David, *Nightmover: How Aldrich Ames Sold the CIA to the KGB for $4.6 Million,* HarperCollins, New York, 1995

APPENDIX A

GLOSSARY OF TERMS USED IN MONEY LAUNDERING CASES

Account — In accounting, each separate type of asset, liability, owner's equity, income, and expense. In banking, an amount of money deposited with the bank.

Adjustable rate mortgage — A mortgage loan in which the interest rate fluctuates. The rate is linked to other interest rates, such as the prime rate.

AMEX — American Stock Exchange. One of the three major exchanges.

Articles of incorporation — Legal documents used to establish a corporation.

Asset — An item of value owned by a business or individual.

Asset-backed bond — Corporate bond backed by the assets of the corporation.

Audit — Analysis of accounting records. The auditor analyzes, scrutinizes, and compares the records.

Audit trail — The books, papers, documents, and records that can be used in the audit process. Standard procedures are used to create the items in the audit trail.

Balance — Equalization of debits and credits in accounts. The books "balance" when the debits equal the credits.

Balance sheet — Fundamental statement of accounting. The balance sheet reflects the net worth of a business at a given point in time. The balance sheet formula is: Assets – Liabilities = Net Worth (Equity).

Bank check — Check drawn on bank funds, such as a cashier's check or a bank draft.

Bank deposits — Indirect method of determining income, involving the analysis of bank records.

Bank draft — A drawing of bank funds held in another bank. Used more often in international transactions or situations where a local check is preferred. Bank A has an account at Bank B, in another city. I give the money to Bank A, which writes me a check on its Bank B account.

Bank holding company — Corporation established to own one or more banks. Regulated by the federal government, bank holding companies can perform certain functions that regular banks cannot. Most bank holding companies "hold" one bank.

Banker's acceptance — Payment method involving a time draft, used for international transactions. Involves a bank in the commercial transaction between two parties. A banker's acceptance is also a financial instrument that can be traded on the open market.

Banking scheme — Money laundering scheme that employs a bank or financial institution to place, layer, or integrate the dirty money.

Barter — A transaction system in which goods and services are directly exchanged for other goods and services without the employment of money.

Bearer bond — A bond that is payable to the bearer. Whoever holds it, owns it. U.S. Savings Bonds are bearer bonds, but corporate bonds in this country are all registered in the name of a specific holder.

Bearer share — A share of stock held in bearer form. Because stock represents ownership of a corporation, whoever holds the majority of a corporation's bearer shares, owns or controls the company. Bearer shares are not used in the United States; some offshore jurisdictions still do.

Bill of lading — Document issued by a shipper describing the goods being shipped, issued on receipt of the goods. The bill of lading is a title document.

Bond — An instrument of debt, issued by a corporation, a government, or another entity. The bond is a promise to repay the investor or lender. Bonds come in various types.

Broker — Licensed agent in securities transactions; the person who manages your money until it's all gone.

Brokerage — Company licensed to deal in securities.

Business cover — Money laundering scheme that involves the use of a business entity (a proprietorship, partnership, or corporation) in the laundering of the dirty money.

Business transaction system — The system of exchange that relies on business, banking, and accounting procedures to conduct financial transactions. Movement from the cash transaction system to the business or financial transaction system is an essential part of money laundering operations.

Buy-back — Money laundering scheme that involves a contrived purchase of goods or services, or even a business, in order to move funds.

Capital — Money. See also *Net worth, Equity.*

Casa de Cambio — "House of Exchange." A currency exchange operation that may also remit funds by wire or perform other services.

Cash — Variety of meanings. Could be coin or currency, as on the Currency Transaction Report form. Could be any form of direct payment other than credit, as at a car dealership. Generally, coin or negotiable paper.

Cash transaction system — The system of exchange that deals exclusively in currency, without the involvement of banks or formalized financial accounting procedures. The drug traffic and most other illegal markets, especially at the lower levels, are all cash transaction systems.

Cash item — Term used in banking to connote currency or another instrument that can be quickly converted to cash.

Cashier's check — A check drawn on the funds of the bank, signed by a cashier or another bank official. The recipient of the check has the security of knowing that the bank is backing up the check with its own money.

CD — Certificate of deposit; a time deposit at a bank, earning interest for a specific period of time.

Central bank — A country's primary banking authority. A central bank serves as the bank for the government, as well as setting monetary policy. In the United States, the Federal Reserve System fills this role.

Certified check — A check drawn on a customer's account, for which the bank, for a fee, certifies that there are funds available on deposit to cover the face amount.

Chain of custody — In a legal case, the passage of evidentiary items from their initial production to their presentation in court. Each stage of possession must be documented to establish a continuous chain.

Check — A written order, usually on a printed form, directing a bank to pay money. Also *cheque.*

CHIPS — Clearing House Interbank Payments System, a system that processes electronic funds transfers, operated by the New York Clearinghouse System. Of all international interbank transfers, 95% go by CHIPS.

Class — Type of stock. Stock may be either common (voting) or preferred.

Classification — In accounting, the process of separating out the various transactions conducted by a business and placing them in assigned categories or accounts.

CMIR — Currency and Monetary Instruments Report, FinCEN Form 105. Required by the Bank Secrecy Act in all cases where a person is transporting more than $10,000 in currency or negotiable monetary instruments into or out of the United States.

Collateral — The property used to secure a loan; something that can be taken by the lender and sold if the borrower fails to pay.

Commercial paper — Negotiable paper, such as drafts, bills of exchange, and so forth, given in the course of business. These can be bought and sold by banks and others.

Confirmation slip — A statement issued by a securities brokerage, advising of some transaction involving securities.

Contract — In commodities trading, an agreement to purchase a commodity at a given future price. The size of the individual contracts vary with the commodity. Wheat contracts are for 5,000 bushels; gasoline contracts are for 42,000 gallons; sugar contracts are for 112,000 pounds; and contracts for British Sterling are for 62,500 pounds.

Cooperative — Form of property ownership.

Corporate bylaws — Legal supplement to the articles of incorporation, setting forth the operating rules for a corporation.

Corporate charter — The "birth certificate" for this artificial person, issued by the state; the legal authority for the corporation to exist and function.

Corporation — An association of individuals, created by law or under authority of law, having a continuous existence apart from the existence of its members and powers and liabilities distinct from those of its members.

Correspondent bank — A bank that has a regular relationship with another bank, keeping funds on deposit with the other bank so that it can conduct banking transactions away from its home area.

Credit — In accounting, the entry on the right side of the account or ledger. Also means the time allowed for payment of goods or services obtained on trust, or the seller's confidence that the purchaser can and will pay money owed.

Credit union — A financial institution made up of "members," affiliated through employment or some other relationship, who invest together and loan money to each other.

CTR — Currency Transaction Report, FinCEN Form 104. Required by banks and financial institutions for all cash transactions over $10,000.

CTRC — Currency Transaction Report for Casinos, FinCEN Form 103. Must be prepared by larger casinos in any cash transaction involving more than $10,000. Nevada casinos file an identical form with the State Gaming Commission; everybody else files with IRS.

Currency exchange — An exchange of one country's money for that of another country. Also the business where this is done, which is considered a nonbank financial institution. Currency exchanges can also involve attempts to reduce the bulk of currency by changing many small-denomination bills for fewer large-denomination ones.

Current asset — In accounting, cash or any other asset that is expected to be converted to cash within a year.

Cyber bank — A recent creation of the Internet. Cyber banks do business using the World Wide Web and purport to offer a range of banking services for their customers. Security is a problem, but these banks are working on it. Being unregulated, these banks could be trouble in the future.

Debenture — A corporate bond, unsecured by a mortgage and dependent on the credit of the issuer.

Debit — In accounting, the entry on the left side of the ledger.

Deep discount — Refers to a financial instrument sold at a fraction of its face value, to be redeemed some time later at that face value.

Demand deposit — Bank account in which the customer can "demand" or withdraw the money immediately or with very short notice (e.g., checking accounts).

Deposit — The placement of money in a bank.

Deposit ticket — The record that documents a deposit. Usually prepared by the customer, listing the items to be deposited, including coins, currency, and checks.

Depreciation — Decrease in value of a business asset due to wear and tear, decay, or decline in price. Calculated on a schedule for tax purposes, depending on the type of asset.

Discount — Refers to a financial instrument, such as a bond or other type of indebtedness, sold at less than its face value, to be redeemed later for full value.

Discount rate — One of the rates at which banks can borrow money from the Federal Reserve; also the rate of interest charged in discounting commercial paper.

Distribution — An allocation of the profits of a partnership or corporation.

Dividend — A sum of money paid to shareholders out of the earnings of the corporation. Dividends can be in the form of cash, stock, or property.

Dividend disbursing agent — The individual or business (often a bank) charged by a corporation with the payment of its dividends. The agent has a record of all shareholders, information you may need to know.

Document collection — In international trade, the process of exchanging the documents that provide ownership in items for the money used to pay for them. An actual exchange involving a buyer, a seller, and two banks.

Documentary evidence — Documents used in court to prove a fact in issue. Documentary evidence may fall under a limited exception to the hearsay rule, but it still must be introduced by a witness.

EFT — Electronic funds transfer. Sending money by wire, in large interbank transfers, or by Western Union.

Electronic funds transfer — See *EFT*.

Equity — What a person owns. See *Net worth*.

Escrow — The period in a real estate transaction when a third party acts as an impartial agent for both buyer and seller. The escrow agent or company handles payment and transfer of title.

Escrow file — A complete record of a real estate transaction, generally held by the escrow agent or company.

Exchange instrument — An instrument or document used in international trade or in commerce.

Expense — A cost or charge.

FBAR — Foreign Bank Account Report, Form TD 90-22.1. Required to be filed by individuals who control foreign bank accounts with more than $10,000 during the year. One of the forms required by the BSA.

Fed — The Federal Reserve System. Sets monetary policy, acts as the banker for the U.S. government, and authorizes the printing of money.

Federal Reserve Bank — One of the regional banks that make up part of the Federal Reserve System. The entire system is controlled by a Board of Governors, and each FRB has its own governor.

Federal Savings Bank — A financial institution that is supposed to focus mainly on home and mortgage lending. Also known as a savings and loan or thrift. Lots of them went under in the 1980s because they were branching out into other fields. Deposits were formerly insured by the FSLIC. FSBs are regulated by the Federal Home Loan Bank Board.

Fedwire — Electronic funds transfer system operated by the Federal Reserve. Used for transfer of funds between domestic banks in the United States.

Fei chi'en — The Chinese version of an informal value transfer system, sometimes known as an underground banking system. Means literally "flying money." Underground banks such as *fei chi'en* and *hawala* operate through a network of personal connections and trust and can move large amounts of money from country to country very quickly.

Finance charge — The interest on a loan.

FinCEN — The Financial Crimes Enforcement Network of the U.S. Department of the Treasury; America's leader in money laundering policy. Good source of information in financial cases, especially with regard to Bank Secrecy Act data.

Fixed asset — An asset that isn't going anywhere, such as a building or land; tangible property of long life.

Float — In banking, the time it takes for customers' checks to go through the clearing process, during which time the bank has the use of that money and can earn interest on it. In securities, to "float an issue" is to market a security, usually for the first time. In commerce, a float is an acceptance awaiting maturity.

Franchise — An arrangement between a big business and a small one, in which the smaller one gets the right to use the larger's name and products for a fee.

Futures — Speculative purchases or sales of commodities for future receipt or delivery. As in, "I heard she hit the jackpot in cattle futures."

General ledger — The final book of consolidation of all the preceding books of accounts; the source of financial reports.

Grantee — The person receiving title to property; the buyer.

Grantor — The owner of a piece of real property who is "granting" title to a buyer.

Growth stock — A stock that doesn't pay dividends and is purchased because the company is using that money to grow and expand, which should, if all goes well, make the stock's value rise.

Hawala — Another version of an informal value transfer system or underground banking system, originating on the Indian subcontinent but very popular in Islamic and Indian communities around the world.

Hawaladar — The operator of a *hawala*.

Holding corporation — A corporation that exists to own another corporation. Bank holding corporations own one or more banks.

Hundi — The hundi is an Indian version of the *Hawala* IVT. See *hawala* and *fei chi'en*.

Income — Also known as revenue; money earned or received.

Income statement — One of the two basic financial statements (with the balance sheet). The income statement addresses income and expenses to determine net income (or loss) for a given period of time.

Income stock — A stock that pays a dividend, usually issued by an established corporation.

Indirect method — A court approved method of determining a person's income from unexplained sources when his or her books and records are not available. The net worth, bank deposits, and source and application of funds or expenditures methods are the most common.

Installment — Payment of a loan made on a recurring basis. For example, "She pays the loan in monthly installments."

Intangible — An asset that does not have a physical value but is still worth something. Patents, goodwill, and copyrights are examples.

Integration — The stage in the money laundering cycle in which the clean-looking funds are brought back into the financial system for the criminal's use. Follows placement and layering.

Interest — The fee charged by a lender for the use of its money.

Investment bank — An entity that exists to finance the issuance of securities. Not really a financial institution in the same sense as a commercial bank.

Invoice — An itemization of goods purchased or services provided, together with the charges and terms; an itemized bill containing the prices that comprise the total charge.

IPO — Initial public offering; the first time a new stock is placed on the market. Investment banks underwrite the entire issue and then put it up for public sale.

Joint venture — A partnership arrangement, usually for a limited term and a specific purpose, such as a real estate development project.

Journal — A book of original entry and chronological listing of transactions.

Layering — The second stage of the money laundering process, in which multiple transactions are conducted to conceal the origin of the dirty money. May involve a variety of mechanisms, including shell corporations and wire transfers.

Ledger — A group of accounts.

Letter of credit — An order issued by a banker allowing a person named to draw money to a specified amount from correspondents of the issuer. An instrument issued by a banker authorizing a person named to make drafts upon the issuer up to a specified amount. Used in international commerce.

Leverage — Pure speculation. Leverage is the difference between the purchase price of a security and the money you put up to buy it. To invest with borrowed money.

Liability — The equity of a creditor; something you owe somebody else. An obligation.

Liability ledger — In banking, the part of a customer's loan file that records the payments on the customer's loan and the current status of the liability.

Line of credit — An offer or agreement to lend money, which the customer can draw on when needed. Lines of credit are "opened" so that a business can have the credit available when the time comes to move on a purchase or action.

Load — In securities, loads are the commissions charged in connection with mutual funds or other investments. These commissions may be "front loaded" or "back-end loaded," depending on whether they are paid at the time of purchase or later.

Loan-back — A money laundering scheme in which the launderer appears to be involved in a real loan but is really borrowing from (and repaying) him- or herself.

M1 — Money Supply 1. As tracked by the Federal Reserve, M1 consists of all currency and demand account deposits in the American economy.

Margin account — Basically a loan from your broker. In margin trading, the investor can borrow up to 50% of the purchase price of an investment from the broker. You pay the broker interest, but you don't have to pay the loan back until the stock is sold, and you get to keep all the profits if the security does what you thought it would. If it doesn't, you get a …

Margin call — If the value of your investment falls below 75% of the original value, you'll get called by the broker to put up additional funds. If you can't "meet the call," the stock has to be sold to pay the broker.

Maturity date — The date on which a security, such as a bond, is due and payable.

Money — Any article or substance used as a medium of exchange, store of wealth, or means of payment.

Money laundering — The process of making money derived from criminal activity appear to be from a legal source. Making dirty cash seem clean.

Money market account — Account at a securities brokerage resembling a bank savings account, only containing securities as well as cash. Some money market accounts include provisions for check writing, which makes the banks nervous.

Money order — A draft on bank funds, resembling a cashier's check, but in a small amount. Money orders are also used by the U.S. Postal Service, Western Union, and other NBFIs. Postal money orders are limited to $700.

Mortgage — Conveyance of property to a creditor as security for a loan.

Mortgage-backed bond — An instrument of debt backed by a pool of mortgage loans.

Municipal bond — Instrument of debt issued by a city, county, or other public agency. Ordinarily the interest on "munis" is free of federal and most state taxes.

Mutual fund — A collection of stocks, bonds, or other securities owned by a group of investors and managed by a professional investment company.

NASDAQ — The exchange operated by the National Association of Securities Dealers. This exchange is all electronic and offers thousands more issues than the NYSE. A lot of tech stocks are on the NASDAQ.

NBFI — Nonbank financial institution. Certain of these businesses, also known as money services businesses, are considered financial institutions by federal law, including currency exchangers, money remitters, casinos, and even, in some cases, car dealerships.

Net worth — What you own. All of your assets, minus all of your liabilities; your equity or capital. Also, the indirect method of proving income that involves calculating differences in a person's net worth from year to year.

No load — An investment (usually a mutual fund) that requires no payment of a commission.

Nominee — A person who is representing another in a transaction and who may appear to be the owner or purchaser or seller.

NYSE — New York Stock Exchange. The oldest and most prestigious of the exchanges. Not the biggest anymore, but the one everybody watches.

Odd lot — A "round lot" is 100 shares of stock. An odd lot is anything else.

Offset — In double-entry bookkeeping, the entry made on the other side of the account (for every debit, there has to be a credit). In securities, a transaction that counterbalances a previous one, such as with commodities trading, where an order to buy cattle contracts needs to be offset with an order to sell, before somebody delivers all those steers to your home.

Offshore — Anywhere other than the United States (or the country you're in).

Offshore bank — Any bank operating outside the United States; usually refers to foreign banks in foreign countries (although American banks operate offshore as well).

Offshore company/corporation — A business entity with its charter issued in a foreign jurisdiction.

Option — In securities, the legal right to buy or sell a security at a given price in a given time period. Relates to stocks and commodities. Stock options are traded on the exchanges just like the stocks themselves.

OTC — Over the counter; relating to stocks and the market in which they are sold. Not an exchange, the market consists of (usually cheaper) stocks not listed on the exchanges.

Overinvoicing — A money laundering scheme that involves the inflation of invoice amounts.

Overdraft — What happens when you write a check for which there isn't enough money in your account. Some banks will loan you the difference automatically, at a substantial fee.

Paper — Usually relates to a debt or a note, as in "commercial paper."

Par value — In bonds, the face value of a bond. It may be sold at a discount of the par value. In stocks, the par value is the original stated price.

Partnership — A contractual arrangement between two or more people acting in a common business association.

Partnership agreement — The written contract that sets up the partnership, as prescribed by the Uniform Partnership Act.

Placement — The initial phase of the money laundering cycle, in which the transition is made from the cash transaction system to the business transaction system. Placement involves the conversion of currency into another form or at least its reduction in bulk or transportation.

Point — Could be a dollar, as in the stock market, or a fraction of a unit of currency, as in the foreign exchange market. You wouldn't want to get the two mixed up, as this could cost a lot of money.

Prime rate — The interest rate at which banks loan money to their largest corporate customers. Many other interest rates, mortgages, and so forth are tied to fluctuations in the prime rate.

Principal — The amount of money borrowed that will ultimately be paid back.

Private bank — Usually one that does not take deposits from the general public. Some large banks offer private banking for special customers, which includes money management and red carpet treatment.

Promissory note — Written confirmation of a loan and a promise by the borrower to repay; an IOU.

Property — That which a person owns. May be chattel (personal) property or real. Estate property is that which can be handed down from one generation to the next.

Proprietorship — A business that is owned and operated by one person. Any business not a partnership or a corporation is automatically considered a proprietorship.

Revenue — An increase in owner's equity or net worth arising from operations. See *Income*.

Revolving credit — Credit available for reuse, as opposed to a one-time loan. Credit cards are the best example.

Round lot — In securities, 100 shares.

Safe deposit — Service offered by a bank to hold property for customers in its vault. The bank rents the safe deposit boxes and has no knowledge of the contents.

Safekeeping — In securities, the maintenance of an investor's securities at the brokerage.

SAR — Suspicious Activity Report. The transaction reporting form used by financial institutions to notify a number of government agencies of suspicious or possibly illegal activity. Replaced the Suspicious Transaction Report and several Criminal Referral Forms. Good source of information about possible structuring of cash transactions.

Savings bond — A U.S. government security sold at a discount of its face value, sold in denominations from $50 to $10,000, and not permitted to be marketed or traded among investors.

Securities manipulation — A type of money laundering scheme that involves the use of securities in various ways to move the money or conceal the source or control of the money.

Security — In banking, the property put up as collateral for a loan, forming the basis for the bank's belief that it will be repaid. In investments, a security is anything that provides evidence of either debt (as in bonds) or property (as in stocks).

Segregation — The holding by a brokerage of investors' securities in the brokerage's street name.

Selling short — A credit-type transaction in which the investor bets that a stock will go down. For example, I borrow money from my broker to sell a given number of shares at the current price. When the stock goes down, I buy an equal number of shares at the new low price, give these to the broker, and pocket the balance of the money the broker loaned me.

Share — One piece of an entire corporation. Represents a percentage of ownership, based on the total number of shares outstanding.

Shareholder — An owner of a corporation. AT&T has more than a million such owners.

Shell corporation — A corporation that has no assets, other than a bank account or two.

Shop book rule — The rule of evidence that allows business records to be admitted as an exception to the hearsay rule if they can be properly authenticated.

Short — In commodities, to "go short" is to sell. See *Selling short* for the relationship to stocks.

Sight draft — A bank draft payable "on sight" or when presented. See *Time draft*.

Signature card — The initial document used to open a bank account, listing all those persons whose signatures allow them to take actions regarding the account.

Smurf — A person who engages in multiple cash transactions to avoid reporting requirements by conducting the transactions in amounts under $10,000.

Société anonyme — French form of a corporation. In Spanish, *sociedad anónima*. Abbreviated S.A. at the end of the corporate name, e.g., Bank of America Switzerland S.A.

Spot market — In commodities, the market that deals in commodities selling now, as opposed to in the future.

Stock — A piece of the corporate pie. The equity of a corporation, divided up into ownership shares among the holders of the stock. Stock may be common (voting) or preferred.

Stock option — In securities, the legal right to buy or sell a stock at a given price in a given time period. Stock options are traded on the exchanges just like the stocks themselves.

Stock warrant — A stock warrant allows an investor to buy a stock for a given price for a certain period. You would buy a warrant if you thought that the stock was going to go up. The fee is a percentage of the stock price.

Stockbroker — See *Broker*.

Stop loss order — An instruction filed by an investor to sell a security when the price falls to a certain level.

Street name — The brokerage's name, under which securities owned by an investor may be held or registered. The brokerage would receive the dividends and forward them to the investor.

Structure — To arrange a financial transaction in such a way that a currency reporting requirement is avoided. This usually entails breaking up a large cash transaction into a series of smaller ones. Depending on how it's done, structuring could be a violation of federal law.

SUA — Specified Unlawful Activity; any of the listed crimes that may form the basis for a money laundering prosecution under Title 18 U.S.C. Section 1956.

Subsidiary ledger — In accounting, any of the books that support the general ledger.

Substitution of assets — In criminal forfeiture cases, the substitution of an asset of equal value for one that has been forfeited but cannot be located.

SWIFT — The Society for Worldwide Interbank Financial Telecommunications, based in Belgium. It has 2600 member institutions and functions as a communications service to initiate funds transfers.

Syndicate — A type of business entity in which participants join together to act with one purpose. Syndicates are often used in connection with investment opportunities. Several investment banks may form a syndicate to underwrite an initial public offering of stock.

TECS — Treasury Enforcement Communications System; contains Bank Secrecy Act information.

Teller tape — The record generated by the computer or calculating device at each bank teller's station. The teller tape will have a record of all the transactions conducted by that teller during the day.

Terms — The conditions under which a loan is made.

Testimonial evidence — Testimony of a live witness. Must accompany the documentary sort of evidence used in a financial case. Also critical in money laundering cases in proving up the Specified Unlawful Activity.

Time deposit — A savings account or another bank deposit, intended to be left at the bank for an extended period. Opposed to demand deposits, such as checking accounts, in which the money comes and goes.

Time bill — A bill of exchange payable at a specified date.

Time draft — A bank draft payable in a certain number of days or on a specified date after it is presented. Used in international commerce.

Transfer agent — In securities, the individual or institution, often a bank, appointed by a corporation to handle matters relating to its stock.

Traveler's check — A check, usually one of a set, sold by a bank or some similar company that is cashed by countersigning in the presence of the payee. Widely accepted, especially in international travel settings.

Treasury bond — A type of U.S. government security; the instruments of our national debt.

Trust — A fiduciary relationship in which one person (the trustee) holds the title to property (the trust estate or trust property) for the benefit of another (the beneficiary).

Trust Services — The department of a bank that handles matters relating to trusts. The bank may act as a trustee for individual trusts.

Underinvoicing — A money laundering scheme in which the value of merchandise being exchanged is substantially greater than the amount shown on the invoice.

Usury — Lending at an excessive rate of interest. Frowned upon by moralists and prohibited by some statutes. Described as one of the surest ways to wealth, and one of the worst.

Wire transfer — See *Electronic funds transfer*.

Zero-coupon bond — A bond sold at a discount of its face value, to be redeemed at par. A U.S. Savings Bond is a zero-coupon bond.

APPENDIX B

SOURCE DEBRIEFING GUIDE

This source debriefing guide was obtained from the *Financial Investigations Checklist* published by the United States Department of Justice, June 1992.

1. Who are the members of the group?
   a. How do you know?
   b. What evidence do you have?
      i. Phone books
      ii. Toll records
      iii. Photographs
   c. What role does each member have?
   d. What are the relationships among the members?
   e. Who are the key people?
   f. Who are their friends?
   g. Who are their girlfriends or boyfriends?
2. What are the criminal enterprises of the group?
   a. Critical to know for affidavit wording:
      i. Money launderers have certain records.
      ii. Traffickers have different records.
   b. The affiant's experience identifies which types of records are maintained by which type of criminal enterprise.
3. What are the receipts of the criminal enterprise?
   a. What volume of drugs is distributed per week/month/year?
   b. What are the expenses?
      i. Personnel
      ii. Stash house
      iii. Car rentals
      iv. Cellular phones, etc.
   c. Gross receipts (or cash on hand) = Drugs sold per week — (Cost of drugs + Additional expenses)
      i. Use to show probable cause that cash will be on premises.
   d. What is the purity of the drugs received from the source?
   e. What is the purity of the drugs when sold?
   f. On what days are collections of drug proceeds made?
      i. Where are collections made?
      ii. From whom are collections made?
      iii. Who makes the collections?
      iv. What denominations of currency are received?
      v. What does the organization do with the collections?
         A. Is there a counting house?
         B. Does the organization use a launderer?
         C. Is the currency converted to larger bills?
         D. Is the currency converted to money orders, checks, or other financial instruments?
         E. Is the currency deposited into bank accounts or through other financial institutions?

F. Name and address of institution
G. Account numbers
H. Office or branch used
I. Is the currency negotiated through one or more businesses?
4. What front companies are used?
   a. Where do they bank?
   b. Who is their accountant?
   c. Who is their bookkeeper?
   d. Who is their stockbroker?
   e. Who is their real estate broker?
   f. Where do they receive their mail from?
   g. Who is their attorney?
      i. Does the same attorney represent all the companies?
      ii. Is the attorney compromised?
         A. How is he or she compromised?
         B. How is the attorney paid?
5. What records do the companies or principals maintain?
   a. What computers do they use?
   b. What computer software do they use?
   c. Where are the records kept?
      i. Where did the informant see the records?
      ii. Who else was present?
   d. Who keeps the records?
   e. Who are the company's customers?
   f. Who are the company's suppliers?
   g. Who hauls the company's trash?
   h. Do any of the subjects carry phone directories or computer data banks on their persons?
   i. What is their beeper or cellular telephone number?
6. What assets do the subjects or their companies own?
   a. Real estate
      i. Who owns it?
      ii. Who is the registered owner?
         A. When was the property bought?
         B. Who was it purchased from?
         C. How was it paid for?
      iii. What cars visit the property?
      iv. Is there evidence of the subjects' arrivals and departures?
      v. Where does the mail to the property come from?
      vi. Who uses the property as a return address?
      vii. Who pays for the phone and utilities?
   b. Do any of the subjects own:
      i. Expensive jewelry
      ii. Furs
      iii. Cars
      iv. Boats
      v. Airplanes
      vi. Gold or other precious metals
      vii. Artwork
      viii. Antiques
      ix. What are the details of the purchase?
         A. When did they buy it?
         B. Where did they buy it?
         C. From whom did they buy it?
         D. How did they pay for it?
         E. Where is the property stored?
         F. Who is the registered owner?
   c. Do any of the subjects keep large amounts of cash:
      i. On their person
      ii. In their house
      iii. In their office
      iv. In their vehicle
      v. In a bank safe deposit box
      vi. Elsewhere?
         A. Is the cash hidden?
         B. Have they built hidden stash locations in their house, car, or office?
7. What are their favorite places of entertainment?
   a. What credit cards do the subjects use?
   b. What are their shopping habits?
   c. What stores do they frequent?

d. Do they buy with cash, check, or credit card?
e. What trips have they taken?
f. Do they gamble?
g. What types of gambling are they involved in?
    A. Casinos
    B. Sports
    C. Floating crap games
    D. Other bookmaking
h. Do they have a favorite bookie?
    i. Do they have casino accounts?
i. Where do they go on vacation?
j. What travel agent do they use?
k. Where did they go?
l. When did they go?
m. What is their favorite vacation spot?
i. What airlines do they use?
n. What rental car companies do they use?

In addition to the above questions, we would suggest that informants or witnesses also be asked questions about other sources of funds, in anticipation of potential defenses raised by the subjects.

1. What legitimate income has the subject had over the past five years?
    a. Income from legitimate employment
    b. Income from trusts, gifts, insurance, or legal claims
    c. Income from foreign countries
    d. Proceeds of loans

APPENDIX C

SUBPOENA TEMPLATES

AIRLINE COMPANY

Any and all original documents (or microfilm copies where originals are not available), in your custody or subject to your control, that in any way relate to _____,
or on behalf of them either individually, or on behalf of, in trust for, or in combination with any other person or entity for the period _____ through _____, inclusive, including but not limited to, the following:

1. Copies of airline tickets
2. Passenger manifests
3. Receipts
4. Frequent flier or benefit program summaries
5. Monthly, quarterly, or other frequent flier program statements
6. Correspondence

AUTOMOBILE DEALERSHIP

Any and all original documents (or microfilm copies where originals are not available), in your custody or subject to your control, that in any way relate to _____,
or on behalf of them either individually, or on behalf of, in trust for, or in combination with any other person or entity for the period _____ through _____, inclusive, including but not limited to, the following:

1. Purchase orders, invoices, receipts, applications for title, and any miscellaneous records or correspondence, and the identity of the salesperson for any new or used vehicles (including autos, trucks, or recreational vehicles) sold, including:
   a. Deal files or folders
   b. Credit applications
   c. Registration and title documents
2. Any and all records and/or correspondence pertaining to any vehicles of any kind purchased by the dealership or taken in trade
3. Invoices, ledgers, receipts, or service records relating to any repairs or servicing performed
4. Contracts, leases, ledgers, receipts, terms and manner of payment for and vehicles leased
5. Copies of any IRS Forms 8300 prepared in connection with receipt of currency from the above described persons or entities

BAIL BOND COMPANY

Any and all original documents (or microfilm copies where originals are not available), in your custody or subject to your control, that in any way relate to _____,
or on behalf of them either individually, or on behalf of, in trust for, or in combination with any other person or entity for the period _____ through _____,

inclusive, including but not limited to, the following:

1. Account ledgers and receipts indicating dates and amount of all bonding fees or premiums, and manner of payment
2. Invoices
3. Receipts
4. Applications
5. Correspondence
6. Notes, memos of contact or conversation

BANK — COMPREHENSIVE

The following documents for all accounts bearing the signatory authority of _____, and/or in the name(s) of _____, and/or bearing the account number(s) _____ for the period _____ to _____, including but not limited to:

1. All documents pertaining to all open or closed checking, savings, NOW, time, or other deposit or checking accounts in the name of or under signature authority of any of the named parties or entities, including but not limited to:
   a. Signature cards
   b. Corporate board authorization minutes or partnership resolutions
   c. Bank statements
   d. Canceled checks
   e. Deposit tickets
   f. Items deposited
   g. Credit and debit memos
   h. Forms 1099, 1089, or back-up withholding documents
2. All documents pertaining to open or closed bank loans or mortgage documents, reflecting loans made to or co-signed by any of the named parties or entities, including but not limited to:
   a. Loan applications, and related documents, including copies of income tax returns
   b. Corporate board authorization minutes or partnership resolutions
   c. Loan ledger sheets
   d. Documents (checks, debit memos, cash-in tickets, wires in, etc.) reflecting the means by which loan repayments were made
   e. Documents (checks, debit memos, cash-in tickets, wires in, etc.) reflecting disbursement of the loan proceeds
   f. Loan correspondence files, including but not limited to:
      Letters to the bank
      Letters from the bank
      Notes, memoranda, etc. to the file
   g. Collateral agreements and documents
   h. Credit reports
   i. Financial statements
   j. Notes or other instruments reflecting the obligation to pay
   k. Real estate mortgages, chattel mortgages, or other security instruments for loans
   l. Forms 1099, 1089, or back-up withholding documents
   m. Loan amortization statements
3. All documents pertaining to certificates of deposit purchased or redeemed by any of the named parties or entities, including but not limited to:
   a. Copies of the certificates
   b. Corporate board authorization minutes or partnership resolutions
   c. Documents (checks, debit memos, cash-in tickets, wires in, etc.) reflecting the means by which CDs were purchased
   d. Documents (bank checks, credit memos, cash-out tickets, wires out, etc.) reflecting disbursements of the proceeds of any negotiated CDs
   e. Records reflecting rollovers, or interest earned, withdrawn, or reinvested
   f. Forms 1099, 1089, or back-up withholding documents

4. All documents pertaining to open or closed investment or security custodian accounts, IRA, Keogh, or other retirement plans in the name of or for the benefit of any of the named parties or entities, including but not limited to:
   a. Documents (checks, debit memos, cash-in tickets, wires in, etc.) reflecting the means by which the securities were purchased
   b. Documents (bank checks, credit memos, cash-out tickets, wires out, etc.) reflecting disbursement of the proceeds of any negotiated securities
   c. Confirmation slips
   d. Monthly statements
   e. Payment receipts
   f. Safekeeping records and logs
   g. Receipts for receipt or delivery of securities
   h. Forms 1099, 1089, or back-up withholding documents
5. All documents pertaining to all cashier's, manager's, or bank checks, traveler's checks, and money orders purchased or negotiated by any of the named parties or entities, including but not limited to:
   a. Documents (checks, debit memos, cash-in tickets, wires in, etc.) reflecting the means by which the checks or money orders were purchased
   b. Documents (bank checks, credit memos, cash-out tickets, wires out, etc.) reflecting disbursement of the proceeds of any negotiated checks or money orders
   c. Applications for purchase of checks or money orders
   d. Retained copies of negotiated checks or money orders
6. Customer correspondence files for each of the named parties and entities
7. All documents pertaining to wire transfers sent or received by any of the named parties or entities, including but not limited to:
   a. Fedwire, CHIPS, SWIFT, or other money transfer or message documents
   b. Documents (checks, debit memos, cash-in tickets, wires in, etc.) reflecting the source of the funds wired out
   c. Documents (bank checks, credit memos, cash-out tickets, wires out, etc.) reflecting the ultimate disposition within the institution of the funds wired
   d. Notes, memoranda or other writings pertaining to the sending or receipt of wire transfers
8. All documents pertaining to current or expired safe deposit box rentals by or under the signatory authority of any of the named parties or entities, including but not limited to:
   a. Contracts
   b. Signature cards
   c. Entry records
9. All documents pertaining to open or closed bank credit cards in the name of or under the signatory authority of any of the named parties or entities, including but not limited to:
   a. Applications for credit
   b. Corporate board authorization minutes or partnership resolutions
   c. Credit reports
   d. Monthly statements
   e. Financial statements
   f. Charge tickets
   g. Documents (checks, debit memos, cash-in tickets, wires in, etc.) reflecting payments on the account
   h. Correspondence files
10. Teller tapes reflecting all transactions between the institution and any of the parties or entities named.
11. All CTRs (Form 104) and CMIRs (Form 105) filed with the Department of the Treasury, Internal Revenue Service FinCEN, or United States Customs by the (Institution Name) between (dates) concerning currency transac-

tions conducted by or on behalf of the named parties or entities.
12. Copies of bank surveillance film or videotape reflecting all transactions between the institution and any of the parties or entities named.
13. Copies of the following documents, if any, filed by the (Institution Name) with the aforementioned federal agencies, the Drug Enforcement Administration, the Federal Bureau of Investigation, the Justice Department, or any bank regulatory agency, concerning transactions by, on behalf of, or involving the named parties or entities:
    a. Suspicious Activity Report, FinCEN Form TD F 90-22.47
14. Any and all "exemption lists," requests for exemptions, and statements submitted in support of such requests filed with the Internal Revenue Service pursuant to 31 U.S.C. 103.22 concerning the named parties or entities.
15. Any and all correspondence, letters, or documents reflecting telephone conversations or meetings between the (Institution Name) and any bank regulatory or federal law enforcement agency regarding suspicious transactions, pending investigations, or ongoing investigations relating to any of the named parties or entities.

BANK — ACCOUNT INFORMATION

You are requested to bring with you and produce:
Account number or other identifying data that would tend to establish whether _____ holds or has held in the period from _____ to _____, any of the following:

1. Checking accounts
2. Savings accounts
3. NOW accounts
4. Time accounts
5. Other deposit or checking accounts
6. Bank loans, mortgages, or other loans
7. Certificates of deposit
8. Investment or security accounts
9. Safe deposit boxes

whether open, closed, or expired, or over which the above named parties or entities has exercised control or held signature authority.

This request includes, but is not limited to the production of account numbers, a record of the dates in which the account or service was active or open, and such information that would tend to establish the identities of those parties or entities which exercise control or hold signature authority over the account or service, and further, this request shall be construed to include all branches, offices, or divisions of _____ Bank.

BANK —

The following documents for all accounts bearing the signatory authority of _____, and/or in the name(s) of _____, and/or bearing the account number(s) _____ for the period _____ to _____, including but not limited to:

1. Demand (checking) account records, including:
    a. New account sheet
    b. Signature card
    c. Corporate resolution or partnership agreement (if applicable)
    d. Customer ledger
    e. Deposit tickets
    f. Canceled checks
    g. Copies of transit, clearing, or "on us" items, or credit memoranda deposited to the account
2. Time (savings) account records, including:
    a. New account sheet
    b. Signature card
    c. Corporate resolution or partnership agreement (if applicable)

d. Customer ledger
e. Deposit tickets
f. Withdrawal slips and supporting canceled checks, if any
g. Copies of all items deposited into the account
h. Copies of negotiable orders of withdrawal

3. Loan records, including:
   a. Loan file, including:
      Lending office memoranda
      Financial statements
      Outside audits
      Loan committee action reports
      Appraisals
      Miscellaneous information
   b. Applications for loans granted or rejected
   c. Customer liability ledger
   d. Checks or deposit items representing the disbursement of principal
   e. Collateral ledger
   f. Loan guarantees or hypothecation agreements
   g. Letters of credit

4. Trust records, including:
   a. Trust agreement, or other evidence of authority to act in a fiduciary capacity
   b. Trust asset ledger
   c. Cash ledger
   d. Investment ledger
   e. Stock ledger
   f. Safekeeping records
   g. Buy and sell orders, and their confirmations
   h. Income and expense ledger
   i. Trust checks or drafts paid

5. Other bank records, including:
   a. Money orders, cashier's checks, and drafts, with application or requisition forms
   b. Certified checks
   c. Wire transfers
   d. Collection items
   e. Insurance records
   f. Travel agency records
   g. Safe deposit box records
   h. Copies of any negotiable instruments cashed or paid by the bank without entry to any depository account
   i. Copies of Currency Transaction Reports, FinCEN Form 104, or Suspicious Activity Reports
   Cash transactions exempt log or register

CASINO

Any and all original documents (or microfilm copies where originals are not available), in your custody or subject to your control, that in any way relate to _____, or on behalf of them either individually, or on behalf of, in trust for, or in combination with any other person or entity for the period _____ through _____, inclusive, including but not limited to, the following documents, computer printouts, or non-printer equipped computer displays:

1. Gambling or gaming credit cards
2. Hotel folios
3. Amounts of payments
4. Methods of payments
5. Financial statements and credit reports
6. Applications for credit
7. Player rating schedule
8. Gambling history, including:
   a. Year to date win/loss
   b. Last four visits win/loss
   c. Total complimentary values
   d. Total action to date
   e. Current rating
9. Results of video or other electronic surveillance or monitoring

CELLULAR TELEPHONE COMPANY

All cellular telephone subscriber information for cellular telephone numbers _____, or in the name(s) of _____, for the period _____ to _____, including but not limited to:

1. Applications for cellular telephone service
2. Credit information
3. Monthly billings
4. Documentation listing all toll calls and/or long-distance calls, including dates, number called or calling, duration of call, and cost of call
5. Information concerning the cellular telephone equipment purchased or rented for use in connection with this account
6. Correspondence

CORPORATION — GENERAL

The following documents for the period _____ to _____, including but not limited to retained copies of all documents relating to (corporate name) banking transactions, including, but not limited to:

1. All documents pertaining to all open or closed checking, savings, NOW, time, or other deposit or checking accounts held in the name of, for the benefit of, or under the control of (corporate name), including but not limited to:
   a. Retained copies of signature cards
   b. Corporate board authorization minutes or partnership resolutions
   c. Bank statements
   d. Canceled checks
   e. Deposit tickets
   f. Retained copies of items deposited
   g. Retained copies of credit and debit memos
   h. Forms 1099, 1089, or back-up withholding documents
2. All documents to open or closed bank loans or mortgage documents, reflecting loans made to, cosigned by, or made for the benefit of (corporate name), including but not limited to:
   a. Loan applications
   b. Corporate board authorization minutes or partnership resolutions
   c. Loan statements
   d. Documents (checks, debit memos, cash-in tickets, wire transfer documents, etc.) reflecting the means by which loan repayments were made
   e. Retained copies of documents (checks, debit memos, cash-in tickets, wire transfer documents, etc.) reflecting disbursement of the loan proceeds
   f. Copies of loan correspondence, including but not limited to:
   Letters to the bank
   Letters from the bank
   Notes, memoranda, etc. to the file
   g. Collateral agreements and documents
   h. Credit reports
   i. Financial statements
   j. Notes or other instruments reflecting the obligation to pay
   k. Real estate mortgages, chattel mortgages, or other security instruments for loans
   l. Forms 1099, 1089, or back-up withholding documents
   m. Loan amortization statements
3. All documents pertaining to certificates of deposit purchased or redeemed by the corporation, including but not limited to:
   a. Copies of the certificates
   b. Corporate board authorization minutes or partnership resolutions
   c. Documents (checks, debit memos, cash-in tickets, wire transfer documents, etc.) reflecting the means by which CDs were purchased
   d. Retained copies of documents (bank checks, credit memos, cash-out tickets, wires out, etc.) reflecting disbursements of the proceeds of any negotiated CDs
   e. Records reflecting rollovers, or interest earned, withdrawn, or reinvested
   f. Forms 1099, 1089, or back-up withholding documents

4. All documents pertaining to open or closed investment or security custodian accounts, IRA, Keogh, or other retirement plans in the name of or for the benefit of any of the corporation, including but not limited to:
   a. Documents (checks, debit memos, cash-in tickets, wire transfer documents, etc.) reflecting the means by which the securities were purchased
   b. Retained copies of documents (bank checks, credit memos, cash-out tickets, wire transfer documents, etc.) reflecting disbursement of the proceeds of any negotiated securities
   c. Confirmation slips
   d. Monthly statements
   e. Payment receipts
   f. Safekeeping records and logs
   g. Receipts for receipt or delivery of securities
   h. Forms 1099, 1089, or back-up withholding documents
5. Bank correspondence files
6. All documents pertaining to all cashier's, manager's, or bank checks, traveler's checks, and money orders purchased or negotiated by the corporation, including but not limited to:
   a. Documents (checks, debit memos, cash-in tickets, wire transfer documents, etc.) reflecting the means by which the checks or money orders were purchased
   b. Retained copies of documents (bank checks, credit memos, cash-out tickets, wires out, etc.) reflecting disbursement of the proceeds of any negotiated checks or money orders
   c. Applications for purchase of checks or money orders
   d. Retained copies of checks or money orders
7. All documents pertaining to wire transfers sent or received by the corporation, including but not limited to:
   a. Retained copies of Fedwire, CHIPS, SWIFT, or other money transfer or message documents
   b. Documents (checks, debit memos, cash-in tickets, wire transfer documents, etc.) reflecting the source of the funds wired out
   c. Documents (bank checks, credit memos, cash-out tickets, wire transfer documents, etc.) reflecting the ultimate disposition of the funds wired in
   d. Notes, memoranda, or other writings pertaining to the sending or receipt of wire transfers
8. All documents pertaining to current or expired safe deposit box rentals by or under the signatory authority of the corporation, including but not limited to:
   a. Contracts
   b. Signature cards
   c. Entry records
9. All documents pertaining to open or closed bank credit cards in the name of the corporation, including but not limited to:
   a. Applications for credit
   b. Corporate board authorization minutes or partnership resolutions
   c. Retained copies of credit reports
   d. Monthly statements
   e. Financial statements
   f. Charge tickets
   Documents (checks, debit memos, cash-in tickets, wire transfer documents, etc.) reflecting payments on the account

CORPORATION — SUSPECT

All books and records of _____
and its affiliate or subsidiary companies, including, but not limited to the following:

1. Corporate charter
2. Articles of incorporation
3. Declaration of paid-in-capital

4. Corporate minute book
5. Stock ledger book
6. General journal
7. General ledger
8. Cash receipts journal
9. Cash disbursements journal
10. Contracts
11. Invoices
12. Billings
13. Investment records for both real and personal property
14. Adjusting entries
15. Bank statements with deposit tickets and canceled checks
16. Loan records
17. Copies of cashier's checks, money orders, drafts, or certified checks
18. Financial statements
19. Annual reports
20. Federal and state tax returns
21. General excise tax returns
22. Internal and independent audits
23. All correspondence and internal memoranda
24. IRS Forms 1099, 1089, or forms relating to distributions to officers or shareholders
25. IRS Forms 10Q, 10K, or 8K

all of which relate to the period from _____ through _____, inclusive.

CREDIT BUREAU

Any and all original documents (or microfilm copies where originals are not available), in your custody or subject to your control, that in any way relate to _____, or on behalf of them either individually, or on behalf of, in trust for, or in combination with any other person or entity for the period _____ through _____, inclusive, including but not limited to, the following documents, computer printouts, or non-printer equipped computer displays:

1. Identifying information, including:
   a. Full name
   b. Social Security number
   c. Address
   d. Telephone number
   e. Spouse's name
2. Credit bureau reports, applications or forms
3. Copies of applications for credit
4. Financial status and employment information, including:
   a. Income
   b. Spouse's income
   c. Place, position, and tenure of employment
   d. Other sources of income
   e. Duration and income in former employment
5. Credit history, including:
   a. Types of credit previously obtained
   b. Names of previous credit grantors
   c. Extent of previous credit
   d. Complete payment history
6. Existing lines of credit, including:
   a. Payment records
   b. Outstanding obligations
7. Public record information, including:
   a. Newspaper clippings
   b. Arrest and conviction records
   c. Bankruptcies, tax liens, judgments, or lawsuits
8. Listing of credit agency subscribers that have previously requested a credit report or other information concerning the above listed person or entity

CREDIT CARD COMPANY

The following documents for all open or closed credit card accounts bearing the signatory authority of and/or in the name of _____, and credit card number(s) _____, for the period _____ to _____, including but not limited to:

1. Applications for credit

2. Corporate board authorization minutes or partnership resolutions
3. Financial statements
4. Monthly statements
5. Charge tickets
6. Documents (bank checks, personal checks, money orders, wire transfers in, etc.) reflecting payments on the account
7. Correspondence files

ESCROW COMPANY

Any and all original documents (or microfilm copies where originals are not available), in your custody or subject to your control, that in any way relate to _____, or on behalf of them either individually, or on behalf of, in trust for, or in combination with any other person or entity for the period _____ through _____, inclusive, including but not limited to, the following:

1. Escrow files
2. Title search and verification documents
3. Mortgage, loan, and financing documents
4. Quitclaim, warranty, or other deeds
5. Copies of checks, cashier's checks, money orders, drafts or other items reflecting payments
6. Escrow instruction agreements and settlements
7. Correspondence

HOTEL

Any and all original documents (or microfilm copies where originals are not available), in your custody or subject to your control, that in any way relate to _____, or on behalf of them either individually, or on behalf of, in trust for, or in combination with any other person or entity for the period _____ through _____, inclusive, including but not limited to, the following:

1. Guest folios
2. Registration cards
3. Billing statements
4. Records relating to guest charges, including:
   a. Telephone calls made or received
   b. Charges on the room
5. Retained copies of canceled checks, credit card slips, or other records reflecting payment on the account

INSURANCE COMPANY

Any and all original documents (or microfilm copies where originals are not available), in your custody or subject to your control, that in any way relate to _____, or on behalf of them either individually, or on behalf of, in trust for, or in combination with any other person or entity for the period _____ through _____, inclusive, including but not limited to, the following:

1. Applications for insurance, including background and financial information, as well as insurance carried by other companies
2. Appraisals and descriptions of appraised property
3. Customer ledger
4. Policy and loan records
5. Dividend payment record, including canceled checks, if applicable
6. Payment records on termination (if life), losses (if casualty), or refunds on cancellations, including canceled checks
7. Correspondence files

LAWYER — FEE INFORMATION

Any and all original documents (or microfilm copies where originals are not available), in your custody or subject to your control, that in any way relate to _____, or on behalf of them either individually, or on behalf of, in trust for, or in combination with any other person or entity for the period _____ through _____, inclusive, including but not limited to, the following:

1. Legal fee information, including:
   a. Receipts
   b. Client account ledgers
   c. Records indicating dates and amounts of all legal fees paid and manner of payment, and the purpose of the payment
2. Bail bond fee information, including:
   a. Receipts
   b. Ledgers
   c. Deposit tickets
   d. Retained copies of canceled checks
   e. Any records indicating dates and amounts of any bail bond paid and the manner and purpose of the payment
3. Trust fund information, including:
   a. Receipts
   b. Ledgers
   c. Deposit tickets
   d. Retained copies of canceled checks
   e. Any records indicating dates and amounts of any trust funds either held by the law firm or channeled through the firm, and the purpose of those funds
4. Other records pertaining to the purchase or sale of real or personal property, including:
   a. Receipts
   b. Ledgers
   c. Canceled checks
   d. Correspondence
5. Copies of IRS Forms 8300 made in connection with any transaction

LONG-DISTANCE TELEPHONE SERVICE PROVIDER

All telephone subscriber information for telephone numbers _____, or in the name(s) of _____, for the period _____ to _____, including but not limited to:

1. Applications for telephone service
2. Credit information
3. Monthly billings
4. Documentation listing all toll calls and/or long-distance calls, including dates, number called or calling, duration of call, and cost of call

REAL ESTATE BROKER

Any and all original documents (or microfilm copies where originals are not available), in your custody or subject to your control, that in any way relate to _____, or on behalf of them either individually, or on behalf of, in trust for, or in combination with any other person or entity for the period _____ through _____, inclusive, including but not limited to, the following:

1. Authority to act as an agent for _____ or his/her designee
2. Propositions or offers
3. Closing statements
4. DROA (Deposit Received — Offer Acceptance) forms and accompanying documents
5. Canceled checks
6. Correspondence
7. Descriptions of real property purchased or sold

RETAILER

Any and all original documents (or microfilm copies where originals are not available), in your custody or subject to your control, that in any way relate to _____, or on behalf of them either individually, or on behalf of, in trust for, or in combination with any other person or entity for the period _____ through _____, inclusive, including but not limited to, the following:

1. Invoices
2. Accounts receivable ledger
3. Manner of payment
4. Retained copies of canceled checks
5. Credit applications
6. Copies of receipts or purchase orders
7. Correspondence
8. Copies of IRS Forms 8300 that were prepared in connection with the receipt of funds from the above described person or entity

SECURITIES BROKER

Retained copies of all documents relating to any and all securities transactions in the name(s) of _____ or under the account number(s) of _____, for the period _____ to _____, including but not limited to:

1. Account statements for all accounts including but not limited to:
   a. Cash accounts
   b. Margin accounts
   c. Mutual fund accounts
   d. Limited partnership accounts
   e. IRA accounts
   f. Keogh accounts
   g. Cash management accounts
2. Applications to open accounts
3. Cash received and delivered blotters
4. Confirmation slips
5. Corporate board/partnership resolutions
6. CTRs and CMIRs
7. Customer correspondence files
8. Payment receipts
9. Securities position records
10. Stock certificates or bonds
11. Stock delivery receipts

TELEPHONE COMPANY

All subscriber or account information for (address) _____, or in the name(s) of _____, for the period _____ to _____, including but not limited to:

1. Applications for service
2. Credit information
3. Monthly billings
4. Information concerning the type of equipment purchased or rented for use in connection with this account
5. Correspondence

TRAVEL AGENCY

Any and all original documents (or microfilm copies where originals are not available), in your custody or subject to your control, that in any way relate to _____, or on behalf of them either individually, or on behalf of, in trust for, or in combination with any other person or entity for the period _____ through _____, inclusive, including but not limited to, the following:

1. Copies of written agreements or contracts documenting authority to act as an agent for _____ or his designee
2. Travel files and documents, including:
   a. Schedules or itineraries
   b. Retained copies of airline, rail, bus, ship, or other tickets
   c. Copies of confirmation slips, numbers, or notifications
   d. Rental car reservations or records
   e. Hotel or lodging reservations or records
   f. Other visitor attraction reservations or records
3. Records of payment, including:
   a. Retained copies of canceled checks
   b. Credit card slips or vouchers
4. Correspondence

APPENDIX D

DOCUMENT SEARCH WARRANT EXAMPLE

This Affidavit for Search Warrant is presented for use as a guide in the preparation of a "documents only" search warrant. The scenario and the characters in it are fictional. Any resemblance to a real person, living or dead, is purely coincidental. The language in this affidavit, especially that relating to the seizing of computer equipment and media, was reviewed and approved by the United States Attorney's office, and something similar worked once in court. Every case is different, and practices differ from district to district.

AFFIDAVIT OF JOHN SMITH

Special Agent JOHN SMITH, affiant, being duly sworn on oath, deposes and says:

AFFIANT'S BACKGROUND

1. *In this section, the affiant documents his or her employment, training, education, and experience. These are factors that may assist the judicial officer in finding that any of the affiant's conclusions presented in the affidavit are based on special knowledge or expertise.*

2. I have had extensive communication with other state and federal narcotics investigators who specialize in the investigation of methamphetamine distribution, and who have had experience in the investigation of the laundering of the proceeds of methamphetamine and other drug trafficking, as well as interviewing, interrogating, and debriefing defendants, participant witnesses, informants, and other persons who have had personal knowledge and experience of drug trafficking and money laundering.

3. My awareness of these drug trafficking and money laundering practices arises from the following: (a) my involvement in prior drug-related investigations and searches during my career as a law enforcement officer, as previously described, (b) my involvement on a number of occasions in debriefing confidential informants and cooperating individuals in prior drug and money laundering investigations, as well as what other agents and police officers have advised me when relating the substance of their similar debriefings, and the results of their own investigations, and (c) other intelligence information provided through law enforcement channels.

PREMISES TO BE SEARCHED

4. This affidavit is submitted in support of a request for separate search warrants for (1) the residence of Jan and Nadia BROWN located at 1234 Pacific Avenue, Kailua (further described *infra*, and (2) the office area of the premises of MANGO BLOSSOM RECORDS located at 5440 Kalakaua Avenue, Suite 1820, Honolulu (further described *infra*), for records and items of evidence as described in Exhibit B hereto.

PROBABLE CAUSE

5. In this section you summarize the facts that lead you to conclude that evidence, in the form of documents or financial records, is located at the premises you describe. Because

the facts are different in every case, there's no need to set any out here. You will want to hit several points, however, including:

- Informant information about the underlying SUA
- Informant information about records or documents at the location
- Anything the informant said about specific items or containers where evidence might be found
- Information about the informant's reliability and credibility
- Corroborative information, especially that from government business records, which is inherently reliable
- Anything that ties in specific people, events, or items of evidence (For example, you want to seize any computers or computer media, so include any information you have that tends to show computers are kept at the location.)

Following the probable cause facts, include a section summarizing the affiant's background or track record regarding similar searches. This also contributes to the judge's ability to conclude that maybe the officer knows what he or she is talking about. If this is your first-ever document warrant, go find somebody who's done a bunch of them and use him or her as your expert. It's a simple matter to change all of the wording below to say, "I spoke with Officer Doe, who advised me that she has been involved in, initiated, or otherwise participated...."

6. In the course of my career as a Special Agent and a State Narcotics Agent, I have been involved in, initiated, or otherwise participated in the execution of at least two hundred (200) residential search warrants in cases involving drug trafficking, money laundering, or tax fraud. As a result of my participation in the searches of these residences, as well as my other experience as a Criminal Investigator, I have observed and know that it is a common practice for persons engaged in a trade or business to keep and maintain books and records at their location of business. I have further found that it is common practice in the business community to maintain journals, ledgers, and other records showing the receipt and disposition of funds. I have also found in my experience in dealing with business records that the flow of funds into and out of a company can be tracked by tracing the "paper trail" created by the entries into the business records and bank accounts, and by the documents received or prepared to support a transaction.

7. I have further found that the business records of individuals, businesses, and companies are used as a basis for the preparation of business, corporate, or personal income tax returns. I also have found that business records are ordinarily kept and maintained at the place of business for extended periods of time, often several years, in order to provide support for revenue and expense transactions if questioned by IRS examiners at a later date, among other reasons.

8. Further, I am aware that some persons may keep some of these records at their personal residence, and that in cases involving small, closely held, or family-owned businesses, certain documents, books, papers, and records are likely to also be found at a person's residence due to the person's relationship to the business, or their personal nature. These records include (a) Articles of incorporation, corporate resolutions, corporate minute books, corporate stock books, corporate state charters, and records of corporate taxes paid; (b) General journals, cash receipt journals, cash disbursement journals, and sales journals; (c) General ledgers and subsidiary ledgers, which include notes receivable, accounts receivable, accounts payable, notes payable, and closing ledgers; (d) Bank statements, deposit slips, withdrawal slips, and canceled checks, savings account passbooks, and certificates of deposit; (e) Receipts, invoices, and other documents reflecting purchases or expenditures; (f) Copies of federal income tax returns, Forms 1040, 1120, 1120S, 940, and 941, filed or not filed, and supporting work papers, summary sheets, and analyses used in the preparation of these returns; (g) Financial statements, budgets,

and operating plans; (h) Records relating to investments in securities, mutual funds, commodities, or other assets; (i) Records relating to the purchase, ownership, and sale of real estate or real property, including contracts, deeds, mortgage loan documents, title reports, DROA documents, escrow papers, and related correspondence; (j) State income tax and general excise tax returns and related documents; (k) Employee wage, salary, and benefit information.

9. Based upon my experience as a Special Agent and a narcotics investigator, I am aware that people who keep personal financial records and records relating to their business at their residence generally keep these in a central location, such as a "home office," desk area, or study. I have also observed and am aware that older and/or noncurrent records may be boxed and stored elsewhere in the residence, such as in an enclosed garage, storage area, attic, or basement.

Now, include a section on computerized records. Because you probably won't have the expertise, you qualify another expert who tells you what he or she thinks you should be looking for. You're also asking for permission to take the computers and computer media off-site to let the experts search them, since doing it at the scene would take too long.

SEARCH FOR COMPUTERIZED RECORDS; REMOVAL FOR "OFF-SITE" SEARCH

10. I know that almost all of the records and documents that this affidavit seeks authorization to search for can be made/stored/kept electronically on a personal computer and/or computer hardware and software. Since other persons involved in this investigation have maintained records of their activities in electronic form, it will also be necessary to search the personal computer(s) located at described premises, and computer hardware and software, for electronically made/kept/stored documents/records.

11. I have consulted with Special Agent James Chan of the Internal Revenue Service, Criminal Investigation Division, who is a Special Agent of approximately eleven (11) years' experience, and who is trained as a Seized Computer and Evidence Recovery Specialist, having attended both the Basic and Advanced Training Classes sponsored by IRS in that subject. Special Agent Chan advised me that he has been involved in approximately five (5) previous cases in which computers and computer-related evidence have been seized, including one case that involved associates of Jan and Nadia BROWN.

12. Based upon my knowledge, training and experience, and that of Special Agent Chan, I know that searching and seizing information from computers usually requires agents to seize most or all electronic storage devices (along with related peripherals) to be searched later by a qualified computer expert in a laboratory or other controlled environment. This is true because of the following:

a. *The volume of evidence.* Computer storage devices (like hard disks, diskettes, tapes, laser disks, USB drives, storage devices, Bernoulli drives) can store the equivalent of thousands of pages of information. Additionally, a suspect may try to conceal criminal evidence; he or she might store it in random order with deceptive file names. This may require searching authorities to examine all the stored data to determine which particular files are evidence or instrumentalities of crime. This sorting process can take weeks or months, depending on the volume of data stored, and it would be impractical to attempt this kind of data search on site.

b. *Technical requirements.* Searching computer systems for criminal evidence is a highly technical process requiring expert skill and a properly controlled environment. The vast array of computer hardware and software available requires even computer experts to specialize in some systems and applications, so it is difficult to know before a search which expert is qualified to analyze the system and its data. In any event, however, data search protocols are exacting scientific procedures designed to protect the integrity of the evidence and to recover even "hidden," erased, compressed, password-protected, or encrypted files. Since computer evidence is extremely vulnerable to inadvertent or intentional modification or destruction (both from external sources or from destructive code imbedded in the system as a "booby trap"), a controlled environment is essential to a complete and accurate search and analysis.

13. Based upon my knowledge, training, and experience, and that of Special Agent Chan, I also know that searching computerized information for evidence of a crime commonly requires agents to seize most or all of a computer system's input/output peripheral devices, related software, documentation, and data security devices (including passwords) so that a qualified computer expert can accurately retrieve the system's data in a laboratory or other controlled environment. This is true because the peripheral devices that allow users to enter or retrieve data from the storage devices vary widely in their compatibility with other hardware and software. Many system storage devices require particular input/output (or "I/O") devices in order to read the data on the system. It is important that the analyst be able to properly reconfigure the system as it now operates in order to accurately retrieve the evidence listed above. In addition, the analyst needs the relevant system software (operating systems, interfaces, and hardware drivers) and any applications software that may have been used to create the data (whether stored on hard drives or on external media), documentation, and security devices.

14. Accordingly, for the reasons described herein, it will be necessary to remove the computer(s), peripheral devices, related software, documentation, and other data security devices from the described premises in order to execute this search warrant as to the search for electronic records/data. If, after inspecting the I/O devices, software, documentation, and data security devices, the analyst determines that these items are no longer necessary to retrieve and preserve the data evidence, your affiant represents that he will return them within a reasonable time.

Affiant's Conclusions

This section concludes your affidavit. Note that your conclusions are clearly labeled as such, but the groundwork for qualifying you to make those conclusions has already been laid. This is also the section where you would make your case that the entire enterprise was "permeated with fraud." If the judge finds that this is so, virtually all of the records on the premises that relate to the enterprise can be seized. It will certainly broaden the scope of the warrant. The facts leading you to make this conclusion need to be stated above.

15. Based upon the statements of the sources identified above, and my review of the records obtained in connection with this case, and described herein, I believe that probable cause exists to believe that Jan and Nadia BROWN were involved in drug trafficking activity during a period from at least 1992 and continuing through at least 1995. I believe that as a result of this activity, Jan and Nadia BROWN received monies from the sale of illicit drugs, and that this money was invested in at least three (3) enterprises, to wit, a recording company known as "MANGO BLOSSOM RECORDS," an equipment leasing company known as "JNB EQUIPMENT LEASING," and cash loans, made to associates. I further believe that these activities generated additional income in the form of record sales, payment for musical performances, rental fees for the leasing of heavy equipment, and interest payments on loans. Based upon the records of the Internal Revenue Service, it appears that no tax returns were filed by either Jan or Nadia BROWN in connection with receipt of the above described income. I further believe that the evidence adduced in this case supports

my conclusion that the business affairs of Jan and Nadia BROWN, from the generation of illegal income, to the laundering of this income through otherwise "legitimate"-appearing businesses, to the concealment of all income from whatever source by failing to file tax returns, are completely permeated with fraud.

Statement of Probable Cause

16. Based upon the above, I am informed and believe that there is probable cause to believe that the items described in the list attached hereto as Exhibit B constitute evidence of violations of Title 18 U.S.C. Sections 371, 1956, and 1957; Title 21 U.S.C. Sections 841 and 846; and Title 26 U.S.C. Sections 6050I, 7201, and 7203, and are located in the premises described as (1) the residence at 1234 Pacific Avenue, further described as a brownish-color one-story wooden structure, with a garage facing Pacific Avenue and a mailbox bearing the number 1234, all of which is depicted on the photograph attached as Exhibit A, and all of which is located in Kailua, in the City and County of Honolulu, District and State of Hawaii.

I declare under penalty of perjury that the foregoing is true and correct to the best of my knowledge and belief.

EXHIBIT B

1. Items of evidence which relate to MANGO BLOSSOM RECORDS and JNB EQUIPMENT LEASING, during the period January 1995 through September 1997, including the following:

a. Articles of incorporation, corporate resolutions, corporate minute books, corporate stock books, corporate state charters, and records of corporate taxes paid;

b. General journals, cash receipt journals, cash disbursement journals, and sales journals;

c. General ledgers and subsidiary ledgers, which include notes receivables, accounts receivables, accounts payable, notes payable, and closing ledgers;

d. Bank statements, deposit slips, withdrawal slips, canceled checks, cashier's check receipts or copies, savings account passbooks, and certificates of deposit;

e. Receipts, invoices, and other documents reflecting purchases or expenditures;

f. Copies of federal income tax returns, Forms 1120, 1120S, 940, and 941, filed or not filed, and supporting work papers, summary sheets, and analyses used in the preparation of these returns;

g. Financial statements, budgets, and operating plans;

h. Records relating to investments in securities, mutual funds, commodities, or other assets;

i. Records relating to the rental, leasing, purchase, ownership, and sale of real estate or real property, including rental agreements, leases, contracts, deeds, mortgage loan documents, title reports, DROA documents, escrow papers, and related correspondence;

j. State income tax and general excise tax returns, personal and corporate, and related documents;

k. Employee wage, salary, and benefit information;

l. Canceled checks, check register(s), and a monthly book or schedule of receipts (cash receipts journal);

m. Computer equipment, including CPU, disk or tape drives, monitors, printers, CD-ROM and other media, including diskettes, tapes, or other storage devices, which is used in the preparation or storage of the above described records;

n. Correspondence, promissory notes, loan payment schedules, or other records reflecting the making of loans by or to Jan K. BROWN, Nadia BROWN, a.k.a. Nadia KELLY,

MANGO BLOSSOM RECORDS, or JNB EQUIPMENT LEASING;

o. Records relating to the rental, leasing, purchase, ownership, and sale of heavy or construction-type equipment, including rental agreements, leases, contracts, deeds, loan documents, title reports, and maintenance records.

2. Items of evidence which relate to Jan and Nadia BROWN personally, or in their capacities as officers and directors of MANGO BLOSSOM RECORDS, LTD., or JNB EQUIPMENT LEASING during the period January 1993 through September 1997, including the following:

a. Bank statements, deposit slips, withdrawal slips, canceled checks, cashier's check receipts or copies, savings account passbooks, and certificates of deposit;
b. Receipts, invoices, and other documents reflecting purchases or expenditures;
c. Copies of federal income tax returns, Forms 1040, filed or not filed, and information returns, supporting work papers, summary sheets, and analyses used in the preparation of these returns;
d. Records relating to investments in securities, mutual funds, commodities, or other assets;
e. Records relating to the rental, leasing, purchase, ownership, and sale of real estate or real property, including rental agreements, leases, contracts, deeds, mortgage loan documents, title reports, DROA documents, escrow papers, and related correspondence;
f. State income tax and general excise tax returns, personal and corporate, and related documents;
g. Canceled checks, check register(s), and a monthly book or schedule of receipts (cash receipts journal);
h. Computer equipment, including CPU, disk or tape drives, monitors, printers, CD-ROM and other media, including diskettes, tapes, or other storage devices, which is used in the preparation or storage of the above described records;
i. Correspondence, promissory notes, loan payment schedules, or other records reflecting the making of loans by or to Jan K. BROWN, Nadia BROWN, a.k.a. Nadia KELLY, MANGO BLOSSOM RECORDS, or JNB EQUIPMENT LEASING;
j. Stock certificates in the name of "Wave Crest, Inc." or containing references to Jack Smythe, which have been used to secure loans. Promissory notes or other agreements relating to loans to Jack Smythe, Wave Crest, Inc., or enterprises affiliated with those two entities;
k. Address books, telephone bills, cellular telephone billing records, and other records showing communication between Jan and Nadia BROWN, and other persons.

3. Items of personal property which tend to identify the person(s) in residence, occupancy, control or ownership of the premises that are the subject of this warrant, including but not limited to canceled mail, deeds, leases, rental agreements, photographs, personal telephone books, utility and telephone bills, statements, identification documents, and keys.

APPENDIX E

FORMS

FINCEN Form 103
(Formerly Form 8362)
(Rev. March 2003)
Department of the Treasury
FINCEN

Currency Transaction Report by Casinos

▶ Previous editions will not be accepted after September 30, 2003.
▶ Please type or print.
(Complete all applicable parts--See Instructions)

OMB No. 1506-0005

1 If this Form 103 (CTRC) is submitted to **amend a prior report** check here: ☐ and attach a copy of the original CTRC to this form.

Part I — Person(s) Involved in Transaction(s)

Section A--Person(s) on Whose Behalf Transaction(s) Is Conducted (Customer)   **2** ☐ Multiple persons

3 Individual's last name or Organization's name

4 First name

5 M.I.

6 Permanent address (number, street, and apt. or suite no.)

7 SSN or EIN

8 City

9 State

10 ZIP code

11 Country (if not U.S.)

12 Date of birth MM / DD / YYYY

13 Method used to verify identity: **a** ☐ Examined identification credential/document   **b** ☐ Known Customer - information on file   **c** ☐ Organization

14 Describe identification credential: **a** ☐ Driver's license/State ID **b** ☐ Passport **c** ☐ Alien registration **d** ☐ Other _____

   e Issued by: _____   **f** Number: _____

15 Customer's Account Number

Section B--Individual(s) Conducting Transaction(s) - If other than above (Agent)   **16** ☐ Multiple agents

17 Individual's last name

18 First name

19 M.I.

20 Address (number, street, and apt. or suite no.)

21 SSN

22 City

23 State

24 ZIP code

25 Country (if not U.S.)

26 Date of birth MM / DD / YYYY

27 Method used to verify identity: **a** ☐ Examined identification credential/document   **b** ☐ Known Customer - information on file

28 Describe identification credential: **a** ☐ Driver's license/State ID **b** ☐ Passport **c** ☐ Alien registration **d** ☐ Other _____

   e Issued by: _____   **f** Number: _____

Part II — Amount and Type of Transaction(s). Complete all items that apply.   **29.** ☐ Multiple transactions

30 CASH IN: (in U.S. dollar equivalent)
   a Purchase(s) of casino chips, tokens, and other gaming instruments $_____ .00
   b Deposit(s) (front money or safekeeping) _____ .00
   c Payment(s) on credit (including markers) _____ .00
   d Currency wager(s) _____ .00
   e Currency received from wire transfer(s) out _____ .00
   f Purchase(s) of casino check(s) _____ .00
   g Currency exchange(s) _____ .00
   h Other (specify): _____ _____ .00

   i Enter total of CASH IN transaction(s) $_____ .00

31 CASH OUT: (in U.S. dollar equivalent)
   a Redemption(s) of casino chips, tokens, and other gaming instruments $_____ .00
   b Withdrawal(s) of deposit (front money of safekeeping) _____ .00
   c Advance(s) on credit (including markers) _____ .00
   d Payment(s) on wager(s), including slot jackpot(s) _____ .00
   e Currency paid from wire transfer(s) in _____ .00
   f Negotiable instrument(s) cashed (including checks) _____ .00
   g Currency exchange(s) _____ .00
   h Travel and complimentary expenses and gaming incentives _____ .00
   i Payment for tournament, contest or other promotions _____ .00
   j Other (specify): _____ _____ .00

   K Enter total of CASH OUT transaction(s) $_____ .00

32 Date of transaction (see instructions) MM / DD / YYYY

33 Foreign currency used: _____ (Country)

Part III — Casino Reporting Transactions

34 Casino's trade name

35 Casino's legal name

36 Employer identification number (EIN)

37 Address (number, street, and apt. or suite no.) where transaction occurred

38 City

39 State

40 ZIP code

Sign Here ▶

41 Title of approving official

42 Signature of approving official

43 Date of signature MM / DD / YYYY

44 Type or print preparer's name

45 Type or print name of person to contact

46 Contact telephone number (___) ___ – ____

For Paperwork Reduction Act Notice, see page 4.   Cat. No. 37041B   FinCEN Form **103** (Rev. 3-03) (Formerly Form 8362)

FinCEN Form 103 (Rev. 3-03) (Formerly Form 8362)   Page **2**

Multiple Persons or Multiple Agents
(Complete applicable parts below if box 2 or box 16 on page 1 is checked.)

Part I — Person(s) Involved in Transaction(s)

Section A—Person(s) on Whose Behalf Transaction(s) Is Conducted (Customer)

3 Individual's last name or Organization's name	4 First name	5 M.I.

6 Permanent address (number, street, and apt. or suite no.)	7 SSN or EIN

8 City	9 State	10 ZIP code	11 Country (if not U.S.)	12 Date of birth MM/DD/YYYY

13 Method used to verify identity: **a** ☐ Examined identification credential/document   **b** ☐ Known Customer - information on file   **c** ☐ Organization

14 Describe identification credential: **a** ☐ Driver's license/State ID   **b** ☐ Passport   **c** ☐ Alien registration   **d** ☐ Other _____
    e Issued by: _____   **f** Number: _____

15 Customer's Account Number

Section B—Individual(s) Conducting Transaction(s) - If other than above (Agent)

17 Individual's last name	18 First name	19 M.I.

20 Address (number, street, and apt. or suite no.)	21 SSN

22 City	23 State	24 ZIP code	25 Country (if not U.S.)	26 Date of birth MM/DD/YYYY

27 Method used to verify identity: **a** ☐ Examined identification credential/document   **b** ☐ Known Customer - information on file

28 Describe identification credential: **a** ☐ Driver's license/State ID   **b** ☐ Passport   **c** ☐ Alien registration   **d** ☐ Other _____
    e Issued by: _____   **f** Number: _____

General Instructions

Form 103. Use this revision of Form 103 (formerly 8362) for filing on reportable transactions. However, the July 1997 version of Form 8362, Currency Transaction Report by Casinos (also referred to as a CTRC), can still be used until September 30, 2003.

Suspicious Transactions. If a transaction is greater than $10,000 in currency as well as suspicious, casinos must file a Form 103 and must report suspicious transactions and activities on FinCEN Form 102, Suspicious Activity Report by Casinos (SARC). Also, casinos are required to use the SARC form to report suspicious activities involving or aggregating at least $5,000 in funds. **Do not** use Form 103 to (a) report suspicious transactions involving $10,000 or less in currency or (b) indicate that a transaction of more than $10,000 is suspicious.

When a suspicious activity requires immediate attention, casinos should call 1-800-800-2877, Monday through Friday, from 9:00a.m. to 6:00p.m. Eastern Standard Time (EST). An Internal Revenue Service (IRS) employee will direct the call to the local office of the IRS Criminal Investigation (CI). In an emergency, consult directory assistance for the local IRS CID office.

Who must file. Any organization duly licensed or authorized to do business as a casino, gambling casino, or card club in the United States (except casinos located in Nevada) and having gross annual gaming revenues in excess of $1 million must file Form 103. This includes the principal headquarters and every domestic branch or place of business of the casino or card club. The requirement includes state-licensed casinos (both land-based and riverboat), tribal casinos, and state-licensed and tribal card clubs. Since card clubs are subject to the same reporting rules as casinos, the term "casino" as used in these instructions refers to both a casino and a card club.

Note: Nevada casinos must file Form 103N, Currency Transaction Report by Casinos - Nevada (CTRC-N), to report transactions as required under Nevada Regulation 6A.

What to file. A casino must file Form 103 for each transaction involving either currency received (Cash In) or currency disbursed (Cash Out) of more than $10,000 in a gaming day. A gaming day is the normal business day of the casino by which it keeps its books and records for business, accounting, and tax purposes. Multiple transactions must be treated as a single transaction if the casino has knowledge that: (a) they are made by or on behalf of the same person, and (b) they result in either Cash In or Cash Out by the casino totaling more than $10,000 during any one gaming day. Reportable transactions may occur at a casino cage, gaming table, and/or slot machine. The casino should report both Cash In and Cash Out transactions by or on behalf of the same customer on a single Form 103. **Do not** use Form 103 to report receipts of currency in excess of $10,000 by non-gaming businesses of a casino (e.g., a hotel); instead, use **Form 8300,** Report of Cash Payments Over $10,000 Received in a Trade or Business.

Exceptions. A casino does not have to report transactions with domestic banks, currency dealers or exchangers, or commercial check cashers.

Identification requirements. All individuals (except employees conducting transactions on behalf of armored car services) conducting a reportable transaction(s) for themselves or for another person must be identified by means of an official or otherwise reliable record.

Acceptable forms of identification include a driver's license, military or military dependent identification card, passport, alien registration card, state issued identification card, cedular card (foreign), or a combination of other documents that contain an individual's name and address and preferably a photograph and are normally acceptable by financial institutions as a means of identification when cashing checks for persons other than established customers.

For casino customers granted accounts for credit, deposit, or check cashing, or on whom a CTRC containing verified identity has been filed, acceptable identification information obtained previously and maintained in the casino's internal records may be used as long as the following conditions are met. The customer's identity is re-verified periodically, any out-of-date identifying information is updated in the internal records, and the date of each re-verification is noted on the internal record. For example, if documents verifying an individual's identity were examined and recorded on a signature card when a deposit or credit account was opened, the casino may rely on that information as long as it is re-verified periodically.

When and where to file: File each Form 103 by the 15th calendar day after the day of the transaction with the:

    IRS Detroit Computing Center
    ATTN: CTRC
    P.O. Box 32621
    Detroit, MI 48232

A casino must retain a copy of each Form 103 filed for 5 years from the date of filing.

Penalties. Civil and/or criminal penalties may be assessed for failure to file a CTRC or supply information, or for filing a false or fraudulent CTRC. See 31 U.S.C. 5321, 5322, and 5324.

FinCEN Form 103 (Rev. 3-03)

Definitions. For purposes of Form 103, the terms below have the following meanings:

Agent. Any individual who conducts a currency transaction on behalf of another individual or organization.

Currency. The coin and paper money of the United States or of any other country that is circulated and customarily used and accepted as money.

Customer. Any person involved in a currency transaction whether or not that person participates in the casino's gaming activities

Person. An individual, corporation, partnership, trust or estate, joint stock company, association, syndicate, joint venture, or any other unincorporated organization or group.

Organization. Person other than an individual.

Transaction In Currency (Currency Transaction). The **physical** transfer of currency from one person to another.

Negotiable Instruments. All checks and drafts (including business, personal, bank, cashier's, and third-party), traveler's checks, money orders, and promissory notes, whether or not they are in bearer form.

Specific Instructions

Note: Additional information that cannot fit on the front and back of Form 103 must be submitted on plain paper attached to Form 103. Type or print the individual's or organization's name and identifying number, date of transaction, and casino's name and employer identification number (i.e., Items 3, 4, 5, 7, 32, 34, 35, and 36) as well as identify the specific item number on all additional sheets. This will ensure that if a sheet becomes separated, it will be associated with the appropriate Form 103.

Item 1. Amends prior report.—Check Item 1 if this Form 103 amends a previously filed report. Staple a copy of the original report behind the amended one. Complete Part III in its entirety, but complete only those other entries that are being amended.

Part I. Person(s) Involved in Transaction(s)

Note: Section A must be completed in all cases. If an individual conducts a transaction on his/her own behalf, complete only section A; leave Section B BLANK. If a transaction is conducted by an individual on behalf of another person(s), complete Section A for each person on whose behalf the transaction is conducted; complete Section B for the individual conducting the transaction.

Section A. Person(s) on Whose Behalf Transaction(s) Is Conducted (Customer)

Item 2. Multiple persons.—Check Item 2 if this transaction is being conducted on behalf of more than one person. For example, if John and Jane Doe cash a check made out to them jointly at the casino, more than one individual has conducted the transaction. Enter information in Section A for one of the individuals; provide information for the other individual on page 2, Section A. Attach additional sheets as necessary.

Items 3, 4, and 5. Individual/Organization name.—If the person on whose behalf the transaction(s) is conducted is an individual, put his/her last name in Item 3, first name in Item 4 and middle initial in Item 5. If there is no middle initial, leave Item 5 BLANK. If the transaction is conducted on behalf of an organization, enter the name in Item 3 and leave Items 4 and 5 BLANK, but identify the individual conducting the transaction in Section B. If an organization has a separate "doing business as (DBA)" name, enter in Item 3 the organization's legal name (e.g., Smith Enterprises, Inc.) followed by the name of the business (e.g., DBA Smith Casino Tours). In this case, use Items 4 and 5 if more space is needed.

Items 6, 8, 9, 10, and 11. Address.—Enter the permanent street address, city, two-letter state abbreviation used by the U.S. Postal Service, and ZIP code of the person identified in Item 3. Also, enter in Item 6 the apartment or suite number and road or route number. Do not enter a P.O. box number unless the person has no street address. If the person is from a foreign country, enter any province name as well as the appropriate two-letter country code (e.g., "CA" for Canada, "JA" for Japan, etc.). If the country is the United States, leave Item 11 BLANK.

Item 7. Social security number (SSN) or Employer identification number (EIN).—Enter the SSN (if an individual) or EIN (if other than an individual) of the person identified in Items 3 through 5. If that individual is a nonresident alien individual who does not have an SSN, enter "NONE" in this space.

Item 12. Date of birth.—Enter the customer's date of birth (DOB) if it is known to the casino through an existing internal record or reflected on an appropriate identification document or credential presented to the casino to verify the customer's identity (see **Identification Requirements** above). Internal casino records can include those for casino customers granted accounts for credit, deposit, or check cashing, or on whom a CTRC containing verified identity has been filed. If such records do not indicate the DOB, a casino should ask the customer for the DOB. If the DOB is not available from any of these sources, the casino should enter NOT AVAILABLE in the space. Eight numerals must be inserted for each date. Enter the date in the format "mmddyyyy", where "mm" is the month, "dd" is the day, and "yyyy" is the year. Zero (0) should precede any single-digit number. For example, if the individual's birth date is June 1, 1948, enter "06 01 1948" in Item 12.

Item 13. Method used to verify identity.—If an individual conducts the transaction(s) on his/her own behalf, his/her name and address **must** be verified by examination of an official credential/document or internal record containing identification information on a known customer (see **Identification Requirements** above). Check box **a** if you examined an official identification credential/document. Check box **b** if you examined an acceptable internal casino record (i.e., credit, deposit, or check cashing account record, or a CTRC worksheet) containing previously verified identification information on a "known customer." Check box **c** if the transaction is conducted on behalf of an organization. If box **a** or **b** is checked, you **must** complete Item 14. If box **c** is checked, do not complete Item 14.

Item 14. Describe identification credential.— If a driver's license, passport, or alien registration card was used to verify the individual's identity, check as appropriate box **a, b**, or **c**. If you check box **d**, you must specifically identify the type of document used (e.g., enter "military ID" for a military or military/dependent identification card). A statement such as "known customer" in box **d** is **not** sufficient for completion of Form 103. Enter in Item 14e the two-letter state postal code, two-letter country code, or the name of the issuer for that document, and enter in Item 14f the number shown on that official document.

Item 15. Customer account number.—Enter the account number which corresponds to the transaction being reported and which the casino has assigned to the person whose name is entered in Item 3. If the person has more than one account number affected by the transaction, enter the account number that corresponds to the majority of currency being reported.

If the transaction does not involve an account number, enter "NOT APPLICABLE" in the space.

Section B. Individual(s) Conducting Transaction(s) – If Other Than Above (Agent)
Complete Section B if an individual conducts a transaction on behalf of another person(s) listed in Section A. If an individual conducts a transaction on his/her own behalf, leave Section B BLANK.

Item 16. Multiple agents.—If, during a gaming day, more than one individual conducts transactions on behalf of an individual or organization listed in Section A, check this box and complete Section B. List one of the individuals on the front of the form and the other individual(s) on page 2, Section B. Attach additional sheets as necessary.

Items 17, 18, and 19. Name of individual.— Enter the individual's last name in Item 17, first name in Item 18, and middle initial in Item 19. If there is no middle initial, leave Item 19 BLANK. For example, if John Doe, an employee of the Error Free Rock Band, cashes an $11,000 check for the band, Error Free Rock Band is identified in Section A, and John Doe is identified in Section B.

Items 20, 22, 23, 24, and 25. Address.— Enter the permanent street address, including ZIP code, of the individual conducting the transaction. If the individual is from a foreign country, enter any province name and the appropriate two-letter country code.

Item 21. Social security number (SSN).—
Enter the SSN of the individual identified in Items 17 through 19. If that individual is a nonresident alien who does not have an SSN, enter "NONE" in the space.

Item 26. Date of birth.—Enter the individual's date of birth. For proper format, see the instructions under **Item 12** above.

Item 27. Method used to verify identity.—Any individual listed in Items 17 through 19 must present an official document to verify his/her name and address. See the instructions under **Item 13** above for more information. After completing Item 27, you must also complete Item 28.

Item 28. Describe identification credential.—Describe the identification credential used to verify the individual's name and address. See the instructions under **Item 14** above for more information.

Part II. Amount and Type of Transaction(s)
Part II identifies the type of transaction(s) reported and the amount(s) involved. You must complete all items that apply.

Item 29. Multiple transactions.—Check this box if multiple currency transactions, none of which individually exceeds $10,000, comprise this report.

Items 30 and 31. Cash in and cash out.— Enter in the appropriate spaces provided in Items 30 and/or 31, the specific currency amount for each "type of transaction" for a reportable Cash In or Cash Out. If the casino engages in a Cash In or a Cash Out transaction that is not listed in Items 30a through 30g

FinCEN Form 103 (Rev. 3-03) Page 4

or Items 31a through 31i, specify the type of transaction and the amount of currency in Item 30h or 31j, respectively. Enter the total amount of the reportable Cash In transaction(s) in Item 30i. Enter the total amount of the reportable Cash Out transaction(s) in Item 31k.

If less than a full dollar amount is involved increase the figure to the next higher dollar. For example, if the currency total is $20,500.25, show it as $20,501.00.

If there is a currency exchange, list it separately with both the Cash In and Cash Out totals. If foreign currency is exchanged, use the U.S. dollar equivalent on the day of the transaction.

Payment(s) on credit, Item 30c, includes all forms of cash payments made by a customer on a credit account or line of credit, or in redemption of markers or counter checks. Currency received from wire transfer(s) out, Item 30e, applies to cash received from a customer when the casino sends a wire transfer on behalf of a customer.

Currency paid from wire transfer(s) in, Item 31e, applies to cash paid to a customer when the casino receives a wire transfer on behalf of a customer. Travel and complimentary expenses and gaming incentives, Item 31h, includes reimbursements for a customer's travel and entertainment expenses and cash complementaries ("comps").

Determining Whether Transactions Meet The Reporting Threshold

Only cash transactions that, alone or when aggregated, exceed $10,000 should be reported on Form 103. A casino must report multiple currency transactions when it has knowledge that such transactions have occurred. This includes knowledge gathered through examination of books, records, logs, information retained on magnetic disk, tape or other machine-readable media, or in any manual system, and similar documents and information that the casino maintains pursuant to any law or regulation or within the ordinary course of its business.

Cash In and Cash Out transactions for the same customer are to be aggregated separately and must not be offset against one another. If there are both Cash In and Cash Out transactions which **each** exceed $10,000, enter the amounts in Items 30 and 31 and report on a single Form 103.

Example 1. Person A purchases $11,000 in chips with currency (one Cash In entry); and later receives currency from a $6,000 redemption of chips and a $2,000 slot jackpot win (two Cash Out entries). Complete Form 103 as follows:

Cash In of "$11,000" is entered in Item 30a (purchase of chips) and Cash In Total of "$11,000" is entered in Item 30i. No entry is made for Cash Out. The two Cash Out transactions equal only $8,000, which does not meet the BSA reporting threshold.

Example 2. Person B deposits $5,000 in currency to his front money account and pays $10,000 in currency to pay off an outstanding credit balance (two Cash In entries); receives $7,000 in currency from a wire transfer (one Cash Out entry); and presents $2,000 in small denomination U.S. currency to be exchanged for an equal amount in U.S. $100 bills. Complete Form 103 as follows:

Cash In of "$5,000" is entered in Item 30b (deposit), "$10,000" is entered in Item 30c (payment on credit), "$2,000" is entered in Item 30g (currency exchange), and Cash In Total of "$17,000" is entered in Item 30i. In determining whether the transactions are reportable, the currency exchange is aggregated with both the Cash In and the Cash Out amounts. The result is a reportable $17,000 Cash In transaction. No entry is made for Cash Out. The total Cash Out amount only equals $9,000, which does not meet the BSA reporting threshold.

Example 3. Person C deposits $7,000 in currency to his front money account and pays $9,000 in currency to pay off an outstanding credit balance (two Cash In entries); receives $2,500 in currency from a withdrawal from a safekeeping account, $2,500 in currency from a wire transfer and cashes a personal check of $7,500 (three Cash Out entries); and presents Canadian dollars which are exchanged for $1,500 in U.S. dollar equivalent. Complete Form 103 as follows:

Cash In of "$7,000" is entered in Item 30b (deposit), "$9,000" is entered in Item 30c (payment on credit), "$1,500" is entered in Item 30g (currency exchange), and a Cash In total of "$17,500" is entered in Item 30i. Cash Out of "$2,500" is entered in Item 31b (withdrawal of deposit), "$2,500" is entered in Item 31e (wire transfer), "$7,500" is entered in Item 31f (negotiable instrument cashed), "$1,500" is entered in Item 31g (currency exchange) and a Cash Out Total of "$14,000" is entered in Item 31k. In this example, both the Cash In and Cash Out totals exceed $10,000, and each must be reflected on Form 103.

Example 4. Person D purchases $10,000 in chips with currency and places a $10,000 cash bet (two Cash In entries); and later receives currency for an $18,000 redemption of chips and $20,000 from a payment on a cash bet (two Cash Out entries). Complete Form 103 as follows:

Cash In of "$10,000" is entered in Items 30a and 30d and a Cash In total of "$20,000" is entered in Item 30i. Cash Out of "$18,000" is entered in Item 31a (redemption of chips), "$20,000" is entered in Item 31d (payment on bets) and a Cash Out Total of "$38,000" is entered in Item 31k. In this example, both the Cash In and Cash Out totals exceed $10,000, and each must be reflected on Form 103.

Item 32. Date of transaction.—Enter the gaming day on which the transaction occurred (see **What To File** above). For proper format, see the instructions for**Item 12** above.

Item 33. Foreign currency.—If foreign currency is involved, identify the country of issuance by entering the appropriate two-letter country code. If multiple foreign currencies are involved, identify the country for which the largest amount in U.S. dollars is exchanged.

Part III. Casino Reporting Transaction(s)

Item 34. Casino's trade name.—Enter the name by which the casino does business and is commonly known. Do not enter a corporate, partnership, or other entity name, unless such name is the one by which the casino is commonly known.

Item 35. Casino's legal name.—Enter the legal name as shown on required tax filings, only if different from the trade name shown in Item 34. This name will be defined as the name indicated on a charter or other document creating the entity, and which is identified with the casino's established EIN.

Item 36. Employer identification number (EIN).—Enter the casino's EIN.

Items 37, 38, 39, and 40. Address.—Enter the street address, city, state, and ZIP code of the casino (or branch) where the transaction occurred. **Do not** use a P.O. box number.

Items 41 and 42. Title and signature of approving official.—The official who is authorized to review and approve Form 103 must indicate his/her title and sign the form.

Item 43. Date the form is signed.—The approving official must enter the date the Form 103 is signed. For proper format, see the instructions for **Item 12** above.
Item 44. Preparer's name.—Type or print the full name of the individual preparing Form 103. The preparer and the approving official may be different individuals.

Items 45 and 46. Contact person/telephone number.—Type or print the name and commercial telephone number of a responsible individual to contact concerning any questions about this Form 103.

Paperwork Reduction Act Notice.—The requested information is useful in criminal, tax, and regulatory investigations and proceedings. Financial institutions are required to provide the information under 31 U.S.C. 5313 and 31 CFR Part 103, commonly referred to as the Bank Secrecy Act (BSA).

The BSA is administered by the U.S. Department of the Treasury's Financial Crimes Enforcement Network (FinCEN). You are not required to provide the requested information unless a form displays a valid OMB control number. The time needed to complete this form will vary depending on individual circumstances. The estimated average time is 19 minutes. Send comments regarding this burden estimate, including suggestions for reducing the burden, to the Office of Management and Budget, Paperwork Reduction Project, Washington, DC 20503 and to the Financial Crimes Enforcement Network, Attn.: Paperwork Reduction Act, P.O. Box 39, Vienna VA 22183-0039.

TD F 90-22.56
Treasury Form
October 2002

Suspicious Activity Report by Money Services Business

▶ Please type or print. Always complete entire report (see instructions).

OMB No. 1506-0015

1 Check the box if this report corrects a prior report. (See instructions, page 7) ☐

2 Type of filer (check **all** financial services/products offered)
- a ☐ Issuer of money order(s)
- b ☐ Redeemer of money order(s)
- c ☐ Seller of money order(s)
- d ☐ Issuer of traveler's check(s)
- e ☐ Redeemer of traveler's check(s)
- f ☐ Seller of traveler's check(s)
- g ☐ Money transmitter
- h ☐ U.S. Postal Service (see instructions)
- i ☐ Other _____

Part I — Subject Information

3 ☐ Multiple subjects (See instructions, page 7)

4 Subject type (check only one box)
- a ☐ Purchaser/Sender
- b ☐ Payee/Receiver
- c ☐ Both ("a" & "b")
- d ☐ Other

5* Individual's last name or Entity's full name

6* First name

7* Middle initial

8* Address

9* City

10* State

11* Zip code

12* Country (if not U.S.)

13* Government issued identification (if available)
- a ☐ Driver's license/State I.D.
- b ☐ Passport
- c ☐ Alien registration
- d ☐ Other _____
- e Number
- f Issuing state or country _____

14* SSN/ITIN (individual) or EIN (entity)

15 Date of birth __/__/____ MM DD YYYY

16 Phone number (include area code)

17 Vehicle Lic.# / State (Optional)
  a number   b state

18 Customer number, if any

19 Occupation/Type of business

20* Endorser's (individual or Entity) name, if any

21* Bank account number of endorser, if any

22* Bank of first deposit, if any

Part II — Suspicious Instrument/Money Transfer Information

23 Financial services involved in suspicious transaction(s) (Check **all** that apply.)
- a ☐ Money Order
- b ☐ Traveler's Check
- c ☐ Money Transfer
- d ☐ Other _____

24* Date or date range of suspicious activity
From __/__/____ To __/__/____
    MM DD YYYY   MM DD YYYY

25 Total dollar amount involved in suspicious activity
$ _____.00

26.1* Serial number(s) of [a] money order(s) ☐ or [b] traveler's check(s) ☐ c Issuer name _____
d Starting No. _____ e Ending No. _____

26.2 Serial number(s) of [a] money order(s) ☐ or [b] traveler's check(s) ☐ c Issuer name _____
d Starting No. _____ e Ending No. _____

26.3 Serial number(s) of [a] money order(s) ☐ or [b] traveler's check(s) ☐ c Issuer name _____
d Starting No. _____ e Ending No. _____

27.1* Money transfer number
  a Issuer name _____
  b No. _____

27.2 Money transfer number
  a Issuer name _____
  b No. _____

Catalog No. 34944N

27.3 Money transfer number	27.4 Money transfer number
a Issuer name _____	a Issuer name _____
b No. ┆ ┆ ┆ ┆ ┆ ┆ ┆ ┆ ┆ ┆ ┆ ┆ ┆ ┆ ┆	b No. ┆ ┆ ┆ ┆ ┆ ┆ ┆ ┆ ┆ ┆ ┆ ┆ ┆ ┆ ┆
27.5 Money transfer number	27.6 Money transfer number
a Issuer name _____	a Issuer name _____
b No. ┆ ┆ ┆ ┆ ┆ ┆ ┆ ┆ ┆ ┆ ┆ ┆ ┆ ┆ ┆	b No. ┆ ┆ ┆ ┆ ┆ ┆ ┆ ┆ ┆ ┆ ┆ ┆ ┆ ┆ ┆

28* Category of suspicious activity (Check **all** that apply.)
  a ☐ Money laundering   b ☐ Structuring   c ☐ Terrorist financing   d ☐ Other (specify)_____

29* Character of suspicious activity (check only one box "a, b, or c", then check **all** of (1) through (9) that apply)
  a ☐ Unusual use of money order(s) or traveler's check(s)   b ☐ Unusual use of money transfer(s)   c ☐ Both
  Check all of the following that apply
  (1) ☐ Alters transaction to avoid completion of funds transfer record or money order or traveler's check record ($3,000 or more)
  (2) ☐ Alters transaction to avoid filing a CTR form ($10,000 or more)
  (3) ☐ Comes in frequently and purchases less than $3,000
  (4) ☐ Changes spelling or arrangement of name
  (5) ☐ Individual(s) using multiple or false identification documents
  (6) ☐ Two or more individuals using the similar/same identification
  (7) ☐ Two or more individuals working together
  (8) ☐ Same individual(s) using multiple locations over a short time period
  (9) ☐ Offers a bribe in the form of a tip/gratuity

Part III — Transaction Location Information

30 ☐ Multiple selling and/or paying business locations

31 Type of business location (check only one box)
  a ☐ Selling business location   b ☐ Paying business location   c ☐ Both

32* Legal name of business

33 Doing business as

34* Permanent address (number, street, and suite no.)

35* City

36* State   37* Zip code

38* EIN (entity) or SSN/ITIN (individual)

39* Business phone number (include area code)

40 Country (if not U.S.)

Part IV — Law Enforcement Agency Information

41 If a law enforcement agency has already been contacted (excluding submission of a SAR-MSB), check **the** appropriate box.
  a ☐ DEA   d ☐ U.S. Customs Service   g ☐ Other Federal   i ☐ Local law enforcement
  b ☐ FBI   e ☐ U.S. Postal Inspection Service h ☐ State law enforcement j ☐ Tribal law enforcement
  c ☐ IRS   f ☐ U.S. Secret Service
  Include agency name when box g, h, i, or j is checked _____

42 Name of person contacted at law enforcement agency

43 Phone number (include area code)

44 Date contacted   MM/DD/YYYY

Part V — Reporting Business Information (if *different* from Location Information in Part III)

45* Legal name of business

46 Doing business as

47* Permanent address (number, street, and suite no.)

48* City

49* State   50* Zip code

51* EIN (entity) or SSN/ITIN (individual)

52* Business phone number (include area code)

53 Country (if not U.S.)

Part VI — Contact for Assistance

54* Last name of individual to be contacted regarding this report

55* First name

56 Middle initial

57* Title/Position

58* Work phone number (include area code)

59 Date report prepared   MM/DD/YYYY

Paperwork Reduction Act Notice: The purpose of this form is to provide an effective means for a money services business (MSB) to notify appropriate law enforcement agencies of suspicious transactions and activities that occur by, through, or at a MSB. This report is authorized by law, pursuant to authority contained in 31 U.S.C. 5318(g). Information collected on this report is confidential (31 U.S.C. 5318(g)). Federal regulatory agencies, State law enforcement agencies, the U.S. Departments of Justice and Treasury, and other authorized authorities may use and share this information. Public reporting and recordkeeping burden for this form is estimated to average 35 minutes per response, and includes time to gather and maintain information for the required report, review the instructions, and complete the information collection. Send comments regarding this burden estimate, including suggestions for reducing the burden, to the Office of Management and the Budget, Paperwork Reduction Project, Washington, DC 20503 **and** to the Financial Crimes Enforcement Network, Attn.: Paperwork Reduction Act. P.O. Box 39, Vienna VA 22183-0039. The agency may not conduct or sponsor, and an organization (or a person) is not required to respond to, a collection of information unless it displays a currently valid OMB control number.

Part VII — Suspicious Activity Information - Narrative*

Explanation/description of suspicious activity. This section of the report is <u>critical</u>. The care with which it is completed <u>may determine whether or not the described activity and its possible criminal nature are clearly understood by investigators</u>. Provide a clear, complete and chronological description of the activity, including what is unusual, irregular or suspicious about the transaction(s). Use the checklist below, <u>as a guide,</u> as you prepare your description. The description should cover the material indicated in Parts I, II and III, but the money services business (MSB) should describe any other information that it believes is necessary to better enable investigators to understand the suspicious activity being reported.

a. **Describe** conduct that raised suspicion.
b. **Explain** whether the transaction(s) was completed or only attempted.
c. **Describe** supporting documentation and retain such documentation for your file for five years.
d. **Indicate** a time period, if it was a factor in the suspicious transaction(s), for example, specify the time and whether it occurred during AM or PM. If the activity covers more than one day, identify the time of day when such activity occurred most frequently.
e. **Retain** any admission or explanation of the transaction(s) provided by the subject(s), or other persons. Indicate when and to whom it was given.
f. **Retain** any evidence of cover-up or evidence of an attempt to deceive federal or state examiners, or others.
g. **Indicate** where the possible violation of law(s) took place (e.g., main office, branch, agent location, etc.).
h. **Indicate** whether the suspicious activity is an isolated incident or relates to another transaction.
i. **Indicate** for a foreign national any available information on subject's passport(s), visa(s), and/or identification card(s). Include date, country, city of issue, issuing authority, and nationality.
j. **Indicate** whether any information has been excluded from this report; if so, state reasons.
k. **Indicate** whether any U.S. or foreign instrument(s) were involved. If so, provide the amount, name of currency, and country of origin.

l. **Indicate** whether any transfer of money to or from a foreign country, or any exchanges of a foreign currency were involved. If so, identify the currency, country, and sources and destinations of money.
m. **Indicate** any additional account number(s), and any foreign bank(s) account numbers which may be involved in transfer of money.
n. **Identify** any employee or other individual or entity (e.g., agent) suspected of improper involvement in the transaction(s).
o. **For issuers, indicate** if the endorser of money order(s) and/or traveler's check(s) is different than payee. If so, provide the individual's name or entity name; bank's name, city, state and country; ABA routing number; endorser's bank account number; foreign non-bank name (if any); correspondent bank name and account number (if any); etc.
p. **For selling or paying locations, indicate** if there is a video recording medium or surveillance photograph of the customer.
q. **For selling or paying locations,** if you do not have a record of a government issued identification document, <u>describe</u> the type, issuer and number of any alternate identification that is available (e.g., for a credit card specify the name of the customer and credit card number.)
r. **For selling or paying locations, describe** the subject(s) if you do not have the identifying information in Part I or if multiple individuals use the same identification. Use descriptors such as male, female, age, etc.
s. <u>If correcting a prior report, complete the form in its entirety and note the changes here in Part VII.</u>

Information already provided in earlier Parts of this form need not necessarily be repeated if the meaning is clear.

Supporting documentation should not be filed with this report. <u>Maintain the information for your files.</u>

Enter explanation/description in the space below. If necessary, continue the narrative on a duplicate of this page or a blank page.

FinCEN Form 104
(Formerly Form 4789)
(Eff. December 2003)
Department of the Treasury
FinCEN

Currency Transaction Report

▶ Previous editions will not be accepted after August 31, 2004.

▶ Please type or print.

(Complete all parts that apply--See Instructions)

OMB No. 1506-0004

1. Check all box(es) that apply: a ☐ Amends prior report   b ☐ Multiple persons   c ☐ Multiple transactions

Part I — Person(s) Involved in Transaction(s)

Section A--Person(s) on Whose Behalf Transaction(s) Is Conducted

2. Individual's last name or entity's name
3. First name
4. Middle initial
5. Doing business as (DBA)
6. SSN or EIN
7. Address (number, street, and apt. or suite no.)
8. Date of birth __/__/____ MM DD YYYY
9. City
10. State
11. ZIP code
12. Country code (if not U.S.)
13. Occupation, profession, or business
14. If an individual, describe method used to verify identity: a ☐ Driver's license/State I.D.   b ☐ Passport   c ☐ Alien registration
    d ☐ Other _____   e Issued by: _____   f Number: _____

Section B--Individual(s) Conducting Transaction(s) (if other than above).

If Section B is left blank or incomplete, check the box(es) below to indicate the reason(s)

a ☐ Armored Car Service   b ☐ Mail Deposit or Shipment   c ☐ Night Deposit or Automated Teller Machine   d ☐ Multiple Transactions   e ☐ Conducted On Own Behalf

15. Individual's last name
16. First name
17. Middle initial
18. Address (number, street, and apt. or suite no.)
19. SSN
20. City
21. State
22. ZIP code
23. Country code (If not U.S.)
24. Date of birth __/__/____ MM DD YYYY
25. If an individual, describe method used to verify identity: a ☐ Driver's license/State I.D.   b ☐ Passport   c ☐ Alien registration
    d ☐ Other _____   e Issued by: _____   f Number: _____

Part II — Amount and Type of Transaction(s). Check all boxes that apply.

26. Total cash in $ _____ .00
27. Total cash out $ _____ .00
28. Date of transaction __/__/____ MM DD YYYY
26a. Foreign cash in _____ .00 (see instructions, page 3)
27a. Foreign cash out _____ .00 (see instructions, page 3)
29. ☐ Foreign Country _____
30. ☐ Wire Transfer(s)
31. ☐ Negotiable Instrument(s) Purchased
32. ☐ Negotiable Instrument(s) Cashed
33. ☐ Currency Exchange(s)
34. ☐ Deposit(s)/Withdrawal(s)
35. ☐ Account Number(s) Affected (if any): _____
36. ☐ Other (specify) _____

Part III — Financial Institution Where Transaction(s) Takes Place

37. Name of financial institution
    Enter Regulator or BSA Examiner code number ▶ (see instructions)
38. Address (number, street, and apt. or suite no.)
39. EIN or SSN
40. City
41. State
42. ZIP code
43. Routing (MICR) number

Sign Here ▶

44. Title of approving official
45. Signature of approving official
46. Date of signature __/__/____ MM DD YYYY
47. Type or print preparer's name
48. Type or print name of person to contact
49. Telephone number (___) ___ - ____

▶ For Paperwork Reduction Act Notice, see page 4.   Cat. No. 37683N   FinCEN Form 104 (Formerly Form 4789) (Rev. 8-03)

FinCEN Form 104 (formerly Form 4789) (Rev. 8-03)   Page 2

Multiple Persons
Complete applicable parts below if box 1b on page 1 is checked

Part I Person(s) Involved in Transaction(s)

Section A--Person(s) on Whose Behalf Transaction(s) Is Conducted

2 Individual's last name or entity's name | 3 First name | 4 Middle initial

5 Doing business as (DBA) | 6 SSN or EIN

7 Address (number, street, and apt. or suite no.) | 8 Date of birth ___/___/_____ MM DD YYYY

9 City | 10 State | 11 ZIP code | 12 Country code (if not U.S.) | 13 Occupation, profession, or business

14 If an individual, describe method used to verify identity: a ☐ Driver's license/State I.D. b ☐ Passport c ☐ Alien registration
   d ☐ Other _____ e Issued by: _____ f Number: _____

Section B--Individual(s) Conducting Transaction(s) (if other than above).

15 Individual's last name | 16 First name | 17 Middle initial

18 Address (number, street, and apt. or suite no.) | 19 SSN

20 City | 21 State | 22 ZIP code | 23 Country code (if not U.S.) | 24 Date of birth ___/___/_____ MM DD YYYY

25 If an individual, describe method used to verify identity: a ☐ Driver's license/State I.D. b ☐ Passport c ☐ Alien registration
   d ☐ Other _____ e Issued by: _____ f Number: _____

Part I Person(s) Involved in Transaction(s)

Section A--Person(s) on Whose Behalf Transaction(s) Is Conducted

2 Individual's last name or entity's name | 3 First name | 4 Middle initial

5 Doing business as (DBA) | 6 SSN or EIN

7 Address (number, street, and apt. or suite no.) | 8 Date of birth ___/___/_____ MM DD YYYY

9 City | 10 State | 11 ZIP code | 12 Country code (if not U.S.) | 13 Occupation, profession, or business

14 If an individual, describe method used to verify identity: a ☐ Driver's license/State I.D. b ☐ Passport c ☐ Alien registration
   d ☐ Other _____ e Issued by: _____ f Number: _____

Section B--Individual(s) Conducting Transaction(s) (if other than above).

15 Individual's last name | 16 First name | 17 Middle initial

18 Address (number, street, and apt. or suite no.) | 19 SSN

20 City | 21 State | 22 ZIP code | 23 Country code (if not U.S.) | 24 Date of birth ___/___/_____ MM DD YYYY

25 If an individual, describe method used to verify identity: a ☐ Driver's license/State I.D. b ☐ Passport c ☐ Alien registration
   d ☐ Other _____ e Issued by: _____ f Number: _____

FinCEN Form 104 (Formerly Form 4789) (Rev. 8-03)   Page 3

Suspicious Transactions

This Currency Transaction Report (CTR) should NOT be filed for suspicious transactions involving $10,000 or less in currency OR to note that a transaction of more than $10,000 is suspicious. Any suspicious or unusual activity should be reported by a financial institution in the manner prescribed by its appropriate federal regulator or BSA examiner. (See the instructions for Item 37.) If a transaction is suspicious and in excess of $10,000 in currency, then both a CTR and the appropriate Suspicious Activity Report form must be filed.

Should the suspicious activity require immediate attention, financial institutions should telephone 1-800-800-CTRS. An Internal Revenue Service (IRS) employee will direct the call to the local office of the IRS Criminal Investigation Division (CI). This toll-free number is operational Monday through Friday, from approximately 9:00 am to 6:00 pm Eastern Standard Time. If an emergency, consult directory assistance for the local IRS CID Office.

General Instructions

Who Must File. Each financial institution (other than a casino, which instead must file FinCEN Form 103, and the U.S. Postal Service for which there are separate rules) must file FinCEN Form 104 (formerly 4789) (CTR) for each deposit, withdrawal, exchange of currency, or other payment or transfer, by, through, or to the financial institution which involves a transaction in currency of more than $10,000. Multiple transactions must be treated as a single transaction if the financial institution has knowledge that (1) they are by or on behalf of the same person, and (2) they result in either currency received (Cash In) or currency disbursed (Cash Out) by the financial institution totaling more than $10,000 during any one business day. For a bank, a business day is the day on which transactions are routinely posted to customers' accounts, as normally communicated to depository customers. For all other financial institutions, a business day is a calendar day.

Generally, financial institutions are defined as banks, other types of depository institutions, brokers or dealers in securities, money transmitters, currency exchangers, check cashers, and issuers and sellers of money orders and traveler's checks. Should you have questions, see the definitions in 31 CFR Part 103.

When and Where To File. File this CTR by the 15th calendar day after the day of the transaction with the:

IRS Detroit Computing Center
ATTN: CTR
P.O. Box 33604
Detroit, MI 48232-5604

Keep a copy of each CTR for five years from the date filed.

A financial institution may apply to file the CTRs magnetically. To obtain an application to file magnetically, write to the:

IRS Detroit Computing Center
ATTN: CTR Magnetic Media Coordinator
P.O. Box 33604
Detroit, MI 48232-5604

Identification Requirements. All individuals (except employees of armored car services) conducting a reportable transaction(s) for themselves or for another person, must be identified by means of an official document(s). Acceptable forms of identification include a driver's license, military and military/dependent identification cards, passport, state issued identification card, cedular card (foreign), non-resident alien identification cards, or any other identification document or documents, which contain name and preferably address and a photograph and are normally acceptable by financial institutions as a means of identification when cashing checks for persons other than established customers.

Acceptable identification information obtained previously and maintained in the financial institution's records may be used. For example, if documents verifying an individual's identity were examined and recorded on a signature card when an account was opened, the financial institution may rely on that information. In completing the CTR, the financial institution must indicate on the form the method, type, and number of the identification. Statements such as "known customer" or "signature card on file" are not sufficient for form completion.

Penalties. Civil and criminal penalties are provided for failure to file a CTR or to supply information or for filing a false or fraudulent CTR. See 31 U.S.C. 5321, 5322 and 5324.

For purposes of this CTR, the terms below have the following meanings:

Currency. The coin and paper money of the United States or any other country, which is circulated and customarily used and accepted as money.

Person. An individual, corporation, partnership, trust or estate, joint stock company, association, syndicate, joint venture or other unincorporated organization or group.

Organization. Entity other than an individual.

Transaction in Currency. The **physical** transfer of currency from one person to another. This does not include a transfer of funds by means of bank check, bank draft, wire transfer or other written order that does not involve the physical transfer of currency.

Negotiable Instruments. All checks and drafts (including business, personal, bank, cashier's and third-party), money orders, and promissory notes. For purposes of this CTR, all traveler's checks shall also be considered negotiable instruments whether or not they are in bearer form.

Foreign exchange rates. If completing items 26a/27a, use the exchange rate in effect for the business day of the transaction. The source of the exchange rate that is used will be determined by the reporting institution.

Specific Instructions

Because of the limited space on the front and back of the CTR, it may be necessary to submit additional information on attached sheets. Submit this additional information on plain paper attached to the CTR. Be sure to put the individual's or entity's name and identifying number (items 2, 3, 4, and 6 of the CTR) on any additional sheets so that if it becomes separated, it may be associated with the CTR.

Item 1a. Amends Prior Report. If this CTR is being filed because it amends a report filed previously, check Item 1a. Staple a copy of the original CTR to the amended one, complete Part III fully and only those other entries which are being amended.

Item 1b. Multiple Persons. If this transaction is being conducted by more than one person or on behalf of more than one person, check Item 1b. Enter information in Part I for one of the persons and provide information on any other persons on the back of the CTR.

Item 1c. Multiple Transactions. If the financial institution has knowledge that there are multiple transactions, check Item 1c.

PART I - Person(s) Involved in Transaction(s)

Section A **must** be completed. If an individual conducts a transaction on his own behalf, complete Section A and leave Section "B" BLANK. If an individual conducts a transaction on his own behalf and on behalf of another person(s), complete Section "A" for each person and leave Section "B" BLANK. If an individual conducts a transaction on behalf of another person(s), complete Section "B" for the individual conducting the transaction, and complete Section "A" for each person on whose behalf the transaction is conducted of whom the financial institution has knowledge.

Section A. Person(s) on Whose Behalf Transaction(s) Is Conducted. See instructions above.

Items 2, 3, and 4. Individual/Organization Name. If the person on whose behalf the transaction(s) is conducted is an individual, put his/her last name in Item 2, first name in Item 3, and middle initial in Item 4. If there is no middle initial, leave item 4 BLANK. If the transaction is conducted on behalf of an entity, put its name in Item 2 and leave Items 3 and 4 BLANK.

Item 5. Doing Business As (DBA). If the financial institution has knowledge of a separate "doing business as" name, enter it in Item 5. For example, Smith Enterprise DBA MJ's Pizza.

Item 6. SSN/ITIN or EIN. Enter the Social Security Number (SSN) or Individual Taxpayer Identification Number (ITIN) or Employer Identification Number (EIN) of the person or entity identified in Item 2. If none, write NONE.

Items 7, 9, 10, 11, and 12. Address. Enter the permanent address including ZIP Code of the person identified in Item 2. Use the U.S. Postal Service's two letter state abbreviation code. A P. O. Box should not be used by itself, and may only be used if there is no street address. If a P. O. Box is used, the name of the apartment or suite number, road or route number where the person resides must also be provided. If the address is outside the U.S., provide the street address, city, province or state, postal code (if known), and the two letter country code. For country code list go to www.fincen.gov/reg_bsaforms.html or telephone 1-800-949-2732 and select option number 5. If U.S., leave item 12 blank.

Item 8. Date of Birth. Enter the date of birth. Eight numerals must be inserted for each date. The first two will reflect the month, the second two the day, and the last four the year. A zero (0) should precede any single digit number. For example, if an individual's birth date is April 3 1948, Item 8 should read 04 03 1948.

Item 13. Occupation, Profession, or Business. Identify the occupation, profession, or business of the person on whose behalf the transaction was conducted. For example: secretary, shoe salesman, carpenter, attorney, housewife, restaurant, liquor store,etc. Do not use non-specific terms such as merchant, self-employed, businessman, etc.

Item 14. If an Individual, Describe Method Used To Verify Identity. If an individual conducts the transaction(s) on his/her own behalf, his/her identity must be verified by examination of an acceptable document (see **General Instructions**). For example, check box **a** if a driver's license is used to verify an individual's identity, and enter the state that issued the license and the number in items **e** and **f**. If the transaction is conducted by an individual on behalf of another individual not present or on behalf of an entity, enter N/A in Item 14.

Section B. Individual(s) Conducting Transaction(s) (if other than above). Financial institutions should enter as much information as is available.

FinCEN Form 104 (Formerly 4789) (Rev. 8-03)

However, there may be instances in which Items 15-25 may be left BLANK or incomplete. If Items 15-25 are left BLANK or incomplete, check one or more of the boxes provided to indicate the reasons.

Example: If there are multiple transactions that, if only when aggregated, the financial institution has knowledge the transactions exceed the reporting threshold, and therefore, did not identify the transactor(s), check box **d** for Multiple Transactions.

Items 15, 16, and 17. Individual's Name. Complete these items if an individual conducts a transaction(s) on behalf of another person. For example, if John Doe, an employee of XYZ Grocery Store, makes a deposit to the store's account, XYZ Grocery Store should be identified in Section A and John Doe should be identified in section B.

Items 18, 20, 21, 22, and 23. Address. Enter the permanent street address including ZIP Code of the individual. (See the instructions for Items 7 and 9 through 12.) Enter country code if not U.S. (Reference item 12).

Item 19. SSN/ITIN. If the individual has a Social Security Number, or Individual Taxpayer Indentification Number, enter it in Item 19. If the individual does not have an SSN/ITIN, enter NONE.

Item 24. Date of Birth. Enter the individual's date of birth. (See the instructions for Item 8.)

Item 25. If an Individual, Describe Method Used To Verify Identity. Enter the method used to identify the individual's identity. (See **General Instructions** and the instructions for Item 14.)

PART II - Amount and Type of Transaction(s)
Complete Part II to identify the type of transaction(s) and the amount(s) involved.

Items 26 and 27. Total Cash In/Total Cash Out. In the spaces provided, enter the total amount of currency received (Total Cash In) or total currency disbursed (Total Cash Out) by the financial institution. If foreign currency is exchanged, use the U.S. dollar equivalent on the day of the transaction (See "Foreign exchange rates"), and complete item 26a or 27a, whichever is appropriate.

If less than a full dollar amount is involved, increase that figure to the next highest dollar. For example, if the currency totals $20,000.05, show the total as $20,001.00.

Items 26a and 27a. Foreign cash in/Foreign cash out. If foreign currency is exchanged, enter the amount of foreign currency in items 26a and 27a. Report country of origin in item 29.

Item 28. Date of Transaction. Insert eight numerals for each date. (See instructions for Item 8.)

Item 29. Foreign Country. If items 26a and/or 27a are completed indicating that foreign currency is involved, check Item 29 and identify the country. If multiple foreign currencies are involved, check box 36 and identify the additional country(s) and/or currency(s) involved.

Determining Whether Transactions Meet the Reporting Threshold.

Only cash transactions that, if alone or when aggregated, exceed $10,000 should be reported on the CTR. Transactions shall not be offset against one another.

If there are both Cash In and Cash Out transactions that are reportable, the amounts should be considered separately and not aggregated. However, they may be reported on a single CTR.

If there is a currency exchange, it should be aggregated separately with each of the Cash In and Cash Out totals.

Example 1: A person deposits $11,000 in currency to his savings account and withdraws $3,000 in currency from his checking account. The CTR should be completed as follows:
Cash In $11,000 and no entry for Cash Out. This is because the $3,000 transaction does not meet the reporting threshold.

Example 2: A person deposits $11,000 in currency to his savings account and withdraws $12,000 in currency from his checking account. The CTR should be completed as follows:
Cash In $11,000, Cash Out $12,000. This is because there are two reportable transactions. However, one CTR may be filed to reflect both.

Example 3: A person deposits $6,000 in currency to his savings account and withdraws $4,000 in currency from his checking account. Further, he presents $5,000 in currency to be exchanged for the equivalent in French Francs. The CTR should be completed as follows:
Cash In $11,000 and no entry for Cash Out. This is because in determining whether the transactions are reportable, the currency exchange is aggregated with each of the Cash In and Cash Out amounts. The result is a reportable $11,000 Cash In transaction. The total Cash Out amount is $9,000, which does not meet the reporting threshold. Therefore, it is not entered on the CTR.

Example 4: A person deposits $6,000 in currency to his savings account and withdraws $7,000 in currency from his checking account. Further, he presents $5,000 in currency to be exchanged for the equivalent in French francs. The CTR should be completed as follows:
Cash In $11,000, Cash Out $12,000. This is because in determining whether the transactions are reportable, the currency exchange is aggregated with each of the Cash In and Cash Out amounts. In this example, each of the Cash In and Cash Out totals exceed $10,000 and must be reflected on the CTR.

Items 30-33. Check the appropriate item(s) to identify the following type of transaction(s):
30. Wire Transfer(s)
31. Negotiable Instrument(s) Purchased
32. Negotiable Instrument(s) Cashed
33. Currency Exchange(s)

Item 34. Deposits/Withdrawals. Check this item to identify deposits to or withdrawals from accounts, e.g. demand deposit accounts, savings accounts, time deposits, mutual fund accounts, or any other account held at the financial institution. Enter the account number(s) in Item 35.

Item 35. Account Numbers Affected (if any). Enter the account numbers of any accounts affected by the transactions that are maintained at the financial institution conducting the transaction(s). If necessary, use additional sheets of paper to indicate all of the affected accounts.

Example 1: If a person cashes a check drawn on an account held at the financial institution, the CTR should be completed as follows:
Indicate negotiable instrument(s) cashed and provide the account number of the check.

If the transaction does not affect an account, make no entry.

Example 2: A person cashes a check drawn on another financial institution. In this instance, negotiable instrument(s) cashed would be indicated, but no account at the financial institution has been affected. Therefore, Item 35 should be left BLANK.

Item 36. Other (specify). If a transaction is not identified in Items 30-34, check Item 36 and provide an additional description. For example, a person presents a check to purchase "foreign currency." Also list multiple foreign currencies from item 29.

PART III - Financial Institution Where Transaction(s) Take Place

Item 37. Name of Financial Institution and Identity of Regulator or BSA Examiner. Enter the financial institution's full legal name and identify the regulator or BSA examiner, using the following codes:

Regulator or BSA Examiner	CODE
Comptroller of the Currency (OCC)	1
Federal Deposit Insurance Corporation (FDIC)	2
Federal Reserve System (FRS)	3
Office of Thrift Supervision (OTS)	4
National Credit Union Administration (NCUA)	5
Securities and Exchange Commission (SEC)	6
Internal Revenue Service (IRS)	7
U.S. Postal Service (USPS)	8
Commodity Futures Trading Commission (CFTC)	9
State Regulator	10

Items 38, 40, 41, and 42. Address. Enter the street address, city, state, and ZIP Code of the financial institution where the transaction occurred. If there are multiple transactions, provide information of the office or branch where any one of the transactions has occurred.

Item 39. EIN or SSN. Enter the financial institution's EIN. If the financial institution does not have an EIN, enter the SSN of the financial institution's principal owner.

Item 43. Routing (MICR) Number. If a depository institution, enter the routing (Magnetic Ink Character Recognition (MICR)) number.

SIGNATURE

Items 44 and 45. Title and signature of Approving Official. The official who reviews and approves the CTR must indicate his/her title and sign the CTR.

Item 46. Date of Signature. The approving official must enter the date the CTR is signed. (See the instructions for Item 8.)

Item 47. Preparer's Name. Type or print the full name of the individual preparing the CTR. The preparer and the approving official may not necessarily be the same individual.

Items 48 and 49. Contact Person/Telephone Number. Type or print the name and telephone number of an individual to contact concerning questions about the CTR.

Paperwork Reduction Act Notice. The requested information is useful in criminal, tax, and regulatory investigations and proceedings. Financial institutions are required to provide the information under 31 U.S.C. 5313 and 31 CFR Part 103, commonly referred to as the Bank Secrecy Act (BSA). The BSA is administered by the U.S. Department of the Treasury's Financial Crimes Enforcement Network (FinCEN). You are not required to provide the requested information unless a form displays a valid OMB control number.

The time needed to complete this form will vary depending on individual circumstances. The estimated average time is 19 minutes. If you have comments concerning the accuracy of this time estimate or suggestions for making this form simpler, you may write to the **Financial Crimes Enforcement Network, P. O. Box 39, Vienna, VA 22183. Do not** send this form to this office. Instead, see **When and Where to File** in the instructions.

DEPARTMENT OF THE TREASURY
FINANCIAL CRIMES ENFORCEMENT NETWORK

REPORT OF INTERNATIONAL TRANSPORTATION OF CURRENCY OR MONETARY INSTRUMENTS

FinCEN Form **105**
(Formerly Customs Form 4790)
(Rev. July 2003)
Department of the Treasury
FinCEN

OMB NO. 1506-0014

▶ To be filed with the Bureau of Customs and Border Protection
▶ For Paperwork Reduction Act Notice and Privacy Act Notice, see back of form.

31 U.S.C. 5316; 31 CFR 103.23 and 103.27

▶ Please type or print.

PART I — FOR A PERSON DEPARTING OR ENTERING THE UNITED STATES, OR A PERSON SHIPPING, MAILING, OR RECEIVING CURRENCY OR MONETARY INSTRUMENTS. (IF ACTING FOR ANYONE ELSE, ALSO COMPLETE PART II BELOW.)

1. NAME (Last or family, first, and middle)
2. IDENTIFICATION NO. (See instructions)
3. DATE OF BIRTH (Mo./Day/Yr.)
4. PERMANENT ADDRESS IN UNITED STATES OR ABROAD
5. YOUR COUNTRY OR COUNTRIES OF CITIZENSHIP
6. ADDRESS WHILE IN THE UNITED STATES
7. PASSPORT NO. & COUNTRY
8. U.S. VISA DATE (Mo./Day/Yr.)
9. PLACE UNITED STATES VISA WAS ISSUED
10. IMMIGRATION ALIEN NO.
11. IF CURRENCY OR MONETARY INSTRUMENT IS ACCOMPANIED BY A PERSON, COMPLETE 11a OR 11b

A. EXPORTED FROM THE UNITED STATES
Departed From: (U.S. Port/City in U.S.)
Arrived At: (Foreign City/Country)

B. IMPORTED INTO THE UNITED STATES
Departed From: (Foreign City/Country)
Arrived At: (City in U.S.)

12. IF CURRENCY OR MONETARY INSTRUMENT WAS MAILED OR OTHERWISE SHIPPED, COMPLETE 12a THROUGH 12f

12a. DATE SHIPPED (Mo./Day/Yr.)
12b. DATE RECEIVED (Mo./Day/Yr.)
12c. METHOD OF SHIPMENT (e.g. U.S. Mail, Public Carrier, etc.)
12d. NAME OF CARRIER

12e. SHIPPED TO (Name and Address)

12f. RECEIVED FROM (Name and Address)

PART II — INFORMATION ABOUT PERSON(S) OR BUSINESS ON WHOSE BEHALF IMPORTATION OR EXPORTATION WAS CONDUCTED

13. NAME (Last or family, first, and middle or Business Name)
14. PERMANENT ADDRESS IN UNITED STATES OR ABROAD
15. TYPE OF BUSINESS ACTIVITY, OCCUPATION, OR PROFESSION
15a. IS THE BUSINESS A BANK? ☐ Yes ☐ No

PART III — CURRENCY AND MONETARY INSTRUMENT INFORMATION (SEE INSTRUCTIONS ON REVERSE) (To be completed by everyone)

16. TYPE AND AMOUNT OF CURRENCY/MONETARY INSTRUMENTS

Currency and Coins ▶ $
Other Monetary Instruments (Specify type, issuing entity and date, and serial or other identifying number.) ▶ $
(TOTAL) ▶ $

17. IF OTHER THAN U.S. CURRENCY IS INVOLVED, PLEASE COMPLETE BLOCKS A AND B.
A. Currency Name
B. Country

PART IV — SIGNATURE OF PERSON COMPLETING THIS REPORT

Under penalties of perjury, I declare that I have examined this report, and to the best of my knowledge and belief it is true, correct and complete.

18. NAME AND TITLE (Print)
19. SIGNATURE
20. DATE OF REPORT (Mo./Day/Yr.)

CUSTOMS AND BORDER PROTECTION USE ONLY

| DATE | AIRLINE/FLIGHT/VESSEL | LICENSE PLATE STATE/COUNTRY | NUMBER |

COUNT VERIFIED   Yes ☐ No ☐
VOLUNTARY REPORT   Yes ☐ No ☐
INSPECTOR (Name and Badge Number)

FinCEN FORM 105
(Formerly Customs Form 4790)

GENERAL INSTRUCTIONS

This report is required by 31 U.S.C. 5316 and Treasury Department regulations (31 CFR 103).

WHO MUST FILE:

(1) Each person who physically transports, mails, or ships, or causes to be physically transported, mailed, or shipped currency or other monetary instruments in an aggregate amount exceeding $10,000 at one time from the United States to any place outside the United States or into the United States from any place outside the United States, and

(2) Each person who receives in the United States currency or other monetary instruments In an aggregate amount exceeding $10,000 at one time which have been transported, mailed, or shipped to the person from any place outside the United States.

A TRANSFER OF FUNDS THROUGH NORMAL BANKING PROCEDURES, WHICH DOES NOT INVOLVE THE PHYSICAL TRANSPORTATION OF CURRENCY OR MONETARY INSTRUMENTS, IS NOT REQUIRED TO BE REPORTED.

Exceptions: Reports are not required to be filed by:

(1) a Federal Reserve bank,

(2) a bank, a foreign bank, or a broker or dealer in securities in respect to currency or other monetary instruments mailed or shipped through the postal service or by common carrier,

(3) a commercial bank or trust company organized under the laws of any State or of the United States with respect to overland shipments of currency or monetary instruments shipped to or received from an established customer maintaining a deposit relationship with the bank, in amounts which the bank may reasonably conclude do not exceed amounts commensurate with the customary conduct of the business, industry, or profession of the customer concerned,

(4) a person who is not a citizen or resident of the United States in respect to currency or other monetary instruments mailed or shipped from abroad to a bank or broker or dealer in securities through the postal service or by common carrier,

(5) a common carrier of passengers in respect to currency or other monetary instruments in the possession of its passengers,

(6) a common carrier of goods in respect to shipments of currency or monetary instruments not declared to be such by the shipper,

(7) a travelers' check issuer or its agent in respect to the transportation of travelers' checks prior to their delivery to selling agents for eventual sale to the public,

(8) a person with a restrictively endorsed traveler's check that is in the collection and reconciliation process after the traveler's check has been negotiated, nor by

(9) a person engaged as a business in the transportation of currency, monetary instruments and other commercial papers with respect to the transportation of currency or other monetary instruments overland between established offices of banks or brokers or dealers in securities and foreign persons.

WHEN AND WHERE TO FILE:

A. Recipients—Each person who receives currency or other monetary instruments in the United States shall file FinCEN Form 105, within 15 days after receipt of the currency or monetary instruments, with the Customs officer in charge at any port of entry or departure or by mail with the **Commissioner of Customs, Attention: Currency Transportation Reports, Washington DC 20229.**

B. Shippers or Mailers—If the currency or other monetary instrument does not accompany the person entering or departing the United States, FinCEN Form 105 may be filed by mail on or before the date of entry, departure, mailing, or shipping with the **Commissioner of Customs, Attention: Currency Transportation Reports, Washington DC 20229.**

C. Travelers—Travelers carrying currency or other monetary instruments with them shall file FinCEN Form 105 at the time of entry into the United States or at the time of departure from the United States with the Customs officer in charge at any Customs port of entry or departure.

An additional report of a particular transportation, mailing, or shipping of currency or the monetary instruments is not required if a complete and truthful report has already been filed. However, no person otherwise required to file a report shall be excused from liability for failure to do so if, in fact, a complete and truthful report has not been filed. Forms may be obtained from any Bureau of Customs and Border Protection office.

PENALTIES: Civil and criminal penalties, including under certain circumstances a fine of not more than $500,000 and Imprisonment of not more than ten years, are provided for failure to file a report, filing a report containing a material omission or misstatement, or filing a false or fraudulent report. In addition, the currency or monetary instrument may be subject to seizure and forfeiture. See 31 U.S.C.5321 and 31 CFR 103.57; 31 U.S.C. 5322 and 31 CFR 103.59; 31 U.S.C. 5317 and 31 CFR 103.58, and U.S.C. 5332.

DEFINITIONS:

Bank—Each agent, agency, branch or office within the United States of any person doing business in one or more of the capacities listed: (1) a commercial bank or trust company organized under the laws of any State or of the United States; (2) a private bank; (3) a savings association, savings and loan association, and building and loan association organized under the laws of any State or of the United States; (4) an insured institution as defined in section 401 of the National Housing Act; (5) a savings bank, industrial bank or other thrift institution; (6) a credit union organized under the laws of any State or of the United States; (7) any other organization chartered under the banking laws of any State and subject to the supervision of the bank supervisory authorities of a State other than a money service business; (8) a bank organized under foreign law; and (9) any national banking association or corporation acting under the provisions of section 25A of the Federal Reserve Act (12 U.S.C. Sections 611-632).

Foreign Bank—A bank organized under foreign law, or an agency, branch or office located outside the United States of a bank. The term does not include an agent, agency, branch or office within the United States of a bank organized under foreign law.

Broker or Dealer in Securities—A broker or dealer in securities, registered or required to be registered with the Securities and Exchange Commission under the Securities Exchange Act of 1934.

Identification Number—Individuals must enter their social security number, if any. However, aliens who do not have a social security number should enter passport or alien registration number. All others should enter their employer identification number.

Monetary Instruments— (1) Coin or currency of the United States or of any other country, (2) traveler's checks in any form, (3) negotiable instruments (including checks, promissory notes, and money orders) in bearer form, endorsed without restriction, made out to a fictitious payee, or otherwise in such form that title thereto passes upon delivery, (4) incomplete instruments (including checks, promissory notes, and money orders) that are signed but on which the name of the payee has been omitted, and (5) securities or stock in bearer form or otherwise in such form that title thereto passes upon delivery. Monetary instruments do not include (i) checks or money orders made payable to the order of a named person which have not been endorsed or which bear restrictive endorsements, (ii) warehouse receipts, or (iii) bills of lading.

Person—An individual, a corporation, a partnership, a trust or estate, a joint stock company, an association, a syndicate, joint venture or other unincorporated organization or group, an Indian Tribe (as that term is defined in the Indian Gaming Regulatory Act), and all entities cognizable as legal personalities.

SPECIAL INSTRUCTIONS

You should complete each line that applies to you. **PART II.** -Block 13; provide the complete name of the shipper or recipient on whose behalf the exportation or importation was conducted. **PART III.** — Specify type of instrument, issuing entity, and date, serial or other identifying number, and payee (if any). **PART IV.** — Block 22A and 22B; enter the exact date you shipped or received currency or monetary instrument(s). Block 21, if currency or monetary instruments of more than one country is involved, attach a list showing each type, country or origin and amount.

PRIVACY ACT AND PAPERWORK REDUCTION ACT NOTICE:

Pursuant to the requirements of Public law 93-579 (Privacy Act of 1974), notice is hereby given that the authority to collect information on Form 4790 in accordance with 5 U.S.C. 552a(e)(3) is Public law 91-508; 31 U.S.C. 5316; 5 U.S.C. 301; Reorganization Plan No.1 of 1950; Treasury Department Order No. 165, revised, as amended; 31 CFR 103; and 44 U.S.C. 3501.

The principal purpose for collecting the information is to assure maintenance of reports or records having a high degree of usefulness in criminal, tax, or regulatory investigations or proceedings. The information collected may be provided to those officers and employees of the Bureau of Customs and Border Protection and any other constituent unit of the Department of the Treasury who have a need for the records in the performance of their duties. The records may be referred to any other department or agency of the Federal Government upon the request of the head of such department or agency. The information collected may also be provided to appropriate state, local, and foreign criminal law enforcement and regulatory personnel in the performance of their official duties.

Disclosure of this information is mandatory pursuant to 31 U.S.C. 5316 and 31 CFR Part 103 (See Penalities).

Disclosure of the social security number is mandatory. The authority to collect this number is 31 U.S.C. 5316(b) and 31 CFR 103.27(d). The social security number will be used as a means to identify the individual who files the record.

An agency may not conduct or sponsor, and a person is not required to respond to, a collection of information unless it displays a currently valid OMB control number. The collection of this information is mandatory pursuant to 31 U.S.C. 5316.

Statement required by 5 CFR 1320.8(b)(3)(iii): The estimated average burden associated with this collection of information is 11 minutes per respondent or record keeper depending on individual circumstances. Comments concerning the accuracy of this burden estimate and suggestions for reducing this burden should be directed to the Department of the Treasury, Financial Crimes Enforcement Network, P.O. Box 39 Vienna, Virginia 22183. **DO NOT send completed forms to this office—See When and Where To File above.**

FinCEN FORM 105
(Formerly Customs Form 4790)

| IRS Form **8300** (Rev. December 2001) OMB No. 1545-0892 Department of the Treasury Internal Revenue Service | **Report of Cash Payments Over $10,000 Received in a Trade or Business** ▶ See instructions for definition of cash. ▶ Use this form for transactions occurring after December 31, 2001. Do not use prior versions after this date. For Privacy Act and Paperwork Reduction Act Notice, see page 4. | FinCEN Form **8300** (December 2001) OMB No. 1506-0018 Department of the Treasury Financial Crimes Enforcement Network |

1 Check appropriate box(es) if: **a** ☐ Amends prior report; **b** ☐ Suspicious transaction.

Part I — Identity of Individual From Whom the Cash Was Received

2 If more than one individual is involved, check here and see instructions . . . . ▶ ☐

3 Last name | **4** First name | **5** M.I. | **6** Taxpayer identification number

7 Address (number, street, and apt. or suite no.) | **8** Date of birth ▶ M M D D Y Y Y Y (see instructions)

9 City | **10** State | **11** ZIP code | **12** Country (if not U.S.) | **13** Occupation, profession, or business

14 Document used to verify identity: **a** Describe identification ▶ ....
 b Issued by .... **c** Number ....

Part II — Person on Whose Behalf This Transaction Was Conducted

15 If this transaction was conducted on behalf of more than one person, check here and see instructions . . . . . ▶ ☐

16 Individual's last name or Organization's name | **17** First name | **18** M.I. | **19** Taxpayer identification number

20 Doing business as (DBA) name (see instructions) | Employer identification number

21 Address (number, street, and apt. or suite no.) | **22** Occupation, profession, or business

23 City | **24** State | **25** ZIP code | **26** Country (if not U.S.)

27 Alien identification: **a** Describe identification ▶ ....
 b Issued by .... **c** Number ....

Part III — Description of Transaction and Method of Payment

28 Date cash received M M D D Y Y Y Y | **29** Total cash received $ .00 | **30** If cash was received in more than one payment, check here . . . ▶ ☐ | **31** Total price if different from item 29 $ .00

32 Amount of cash received (in U.S. dollar equivalent) (must equal item 29) (see instructions):
 a U.S. currency $ _____ .00 (Amount in $100 bills or higher $ _____ .00)
 b Foreign currency $ _____ .00 (Country ▶ _____)
 c Cashier's check(s) $ _____ .00 ⎫
 d Money order(s) $ _____ .00 ⎬ Issuer's name(s) and serial number(s) of the monetary instrument(s) ▶ ....
 e Bank draft(s) $ _____ .00 ⎪
 f Traveler's check(s) $ _____ .00 ⎭

33 Type of transaction
 a ☐ Personal property purchased
 b ☐ Real property purchased
 c ☐ Personal services provided
 d ☐ Business services provided
 e ☐ Intangible property purchased
 f ☐ Debt obligations paid
 g ☐ Exchange of cash
 h ☐ Escrow or trust funds
 i ☐ Bail received by court clerks
 j ☐ Other (specify) ▶

34 Specific description of property or service shown in 33. (Give serial or registration number, address, docket number, etc.) ▶ ....

Part IV — Business That Received Cash

35 Name of business that received cash | **36** Employer identification number

37 Address (number, street, and apt. or suite no.) | Social security number

38 City | **39** State | **40** ZIP code | **41** Nature of your business

42 Under penalties of perjury, I declare that to the best of my knowledge the information I have furnished above is true, correct, and complete.

Signature ▶ _____ Authorized official   Title ▶ _____

43 Date of signature M M D D Y Y Y Y | **44** Type or print name of contact person | **45** Contact telephone number ( )

IRS Form **8300** (Rev. 12-2001)   Cat. No. 62133S   FinCEN Form **8300** (12-2001)

IRS Form 8300 (Rev. 12-2001)   Page **2**   FinCEN Form 8300 (12-2001)

Multiple Parties
(Complete applicable parts below if box 2 or 15 on page 1 is checked)

Part I — Continued—Complete if box 2 on page 1 is checked

3 Last name	4 First name	5 M.I.	6 Taxpayer identification number
7 Address (number, street, and apt. or suite no.)		8 Date of birth (see instructions) ▶	M M D D Y Y Y Y
9 City	10 State	11 ZIP code	12 Country (if not U.S.)	13 Occupation, profession, or business

14 Document used to verify identity: **a** Describe identification ▶ ....
   b Issued by   **c** Number

3 Last name	4 First name	5 M.I.	6 Taxpayer identification number
7 Address (number, street, and apt. or suite no.)		8 Date of birth (see instructions) ▶	M M D D Y Y Y Y
9 City	10 State	11 ZIP code	12 Country (if not U.S.)	13 Occupation, profession, or business

14 Document used to verify identity: **a** Describe identification ▶ ....
   b Issued by   **c** Number

Part II — Continued—Complete if box 15 on page 1 is checked

16 Individual's last name or Organization's name	17 First name	18 M.I.	19 Taxpayer identification number
20 Doing business as (DBA) name (see instructions)			Employer identification number
21 Address (number, street, and apt. or suite no.)			22 Occupation, profession, or business
23 City	24 State	25 ZIP code	26 Country (if not U.S.)

27 Alien identification: **a** Describe identification ▶ ....
   b Issued by   **c** Number

16 Individual's last name or Organization's name	17 First name	18 M.I.	19 Taxpayer identification number
20 Doing business as (DBA) name (see instructions)			Employer identification number
21 Address (number, street, and apt. or suite no.)			22 Occupation, profession, or business
23 City	24 State	25 ZIP code	26 Country (if not U.S.)

27 Alien identification: **a** Describe identification ▶ ....
   b Issued by   **c** Number

IRS Form **8300** (Rev. 12-2001)   FinCEN Form **8300** (12-2001)

IRS Form 8300 (Rev. 12-2001)   Page **3**   FinCEN Form 8300 (12-2001)

Section references are to the Internal Revenue Code unless otherwise noted.

Changes To Note

- Section 6050I (26 United States Code (U.S.C.) 6050I) and 31 U.S.C. 5331 require that certain information be reported to the IRS and the Financial Crimes Enforcement Network (FinCEN). This information must be reported on **IRS/FinCEN Form 8300.**
- Item 33 box **i** is to be checked **only** by clerks of the court; box **d** is to be checked by bail bondsmen. See the instructions on page 4.
- For purposes of section 6050I and 31 U.S.C. 5331, the word "cash" and "currency" have the same meaning. See **Cash** under **Definitions** below.

General Instructions

Who must file. Each person engaged in a trade or business who, in the course of that trade or business, receives more than $10,000 in cash in one transaction or in two or more related transactions, must file Form 8300. Any transactions conducted between a payer (or its agent) and the recipient in a 24-hour period are related transactions. Transactions are considered related even if they occur over a period of more than 24 hours if the recipient knows, or has reason to know, that each transaction is one of a series of connected transactions.

Keep a copy of each Form 8300 for 5 years from the date you file it.

Clerks of Federal or State courts must file Form 8300 if more than $10,000 in cash is received as bail for an individual(s) charged with certain criminal offenses. For these purposes, a clerk includes the clerk's office or any other office, department, division, branch, or unit of the court that is authorized to receive bail. If a person receives bail on behalf of a clerk, the clerk is treated as receiving the bail. See the instructions for **Item 33** on page 4.

If multiple payments are made in cash to satisfy bail and the initial payment does not exceed $10,000, the initial payment and subsequent payments must be aggregated and the information return must be filed by the 15th day after receipt of the payment that causes the aggregate amount to exceed $10,000 in cash. In such cases, the reporting requirement can be satisfied either by sending a single written statement with an aggregate amount listed or by furnishing a copy of each Form 8300 relating to that payer. Payments made to satisfy separate bail requirements are not required to be aggregated. See Treasury Regulations section 1.6050I-2.

Casinos must file Form 8300 for nongaming activities (restaurants, shops, etc.).

Voluntary use of Form 8300. Form 8300 may be filed voluntarily for any suspicious transaction (see **Definitions**) for use by FinCEN and the IRS, even if the total amount does not exceed $10,000.

Exceptions. Cash is not required to be reported if it is received:

- By a financial institution required to file **Form 4789,** Currency Transaction Report.
- By a casino required to file (or exempt from filing) **Form 8362,** Currency Transaction Report by Casinos, if the cash is received as part of its gaming business.
- By an agent who receives the cash from a principal, if the agent uses all of the cash within 15 days in a second transaction that is reportable on Form 8300 or on Form 4789, and discloses all the information necessary to complete Part II of Form 8300 or Form 4789 to the recipient of the cash in the second transaction.
- In a transaction occurring entirely outside the United States. See **Pub. 1544,** Reporting Cash Payments Over $10,000 (Received in a Trade or Business), regarding transactions occurring in Puerto Rico, the Virgin Islands, and territories and possessions of the United States.
- In a transaction that is not in the course of a person's trade or business.

When to file. File Form 8300 by the 15th day after the date the cash was received. If that date falls on a Saturday, Sunday, or legal holiday, file the form on the next business day.

Where to file. File the form with the Internal Revenue Service, Detroit Computing Center, P.O. Box 32621, Detroit, MI 48232.

Statement to be provided. You must give a written statement to each person named on a required Form 8300 on or before January 31 of the year following the calendar year in which the cash is received. The statement must show the name, telephone number, and address of the information contact for the business, the aggregate amount of reportable cash received, and that the information was furnished to the IRS. Keep a copy of the statement for your records.

Multiple payments. If you receive more than one cash payment for a single transaction or for related transactions, you must report the multiple payments any time you receive a total amount that exceeds $10,000 within any 12-month period. Submit the report within 15 days of the date you receive the payment that causes the total amount to exceed $10,000. If more than one report is required within 15 days, you may file a combined report. File the combined report no later than the date the earliest report, if filed separately, would have to be filed.

Taxpayer identification number (TIN). You must furnish the correct TIN of the person or persons from whom you receive the cash and, if applicable, the person or persons on whose behalf the transaction is being conducted. **You may be subject to penalties for an incorrect or missing TIN.**

The TIN for an individual (including a sole proprietorship) is the individual's social security number (SSN). For certain resident aliens who are not eligible to get an SSN and nonresident aliens who are required to file tax returns, it is an IRS Individual Taxpayer Identification Number (ITIN). For other persons, including corporations, partnerships, and estates, it is the employer identification number (EIN).

If you have requested but are not able to get a TIN for one or more of the parties to a transaction within 15 days following the transaction, file the report and attach a statement explaining why the TIN is not included.

Exception: *You are not required to provide the TIN of a person who is a nonresident alien individual or a foreign organization if that person does not have income effectively connected with the conduct of a U.S. trade or business and does not have an office or place of business, or fiscal or paying agent, in the United States. See Pub. 1544 for more information.*

Penalties. You may be subject to penalties if you fail to file a correct and complete Form 8300 on time and you cannot show that the failure was due to reasonable cause. You may also be subject to penalties if you fail to furnish timely a correct and complete statement to each person named in a required report. A minimum penalty of $25,000 may be imposed if the failure is due to an intentional or willful disregard of the cash reporting requirements.

Penalties may also be imposed for causing, or attempting to cause, a trade or business to fail to file a required report; for causing, or attempting to cause, a trade or business to file a required report containing a material omission or misstatement of fact; or for structuring, or attempting to structure, transactions to avoid the reporting requirements. These violations may also be subject to criminal prosecution which, upon conviction, may result in imprisonment of up to 5 years or fines of up to $250,000 for individuals and $500,000 for corporations or both.

Definitions

Cash. The term "cash" means the following:

- U.S. and foreign coin and currency received in any transaction.
- A cashier's check, money order, bank draft, or traveler's check having a face amount of $10,000 or less that is received in a **designated reporting transaction** (defined below), or that is received in any transaction in which the recipient knows that the instrument is being used in an attempt to avoid the reporting of the transaction under either section 6050I or 31 U.S.C. 5331.

Note: *Cash does not include a check drawn on the payer's own account, such as a personal check, regardless of the amount.*

Designated reporting transaction. A retail sale (or the receipt of funds by a broker or other intermediary in connection with a retail sale) of a consumer durable, a collectible, or a travel or entertainment activity.

Retail sale. Any sale (whether or not the sale is for resale or for any other purpose) made in the course of a trade or business if that trade or business principally consists of making sales to ultimate consumers.

Consumer durable. An item of tangible personal property of a type that, under ordinary usage, can reasonably be expected to remain useful for at least 1 year, and that has a sales price of more than $10,000.

Collectible. Any work of art, rug, antique, metal, gem, stamp, coin, etc.

Travel or entertainment activity. An item of travel or entertainment that pertains to a single trip or event if the combined sales price of the item and all other items relating to the same trip or event that are sold in the same transaction (or related transactions) exceeds $10,000.

Exceptions. A cashier's check, money order, bank draft, or traveler's check is not considered received in a designated reporting transaction if it constitutes the proceeds of a bank loan or if it is received as a payment on certain promissory notes, installment sales contracts, or down payment plans. See Pub. 1544 for more information.

Person. An individual, corporation, partnership, trust, estate, association, or company.

Recipient. The person receiving the cash. Each branch or other unit of a person's trade or business is considered a separate recipient unless the branch receiving the cash (or a central office linking the branches), knows or has reason to know the identity of payers making cash payments to other branches.

Transaction. Includes the purchase of property or services, the payment of debt, the exchange of a negotiable instrument for cash, and the receipt of cash to be held in escrow or trust. A single transaction may not be broken into multiple transactions to avoid reporting.

Suspicious transaction. A transaction in which it appears that a person is attempting to cause Form 8300 not to be filed, or to file a false or incomplete form. The term also includes any transaction in which there is an indication of possible illegal activity.

IRS Form 8300 (Rev. 12-2001)   Page **4**   FinCEN Form 8300 (12-2001)

Specific Instructions

You must complete all parts. However, you may skip Part II if the individual named in Part I is conducting the transaction on his or her behalf only. **For voluntary reporting of suspicious transactions, see Item 1 below.**

Item 1. If you are amending a prior report, check box 1a. Complete the appropriate items with the correct or amended information only. Complete all of Part IV. Staple a copy of the original report to the amended report.

To voluntarily report a suspicious transaction (see **Definitions**), check box 1b. You may also telephone your local IRS Criminal Investigation Division or call 1-800-800-2877.

Part I

Item 2. If two or more individuals conducted the transaction you are reporting, check the box and complete Part I for any one of the individuals. Provide the same information for the other individual(s) on the back of the form. If more than three individuals are involved, provide the same information on additional sheets of paper and attach them to this form.

Item 6. Enter the taxpayer identification number (TIN) of the individual named. See **Taxpayer identification number (TIN)** on page 3 for more information.

Item 8. Enter eight numerals for the date of birth of the individual named. For example, if the individual's birth date is July 6, 1960, enter 07 06 1960.

Item 13. Fully describe the nature of the occupation, profession, or business (for example, "plumber," "attorney," or "automobile dealer"). Do not use general or nondescriptive terms such as "businessman" or "self-employed."

Item 14. You must verify the name and address of the named individual(s). Verification must be made by examination of a document normally accepted as a means of identification when cashing checks (for example, a driver's license, passport, alien registration card, or other official document). In item 14a, enter the type of document examined. In item 14b, identify the issuer of the document. In item 14c, enter the document's number. For example, if the individual has a Utah driver's license, enter "driver's license" in item 14a, "Utah" in item 14b, and the number appearing on the license in item 14c.

Part II

Item 15. If the transaction is being conducted on behalf of more than one person (including husband and wife or parent and child), check the box and complete Part II for any one of the persons. Provide the same information for the other person(s) on the back of the form. If more than three persons are involved, provide the same information on additional sheets of paper and attach them to this form.

Items 16 through 19. If the person on whose behalf the transaction is being conducted is an individual, complete items 16, 17, and 18. Enter his or her TIN in item 19. If the individual is a sole proprietor and has an employer identification number (EIN), you must enter both the SSN and EIN in item 19. If the person is an organization, put its name as shown on required tax filings in item 16 and its EIN in item 19.

Item 20. If a sole proprietor or organization named in items 16 through 18 is doing business under a name other than that entered in item 16 (e.g., a "trade" or "doing business as (DBA)" name), enter it here.

Item 27. If the person is not required to furnish a TIN, complete this item. See **Taxpayer Identification Number (TIN)** on page 3. Enter a description of the type of official document issued to that person in item 27a (for example, "passport"), the country that issued the document in item 27b, and the document's number in item 27c.

Part III

Item 28. Enter the date you received the cash. If you received the cash in more than one payment, enter the date you received the payment that caused the combined amount to exceed $10,000. See **Multiple payments** under **General Instructions** for more information.

Item 30. Check this box if the amount shown in item 29 was received in more than one payment (for example, as installment payments or payments on related transactions).

Item 31. Enter the total price of the property, services, amount of cash exchanged, etc. (for example, the total cost of a vehicle purchased, cost of catering service, exchange of currency) if different from the amount shown in item 29.

Item 32. Enter the dollar amount of each form of cash received. Show foreign currency amounts in U.S. dollar equivalent at a fair market rate of exchange available to the public. **The sum of the amounts must equal item 29.** For cashier's check, money order, bank draft, or traveler's check, provide the name of the issuer and the serial number of each instrument. Names of all issuers and all serial numbers involved must be provided. If necessary, provide this information on additional sheets of paper and attach them to this form.

Item 33. Check the appropriate box(es) that describe the transaction. If the transaction is not specified in boxes a–i, check box j and briefly describe the transaction (for example, "car lease," "boat lease," "house lease," or "aircraft rental"). If the transaction relates to the receipt of bail by a court clerk, check box **i**, "Bail received by court clerks." This box is **only** for use by court clerks. If the transaction relates to cash received by a bail bondsman, check box **d**, "Business services provided."

Part IV

Item 36. If you are a sole proprietorship, you must enter your SSN. If your business also has an EIN, you must provide the EIN as well. All other business entities must enter an EIN.

Item 41. Fully describe the nature of your business, for example, "attorney" or "jewelry dealer." Do not use general or nondescriptive terms such as "business" or "store."

Item 42. This form must be signed by an individual who has been authorized to do so for the business that received the cash.

Privacy Act and Paperwork Reduction Act Notice. Except as otherwise noted, the information solicited on this form is required by the Internal Revenue Service (IRS) and the Financial Crimes Enforcement Network (FinCEN) in order to carry out the laws and regulations of the United States Department of the Treasury. Trades or businesses, except for clerks of criminal courts, are required to provide the information to the IRS and FinCEN under both section 6050I and 31 U.S.C. 5331. Clerks of criminal courts are required to provide the information to the IRS under section 6050I. Section 6109 and 31 U.S.C. 5331 require that you provide your social security number in order to adequately identify you and process your return and other papers. The principal purpose for collecting the information on this form is to maintain reports or records where such reports or records have a high degree of usefulness in criminal, tax, or regulatory investigations or proceedings, or in the conduct of intelligence or counterintelligence activities, by directing the Federal Government's attention to unusual or questionable transactions.

While such information is invaluable with regards to the purpose of this form, you are not required to provide information as to whether the reported transaction is deemed suspicious. No penalties or fines will be assessed for failure to provide such information, even if you determine that the reported transaction is indeed suspicious in nature. Failure to provide all other requested information, or the provision of fraudulent information, may result in criminal prosecution and other penalties under Title 26 and Title 31 of the United States Code.

Generally, tax returns and return information are confidential, as stated in section 6103. However, section 6103 allows or requires the IRS to disclose or give the information requested on this form to others as described in the Code. For example, we may disclose your tax information to the Department of Justice, to enforce the tax laws, both civil and criminal, and to cities, states, the District of Columbia, U.S. commonwealths or possessions, and certain foreign governments to carry out their tax laws. We may disclose your tax information to the Department of Treasury and contractors for tax administration purposes; and to other persons as necessary to obtain information which we cannot get in any other way in order to determine the amount of or to collect the tax you owe. We may disclose your tax information to the Comptroller General of the United States to permit the Comptroller General to review the IRS. We may disclose your tax information to Committees of Congress; Federal, state, and local child support agencies; and to other Federal agencies for the purposes of determining entitlement for benefits or the eligibility for and the repayment of loans. We may also disclose this information to Federal agencies that investigate or respond to acts or threats of terrorism or participate in intelligence or counterintelligence activities concerning terrorism.

FinCEN may provide the information collected through this form to those officers and employees of the Department of the Treasury who have a need for the records in the performance of their duties. FinCEN may also refer the records to any other department or agency of the Federal Government upon the request of the head of such department or agency and may also provide the records to appropriate state, local, and foreign criminal law enforcement and regulatory personnel in the performance of their official duties.

You are not required to provide the information requested on a form that is subject to the Paperwork Reduction Act unless the form displays a valid OMB control number. Books or records relating to a form or its instructions must be retained as long as their contents may become material in the administration of any law under Title 26 or Title 31.

The time needed to complete this form will vary depending on individual circumstances. The estimated average time is 21 minutes. If you have comments concerning the accuracy of this time estimate or suggestions for making this form simpler, you can write to the Tax Forms Committee, Western Area Distribution Center, Rancho Cordova, CA 95743-0001. **Do not** send this form to this office. Instead, see **Where To File** on page 3.

Department of the Treasury
TD F 90-22.1
(Rev. 7/00) SUPERSEDES ALL PREVIOUS EDITIONS

REPORT OF FOREIGN BANK AND FINANCIAL ACCOUNTS

Do **NOT** file with your Federal Tax Return

OMB No. 1506-0009

1. Filing for Calendar Year   Y Y Y Y
2. Type of Filer   a ☐ Individual   b ☐ Partnership   c ☐ Corporation   d ☐ Fiduciary
3. Taxpayer Identification Number

Part I — Filer Information

4. Last Name or Organization Name
5. First Name
6. Middle Initial
7. Address (Number, Street, and Apt. or Suite No.)
8. Date of Birth   M M D D Y Y Y Y
9. City
10. State
11. Zip/Postal Code
12. Country
13. Title (Not necessary if reporting a personal account.)
14. Are these accounts jointly owned?   a ☐ Yes   b ☐ No
15. Number of joint owners
16. Taxpayer Identification Number of joint owner (if known)
17. Last Name or Organization Name
18. First Name
19. Middle Initial

Part II — Information on Financial Accounts

20. Number of Foreign Financial Accounts in which a financial interest is held
21. Type of account   a ☐ Bank   b ☐ Securities   c ☐ Other _____
22. Maximum value of account
    a ☐ Under $10,000
    b ☐ $10,000 to $99,999
    c ☐ $100,000 to $1,000,000
    d ☐ Over $1,000,000
23. Account Number or other designation
24. Name of Financial Institution with which account is held
25. Country in which account is held
26. Does the filer have a financial interest in this account?   a ☐ Yes   b ☐ No   If no, complete boxes 27-35.
27. Last Name or Organization Name of Account Holder
28. First Name
29. Middle Initial
30. Taxpayer Identification Number
31. Address (Number, Street, and Apt. or Suite No.)
32. City
33. State
34. Zip/Postal Code
35. Country
36. Signature
37. Date   M M D D Y Y Y Y

This form should be used to report a financial interest in, signature authority, or other authority over one or more financial accounts in foreign countries, as required by the Department of the Treasury Regulations (31 CFR 103). No report is required if the aggregate value of the accounts did not exceed $10,000. **SEE INSTRUCTIONS FOR DEFINITION.** File this form with:

U.S. Department of the Treasury, P.O. Box 32621, Detroit, MI 48232-0621.

PRIVACY ACT NOTIFICATION

Pursuant to the requirements of Public Law 93-579 (Privacy Act of 1974), notice is hereby given that the authority to collect information on TD F 90-22.1 in accordance with 5 USC 522a(e) is Public Law 91-508; 31 USC 5314; 5 USC 301; 31 CFR 103.

The principal purpose for collecting the information is to assure maintenance of reports where such reports or records have a high degree of usefulness in criminal, tax, or regulatory investigations or proceedings. The information collected may be provided to those officers and employees of any constituent unit of the Department of the Treasury who have a need for the records in the performance of their duties. The records may be referred to any other department or agency of the United States upon the request of the head of such department or agency for use in a criminal, tax, or regulatory investigation or proceeding. The information collected may also be provided to appropriate state, local, and foreign law enforcement and regulatory personnel in the performance of their official duties.

Disclosure of this information is mandatory. Civil and criminal penalties, including in certain circumstances a fine of not more than $500,000 and imprisonment of not more than five years, are provided for failure to file a report, supply information, and for filing a false or fraudulent report. Disclosure of the Social Security number is mandatory. The authority to collect is 31 CFR 103. The Social Security number will be used as a means to identify the individual who files the report.

Continuation Page

Form TD F 90-22.1

This side can be copied as many times as necessary in order to provide information on all accounts.

1 Filing for Calendar Year Y Y Y Y	3 Taxpayer Identification Number	4 Filer Last Name or Business Name	Page Number OF

2 Type of Filer
- a ☐ Individual   c ☐ Corporation
- b ☐ Partnership d ☐ Fiduciary

21 Type of Account
- a ☐ Bank   c ☐ Other _____
- b ☐ Securities

22 Maximum value of account
- a ☐ Under $10,000   c ☐ $100,000 to $1,000,000
- b ☐ $10,000 to $99,999   d ☐ Over $1,000,000

23 Account Number, or other designation

24 Name of Financial Institution with which account is held

25 Country in which account is held

26 Does the filer have a financial interest in this account? a ☐ Yes
If no, complete boxes 27-35. b ☐ No

27 Last Name or Organization Name of Account Owner

28 First Name

29 Middle Initial

30 Taxpayer Identification Number

31 Address (Number, Street, and Apt. or Suite No.)

32 City

33 State

34 Zip/Postal Code

35 Country

---

2 Type of Filer
- a ☐ Individual   c ☐ Corporation
- b ☐ Partnership d ☐ Fiduciary

21 Type of Account
- a ☐ Bank   c ☐ Other _____
- b ☐ Securities

22 Maximum value of account
- a ☐ Under $10,000   c ☐ $100,000 to $1,000,000
- b ☐ $10,000 to $99,999   d ☐ Over $1,000,000

23 Account Number, or other designation

24 Name of Financial Institution with which account is held

25 Country in which account is held

26 Does the filer have a financial interest in this account? a ☐ Yes
If no, complete boxes 27-35. b ☐ No

27 Last Name or Organization Name of Account Owner

28 First Name

29 Middle Initial

30 Taxpayer Identification Number

31 Address (Number, Street, and Apt. or Suite No.)

32 City

33 State

34 Zip/Postal Code

35 Country

---

2 Type of Filer
- a ☐ Individual   c ☐ Corporation
- b ☐ Partnership d ☐ Fiduciary

21 Type of Account
- a ☐ Bank   c ☐ Other _____
- b ☐ Securities

22 Maximum value of account
- a ☐ Under $10,000   c ☐ $100,000 to $1,000,000
- b ☐ $10,000 to $99,999   d ☐ Over $1,000,000

23 Account Number, or other designation

24 Name of Financial Institution with which account is held

25 Country in which account is held

26 Does the filer have a financial interest in this account? a ☐ Yes
If no, complete boxes 27-35. b ☐ No

27 Last Name or Organization Name of Account Owner

28 First Name

29 Middle Initial

30 Taxpayer Identification Number

31 Address (Number, Street, and Apt. or Suite No.)

32 City

33 State

34 Zip/Postal Code

35 Country

This form should be used to report a financial interest in, signature authority, or other authority over one or more financial accounts in foreign countries, as required by the Department of the Treasury Regulations (31 CFR 103). No report is required if the aggregate value of the accounts did not exceed $10,000. **SEE INSTRUCTIONS FOR DEFINITION.** File this form with:

U.S. Department of the Treasury, P.O. Box 32621, Detroit, MI 48232-0621.

Paperwork Reduction Act. The estimated average burden associated with this collection of information is 10 minutes per respondent or recordkeeper, depending on individual circumstances. Comments regarding the accuracy of this burden estimate, and suggestions for reducing the burden should be directed to the Department of the Treasury, Financial Crimes Enforcement Network, P.O. Box 39, Vienna, VA 22183. You are not required to provide the requested information unless a form displays a valid OMB control number.

INSTRUCTIONS

General Instructions

Who Must File this Report Each Unites States person, who has a financial interest in or signature authority, or other authority over any financial accounts, including bank, securities, or other types of financial accounts in a foreign country, if the aggregate value of these financial accounts exceeds $10,000 at any time during the calendar year, must report that relationship each calendar year by filing TD F 90-22.1 with the Department of the Treasury on or before June 30, of the succeeding year.

Exceptions

An officer or employee of a bank which is subject to the supervision of the Comptroller of the Currency, the Board of Governors of the Federal Reserve System, the Office of Thrift Supervision, or the Federal Deposit Insurance Corporation need not report that he has signature or other authority over a foreign bank, securities or other financial account maintained by the bank, if the officer of employee has NO personal financial interest in the account.

An officer or employee of a domestic corporation whose equity securities are listed upon national securities exchanges or which has assets exceeding $10 million and 500 or more shareholders of record need not file such a report concerning the other signature authority over a foreign financial account of the corporation, if he has NO personal financial interest in the account and he has been advised in writing by the chief financial officer of the corporation that the corporation has filed a current report, which includes that account.

Report any financial account (except a military banking facility as defined in these instructions) that is located in a foreign country, even if it is held at an affiliate of a United States bank or other financial institution. Do not report any account maintained with a branch, agency, of other office of a foreign bank or other institution that is located in the United States, Guam, Puerto Rico, and the Virgin Islands.

General Definitions

United States Person The term "United States person" means (1) a citizen or resident of the United States, (2) a domestic partnership, (3) a domestic corporation, or (4) a domestic estate or trust.

Financial Account Generally includes any bank, securities, securities derivatives or other financial instruments accounts. Such accounts generally also encompass any accounts in which the assets are held in a commingled fund, and the account owner holds an equity interest in the fund. The term also means any savings, demand, checking, deposit, time deposit, or any other account maintained with a financial institution or other person engaged in the business of a financial institution.

Account in a Foreign Country A "foreign country" includes all geographical areas located outside the United States, Guam, Puerto Rico, and the Virgin Islands.

Financial Interest A financial interest in a bank, securities, or other financial account in a foreign country means an interest described in either of the following two paragraphs:

(1) A United States person has a financial interest in each account for which such person is the owner of record or has legal title, whether the account is maintained for his or her own benefit or for the benefit of others including non-United States persons. If an account is maintained in the name of two persons jointly, or if several persons each own a partial interest in an account, each of those United States persons has a financial interest in that account.

(2) A United States person has a financial interest in each bank, securities, or other financial account in a foreign country for which the owner of record or holder of legal title is: (a) a person acting as an agent, nominee, attorney, or in some other capacity on behalf of the U.S. person; (b) a corporation in which the United States person owns directly or indirectly more than 50 percent of the total value of shares of stock; (c) a partnership in which the United States person owns an interest in more than 50 percent of the profits (distributive share of income); or (d) a trust in which the United States person either has a present beneficial interest in more than 50 percent of the assets or from which such person receives more than 50 percent of the current income.

Signature or Other Authority Over an Account A person has signature authority over an account if such person can control the disposition of money or other property in it by delivery of a document containing his or her signature (or his or her signature and that of one or more other persons) to the bank or other person with whom the account is maintained.

Other authority exists in a person who can exercise comparable power over an account by direct communication to the bank or other person with whom the account is maintained, either orally or by some other means.

Military Banking Facility Do not consider as an account in a foreign country, an account in an institution known as a "United States military banking facility" (or "United States military finance facility") operated by a United States financial institution designated by the United States Government to serve U.S. Government installations abroad, even if the United States military banking facility is located in a foreign country.

Filing Information

When and Where to File - This report must be filed on or before June 30 each calendar year with the Department of the Treasury, Post Office Box 32621, Detroit, MI 48232-0621, or it may be hand carried to any local office of the Internal Revenue Service for forwarding to the Department of the Treasury, Detroit, MI.

EXPLANATIONS FOR SPECIFIC ITEMS

Consolidated Reporting

A corporation which owns directly or indirectly more than 50 percent interest in one or more other entities will be permitted to file a consolidated report on TD F 90-22.1, on behalf of itself and such other entities provided that a listing of them is made part of the consolidated report. Such reports should be signed by an authorized official of the parent corporation.

If the group of entities covered by a consolidated report has a financial interest in 25 or more foreign financial accounts, the reporting corporation need only note that fact on the form in Item 20. It will, however, be required to provide detailed information concerning each account when so requested by the Secretary or his delegate.

Item 14

If the filer owns the account jointly with any other party, then yes should be marked.

Item 15

If the filer holds this account with only one (1) other party, and all accounts listed are held jointly with that party, then complete items 16, 17, 18, and 19. Otherwise leave these items blank.

Item 20

If the filer holds a financial interest in more than 25 foreign financial accounts, indicate the number in this box and do not complete any further items in Part II.

Any person who lists more than 25 foreign financial accounts in item 20 must when requested by the Department of the Treasury provide all the information called for in Part II.

Item 22
Account Valuation

For item 22, the maximum value of an account is the largest amount of currency and non-monetary assets that appear on any quarterly or more frequent account statement issued for the applicable year. If periodic account statements are not so issued, the maximum account asset value is the largest amount of currency and non-monetary assets in the account at any time during the year. Convert foreign currency by using the official exchange rate at the end of the year. In valuing currency of a country that uses multiple exchange rates, use the rate which would apply if the currency in the account were converted into United States dollars at the close of the calendar year.

The value of stock, other securities or other non-monetary assets in an account reported on TD F 90-22.1 is the fair market value at the end of the calendar year, or if withdrawn from the account, at the time of the withdrawal.

For purposes of item 22, if you had a financial interest in more than one account, each account is to be valued separately in accordance with the foregoing two paragraphs. If you had a financial interest in one or more but fewer than 25 accounts, and you are unable to determine whether the maximum value of these accounts exceeded $10,000 at any time during the year, complete Part II or III for each of these accounts.

Item 26

United States Persons with Authority Over but No Financial Interest in an Account - Except as provided in the following paragraph, you must state the name, address, and identifying number of each owner of an account over which you had authority, but if you complete items 27-35 for more than one account of the same owner, you need identify the owner only once. If you complete items 27-35 for one or more accounts in which no United States person had a financial interest, you may state on the first line of this item, in lieu of supplying information about the owner, "No U.S. person had any financial interest in the foreign account." This statement must be based upon the actual belief of the person filing this form after he or she has taken reasonable measures to ensure its correctness.

If you complete Part II for accounts owned by a domestic corporation and its domestic and/or foreign subsidiaries, you may treat them as one owner and write in the space provided, the name of the parent corporation, followed by "and related entities," and the identifying number and address of the parent corporation.

Item 36

Signature

This report must be signed by the person named in Part I. If the report is being filed on behalf of a partnership, corporation, or fiduciary, it must be signed by an authorized individual.

Penalties

For criminal penalties for failure to file a report, supply information, and for filing a false or fraudulent report, see 31 USC 5322(a), 31 USC 5322(b), and 18 USC 1001.

Suspicious Activity Report

July 2003
Previous editions will not be accepted after December 31, 2003

ALWAYS COMPLETE ENTIRE REPORT
(see instructions)

FRB:	FR 2230	OMB No. 7100-0212
FDIC:	6710/06	OMB No. 3064-0077
OCC:	8010-9, 8010-1	OMB No. 1557-0180
OTS:	1601	OMB No. 1550-0003
NCUA:	2362	OMB No. 3133-0094
TREASURY:	TD F 90-22.47	OMB No. 1506-0001

1

1 Check box below only if correcting a prior report.
☐ Corrects Prior Report (see instruction #3 under "How to Make a Report")

Part I — Reporting Financial Institution Information

2 Name of Financial Institution

3 EIN

4 Address of Financial Institution

5 Primary Federal Regulator
a ☐ Federal Reserve   d ☐ OCC
b ☐ FDIC   e ☐ OTS
c ☐ NCUA

6 City   7 State   8 Zip Code

9 Address of Branch Office(s) where activity occurred   ☐ Multiple Branches (include information in narrative, Part V)

10 City   11 State   12 Zip Code   13 If institution closed, date closed ___/___/___ MM DD YYYY

14 Account number(s) affected, if any   Closed?   Closed?
a _____   ☐ Yes ☐ No   c _____   ☐ Yes ☐ No
b _____   ☐ Yes ☐ No   d _____   ☐ Yes ☐ No

Part II — Suspect Information   ☐ Suspect Information Unavailable

15 Last Name or Name of Entity   16 First Name   17 Middle

18 Address   19 SSN, EIN or TIN

20 City   21 State   22 Zip Code   23 Country

24 Phone Number - Residence (include area code)   25 Phone Number - Work (include area code)
(   )   (   )

26 Occupation/Type of Business   27 Date of Birth ___/___/___ MM DD YYYY   28 Admission/Confession?
a ☐ Yes   b ☐ No

29 Forms of Identification for Suspect:
a ☐ Driver's License/State ID   b ☐ Passport   c ☐ Alien Registration   d ☐ Other _____
Number _____   Issuing Authority _____

30 Relationship to Financial Institution:
a ☐ Accountant   d ☐ Attorney   g ☐ Customer   j ☐ Officer
b ☐ Agent   e ☐ Borrower   h ☐ Director   k ☐ Shareholder
c ☐ Appraiser   f ☐ Broker   i ☐ Employee   l ☐ Other _____

31 Is the relationship an insider relationship?   a ☐ Yes   b ☐ No   32 Date of Suspension, Termination, Resignation
If Yes specify: c ☐ Still employed at financial institution   e ☐ Terminated   ___/___/___
                  d ☐ Suspended   f ☐ Resigned   MM DD YYYY

Part III — Suspicious Activity Information

33. Date or date range of suspicious activity
From ___/___/___   To ___/___/___
    MM DD YYYY   MM DD YYYY

34. Total dollar amount involved in known or suspicious activity
$ _____.00

35. Summary characterization of suspicious activity:
- a ☐ Bank Secrecy Act/Structuring/Money Laundering
- b ☐ Bribery/Gratuity
- c ☐ Check Fraud
- d ☐ Check Kiting
- e ☐ Commercial Loan Fraud
- f ☐ Computer Intrusion
- g ☐ Consumer Loan Fraud
- h ☐ Counterfeit Check
- i ☐ Counterfeit Credit/Debit Card
- j ☐ Counterfeit Instrument (other)
- k ☐ Credit Card Fraud
- l ☐ Debit Card Fraud
- m ☐ Defalcation/Embezzlement
- n ☐ False Statement
- o ☐ Misuse of Position or Self Dealing
- p ☐ Mortgage Loan Fraud
- q ☐ Mysterious Disappearance
- r ☐ Wire Transfer Fraud
- t ☐ Terrorist Financing
- u ☐ Identity Theft
- s ☐ Other _____ (type of activity)

36. Amount of loss prior to recovery (if applicable)
$ _____.00

37. Dollar amount of recovery (if applicable)
$ _____.00

38. Has the suspicious activity had a material impact on, or otherwise affected, the financial soundness of the institution?
a ☐ Yes   b ☐ No

39. Has the institution's bonding company been notified?
a ☐ Yes   b ☐ No

40. Has any law enforcement agency already been advised by telephone, written communication, or otherwise?
- a ☐ DEA
- b ☐ FBI
- c ☐ IRS
- d ☐ Postal Inspection
- e ☐ Secret Service
- f ☐ U.S. Customs
- g ☐ Other Federal
- h ☐ State
- i ☐ Local
- j ☐ Agency Name (for g, h or i) _____

41. Name of person(s) contacted at Law Enforcement Agency

42. Phone Number (include area code)
( )

43. Name of person(s) contacted at Law Enforcement Agency

44. Phone Number (include area code)
( )

Part IV — Contact for Assistance

45. Last Name

46. First Name

47. Middle

48. Title/Occupation

49. Phone Number (include area code)
( )

50. Date Prepared
___/___/___
MM DD YYYY

51. Agency (if not filed by financial institution)

Part V — Suspicious Activity Information Explanation/Description

Explanation/description of known or suspected violation of law or suspicious activity.

This section of the report is **critical**. The care with which it is written may make the difference in whether or not the described conduct and its possible criminal nature are clearly understood. Provide below a chronological and **complete** account of the possible violation of law, including what is unusual, irregular or suspicious about the transaction, using the following checklist as you prepare your account. **If necessary, continue the narrative on a duplicate of this page.**

a   **Describe** supporting documentation and retain for 5 years.
b   **Explain** who benefited, financially or otherwise, from the transaction, how much, and how.
c   **Retain** any confession, admission, or explanation of the transaction provided by the suspect and indicate to whom and when it was given.
d   **Retain** any confession, admission, or explanation of the transaction provided by any other person and indicate to whom and when it was given.
e   **Retain** any evidence of cover-up or evidence of an attempt to deceive federal or state examiners or others.
f   **Indicate** where the possible violation took place (e.g., main office, branch, other).
g   **Indicate** whether the possible violation is an isolated incident or relates to other transactions.
h   **Indicate** whether there is any related litigation; if so, specify.
i   **Recommend** any further investigation that might assist law enforcement authorities.
j   **Indicate** whether any information has been excluded from this report; if so, why?
k   If you are correcting a previously filed report, describe the changes that are being made.

For Bank Secrecy Act/Structuring/Money Laundering reports, include the following additional information:

l   **Indicate** whether currency and/or monetary instruments were involved. If so, provide the amount and/or description of the instrument (for example, bank draft, letter of credit, domestic or international money order, stocks, bonds, traveler's checks, wire transfers sent or received, cash, etc.).
m   **Indicate** any account number that may be involved or affected.

Tips on SAR Form preparation and filing are available in the SAR Activity Review at www.fincen.gov/pub_reports.html

Paperwork Reduction Act Notice: The purpose of this form is to provide an effective and consistent means for financial institutions to notify appropriate law enforcement agencies of known or suspected criminal conduct or suspicious activities that take place at or were perpetrated against financial institutions. This report is required by law, pursuant to authority contained in the following statutes. Board of Governors of the Federal Reserve System: 12 U.S.C. 324, 334, 611a, 1844(b) and (c), 3105(c) (2) and 3106(a). Federal Deposit Insurance Corporation: 12 U.S.C. 93a, 1818, 1881-84, 3401-22. Office of the Comptroller of the Currency: 12 U.S.C. 93a, 1818, 1881-84, 3401-22. Office of Thrift Supervision: 12 U.S.C. 1463 and 1464. National Credit Union Administration: 12 U.S.C. 1766(a), 1786(q). Financial Crimes Enforcement Network: 31 U.S.C. 5318(g). Information collected on this report is confidential (5 U.S.C. 552(b)(7) and 552a(k)(2), and 31 U.S.C. 5318(g)). The Federal financial institutions' regulatory agencies and the U.S. Departments of Justice and Treasury may use and share the information. Public reporting and recordkeeping burden for this information collection is estimated to average 30 minutes per response, and includes time to gather and maintain data in the required report, review the instructions, and complete the information collection. Send comments regarding this burden estimate, including suggestions for reducing the burden, to the Office of Management and Budget, Paperwork Reduction Project, Washington, DC 20503 and, depending on your primary Federal regulatory agency, to Secretary, Board of Governors of the Federal Reserve System, Washington, DC 20551; or Assistant Executive Secretary, Federal Deposit Insurance Corporation, Washington, DC 20429; or Legislative and Regulatory Analysis Division, Office of the Comptroller of the Currency, Washington, DC 20219; or Office of Thrift Supervision, Enforcement Office, Washington, DC 20552; or National Credit Union Administration, 1775 Duke Street, Alexandria, VA 22314; or Office of the Director, Financial Crimes Enforcement Network, Department of the Treasury, 2070 Chain Bridge Road, Vienna, VA 22182. The agencies may not conduct or sponsor, and an organization (or a person) is not required to respond to, a collection of information unless it displays a currently valid OMB control number.

> **Suspicious Activity Report**
> **Instructions**

> **Safe Harbor** Federal law (31 U.S.C. 5318(g)(3)) provides complete protection from civil liability for all reports of suspicious transactions made to appropriate authorities, including supporting documentation, regardless of whether such reports are filed pursuant to this report's instructions or are filed on a voluntary basis. Specifically, the law provides that a financial institution, and its directors, officers, employees and agents, that make a disclosure of any possible violation of law or regulation, including in connection with the preparation of suspicious activity reports, "shall not be liable to any person under any law or regulation of the United States, any constitution, law, or regulation of any State or political subdivision of any State, or under any contract or other legally enforceable agreement (including any arbitration agreement), for such disclosure or for any failure to provide notice of such disclosure to the person who is the subject of such disclosure or any other person identified in the disclosure".
> **Notification Prohibited** Federal law (31 U.S.C. 5318(g)(2)) requires that a financial institution, and its directors, officers, employees and agents who, voluntarily or by means of a suspicious activity report, report suspected or known criminal violations or suspicious activities may not notify any person involved in the transaction that the transaction has been reported.

> **In situations involving violations requiring immediate attention, such as when a reportable violation is ongoing, the financial institution shall immediately notify, by telephone, appropriate law enforcement and financial institution supervisory authorities in addition to filing a timely suspicious activity report.**

WHEN TO MAKE A REPORT:

1. All financial institutions operating in the United States, including insured banks, savings associations, savings association service corporations, credit unions, bank holding companies, nonbank subsidiaries of bank holding companies, Edge and Agreement corporations, and U.S. branches and agencies of foreign banks, are required to make this report following the discovery of:

    a. **Insider abuse involving any amount.** Whenever the financial institution detects any known or suspected Federal criminal violation, or pattern of criminal violations, committed or attempted against the financial institution or involving a transaction or transactions conducted through the financial institution, where the financial institution believes that it was either an actual or potential victim of a criminal violation, or series of criminal violations, or that the financial institution was used to facilitate a criminal transaction, and the financial institution has a substantial basis for identifying one of its directors, officers, employees, agents or other institution-affiliated parties as having committed or aided in the commission of a criminal act regardless of the amount involved in the violation.

    b. **Violations aggregating $5,000 or more where a suspect can be identified.** Whenever the financial institution detects any known or suspected Federal criminal violation, or pattern of criminal violations, committed or attempted against the financial institution or involving a transaction or transactions conducted through the financial institution and involving or aggregating $5,000 or more in funds or other assets, where the financial institution believes that it was either an actual or potential victim of a criminal violation, or series of criminal violations, or that the financial institution was used to facilitate a criminal transaction, and the financial institution has a substantial basis for identifying a possible suspect or group of suspects. If it is determined prior to filing this report that the identified suspect or group of suspects has used an "alias," then information regarding the true identity of the suspect or group of suspects, as well as alias identifiers, such as drivers' licenses or social security numbers, addresses and telephone numbers, must be reported.

    c. **Violations aggregating $25,000 or more regardless of a potential suspect.** Whenever the financial institution detects any known or suspected Federal criminal violation, or pattern of criminal violations, committed or attempted against the financial institution or involving a transaction or transactions conducted through the financial institution and involving or aggregating $25,000 or more in funds or other assets, where the financial institution believes that it was either an actual or potential victim of a criminal violation, or series of criminal violations, or that the financial institution was used to facilitate a criminal transaction, even though there is no substantial basis for identifying a possible suspect or group of suspects.

    d. **Transactions aggregating $5,000 or more that involve potential money laundering or violations of the Bank Secrecy Act.** Any transaction (which for purposes of this subsection means a deposit, withdrawal, transfer between accounts, exchange of currency, loan, extension of credit, purchase or sale of any stock, bond, certificate of deposit, or other monetary instrument or investment security, or any other payment, transfer, or delivery by, through, or to a financial institution, by whatever means effected) conducted or attempted by, at or through the financial institution and involving or aggregating $5,000 or more in funds or other assets, if the financial institution knows, suspects, or has reason to suspect that:

   i. The transaction involves funds derived from illegal activities or is intended or conducted in order to hide or disguise funds or assets derived from illegal activities (including, without limitation, the ownership, nature, source, location, or control of such funds or assets) as part of a plan to violate or evade any law or regulation or to avoid any transaction reporting requirement under Federal law;

   ii. The transaction is designed to evade any regulations promulgated under the Bank Secrecy Act; or

   iii. The transaction has no business or apparent lawful purpose or is not the sort in which the particular customer would normally be expected to engage, and the financial institution knows of no reasonable explanation for the transaction after examining the available facts, including the background and possible purpose of the transaction.

   The Bank Secrecy Act requires all financial institutions to file currency transaction reports (CTRs) in accordance with the Department of the Treasury's implementing regulations (31 CFR Part 103). These regulations require a financial institution to file a CTR whenever a currency transaction exceeds $10,000. If a currency transaction exceeds $10,000 and is suspicious, the institution must file both a CTR (reporting the currency transaction) and a suspicious activity report (reporting the suspicious or criminal aspects of the transaction). If a currency transaction equals or is below $10,000 and is suspicious, the institution should only file a suspicious activity report.

2. **Computer Intrusion.** For purposes of this report, "computer intrusion" is defined as gaining access to a computer system of a financial institution to:

   a. Remove, steal, procure, or otherwise affect funds of the institution or the institution's customers;
   b. Remove, steal, procure or otherwise affect critical information of the institution including customer account information; or
   c. Damage, disable or otherwise affect critical systems of the institution.

   For purposes of this reporting requirement, computer intrusion does not mean attempted intrusions of websites or other non-critical information systems of the institution that provide no access to institution or customer financial or other critical information.

3. A financial institution is required to file a suspicious activity report no later than 30 calendar days after the date of initial detection of facts that may constitute a basis for filing a suspicious activity report. If no suspect was identified on the date of detection of the incident requiring the filing, a financial institution may delay filing a suspicious activity report for an additional 30 calendar days to identify a suspect. In no case shall reporting be delayed more than 60 calendar days after the date of initial detection of a reportable transaction.

4. This suspicious activity report does not need to be filed for those robberies and burglaries that are reported to local authorities, or (except for savings associations and service corporations) for lost, missing, counterfeit, or stolen securities that are reported pursuant to the requirements of 17 CFR 240.17f-1.

HOW TO MAKE A REPORT:

1. Send each completed suspicious activity report to:

   Detroit Computing Center, P.O. Box 33980, Detroit, MI 48232-0980

2. For items that do not apply or for which information is not available, leave blank.
3. If you are correcting a previously filed report, check the box at the top of the report (line 1). Complete the report in its entirety and include the corrected information in the applicable boxes. Then describe the changes that are being made in Part V (Description of Suspicious Activity), line k.
4. **Do not include any supporting documentation with the suspicious activity report.** Identify and retain a copy of the suspicious activity report and all original supporting documentation or business record equivalent for five (5) years from the date of the suspicious activity report. All supporting documentation must be made available to appropriate authorities upon request.
5. If more space is needed to report additional suspects, attach copies of page 1 to provide the additional information. If more space is needed to report additional branch addresses, include this information in the narrative, Part V.
6. Financial institutions are encouraged to provide copies of suspicious activity reports to state and local authorities, where appropriate.

FinCEN Form 102

April 2003
Previous editions will not be accepted after December 31, 2003

Suspicious Activity Report by Casinos and Card Clubs

▶ Please type or print. Always complete entire report. Items marked with an asterisk * are considered critical (see instructions).

OMB No. 1506-0006

1 Check the box if this report corrects a prior report (see instructions on page 6) ☐

Part I — Subject Information

2 Check box (a) ☐ if more than one subject   box (b) ☐ subject information unavailable

*3 Individual's last name or entity's full name

*4 First name

*5 Middle initial

*6 also known as (AKA- individual), doing business as (DBA- entity)

7 Occupation / type of business

*8 Address

*9 City

*10 State

*11 ZIP code

*12 Country (if not U.S.)

13 Vehicle license # / state (optional)
 a. number   b. state

*14 SSN / ITIN (individual) or EIN (entity)

*15 Account number   No account affected ☐   Account open? Yes ☐ No ☐

16 Date of birth __/__/____ MM DD YYYY

*17 Government issued identification (if available)
a ☐ Driver's license/state ID   b ☐ Passport   d ☐ Alien registration
d ☐ Other _____
e Number: _____   f Issuing state or country _____

18 Phone number - work (___) ___-____

19 Phone number - home (___) ___-____

20 E-mail address (if available)

21 Affiliation or relationship to casino/card club
a ☐ Customer   b ☐ Agent   c ☐ Junket / tour operator   d ☐ Employee   e ☐ Check cashing operator
f ☐ Supplier   g ☐ Concessionaire   h ☐ Other (Explain in Part VI)

22 Does casino/card club still have a business association and/or an employee/employer relationship with suspect?
a ☐ Yes b ☐ No If **no**, why? c ☐ Barred d ☐ Resigned e ☐ Terminated f ☐ Other (Specify in Part VI)

23 Date action taken(22) __/__/____ MM DD YYYY

Part II — Suspicious Activity Information

*24 Date or date range of suspicious activity   From __/__/____ MM DD YYYY   To __/__/____ MM DD YYYY

*25 Total dollar amount involved in suspicious activity $_____.00

*26 Type of suspicious activity:
a ☐ Bribery/gratuity
b ☐ Check fraud (includes counterfeit)
c ☐ Credit/debit card fraud (incl. counterfeit)
d ☐ Embezzlement/theft
e ☐ Large currency exchange(s)
f ☐ Minimal gaming with large transactions
g ☐ Misuse of position
h ☐ Money laundering
i ☐ No apparent business or lawful purpose
j ☐ Structuring
k ☐ Unusual use of negotiable instruments (checks)
l ☐ Use of multiple credit or deposit accounts
m ☐ Unusual use of wire transfers
n ☐ Unusual use of counter checks or markers
o ☐ False or conflicting ID(s)
p ☐ Terrorist financing
q ☐ Other (Describe in Part VI)

Part III — Law Enforcement or Regulatory Contact Information

27 If law enforcement or a regulatory agency has been contacted (excluding submission of a SARC), check the appropriate box.
a ☐ DEA   e ☐ U.S. Customs Service   i ☐ State law enforcement
b ☐ U.S. Attorney (** 28)   f ☐ U.S. Secret Service   j ☐ Tribal gaming commission
c ☐ IRS   g ☐ Local law enforcement   k ☐ Tribal law enforcement
d ☐ FBI   h ☐ State gaming commission   l ☐ Other (List in item 28)

28 Other authority contacted (for box 27 g through l) ** List U.S. Attorney office here.

29 Name of person contacted (for all of box 27)

30 Telephone number of individual contacted in box 29   (___) ___-____

31 Date Contacted __/__/____ MM DD YYYY

Catalog No. 35636U

Part IV	Reporting Casino or Card Club Information			2

*32 Trade name of casino or card club	*33 Legal name of casino or card club	*34 EIN

35 Address

*36 City	*37 State	*38 ZIP code

39 Type of gaming institution
a ☐ State licensed casino   b ☐ Tribal licensed casino   c ☐ Card club   d ☐ Other (specify)_____

Part V	Contact for Assistance

*40 Last name of individual to be contacted regarding this report	*41 First name	*42 Middle initial

*43 Title/Position	*44 Work phone number	*45 Date report prepared
	( ) —	04/22/2004

Part VI	Suspicious Activity Information - Narrative*

Explanation/description of suspicious activity(ies). This section of the report is <u>critical</u>. <u>The care with which it is completed may determine whether or not the described activity and its possible criminal nature are clearly understood by investigators.</u> Provide a clear, complete and chronological description (**not exceeding this page and the next page**) of the activity, including what is unusual, irregular, or suspicious about the transaction(s), using the checklist below <u>as a guide</u> as you prepare your account.

a. **Describe** the conduct that raised suspicion.
b. **Explain** whether the transaction(s) was completed or only attempted.
c. **Describe** supporting documentation and retain such documentation for your file for five years.
d. **Explain** who benefited, financially or otherwise, from the transaction(s), how much and how (if known).
e. **Describe and retain** any admission or explanation of the transaction(s) provided by the subject(s), witness(s), or other person(s). Indicate to whom and when it was given. Include witness or other person ID.
f. **Describe and retain** any evidence of cover-up or evidence of an attempt to deceive federal or state examiners, or others.
g. **Indicate** where the possible violation of law(s) took place (*e.g.*, branch, cage, specific gaming pit, specific gaming area).
h. **Indicate** whether the suspicious activity is an isolated incident or relates to another transaction.
i. **Indicate** whether there is any related litigation. If so, specify the name of the litigation and the court where the action is pending.
j. **Recommend** any further investigation that might assist law enforcement authorities.
k. **Indicate** whether any information has been excluded from this report; if so, state reasons.
l. **Indicate** whether any U.S. or foreign currency and/or U.S. or foreign negotiable instrument(s) were involved. If foreign, provide the amount, name of currency, and country of origin.
m. **Indicate** whether funds or assets were recovered and, if so, enter the dollar value of the recovery in whole dollars only.
n. **Indicate** any additional account number(s), and any domestic or foreign bank(s) account numbers which may be involved.
o. **Indicate** for a foreign national any available information on subject's passport(s), visa(s), and/or identification card(s). Include date, country, city of issue, issuing authority, and nationality.
p. **Describe** any suspicious activities that involve transfer of funds to or from a foreign country, or any exchanges of a foreign currency. Identify the currency, country, sources and destinations of funds.
q. **Describe** subject(s) position if employed by the casino or card club (*e.g.*, dealer, pit supervisor, cage cashier, host, *etc*.).
r. **Indicate** the type of casino or card club filing this report, if this is not clear from Part IV.
s. **Describe** the subject <u>only</u> if you do not have the identifying information in Part I or if multiple individuals use the same identification. Use descriptors such as male, female, age, etc.
t. **Indicate** any wire transfer in or out identifier numbers, including the transfer company's name.
u. <u>If correcting a prior report, complete the form in its entirety and note the changes here in Part VI.</u>

Information already provided in earlier parts of this form need not necessarily be repeated if the meaning is clear.
Supporting documentation should not be filed with this report. <u>Maintain the information for your files.</u>

Tips on SAR Form preparation and filing are available in the SAR Activity Review at www.fincen.gov/pub_reports.html

Enter explanation/description in the space below. Continue on the next page if necessary.

Suspicious Activity Report Narrative (continued from page 2)

APPENDIX F

FEDERAL STATUTES RELATING TO MONEY LAUNDERING FORFEITURE

18 USC §981. CIVIL FORFEITURE

(**a**) (**1**) The following property is subject to forfeiture to the United States:

(**A**) Any property, real or personal, involved in a transaction or attempted transaction in violation of section 1956, 1957 or 1960 of this title, or any property traceable to such property.

(**B**) Any property, real or personal, within the jurisdiction of the United States, constituting, derived from, or traceable to, any proceeds obtained directly or indirectly from an offense against a foreign nation, or any property used to facilitate such an offense, if the offense—

(**i**) involves the manufacture, importation, sale, or distribution of a controlled substance (as that term is defined for purposes of the Controlled Substances Act), or any other conduct described in section 1956 (c) (7) (B);

(**ii**) would be punishable within the jurisdiction of the foreign nation by death or imprisonment for a term exceeding 1 year; and

(**iii**) would be punishable under the laws of the United States by imprisonment for a term exceeding 1 year, if the act or activity constituting the offense had occurred within the jurisdiction of the United States.

(**C**) Any property, real or personal, which constitutes or is derived from proceeds traceable to a violation of section 215, 471, 472, 473, 474, 476, 477, 478, 479, 480, 481, 485, 486, 487, 488, 501, 502, 510, 542, 545, 656, 657, 842, 844, 1005, 1006, 1007, 1014, 1028, 1029, 1030, or 1344 of this title or any offense constituting "specified unlawful activity" (as defined in section 1956 (c) (7) of this title), or a conspiracy to commit such offense.

(**D**) Any property, real or personal, which represents or is traceable to the gross receipts obtained, directly or indirectly, from a violation of—

(**i**) section 666 (a) (1) (relating to Federal program fraud);

(**ii**) section 1001 (relating to fraud and false statements);

(**iii**) section 1031 (relating to major fraud against the United States);

(**iv**) section 1032 (relating to concealment of assets from conservator or receiver of insured financial institution);

(**v**) section 1341 (relating to mail fraud); or

(**vi**) section 1343 (relating to wire fraud),

if such violation relates to the sale of assets acquired or held by the Resolution Trust Corporation, the Federal Deposit Insurance Corporation, as conservator or receiver for a financial institution, or any other conservator for a financial institution appointed by the Office of the Comptroller of the Currency or the Office of Thrift Supervision or the National Credit Union Administration, as conservator or liquidating agent for a financial institution.

(**E**) With respect to an offense listed in subsection (a) (1) (D) committed for the purpose of executing or attempting to execute any scheme or artifice to defraud, or for obtaining money or property by means of false or fraudulent statements, pretenses, representations or promises, the gross receipts of such an offense shall include all property, real or personal, tangible or intangible, which thereby is obtained, directly or indirectly.

(F) Any property, real or personal, which represents or is traceable to the gross proceeds obtained, directly or indirectly, from a violation of—

(i) section 511 (altering or removing motor vehicle identification numbers);

(ii) section 553 (importing or exporting stolen motor vehicles);

(iii) section 2119 (armed robbery of automobiles);

(iv) section 2312 (transporting stolen motor vehicles in interstate commerce); or

(v) section 2313 (possessing or selling a stolen motor vehicle that has moved in interstate commerce).

(G) All assets, foreign or domestic—

(i) of any individual, entity, or organization engaged in planning or perpetrating any act of domestic or international terrorism (as defined in section 2331) against the United States, citizens or residents of the United States, or their property, and all assets, foreign or domestic, affording any person a source of influence over any such entity or organization;

(ii) acquired or maintained by any person with the intent and for the purpose of supporting, planning, conducting, or concealing an act of domestic or international terrorism (as defined in section 2331) against the United States, citizens or residents of the United States, or their property; or

(iii) derived from, involved in, or used or intended to be used to commit any act of domestic or international terrorism (as defined in section 2331) against the United States, citizens or residents of the United States, or their property.

(H) (1) Any property, real or personal, involved in a violation or attempted violation, or which constitutes or is derived from proceeds traceable to a violation, of section 2339C of this title.

(2) For purposes of paragraph (1), the term "proceeds" is defined as follows:

(A) In cases involving illegal goods, illegal services, unlawful activities, and telemarketing and health care fraud schemes, the term "proceeds" means property of any kind obtained directly or indirectly, as the result of the commission of the offense giving rise to forfeiture, and any property traceable thereto, and is not limited to the net gain or profit realized from the offense.

(B) In cases involving lawful goods or lawful services that are sold or provided in an illegal manner, the term "proceeds" means the amount of money acquired through the illegal transactions resulting in the forfeiture, less the direct costs incurred in providing the goods or services. The claimant shall have the burden of proof with respect to the issue of direct costs. The direct costs shall not include any part of the overhead expenses of the entity providing the goods or services, or any part of the income taxes paid by the entity.

(C) In cases involving fraud in the process of obtaining a loan or extension of credit, the court shall allow the claimant a deduction from the forfeiture to the extent that the loan was repaid, or the debt was satisfied, without any financial loss to the victim.

(b) (1) Except as provided in section 985, any property subject to forfeiture to the United States under subsection (a) may be seized by the Attorney General and, in the case of property involved in a violation investigated by the Secretary of the Treasury or the United States Postal Service, the property may also be seized by the Secretary of the Treasury or the Postal Service, respectively.

(2) Seizures pursuant to this section shall be made pursuant to a warrant obtained in the same manner as provided for a search warrant under the Federal Rules of Criminal Procedure, except that a seizure may be made without a warrant if—

(A) a complaint for forfeiture has been filed in the United States district court and the court issued an arrest warrant in rem pursuant to the

Supplemental Rules for Certain Admiralty and Maritime Claims;

(B) there is probable cause to believe that the property is subject to forfeiture and—

(i) the seizure is made pursuant to a lawful arrest or search; or

(ii) another exception to the Fourth Amendment warrant requirement would apply; or

(C) the property was lawfully seized by a state or local law enforcement agency and transferred to a federal agency.

(3) Notwithstanding the provisions of rule 41 (a) of the Federal Rules of Criminal Procedure, a seizure warrant may be issued pursuant to this subsection by a judicial officer in any district in which a forfeiture action against the property may be filed under section 1355 (b) of title 28, and may be executed in any district in which the property is found, or transmitted to the central authority of any foreign state for service in accordance with any treaty or other international agreement. Any motion for the return of property seized under this section shall be filed in the district court in which the seizure warrant was issued or in the district court for the district in which the property was seized.

(4) (A) If any person is arrested or charged in a foreign country in connection with an offense that would give rise to the forfeiture of property in the United States under this section or under the Controlled Substances Act, the Attorney General may apply to any federal judge or magistrate judge in the district in which the property is located for an ex parte order restraining the property subject to forfeiture for not more than 30 days, except that the time may be extended for good cause shown at a hearing conducted in the manner provided in rule 43 (e) of the Federal Rules of Civil Procedure.

(B) The application for the restraining order shall set forth the nature and circumstances of the foreign charges and the basis for belief that the person arrested or charged has property in the United States that would be subject to forfeiture, and shall contain a statement that the restraining order is needed to preserve the availability of property for such time as is necessary to receive evidence from the foreign country or elsewhere in support of probable cause for the seizure of the property under this subsection.

(c) Property taken or detained under this section shall not be repleviable, but shall be deemed to be in the custody of the Attorney General, the Secretary of the Treasury, or the Postal Service, as the case may be, subject only to the orders and decrees of the court or the official having jurisdiction thereof. Whenever property is seized under this subsection, the Attorney General, the Secretary of the Treasury, or the Postal Service, as the case may be, may—

(1) place the property under seal;

(2) remove the property to a place designated by him; or

(3) require that the General Services Administration take custody of the property and remove it, if practicable, to an appropriate location for disposition in accordance with law.

(d) For purposes of this section, the provisions of the customs laws relating to the seizure, summary and judicial forfeiture, condemnation of property for violation of the customs laws, the disposition of such property or the proceeds from the sale of such property under this section, the remission or mitigation of such forfeitures, and the compromise of claims (19 U.S.C. 1602 et seq.), insofar as they are applicable and not inconsistent with the provisions of this section, shall apply to seizures and forfeitures incurred, or alleged to have been incurred, under this section, except that such duties as are imposed upon the customs officer or any other person with respect to the seizure and forfeiture of property under the customs laws shall be performed with respect to seizures and forfeitures of property under this section by such officers, agents, or other persons as may be authorized or designated for that purpose by the Attorney General, the Secretary of the Treasury, or the Postal Service, as the case may be. The Attorney General shall have sole responsibility for disposing of petitions for remission or mitigation with respect to property involved in a judicial forfeiture proceeding.

(e) Notwithstanding any other provision of the law, except section 3 of the Anti Drug Abuse Act of 1986, the Attorney General, the Secretary of the Treasury, or the Postal Service, as the case may be, is authorized to retain property forfeited pursuant to this section, or to transfer such property on such terms and conditions as he may determine—

(1) to any other federal agency;

(2) to any state or local law enforcement agency which participated directly in any of the acts which led to the seizure or forfeiture of the property;

(3) in the case of property referred to in subsection (a) (1) (C), to any federal financial institution regulatory agency—

(A) to reimburse the agency for payments to claimants or creditors of the institution; and

(B) to reimburse the insurance fund of the agency for losses suffered by the fund as a result of the receivership or liquidation;

(4) in the case of property referred to in subsection (a) (1) (C), upon the order of the appropriate federal financial institution regulatory agency, to the financial institution as restitution, with the value of the property so transferred to be set off against any amount later recovered by the financial institution as compensatory damages in any state or federal proceeding;

(5) in the case of property referred to in subsection (a) (1) (C), to any federal financial institution regulatory agency, to the extent of the agency's contribution of resources to, or expenses involved in, the seizure and forfeiture, and the investigation leading directly to the seizure and forfeiture, of such property;

(6) as restoration to any victim of the offense giving rise to the forfeiture, including, in the case of a money laundering offense, any offense constituting the underlying specified unlawful activity; or

(7) In[1] the case of property referred to in subsection (a) (1) (D), to the Resolution Trust Corporation, the Federal Deposit Insurance Corporation, or any other federal financial institution regulatory agency (as defined in section 8 (e) (7) (D) of the Federal Deposit Insurance Act).

The Attorney General, the Secretary of the Treasury, or the Postal Service, as the case may be, shall ensure the equitable transfer pursuant to paragraph (2) of any forfeited property to the appropriate state or local law enforcement agency so as to reflect generally the contribution of any such agency participating directly in any of the acts which led to the seizure or forfeiture of such property. A decision by the Attorney General, the Secretary of the Treasury, or the Postal Service pursuant to paragraph (2) shall not be subject to review. The United States shall not be liable in any action arising out of the use of any property the custody of which was transferred pursuant to this section to any nonfederal agency. The Attorney General, the Secretary of the Treasury, or the Postal Service may order the discontinuance of any forfeiture proceedings under this section in favor of the institution of forfeiture proceedings by state or local authorities under an appropriate state or local statute. After the filing of a complaint for forfeiture under this section, the Attorney General may seek dismissal of the complaint in favor of forfeiture proceedings under state or local law. Whenever forfeiture proceedings are discontinued by the United States in favor of state or local proceedings, the United States may transfer custody and possession of the seized property to the appropriate state or local official immediately upon the initiation of the proper actions by such officials. Whenever forfeiture proceedings are discontinued by the United States in favor of state or local proceedings, notice shall be sent to all known interested parties advising them of the discontinuance or dismissal. The United States shall not be liable in any action arising out of the seizure, detention, and transfer of seized property to state or local officials. The United States shall not be liable in any action arising out of a transfer under paragraph (3), (4), or (5) of this subsection.

(f) All right, title, and interest in property described in subsection (a) of this section shall vest in the United States upon commission of the act giving rise to forfeiture under this section.

(g) (1) Upon the motion of the United States, the court shall stay the civil forfeiture proceeding if the court determines that civil discovery will adversely affect the ability of the government to conduct a related criminal investigation or the prosecution of a related criminal case.

(2) Upon the motion of a claimant, the court shall stay the civil forfeiture proceeding with respect to that claimant if the court determines that—

(A) the claimant is the subject of a related criminal investigation or case;

(B) the claimant has standing to assert a claim in the civil forfeiture proceeding; and

(C) continuation of the forfeiture proceeding will burden the right of the claimant against self-incrimination in the related investigation or case.

(3) With respect to the impact of civil discovery described in paragraphs (1) and (2), the court may determine that a stay is unnecessary if a protective order limiting discovery would protect the interest of one party without unfairly limiting the ability of the opposing party to pursue the civil case. In no case, however, shall the court impose a protective order as an alternative to a stay if the effect of such protective order would be to allow one party to pursue discovery while the other party is substantially unable to do so.

(4) In this subsection, the terms "related criminal case" and "related criminal investigation" mean an actual prosecution or investigation in progress at the time at which the request for the stay, or any subsequent motion to lift the stay is made. In determining whether a criminal case or investigation is "related" to a civil forfeiture proceeding, the court shall consider the degree of similarity between the parties, witnesses, facts, and circumstances involved in the two proceedings, without requiring an identity with respect to any one or more factors.

(5) In requesting a stay under paragraph (1), the government may, in appropriate cases, submit evidence ex parte in order to avoid disclosing any matter that may adversely affect an ongoing criminal investigation or pending criminal trial.

(6) Whenever a civil forfeiture proceeding is stayed pursuant to this subsection, the court shall enter any order necessary to preserve the value of the property or to protect the rights of lienholders or other persons with an interest in the property while the stay is in effect.

(7) A determination by the court that the claimant has standing to request a stay pursuant to paragraph (2) shall apply only to this subsection and shall not preclude the government from objecting to the standing of the claimant by dispositive motion or at the time of trial.

(h) In addition to the venue provided for in section 1395 of title 28 or any other provision of law, in the case of property of a defendant charged with a violation that is the basis for forfeiture of the property under this section, a proceeding for forfeiture under this section may be brought in the judicial district in which the defendant owning such property is found or in the judicial district in which the criminal prosecution is brought.

(i) (1) Whenever property is civilly or criminally forfeited under this chapter, the Attorney General or the Secretary of the Treasury, as the case may be, may transfer the forfeited personal property or the proceeds of the sale of any forfeited personal or real property to any foreign country which participated directly or indirectly in the seizure or forfeiture of the property, if such a transfer—

(A) has been agreed to by the Secretary of State;

(B) is authorized in an international agreement between the United States and the foreign country; and

(C) is made to a country which, if applicable, has been certified under section 481 (h) of the Foreign Assistance Act of 1961.

A decision by the Attorney General or the Secretary of the Treasury pursuant to this paragraph shall not be subject to review. The foreign country shall, in the event of a transfer of property or proceeds of sale of property under this subsection, bear all expenses incurred by the United States in the seizure, maintenance, inventory, storage, forfeiture, and disposition of the property, and all transfer costs. The payment of all such expenses, and the transfer of assets pursuant to this paragraph, shall be upon such terms and conditions as the Attorney General or the Secretary of the Treasury may, in his discretion, set.

(2) The provisions of this section shall not be construed as limiting or superseding any other authority of the United States to provide assistance to a foreign country in obtaining property related to a crime committed in the foreign country, including property which is sought as evidence of a crime committed in the foreign country.

(3) A certified order or judgment of forfeiture by a court of competent jurisdiction of a foreign country concerning property which is the subject of forfeiture under this section and was determined by such court to be the type of property described in subsection (a) (1) (B) of this section, and any certified recordings or transcripts of testimony taken in a foreign judicial proceeding concerning such order or judgment of forfeiture, shall be admissible in evidence in a proceeding brought pursuant to this section. Such certified order or judgment of forfeiture, when admitted into evidence, shall constitute probable cause that the property forfeited by such order or judgment of forfeiture is subject to forfeiture under this section and creates a rebuttable presumption of the forfeitability of such property under this section.

(4) A certified order or judgment of conviction by a court of competent jurisdiction of a foreign country concerning an unlawful drug activity which gives rise to forfeiture under this section and any certified recordings or transcripts of testimony taken in a foreign judicial proceeding concerning such order or judgment of conviction shall be admissible in evidence in a proceeding brought pursuant to this section. Such certified order or judgment of conviction, when admitted into evidence, creates a rebuttable presumption that the unlawful drug activity giving rise to forfeiture under this section has occurred.

(5) The provisions of paragraphs (3) and (4) of this subsection shall not be construed as limiting the admissibility of any evidence otherwise admissible, nor shall they limit the ability of the United States to establish probable cause that property is subject to forfeiture by any evidence otherwise admissible.

(j) For purposes of this section—

(1) the term "Attorney General" means the Attorney General or his delegate; and

(2) the term "Secretary of the Treasury" means the Secretary of the Treasury or his delegate.

(k) Interbank Accounts.—

(1) In general.—

(A) In general.— For the purpose of a forfeiture under this section or under the Controlled Substances Act (21 U.S.C. 801 et seq.), if funds are deposited into an account at a foreign bank, and that foreign bank has an interbank account in the United States with a covered financial institution (as defined in section 5318 (j) (1) of title 31), the funds shall be deemed to have been deposited into the interbank account in the United States, and any restraining order, seizure warrant, or arrest warrant in rem regarding the funds may be served on the covered financial institution, and funds in the interbank account, up to the value of the funds deposited into the account at the foreign bank, may be restrained, seized, or arrested.

(B) Authority to suspend.— The Attorney General, in consultation with the Secretary of the Treasury, may suspend or terminate a forfeiture under this section if the Attorney General determines that a conflict of law exists between the laws of the jurisdiction in which the foreign bank is located and the laws of the United States with respect to liabilities arising from the restraint, seizure, or arrest of such funds, and that such suspension or termination would be in the interest of justice and would not harm the national interests of the United States.

(2) No requirement for government to trace funds.— If a forfeiture action is brought against funds that are restrained, seized, or arrested under paragraph (1), it shall not be necessary for the government to establish that the funds are directly traceable to the funds that were deposited into the foreign bank, nor shall it be necessary for the government to rely on the application of section 984.

(3) Claims brought by owner of the funds.— If a forfeiture action is instituted against funds restrained, seized, or arrested under paragraph (1), the owner of the funds deposited into the account at the foreign bank may contest the forfeiture by filing a claim under section 983.

(4) Definitions.— For purposes of this subsection, the following definitions shall apply:

(A) Interbank account.— The term "interbank account" has the same meaning as in section 984 (c) (2) (B).

(B) Owner.—

(i) In general.— Except as provided in clause (ii), the term "owner"—

(I) means the person who was the owner, as that term is defined in section 983 (d) (6), of the funds that were deposited into the foreign bank at the time such funds were deposited; and

(II) does not include either the foreign bank or any financial institution acting as an intermediary in the transfer of the funds into the interbank account.

(ii) Exception.— The foreign bank may be considered the "owner" of the funds (and no other person shall qualify as the owner of such funds) only if—

(I) the basis for the forfeiture action is wrongdoing committed by the foreign bank; or

(II) the foreign bank establishes, by a preponderance of the evidence, that prior to the restraint, seizure, or arrest of the funds, the foreign bank had discharged all or part of its obligation to the prior owner of the funds, in which case the foreign bank shall be deemed the owner of the funds to the extent of such discharged obligation.

18 U.S.C. §982

(a) (1) The court, in imposing sentence on a person convicted of an offense in violation of section 1956, 1957, or 1960 of this title, shall order that the person forfeit to the United States any property, real or personal, involved in such offense, or any property traceable to such property.

(2) The court, in imposing sentence on a person convicted of a violation of, or a conspiracy to violate—

(A) section 215, 656, 657, 1005, 1006, 1007, 1014, 1341, 1343, or 1344 of this title, affecting a financial institution, or

(B) section 471, 472, 473, 474, 476, 477, 478, 479, 480, 481, 485, 486, 487, 488, 501, 502, 510, 542, 545, 842, 844, 1028, 1029, or 1030 of this title,

shall order that the person forfeit to the United States any property constituting, or derived from, proceeds the person obtained directly or indirectly, as the result of such violation.

(3) The court, in imposing a sentence on a person convicted of an offense under—

(A) section 666 (a) (1) (relating to federal program fraud);

(B) section 1001 (relating to fraud and false statements);

(C) section 1031 (relating to major fraud against the United States);

(D) section 1032 (relating to concealment of assets from conservator, receiver, or liquidating agent of insured financial institution);

(E) section 1341 (relating to mail fraud); or

(F) section 1343 (relating to wire fraud),

involving the sale of assets acquired or held by the Resolution Trust Corporation, the Federal Deposit Insurance Corporation, as conservator or receiver for a financial institution or any other conservator for a financial institution appointed by the Office of the Comptroller of the Currency or the Office of Thrift Supervision, or the National Credit Union Administration, as conservator or liquidating agent for a financial institution, shall order that the person forfeit to the United States any property, real or personal, which represents or is traceable to the gross receipts obtained, directly or indirectly, as a result of such violation.

(4) With respect to an offense listed in subsection (a) (3) committed for the purpose of executing or attempting to execute any scheme

or artifice to defraud, or for obtaining money or property by means of false or fraudulent statements, pretenses, representations, or promises, the gross receipts of such an offense shall include any property, real or personal, tangible or intangible, which is obtained, directly or indirectly, as a result of such offense.

(5) The court, in imposing sentence on a person convicted of a violation or conspiracy to violate—

(A) section 511 (altering or removing motor vehicle identification numbers);

(B) section 553 (importing or exporting stolen motor vehicles);

(C) section 2119 (armed robbery of automobiles);

(D) section 2312 (transporting stolen motor vehicles in interstate commerce); or

(E) section 2313 (possessing or selling a stolen motor vehicle that has moved in interstate commerce);

shall order that the person forfeit to the United States any property, real or personal, which represents or is traceable to the gross proceeds obtained, directly or indirectly, as a result of such violation.

(6)

(A) The court, in imposing sentence on a person convicted of a violation of, or conspiracy to violate, section 274 (a), 274A (a) (1), or 274A (a) (2) of the Immigration and Nationality Act or section 1425, 1426, 1427, 1541, 1542, 1543, 1544, or 1546 of this title, or a violation of, or conspiracy to violate, section 1028 of this title if committed in connection with passport or visa issuance or use, shall order that the person forfeit to the United States, regardless of any provision of state law—

(i) any conveyance, including any vessel, vehicle, or aircraft used in the commission of the offense of which the person is convicted; and

(ii) any property real or personal—

(I) that constitutes, or is derived from or is traceable to the proceeds obtained directly or indirectly from the commission of the offense of which the person is convicted; or

(II) that is used to facilitate, or is intended to be used to facilitate, the commission of the offense of which the person is convicted.

(B) The court, in imposing sentence on a person described in subparagraph (A), shall order that the person forfeit to the United States all property described in that subparagraph.

(7) The court, in imposing sentence on a person convicted of a federal health care offense, shall order the person to forfeit property, real or personal, that constitutes or is derived, directly or indirectly, from gross proceeds traceable to the commission of the offense.

(8) The court, in sentencing a defendant convicted of an offense under section 1028, 1029, 1341, 1342, 1343, or 1344, or of a conspiracy to commit such an offense, if the offense involves telemarketing (as that term is defined in section 2325), shall order that the defendant forfeit to the United States any real or personal property—

(A) used or intended to be used to commit, to facilitate, or to promote the commission of such offense; and

(B) constituting, derived from, or traceable to the gross proceeds that the defendant obtained directly or indirectly as a result of the offense.

(b)

(1) The forfeiture of property under this section, including any seizure and disposition of the property and any related judicial or administrative proceeding, shall be governed by the provisions of section 413 (other than subsection (d) of that section) of the Comprehensive Drug Abuse Prevention and Control Act of 1970 (21 U.S.C. 853).

(2) The substitution of assets provisions of subsection 413 (p) shall not be used to order a defendant to forfeit assets in place of the actual property laundered where such defendant acted merely as an intermediary who handled but did not retain the property in the course of the money laundering offense unless the defendant, in committing the offense or offenses giving rise to the forfeiture, conducted three or more separate transactions involving a total of $100,000 or more in any 12-month period.

18 USC §984. CIVIL FORFEITURE OF FUNGIBLE PROPERTY

(a) This section shall apply to any action for forfeiture brought by the government in connection with any offense under section 1956, 1957, or 1960 of this title or section 5322 or 5324 of title 31, United States Code.

(b) (1) In any forfeiture action in rem in which the subject property is cash, monetary instruments in bearer form, funds deposited in an account in a financial institution (as defined in section 20 of this title), or other fungible property—

(A) it shall not be necessary for the government to identify the specific property involved in the offense that is the basis for the forfeiture; and

(B) it shall not be a defense that the property involved in such an offense has been removed and replaced by identical property.

(2) Except as provided in subsection (c), any identical property found in the same place or account as the property involved in the offense that is the basis for the forfeiture shall be subject to forfeiture under this section.

(c) No action pursuant to this section to forfeit property not traceable directly to the offense that is the basis for the forfeiture may be commenced more than 1 year from the date of the offense.

(d) (1) No action pursuant to this section to forfeit property not traceable directly to the offense that is the basis for the forfeiture may be taken against funds held by a financial institution in an interbank account, unless the financial institution holding the account knowingly engaged in the offense.

(2) As used in this section, the term "interbank account" means an account held by one financial institution at another financial institution primarily for the purpose of facilitating customer transactions.

APPENDIX G

FEDERAL STATUTES RELATING TO TERRORIST FINANCING

§2339A. PROVIDING MATERIAL SUPPORT TO TERRORISTS

(a) **Offense.**— Whoever provides material support or resources or conceals or disguises the nature, location, source, or ownership of material support or resources, knowing or intending that they are to be used in preparation for, or in carrying out, a violation of section 32, 37, 81, 175, 229, 351, 831, 842 (m) or (n), 844 (f) or (i), 930 (c), 956, 1114, 1116, 1203, 1361, 1362, 1363, 1366, 1751, 1992, 1993, 2155, 2156, 2280, 2281, 2332, 2332a, 2332b, 2332f, or 2340A of this title, section 236 of the Atomic Energy Act of 1954 (42 U.S.C. 2284), or section 46502 or 60123 (b) of title 49, or in preparation for, or in carrying out, the concealment of an escape from the commission of any such violation, or attempts or conspires to do such an act, shall be fined under this title, imprisoned not more than 15 years, or both, and, if the death of any person results, shall be imprisoned for any term of years or for life. A violation of this section may be prosecuted in any federal judicial district in which the underlying offense was committed, or in any other federal judicial district as provided by law.

(b) **Definition.**— In this section, the term "material support or resources" means currency or monetary instruments or financial securities, financial services, lodging, training, expert advice or assistance, safe houses, false documentation or identification, communications equipment, facilities, weapons, lethal substances, explosives, personnel, transportation, and other physical assets, except medicine or religious materials.

§2339B. PROVIDING MATERIAL SUPPORT OR RESOURCES TO DESIGNATED FOREIGN TERRORIST ORGANIZATIONS

(a) **Prohibited Activities.**—

(1) **Unlawful conduct.**— Whoever, within the United States or subject to the jurisdiction of the United States, knowingly provides material support or resources to a foreign terrorist organization, or attempts or conspires to do so, shall be fined under this title or imprisoned not more than 15 years, or both, and, if the death of any person results, shall be imprisoned for any term of years or for life.

(2) **Financial institutions.**— Except as authorized by the Secretary, any financial institution that becomes aware that it has possession of, or control over, any funds in which a foreign terrorist organization, or its agent, has an interest, shall—

(A) retain possession of, or maintain control over, such funds; and

(B) report to the Secretary the existence of such funds in accordance with regulations issued by the Secretary.

(b) **Civil Penalty.**— Any financial institution that knowingly fails to comply with subsection

(a) (2) shall be subject to a civil penalty in an amount that is the greater of—

(A) $50,000 per violation; or

(B) twice the amount of which the financial institution was required under subsection (a) (2) to retain possession or control.

(c) **Injunction.**— Whenever it appears to the Secretary or the Attorney General that any person is engaged in, or is about to engage in, any act that constitutes, or would constitute, a violation of this section, the Attorney General may initiate civil action in a district court of the United States to enjoin such violation.

(d) **Extraterritorial Jurisdiction.**— There is extraterritorial federal jurisdiction over an offense under this section.

(e) **Investigations.**—

(1) **In general.**— The Attorney General shall conduct any investigation of a possible violation of this section, or of any license, order, or regulation issued pursuant to this section.

(2) **Coordination with the Department of the Treasury.**— The Attorney General shall work in coordination with the Secretary in investigations relating to—

(A) the compliance or noncompliance by a financial institution with the requirements of subsection (a) (2); and

(B) civil penalty proceedings authorized under subsection (b).

(3) **Referral.**— Any evidence of a criminal violation of this section arising in the course of an investigation by the Secretary or any other federal agency shall be referred immediately to the Attorney General for further investigation. The Attorney General shall timely notify the Secretary of any action taken on referrals from the Secretary, and may refer investigations to the Secretary for remedial licensing or civil penalty action.

(f) **Classified Information in Civil Proceedings Brought by the United States.**—

(1) **Discovery of classified information by defendants.**—

(A) **Request by United States.**— In any civil proceeding under this section, upon request made ex parte and in writing by the United States, a court, upon a sufficient showing, may authorize the United States to—

(i) redact specified items of classified information from documents to be introduced into evidence or made available to the defendant through discovery under the Federal Rules of Civil Procedure;

(ii) substitute a summary of the information for such classified documents; or

(iii) substitute a statement admitting relevant facts that the classified information would tend to prove.

(B) **Order granting request.**— If the court enters an order granting a request under this paragraph, the entire text of the documents to which the request relates shall be sealed and preserved in the records of the court to be made available to the appellate court in the event of an appeal.

(C) **Denial of request.**— If the court enters an order denying a request of the United States under this paragraph, the United States may take an immediate, interlocutory appeal in accordance with paragraph (5). For purposes of such an appeal, the entire text of the documents to which the request relates, together with any transcripts of arguments made ex parte to the court in connection therewith, shall be maintained under seal and delivered to the appellate court.

(2) **Introduction of classified information; precautions by court.**—

(A) **Exhibits.**— To prevent unnecessary or inadvertent disclosure of classified information in a civil proceeding brought by the United States under this section, the United States may petition the court ex parte to admit, in lieu of classified writings, recordings, or photographs, one or more of the following:

(i) Copies of items from which classified information has been redacted.

(ii) Stipulations admitting relevant facts that specific classified information would tend to prove.

(iii) A declassified summary of the specific classified information.

(B) **Determination by court.**— The court shall grant a request under this paragraph if the court finds that the redacted item, stipulation, or summary is sufficient to allow the defendant to prepare a defense.

(3) Taking of trial testimony.—

(A) Objection.— During the examination of a witness in any civil proceeding brought by the United States under this subsection, the United States may object to any question or line of inquiry that may require the witness to disclose classified information not previously found to be admissible.

(B) Action by court.— In determining whether a response is admissible, the court shall take precautions to guard against the compromise of any classified information, including—

(i) permitting the United States to provide the court, ex parte, with a proffer of the witness's response to the question or line of inquiry; and

(ii) requiring the defendant to provide the court with a proffer of the nature of the information that the defendant seeks to elicit.

(C) Obligation of defendant.— In any civil proceeding under this section, it shall be the defendant's obligation to establish the relevance and materiality of any classified information sought to be introduced.

(4) Appeal.— If the court enters an order denying a request of the United States under this subsection, the United States may take an immediate interlocutory appeal in accordance with paragraph (5).

(5) Interlocutory appeal.—

(A) Subject of appeal.— An interlocutory appeal by the United States shall lie to a court of appeals from a decision or order of a district court—

(i) authorizing the disclosure of classified information;

(ii) imposing sanctions for nondisclosure of classified information; or

(iii) refusing a protective order sought by the United States to prevent the disclosure of classified information.

(B) Expedited consideration.—

(i) In general.— An appeal taken pursuant to this paragraph, either before or during trial, shall be expedited by the Court of Appeals.

(ii) Appeals prior to trial.— If an appeal is of an order made prior to trial, an appeal shall be taken not later than 10 days after the decision or order appealed from, and the trial shall not commence until the appeal is resolved.

(iii) Appeals during trial.— If an appeal is taken during trial, the trial court shall adjourn the trial until the appeal is resolved, and the court of appeals—

(I) shall hear argument on such appeal not later than 4 days after the adjournment of the trial;

(II) may dispense with written briefs other than the supporting materials previously submitted to the trial court;

(III) shall render its decision not later than 4 days after argument on appeal; and

(IV) may dispense with the issuance of a written opinion in rendering its decision.

(C) Effect of ruling.— An interlocutory appeal and decision shall not affect the right of the defendant, in a subsequent appeal from a final judgment, to claim as error reversal by the trial court on remand of a ruling appealed from during trial.

(6) Construction.— Nothing in this subsection shall prevent the United States from seeking protective orders or asserting privileges ordinarily available to the United States to protect against the disclosure of classified information, including the invocation of the military and state secrets privilege.

(g) Definitions.— As used in this section—

(1) the term "classified information" has the meaning given that term in section 1 (a) of the Classified Information Procedures Act (18 U.S.C. App.);

(2) the term "financial institution" has the same meaning as in section 5312 (a) (2) of title 31, United States Code;

(3) the term "funds" includes coin or currency of the United States or any other country, traveler's checks, personal checks, bank checks, money orders, stocks, bonds, debentures, drafts, letters of credit, any other negotiable instrument, and any electronic representation of any of the foregoing;

(4) the term "material support or resources" has the same meaning as in section 2339A;

(5) the term "Secretary" means the Secretary of the Treasury; and

(6) the term "terrorist organization" means an organization designated as a terrorist organization under section 219 of the Immigration and Nationality Act.

§2339C. PROHIBITIONS AGAINST THE FINANCING OF TERRORISM

(a) Offenses.—

(1) In general.— Whoever, in a circumstance described in subsection (b), by any means, directly or indirectly, unlawfully and willfully provides or collects funds with the intention that such funds be used, or with the knowledge that such funds are to be used, in full or in part, in order to carry out—

(A) an act which constitutes an offense within the scope of a treaty specified in subsection (e) (7), as implemented by the United States, or

(B) any other act intended to cause death or serious bodily injury to a civilian, or to any other person not taking an active part in the hostilities in a situation of armed conflict, when the purpose of such act, by its nature or context, is to intimidate a population, or to compel a government or an international organization to do or to abstain from doing any act, shall be punished as prescribed in subsection (d) (1).

(2) Attempts and conspiracies.— Whoever attempts or conspires to commit an offense under paragraph (1) shall be punished as prescribed in subsection (d) (1).

(3) Relationship to predicate act.— For an act to constitute an offense set forth in this subsection, it shall not be necessary that the funds were actually used to carry out a predicate act.

(b) Jurisdiction.— There is jurisdiction over the offenses in subsection (a) in the following circumstances—

(1) the offense takes place in the United States and—

(A) a perpetrator was a national of another state or a stateless person;

(B) on board a vessel flying the flag of another state or an aircraft which is registered under the laws of another state at the time the offense is committed;

(C) on board an aircraft which is operated by the government of another state;

(D) a perpetrator is found outside the United States;

(E) was directed toward or resulted in the carrying out of a predicate act against—

(i) a national of another state; or

(ii) another state or a government facility of such state, including its embassy or other diplomatic or consular premises of that state;

(F) was directed toward or resulted in the carrying out of a predicate act committed in an attempt to compel another state or international organization to do or abstain from doing any act; or

(G) was directed toward or resulted in the carrying out of a predicate act—

(i) outside the United States; or

(ii) within the United States, and either the offense or the predicate act was conducted in, or the results thereof affected, interstate or foreign commerce;

(2) the offense takes place outside the United States and—

(A) a perpetrator is a national of the United States or is a stateless person whose habitual residence is in the United States;

(B) a perpetrator is found in the United States; or

(C) was directed toward or resulted in the carrying out of a predicate act against—

(i) any property that is owned, leased, or used by the United States or by any department or agency of the United States, including an embassy or other diplomatic or consular premises of the United States;

(ii) any person or property within the United States;

(iii) any national of the United States or the property of such national; or

(iv) any property of any legal entity organized under the laws of the United States, including any of its states, districts, commonwealths, territories, or possessions;

(3) the offense is committed on board a vessel flying the flag of the United States or an aircraft which is registered under the laws of the United States at the time the offense is committed;

(4) the offense is committed on board an aircraft which is operated by the United States; or

(5) the offense was directed toward or resulted in the carrying out of a predicate act committed in an attempt to compel the United States to do or abstain from doing any act.

(c) Concealment.— Whoever—

(1)

(A) is in the United States; or

(B) is outside the United States and is a national of the United States or a legal entity organized under the laws of the United States (including any of its states, districts, commonwealths, territories, or possessions); and

(2) knowingly conceals or disguises the nature, location, source, ownership, or control of any material support, resources, or funds—

(A) knowing or intending that the support or resources were provided in violation of section 2339B of this title; or

(B) knowing or intending that any such funds or any proceeds of such funds were provided or collected in violation of subsection (a),

shall be punished as prescribed in subsection (d) (2).

(d) Penalties.—

(1) Subsection (a).—Whoever violates subsection (a) shall be fined under this title, imprisoned for not more than 20 years, or both.

(2) Subsection (c).—Whoever violates subsection (c) shall be fined under this title, imprisoned for not more than 10 years, or both.

(e) Definitions.— In this section—

(1) the term "funds" means assets of every kind, whether tangible or intangible, movable or immovable, however acquired, and legal documents or instruments in any form, including electronic or digital, evidencing title to, or interest in, such assets, including coin, currency, bank credits, traveler's checks, bank checks, money orders, shares, securities, bonds, drafts, and letters of credit;

(2) the term "government facility" means any permanent or temporary facility or conveyance that is used or occupied by representatives of a state, members of a government, the legislature, or the judiciary, or by officials or employees of a state or any other public authority or entity or by employees or officials of an intergovernmental organization in connection with their official duties;

(3) the term "proceeds" means any funds derived from or obtained, directly or indirectly, through the commission of an offense set forth in subsection (a);

(4) the term "provides" includes giving, donating, and transmitting;

(5) the term "collects" includes raising and receiving;

(6) the term "predicate act" means any act referred to in subparagraph (A) or (B) of subsection (a) (1);

(7) the term "treaty" means—

(A) the Convention for the Suppression of Unlawful Seizure of Aircraft, done at The Hague on December 16, 1970;

(B) the Convention for the Suppression of Unlawful Acts against the Safety of Civil Aviation, done at Montreal on September 23, 1971;

(C) the Convention on the Prevention and Punishment of Crimes against Internationally Protected Persons, including Diplomatic Agents, adopted by the General Assembly of the United Nations on December 14, 1973;

(D) the International Convention against the Taking of Hostages, adopted by the General Assembly of the United Nations on December 17, 1979;

(E) the Convention on the Physical Protection of Nuclear Material, adopted at Vienna on March 3, 1980;

(F) the Protocol for the Suppression of Unlawful Acts of Violence at Airports Serving International Civil Aviation, supplementary to the Convention for the Suppression of Unlawful Acts against the Safety of Civil Aviation, done at Montreal on February 24, 1988;

(G) the Convention for the Suppression of Unlawful Acts against the Safety of Maritime Navigation, done at Rome on March 10, 1988;

(H) the Protocol for the Suppression of Unlawful Acts against the Safety of Fixed Platforms located on the Continental Shelf, done at Rome on March 10, 1988; or

(I) the International Convention for the Suppression of Terrorist Bombings, adopted by the General Assembly of the United Nations on December 15, 1997;

(8) the term "intergovernmental organization" includes international organizations;

(9) the term "international organization" has the same meaning as in section 1116 (b) (5) of this title;

(10) the term "armed conflict" does not include internal disturbances and tensions, such as riots, isolated and sporadic acts of violence, and other acts of a similar nature;

(11) the term "serious bodily injury" has the same meaning as in section 1365 (g) (3) of this title;

(12) the term "national of the United States" has the meaning given that term in section 101 (a) (22) of the Immigration and Nationality Act (8 U.S.C. 1101 (a) (22)); and

(13) the term "state" has the same meaning as that term has under international law, and includes all political subdivisions thereof.

(f) Civil Penalty.— In addition to any other criminal, civil, or administrative liability or penalty, any legal entity located within the United States or organized under the laws of the United States, including any of the laws of its states, districts, commonwealths, territories, or possessions, shall be liable to the United States for the sum of at least $10,000, if a person responsible for the management or control of that legal entity has, in that capacity, committed an offense set forth in subsection (a).

TITLE 50 UNITED STATES CODE, CHAPTER 35. INTERNATIONAL EMERGENCY ECONOMIC POWERS

Sec. 1701. Unusual and extraordinary threat; declaration of national emergency; exercise of presidential authorities

(a) Any authority granted to the President by section 1702 of this title may be exercised to deal with any unusual and extraordinary threat, which has its source in whole or substantial part outside the United States, to the national security, foreign policy, or economy of the United States, if the President declares a national emergency with respect to such threat.

(b) The authorities granted to the President by section 1702 of this title may only be exercised to deal with an unusual and extraordinary threat with respect to which a national emergency has been declared for purposes of this chapter and may not be exercised for any other purpose. Any exercise of such authorities to deal with any new threat shall be based on a new declaration of national emergency which must be with respect to such threat.

Sec. 1702. Presidential authorities

(a) (1) At the times and to the extent specified in section 1701 of this title, the President may, under such regulations as he may prescribe, by means of instructions, licenses, or otherwise—

(A) investigate, regulate, or prohibit—

(i) any transactions in foreign exchange,

(ii) transfers of credit or payments between, by, through, or to any banking institution, to the extent that such transfers or payments involve any interest of any foreign country or a national thereof,

(iii) the importing or exporting of currency or securities; and

(B) investigate, regulate, direct and compel, nullify, void, prevent or prohibit, any acquisition, holding, withholding, use, transfer, withdrawal, transportation, importation or exportation of, or dealing in, or exercising any right, power, or privilege with respect to, or transactions involving, any property in which any foreign country or a national thereof has any interest; by any person, or with respect to any property, subject to the jurisdiction of the United States.

(2) In exercising the authorities granted by paragraph (1), the President may require any person to keep a full record of, and to furnish under oath, in the form of reports or otherwise, complete information relative to any act or transaction referred to in paragraph (1) either before, during, or after the completion thereof, or relative to any interest in foreign property, or relative to any property in which any foreign country or any national thereof has or has had any interest, or as may be otherwise necessary to enforce the provisions of such paragraph.

In any case in which a report by a person could be required under this paragraph, the President may require the production of any books of account, records, contracts, letters, memoranda, or other papers, in the custody or control of such person.

(3) Compliance with any regulation, instruction, or direction issued under this chapter shall to the extent thereof be a full acquittance and discharge for all purposes of the obligation of the person making the same. No person shall be held liable in any court for or with respect to anything done or omitted in good faith in connection with the administration of, or pursuant to and in reliance on, this chapter, or any regulation, instruction, or direction issued under this chapter.

(b) The authority granted to the President by this section does not include the authority to regulate or prohibit, directly or indirectly—

(1) any postal, telegraphic, telephonic, or other personal communication, which does not involve a transfer of anything of value;

(2) donations, by persons subject to the jurisdiction of the United States, of articles, such as food, clothing, and medicine, intended to be used to relieve human suffering, except to the extent that the President determines that such donations (A) would seriously impair his ability to deal with any national emergency declared under section 1701 of this title, (B) are in response to coercion against the proposed recipient or donor, or (C) would endanger Armed Forces of the United States which are engaged in hostilities or are in a situation where imminent involvement in hostilities is clearly indicated by the circumstances; or

(3) the importation from any country, or the exportation to any country, whether commercial or otherwise, regardless of format or medium of transmission, of any information or informational materials, including but not limited to, publications, films, posters, phonograph records, photographs, microfilms, microfiche, tapes, compact disks, CD ROMs, artworks, and news wire feeds. The exports exempted from regulation or prohibition by this paragraph do not include those which are otherwise controlled for export under section 2404 of the Appendix to this title, or under section 2405 of the Appendix to this title to the extent that such controls promote the nonproliferation or antiterrorism policies of the United States, or with respect to which acts are prohibited by chapter 37 of title 18; or

(4) any transactions ordinarily incident to travel to or from any country, including importation of accompanied baggage for personal use, maintenance within any country including payment of living expenses and acquisition of goods or services for personal use, and arrangement or facilitation of such travel including nonscheduled air, sea, or land voyages.

Sec. 1703. Consultation and reports

(a) Consultation with Congress

The President, in every possible instance, shall consult with the Congress before exercising any of the authorities granted by this chapter and shall consult regularly with the Congress so long as such authorities are exercised.

(b) Report to Congress upon exercise of presidential authorities

Whenever the President exercises any of the authorities granted by this chapter, he shall immediately transmit to the Congress a report specifying—-

(1) the circumstances which necessitate such exercise of authority;

(2) why the President believes those circumstances constitute an unusual and extraordinary threat, which has its source in whole or substantial part outside the United States, to the national security, foreign policy, or economy of the United States;

(3) the authorities to be exercised and the actions to be taken in the exercise of those authorities to deal with those circumstances;

(4) why the President believes such actions are necessary to deal with those circumstances; and

(5) any foreign countries with respect to which such actions are to be taken and why such actions are to be taken with respect to those countries.

(c) Periodic follow-up reports

At least once during each succeeding six-month period after transmitting a report pursuant to subsection (b) of this section with respect to an exercise of authorities under this chapter, the President shall report to the Congress with respect to the actions taken, since the last such report, in the exercise of such authorities, and with respect to any changes which have occurred concerning any information previously furnished pursuant to paragraphs (1) through (5) of subsection (b) of this section.

(d) Supplemental requirements

The requirements of this section are supplemental to those contained in title IV of the National Emergencies Act (50 U.S.C. 1641).

Sec. 1704. Authority to issue regulations

The President may issue such regulations, including regulations prescribing definitions, as may be necessary for the exercise of the authorities granted by this chapter.

Sec. 1705. Penalties

(a) A civil penalty of not to exceed $10,000 may be imposed on any person who violates any license, order, or regulation issued under this chapter.

(b) Whoever willfully violates any license, order, or regulation issued under this chapter shall, upon conviction, be fined not more than $50,000, or, if a natural person, may be imprisoned for not more than 10 years, or both; and any officer, director, or agent of any corporation who knowingly participates in such violation may be punished by a like fine, imprisonment, or both.

Sec. 1706. Savings provisions

(a) Termination of national emergencies pursuant to National Emergencies Act

(1) Except as provided in subsection (b) of this section, notwithstanding the termination pursuant to the National Emergencies Act (50 U.S.C. 1601 et seq.) of a national emergency declared for purposes of this chapter, any authorities granted by this chapter, which are exercised on the date of such termination on the basis of such national emergency to prohibit transactions involving property in which a foreign country or national thereof has any interest, may continue to be so exercised to prohibit transactions involving that property if the President determines that the continuation of such prohibition with respect to that property is necessary on account of claims involving such country or its nationals.

(2) Notwithstanding the termination of the authorities described in section 101 (b) of this act, any such authorities, which are exercised with respect to a country on the date of such termination to prohibit transactions involving any property in which such country or any national thereof has any interest, may continue to be exercised to prohibit transactions involving that property if the President determines that the continuation of such prohibition with respect to that property is necessary on account of claims involving such country or its nationals.

(b) Congressional termination of national emergencies by concurrent resolution

The authorities described in subsection (a) (1) of this section may not continue to be exercised under this section if the national emergency is terminated by the Congress by concurrent resolution pursuant to section 202 of the National Emergencies Act (50 U.S.C. 1622) and if the Congress specifies in such concurrent resolution that such authorities may not continue to be exercised under this section.

(c) Supplemental savings provisions; supersedure of inconsistent provisions

(1) The provisions of this section are supplemental to the savings provisions of paragraphs (1), (2), and (3) of section 101 (a) (50 U.S.C. 1601 (a) (1), (2), (3)) and of paragraphs (A), (B), and (C) of section 202 (a) (50 U.S.C. 1622 (a) (A), (B), and (C)) of the National Emergencies Act.

(2) The provisions of this section supersede the termination provisions of section 101 (a) (50

U.S.C. 1601 (a)) and of title II (50 U.S.C. 1621 et seq.) of the National Emergencies Act to the extent that the provisions of this section are inconsistent with these provisions.

(d) Periodic reports to Congress

If the President uses the authority of this section to continue prohibitions on transactions involving foreign property interests, he shall report to the Congress every six months on the use of such authority.

INDEX

A

ABA Transit Number, 195, 197
Accardo, Tony, 17
Acceptance D/P, 214
Accounting
    balance sheets, 113, 131–132, 136–137
    basic definitions in, 112–113
    debit and credit, 136–139
    fundamental equation, 135–136
    generally accepted accounting principles, 107–108, 135–139
    income statements, 113, 133, 137, 140–143
    journals, 138–139, 142–143
    ledgers, 143
    single-entry *vs.* double-entry bookkeeping, 135, 138
    source documents, 138–139
Accounts payable, 140
Accounts receivable, 139
Accumulated retained earnings, 140
Adjustable rate mortgages (ARMs), 188
Administrative forfeiture, 71–72
Administrative subpoenas, 285–286
Advice, in international payments, 210
Agency bonds, 261
Agent services, 206
Agriculture Department, 297–298
Aircraft sales, information from, 309
Air Force, 298
Airlines, information from, 309, 443
Alcohol and Tobacco Trade Bureau, 300
Alexander v. Thornburgh (1991), 340
Allen, Robert, 22
Alphonse Capone Second Hand Furniture, Inc., 117–135; *see also* Capone, Alphonse
Al Qaeda
    drug trade and, 377
    hawala schemes, 389–391
    money trail of, 384–387
    state sponsorship of, 376
Al-Sadawai, Alaa, 63
Amendment, in international payments, 210
American Airlines, money laundering by, 26–27
American Shipbuilding, money laundering by, 28–30
American Stock Exchange (AMEX), 254, 255
Ames, Aldrich, 108–111, 272, 277

Anastasia, Albert, 17
The Anderson Tapes (Sanders), 267
Andreas, Dwayne, 21, 22, 24
Andresen v. Maryland (1976), 283
Annual reports, 117, 119–135, 342
Annunzio–Wylie Anti–Money Laundering Act of 1992, 33
Anti-Drug Abuse Act of 1988, 33
ARMs (adjustable rate mortgages), 188
Army, 298
Articles of incorporation, 165–166
Assessment records, 304
Asset-backed bonds, 261
Asset Forfeiture Manual (IRS), 75
Assets
    asset substitution, 66, 73–74
    classification of, 139–140
    debit and credit and, 137, 139
    definition of, 112, 135–136
    depreciation of, 140
    forfeiture of (*see* Forfeiture)
    intangible, 140
    jointly held, 151
Asset substitution, 66, 73–74
Attorneys, *see* Lawyers
Audits, 116, 143–144
Authorization to Sell, 244
Auto finance corporations, 185
Automatic teller machines (ATMs), 194
Automobile dealers, 309, 443
Avocat, 222–223

B

Babylonian clay tablets, 6, 8
Back-to-back letter of credit, 214
Bacon, Francis, 174
Bail bond company, subpoena template for, 443–444
Balance sheets
    of Alphonse Capone Second Hand Furniture, Inc., 131–132
    analyzing, 139–140, 142
    debit and credit in, 136–138
    equation for, 113
    of shell corporations, 342
Bank cards, *see* Credit cards

Bank deposits method, 152–153, 157–159
Bank drafts, 202
Banker's acceptance, 176, 209, 215–216
Bank examinations, 179
Bank holding companies, 185
Banking–business combination scheme, 326–330, 335–339
Banking operations, 187–207
   business services, 205
   Check 21 and, 199
   consumer loans, 188–190
   currency exchange, 205
   holding and administering property, 203–204
   loan processes, 190
   monthly account statements, 199
   paying checks, 195–199
   receiving deposits, 181–182, 191–192
   record-keeping and reporting, 60–61, 206–207
   teller's tapes, 193
   transferring funds, 200–203
   trust department services, 205–206
"Bank money," 176
Bank money orders, 83, 202
Bank of Credit and Commerce International (BCCI), 98
Bank of New England, 169
Bank records
   customer notification of disclosure of, 207
   required availability of, 60–61
   requirements for, 206–207
   retention requirements, 206
Bankruptcy Court, 301
Bankruptcy records, 149, 301
Banks; *see also* banking operations; financial institutions; International banking
   central, 184
   charter revocation, 91
   correspondent, 59–61, 60, 184, 198, 220
   credit unions, 180, 184–185
   cyber, 184
   definition of, 81–82
   deposits to, 181–182, 191–192
   Federal Reserve, 177, 184 (*see also* Federal Reserve System)
   federal savings, 183–184
   functions of, 180
   fund measurements, 177
   history of banking, 174–176, 187
   in holding companies, 185
   investment, 183
   lending by, 179, 180–181
   management and operation of, 179–180
   national, 176
   offshore, 42–44, 183, 218–219, 291
   records, 60–61, 206–207
   regulation and control of, 178–179
   Report of Condition of, 186
   reserve requirements, 178
   resources on, 185–186
   robberies, 377
   subpoena template for, 444–447
   teller's tapes, 193
   trust services of, 182–183
Bank Secrecy Act (BSA) of 1970, 80–92
   bank compliance officers, 79
   bank records requirements, 206–207
   criminal penalties in, 9, 18, 33, 62, 89–91
   Currency and Monetary Instruments Report, 84
   Currency Transaction Report, 83–84
   Currency Transaction Report by Casinos, 84–85
   false statements, 95–96
   focus of, 32
   Foreign Bank Account Reports, 85
   foreign bank accounts, 33, 85
   forfeiture provisions, 68, 491–499
   money-transmitting business registration, 88–89, 91
   number of reports received from, 81
   reporting threshold of, 33
   Report of Cash Payments Over $10,000 Received in a Trade or Business, 87–88, 475–478
   reports required by, 83–88
   Section 5313, 32
   Suspicious Activity Reports, 85–87
   Title I, 80
   Title II, 80
   Title 18, 35–36
   Title 31, 81, 91–92
Bank tellers, not used as informants, 269
Barker, Bernard, 20, 22, 23, 24–26
Barrera, Alberto, 332–333, 398
Bartering, 2, 174
Basis for the investigation, 397–398; *see also* Case management
BBI (Bank-to-Bank Information), 236
BCCI (Bank of Credit and Commerce International), 98
Bearer bonds, 261
Bearer share corporations, 170
Beneficiaries, of trusts, 248
Benevolence International Foundation, 56
Bill of exchange, 212
Bill of lading, 211
bin Laden, Osama, 384
Black market peso exchange (BMPE) schemes, 335–339
Boat dealers, information from, 309
Bond coupons, 194
Bonds, 260–262; *see also* Securities
Book entry bonds, 261
Book transfers, 237
Braniff Airlines, money laundering by, 28–29
Braswell v. United States (1984), 168, 279
Bribery of foreign officials, 18

British Commonwealth, 99–100
Brokerage houses
  buying and selling stocks through, 256–257
  information from, 258–259, 262, 263
  money laundering through, 265–266
Brokers
  real estate, 244, 452
  securities, 62, 94, 185, 263
  stock, 256–257
BSA, *see* Bank Secrecy Act (BSA) of 1970
Building permits, 249
Bureau of Alcohol, Tobacco, Firearms and Explosives, 300
Bureau of Customs and Border Protection, 84
Bureau of Immigration and Customs Enforcement, 91
Bureau of Indian Affairs, 299
Business–banking combination scheme, 326–330, 335–339
Business cards, giving and getting, 312–313
Business day, definition of, 83
Businesses; *see also* Business organization
  business transaction systems, 7–9
  money-transmitting, 88–89, 91, 93–94, 227, 238–240
  questions to ask, 313
  racketeering in acquisition of, 93
  simple business cover scheme, 319–323, 324
  as sources of information, 308–312
  subpoenas of records from, 269–270
  Suspicious Activity Reports filed by, 62
  terrorist financing from, 376
Business organization, 161–172
  comparison of, 170
  cooperatives, 171
  corporations, 165–169, 170
  foreign corporations, 170
  franchises, 171
  holding corporations, 169–170
  joint ventures, 171
  mutual companies, 171
  nonprofit corporations, 171
  offshore corporations, 170
  partnerships, 162–165, 170
  proprietorships, 161–162, 170
  shell corporations, 170–171, 339–344
  société anonyme, 171–172
  syndicates, 171
Business transaction systems, 7–9
Buy-back schemes, 361–364

C

CAFRA (Civil Asset Forfeiture Reform Act of 2000), 65, 67, 70, 74, 406
California Bankers Association v. Shultz (1974), 32–33, 80

CAMFAB, 28
Campaign financing
  American Airlines and, 26–27
  Braniff Airlines and, 28–29
  George Steinbrenner III and, 28–30
  legislation on, 17–18
  Watergate scandal and, 20–26
Cantonal (Swiss) banks, 221, 222
Capacity, on loan applications, 190
Capital
  definition of, 135
  as equity, 140
  flight of, 359
Capone, Alphonse, 117–135
  annual report made from books of, 117, 118–135
  case study of, 411–416, 421–423
  importance of, 15–16
  organization of, 117–118
Casas de cambio, 205
Case development process, 394–396
Case examples
  Al Qaeda, 384–387, 389–391
  Ames, Aldrich, 108–111, 272, 277
  banking–business combination scheme, 327
  black market peso exchange scheme, 335–337
  buy-back scheme, 362–363
  Capone, Alphonse, 411–416, 421–423
  of case development process, 396, 398, 401, 403–408
  Daley, Wallace J., 396, 398, 401, 403–408
  hawala system, 389–391
  loan-back schemes, 346–347, 349–350
  of the money laundering cycle, 10–11
  overinvoicing scheme, 358–359, 360–361
  Provisional Irish Republican Army, 370–378
  securities manipulation, 365–367
  shell corporations, 339–344
  simple banking operation scheme, 323–325
  simple business cover scheme, 320–321, 324
  of structuring, 332–333
  underinvoicing scheme, 357
  use of nominees scheme, 317–318, 414
  Watergate, 19–24
  of wire transfer scenario, 226–227
Case file, 411–423; *see also* Case management
  case report, 419–420
  chain of custody, 415
  document control, 416–419
  exhibits and exhibit lists, 419–421
  introducing documentary evidence, 414–415
  presentation of evidence, 405–407, 419
  types of documentary evidence, 412–414
Case initiation, 396–397; *see also* Case management
Case management; *see also* Case file
  agency jurisdiction in, 398
  basis for the investigation, 397–398

case development process, 394–396
case example of, 396, 398, 401, 403–408
case file location, 399
case initiation, 396–397
case organization, 398–399
chain of custody, 415
covert evidence collection, 401, 403
document control, 416–419
evidence analysis, 404–406, 418
evidence collection, 400–401
evidence logs, 417
integrated approach in, 394
investigative plan, 399–407
overt evidence collection, 403–404
presentation of evidence, 405–407, 419
profiling, 401–402
prosecutor involvement, 399
Case organization, 398–399; *see also* Case management
Case report, 419–420; *see also* Case file
Cash Disbursements journals, 138, 142–143
Cashier's checks, 83, 200–201
Cash in advance, 210–211
Cash on hand, 149, 150
Cash smuggling, 58–59
Cash transactions
bank deposits of cash, 193–195
cashing checks, 200
Currency and Monetary Instrument Reports (*see* Currency and Monetary Instrument Report)
Currency Transaction Reports (*see* Currency Transaction Reports)
recordkeeping for, 138
Report of Cash Payments Over $10,000 Received in a Trade or Business, 87–88, 475–478
Report of International Transportation of Currency or Monetary Instruments, 473–474
required records for, 9, 32, 87–88
for services, 88
smurfing, 33 (*see also* Structuring)
systems compared with business transaction systems, 7–8
teller's tapes, 193
transporting cash across borders, 9, 359 (*see also* Currency exchange)
Casinos
Currency Transaction Reports by, 84–85, 311, 462–465
as financial institutions, 82
information from, 311
in Nevada, 85
subpoena template for, 447
Suspicious Activity Report by Casinos and Card Clubs, 488–490
Cayman Islands, 291
CBP (Customs and Border Protection), 299
CDs (certificates of deposit), 182, 192–193

Cellular telephone companies, 309
Central banks, 184
Certificates of deposit (CDs), 182, 192–193
Certificates of inspection, 211
Certificates of manufacture, 212
Certificates of origin, 212
Certified checks, 202
Chain of custody, 415
Character, in loan applications, 190
Check 21, 199
Check Clearing for the 21st Century Act of 2004 (Check 21), 199
Checks, paying process for, 195–199
CHIPS (Clearing House Interbank Payments System), 231, 236–238
Choice-Point, 302
"Churning," 323
CICAD (Inter-American Drug Abuse Control Commission), 101–102
CID (Criminal Investigation Division), 298
Circuit Courts (state), 302
Circumstantial evidence, 37
Civil Asset Forfeiture Reform Act of 2000 (CAFRA), 65, 67, 70, 74, 406
Civil forfeiture; *see also* Forfeiture
administrative procedures, 71–72
advantages of, 70
criminal compared with, 66, 70
procedures for, 70–71
statutes on, 65–66, 491–497, 499
what can be seized, 70
Closed-end mutual funds, 262
CMIR, *see* Currency and Monetary Instrument Report
Cohen, Mickey, 17
Coins, ancient, 3–4, 14, 176
Collateral, on loan applications, 181, 190
Collateralized loans, 181
Collection with acceptance (acceptance D/P), 214
Colombian cocaine trafficking, 377–378
Commerce Department, 298, 361
Commercial invoice, 212
Commercial paper, 176, 177, 355
Commingling funds
court cases on, 41
forfeiture and, 68, 69
in Section 1957 monetary transaction, 47
Committee on Uniform Securities Identification of the American Bankers Association (CUSIP) numbers, 254
Committee to Re-Elect the President (CRP)
American Airlines and, 26–27
American Shipbuilding and, 28–30
Braniff Airlines and, 28–29
Watergate scandal, 20–26
Commodities, 264

Common stock, 252
Commonwealth Scheme for Mutual Assistance in Criminal Matters, 99–100
Communications
    companies as sources of information, 309–310
    subpoena template for companies, 447–448
    by terrorists, 373–374
Community property, 247
Community property states, 247
Comptroller of the Currency, 178–179, 185
Conditions, on loan applications, 190
Condominiums, 247
Conducts, definition of, 35
Confederate currency, 5
Confirmation slips, for securities transactions, 258–259
Consolidation loans, 190
Conspiracy, statutes on, 47, 93
Constitutional rights
    Fourth Amendment rights, 280, 286
    Fifth Amendment, 162, 165, 168, 278–279, 290–291
    Eighth Amendment, 67, 68
Continental Baking Co. v. United States (1960), 169
Convertible bonds, 261
Conveyance tax, 250
Cooperatives, 171
Corporate bylaws, 166
Corporate charters, 166
Corporations, 165–169
    accounting departments of, 167
    advantages and disadvantages of, 166–168, 170
    articles of, 165–166
    bond issuance, 260–262
    criminal liability in, 168–169
    foreign, 170
    holding, 169–170
    nonprofit, 171
    offshore, 170, 343–345
    organizational chart of, 167
    real estate owned by, 247
    S corporations, 168
    shell, 170–171, 339–344
    subpoena template for, 448–450
Correspondent banks
    check paying and, 198
    due diligence for, 61
    forfeiture and, 59–60
    function of, 184
    shell banks and, 60
    vostro and nostro accounts in, 220
    wire transfers and, 237
Cost bonds, 71
Costello, Frank, 17
Cost of goods sold, 141
Cost of services, 141
Court decisions, *see under names of individual court cases*

Court records, 301–303
Covers, 271–277
Credit
    credit agency resources, 305–308, 450
    credit reports, 269, 305
    definition of, 174–175
    importance of, 175
    origin of, 174
    revolving, 189
Credit agencies, 305–306, 450
Credit cards
    information from issuers of, 306–308
    interest on, 181
    loans on, 189
    subpoena templates for companies, 450–451
Credit reports, 269, 305
Credits and debits, in accounting, 136–139, 199
Credit unions, 180, 184–185
Criminal forfeiture, 66, 72–74, 497–498; *see also* Forfeiture
Criminal Investigation Division (CID), 298
"Criminally derived property," 46
Criminal penalties
    in Bank Secrecy Act, 62
    for false statements, 95–96
    in Money Laundering Control Act of 1986, 49
    in USA Patriot Act of 2001, 57–58
Criminal Referrals, 207
CRP, *see* Committee to Re-Elect the President
CTR, *see* Currency Transaction Reports
CTRC (Currency Transaction Report by Casinos), 84–85, 311, 462–465
Currency; *see also* Cash transactions
    capital flight, 359
    controls on, 290
    currency exchange, 205, 216–218, 335–339
    Eurodollars, 218
    red seal *vs.* green seal, 218
    smuggling of, 58–59
Currency and Monetary Instrument Report (CMIR)
    currency controls compared with, 290
    data on TECS, 295
    forfeiture and, 67
    form number, 81
    number filed annually, 91
    penalties for failure to file, 90
    requirements for, 84
    used in net worth method, 151
    in Watergate scandal, 26
Currency controls, 290
Currency dealers, as financial institutions, 82
Currency exchange, 205, 216–218, 335–339
Currency Transaction Report by Casinos (CTRC), 84–85, 311, 462–465

Currency Transaction Reports (CTR)
    by casinos, 84–85
    data on TECS, 295
    form for, 469–472
    form number, 81, 83
    penalties for failure to file, 89–90
    requirements for, 83–84
    structuring to avoid, 83–84 (*see also* Structuring)
    in the Watergate scandal, 26
    for wired money transfer, 229
Currency transactions, definition of, 83; *see also* Cash transactions
Current accounts (Swiss), 222
CUSIP (Committee on Uniform Securities Identification of the American Bankers Association) numbers, 254
Customs and Border Protection (CBP), 299
Customs Cooperation Agreements, 291
Customs Court, 301
Cyber banks, 184

D

D/A (documents against acceptance), 211
Dahlberg, Kenneth, 21, 22, 24, 26
Daley, Wallace J., 396, 398, 401, 403–408
Databases
    commercial, 302, 303–304
    federal, 294, 295
"dba," 162
DC (documentary collections), 211, 214–216
DEA (Drug Enforcement Administration), 286, 295, 300
Dean, John, 15
Debenture, 261
Debit cards, 195, 307
Debits and credits, in accounting, 136–139, 199
Debray, Regis, *Revolution in the Revolution*, 377
Declaration of Forfeiture, 71
Defense Criminal Investigation Service, 298
Defense Department, 298
Defense Investigative Service, 298
Demand accounts, 182, 192
Department of Agriculture, 297–298
Department of Commerce, 298, 361
Department of Defense (DOD), 298
Department of Health, Education, and Welfare, 298
Department of Homeland Security, 294, 299
Department of Justice, 300, 401
Department of State, 300
Department of the Air Force, 298
Department of the Army, 298
Department of the Interior, 299–300
Department of the Navy, 300
Department of the Treasury, 300
Department of Veterans Affairs (DVA), 301

Deposit Receipt Offer and Acceptance (DROA), 244
Deposits, bank, 181–182, 191–192, 200
Deposit tickets, 194
Depreciation, 140
Dialed number recorders (DNRs), 277
Direct Sales Company, Inc. v. United States (1943), 32
Disbursing agents, 260
Discount rate, 177
Discrepancy, in international payments, 210
District Courts, state, 302
District Courts, U. S., 301
Dividends, 252, 253
Divorce courts, 302
Divorce records, use of, 147, 302
DJIA (Dow Jones Industrial Average), 256
DNRs (dialed number recorders), 277
Documentary collections (DC), 211, 214–216
Documentary evidence, 412–419
    chain of custody on, 415
    document control, 416–419
    grand jury material, 418
    introducing, 414–415
    security of, 418
    types of, 412–414
Documentary letters of credit, 213–214, 216, 217
Document control, 416–419
Documents against acceptance (D/A), 211, 214
Documents against payment (D/P), 211, 214, 215
Document warrants, 279–284
    affidavit information for, 281
    description of items to be seized, 283–285
    evidence of financial activity, 282
    evidence of lack of employment, 282
    example, 455–460
    in *hawala* schemes, 391
    particularity in, 280
    probable cause in, 280–282
    scope of search, 281
    time limits in, 281
    in zakat schemes, 389
DOD (Department of Defense), 298
Double-entry bookkeeping, 135–136, 138
Double invoicing technique, 101
Dow Jones Industrial Average (DJIA), 256
Down payments, 245
D/P (documents against payment), 211, 215
Drafts, 212
DROA (Deposit Receipt Offer and Acceptance), 244
Drug Enforcement Administration (DEA), 286, 295, 300
Drug trafficking
    authentication of subject's records, 271
    bulk cash smuggling in, 58–59
    case example of, 396, 398, 401, 403–408
    Colombian, 377–378
    extortion of traffickers, 377

fei chi'en and *hawala* in, 238–240
Financial Action Task Force and, 100–101
forfeiture in, 66
international movement of currency in, 42–44
investment of profits of, 94–95
mutual assistance treaties and, 291
OAS model regulations on, 102
single-entry bookkeeping in, 135
terrorist financing and, 377–378, 386
use of dollars in, 218
wire transfer scenario, 226–227, 229–230
Duces tecum, 283, 286
Due diligence for banking, 61
Dun & Bradstreet (D&B), 305–306, 342
Dutch Sandwich scheme, 348–351
DVA (Department of Veterans Affairs), 301

E

EFT, *see* Electronic funds transfer
Egmont Group, 102
Egyptian money, ancient, 2
Eighth Amendment rights, 67, 68
Electricity companies, 310
Electronic funds transfer (EFT), 231–236
    book transfers, 237
    Fedwire, 231, 232–236
    forms used in, 233–236
    major systems of, 231
    in money laundering scheme, 226–227
    procedure for, 232
    records generated in, 232–233
    SWIFT and CHIPS, 236–238
    volume of, 225, 231
El Paso Intelligence Center (EPIC), 295
Emerson, Steven, 382
EOAF (Executive Offices for Asset Forfeiture), 77
Equitable sharing, 77
Equity
    calculating, 140
    definition of, 135
    of shareholders, 252
    use in determining income, 146
Escrow companies, 206, 451
Escrow papers, 245–246
Estate settling, 205
Eurodollars, 218
Evidence, *see* Financial information, obtaining
Evidence analysis, 404–406, 418; *see also* Case management
Excessive fines, 67
Exchange instruments, 200–203
Executive Offices for Asset Forfeiture (EOAF), 77
Exhibits and exhibit lists, 419–421
Ex parte court orders, 165, 266, 283, 289–290

Expenditures method, 151–152
Export licenses, 212
Express private trusts, 248
Extortion racket, 377

F

Fabrega, Camilo, 28
Facilitation, forfeiture of property used in, 69
Failure to maintain records, 90
Fair Credit Reporting Act of 1971 (FCRA), 305
False statements, 95–96
Family courts, 302
FARC (Revolutionary Armed Forces of Colombia), 63
FATF (Financial Action Task Force), 100–101, 372–373
Fax intercept orders, 277
FBAR, *see* Foreign Bank Account Report
FDA (Food and Drug Administration), 298
FDIC (Federal Deposit Insurance Corporation), 178–179, 185–186
Federal Aviation Administration (FAA), 300
Federal Bureau of Investigation (FBI), 300
Federal databases
    Narcotics and Dangerous Drugs Information System, 295
    National Crime Information Center, 294, 295
    National Law Enforcement Telecommunications System, 295
    Treasury Enforcement Communications System, 294
Federal Deposit Insurance Corporation (FDIC), 178–179, 185–186
Federal Maritime Commission (FMC), 300–301
Federal National Mortgage Association, 188
Federal Reserve notes, 4
Federal Reserve System
    address of, 185
    check paying and, 198
    Fedwire, 231, 232–236
    fund measurements by, 177
    interest rates and, 178
    money supply and, 177
    structure of, 177, 184
Federal Savings and Loan Insurance Corporation (FSLIC), 183–184
Federal savings banks, 183–184
Fedwire, 231, 232–236
Fee simple owners, 246
Fei chi'en, 94, 238–239; *see also hawala*
Fifth Amendment rights
    in business partnerships, 165, 279
    in corporations, 168
    in offshore third party records, 290–291
    in sole proprietorships, 162, 279
    subject's records and, 278–279, 413
Fifth Amendment rule, 15

Financial Action Task Force (FATF), 100–101, 372–373
Financial Crimes Enforcement Network (FinCEN)
    Bank Secrecy Act and, 80
    Currency and Monetary Instrument Reports and, 84
    Financial Action Task Force and, 100
    information in, 296–297
    on money laundering stages, 7, 10
    profiling by, 401
    as representative to Egmont Group, 102
Financial information, obtaining, 267–292; *see also* Financial investigation techniques; Sources of information
    from abroad, 290–292
    asking subject for, 278
    document search warrants, 279–284
    financial search warrants, 279, 288–289
    informants, 269–270
    interviews, 270–271
    letters rogatory, 291–292
    mail covers, 272, 273–276
    pen registers, 277
    physical surveillance, 271–272
    risk of premature disclosure, 268–269
    second party access to subject's records, 278
    subpoenas of business records, 269–270
    tax and mutual legal assistance treaties, 291
    tax returns, 289–290
    third-party records, 285–290
    trash covers, 272, 277
    undercover agents, 270, 407–409
Financial institutions; *see also* Banks
    anti–money laundering program requirements, 62
    BSA compliance officers in, 79
    definition of, 35, 39, 46, 81–82
    identification verification standards, 61
    interbank account forfeitures, 62
    nonbank, 80
    notification to subject of request for records, 287–288
    obtaining information from, 75–76
    records availability requirements, 60–61
    regulated by BSA, 80–81
    regulation and control of, 178–179
    relationship information from, 192, 285
    Right to Financial Privacy Act and, 285
    seizure of, 72
Financial Intelligence Units (FIUs), 102
Financial investigation techniques; *see also* Case management; Financial information, obtaining; Sources of information
    in Ames case, 110, 272, 277
    awards to informants, 270
    balance sheets, 113, 139–140
    bank deposits, 152–153, 192
    in banking–business combination scheme, 329–330
    in black market peso exchange operation, 336–339
    business cards from contacts in, 312–313
    in buy-back schemes, 364
    in Capone case, 117–135
    cashier's checks, 201
    creating audit trails, 116–117
    direct *vs.* indirect methods, 146, 154
    income statements, 113, 140–143
    in invoice scams, 361
    in Lindbergh kidnapping, 154–160
    loan applications, 190–191
    in loan-back schemes, 348, 349–351
    net worth method, 146–151
    protective orders, 207
    in real property, 250
    red flags in analyzing records, 144
    for safe deposit boxes, 204
    in secured property loans, 188–189
    in securities manipulations, 367
    of shell corporations, 340–343
    in simple banking scheme, 325–326
    in simple business cover scheme, 322–323, 324
    in smurfing operations, 333–335
    source and application of funds, 151–152
    in terrorist financing, 378–384
    in transfer of funds, 202–203
    undercover operations, 407–409
    unit and volume method, 153
    in use of nominee schemes, 318–319
    when and how to use sources, 268–269
    for wire transfers, 240–242
    in zakat schemes, 389
Financial search warrants, 279, 288–289
Financial transactions; *see also* Cash transactions; Money transfers
    definition of, 35, 38, 39
    intent to avoid reporting requirements, 42
    international, 210–211 (*see also* International banking)
    Section 1957 and, 45–47
    in sting operations, 44–45, 409
FinCEN, *see* Financial Crimes Enforcement Network
Fitzgerald, Patrick, 56
FIUs (Financial Intelligence Units), 102
Fixed-income securities, 260–262
Flimsies, of cashier's checks, 201
Float, 193, 199
Floor brokers, 256–257
Florez-Gomez, Libardo, 63
FMC (Federal Maritime Commission), 300–301
Food and Drug Administration (FDA), 298
Food and Nutritional Services Agency, 297–298
Food stamps, 297–298
Foreign Bank Account Report (FBAR)
    data on TECS, 295
    form number, 81

penalties for failure to file, 91
requirements of, 85, 221
Foreign banks; *see also* International banking
advantages of, 219
definition of, 82
Eurodollars in, 218
Fifth Amendment rights and records from, 291
Foreign Bank Account Reports, 81, 85, 91, 221, 295
international transportation offense, 42–44
Meyer Lansky and, 16
record availability in, 60–61
reporting requirements for, 9, 33
Report of Foreign Bank and Financial Accounts, 479–482
secrecy laws in, 183
smurfing operations in, 332–333, 334
Foreign branches of U.S. banks, 221
Foreign corporations, 170
Foreign exchange, 205, 216–218
Foreign terrorist organizations (FTOs), 380–381; *see also* Terrorist financing
Forest Service, 297
Forfeiture, 65–77
administrative, 71–72
civil, 65–66, 70–72, 491–497, 499
Civil Asset Forfeiture Reform Act of 2000, 65, 67, 70, 74, 406
civil *vs.* criminal forfeiture, 66
commingling funds and, 68, 69
criminal, 66, 72–74, 497–498
double jeopardy issue in, 66
Eighth Amendment and, 67
equitable sharing of proceeds from, 77
forfeiture of laundered assets, 67–70
forfeiture of proceeds of criminal activity, 66
grand jury information, 75
from intermediaries, 73–74
international cooperation in, 98, 100
non–grand jury information, 75–76
power of, 18
preseizure planning, 74–75, 76, 406
principle behind, 65–66
problems with, 67
procedures for, 70–73
of property exchanged for assets, 68–69
of property used in facilitation, 69
of real property, 69, 71, 72, 76
statutes on, 491–499
of substitute assets, 66, 73–74
in the USA PATRIOT Act, 58–60, 62
Forms, 461–490
Currency Transaction Report, 469–472
Currency Transaction Report by Casinos, 462–465
Report of Cash Payments Over $10,000 Received in a Trade or Business, 475–478

Report of Foreign Bank and Financial Accounts, 479–482
Report of International Transportation of Currency or Monetary Instruments, 473–474
Suspicious Activity Report, 483–487
Suspicious Activity Report by Casinos and Card Clubs, 488–490
Suspicious Activity Report by Money Services Business, 466–468
Forward foreign exchange, 210
Forward prices, 218
FOSF (Friends of Sinn Fein), 375
"Four name paper" (banker's acceptance), 176, 209
Fourth Amendment rights, 280, 286
Franchises, 171
Frank, William, 153, 157
Freehold estates, 246
Friends of Sinn Fein (FOSF), 375
FSLIC (Federal Savings and Loan Insurance Corporation), 183–184
FTOs (foreign terrorist organizations), 380–381; *see also* Terrorist financing
Fund measurements, 177
Funds, definition of, 381
Futures contracts, 263–264, 265

G

Gambling violations, 53
General ledger, 143
Generally Accepted Accounting Principles (GAAP), 107–108, 116
General Motors Acceptance Corporation (GMAC), 185
General partnerships, 164, 170
Geographic Targeting Orders (GTOs), 241
Gibson, James, 63
Gifts, as defense to net worth, 150
Glossary of terms, 429–437
GMAC (General Motors Acceptance Corporation), 185
GNMA (Government National Mortgage Association), 188
Gold, as money, 3
"Gold backs," 4
Gold certificates, 155–156
Golden Rule, "other," 176
Good Till Canceled (GTC), 256
Goodwill, as asset, 140
Government agencies
county, 302–303
courts, 301–303
Department of Agriculture, 297–298
Department of Commerce, 298
Department of Defense, 298
Department of Health, Education, and Welfare, 298
Department of Homeland Security, 294, 299

Department of Justice, 300, 401
Department of State, 300
Department of the Air Force, 298
Department of the Army, 298
Department of the Interior, 299–300
Department of the Navy, 300
Department of the Treasury, 300
Department of Veterans Affairs, 301
Federal Aviation Administration, 300
Federal Maritime Commission, 300–301
FinCEN, 296–297 (*see also* Financial Crimes Enforcement Network)
Immigration and Customs Enforcement, 299
municipal, 302–303
Postal Service, 300
Securities and Exchange Commission, 301
Small Business Administration, 301
Social Security Administration, 298
state, 302–303
Government National Mortgage Association (GNMA), 188
Grand jury
  in forfeiture cases, 75
  storage of material from, 418
  subpoenas, 286–288
Grantee–Grantor Index, 248–249
Green funds, 262
Gross annual gaming revenue, 82
Growth stocks, 253
GTC (Good Till Canceled), 256
GTOs (Geographic Targeting Orders), 241
Guide to Routing Codes, 186
Gulf Resources, 21–23, 24–25
Guzik, Jake "Greasy Thumb," 416

H

Haldeman, H. R., 26
HAMAS, 374, 378, 380, 387–389
Hauptmann, Bruno, 150, 154–160, 397–398
Hawaii, real estate records in, 248
hawala
  in Al Qaeda money trail, 385–386
  case example of, 389–391
  money transfer process in, 238, 239
  Title 18 and, 94
Hazardous chemicals, real property seizures and, 76
Health Insurance Portability and Accountability Act of 1996, 33
HELs (home equity loans), 190
Hezbollah, 374, 378, 380
High Intensity Financial Crimes Area (HIFCA) task forces, 19
HLF (Holy Land Foundation for Relief and Development), 387–388

Holding corporations, 169–170
Holland v. United States (1954), 151
Holy Land Foundation for Relief and Development (HLF), 387–388
Home equity loans (HELs), 190
Home improvement loans, 190
Homeland Security Department, 294, 299
Hooper-Holmes Bureau, Inc., 306
Horgan, John, 376
Hotels, information from, 308–309, 451
Houses, *see* Real property
Hundi, 94
Hussein, Mohammed, 63

I

Identification verification standards, 61
Immigration and Customs Enforcement (ICE), 299
Import licenses, 212
INAC (Irish Northern Aid Committee, Inc.), 375
Income statements, 113, 133, 140–143
Indirect methods of proving income, 145–160
  bank deposits method, 152–153, 157–159
  direct *vs.* indirect methods, 146, 154
  in Lindbergh kidnapping, 154–160
  net worth method, 146–151
  source and application of funds technique, 151–152
  unit and volume method, 153
Inflation, paper money and, 5
Informal value transfer system (IVTS), 94, 391–392; *see also hawala*
Informants, 269–270
Information, obtaining, *see* Financial information, obtaining
Inheritances, as defense to net worth, 150
Initial public offerings (IPOs), 183, 252, 255
in personam actions, 66
in rem actions, 66
Insurance companies, 212, 310, 451
Intangible assets, 140
Integration stage, 10, 11, 354
Intelligence Unit of the Bureau of Internal Revenue, 31
Intent of defendant, 40–42
Inter-American Drug Abuse Control Commission (CICAD), 101–102
Interbank accounts, forfeiture of funds in, 62
Interest
  on bank loans, 181, 188
  Federal Reserve control over rates, 178
  importance of, 175
  origin of, 174
Interior Department, 299–300
Intermediaries, forfeiture by, 73–74
Internal Revenue Service (IRS)
  Bank Secrecy Act and, 80, 91

Intelligence Unit, 31
intent requirement, 40–41
MSB oversight by, 229
taxes on illegal businesses, 15–17
tax returns, 149, 283, 289–290
International Asian Organized Crime Conference, 290
International banking, 209–224
    advantages of offshore banks, 219
    basic trade documents, 211–212
    cash in advance, 210–211
    documentary collections, 211, 214–216
    documentary letters of credit, 211, 212–214
    documents available from foreign banks, 223
    foreign exchange, 216–218
    open account, 211
    in Switzerland, 221–224
    terminology in, 210
    types of banks, 219–220
    by U.S. banks, 220–221
International controls, 97–106
    British Commonwealth, 99–100
    Egmont Group, 102
    Financial Action Task Force, 100–101
    impact of, 102–103
    INTERPOL, 99
    motivation for, 97–98
    Mutual Legal Assistance Treaties, 103–106
    Organization of American States, 101–102
    regional initiatives, 102
    U. N. Narcotics Convention of 1988 (Vienna Convention), 99
International Money Laundering Abatement and Anti-Terrorist Financing Act of 2001, 57; *see also* USA PATRIOT Act of 2001
International trade documents, 211–212
International Transportation of Currency or Monetary Instruments, 473–474
International transportation offense, 42–44
Internet
    cyber banks, 184
    offshore corporations and, 343, 345
    research on, 304–305
INTERPOL (International Criminal Police Organization), 99
Interstate commerce requirement, 40
Interstate Identification Index File, 295
Interstate or Foreign Travel and Transportation in Aid of Racketeering Enterprises (ITAR) Act, 53
Interviews, 270
Inventories, 139
Investigation techniques, *see* Financial investigation techniques
Investigative Checklist, 401
Investigative plan, 399–407
Investment banks, 183

Invoices, 354–355
Invoice schemes, 354–361
    overinvoicing, 358–361
    underinvoicing, 355–358
    in Watergate scandal, 27
IPOs (initial public offerings), 183, 252, 255
Irish Northern Aid Committee, Inc. (INAC), 375
Irish Republican Army, *see* Provisional Irish Republican Army
Irrevocable credits, 213, 214, 217
IRS, *see* Internal Revenue Service
ITAR (Interstate or Foreign Travel and Transportation in Aid of Racketeering Enterprises), 53
IVTS (informal value transfer system), 94, 391–392; *see also hawala*

J

John Doe subpoenas, 413
John Doe v. United States (1988), 290–291
Jointly held assets, 151
Joint tenancy, 247
Joint ventures, 171
Journals
    bank, 194
    financial statements and, 138–139, 142–143
    of money transfers, 235
Justice Department, 300, 401

K

Kidd, Capt. William, 11–14
"Know Your Customer rule," 83

L

Land, *see* Real property
Lansky, Meyer, 16–17, 32
Lawyers
    reporting cash payments for, 88
    Strike Force, 93
    subpoena template for, 451–452
Layering stage, 9–10, 11, 354
Lead charts, 405
Leasehold estates, 246
Ledgers, 143
Legislation, *see* Statutes
Lethal Weapon 2, 345–348
Letter box companies, 101
Letters of credit, 213–214, 216, 217
Letters rogatory, 291–292
Lexis-Nexis, 248, 302–304
Liabilities
    classification of, 140

debit and credit and, 137
definition of, 112, 135–136
Liability
of bankers for loans, 179
in corporations, 166, 168–169
in partnerships, 164
in sole proprietorships, 162
Liddy, G. Gordon, 22–25
Life estates, 246
Limited partnerships, 163, 164–165
Limit orders, 256
Lindbergh kidnapping, 154–160
Link analysis, 404–405
lis pendens, 76
Living expenses, estimating, 149–150
Loan applications, false statements on, 95–96
Loan-back schemes, 345–351
Loans
collateralized, 181
consolidation, 190
credit card, 189
in defense to net worth, 150
false statements on applications, 190
home equity, 190
home improvement, 190
liability of bankers for, 179
mortgage, 188
overdraft protection, 189
personal lines of credit, 189
process for, 190
secured cash, 189
secured property, 188
student, 189–190
terms of, 188
use of records in financial investigations, 190–191
Loan Sandwich scheme, 348–351
Lock box banking, 205
Logs, on money transfers, 235–236
Lombard loans, 175
Long-distance communications providers, 310, 452
Louis XVI (king of France), 3
"L.P.," 165
"Ltd.," 165
Luciano, Charles "Lucky," 16

M

M1 (Money Supply 1), 177
M2 (Money Supply 2), 177
Machine stamps, on checks, 200
Mail covers, 272
Margin calls, 257
Margin loans, 185
Margin trading, 257
Market orders, 256

Material support, definition of, 379
McCord, James, 20
McFee v. United States, 151
Metals, precious, as money, 3
MICR numbers, 196–197
Microfilm photographs of checks, 197, 206
Military personnel, records of, 298
MLATs, *see* Mutual Legal Assistance Treaties
MLCA, *see* Money Laundering Control Act (MLCA) of 1986
MLS (Multiple Listing Service), 244
Model Regulations on Crimes Related to Laundering... (OAS), 102
Mohammed, Khalid Sheikh, 386
Monetary instruments, definition of, 35, 84
Monetary transactions, 45–47; *see also* Cash transactions; Financial transactions
Money
coins, 3–4, 14, 176
evolution of, 2–6
forms in money laundering, 5–6
nature of, 1–2
paper, 4–5
process stages in, 7–10
Money changers, 4
Money laundering; *see also* Case examples; Money laundering schemes
by Al Qaeda, 384–387
by American Airlines, 26–27
by Capone, 117–135
case study in, 10–11
cycle in, 10–11
by Daley, 396, 398, 401, 403–408
definition of, 6–7
forms of currency in, 5–6
by Hauptmann, 150, 154–160, 397–398
international control, 97–106
by organized crime, 15–17, 117–135
by pirates, 11–14
by Provisional Irish Republican Army, 370–378
by Steinbrenner III, 28–30
terrorist financing and, 57, 381–392
in Watergate scandal, 19–24
Money Laundering Alert, 358
Money Laundering Control Act (MLCA) of 1986
conspiracy provision, 47
defendant acting with intent to conceal, 40–42
defendant conducting a financial transaction, 38–40
defendant's knowledge of money from SUA, 37–38
definitions in, 35
intent to avoid transaction-reporting requirement, 42
international transportation offense, 42–44
interstate commerce requirement, 40
language of statute, 34–35
legislative amendments to, 33

listing of SUAs, 49–51
money as proceeds of an SUA, 36–37
money from felonies, 38
money-transmitting businesses, 93–94
overview of, 35–36
passage of, 31
Section 1957, 45–47
sentencing provisions, 49
statute of limitations in, 48–49
"sting" provision, 44–45, 270, 409
venue in, 47–48
Money laundering cycle, 10–11
Money laundering schemes
   banking–business combination, 326–330
   black market peso exchange, 335–339
   buy-backs, 361–364
   components of, 353–354
   key to graphics in charts, 316
   loan-back, 345–351
   overinvoicing, 358–361
   securities manipulation, 364–367
   shell corporations, 339–344
   simple banking operation, 323–326
   simple business cover, 319–323, 324
   smurfing, 331–335
   underinvoicing, 354–358
   use of nominee, 316–319, 414
   using letters of credit, 213–214
   by wire transfer, 226–227, 229–230, 240–242
Money Laundering Suppression Act of 1994, 33
Money market funds, 262–263
Money orders, 83, 202
Money services businesses (MSB), 227, 466–468
Money transfers, 225–242
   book transfers, 237
   CHIPS (Clearing House Interbank Payments System), 231, 236–238
   electronic funds transfer, 225, 231–236
   forms used in, 233–236
   informal banking systems, 238–240
   licensed money transmitters, 227–228
   money laundering schemes by, 226–227, 229–230, 240–242
   operation, 228–229
   records of, 229, 232–233
   sources of information on, 240–242
   SWIFT (Society for Worldwide Interbank Financial Telecommunications), 231, 236–238
   Western Union money transfer slip, 230
Money-transmitting businesses; *see also* Money transfers
   current listing of, 227
   definition of, 89
   illegal, 93–94
   IRS oversight of, 229
   registration requirements of, 88–89, 91

Title 18 violations by, 94
   unregulated and undocumented, 238–240
Monthly account statements
   from banks, 199
   from brokerage houses, 259
Moody's Bank and Finance, 186
Mortgage-backed bonds, 261
Mortgage loans, 188
MSB (money services businesses), 227, 466–468
Multiple Listing Service (MLS), 244
Municipal bonds, 261
Mutual companies, 171
Mutual funds, 262–263
Mutual Legal Assistance Treaties (MLATs)
   countries with, 103
   diplomatic efforts towards, 98
   drug trafficking and, 291
   obtaining information from, 291
   Swiss MLAT exemplar, 104–106

N

Narco-terrorism, 377–378
Narcotics and Dangerous Drugs Information System (NADDIS), 295
NASDAQ, 254, 255
National Association of Secretaries of State, 166
National Crime Information Center (NCIC), 294, 295
National Law Enforcement Telecommunications System (NLETS), 294, 295
National Marine Fisheries Service, 298
National Park Service, 300
Naval Criminal Investigative Service, 300
Navy, 300
NBFI (nonbank financial institutions), 80
NCIC (National Crime Information Center), 294, 295
Negotiation letter of credit, 214
Net income, 141
Net sales, 141
Net worth
   debit and credit and, 137
   definition of, 112, 135–136
   use in establishing income, 146–151
Net worth method, 146–151
   cash on hand in, 149, 150
   defenses to, 150–151
   formula for, 147
   funds from known sources, 150
   in Lindbergh kidnapping case, 157
   living expenses in, 149–150
   rules for application of, 148–149
   sample calculation, 148
   sources of information for, 147
Nevada casinos, 85
Newspapers, information from, 312

New York Stock Exchange (NYSE), 254, 255
Nitti, Frank, 16, 423
Nixon, Richard, Watergate scandal and, 19–26
NLETS (National Law Enforcement Telecommunications System), 294, 295
No-load mutual funds, 263
Nominees, in money laundering scheme, 316–319, 414
Nonbank financial institutions (NBFI), 80
Nondisclosure orders, 277
Non-freehold estates, 246
Nonprofit corporations, 171
Nonprofit organizations, 171, 382
Northern Aid Committee (NORAID), 375
Northern Bank, Ulster, robbery of, 377
Nossen, Richard, *The Seventh Basic Investigative Technique,* 393
Nostro accounts, 220
Notes Payable, 140
Notes Receivable, 139
NYSE (New York Stock Exchange), 254, 255

O

OAS (Organization of American States), 101–102
OBI (Other Bank Information), 236
Obtaining financial information, *see* Financial information, obtaining
Odd lots, 255
Office of Foreign Assets Control, 300
Office of Inspector General (OIG), 297, 299
Office of International Affairs (OIA), 290
Office of Special Investigations (OSI), 298
Offsets, 264
Offshore banks, *see* Foreign banks
Offshore corporations, 170, 343–345
Ogarrio D'Aguerre, Manuel, 21, 23, 25
O'Hare, Eddie, 411–412, 416, 421, 423
O'Hare, Edward H. "Butch," Jr., 423
OIA (Office of International Affairs), 290
OIG (Office of Inspector General), 297, 299
Oklahoma Press Publishing Co. v. Walling (1946), 286
Online research, 304–305
Open account, 211
Open-end mutual funds, 262
Operating revenue, 141
Operation Dinero, 407
Operation Mountain Express II, 378
Options, 263
Order Delaying Notification, 76
Organization of American States (OAS), 101–102
Organized crime, tax evasion by, 15–17; *see also* Capone, Alphonse; Lansky, Meyer
OSI (Office of Special Investigations), 298
Overdraft protection, 189
Overinvoicing schemes, 358–361
Over the Counter (OTC) market, 254
Owe–pay sheets, 415

P

Pak, Simon, 358
Paper, in banking, 176
Paper money, 4–5
Parallel exchange rate, 336
"Particularity," 280
Partnerships, 162–165, 170, 279
Passbook accounts, 182
Patents, 140
Patriot Act, *see* USA PATRIOT Act of 2001
Pay and owe sheets, 415
P.E.G. (prior endorsement guaranteed), 198
Penalties, *see* Criminal penalties
Pen registers, 277
"Permeated with fraud," 284–285
Pershing, Gen. "Black Jack," 4
Personal lines of credit (PLC), 189
Persons
    corporations as, 165
    definition of, 82, 85
Pesci, Joe, 345
Philipse, Frederick, 13
Physical surveillance, 271–272; *see also* Surveillance
Pieces of eight, 13–14
Piracy, money laundering in, 4, 11–14
Placement stage, 7–8, 11, 353–354
PLC (personal lines of credit), 189
Plea agreements, 73
"Plumbers" (Special Investigations Unit), 24; *see also* Watergate scandal of 1972
Politicians, influencing, 265
Post offices
    as financial institutions, 80, 82
    information from, 300
    mail covers, 272, 273–276
    money orders from, 202
Predicate offenses, 36, 51–53, 93, 505; *see also* Racketeer Influenced and Corrupt Organizations
Preferred stock, 252–253
Premature disclosure, 268–269
Preseizure planning, 74–75, 76, 406
Presentation of evidence, 405–407, 419; *see also* Case management
Prime rate, 177–178
Principal, 175, 188
Private banks
    due diligence in, 61
    function of, 184
    in Switzerland, 222
Privilege, attorney–client, 271
"Probable cause," 280–282

Probate courts, 302
Profiling, 401–402
Profit and loss statements, 113, 133, 140–143
Property dividends, 253
Proprietorships, 161–162, 170, 279
Prosecutor involvement, 399
Prostitution, 53
Protective orders, 207
Provisional Irish Republican Army (PIRA), 370–378
    funding needs of, 370–374
    sources of funding for, 374–378
Public Law 91-508, *see* Bank Secrecy Act (BSA) of 1970
Public utilities, 310
PUPID (Pick Up with Proper ID), 241
Purchase invoices, 354

Q

Qualified fee estates, 246

R

Racketeer Influenced and Corrupt Organizations (RICO)
    BSA violations and, 33
    forfeiture under, 18
    predicate offenses under, 36, 51–53, 93, 505
    racketeering acts in, 92–93
Real Estate Investment Trust (REIT), 248
Real Estate Limited Partnership (RELP), 165
Real property, 243–250
    assessment records, 304
    Authorization to Sell, 244
    in balance sheets, 139
    conveyance tax on, 250
    of corporations, 247
    Deposit Receipt Offer and Acceptance, 244
    escrow papers, 245–246
    forfeiture of, 69, 71, 72, 76
    hidden assets, 249–250
    mortgage loans on, 188
    Multiple Listing Service, 244
    ownership methods, 246–247
    records from transactions, 246
    researching records of, 248–250
    seller approval, 245
    subpoena template for brokers, 452
    of trusts, 248
Rebozo, Charles G. "Bebe," 364–365
Red clause letter of credit, 214
REIT (Real Estate Investment Trust), 248
Relationship information, from banks, 192, 285
RELP (Real Estate Limited Partnership), 165
Remittance corporations, 229; *see also* Money-transmitting businesses

Report of Cash Payments Over $10,000 Received in a Trade or Business, 87–88, 475–478
Report of Foreign Bank and Financial Accounts, 479–482
Report of International Transportation of Currency or Monetary Instruments, 473–474; *see also* Currency and Monetary Instrument Report
Report on Money Laundering Typologies, 338
Reserve requirements, 178
Resources, *see* Sources of information
Retailers, subpoena template for, 452–453
Revocable credits, 212–213, 214
Revolutionary Armed Forces of Colombia (FARC), 63
Revolution in the Revolution (Debray), 377
Revolving credit, 189
Rex v. William Kidd, et al., 11–14
RICO, *see* Racketeer Influenced and Corrupt Organizations
Ries, Fred, 416, 423
Right to Financial Privacy Act (RTFPA), 285, 287
Rothstein, Arnold "The Big Bankroll," 16
Round lots, 255
Royal Bank of Scotland notes, 4–5
RTFPA (Right to Financial Privacy Act), 285, 287

S

Safe deposit boxes, 39, 181–182, 203–204
Safekeeping, of securities, 258
Sales invoices, 354
Salt, as money, 3
Sanders, Lawrence, *The Anderson Tapes,* 267
SARs, *see* Suspicious Activity Reports
Saudi Arabia, 386
Savings accounts, 182, 192, 222
Savings and loans, 183–184
Savings bonds, 261–262
S corporations, 168
Search engines, 304
Search warrants, 279–284
    document, 279–284, 455–460
    example, 455–460
    financial, 279, 288–289
    "permeated with fraud" phrase in, 284–285
    preparing list of items to be seized, 283–285
SEC (Securities and Exchange Commission), 301
Secrecy rules, for grand jury subpoenas, 287–288
Section 1956, *see* Money Laundering Control Act (MLCA) of 1986
Section 1957, 45–47
Section 5313, 32
Section 5330, 89
Section 2339A, 379
Secured cash loans, 189
Secured property loans, 188

Securities, 251–266; *see also* Stocks
   bondholder information, 262
   bonds, 260–262
   buying and selling stocks, 256–260
   definition of, 251
   disbursing agents, 260
   information available about, 258–260, 262–263
   making money on stocks, 253–254
   manipulation schemes, 364–367
   money laundering and, 265–266
   mutual funds, 262–263
   segregation of stocks, 258
   stockholder information, 258–260
   stock market operations, 254–256
   stock markets, 254
   stock types, 252–253
   subpoena template for brokers, 453
   transfer agents, 259–260
Securities and Exchange Commission (SEC), 301
Securities brokers
   functions of, 185
   information from, 263
   investment of illicit drug profits by, 94
   Suspicious Activity Reports filed by, 62
Segregation, of securities, 258
Seizure warrants, 70–71, 73, 75
Selling short, 257
Sentencing, *see* Criminal penalties
September 11, 2001 terrorist attacks; *see also* USA PATRIOT Act of 2001
   Al Qaeda money trail, 384–387
   impact on money laundering legislation, 79, 87, 378
   SAR activity following, 382–383
The Seventh Basic Investigative Technique (Nossen), 393
Shareholders, of corporations, 166, 252, 343
Shares, *see* Stocks
Shell banks, 60
Shell branch offices, 220–221
Shell corporations, 170–171, 339–344
Shop book rule, 271, 285, 415
Shumway, Leslie, 414–416, 423
Siegel, Benjamin "Bugsy," 16, 32
Sight drafts, 212
Signature cards, 192
Silver certificates, 4
Simple banking operation scheme, 323–326
Simple business cover schemes, 319–323, 324
Single-entry bookkeeping, 135
Single proprietorships, 161–162, 170, 279
Sinn Fein, 374–375
Small Business Administration, 301
Smart cards, 225, 307
Smuggling, of currency, 58–59
Smurfing, *see* Structuring
Social Security Administration (SSA), 298

Social Security Death Index, 299, 302
Sociedad anónima, 172
Société anonyme (S.A.), 171–172
Society for Worldwide Interbank Financial Telecommunications (SWIFT), 231, 236–238
Sole proprietorships, 161–162, 170, 279
Source and application of funds technique, 151–152
Source documents, 138–139
Sources of information, 293–313
   businesses and industry, 308
   commercial databases, 303–304
   communication companies, 309–310
   court records, 301–303
   credit card issuers, 306–308
   credit-related, 305–308
   entertainment, 311
   FinCEN, 296–297
   government agencies, 297–301
   insurance companies, 310
   international business ratings, 306
   libraries, 311–312
   on money transfers, 240–242
   Narcotics and Dangerous Drugs Information System, 295
   National Crime Information Center, 295
   National Law Enforcement Telecommunications System, 295
   for net worth method, 147
   newspapers, 312
   online research, 304–305
   public utilities, 310
   travel and transportation, 308–309
   Treasury Enforcement Communications System, 294
Sources of Information from Abroad (IRS), 290
Specified Unlawful Activities (SUAs)
   circumstantial evidence of, 37
   establishing money as proceeds of, 36–37
   exclusion of tax evasion, 41
   forfeiture of proceeds from, 68
   frequently asked questions about, 53
   intent to conceal nature of proceeds of, 41–42
   listing of, 49–53
   monetary transactions from, 45–47
   scope of statute, 19, 24
   in sting operations, 45, 409
   in terrorist financing, 381
Spot market, 264
Spot prices, 218
SSA (Social Security Administration), 298
Standard settlement instructions (SSI), 186
Stans, Maurice, 21, 28
State Department, 300
Statement of hardship, 193
State sponsorship of terrorism, 374, 375–376
Statute of limitations, 48

Statutes
    Annunzio–Wylie Anti–Money Laundering Act of 1992, 33
    Anti-Drug Abuse Act of 1988, 33
    Bank Secrecy Act of 1970, 9, 18, 32, 80–92
    Check Clearing for the 21st Century Act of 2004, 199
    Civil Asset Forfeiture Reform Act of 2000, 65, 67, 70, 74, 406
    civil forfeiture, 65–66, 491–497, 499
    criminal forfeiture, 65–66, 497–499
    Fair Credit Reporting Act of 1971, 305
    Health Insurance Portability and Accountability Act of 1996, 33
    Interstate or Foreign Travel and Transportation in Aid of Racketeering Enterprises Act, 53
    Money Laundering Control Act of 1986, 31, 34–47
    Money Laundering Suppression Act of 1994, 33
    Racketeer Influenced and Corrupt Organizations, 92–93
    Right to Financial Privacy Act, 285, 287
    Terrorism Prevention Act of 1996, 33
    terrorist financing, 378–381, 501–509
    Title 21, investment of illicit drug profits, 94–95
    Uniform Partnership Act, 162
    USA PATRIOT Act of 2001, 55–63
Steinbrenner, George, III, money laundering by, 28–30
"Sting" operations, 44–45, 270, 409
Stock certificates, 254–255
Stock dividends, 253
Stocks; *see also* Securities
    buying and selling, 256–260
    disbursing agents, 260
    getting information about, 258–260, 263
    making money on, 253–254
    market operations, 254–256
    money laundering and, 265–266
    stock markets, 254
    transfer agents, 259–260
    types of, 252–253
Stock warrants, 258
Stop-loss orders, 256
Straw man schemes, 319
Strips, 261
Structuring (smurfing)
    black market peso exchange schemes, 335–339
    case examples of, 332–334
    Currency Transaction Reports and, 83–84
    definition of, 33, 82–83
    each transaction as separate violation, 39
    intent to conceal nature of proceeds through, 41
    investigation of, 333–335
    of legally earned money, 53
    in offshore transactions, 332–333, 334
    penalties for, 89–90
    in the 1990s, 332–333
    in simple banking operation scheme, 323
    simple scheme, 332
    undercover operations in, 407–409
Student loans, 189–190
SUA, *see* Specified Unlawful Activities
Subject's records, 277–285
    asking for, 278
    business records, 269–270, 413
    as documentary evidence, 412–413
    obtained through second party, 278
    preparing list of items to be seized, 284–285
    search warrants for, 279–284
    subpoenas for, 278–279
Subpoenas
    administrative, 285–286
    in case files, 417
    by the DEA, 286
    duces tecum, 283, 286
    "for records," 288
    grand jury, 286–288
    for information from abroad, 292
    John Doe, 413
    search warrants *vs.,* 288–289
    service of, 287
    of subject's business records, 269–270
    templates for, 443–453
Subsidiary ledgers, 143
"Substantial penalty for early withdrawal," 193
Substitute assets, 66, 73–74
Substitute checks, 199
Sullivan, Manley, 15
Surveillance
    asset information from, 148
    importance of, 271
    in Lindbergh kidnapping case, 156
    mail covers, 272, 273–276
    pen registers, 277
    physical, 271–272
    trash covers, 272, 277
Suspicious Activity Report by Casinos and Card Clubs, 488–490
Suspicious Activity Reports (SARs)
    by casinos and card clubs, 488–490
    confidentiality of, 86
    form number, 81, 207
    forms for, 466–468, 483–490
    frequency distribution of filings of, 86
    in *hawala* transfers, 391
    requirements of, 85–87
    by securities brokers and dealers, 62
    in terrorist financing, 382–383, 387, 389
    USA PATRIOT Act requirements for, 61–62
    in the Watergate scandal, 26
Suspicious Transaction Reports, 207
Sussman, Barry, 24

SWIFT (Society for Worldwide Interbank Financial Telecommunications), 231, 236–238
Switzerland
   account identification, 223
   account types in, 222
   American banks in, 221–222
   documents available from banks in, 223
   exemplar MLAT, 104–106
   forfeiture sharing by, 98, 103
   international assistance from, 103
   names of banks in, 221
   opening an account in, 222–224
   types of banks in, 221
Syndicates, 171

T

Tabourian, Andre, 26–27
Tape, ticker, 256
Tax Court, U. S., 301–302
Tax fraud
   money laundering statutes and, 41, 53
   requirement of intent, 40–41
   taxes on illegal businesses, 15–17
Tax returns
   ex parte orders for, 266, 283, 289–290
   as financial records, 149, 266, 283
   for partnerships, 165
   terrorist financing and, 382–384, 389
Taylor, Max, 376
T-bills, 261
TECS (Treasury Enforcement Communications System), 294
Telephone companies, 309
Telex, 231
Teller's tapes, 193
Temporary restraining order (TRO), 73
Tenancy by the entirety, 246–247
Tenancy in common, 247
Tenancy in partnership, 247
Tenancy in severalty, 246
TEOAF (Treasury Executive Offices for Asset Forfeiture), 77
Terrorism Prevention Act of 1996, 33
Terrorist financing, 369–392; *see also* USA PATRIOT Act of 2001
   for Al Qaeda, 384–387
   for communications, 373–374
   designated foreign terrorist organizations, 380–381
   FATF 8 Special Recommendations on, 372–373
   Financial Action Task Force and, 100
   by *hawala* schemes, 389–391
   for Holy Land Foundation for Relief and Development, 387–389
   money laundering and, 57, 381–384
   for personnel, 374
   for Provisional Irish Republican Army, 370–378
   for security, 373
   sources of funding, 374–378
   state sponsorship, 374, 375–376
   statutes against, 378–381, 501–509
   U.N. Convention on, 371
   for weapons, 370, 373
Terrorist organizations, 380–381
Testimonial evidence, 412
Third-party records, 285–290
   administrative subpoena for, 285–286
   costs of, 286, 288
   as documentary evidence, 413
   financial search warrants, 279, 288–289
   grand jury subpoenas, 286–287
   legal considerations in, 285
   requesting, 285, 287, Appendix C
   service of subpoenas for, 287
Thomson Bank Directory, 186
Time bill of exchange, 212, 215–216
Time deposits, 177, 182, 192
Time drafts, 212, 215–216
Timelines, case, 404
Titles I and II of Public Law 91-508, *see* Bank Secrecy Act (BSA) of 1970
Title 18, 93–94, 95
Title 21, 94–95
Title 26, 87
Title 31, 89–92; *see also* Bank Secrecy Act (BSA) of 1970
Traders, 256
Transaction, definition of, 35, 38, 39; *see also* Cash transactions; Financial transactions
Transaction in currency, definition of, 83; *see also* Cash transactions
Transaction systems, money laundering and, 7–8
Transportation of funds within the U. S., 39
Trash covers, 272, 277
Travel agencies, information from, 309, 453
Travel and Entertainment Card (T&E), 307
Travelers checks
   "bank money" as early, 176
   Currency Transaction Reports for, 83
   in structuring, 83–84
   tracing, 202
Treason, in case of Aldrich Ames, 108–111
Treasury bonds, 261
Treasury Department
   Alcohol and Tobacco Trade Bureau, 300
   Comptroller of the Currency, 178–179
   Financial Crimes Enforcement Network, 296
   Office of Foreign Assets Control, 300
Treasury Enforcement Communications System (TECS), 294

Treasury Executive Offices for Asset Forfeiture (TEOAF), 77
TRO (temporary restraining order), 73
Trust deeds, 245
Trust department services, 182–183, 205–206
Trusts, 248

U

Undercover operations, 270, 407–409
Underinvoicing schemes, 355–358
Uniform Agreement of Sale and Deposit Receipt, 244
Uniform Customs and Practices for Documentary Credits, 212
Uniform Partnership Act (UPA), 162
Unit and volume method, 153
United Nations International Convention for the Suppression of the Financing of Terrorism (1999), 371
United Nations Narcotics Convention of 1988 (Vienna Convention), 99
United States, *see* Government agencies
United States person, definition of, 85
United States of America v. Bank of New England (1987), 169
United States v. Adams (1996), 47
United States v. All Assets of G.P.S. Automotive Corp., 69
United States v. All of the Inventories of the Businesses Known as Khalife Brothers Jewelry (1992), 69
United States v. Angulo-Lopez (1986), 280
United States v. Bajakajian (1998), 58, 59, 67
United States v. Barnes (1979), 282, 289, 290
United States v. Belcher (1991), 88
United States v. Bieganowski (2002), 39
United States v. Bornfield (1998), 38
United States v. Bowman (2000), 41, 42
United States v. Breque (1992), 45
United States v. Brown (1991), 37
United States v. Brown (1994), 39
United States v. Cabrales (1998), 48
United States v. Campbell (1992), 38
United States v. Carcione (2001), 37
United States v. Carr (1994), 44
United States v. Contents of Account Numbers 208-06070 and 208-06068-1-2 (1994), 69
United States v. Crisp (1970), 282
United States v. Cruz (1993), 37
United States v. Davis (2000), 37
United States v. Delgado (1997), 68
United States v. Doe (1984), 279
United States v. Estacio (1996), 37
United States v. Falcone (1940), 32
United States v. Falley (1973), 289
United States v. Fannin (1987), 281, 283
United States v. Farese (2001), 41
United States v. Fields (1996), 41
United States v. Gaytan (1996), 39
United States v. Golb (1996), 48
United States v. Goldberger and Dubin (1991), 88
United States v. Gonzalez-Rodriguez (1992), 39
United States v. Grey (1995), 40
United States v. Griffith (1994), 37
United States v. Hamilton, (1991), 42
United States v. Hinton (1976), 283, 289
United States v. Hollingsworth (1994), 45
United States v. Hunt (2001), 41
United States v. Jackskion (1939), 88, 282
United States v. Jackson (1991), 39, 41
United States v. James Daniel Good Real Property (1993), 71, 76
United States v. Kaufmann (1993), 42, 45
United States v. Kaufmann (1995), 45
United States v. Koller (1992), 39
United States v. Kow (1995), 283
United States v. Loehr (1992), 45
United States v. Long (1990), 38
United States v. Magano (1976), 88
United States v. Misher (1996), 37
United States v. Monies in Account No. 90-3617-3 (1991), 69
United States v. Monroe (1991), 43
United States v. Montague (1994), 38
United States v. Montoya (1991), 40
United States v. Ness (2003), 41
United States v. Offices Known as 50 State Distribution, Co. (1983), 284–285
United States v. Omoruyi (2001), 41
United States v. One 1989 Jaguar XJ6 (1993)
United States v. One 1988 Prevost Liberty Motor Home, 67
United States v. Paramo (1993), 40
United States v. Piervinanzi (1994), 43
United States v. Prince (2000), 41
United States v. Puche (2003), 38
United States v. Puig-Infante (1994), 39
United States v. Ramirez (1995), 39
United States v. Real Property at 874 Gartel Drive (1996), 68
United States v. Real Property in Mecklenburg County (1993), 69
United States v. Reed (1996), 39
United States v. Rodriguez (1995), 68
United States v. Rounsvall (1997), 37
United States v. Saccoccia (1995), 37
United States v. Sanders (1991), 42, 247
United States v. Santos (1994), 42
United States v. Short (1999), 39
United States v. Sokolow (1996), 47
United States v. Starke (1995), 45
United States v. Stavroulakis (1992), 47

United States v. Voigt (1996), 72
United States v. Washington (1986), 280
United States v. Werber (1992), 37
UPA (Uniform Partnership Act), 162
U.S. Bankruptcy Court, 301
U.S. banks, international banking by, 220–222
U.S. Citizenship and Immigration Services (USCIS), 299
U.S. Coast Guard, 299
U.S. Customs Court, 301
U.S. District Courts, 301
U.S. Tax Court, 301–302
USA PATRIOT Act of 2001, 55–63
    background on, 19, 55–57
    criminal sanctions in, 57–58
    currency smuggling, 58–59
    effects of, 62–63
    forfeiture in, 58–60
    on illegal money transmitter businesses, 240
    money laundering *vs.* terrorist financing, 57
    regulatory action in, 60–62
    "special measures" in, 61
    sunset provisions, 62
    Title 18, 93
    Title 26, 87
Use immunity, 279
Use of nominee scheme, 316–319, 414
Usury, definition of, 174

V

Validity, in international payments, 210
Veterans Affairs Department, 301
Vienna Convention, 99
Vostro accounts, 220

W

Wagering, 311
Warrants
    document, 279–284, 455–460
    financial, 279, 288–289
    preparing list of items to be seized, 283–285
    seizure, 70–71, 73, 75
    stock, 258
Water companies, 310
Watergate scandal of 1972, 19–26, 24–26
Weapons, money for, 370, 373
Web sites
    on Fedwire transfers, 236
    for listing of current MSBs, 227
    for search engines, 304
    support of terrorist organizations and, 375
Wells, H. G., 1
Western Union, 229, 230
Wilson, Frank, 411, 415–416, 423
Wiretap orders, 277
Wiring money, 94, 194; *see also* Money transfers
Withdrawals, bank, 200
Witness statements, 270–271
World Bank Directory, 186

Z

Zakat donations, 384–385, 388–389
al Zawahiri, Ayman, 384
Zdanowicz, John, 358
Zero-coupon bonds, 194, 261